Gardeners' Question Time

plant chooser

Gardeners' Question Time
plant chooser

inspired by the popular 'Plant of the Week' feature

Matthew Biggs,
John Cushnie,
Bob Flowerdew
& Bunny Guinness

Kyle Cathie Ltd

Dedication

To Jo, the assistant producer of *GQT*,
who somehow manages to keep all of us
happy and prevent any duplication of
Plant of the Week. Since we don't know
the questions in advance, it is nice to
have something we can talk about.
Thanks, Jo.

First published in Great Britain in 2003 by
Kyle Cathie Limited
122 Arlington Road
London NW1 7HP
general.enquiries@kyle-cathie.com
www.kylecathie.com

by arrangement with the BBC

This paperback edition published in 2008

BBC logo © BBC 1996

The BBC logo is a registered trademark of the British
Broadcasting Corporation and is used under licence

10 9 8 7 6 5 4 3 2 1

ISBN 978 1 85626 785 4

Project editor Caroline Taggart
Design by Geoff Hayes
Picture research by Jess Walton
Text edited by Selina Mumford & Gail Dixon-Smith
Editorial assistant Vicki Murrell
Production by Sha Huxtable

Matthew Biggs, John Cushnie, Bob Flowerdew &
Bunny Guinness are hereby identified as the authors
of this work in accordance with Section 77 of the
Copyright, Designs and Patents Act 1988.

A Cataloguing in Publication record for this title is
available from the British Library.

Printed in Singapore through Tien-Wah Press

Half-title page: *Lysichiton americanus;*
Title spread: *Papaver orientalis;*
This page: *Prunus avium*

contents

notes on the text

acknowledgements

AGM

The abbreviation AGM, used throughout the text, means the Royal Horticultural Society's Award of Garden Merit, one of the highest accolades the RHS can give a plant. Every AGM plant should have outstanding excellence for garden decoration or use; be available in the trade; be of good constitution; and require neither highly specialist growing conditions nor care.

North American hardiness zones:

The zones quoted in each entry are those established by the US Department of Agriculture, and refer to the maximum and minimum temperatures in which the plants will survive.

1	Below −50°F	Below −45.6°C
2a	−50 to −45°F	−42.8 to −45.5°C
2b	−45 to −40°F	−40.0 to −42.7°C
3a	−40 to −35°F	−37.3 to −39.9°C
3b	−35 to −30°F	−34.5 to −37.2°C
4a	−30 to −25°F	−31.7 to −34.4°C
4b	−25 to −20°F	−28.9 to −31.6°C
5a	−20 to −15°F	−26.2 to −28.8°C
5b	−15 to −10°F	−23.4 to −26.1°C
6a	−10 to −5°F	−20.6 to −23.3°C
6b	−5 to 0°F	−17.8 to −20.5°C
7a	0 to 5°F	−15.0 to −17.7°C
7b	5 to 10°F	−12.3 to −14.9°C
8a	10 to 15°F	−9.5 to −12.2°C
8b	15 to 20°F	−6.7 to −9.4°C
9a	20 to 25°F	−3.9 to −6.6°C
9b	25 to 30°F	−1.2 to −3.8°C
10a	30 to 35°F	1.6 to −1.1°C
10b	35 to 40°F	4.4 to 1.7°C
11	above 40°F	above 4.5°C

Gardeners' Question Time is a team effort and the production of this book has been the same.

Our thanks go to our editor, Caroline Taggart, who has skilfully steered a safe course through some troubled waters. To our designer, Geoff Hayes, for creating such a good-looking book, and picture researcher Jess Walton, for unearthing some terrific images. To Kyle Cathie for recognizing the potential to transform the weekly radio slot into a book for life.

And finally to our loyal listeners, without whom none of this would be possible.

Matthew Biggs, John Cushnie, Bob Flowerdew, Bunny Guinness and Trevor Taylor

Right: Taxus baccata

introduction

Gardeners' Question Time was first broadcast in 1947 and it's been on the air every week since. Without a gap. Now it's a foolhardy producer who tinkers with the format of a programme that's one of the world's great broadcasting successes, so it was with some trepidation that I introduced the 'Plant of the Week' feature into the programme in October 2000. The reason I did it was simple: the team was brimming over with great plants they'd like to talk about, but if no one asked the right question they did not have an opportunity to tell us about them.

At production meetings, backstage before a recording and even over a meal after a show I'd hear panel members get really excited as they swapped stories about some new discovery or other. If you could have captured the excitement and enthusiasm, bottled it and sold it, you'd have made a fortune. But without the right questions those plants would remain a green-room secret forever.

Contrary to popular belief, the team don't know the questions in advance. The audience pop their questions in a giant flowerpot when they arrive and I select what is going to be asked on the programme in the half-hour before we record. The first the team knows of a question is when it's asked. We are, therefore, totally dependent upon the topics on the minds of our audience on the day. I may be a gardening producer, but I don't plant questions.

Although this preserved the integrity of the programme it did mean some plants, some really great plants, plants the team were itching to talk about, never got a mention.

'Plant of the Week' changed all that. Here was a slot in the programme where a member of the panel could be totally self-indulgent. Without needing an excuse, except the relevance to the week, our experts could pick a plant, eulogize about it, and commend it to our two million listeners.

The team loved it. Nothing makes a gardener happier than to be able to extol the virtues of his or her favourite plants and persuade others to grow them. Imagine the thrill, therefore, of being able to drop a word in the ear of two million keen gardeners. It was horticultural heaven.

If the team was in heaven then, not surprisingly, the horticultural trade thought they were angels. We'd hear stories of nurseries and garden centres tuning in on a Sunday afternoon; within half an hour signs would be erected pointing customers to that week's '*Gardeners' Question Time* Plant of the Week'. Stocks would vanish and fresh supplies would be hard to find. Retailers would launch searches to locate the current 'Plant of the Week' as customers, our listeners, would be queuing up to buy the team's latest hot tip.

It made us realize just how powerful an influence we had. And with that power came responsibilities. Suppliers would lobby me and panel members seeking to get their plant selected as a 'Plant of the Week'. Inducements were even offered. They were all refused. There were, of course, temptations. When the programme fell on 1st April we mischievously mused about the possibility of inventing a genus with amazing characteristics and letting the horticultural trade sort that one out. We haven't done it…yet.

There are more than a third of a million different plants in the world. Members of the team have met most and are on first-name terms with the majority. In this book they share with you their enthusiasm for the best plants on the planet. Of course there are many more plants here than there are weeks in a year. We've taken the successful 'Plant of the Week' theme and given the team full rein to indulge themselves. From stunning annuals to scrummy fruits, from delicate alpines to perennial thugs, this book contains more than 700 of the team's favourite plants.

You cannot get better advice than from this quartet of Bob Flowerdew, Bunny Guinness, John Cushnie and Matthew Biggs. Read the text and you'll hear their voices. Of course, as on the programme, they do not all agree. Gardening's like that. But one thing they do all agree on, and that is within these two covers you'll find a Plant of the Week for a lifetime of gardening.

Trevor Taylor
Producer
Gardeners' Question Time

Gardeners' Question Time can be heard on BBC Radio 4 (92–95 VHF and 198 LW) on Sundays at 2 p.m. and Wednesdays at 3 p.m.

a note from the authors

John

Choosing my Plant of the Week for *Gardeners' Question Time* is great fun. There is always a plant exactly right for the week the programme is going out. My problem is that I am fickle. I love them all. So many plants, so little space… Seasonally I have favourites that change almost as quickly as new plants come into flower.

My all-time, permanent, 'wouldn't be without them' plants come about because of their colour, texture, shape, fragrance or flavour. Those that bring back childhood memories, such as old-fashioned roses, *Daphne mezereum* and honeysuckle, score well, as do all those associated with relatives and friends. My father loved the 'Peace' rose, Mum liked anemones and sweet William.

Then there are the plants I can't succeed with because of climatic conditions. I keep trying, often winning for a season or two before Jack Frost has his way. That is frustrating, but I appreciate these plants all the more when I see them in their natural habitat. I have grown and love every one of the plants I have recommended and I know that if you have a go you will love them too.

Bunny

Plants are the furniture of the garden and as such they should not only thrive in their situation, but must also provide much of its personality.

In my garden I grow nearly all the plants that I have selected for this book. Some I've had for many years, some I've acquired only recently. The remainder are plants that I have been meaning to get for ages and have used fairly extensively in gardens for other people or have observed in different situations.

It is an exacting and challenging job looking for just the right plant for specific spaces and functions. I am extremely lucky in having several members of my close family who have extensive nurseries specializing in different areas and continually sourcing and refining their stock. They are a great pool of knowledge to draw on and I am grateful to them all.

Bob

I hope you enjoy reading about my favourite plants. In many ways these are my greatest friends; I'm more interested in them, their history and eccentricities, and I take more effort to care for their needs and well being than anything else in the world. I spend most of my life with them and I can thoroughly recommend their company in your garden or greenhouse. I hope you too will take some, if not all, of them into your lives to love and cherish as much as I have done – and to get as much pleasure in return. And then to lop off their heads and eat their roots or stick them in a vase – they are just plants, after all.

I also hope you enjoy the rest of the book; I'd skip what the others have written but their pictures are quite good!

Matt

The opportunity to select some of my favourite plants sent a zing of excitement up my spine; it's the request that every plant-lover dreams of. I am in awe of the plant world – they are essential for survival, they clothe and feed us, provide shelter and medicines too, yet also offer something spiritual. Plants create the robes that clothe the earth and gardeners have the privilege of selecting the finest and weaving them into a tapestry that is wrapped around our dwellings to improve our quality of life.

I've chosen plants that quicken the pulse or leave me spellbound by their beauty. It's gratifyingly self-indulgent, but I hope you will be inspired by the selection and enjoy wallowing in pools of pleasure as they grow in your garden. Life would be impossible without them, so don't resist, go out, enjoy and feel the power of plants!

our top twelves

Choosing the plants to include in this book wasn't easy. One of the biggest difficulties was limiting ourselves to about 175 each when there are literally thousands to choose from. We compiled our first lists without consulting each other and inevitably there was overlap. All four of us originally put down *Cytisus battandieri*; three of us chose *Crambe maritima* – that's why there is the occasional 'PS', where one of us wanted to add to what another had written. And while we all have our favourite varieties, you'll see that there are lots of roses, lots of salvias, hydrangeas, daphnes and honeysuckles. They are all such great plants.

The 'plants of the week' scattered through the book are our crème de la crème, but then we had to ask ourselves why? Was it because the flowers were followed by attractive fruit and stunning autumn colour; or because an evergreen looked terrific whatever the season? So here are some of our favourite plants for different seasons, different parts of the garden and different purposes.

Spring interest

John
Amelanchier 'Ballerina' A great all-round small tree with spring leaf colour and flower.
Camellia x *williamsii* 'Anticipation' Glossy, dark green foliage with large, double, deep rose-pink flowers in spring.
Ulex europaeus 'Flore Pleno' This variety doesn't produce seedlings. The flowers have a coconut fragrance.
Daphne odora 'Aureomarginata' Fabulous foliage, knock-out scent, long-lasting foliage.

Bunny
Allium hollandicum 'Purple Sensation' Great colour and highly useful form for threading through planting.
Tulipa 'Magier' Exquisite flowers, which are fascinatingly marked
Akebia quinata Beautiful in leaf and best value of all spring flowers

Bob
Smilacina racemosa Better than a hosta and gorgeously scented.
Convallaria Just divine scent and good ground cover in damp places.

Matt
Ribes laurifolium Unusual greenish flowers in early spring are certainly a talking point.
Anemone nemorosa 'Robinsoniana' One of the stars in the firmament of spring; a delicious blue.
Arisarum proboscideum The 'mouse plant', its chocolate flowers have long wispy 'tails'.

Summer interest

John
Fabiana imbricata f. *violacea* Evergreen with mauve-lavender flowers in summer. Ideal for impoverished acid soil.
Philadelphus 'Belle Etoile' Guaranteed to flower every summer with masses of fragrant, white flowers.
Hydrangea sargentiana Clusters of blue fertile flowers surrounded by a ring of pure white sterile flowers.

Bunny
Salvia sclarea var. *turkestanica* Long-lasting, extraordinary flowers with bags of personality.
Salvia patens The intense blue is unbeatable and gives months of colour – a strong favourite.
Rosa 'Ferdinand Pichard' Wonderful stripy roses, with form and good foliage.

Bob
Mathiola bicornis Scent to die for.
Lathyrus odoratus Scent to live for.
Strawberries!!!!!!!!!!!!!!!!!!

Matt
Molinia caerulea 'Transparent' Floating on a late summer breeze, the seedheads and foliage look magnificent.
Dahlia imperialis By late summer, its long leafy stems are starting to create an impact.
Ceratostigma willmottianum The flowers are mid-blue and last from mid-summer to autumn. What more can I say?

Autumn interest

John
Liquidambar styraciflua 'Worplesdon' Autumn leaf colour changes from green through purple to orange-yellow.

Yucca gloriosa Enormous, upright spikes of hundreds of pendant, bell-shaped white flowers.
Gladiolus callianthus Spikes of highly fragrant, tubular, white flowers with a deep crimson centre.

Bunny
Cotinus coggygria Unbeatable tree/shrub for smoky flowers and autumnal foliage.
Anemone x *hybrida* 'Honorine Joubert' Excellent plant all round, but colour is long lasting and very fresh.
Brugmansia arborea 'Aurea' Exotic flowers that knock you out with their size, colour and profusion.

Bob
Grapes (*Vitis* spp.) All of them one after the other, oh I love eating them .
King Edward potatoes (*Solanum tuberosum*) Chips, chips and more chips all winter through.
'Doyenne du Comice' pears (*Pyrus*) Can't live without them.

Matt
Rhus glabra 'Laciniata' Autumn colour with a crackle and a roar! '
Cercidiphyllum japonicum You can smell the autumn colour and the fragrance is vanilla!
Aster x *frikartii* 'Monch' A very early starter and one of the best for an autumn display.

Winter interest

John
Betula utilis var. *jacquemontii* Its pure white bark puts this birch in a class of its own.
Taxus baccata 'Fastigiata Aurea' A beautiful, well-behaved, upright conifer with golden-yellow foliage.
Cornus alba 'Sibirica' Bright red bark on new growths to brighten a dull winter day.

Bunny
Taxus baccata I never tire of looking at its many different structural forms, which are outstanding 12 months a year.
Choisya ternata Dependable, well behaved and ever glossy.
Rosmarinus spp. Form, scent, flowers especially in winter and the original Christmas tree.

Bob

Claytonia (*Claytonia perfoliata*) As I would feel starved without its fresh leaves.
Pak-choi (*Brassica rapa chinensis*) As I would starve without its winter long supplies.
Lemons (*Citrus* spp.) For leaf, flower and fruit all winter through.

Matt

Chimonanthus praecox One of the great olfactory pleasures of the plant world.
Edgeworthia chrysantha Fragrant rich yellow flowers cloaked in silvery yellow hairs are my heart's desire.
Acacia dealbata Decked with bright yellow flowers in late winter, at the time when we all need some sunshine.

Fragrance

John

Hyacinthus orientalis 'Lady Derby' A single stem of this pink hyacinth is sufficient to fill a room with perfume.
Sarcococca confusa In winter the small white flowers manufacture unending supplies of incredible fragrance.
Hamamelis mollis 'Coombe Wood' Highly fragrant, bright- yellow flowers in the dead of winter.

Bunny

Mathiola incana Unbeatable fragrance which fills huge spaces for months in summer.
Myrtus communis Rich, spicy fragrance, a plant with romantic associations…the ideal wedding present.
Rosa 'Golden Celebration' You can virtually drink in this scent, a mix of sauterne wine and strawberry.

Bob

Gardenia augusta It is thoroughly decadent.
Cereus grandiflorus The perfume drives me crazy.
Rosa 'Etoile de Hollande' A positively erotic fragrance.

Matt

Zaluizianskia ovata Has an evening and night-time fragrance to make you swoon!
Trachelospermum jasminoides Sensual and exotic; one breath and you're transported to the tropics!
Daphne bholua 'Jacqueline Postill' A fragrance that every aristocratic perfumier would love to have created, but nature got there first!

Tulipa 'Magier' *and T.* 'Queen of the Night' *with Myosotis* 'Blue Ball'

Dark damp corners

John

Sarcococca confusa It enjoys a shady site protected from cold winds where its perfume will linger.
Gaultheria mucronata Evergreen with masses of beautifully coloured fruit throughout the winter.
Galanthus 'S. Arnott' Flowering in winter and early spring the white flowers of this snowdrop are honey scented.

Bunny

Dicksonia antartica Ideal for adding an unbeatable, lush dimension, but also dramatic.
Dryopteris felix mas The lime-coloured fresh leaves will revive many awkward spaces.
Asplenium scolopendrium An unsophisticated native fern that has a useful and attractive leaf for contrasting with other ferns.

Bob

A shed. Why beat your head against a brick wall?

Matt

Rhodotypos scandens Will survive in the most inhospitable conditions. The flowers are exquisite.
Vinca minor 'Atropurpurea' Deep purple flowers hide among the tangled, scrambling stems.
Dryopteris wallichiana Prefers it not too dark but loves the damp; a remarkably beautiful fern.

Sunny sites

John

Convolvulus cneorum A bushy, silvery shrub plastered with ivory-white flowers in early summer.
Genista lydia Masses of bright yellow pea-like flowers smother the plant in early summer.
Callistemon 'Australflora Firebrand' Bright crimson 'bottlebrush'-shaped flowers in summer. A real beauty, sport.

Bunny

Buddleia x *Lochinch* Beautiful foliage, good form, superbly coloured blue flowers.
Rosa 'Marie Pavie' Non-stop, beautiful flowers, provides useful low height for action-packed front-of-border positions.
Salvia indica 'Indigo Spires' Unbeatable – reliable but restful, non-stop wands of blue flowers all summer.

Bob

Grapes (*Vitis* spp.) Because I love them so much.
More grapes Because one lot is not enough.
Even more grapes As I never know when to stop.

Matt

Cistus ladanifer A charming plant whose flower and fragrance evoke Mediterranean memories.
Iris 'Brown Lasso' Even among the beautiful iris family, this is outstanding.
Lobelia tupa Wild and wonderful, it illustrates the extraordinary diversity among the relatives of the hanging-basket favourite.

Dry shade

John

Convallaria majalis 'Flore Pleno' For spring fragrance – its common name of lily-of-the-valley says it all. Plant it.

Kniphofia rooperi Strap-like, evergreen leaves and tall 'pokers' of orange-red flowers in autumn.

Tricyrtis formosana Pinkish purple-speckled flowers on a white background with a splash of yellow best describes these late autumn bloomers.

Bunny

Euphorbia amygdaloides 'Purpurea' Great foliage, pungent long-lasting lime flowers, fabulous and easy.

Euonymus fortunei 'Silver Queen' Only boring if you use it predictably; a great performer.

Buxus sempervirens There are limitless possibilities for this plant, but do not let it become a cliché.

Bob

Another shed.

Matt

Fascicularia bicolor Grows in some shade but prefers a little sun; an intriguing spidery specimen.

Helleborus foetidus Wester Flisk Group Unusual, with fascinating red markings.

Buxus sempervirens 'Handsworthiensis' Remarkably tolerant plant with dark green, leathery leaves.

Crataegus laevigata 'Paul's Scarlet'

Heavy clay soils

John

Alnus cordata A fast-growing tree with glossy green leaves and attractive male catkins.

Crataegus laevigata 'Paul's Scarlet' As tough as an old boot, this thorn has deep pink, double flowers.

Ilex aquifolium 'J. C. van Tol' Bright red holly berries every Christmas.

Bunny

Salix eleagnos Beautiful silver grey foliage that will star in this situation.

Crataegus monogyna Be it a tree, shrub, hedge, clipped standard, thicket plant or woodland edge specimen, you know it will be a great performer.

Digitalis purpurea A real survivor to add natural charm in spades.

Bob

Cabbages (*Brassica oleracea*) They grow so well in it.

Romanesco (*Brassica oleracea* var. *italica*) As I might then get a big head!

Nothing that needs annual planting or sowing.

Matt

Berberis darwinii Gorgeous orange flowers, attractive holly-like leaves and clay-tolerant. No wonder it's a winner!

Rudbeckia fulgida var. *sullivantii* 'Goldsturm' Many ornamental daisies tolerate clay but this is the best.

Rosa canina Our beautiful native dog rose.

Alkaline soils

John

Dianthus gratianopolitanus Forms a carpet of deep pink, fragrant, single flowers in summer.

Spartium junceum Masses of fragrant, golden yellow flowers throughout summer and autumn.

Syringa vulgaris 'Katherine Havemeyer' Highly fragrant, this lilac has double, lavender-blue flowers.

Bunny

Clematis 'Warsaw Nike' Wonderful, rich purple, bold but beautiful flowers that last.

Clematis heracleifilia 'Wyevale' Late blue flowers with personality; great herbaceous ground cover.

Verbascum bombyciferum 'Polarsommer' Outstanding plant for form, colour and ability to find the most scenic place to set seed.

Bob

Anything other than those miserable ericaceous plants that never give a decent fruit or much perfume – and wouldn't grow on this soil anyway, even if you added an entire peat bog to it.

Matt

Hermodactylus tuberosus Subtle flower colour and fragrance to match. A welcome sight in spring.

Sedum spectabile A jolly autumn plant with fine winter form. Great for butterflies.

Helleborus x *sternii* Unusual pink flowers and bold form make this a striking addition to the garden.

Acid soils

John

Kalmia latifolia 'Olympic Fire' Large clusters of pink flowers from crimped, dark red buds in spring.

Pieris formosa var. *forrestii* 'Wakehurst' Looks magical in spring with red leaves and white flowers.

Rhododendron 'Christmas Cheer' Funnel-shaped, pale pink flowers early in the new year.

Bunny

Amelanchier lamarckii Flowers, form, autumn colour all to die for and in one plant!

Camellia 'Cornish Snow' Fabulous flowers, superb foliage.

Magnolia liliiflora 'Nigra' Long-flowering and flowers early on in life.

Bob

I'd lime it so I could grow some decent vegetables and fruits instead of all those miserable acid lovers!

Matt

Vaccinium corymbosum 'Blue Crop' Tasty blue berries and good autumn colour for a 'double whammy' of pleasure!

Rhododendron x *praecox* The cerise-pink flowers very early in the year are a welcome reminder that spring is not far away!

Hacquetia epipactis Unusual lime-coloured bracts are a feature on this curious relative of celery.

Sandy soils

John

Tamarix tetandra Ferny foliage follows clouds of light pink flowers in spring.

Fuchsia magellanica 'Riccartonii' It makes a wonderful hedge for coastal gardens with scarlet and purple flowers all summer.

Lavandula angustifolia 'Twickel Purple' The fragrance of lavender in summer brings back childhood memories.

Bunny

Lavandula 'Sawyers' A lavender that actually looks good in winter, and just needs three things: drainage, drainage and drainage.

Galactites tomentosa Superb exotic foliage, beautiful thistly flowers and a controllable self-seeder.

Hebe x *andersonii* Variegated striking foliage to liven awkward spaces.

Bob

Anything I wanted as long as I watered and mulched it well, and especially a lot of asparagus.

Matt

Eryngium bourgatii 'Picos Blue' Beautiful metallic blue flowers and stems await your adoration.

Cytisus battandieri Bright yellow flowers, reflecting the colour of sunshine, and silky leaves and stems ensure that this majestic Moroccan a must for the garden.

Perovskia atriplicifolia A lovely plant in all its forms, with delicate foliage and beautiful blue flowers. Wow!

Exposed sites

John

Arbutus unedo 'Elfin King' The white, urn-shaped flowers and red 'strawberry' fruit appear together in the autumn.

Hippophae rhamnoides Tolerates seaside conditions with bright orange-yellow berries in winter.

Pyracantha atalantioides Evergreen with large clusters of bright orange-red berries throughout the winter.

Bunny

Hebe albicans Well-rounded form with grey-blue foliage that looks neat and prosperous even after a gale – rarely has a bad hair day.

Brachyglottis monroi A wonderful foliage plant with neat but unusual grey/green leaves.

Ligustrum vulgare Far superior to 'hedging privet', this is a useful tough, native plant.

Bob

Anything I wanted as I'd make windbreaks

Matt

Crataegus monogyna 'Biflora' You cannot beat hawthorns for toughness and this one's made more attractive by its quirky flowering habits.

Fuchsia procumbens If it gets too windy, you can always hide, like this pretty, slightly tender New Zealander.

Sorbus cashmiriana The mountain ash and its relatives are bone hardy and beautiful; this is an excellent example.

Urban sites

John

Skimmia japonica subsp. *reevesiana* Evergreen with white flowers in spring and long-lasting, bright red berries.

Laburnum x *watereri* 'Vossii' Long, trailing racemes of bright golden flowers in early summer.

Cotoneaster 'Rothschildianus' Large clusters of golden berries in autumn and winter.

Bunny

Buddleja globosa A great little goer, and I even quite like its orange flowers.

Salix viminalis Extremely fast-growing plant which tolerates many difficult conditions.

Prunus subhirtella 'Autumnalis' Attractive intermittent flowers appearing through the winter are always appreciated.

Matt

Cotoneaster bullatus Will grow anywhere, in anything; a fine example of horticultural machismo.

Amelanchier 'Ballerina' Beautiful but tough – I've met several ladies like that!

Mespilus germanica A robust tree that's been grown for centuries and has bags of character.

Ground cover

John

Erica carnea 'December Red' This heather is covered from mid-winter until spring with rose-red flower spikes.

Pachysandra terminalis 'Variegata' A low, fast-growing variegated evergreen with white flowers in early summer.

Lithodora diffusa 'Heavenly Blue' Prostrate evergreen covered in azure blue flowers in summer.

Bunny

Geranium renardii Beautiful sheets of velvety foliage, pretty flowers.

Pulmonaria 'Sissinghurst White' Simple, attractive, tolerant and a great performer.

Omphaloides Good foliage but stunning early flowers.

Bob

Hedera spp. So good in shade and good for wildlife.

Limnanthes douglasii Cheap, cheerful and also good for wildlife.

Strawberries (*Fragaria* spp.) Well, why not?

Matt

Gaultheria procumbens One of my favourite plants – it's simple, understated, cheeky and fun.

Daphne blagayana Not your traditional ground cover, but when it's happy it will spread and spread!

Gentiana sino-ornata Perfect if you like deep blue carpets.

Hedging

John

Buxus sempervirens 'Handsworthiensis' Forms a tall, dense, evergreen screen.

x *Cuprocyparis leylandii* There is nothing to beat it for speed of growth. If well maintained it makes a wonderful screen.

Escallonia 'Pride of Donard' Ideal as a hedge with evergreen foliage and pink-red flowers in summer.

Bunny

Carpinus betulus Ideal for many conditions, fastish-growing, tolerant and smart.

Taxus baccata In many cases my first choice for unbeatable structure.

Crataegus monogyna A great native, stockproof, excellent for wildlife and tolerates many situations.

Bob

Crataegus spp. Traditional and the finest formal hedge.

Worcesterberry (*Ribes* hybrid) A brutal statement and good for wildlife and jam.

x *Cuprocyparis leylandii* Much abused, but a fine hedge.

Matt

Colletia hystrix A combination of contemporary sculpture and burglar-proof barrier. How desperately do they want your Rolex?

Ilex aquifolium 'J. C. van Tol' Self-pollination guarantees a regular supply of berries. If only everything in life was that easy!

Escallonia 'Pride of Donard' Glossy leaves and rose-pink flowers; it loves to be by the sea.

Climbers

John

Rosa 'Dublin Bay' A climber with fragrant, crimson, double flowers all summer.

Solanum crispum 'Glasnevin' Clusters of dark blue flowers with golden stamens during summer.

Wisteria sinensis 'Sierra Madre' In late spring and early summer a mass of pendant lavender-blue fragrant flowers flushed white.

Bunny

Trachelospermum jasminoides Brilliant plant, great foliage, superb flowers and good growth rate for an evergreen.

Solanum laxum 'Album' Flowers borne in profusion over a long period.

Rosa 'Mme Alfred Carrière' Outstanding repeat-flowering white rose, with high disease resistance.

Bob

Grapevines (*Vitis* spp.) Surprise, surprise.

Kiwi (*Actinidia chinensis*) Only if there is a sunny spot where it can ramble.

Lonicera etrusca Oh the scent is divine.

Matt

Vitis cognetiae Huge leaves and rich autumn colour; to say it's vigorous is an understatement!

Lonicera periclymenum 'Graham Thomas' Tumbling cascades of flowers with a fragrance that soothes.

Rosa banksiae 'Lutea' Beautiful, elegant and tender. I once saw it growing as a hedge in New Zealand!

For containers

John

Nerine bowdenii Shocking pink flowers on long stems in autumn before the leaves appear.

Gazania Daybreak Series A fantastic range of brightly coloured flowers from summer till autumn.

Helianthus annuus 'Teddy Bear' A dwarf sunflower with big, double, golden yellow flowers ideal for children.

Bunny

Agave americana Sculptural plant that requires minimal watering.

Trachycarpus fortunei Hardy palm that will add a touch of paradise for 12 months of the year.

Buxus sempervirens Well used, but that is not surprising as it looks tip-top all year round.

Bob

Citrus spp. Any of them is amazing value.

Grapevines (*Vitis* spp.) Well of course.

Peaches (*Prunus persica*) Cos this is the only way to get them regularly.

Matt

Astelia chathamica Silvery swords for dappled shade, it's perfect for contemporary style.

Pelargonium 'Lord Bute' A burgundy flower with orange anthers. Now that's class!

Citrus limon 'Garey's Ureka' A regular supply for g & t, and pies submerged in frothy meringue!

Fruits and berries

John

Malus 'John Downie' A charming garden tree with highly ornamental, edible crab apples.

Nicandra physalodes 'Violacea' In autumn the blue flowers are replaced by brown fruit enclosed in papery, purple calyces.

Callicarpa bodinieri var. *giraldii* 'Profusion' Incredible, small, metallic-looking, violet fruit in autumn.

Bunny

Ficus carica 'Brown Turkey' Delicious fruits, stunning foliage and easy to please in dry, hot spaces with next to no soil.

Cydonia oblonga My favourite tree, addictive fruit, superb flowers, beautiful early foliage and just charming for the remaining months.

Fragaria vesca Charming and delicious, neat and unassuming but highly useful.

Bob

My favourite category, so I demanded at least six!

Strawberries (*Fragaria* spp.) For their perfume brought out with cream.

Raspberries (*Rubus idaeus*) For sorbets and jams.

Pineapples (*Ananas comosus*) For the achievement, and perfection of flavour.

Grapes (*Vitis* spp.) For their delight and variety.

Peaches and pears (*Prunus persica* and *Pyrus communis*) For their lusciousness.

Apricots (*Prunus armeniaca*) For their tart melt-in-the-mouth scrumptiousness.

Matt

Callicarpa bodinieri var. *giraldii* 'Profusion' Lilac flowers and funky purple fruits. Flash or what?

Sorbus 'Joseph Rock' Primrose-yellow berries from one of the most gorgeous trees on earth.

Malus 'John Downie' An excellent garden tree with fabulous flowers and cheerful fruits for jellies and wine.

Evergreens

John

Embothrium coccineum Brilliant scarlet flowers in early summer with a backdrop of deep, evergreen leaves.

Juniperus communis 'Compressa' A truly dwarf conifer forming a compact column of needle-like mid-green leaves.

Eleagnus pungens 'Maculata' Dark evergreen leaves splashed with golden yellow.

Bunny

Taxus baccata Love it as a tree, hedge, sculpture – you name it, it will do it.

Astelia chamanica Much hardier than is often supposed (I know one thriving in Yorkshire), and is different but great too.

Cedrus lebani I rarely get to use this, but what a statement when well placed!

Bob

Rosmarinus spp. Useful, edible, scented, easy and pretty

x *Cuprocyparis leylandii* They screen out eyes so well, even upstairs eyes.

Cordyline australis For its head of flowers of gorgeous scent.

Matt

Hoheria sexstylosa 'Stardust' Has elegant leaves, a profusion of starry flowers and is very pretty.

Crinodendron hookerianum Beautiful flowers hang like crimson lanterns against the dark green leaves.

Desfontainia spinosa   A Chilean 'wonder plant' with holly-like leaves and brightly coloured flowers.

Bright colours

John

Ceanothus 'Concha'   Deep, non-fading, Oxford blue flowers open from deep red buds.
Cotinus 'Flame'   Hard to beat when you want brilliant red foliage.
Meconopsis x *sheldonii* 'Slieve Donard'   The very best true blue poppy.

Bunny

Canna iridiflora   Wonderfully vibrant and exotic.
Cosmos atrosanguineus   Freely produced rich velvety maroon red flowers adding a tropical feel
Salvia involucrata 'Bethellii'   Amazing bright flowers all summer – they go on and on and on…

Matt

Forsythia x *intermedia* 'Lynwood'   Not as bright as some, but you may still need your sunglasses.
Euonymus europeaus 'Red Cascade'   Fiery red autumn colour looks great bathed in sunshine.
Schisandra rubriflora   Clusters of bright red berries leap into vision during early autumn.

For tiny gardens

John

Cyclamen hederifolium   Tiny, perfectly formed and scented flowers in shades of pink in autumn.
Sorbus reducta   A miniature rowan tree complete with autumn colour and berries.
Ledum groenlandicum   A tough little evergreen with white flowers in late spring/early summer.

Bunny

Thymus minimus   Green paving but with scent, dynamic colour and adored by bees.
Galactites tomentosa   Magnificent foliage, charming flowers, pops up to surprise you in the best places.
Cynara cardunculus   Looks sensational and tastes even better.

Matt

Leucojum autumnale   Delicate white flowers in autumn: they don't come much smaller than this!
Carex comans 'Frosted Curls'   A swirling leaved sensation for borders or pots.
Clematis x *durandii*   Indigo blue flowers to create an aura of calm.

To attract wildlife

John

Buddleia x *weyeriana* 'Sungold'   Unusual variety with orange-yellow flowers that attract butterflies.
Leycesteria formosa   Birds love the trailing strings of purple fruit in autumn.
Lonicera periclymenum 'Graham Thomas'   White summer flowers and red autumn berries attract birds and bees.

Bunny

Crataegus monogyna   Hums with life through much of the year. Aesthetically adaptable – ideal for a chic minimalist city plot or rugged, windswept moors.
Ligustrum vulgare   Flowers and fruit but also shelter in winter.
Viburnum opulus   A very pretty native with massive appeal to us and them.

Bob

Blackberries (*Ribes* spp.)   More use to more creatures than any other garden plant.
Limnanthes douglassii   As it is also scented, pretty, easy, good ground cover.
Kniphofia spp.   To see the birds taking their nectar.

Matt

Ilex aquifolium 'J. C. van Tol'   Food for the birds and holly blue butterflies.
Buddleja 'Lochinch'   Please plant buddlejas for butterflies. Thank you.
Foeniculum vulgare 'Purpureum'   Flowers are a magnet to a multitude of insects.

For sheltered sites

John

Hebe x *andersonii* 'Variegata'   Long, grey-green leaves margined creamy white; spikes of violet flowers in summer.
Clianthus puniceas 'Red Cardinal'   Brilliant scarlet 'lobster claw' flowers in summer followed by pea-like seed pods.
Akebia quinata   Purple-brown fragrant flowers in early spring followed by odd, sausage-like fruits in autumn.

Bunny

Olea europea   Evergreen, beautiful, clippable, evocative, tolerant of dire soil – well, it's just outstanding.
Aloysia triphylla   Scented leaves, perfumed flowers – very special.

Pyrus 'Doyenne de Comice'

Pelargonium tomentosum   Beautiful form and foliage, with exquisitely scented leaves.

Bob

Banana (*Musa chinensis*)   As it's just such a challenge and talking point.
Lemon verbena (*Aloysia triphylla*)   For the absolutely gorgeous scent of the leaves.
Loquat (*Eriobotrya japonica*)   Should do well and has such big leaves!

Matt

Jeffersonia dubia   Dainty and exquisitely beautiful; a plant to savour.
Sanguinaria canadensis   A gorgeous yet fleeting flower, it's another to add to your wish list.
Arisaema sikokianum   So gorgeous and sumptuously coloured that every garden should have one!

Cornus alba 'Sibirica'

RED-BARKED DOGWOOD

Type: fully hardy, deciduous, spreading shrub
Soil & situation: moist, fertile soil/tolerates heavy, wet ground/full sun
Hardiness zone: 2–8
Height: 2.5m (8ft)
Spread: 2m (6½ft)
Grow for: bright red bark which is one of the joys of midwinter; red autumn leaves; AGM

A clump of leafless, red-stemmed dogwood growing at the edge of a lake and reflected in the surface of the water is a memorable sight. There are *Cornus* with variegated leaves (*C. alba* 'Gouchaultii'), others with yellow (*C. sericea* 'Flaviramea') or purple-black (*C. a* 'Kesselringii') stems, but *C. a.* 'Sibirica' (sometimes listed as *C. a.* 'Westonbirt') is the most accommodating and reliable, medium-sized variety.

The dark green leaves colour to a deep red before they fall, revealing the winter show. Small white flowers in spring and early summer are followed by white fruit, sometimes tinged with blue.

While it is content to grow in marshy and heavy clay sites, it will be more generous in its display if planted in fertile, moist, well-drained soil. It is the young growths that have the brightest bark colour. However, these should be removed close to ground level in spring to encourage new shoots for next winter's display. The bark on older stems fades to a dull, muddy brown-red. Neglected plants can be rejuvenated by a hard pruning in late winter or early spring.

Propagating is simple. A branch will root where it touches the ground and can be removed by taking 30cm (12in) long hardwood cuttings in winter. Insert them 15cm (6in) deep outside, in a trench lined with sand. They will be well rooted within 12 months ready for planting out. **JC**

Abelia x *grandiflora*

Type: hardy, evergreen shrub
Soil & situation: fertile, well-drained soil/full sun/shelter from cold winds
North American hardiness zone: 6–9
Height: 3m (10ft)
Spread: 4m (13ft)
Grow for: arched branches laden with fragrant white flowers in summer and autumn; AGM

An easily managed, evergreen plant that flowers over a long period and, as such, finds its way into lots of my garden designs.

When mature it forms a rounded shrub with arching branches. The glossy, dark green leaves are 5cm (2in) long. It is in flower continuously from mid-summer to the first frosts in autumn. The panicles of funnel-shaped, fragrant, white flowers are tinged pink with deeper pink calyces.

Plant in a sunny site well protected from cold, drying winds, which tend to scorch the new growths. It is a vigorous shrub needing its fair share of the bed. Where close planting causes congestion it loses its leaves and the crowded branches die. The variety *Abelia* x *grandiflora* 'Francis Mason' is less vigorous, growing to 1.5m (5ft) in height with a spread of 2m (6½ft). The leaves are yellow splashed with deep green.

A light pruning immediately after flowering to remove the old flowerheads will keep the plant in shape and encourage next year's flowers. Propagation is easy, either as softwood cuttings in early summer or semi-ripe taken with a heel in early autumn. Remove the tip of the cutting to prevent it flowering. Those rooted in autumn can be potted up in the following spring. **JC**

Abelia x *grandiflora*

Abeliophyllum distichum

Abeliophyllum distichum
WHITE FORSYTHIA

Type: hardy, deciduous shrub
Soil & situation: fertile, free-draining soil/full sun/sheltered site
North American hardiness zone: 5–9
Height & spread: 3m (10ft); 1.5m (5ft) as a border shrub
Grow for: white, pink-tinged, sweetly fragrant flowers in late winter; leaves sometimes turn purple in autumn

It is hard to believe that this elegant, slow-growing shrub, with clusters of dainty white flowers lining its leafless purple-black stems, is a relative of the more familiar yellow-flowered forsythia. Appearing in late winter when little else is in flower, its blooms are deliciously understated. The impact of a single plant is impressive; imagine the delight of a friend of mine who saw thickets of it flowering in the oak forests of South Korea.

Remarkably, in the wild it is scarce; even in 1948 it was noted that 'the distribution was confined to an exceedingly small area, had it not been brought into cultivation, it might easily have become extinct'. Now it is listed as 'critically endangered' – what better incentive to grow one of these treasures in your garden! The cultivar 'Roseum', sometimes called the Roseum Group, has pale pink flowers.

Although hardy, it needs a sunny wall, fence or border to ripen young growths and protect flowers from frost. It should be grown in a well-drained, fertile soil. Prune after flowering. If you are growing it as a wall shrub, cut back flowering shoots to two to three buds; in borders, cut them back to a vigorous branch lower down on the main stem; cut out any weak growth. If the plant is congested remove up to a quarter of the older wood at the base. Propagate by semi-ripe cuttings in mid-summer or by layering. The arching branches layer naturally and can be transplanted a year later. **MB**

Abies koreana
KOREAN FIR

Type: hardy, evergreen conifer
Soil & situation: deep, moist, fertile, well-drained, alkaline soil/full sun
North American hardiness zone: 5–6
Height: 10m (33ft)
Spread: 6m (20ft)
Grow for: a mass of purple-blue cones in winter

I just love to see cones on conifers. With some species they are formed so high up the mature tree you need binoculars, but this plant will oblige by producing cones on plants that are barely 1m (3ft) high.

Small, dark green, upward curving leaves cover the upper part of the stem. On the underside of the leaf there are two broad, silver-white lines.

The insignificant male flowers are deep red and the female purple or pink followed by upright, cylindrical, candle-like, purple or deep blue cones, 5–8cm (2–3½in) long. They exude beads of clear resin like wax dripping down the side of a candle. Eventually they turn a rich brown and break up. *Abies koreana* 'Silberlocke' has leaves that twist upwards revealing their silver undersides.

It is totally hardy, although the foliage of young plants may be scorched by cold, biting winds. It makes a wonderful specimen conifer especially in winter when laden with cones and sprinkled with a dusting of snow.

Propagation is by seed sown fresh in late autumn in a cold frame. Stratify for at least one month. Grow the young seedlings under cover for the first season. Container-grow the plants for their first full year. **JC**

Abies koreana

Abutilon x *hybridum* 'Kentish Belle'

Abutilon x hybridum 'Kentish Belle'
FLOWERING MAPLE, PARLOUR MAPLE, INDIAN MALLOW

Type: frost-hardy, semi-evergreen shrub
Soil & situation: well-drained fertile soil/sun or partial shade/best when trained against, or grown beside, a protective wall or fence
North American hardiness zone: 8–10
Height & spread: 2.5m (8ft)
Grow for: extremely long flowering period, sometimes continuously, from early spring to autumn; attractive and unusual mix of warm apricot-yellow and orangey-red flowers; AGM

As these plants are a little on the tender side, both the flowers and the foliage do really benefit from the shelter and warmth of a wall, often trained as an informal fan. I have seen one smothered in flowers, in Bath, just after Christmas, propped up against a slatted fence. It must have been a mild year as they usually stop with the frosts. The flowers are produced singly and are large, bell-shaped and hang from the dark brown/purple shoots. They stand out far more and are better displayed when trained against a wall, particularly a pale-coloured wall.

The young plants benefit from some tip pruning to encourage a good bushy habit. Mature plants can be cut back hard in early to mid-spring to stop them getting over-large or gangly. Dead-heading helps prolong the flowering period, preventing too much energy being taken up with seed production. Abutilons are easy to propagate from either softwood or semi-ripe cuttings in summer. **BG**

Abutilon 'Souvenir de Bonne'

Abutilon
'Souvenir de Bonne'

Type: half-hardy, evergreen shrub
Soil & situation: free-draining soil/full sun or part day sun/winter protection/cannot withstand temperatures below 0°C (32°F)
North American hardiness zone: 8–10
Height: up to 3.5m (11ft)
Spread: 3m (10ft)
Grow for: amazing foliage margined and sometimes mottled in a creamy white, the leaves are a maple shape; soft orange-apricot flowers from late spring to autumn; AGM

I do appreciate the flowers – they are a fabulous colour – but compared to the really over-the-top foliage they rather pale into insignificance. I am not usually a huge fan of rashly variegated plants but this I find agreeable. Generally they are planted out in the late spring, having been heavily cut back, and are almost invariably nearly leafless with me, due to long periods of 0°C (32°F) over winter.

But they quickly gather pace, spread and flower, contributing a fair amount of impact to my sheltered, walled garden. They have other exotic near neighbours – bananas, brugmansias, melianthus and palms – and it is easy to forget that this is the sunny East Midlands.

My specimens generally reach about 1.8m (6ft) by the end of the summer, due to a good cutting back in the spring. Otherwise they would tend to get extremely leggy. As the plants become older, they become less floriferous, so ideally replacement cuttings are taken every four years or so. These are as for *A.* x *hybridum* 'Kentish Belle' (see previous entry). **BG**

Acacia dealbata
MIMOSA OR SILVER WATTLE

Type: half-hardy, evergreen tree
Soil & situation: well-drained, fertile, neutral to acid soil/sheltered site in full sun
North American hardiness zone: 9–10
Height: 6–15m (20–50ft)
Spread: 5–8m (16–25ft)
Grow for: scented winter and spring flowers; AGM

This is the flowering tree the British have nicknamed the 'florist's mimosa'. Its delicate, buttercup-yellow racemes are made up of hundreds of small, rounded, highly fragrant flowers appearing in winter and early spring. When I was a boy every 'decent' bunch of flowers contained some mimosa and it certainly wasn't grown in quantity locally. I used to think it had been sent from Australia, but Cornwall was probably more accurate.

The 12cm (5in) long, fern-like foliage is silvery-green and made up of around 80 leaflets. It dislikes being transplanted so choose a small tree and plant it in its permanent position. A sheltered, sunny wall is ideal. Additional protection from winter wind and frost in the form of a removable screen of horticultural fleece or bubble wrap will guarantee flowers every winter.

In Australia it may grow to 15m (50ft) with a spread of 8m (25ft), but in most northern hemisphere gardens 6m (20ft) in height with a spread of 5m (16ft) is more realistic. **JC**

Bunny adds:
This is a wonderful wall plant, and I find it worth growing even in the East Midlands. It establishes quickly, so if I did lose it in an exceptionally hard winter, its hole could soon be filled with a replacement.

Acanthus mollis
BEAR'S BREECHES

Type: semi-evergreen, hardy perennial
Soil & situation: tolerates a wide range of soils/dislikes the wettest soil/sun or light shade
North American hardiness zone: 7–10
Height: to 1.5m (5ft)
Spread: to 90cm (36in)
Grow for: a superb plant with a bold habit; white flowers with purple-shaded bracts in summer; large, glossy-green basal leaves, evergreen (in most winters) up to 1m (3ft)

This perennial has the rare quality of looking striking throughout the year. Its opulent, shiny leaves remain a feature for most or all of the winter unless you have exceptionally hard frosts. It has the added benefit of producing robust, but delicately coloured flower spikes for several weeks in the summer. These may well be 1.5m (5ft) high and are excellent for dried, winter decorations. *Acanthus spinosus* is famous for the shape of its leaves, which are similar to those of *A. mollis*, but spiny and deeply cut. A stylized form of these leaves is used as a motif in classical and neo-classical ornamentation. *A. spinosus* is generally freer flowering, but tends to die right back in winter.

This plant requires little attention except division and replanting, when necessary, in autumn or early spring. In my experience this is needed only infrequently. I grow them, in repeated clumps, against a 6m (20ft), north-facing, stone-buttressed wall. The lack of sun reduces the quantity of flowers, but not to a worrying extent. The leaves can suffer from slugs and mildew in early summer. If they look unacceptable I remove them and new, perfect specimens replace them swiftly. The spikes are best removed after flowering. These plants can become rampant, so they are best used surrounded by suitable neighbours, as solo performers or in large tubs where they will thrive. When you move clumps of plants, the fleshy roots, which become severed and left behind, may well strike out again on their own so propagation is easy from root cuttings in autumn. Alternatively, seeds can be sown in spring. **BG**

Right: Acanthus mollis

Left: Acacia dealbata

Acanthus sennii

Acanthus sennii
BEAR'S BREECHES

Type: half-hardy, evergreen perennial
Soil & situation: free-draining soil/full sun
North American hardiness zone: 7–10
Height & spread: 1.8m (6ft)
Grow for: flowers from mid-summer to autumn

I've only seen this once and it is absolutely incredible. Rarely mentioned in literature, *Acanthus sennii* grows at Oxford University Botanic Garden and Chelsea Physic Garden, London, is offered by a couple of nurseries and remains a mystery plant. Named in 1940 by an Italian taxonomist Emilio Chiovenda, it is endemic to the Ethiopian highlands between 1,500 and 3,200m (5,000 and 10,500ft), by streams and river banks, in dry forest margins and on open hillsides. The stiff, glossy, dark green leaves in opposite pairs have wavy margins of spiky teeth and prominent veins but it's the striking black bracts and pink to vermilion flowers in clusters towards the top of the stem that are so unusual and eye-catching. I tried to propagate it but failed, now I'm on the hunt for a plant of my own; it's my horticultural Holy Grail!

Look out also for *A. hirsutus*, whose pale greenish-white flowers peep from hairy green bracts; *A. hungaricus* with dense clusters of pink-purple spikes above dull green leaves; *A. dioscoridis* – low growing with beautiful, broad, pink to purplish flowers and long, narrow, grey-green, downy leaves; and *A. d.* var. *perringii* with deeply divided and slightly spiny foliage, grey-green flower spikes and flowers of delicate pink. They all flower from early to late summer. There are several forms in cultivation.

Grow *A. sennii* in milder areas of the UK at the base of a sunny wall, where it may still need winter protection and a 'dry' mulch like bracken in autumn. It is much better grown in a container and over-wintered indoors to protect from frost. It prefers sunshine and deep, fertile, well-drained soil or a loam-based compost. To propagate take root cuttings in winter. **MB**

Acer capillipes

Acer capillipes
SNAKEBARK MAPLE

Type: hardy, deciduous tree
Soil & situation: ordinary garden soil/sun or partial shade
North American hardiness zone: 5–7
Height & spread: 9–14m (30–46ft)
Grow for: curiously striped bark; bright green leaves, attractive form and autumn tints extend its high points to 12 months in a year; AGM

I planted this tree adjacent to our eating-out area and the canopy, although fairly upright and contained, has a few lazier branches, which shade the table like an umbrella. With maturity, it will spread further. It is an undemanding tree but I think quite a special one. It has settled into this dry corner and is a fine young specimen having reached a height of some 6m (20ft) after about 17 years. The bark has vertical, chalky-white stripes running all the way down the trunk, which are always noticeable. They are painted on a green-brown background. The leaves have three pointed lobes and coral-red stems – the same colour as the new young growth. The flowers open in late spring in the form of hanging racemes of a greenish-white colour and are followed by long, drooping bunches of fruit with keys and wings. It is a suitable tree for a medium-sized or, very possibly, even a small garden, depending on position. It is also adaptable – you occasionally see it as a successful street tree.

I, as always, like to see this tree planted small, certainly no bigger than 1.2m (4ft) high if you can get it that size, and with no stake. This way it will quickly overtake any that were planted at a larger size and will form a much better-shaped tree. It is also far less expensive. Bare-rooted trees establish better than container-grown ones. It needs little aftercare, though make sure that there are no grass or weeds growing within 1m (3ft) diameter around the base of the trunk. This way there is no moisture competition and it will grow far faster. Watering in dry periods in the first two to three years after planting, makes all the difference. Feed is much less critical in this initial period. If the bark becomes covered with green algae, a light wash now and again will make the stripes stand out. **BG**

Acer davidii subsp. grosseri
SNAKEBARK MAPLE

Type: hardy, deciduous tree
Soil & situation: moist, well-drained, fertile soil/full sun or light shade
North American hardiness zone: 5–7
Height & spread: 14m (46ft)
Grow for: size, shape and bark

Some trees have all the luck and this is one of them. It is trouble-free, grows to a reasonable size, is usually well shaped and has one of the finest barks of any maple.

The green-barked trunk and main branches are streaked with pure white stripes. Mid-green leaves turn to orange and then a buttery-yellow in autumn. Pendent racemes of pale yellow flowers appear in spring and are followed, in autumn, by long, trailing clusters of pink-brown, winged keys or seeds.

Acer davidii subsp. *grosseri*

It will grow well on most fertile soils but the young shoots suffer dieback when planted in waterlogged ground. Large plants transplant well providing they are lifted in late autumn with a good rootball and are watered regularly during the first season after moving.

Occasionally it will produce double leader branches which form a narrow angle. Remove the weakest stem with sharp secateurs and train the remaining leader upright by tying it with raffia to a bamboo cane. Cleaning the bark of a mature tree with a power hose or rubbing with a wet piece of hessian will remove the grime and algae leaving the stripes very obvious. Propagation is by grafting in late summer. **JC**

Acer griseum

Acer griseum
PAPERBARK MAPLE

Type: hardy, deciduous tree
Soil & situation: fertile, well-drained, neutral to alkaline soil/full sun or partial shade
North American hardiness zone: 4–8
Height & spread: 10m (33ft)
Grow for: rich autumn leaf colour irrespective of weather conditions; the spectacular mahogany coloured, peeling bark makes this a 'must-have' tree; AGM

There are too many acers available to select and highlight just one but, for me, weak winter sunlight makes this tree's bark glow. The tissue-thin curls of bark demand little (and large) fingers to peel them off. As the older mahogany bark is stripped the under-layer of cinnamon is revealed. The very thing to perk you up in mid-winter.

Left: Acer palmatum var. *heptalobum*

Achillea ptarmica 'Taygetea'

Type: hardy, evergreen perennial
Soil & situation: any well-drained garden soil/ flowers better and lives longer on poorer soils/ full sun
North American hardiness zone: 3–8
Height & spread: 60cm (24in)
Grow for: a good border mainstay; the pale lemon-yellow to cream flowers last from summer till early autumn

The name comes from Achilles who, it is said, discovered its medicinal qualities. If you add this plant to an area of planting it scores on several points, adding both good form and colour. The foliage is produced in hummocks of finely cut, long grey-green leaves. When the mass of flowers arrives in summer they are held high above the foliage – on show for all to see. They are very attractive to bees and butterflies. The roots are rhizomatous so it will spread and this can be to its advantage in more natural, larger-scale perennial and grass plantings. Its tolerance of drier conditions also makes it well suited to the hurly-burly of this type of situation. In more traditional border positions, its neighbours should be planned carefully or it may tend to invade them if not kept in check. Another favourite achillea, which is taller (up to 1.2m/4ft) and has flat flowerheads with a strong, gold-yellow colour is *A. filipendulina* 'Gold Plate' (AGM).

This plant does not need staking. It tends to be fairly short-lived but is easy to propagate from division. Unfortunately it can suffer from powdery mildew. It is a fabulous plant for cutting and drying – flowers are best cut when young so that they retain their colour. If you cut them early the plant may well produce a second flush of flowers. **BG**

Achillea ptarmica 'Taygetea'

The dark green leaves are made up of three leaflets, which turn to bright orange, scarlet and crimson in autumn and remain until late in the season. The bright yellow flowers droop gracefully in spring but, because *A. griseum* has separate male and female flowers, the seed is often without an embryo and cannot germinate.

A tree is for life, so don't rush the planting. Dig in lots of old manure or compost. Spread the roots and plant at the same depth as before. Remove low branches if they get in the way of grass cutting or other plants. If they are allowed to thicken then their late removal will result in scarring on the trunk. **JC**

Acer palmatum var. *heptalobum*
JAPANESE MAPLE

Type: hardy, deciduous tree
Soil & situation: moist, humus-rich, well-drained soil/full sun or partial shade
North American hardiness zone: 5–8
Height: 5m (16ft)
Spread: 6m (20ft)
Grow for: elegant form; amazing autumn colour

Every garden should have a Japanese maple. Where there is sufficient space this is one I would recommend for shape and autumn colour.

The 5–12cm (2–5in) long, palmate leaves have seven to nine long, tapering lobes with finely toothed margins. In autumn the bright green leaves turn orange and finally scarlet. The foliage is held until late autumn. Small, pendent, purple-red flowers are followed by red-winged fruit in early autumn.

Like most Japanese maples this variety will tolerate alkaline or acid soils providing they are deep and retain moisture. Avoid planting in sites exposed to cold spring winds, which will scorch the young foliage. A woodland situation with partial shade is ideal. Mulch with leafmould every autumn after leaf fall. It is possible to transplant large specimens providing the rootball has been prepared the previous year. Dig a trench 30cm (12in) deep and wide around the plant directly below the outside spread of the tree. Cut any roots and backfill the trench with peat or old compost.

Pruning is only necessary to shape the plant and should be carried out in late summer or early autumn when the sap is falling. Young, strong sideshoots should be shortened in spring. Propagation is by grafting in late winter or budding in late summer. Seed will not come true and the resulting plants will be variable. **JC**

Acer pensylvanicum
Plant of the Week (see page 397)

Coffea arabica

COFFEE

Type: tender evergreen shrub to small tree
Soil & situation: moist, humus-rich soil/light shade/ under cover
Hardiness zone: 10–11
Height: 7m (23ft)
Spread: 3m (10ft)
Grow for: white, jasmine-like scented flowers and red cherry-like berries – you may even gather enough to make a cup of coffee! A striking evergreen subject for the conservatory or greenhouse, and a breath of fresh air in January when not much else is cheerful.

Of great educational interest, as well as being really attractive in leaf and flower, coffee is one of the plants that almost everyone wants to see when I mention I grow it in my greenhouse. To make coffee the berries need to be fermented, cured and roasted in fairly large batches, so one or two plants are unlikely to furnish enough to make a properamount, but it is still really interesting to see the berries form. Some of the original cultivators in Africa ate the berry raw and in the Far East the leaves were used to make coffee, but I can't vouch for the safety of these practices. *C. liberica* is similar and equally worth growing.

Native to the African and Arabian tropics, coffee once formed wild forests in Abyssinia and the Sudan, yet apparently remained unknown to the ancients. First used by the Arabs, it was noted by travellers in the 15th century and introduced to London in the middle of the 17th. Taking coffee quickly became a national vice, to be rivalled – and in the UK outdone – only by tea, which arrived about a decade later and for some reason displaced its forerunner, whereas in the rest of the world coffee triumphed.

Coffee must be grown in a warm greenhouse or conservatory where, like gardenias (see page 187), it likes bright light but not direct sun. It can be quite long-lived – perhaps 25 years – if the cold or mealy bug does not get it. Coffee can be hard pruned in spring when too large.

Sow in warmth with *fresh* seed – old seed is hard to germinate and roasted coffee beans are roasted! The main and most consistent problem is mealy bug – regular jetting down on warm days using a high-pressure hose and a soapy spray will control them.   **BF**

Achillea 'Terracotta'

Achillea 'Terracotta'
YARROW, MILLFOIL

Type: hardy, herbaceous perennial
Soil & situation: free-draining soil/sun
North American hardiness zone: 3–8
Height: 75cm (30in)
Spread: 60cm (24in)
Grow for: form and flowers from early summer to early autumn

It's a spectacular change in fortune to rise from being a scruffy lawn weed to become the star of the summer border, yet it's exactly what the yarrow has done. It's mainly because of the interest in natural planting led by the Dutch garden designer Piet Oudolf and others who use the flat flowerheads to provide dabs of colour and form to contrast with other architectural plants like grasses and sea holly (*Eryngium bourgatii*, see page 166). Some achilleas are in single colours, others have flowers with a central eye and many change colour with age. The colour ranges from purple to pale pink, orange, salmon and pale yellow, all with stiff stems and feathery foliage. They are good for cutting and drying; some are fascinating, while others are beautiful!

Achillea 'Terracotta' with its orange-yellow flowers fading to cream is my favourite, but there are lots

Achillea 'Gold Plate'

of others worth trying. *A.* 'Inca Gold' is bright yellow with an orange flush, fading through yellow with pale orange petal tips to pale lemon. *A.* 'Lachsschönheit' is salmon-pink through pale yellow to white-flushed pale pink! It grows to 1.2m (4ft) and needs staking, as does *A.* 'Christine's Pink', which is pink, fading to white with pink eyes. *A.* 'Belle Epoque' is bright red, with faint yellow streaks and a pinkish-white 'eye', it fades through pale yellow flushed dark pink to pale yellow.

In the rush for the 'new' we shouldn't forget *A. filipendulina* 'Gold Plate' and *A. f.* 'Cloth of Gold' with their huge bright yellow flowerheads and pale lemon *A.* 'Moonshine', which have been loyal servants for years.

They need full sun in poor, well-drained soil; dead-head after flowering. *A. filipendulina* and its cultivars are useful plants to give structure in the winter garden. Divide in spring.   **MB**

Aconitum carmichaelii

Type: hardy, herbaceous perennial
Soil & situation: prefers moist but well-drained soils/shade or sun
North American hardiness zone: 3–7
Height: 1.5–1.8m (5–6ft)
Spread: 30–40cm (12–16in)
Grow for: exceptionally handsome plants; their strong blue spikes add stature and good strong colour to any border

I think many people are wary of aconitums because of the poison they contain. It is in fact an alkaloid called aconitine, which is one of the most toxic substances found in plants. But strangely enough, compounds derived from *A. carmichaelii* have long been used for medicinal purposes too. (It was mentioned in Chinese literature in AD 200.) Extracts from the roots are used as stimulants for the heart, pain killers and for anti-rheumatic effects. So it's not all evil and it certainly is beautiful.

There are several different forms of *A. carmichaelii*. (*A. fischeri* was the form grown in many gardens as this plant and now is just known as *A. carmichaelii*.) Plant names have never been easy, now they are highly mobile too. Anyway, *A. fischeri* that was is easy, good looking and vigorous, it flowers late, sometimes in October by which time the leaves are just starting to turn. *A. c.* 'Kelmscott' has been awarded an AGM, so it

is a safe bet that it is a reliably good plant. It produces tall spires of lavender-blue flowers in early to mid-autumn.

Aconites can sometimes become too crowded and when that happens their propensity for flowering is reduced. However, they do not respond well to being disturbed so only divide them when extra feed and moisture are not triggering a better performance. Division is best done in autumn. They are often quick off the mark in spring so they tend to catch you out if you leave it till then. An annual mulch is good – it helps to retain moisture, which is always appreciated.   **BG**

Aconitum carmichaelii

Aconitum hemsleyanum

Aconitum hemsleyanum

Type: hardy, climbing perennial
Soil & situation: moist, humus-rich soils which do not dry out/partial shade or full sun.
North American hardiness zone: 4–7
Height: 2–3m (6½–10ft)
Spread: 45cm (18in)
Grow for: racemes of beautiful, indigo-violet flowers in mid-summer to autumn; scrambling and twining stems

The majority of aconitums are non-climbing but this unusual plant is one of the exceptions, able to climb and intermingle amongst large shrubs in a relaxed, informal way. The intense deep colour of their flowers looks even more vivid when scrambling through a white-flowered plant such as lacecap hydrangea. I always find this an irresistible colour combination. I keep meaning to acquire some *A.* 'Bressingham Spire' (AGM) which has violet-blue flowers, is a non-climbing aconitum and flowers from mid-summer to early autumn. The flowering can be prolonged further by removing the flower spikes once they are past it. It is worth being aware that every part of the aconitum family is highly toxic to people and animals.

As this plant appreciates moisture it is generally far better planted in the autumn. Mulch each spring to help keep soil moisture levels high. Once established these plants will do far better if left undisturbed as their tuberous roots resent movement. Propagate carefully by division; or alternatively it is extremely easy from seed. The colour of the flower varies when it is grown from seed, though you will have to wait until its second year when it starts to flower to find out. I was lucky – mine came a good, strong colour – but do not be dissuaded from having a second try if the first batch are rather a wishy-washy blue. **BG**

Actaea simplex Atropurpurea Group (syn. *Cimicifuga simplex*)
BUGBANE

Type: hardy perennial
Soil & situation: happiest in rich, moist soils, it should not be allowed to dry out during the growing season/prefers light shade
North American hardiness zone: 4–8
Height: 1.5m (5ft)
Spread: 60cm (24in)
Grow for: dramatic foliage plant, with purple leaves, stems and buds; furry, bottle-brush-like, white flowers in autumn

Another of those high-value plants but this one is fussy about moisture levels. My mother grows it in her garden (thin, limestone brash, but heavily adulterated) but she has irrigation, and she is in the wet West Country. In the vast stock beds in her perennial nursery it looks out of this world in the autumn. It has tall, furry, white pokers of see-through flowers and rich, dark purple stems carrying the shiny, green-purple, slightly incised leaves. It is definitely architectural, yet possesses colour, form and flowers – quite a combination.

In less than perfect conditions do what you can to improve the moisture conditions: mulches in spring, organic matter on planting, sheltered site and be at the ready with the watering can when it looks even slightly in want of a drink. To some degree you can mollycoddle it through the first couple of years in less than perfect conditions and then leave it to it, but not if your soil is too sharp-draining and your rainfall low to boot. Apart from this, there is not a lot to be done. It does not require staking despite its stature. It has attractive seedheads, so leave these on so you can enjoy its winter performance too. It is also appealing in flower arrangements. Cut it back when it looks too ragged in late winter/spring. Divide in spring when you have to, which is infrequently. Propagation is often from seed, but the foliage colour will vary, so select out the stunners. **BG**

Actea simplex Atropurpurea Group

Actinidia chinensis

Actinidia chinensis
KIWI/CHINESE GOOSEBERRY

Type: frost-hardy, deciduous, woody, perennial climber
Soil & situation: most soils, moist but not wet/full sun to light shade/prefers warm, sheltered gardens
North American hardiness zone: 7–9
Height: can reach 9m (30ft)
Spread: to 4.5–5m (15–16ft)
Grow for: masses of creamy buff-coloured scented flowers in summer; edible, brown, furry-covered fruits with green flesh in late autumn

The kiwi is firstly a fruiting plant but it has very beautiful young pink shoots; attractive, large, heart-shaped leaves; and such good flowers that it deserves a place in the flower garden. Other species such as *Actinidia arguta* and *A. kolomikta* are similar. They are all closely related to camellias and although the flowers are not as showy, those of most species are sweetly scented – and the edible fruits are rich in vitamins. Coming from China and the Far East, the kiwi has become a major greenhouse crop in many countries where it is grown in surplus tomato houses, but it has been a garden plant for a hundred years. Although normally left to ramble, it can be trained as an espalier, which I have seen done in France.

It needs a tree or strong supports to climb, with tying in and removal of dead wood in winter. To ensure fruiting, you must have both a male and female plant – or buy a new hermaphrodite variety. It can be grown from seed and will fruit in five to ten years. Layer in autumn or take half-ripe cuttings in late summer. Late frosts tend to take off flowers. **BF**

Actinidia kolomikta

Type: hardy, deciduous, climbing shrub
Soil & situation: fertile, well-drained soil/full sun
North American hardiness zone: 5–8
Height: 9m (30ft)
Spread: to 4.5–5m (15–16ft)
Grow for: slightly exotic leaf colouring; fast growing; AGM

I don't really want everyone to plant this climber. It would become common and cease to be a talking point for visitors. Serious questions from adults include queries as to my reasons for painting the leaves.

It is a fast-growing, vigorous, twining climber with 15cm (6in) long, dark green leaves which, when they first emerge, are tinged purple. The top half of the leaf becomes variegated with splashes of white and bright pink. The colour is at its best when grown against a wall in full sun. Clusters of three, fragrant, white flowers appear in early summer. Female plants produce a smooth-skinned, greenish-yellow fruit in autumn.

Keep the root area cool and shaded by mulching annually, in spring, with 10cm (4in) of composted bark. Pruning is usually only carried out to thin the number of climbing stems. When necessary, prune in mid-winter. Plant in a sheltered position, out of the reach of cold winds.

Propagate by softwood cuttings in late summer. Place small cuttings round the inside edge of the pot in an open, gritty compost. They will root quickly, but bear in mind the plant's vigour and don't be tempted to plant out too many. **JC**

Actinidia kolomikta

Aeonium 'Zwartkop'

Aeonium 'Zwartkop'

Type: tender, succulent subshrub
Soil & situation: free-draining soil/partial shade/minimum temperature of 10°C (20°C)
North American hardiness zone: 10–11
Height & spread: up to 2m (6½ft), usually less
Grow for: dramatic purple-black foliage borne in rosettes at the end of branches; AGM

This is a really stunning foliage plant with many uses. It is a good house plant and can be grown in a greenhouse or conservatory, but I think it comes into its own when you put it outside during the warmer months. It looks well in a pot or can be planted into the soil, preferably in a gravel area, so that the distinct form of branches tipped with the amazingly coloured rosettes can be appreciated. *Aeonium arboreum* is similar, but has light green leaves, sometimes they are mottled in a purplish-green. It is not as dramatic but is still a very special foliage plant and may even survive a short, mild frost provided that the compost is on the dry side. It is better in the sun though has a tendency to wilt if very hot.

If growing this in a pot use a gritty, loam-based soil or cactus compost and let it dry out between waterings. When, or if, you plant it outside, plant it in a free-draining moderately fertile soil. To propagate cut off a rosette of leaves, wait till a callus has formed, and then insert the base into a free-draining, gritty compost keeping it on the dry side till it has rooted. **BG**

Aesculus x *carnea* 'Briotii'
RED HORSE CHESTNUT

Type: hardy, deciduous shrub
Soil & situation: deep, moist, fertile, well-drained soil/sun or partial shade
North American hardiness zone: 6–8
Height: 18m (60ft)
Spread: 13m (43ft)
Grow for: wonderful form; autumn leaf colour; eye-catching flowers; AGM

Chestnuts bring back happy childhood memories. The large 'fingered leaves' were probably the first I ever drew (badly) at school; the game of conkers was an important part of playground life; and I was encouraged to grow them from seed with embarrassing results years later when the tree filled our garden and the one on either side.

Aesculus x *carnea* 'Briotii' originated in France and represents beautifully all the charm and grace of the true Parisian. It forms a large spreading tree with glossy, dark green, crinkly edged, overlapping leaflets. Following a hot, dry summer the foliage sometimes displays some red and gold autumn colour. The large, upright, 20–30cm (8–12in) panicles of candle-like flowers appear in early summer. They are deep red with a yellow centre. Very few 'conkers' are produced, the shells of which are less spiny than the white-flowered horse chestnut, *A. hippocastanum*. Warty growths usually appear on the bark of mature trees. They are harmless and should not be removed. When grown as a specimen in parkland the branches will sweep down to ground level. Propagation is usually by bud grafting in summer. **JC**

Aesculus x *carnea* 'Briotii'

Agapanthus praecox subsp. *orientalis*

Agapanthus praecox subsp. *orientalis*

Type: half-hardy, evergreen perennial
Soil & situation: well-drained soil/full sun/some winter protection
North American hardiness zone: 9–11
Height: 90cm (36in)
Spread: 60cm (24in)
Grow for: beautiful blue globe-shaped flowers from mid- to late summer; attractive, glossy leaves

There is quite a variety of different agapanthus; generally the evergreen forms with the broader, strappy bright green leaves are more tender than the hardier forms, such as *Agapanthus* Headbourne hybrids, which are deciduous, and hardy to –15°C (5°F). The flowers of the evergreen forms are bold, beautiful and stunning, whereas the deciduous forms tend to be far less eye-catching, smaller and less freely produced. These plants give an exotic air when shown off in huge tubs, with their sky-blue balls adding a tropical feel. They tell you it really is summer, even when the sky is less than bright blue. The flowers are long-lived and are excellent for cutting.

I grow them in large pots and tend to leave them undivided until they are bursting at the seams. They are said to flower better under crowded conditions, but you do have to make sure that you will be able to get them out without demolishing the pot. (I learnt this one from bitter experience.) In these confined conditions, unless you feed and water them well right up until they have finished flowering, you will find flowering much diminished (also learnt from bitter experience). When you do split them, a simple way is to break the clump into two and re-pot the entire half. This way, flower production the year following splitting is not unduly affected. Winter protection can take the form of a frost-free greenhouse and ensuring that they are watered infrequently, although I tend to just mulch the pots heavily in winter, and provided the position is sheltered, that seems to do the trick. **BG**

Agave americana 'Marginata'

Agave americana

Type: tender, evergreen, succulent perennial
Soil & situation: free-draining soil/sunny position/protection needed in winter, except for large specimens in milder climates
North American hardiness zone: 9–11
Height: 2m (6½ft)
Spread: 3m (10ft)
Grow for: architectural plants with pale green to grey leaves growing in spreading, relaxed rosettes; AGM

I have grown this plant for about four years now, in containers. My specimens are 40cm (16in) high and I have not covered them in winter or even moved the pots back against a wall. I am one of those gardeners who does take chances, but so far I have got away with it in the East Midlands. I am kinder to my variegated version, *A. americana* 'Marginata', also potted, but only a mere 20cm (8in) high, as I pull it in under a south-facing porch when the evening skies and temperatures tell me to watch it. Agaves look perfect in large containers or in gravel. I got sucked into them when I designed a tropical garden for Chelsea, and spent intoxicated hours browsing around specialist nurseries looking at exotica. They are succulents and have characteristic fat, juicy-looking leaves with slightly wavy edges and spines all the way up. Try to avoid coming into too close contact with these if you ever re-pot them. One or two of their leaves bend back, like a swan's neck. As the new leaf slowly opens out it leaves a curious wavy imprint on its old bedfellow. These plants are called 'the century plants', supposedly because they are a great age before they flower. Mine have not yet, but apparently some species take about

eight years, others a mere 30 or 40. I am not sure if I want them to flower though, as the energy required often kills them. The flowers can grow to a height of 9m (30ft), are pale yellow and are borne in panicles.

Grow these plants in bright sunlight, and if potted, feed them with a low nitrogen but high phosphate and potash element. As they grow really large you may need to remove the lower leaves and suckers to balance the look of the plant. Propagation from the suckers is simple – if roots are not already formed they soon do when the base is immersed in a free-draining compost. **BG**

Agrostemma githago
Plant of the Week (see page 193)

Ajuga reptans 'Catlin's Giant'

Type: hardy, evergreen perennial
Soil & situation: any moderately fertile soil/partial shade/will tolerate sun or full shade
North American hardiness zone: 3–9
Height: 1.5m (5ft)
Spread: 1m (3ft)
Grow for: useful, evergreen ground cover which dwarfs other bugles; leaves are a smart shade of purple about 15cm (6in) long; AGM

This is one of those low-maintenance, ground-cover plants. That phrase tends to make me think it should belong in a supermarket car park rather than a garden, but this is not so mundane. I used it in large sheets intermingled with ferns, for the

Ajuga reptans 'Catlin's Giant'

Wind in the Willows garden, my first ever Chelsea garden, and it looked stunning. The flowers are produced on stout spikes, they are a bright, fresh blue set off by the rich, shiny, fluted leaves below. Again it is a plant that you need to be generous with, perhaps as a bold edge to a border or in repetitive clumps. Try mixing it with other higher-accent plants spangled amongst it to really enhance the level of interest – then it really comes into its own.

The leaves do reduce in size after flowering so it is worth cutting off the flowerheads, when they are past it, to negate this effect as far as possible. If the plant starts to run in unwanted directions, it may require reining back every so often. Otherwise it is a simple beast to maintain and look after. To propagate, you simply separate the rooted stems or take softwood cuttings in early summer. **BG**

Akebia quinata

Akebia quinata
CHOCOLATE VINE

Type: hardy, semi-evergreen climber
Soil & situation: moist, well-drained, fertile soil/full sun or partial shade
North American hardiness zone: 5–9
Height: 10m (33ft)
Spread: 9m (30ft)
Grow for: a graceful, fast-growing climber with delicate flowers, semi-evergreen leaves and strangely shaped fruits

Although this climber is a vigorous, rampant grower it gives the appearance of a delicate plant which isn't likely to be invasive. Given the right situation it will out-pace *Clematis montana* and most of the honeysuckles, at the same time managing to look graceful and desirable.

The dark green, rounded leaves are made up of five leaflets notched at their tips. The underside is blue-green turning purple-green in winter. The spicily perfumed clusters of red-purple flowers remind me of vanilla. They appear in late spring and early summer with the male and female flowers in the same 12cm (5in) pendent raceme. The male flowers are paler and are concentrated at the tip of the cluster. After a hot summer it will produce unusual sausage- shaped purple fruits up to 10cm (4in) long with a white pulp holding jet-black seeds.

Pollination will be improved if two plants are growing in the same location. Where there is likely to be late frosts give it some protection to reduce the risk of damage to the early flowers. Pruning is only necessary to tidy the plant and keep it within the available space and should be carried out immediately after flowering has finished. Propagate by sowing seed as soon as it is ripe or by rooting small 5cm (2in) semi-ripe cuttings in summer. Alternatively, where there are suitable low stems, layer some in a peat/grit mixture *in situ*. Large, well-rooted layers should be replanted as soon as possible after digging up. **JC**

Alcea rosea 'Nigra'
Plant of the Week (see page 217)

Alchemilla conjuncta

Type: hardy, herbaceous perennial
Soil & situation: any well-drained soil/sun or partial shade
North American hardiness zone: 3–7
Height: 40cm (16in)
Spread: 30cm (12in)
Grow for: attractive foliage and delicate flowers

Because *Alchemilla mollis* (see next entry), with its lovely lime-green foliage is such an attractive plant and is so easy to grow to the point of being invasive, other related species tend to be overlooked. All of those mentioned below have smaller leaves but still collect the droplets of dew and rain that make them so delectable.

I love pretty little clump-forming *A. conjuncta* with its deeply lobed, mid-green leaves with silvery hairs below, which provide a sheen to the margins. The closely related *A. alpina*, Alpine lady's mantle, is a creeping woody rootstock and forms a dense carpet of rounded leaves with up to seven deep lobes with toothed margins. The tiny yellow-green flowers appear from early to late summer on stems only 12cm (5in) long. It grows to 12cm (5in) x 50cm (20in) and looks very pretty in a rock garden. *A. erythropoda* has grey to blue-green, strongly toothed leaves with deep lobes, dense hair on the leaf stalks and lime-green flowers. It grows to 20cm (8in) each way. These are all worth considering as alternatives. They are ideal for edging or filling gaps in paths and a combination of several species creates an interesting texture.

They need a moist, humus-rich soil in sun or partial shade but tolerate most soils. Divide in early spring or autumn; transplant self-sown seedlings. Dead-head to prevent excessive seeding.
Slugs and snails can damage young foliage. **MB**

Alchemilla mollis
LADY'S MANTLE

Type: hardy, deciduous perennial
Soil & situation: moist, humus-rich soil/full sun or partial shade
North American hardiness zone: 4–7
Height: 60cm (24in)
Spread: 80cm (32in)
Grow for: excellent ground cover making it very useful for the front of the border; the prettiest

Left: Alchemilla conjuncta

Alchemilla mollis

sight after rainfall; AGM
I have a circle of this perennial outside my front door. In summer, after heavy rain, when everything is soggy, it cheers me up. Droplets of water rest and move like beads of mercury on its pale green, pleated leaves with one large drop securely held at the base of each leaf. The masses of frothy, greenish-yellow flowers appear in summer lasting well into autumn. They are carried on long stems, which topple over the foliage like boiling lemon curd.

If you remove the spent flowerheads before seed is set you will save yourself hours of weeding. The seed germinates readily and will grow in every crevice of the garden. Remove all of the foliage at the same time cutting it close to the ground. Water and feed with a liquid tomato fertilizer, then sit back and watch a second batch of new leaves unfurl.

This is a good ground-covering plant for impoverished soil and is drought tolerant. Propagation is by seed sown fresh or, where it has self-sown, lift and transplant the young plants in the spring. Large clumps may be divided in late autumn or early spring. The flowers are excellent for use in flower arranging. **JC**

Bunny adds:
This adaptable plant may prefer moist, humus-rich soil, but as John says it is also great for impoverished soil and is drought-tolerant. Basically it grows anywhere! Dead-head the flowers to encourage further flushes during the summer.

Mahonia japonica

Type: hardy evergreen shrub
Soil & situation: any well-drained soil/light sun to heavy shade
Hardiness zone: 7–8
Height & spread: may reach 1–2m (3–6½ft) all round
Grow for: glossy, dark green, distinctive evergreen with scented yellow flowers in the depths of winter; occasional blue-black berries; AGM

All the mahonias are good plants, with their fresh, spiky, usually glossy foliage making them look like a holly on steroids, and their cheerful yellow racemes of flowers in mid-winter giving off gorgeous lily-of-the-valley-like perfume. I love the way they perfume my front drive for weeks on end. *M. aquifolium* is a near contender for my favourite as it bears edible blue-black berries more reliably and more prolifically, giving it the name Oregon grape – they make a very tasty jelly.

Originally thought to belong to the genus *Berberis*, the 75 or so species of mahonia are natives of North America and the Far East, and do not have spiny stems like berberis. They are named after Bernard MacMahon, an early American botanist. *M. japonica* is a species but has often been confused with the rarer, similar *M. bealei* and also with many hybrids such as *M. bealei* x *napaulensis*; it makes very little difference which of these you end up with as they are all so similar and delightful. In other words if you can scarcely tell them apart it don't much matter!

As long as the soil is well drained they are happy, even on chalk, but they are not so keen in full sun, really doing best under deciduous trees, which give shelter to their winter flowers. They can be cut back in late spring if getting old and leggy. As this is a species you can sow the seed at just about anytime, take half-ripe cuttings in mid-summer or layers almost anytime. They are usually problem free. **BF**

Allium cepa

Allium cepa
JAPANESE ONION

Type: hardy, biennial, bulbous vegetable
Soil & situation: rich soil with plentiful moisture/full sun, no shade
North American hardiness zone: 5–8
Height: vertical leaves up to knee height
Spread: none, but sow at least 5cm (2in) apart
Grow for: one of the earliest onion crops

I find this an extremely valuable crop, as it ripens weeks before either sets or spring-sown seed, just when the stored onions have run out and the bought ones are at their most expensive.

Japanese onions do not store well themselves, so should be used up first.

Introduced from Japan, these have almost totally replaced traditional autumn-sown onion varieties. In the East it is said that when Satan left the garden of Eden onions sprang from where his right foot stepped and garlic from his left.

Plant in firm, potash-rich soil in full sun with wide spacing. Must be sown in situ in late summer. Give cloche covers in very hard winters, and do not transplant. Slugs love these young onions, so I mix in the seed of Buffalo onion, which they prefer, leaving Japanese sorts relatively untouched. **BF**

Allium hollandicum 'Purple Sensation'

Type: hardy, bulbous perennial
Soil & situation: fertile but well-drained soil/full sun
North American hardiness zone: 4–10
Height: up to 1m (3ft) high
Spread: 7.5cm (3in)
Grow for: dramatic, deep violet 8cm (3½in) spheres on tall green wands in mid-summer, followed by attractive dried heads, which persist well into the winter; AGM

This is another plant with a name change – it was formerly known as *A. flatuense*. I always associate it with the Chelsea Flower Show, where large quantities of them are regularly produced for the occasion. They are breathtaking when they arrive, massed together in the van, with their beautifully dramatic, globular flowers on top of the tall, leafless stems. It is, of course, a luxury to be able to position the flowering plant, threading them through other plants and see the planting being 'lifted' as you work with them. In 'real' gardens they work pretty much the same, except of course, you have to imagine how they will look the following summer. Also as the flowers start to emerge, the silvery-tinted foliage at the base withers, so the ideal is to conceal it with low planting that is not too dense to overly shade it. Thankfully, these plants do not smell too onion-like, because they make an amazing cut flower.

Plant the bulbs about 10cm (4in) deep in the autumn. They will self-seed and spread happily on some soils. On others, like mine, I tend to bulk up the numbers with new bulbs when they start to look thin. Alternatively, for the perfectionist with time, you can use them as bedding, lifting them and drying them off once they are past their best, ready for replanting the following autumn. **BG**

Allium hollandicum 'Purple Sensation'

Allium schoenoprasum
CHIVES

Type: herbaceous, clump-forming, perennial vegetable
Soil & situation: any soil with plentiful moisture/full sun to light shade
North American hardiness zone: 3–9
Height & spread: up to 45cm (18in) in rich soil; less in poor soil
Grow for: good edging plant, beautiful purple flowers, edible

There are few plants that make a quicker or neater edging for a vegetable bed. Chives are very beautiful in flower, which benefits many insects; they are also indispensable in soups, stews and salads, especially when egg is an ingredient, and as a garnish. Incidentally, it is more commonly grown in continental Europe than in the USA.

Chives are remarkably adaptable, but for the best results give them a rich, moist soil with plenty of sun. Dead-heading will prevent self-seeding and encourage more new leaves to appear. Propagate by sowing seed or by dividing clumps in spring. At almost any time it can be forced under cover for an earlier crop. Chives are prone to the same diseases as other alliums, especially rusts and moulds (see under Pest and Diseases, page 404). Dig up and burn infected plants and then start with new stock. **BF**

Allium schoenoprasum

Alnus cordata

Alnus cordata
ITALIAN ALDER

Type: hardy, deciduous tree
Soil & situation: fertile, well-drained soil/full sun
North American hardiness zone: 5–7
Height: 25m (80ft)
Spread: 7m (23ft)
Grow for: an attractive fast-growing tree for shelter; AGM

Of the three alders commonly grown this is the one I would consider attractive. The others, *Alnus glutinosa* (common English alder) and *A. incana* (grey alder) are dull but useful for windbreaks and planting in wet sites. *A. cordata* takes its common name from the fact that its timber was used for the piles that still keep Venice afloat. It grows well along river banks and close to water but unlike the other species it tolerates a dry soil. A fast-growing tree, it makes an excellent shelter belt.

The small, oval, finely toothed leaves are a bright, glossy green. Pendent, brown-yellow, male catkins 7.5cm (3in) long appear before the leaves in late winter and early spring. The cones are green, 3cm (1in) long, egg-shaped and occur in groups of three in summer. By winter they have turned black. Alders are the only broad-leafed trees to produce conifer-like cones.

Pruning is necessary only to maintain the tree's shape. Cutting should be completed by mid-winter before the sap starts to flow. Propagation is by fresh seed or rooting hardwood cuttings in early winter. **JC**

Aloe vera

Aloe vera

Type: long-lived perennial but tender succulent
Soil & situation: well-drained compost/moist in summer, dry in winter/greenhouse, conservatory or windowsill/full sun, no shade
North American hardiness zone: 10–11
Height & spread: in a big pot 60cm–1m (2–3ft)
Grow for: a tough survivor with attractive leaves year round; the rare flower is interesting and impressive; AGM

Aloe is a superb survivor for that sunny windowsill where it will tolerate neglect and yet always be architecturally attractive. Its thorn-free, grey-green, starfish-like appearance makes it interesting in an exotic, tropical sort of way. And, of course, *Aloe vera* is a fantastic plant for medicinal purposes; its soothing sap can be applied to burns, rashes and skin eruptions.

It is native to South America, though its name comes from Arabic. It has been introduced to many countries for its bitter sap, which was exported as a dried brown resin for medicinal use (and for putting on babies' thumbs to discourage sucking).

The site must be frost free, in full sun. Cut leaves for use, leaving a big stump remaining to allow withering and prevent rotting off. The easiest way to propagate is by the frequently found offsets, which can be detached to make new plants. It can also be grown from seed, but with difficulty. Do not let its compost become waterlogged, especially not in winter.   **BF**

Aloysia triphylla (syn. *Lippia citriodora*)
LEMON VERBENA

Type: frost-hardy, deciduous perennial, shrubby but semi-herbaceous in habit
Soil & situation: well-drained soil outdoors or moist compost indoors/full sun outdoors but will tolerate some shade indoors/in a pot give plenty of moisture when in growth
North American hardiness zone: 8–11
Height & spread: forms a clump up to 2m x 1m (6½ft x 3ft)
Grow for: scented foliage throughout spring, summer and autumn; scented flowers in summer; AGM

I just love the true lemon sherbet perfume this plant carries – it is said that a leaf folded away in a book still smells decades later! I like to use small amounts in cookery and I'm always pulling off leaves and sniffing them. It can also be used in potpourris or to make teas and tisanes. It is a native of South America, where more than 30 species exist. *Aloysia triphylla* is the only one that can survive outdoors in more temperate climates.

It is a wonderful plant for a warm site or greenhouse, conservatory or windowsill. Ideally plant in a well-drained soil with some light cover against hard frosts; it will then overwinter and come again in spring, much like many fuchsias. However, it may be lost in hard winters, so take cuttings as back up, either in autumn with heat or in spring once growth commences. It can also be grown from seed. A bit prone to aphids and red spider mites when pot-grown undercover, but these disappear if it is planted out for summer or when it is permanently outdoors.   **BF**

Aloysia triphylla

Amaranthus caudatus 'Fat Spike'

Amaranthus caudatus 'Fat Spike'
LOVE-LIES-BLEEDING OR TASSEL FLOWER

Type: hardy annual
Soil & situation: infertile, moist soil/full sun
North American hardiness zone: annual
Height: 90cm (36in)
Spread: 45cm (18in)
Grow for: a bushy plant with upright spikes of purple-red flowers; very useful for summer bedding

The traditional love-lies-bleeding *Amaranthus caudatus*, with its long, red or yellow tassels of flower is a great plant for summer bedding. This variety is different and eye-catching. The spikes are upright but every bit as showy.

The 15cm (6in) long, light green leaves on pale yellow-green stems form a bushy plant. The small, densely packed, dark purplish-red flowers, produced during summer and autumn, are held in an upright, spike-like cyme 30–45cm (12–18in) long on a branched stalk. The spike of flowers is 7cm (2³/₄in) thick at the base tapering to 2cm (³/₄in) at the tip. It is particularly useful for filling gaps in the border or as a centre dot plant to give height in a bedding scheme. The branched spike is excellent fresh or dried in a flower arrangement.

It will flower better when grown in a poor soil with no added fertilizer. Watering in summer will extend the flowering period. Propagation is by seed sown in a heated propagator in mid-spring. It may also be sown directly into the soil where it is to flower in late spring. Thin the seedlings to 45cm (18in) apart. **JC**

Amelanchier 'Ballerina'
SNOWY MESPILUS, JUNEBERRY

Type: hardy, deciduous tree
Soil & situation: moisture-retentive but not waterlogged, acid soil/sun or partial shade
North American hardiness zone: 5–8
Height: 6m (20ft)
Spread: 7m (23ft)
Grow for: attractive flowers, edible fruit and brightly coloured autumn foliage; AGM

If I had to decide on only one tree for my garden *Amelanchier* 'Ballerina' would be in a short shortlist. It provides interest for most of the year with flower, fruit and leaf colour. The star-shaped, white flowers appear in early spring forming long arching racemes just before, or at the same time as the new, young foliage. Opening a bronze-green the foliage turns a glossy mid-green in summer. In autumn it again changes to deep red-purple lasting until the first hard frost.

The edible fruit is sweet and juicy, red at first, ripening to a dark blue-black. You have to be quick to beat the birds or else net the tree. *A.* 'Ballerina' is a hybrid of *A. laevis*, an open-headed spreading tree which our American cousins call the Allegheny service-berry.

Propagation is by semi-ripe cuttings in summer. Pruning is necessary only to keep a tidy shape. Remove crossing branches in late winter when they are still dormant. This tree is recorded as being prone to fire blight disease, but I have never met anyone who has experienced the problem. Of more importance is its dislike for alkaline soil. **JC**

Amelanchier 'Ballerina'

Ameleanchier lamarckii

Amelanchier lamarckii

Type: hardy, deciduous large shrub or small tree
Soil & situation: moist, rich, well-drained, acid soil/sun or partial shade
North American hardiness zone: 3–7
Height: 10m (33ft)
Spread: 12m (40ft)
Grow for: young leaves, flowers and autumn colour; AGM

Act I begins in spring when the pure white flowers, like a mass of snowflakes, appear in loose open clusters at the same time as the coppery-pink, silky young leaves are emerging. It is a truly magnificent sight, particularly when you consider this plant is not a fancy prima donna but a tough, durable, trouble-free plant that is happy to put on a show anywhere, from cities and industrial sites to soft suburban gardens. As if exhausted by the effort it sits quietly through the summer then emerges again in autumn awash in rich red and orange; its performance in shade where yellow is the dominant colour is comparatively muted. It is rather promiscuous and hybridizes freely with other species, producing sweet black fruits that are devoured by birds. It has been naturalized in the UK for over a century and was once cultivated for its fruit in cottage gardens of Holland and northwest Germany. It is naturalized there too and known as the 'currant tree', as the fruits were dried and used as currants or stewed and made into jam.

It needs moist, well-drained, acid soil in sun or partial shade but tolerates poorer conditions. Pruning is only necessary to keep it within its allotted space. It can be grown as a single or multi-stemmed tree; prune accordingly. Propagate from fresh seed or by semi-ripe cuttings in summer, or by layering. If sowing is delayed it may become dormant and take two years to germinate. **MB**

Amsonia tabernaemontana var. *salicifolia*
BLUE STAR

Type: hardy, herbaceous perennial
Soil & situation: any fertile soil/sun
North American hardiness zone: 3–9
Height: 60cm (24in)
Spread: 40cm (16in)
Grow for: pale blue flowers from mid-spring to
mid-summer

This herbaceous gem produces a clump of dark
green, narrow-leaved stems that are tar-black
towards the tip with slightly drooping, rounded
flowerheads. The powder-blue petals are slate-
blue below but to appreciate their fine qualities
you have to stoop down low! The species, from
eastern North America, has broader leaves and is
more familiar in gardens than *A. t.* var. *salicifolia*;
sadly neither is particularly common. A relative,
Amsonia orientalis from northeast Greece and
northwest Turkey, struggles further still, ironically
it is freely available in commerce – and almost
extinct in the wild!

The reasons for growing it are for its fascinating
colour combination and the interminably long
rambling name; it seems overblown for
something so subdued!

Here's something about its origin. *Amsonia* was
named for Dr Charles Amson, an 18th century-
physician from Virginia, USA. *Tabernaemontana*
was named for Jakob Theodor von Bergzabern,
physician to the Count of Palatine in Heidelberg,
West Germany who Latinized his name to
Tabernaemontanus! He wrote a herbal called
Neu Kreuterbuch (1588–91) and in 1590, published
the illustrations separately using over 1,500
woodcuts copied from illustrations in other

Amsonia tabernaemontana var. *salicifolia*

books! These were later acquired by a London
printer from his colleague in Frankfurt and were
used to illustrate John Gerard's 16th-century
Herball, one of the most famous 'Old English'
writings on medicinal plants.

A. t. var. *salicifolia* (meaning 'willow leaved')
needs moist, well-drained, fertile soil in full sun; it
tolerates some drought. Cut back dead foliage,
feed with general fertilizer and mulch in spring.
Divide in autumn or spring; take basal or
softwood cuttings in early summer. **MB**

Ananas sativus
PINEAPPLE

Type: short-lived, very tender, herbaceous
perennial
Soil & situation: well-drained
compost/warmth/full sun, no shade
North American hardiness zone: 10–11
Height & spread: up to 1m (3ft) each way in a
big pot; in a small pot it will survive and throw
a pineapple chunk!
Grow for: good year-round indoor foliage plant;
staggering red flowerhead with violet petals;
superb fruit

Although it takes three years to flower and fruit
from a rooted crown, it is worth the wait. Few
tasks give as much sense of achievement, or taste
so divine, as growing then eating your own
pineapple! In a big pot kept in a warm
greenhouse or conservatory you can expect to
produce a fruit weighing up to 3–4kg (8lb) and
tasting better than any you have ever bought.

A native of the New World, first seen by
Europeans in 1493, pineapple took the Old
World by storm. It was first successfully grown in
Britain from the beginning of 18th century and is
now grown in all warm countries. Eat it as the last
of all fruits at the table as the flavour makes those
coming after seem insipid.

It needs warmth and a well-drained compost, but
keep it moist during summer heat and dryish for
the rest of the year. After fruiting, remove and
pot up sideshoots to replace old plants; bottom
heat greatly improves rooting, growing and
fruiting performance. Do not water when
ripening. Never grow from seed; instead root the
crown from healthy fruit or use offsets from
existing plants. Pineapples are prone to red
spider mite, scale and mealy bug but can be kept
clean with soapy sprays. Beware – the leaves have
small, sharp thorns. especially near the tips. **BF**

Ananas sativus

Andromeda polifolia
BOG ROSEMARY, MARSH ANDROMEDA

Type: hardy, low-growing, evergreen shrub
Soil & situation: moist, humus-rich, acid soil/sun
or partial shade
North American hardiness zone: 2–6
Height: 40cm (16in)
Spread: 60cm (24in)
Grow for: dainty flowers in late spring or early
summer

In the UK this is a native of squelchy sphagnum
peat bogs in central England, Wales and Scotland,
but rather than tramping through bogs where the
water always goes over your wellies, you may prefer
to grow it in the comfort of your own garden. It's
a low-growing, wiry-stemmed, evergreen shrub
and the clusters of slender, glaucous green foliage
suit the name bog rosemary perfectly. The pretty
white flowers in late spring are enchanting, like
dainty lanterns suffused with a soft pink blush.
They are ideal for moist pockets in rock or
woodland gardens and for the margins by streams

Andromeda polifolia

and ponds. Andromeda was the mythological daughter of Cepheus and Cassiope, who was chained to a rock as an offering to a sea monster but was rescued by Perseus. *Polifolia* means grey-leaved. The first name was given after Carl Linnaeus, who assigned the plant its Latin name, had an amusing experience while discovering the plant – but I can't find out the secret!

Forms of *Andromeda polifolia* include 'Alba', which has a straggly habit, glaucous foliage and pure white flowers; 'Microphylla' with broad leaves and bright pink flowers; and the compact 'Nikko'.

Andromeda needs moist, acid, peaty soil in full sun or partial shade. Protect from scorching summer sun. Mulch annually in spring with leafmould. It succeeds better in the ground, with 3–5cm (1–2in) of sphagnum moss around to act as a sponge. To propagate, sow seed in spring or root softwood cuttings in early to mid-summer. Pot suckers or rooted layers in autumn. **MB**

Anemone blanda

Type: hardy tuberous perennial
Soil & situation: free-draining soil, preferably quite moist and humus-rich/sun or partial shade/after flowering copes well with dry conditions for summer dormancy
North American hardiness zone: 4–8
Height & spread: 15cm (6in)
Grow for: beautiful blue, mauve, white or pink solitary flowers from late winter to spring; will quickly form bright carpets of colour in areas with light, alkaline soil; will naturalize in turf; AGM

Anemone blanda

These delightful, early spring-flowering plants are so easy to grow, and quickly form satisfying, large swathes of colour at a bleak time of year. They are also ideal for colonizing difficult, dry shade. After the flowers die off the whole plant disappears without trace, so ferns, foxgloves and other woodland plants can spread out and fill in the spaces.

If your soil is not too rich but is poor, limy and light, these vigorous plants are well worth establishing in the turf. They appear well before the grass starts to grow and look their best growing in extravagant, colourful drifts. There are many different cultivars. A particularly good white one is 'White Splendour', a good strong grower with punchy, large flowers.

There is not a lot that needs doing to these plants. They can be divided up when they become overcrowded and this should be done in summer when the tubers are dormant. **BG**

Matt adds:
The iridescent pink and blue forms make excellent companion plants for shrubs with grey or silver foliage like lavender and sage. The multi-petalled flowers open only in the sun.

Among the other varieties I would recommend, 'Ingramii' is a sumptuous deep violet-blue, with buttermilk stamens. This is the darkest flowered form, first found on Mount Parnassus in southern Greece. *A. blanda* var. *rosea* is pale pink to purple with darker foliage. 'Radar' has intense magenta flowers with a contrasting magenta centre.

Anemone coronaria Saint Brigid Group

Anemone coronaria Saint Brigid Group

Type: hardy, tuberous perennial
Soil & situation: light, gritty, well-drained soil/full sun
North American hardiness zone: 8–10
Height: 30cm (12in)
Spread: 15cm (6in)
Grow for: pretty flowers in a variety of rich, velvety colours in spring or summer

This plant more than any other reminds me of my youth. Flower sellers used to sit outside the City Hall in Belfast and for 6 old pence (2.5 new pence or about 0.04 euro) you could bring your mother home a mixed bunch of 'Saint Brigid' flowers.

The crinkly foliage looks like parsley and the flowers are carried on long, bare stems. The almost flat flowers have a double layer of petals and are available in deep, velvety shades of red, violet, blue and white with paler zones and a centre 'button' of dark stamens. Anemone De Caen Group are similar but with single flowers. The hard, dark, knobbly tubers should be soaked overnight in water to soften the skin and speed up growth. They can be planted at most times of the year, spring being favoured in colder areas when they will flower in summer. Autumn-planted tubers will flower in early spring. Covering the buds with glass will protect them from the worst of the weather and prevent rain splashing mud onto the flowers. In heavy, wet soil they should be lifted after the foliage has died down and stored in sand. **JC**

Monstera deliciosa

SWISS-CHEESE PLANT

Type: tender, perennial, evergreen climber
Soil & situation: any compost/full sun to heavy shade
Hardiness zone: 10–11
Height & spread: to several hundred feet if you let it…
Grow for: enormous, uniquely holey, glossy leaves; amazing flowers and edible fruits. This is one of the most enduring houseplants, at its best at any time of year.

These are the most abused plants in the world, found in every dark corridor and grim office, every dingy net-curtained alcove and sitting in waiting rooms with their pot full of cigarette butts. Yet they survive, despite the vicissitudes of human nurture being less reliable than the tropical rains. However if you take one of these poor abusees and give it a big tub of good, moist compost and put it in the sun in a frost-free place you get the most amazing, very large, white, arum-like flowers. The flowers die and about a year later the central spathe ripens to become a ceriman. The fruit tastes like a pineapple banana on a stick. It is only edible when fully ripe, when the fruit swells, shedding its skin in little thick platelets, leaving the engorged flesh adhering to the central support – delicious. These can even be hardened off and used for summer bedding – it looked impressive to have a few of these interspersed with sugar cane here in Norfolk!

The Swiss-cheese plant is known for its leaf holes resembling that country's cheese. The Latin name is possibly from *monstrifer* for monster bearing, but that's doubtful. However, the *deliciosa* is for the fruit, which is indeed delicious and enjoyed in many countries. The plant comes from Central America where it climbs tropical trees and covers the rainforest floor like ivy, and in such places it is indeed monstrous.

Ideally this likes a large root run in moist, humus-rich soil in a conservatory or frost-free greenhouse in full sun. It can go out on the patio in summer. Be careful not to sunburn a plant by moving it from cool shade indoors into windswept, full sun; harden it off first. It can be hacked into bits and every chunk with a leaf, and especially those with roots already, will root; it can also be grown from seed with some warmth. Very rarely suffering from any problems, these masochists just ask to be neglected and ignored, but don't let them – drag them into the light.   **BF**

Anemone x *hybrida* 'Honorine Jobert'

Anemone x *hybrida* 'Honorine Jobert'
JAPANESE ANEMONE

Type: hardy, herbaceous perennial
Soil & situation: normal garden soil/prefers moist soil/dappled shade or part sun
North American hardiness zone: 4–8
Height: up to 1.2m (4ft) high
Spread: indefinite
Grow for: copious white flowers from summer to mid-autumn; AGM

This is an invaluable perennial. The vine-shaped leaves form handsome clumps, which come into growth relatively late on in spring. Later, single white flowers with golden stamens are produced on wiry stems, and these charming flowers look fresh and glowing throughout their fabulously long flowering period – most welcome at a time when things tend to look parched. You may wish to utilize the spare soil between the slowly-developing foliage in spring: tulips or alliums are ideal temporary fillers. I also find that it takes a few years for the clumps to fill out and have that fully-established air about them, but that might be because with me they are growing on 15cm (6in) of thin topsoil above hardcore, certainly not what the books recommend. Despite this, they give a magnificent show, without fail. They last long as cut flowers too – a real star. There are other good Japanese anemones in various shades of pink: *A. huphensis* 'September Charm' has soft pink flowers that are freely produced.

This indispensable plant can be left untouched for years; the only time you will probably have to divide it up is when friends are transfixed by it and beg a clump. If you want to propagate, root cuttings are the usual method or, if you can afford the stock, division. **BG**

Anemone nemorosa 'Robinsoniana'
WOOD ANEMONE

Type: hardy, rhizomatous perennial
Soil & situation: organic, rich, free-draining soil/sun or partial shade
North American hardiness zone: 4–8
Height: 15cm (6in)
Spread: 30cm (12in)
Grow for: mid-spring flowers; AGM

It's a pleasure to include a selection of one of my favourite 'native' plants. *Anemone nemorosa* is found throughout the UK carpeting deciduous woodlands before the trees are in leaf. Copy this at home by creating a jewel-spangled carpet under deciduous shrubs or trees or 'naturalizing' them in rough grass that doesn't need to be cut until mid-summer when the leaves die back. The flowers open only in the sun.

There's a host of desirable varieties. 'Royal Blue' is possibly the deepest blue with veronica-blue flowers. 'Robinsoniana' has large flowers of delicate wisteria-blue and deep green leaves. 'Bowles' Purple' has shiny, dark purple buds, paler than 'Allenii', darker than 'Robinsoniana',

Anemone nemorosa 'Robinsoniana'

with a purple exterior. *A. nemorosa* has white flowers, sometimes with a delicate lilac or pink hue, which have the daintiness of snowflakes settled on a filigree of foilage. 'Leeds' Variety' is white with a purple-pink reverse, about 5cm (2in) in diameter. 'Alba Plena' originated before 1771 and has double flowers and a large central cluster of white 'petals'. For nature's aberrations, try 'Green Fingers' – the white flowers have a ruff of tiny green leaves in the centre, as they unfurl the petals become pale pink. 'Virescens' is surreal! Every anther, petal and style has become a finely cut leaflet; it looks like the 'Green Man' of legend. It flowers from early to late spring, survives in dry shade and is sometimes labelled 'Viridiflora'.

They grow in almost any soil or situation, preferring dappled shade and well-drained soil enriched with compost or leafmould. Soak the rhizomes overnight in cool water, before planting horizontally at a depth of 3–5cm (1–2in). They take time to settle and may not bloom well in the first year. Keep the area weed free, top dress in autumn with well-rotted organic matter and leave them undisturbed. Anemones seed freely but can be lifted and divided from late summer to autumn when the soil is warm, or after flowering in spring. **MB**

Anemone rivularis

Type: hardy, herbaceous perennial
Soil & situation: moist soil/sun or dappled shade
North American hardiness zone: 6–8
Height: 60cm (24in)
Spread: 30cm (12in)
Grow for: delightful flowers from early to late summer

This wondrous plant is native from Kashmir and northern India to Tibet and southwest China, and was introduced to the UK in 1840. Mention the name of this unspeakably beautiful plant and I go weak at the knees so let me sit down and describe it to you! They are dazzling, with pure, glossy white flowers about 3cm (1in) across, with steel-blue anthers; the same colour diffuses from the sepals over the back of the flower, which hovers on stiff stems in clusters of three to five above a mass of dark divided leaves.

Phew! I've made it, perhaps you can understand my predicament by looking at the picture. Plant several in a group for added impact or simply plant one and admire it endlessly!

As the name suggests, *rivularis* means growing by streams. This species tolerates most moist garden soils, and flourishes where they are humus-rich and beside water. Dig in plenty of well-rotted organic matter if necessary before planting, keep them moist throughout the year and water during drought. They flourish in conditions from full sun to dappled light, even tolerating shade.

Cut back the foliage when it dies down in autumn and mulch with a thick layer of well-rotted organic matter. Divide every few years to revitalize the plant and share the pleasure by giving pieces to friends! Propagate by sowing seed immediately when it ripens in summer or divide in late summer or early autumn after it dies down.   **MB**

Angelica gigas

Type: hardy biennial
Soil & situation: moist soil/partial shade
North American hardiness zone: 4–7
Height: 2m (6½ft)
Spread: 1.2m (4ft)
Grow for: sculptural form, interesting colour and unusual flowers from early to late summer

It may appear dramatic in the flower border but I wouldn't fancy meeting one on a dark night – it looks like the type of plant that would feature in a

Angelica gigas

cheap Japanese horror movie from the 1950s! It bursts from the ground in a sinister fashion unfurling huge, bright green, deeply lobed leaves; everything else is deep plum-purple – the main stems, sideshoots and flowers. Extraordinary! The sheaths spilt open to reveal a dark compressed bloom that gradually unfolds to a typical domed flowerhead, pale beetroot in colour and up to 20cm (8in) wide.

Good in borders, naturalized or as an architectural specimen plant, it is a native of north China, Korea and Japan, mainly from damp woodland meadows. The great plantsman Dan Hinkley of Heronswood Nursery in the USA suggests planting it with bright yellows and golds, but those of us who are less ambitious should settle for a pale background or leave it lurking against dark backgrounds to surprise passers by. I'd love to have a small group spotlit to create a living nocturnal sculpture; one day, one day!

It needs deep, rich, moist soil in dappled shade or sunshine. It self-seeds, but not to the point of becoming a menace. Sow seed in containers in a cold frame as soon as ripe a few weeks after flowering, transplant while small as older plants resent disturbance; it may take two or more years to reach flowering size. It dies after flowering so plant seeds successively for a regular supply of flowers. It is prone to slug damage.   **MB**

Bunny adds:
This is a great plant visually, but can be awkward to grow well. It seems sometimes to do well and sometimes not, for no apparent reason, so is not that dependable.

Anemone rivularis

Anthemis nobilis 'Treneague' (syn. *Chamaemelum nobile* 'Treneague')
CHAMOMILE

Type: hardy, herbaceous, semi-evergreen, prostrate perennial
Soil & situation: moist soil/full sun to light shade
North American hardiness zone: 6–9
Height & spread: prostrate, especially if walked on; an individual plant will eventually reach 25cm (10in) each way.
Grow for: excellent ground cover for small areas, for example a seat; gorgeous scent; occasional flowers can be used for tea

Other chamomiles (there are more than 80 species in the genus) are more use for medicinal or culinary purposes but this is the one for mixing into a lawn or putting in crazy paving, as it is a creeping prostrate plant, likes being trodden on and rarely flowers. The smell is divine and it is apparently included in the lawns around Buckingham Palace, so ought to be good enough for me!

Native to Britain, it has long been believed to be the 'plant physician' – chamomile is said to heal sickly plants brought near it, and it is still much used in herbal medicine. It also flavoured beer and was smoked before tobacco became available.

Chamomile likes full sun and sandy soil, which needs to be well watered in spring and early summer. Dead-heading is useful as it prevents self-seeding, which produces wrong forms. It must be kept well weeded and rolled if not regularly trodden, and clipped if it gets too straggly. The true sort cannot be grown from seed, it must be propagated by division in spring. It's hard to keep a large area such as a chamomile lawn weed-free as grasses, for instance, creep in. **BF**

Anthemis nobilis 'Treneague'

Anthemis punctata subsp. *cupaniana*

Anthemis punctata subsp. *cupaniana*
DOG FENNEL

Type: frost-hardy, evergreen perennial
Soil & situation: free-draining soils/low or moderate fertility/almost neutral or alkaline/sunny position
North American hardiness zone: 6–9
Height: 30cm (12in)
Spread: 90cm (36in)
Grow for: easy, fast-growing, evergreen ground cover; aromatic, mounded, finely cut leaves; masses of long-lasting, simple, white daisy-like flowers with tight, yellow centres in early summer; AGM

If you are looking for rapid-to-establish, charming ground cover that has a bumper flowering period and evergreen foliage, you may well find this is the one that fits the bill. The pretty flowers are held well above the silver-grey foliage on slender stalks. In winter the foliage is less silver, more grey-green. In one garden, my client did not share my passion for it as she found it swamped too many other plants. As everything was planted in one fell swoop, the anthemis was in overdrive before the other plants had got off the starting blocks. If you pop it into established plantings it is easier to manicure if necessary. I am still a big fan however, and its rampant nature is easy to keep in check with a sharp snip from the secateurs. The flowers, apparently, can be preserved using glycerine.

To keep this plant flowering for even longer periods, cut off the dead heads. If it becomes straggly, trim back the foliage so as to get a more manicured, compact plant.

Being fast-growing, it is also short-lived, often having exhausted itself from over-exertion. Cuttings where the stems root themselves into the soil are easy to establish: I usually do this *in situ*, in spring. Be prepared to give them the odd drink if it is too warm and they look as if they may shrivel. **BG**

Anthemis tinctoria 'Sauce Hollandaise'
YELLOW CHAMOMILE, DYERS' CHAMOMILE

Type: hardy, evergreen perennial
Soil & situation: range of situations/sharp drainage/sunshine
North American hardiness zone: 3–7
Height: to 60cm (24in)
Spread: 40–60cm (16–24in)
Grow for: many pale, lemon-cream flowers which fade to creamy-white from late spring to autumn; attractive finely cut dark green foliage

Anthemis tinctoria is the traditionally used 'dyers' chamomile', also sometimes known as yellow chamomile, the golden marguerite and the ox-eye chamomile. It is a clump-forming perennial, which is naturalized in the UK. It has pungent, bright golden to cream flowers, the foliage is mid-green on top with a greyer green below. Its capacity to compete with the grasses and its long flowering season make it a wonderfully useful plant for growing in flowering meadows.

The variety *A. t.* 'Sauce Hollandaise' is far less vigorous but certainly not timid either. It is often included in mixed or herbaceous borders for its ability to produce copious quantities of flowers of a soft, subtle colour. It makes a superb container plant, where you can see the combination of good foliage and simple, but charming flowers shown off to their full advantage. There are other great forms of *A. tinctoria*, such as 'E.C. Buxton', another strong favourite of mine, with exquisite-coloured, light lemon flowers and mid-green leaves.

Plant care is as for *Anthemis punctata* subsp. *cupaniana* (see previous entry). **BG**

Anthemis tinctoria 'Sauce Hollandaise'

Anthriscus cerefolium
CHERVIL

Type: hardy annual salad herb
Soil & situation: almost any soil, kept moist but not waterlogged/full sun in winter, shade in summer
North American hardiness zone: annual
Height: to 1m (3ft) in good soil when flowering
Spread: 15cm (6in) in good soil
Grow for: incredibly useful culinary herb, with cloche or cover available for 52 weeks of the year

Closely related to the wild cow parsley, chervil has wonderful green leaves with a jagged ferny appearance; if grown as a singleton it can get quite big, but when grown for culinary use it's normally crowded into rows. The sweet, parsley-like flavour has a hint of aniseed and I use chervil in almost every savoury dish I cook – and every salad. It is an essential component of a good bouquet garni and has been in widespread use since Roman times, if not earlier.

A native of Europe and Asia, *Anthriscus cerefolium* is one of 20 species. It is closely related to parsley, but has a sweeter flavour. There is also a rare turnip-rooted variety, which I find easy to grow if I can get the damn seed to germinate! Be warned.

A rich soil is ideal but not essential; too dry a site will cause a miserable red-yellow appearance and rapid bolting, especially in full sun. In winter chervil can be grown under cover, but needs a sunny spot. It can be cut back hard to prevent flowering and also to get a new crop of leaves, if the soil is kept moist. Sow once or twice a month from spring to late summer outdoors, or any time except mid-winter under cover.

Chervil makes poor growth if parched by hot sun or dry soil, and it suffers from carrot root fly in open ground, so grow under horticultural fleece or cloches. **BF**

Anthriscus cerefolium

Antirrhinum majus Tahiti Series

Antirrhinum majus
Tahiti Series
SNAPDRAGON

Type: hardy, short-lived perennial
Soil & situation: fertile, well-drained soil/full sun
North American hardiness zone: 9–11
Height: 20cm (8in)
Spread: 15–30cm (6–12in)
Grow for: summer bedding display

As a child, were you shown how to gently squeeze the sides of the flower with finger and thumb to make its mouth open? Just occasionally I still do.

The 8cm (3½in) long, lance-shaped, glossy, deep green leaves are carried up the branched, stiff stems. The upright racemes of slightly fragrant flowers are produced in summer and autumn. They have two lips with rounded upper and lower lobes in pink, orange, white and red. The variety *Antirrhinum nanum* 'Tequila Sunrise' produces flowers in a range of bright colours all with bronze leaves. The Rocket Series flowers at 1.2m (4ft) and makes excellent cut flowers.

Dead-heading the spent flowers extends the period of flowering. If there is a particular colour you like, leave the plant in the ground. Protect it from winter wet and cold winds with horticultural fleece and it will not only flower next year but it will be earlier.

Sow seed in early spring and harden off in a cold frame before planting out. Autumn sowings can be overwintered and planted out after all risk of frost is over for an early display of flower. The foliage is rust resistant, which is a feature of modern varieties. In the past whole bedding schemes were disfigured by an attack of rust disease. **JC**

Arachis hypogaea

Aquilegia canadensis
Plant of the Week (see page 87)

Arachis hypogaea
GROUNDNUT, PEANUT

Type: tender annual vegetable crop
Soil & situation: almost any loose soil/moist when young/warm position in full sun
North American hardiness zone: annual
Height & spread: can form a clump about 30cm (12in) all round, larger in right conditions
Grow for: great botanical interest; pretty clover-like leaves and yellow flowers; edible nut

Not only are peanuts a useful crop, but they are also one of the prettiest, and as they are legumes they enrich the soil. Most importantly they are one of the few plants that can catch a young person's interest; their unique habit of burying the flowerhead after blooming to swell their seeds underground makes them a good introduction to gardening, even if the yields are small.

A native of South America but now widespread in all warm countries, peanut causes allergic reactions, especially if old and mouldy, in many people. *Arachis* comes from an old Greek word for plant and *hypogaea* means underground.

Start off peanuts in small pots, then plant them out in loose border soil or in very big wide trays or boxes in a greenhouse or conservatory, or possibly in a very warm sheltered garden after the last frost. In a pot the seedhead can't be buried by the plants, so border soil is best if you want to harvest the nuts. Sow in early spring in pots in the warmth. No problems other than cold (and do not try sowing roasted or salted nuts, as only the fresh ones in their husks will be able to grow).
BF

Aralia elata 'Aureovariegata'
JAPANESE ANGELICA TREE

Type: hardy, deciduous tree
Soil & situation: fertile, moist, humus-rich soil/light shade
North American hardiness zone: 4–9
Height & spread: 5m (16ft)
Grow for: dramatic form and foliage, and billowing heads of small flowers

My tree has a bad habit of drawing my blood on its spiny stems, but that is a small price to pay for its bold architectural shape of open, spreading branches and big leaves.

The very spiny stems bear large – 1.2m (4ft) long – two-pinnate leaves made up of as many as 70 leaflets. The mid-green foliage is margined golden-yellow fading to cream as the leaves age. The tiny, white flowers appear in late summer and autumn in large, spreading, open umbels up to 60cm (24in) long and are followed by small, round, black fruit.

This aralia needs a bit of space. It will flourish if sited in woodland or beside a stream or pond. Provide shelter from strong winds, which tend to shred the large leaves. Where plants are growing strongly feed with a high-potash fertilizer in early autumn to firm up the shoots before the winter frosts. Prune in late winter to remove crossing branches. Occasionally it will produce suckers with all green leaves. Dig them out by the root before they become large and a nuisance. Propagation is by grafting onto a rootstock of the green-leafed *Aralia elata*. **JC**

Aralia elata 'Aureovariegata'

Araujia sericifera (syn. *Physianthus albens*)
CRUEL PLANT

Type: perennial, half-hardy to tender, semi-evergreen, twining climber
Soil & situation: well-drained, humus-rich soil, not limy/full sun/moist all summer
North American hardiness zone: 10–11
Height & spread: to 6–7m (20–23ft)
Grow for: very long flowering period; gorgeously scented chalice- to salver-shaped, usually white, moth-catching flowers; attractive pear-sized, pear-shaped, green seedpods burst to release silky stranded seeds

I love this cruel plant, also sometimes wrongly known as the silk vine, as it has good foliage and the most wonderful perfume, one of the strongest. Although it was thought to be tender I have grown it for many years on a warm wall where it has withstood a fair few hard frosts. The habit of trapping moths by their tongues and holding them until late morning seems cruel, but ensures pollination and the moths seem to come to no actual harm. A fascinating bit of natural history in action.

Araujia comes from Brazil and the Argentines, and is one of a group of tender climbers to which it is worth giving hothouse treatment. However, grown from seed you can select far hardier strains that can endure outdoors or grace a conservatory year round.

It prefers loamy, peaty soils and some frost protection in exceptionally hard winters. Remove dead wood and seedpods, and if grown in pots nip out tips in spring and early summer to keep bushy. Sow in early spring, grow on under cover and plant out several seedlings the following year in late spring; hardy ones will survive if lucky or grow in a big pot under cover. *Araujia* suffers no common problems other than disliking cold winters. **BF**

Araujia sericifera

Arbutus unedo 'Elfin King'

Arbutus unedo 'Elfin King'
STRAWBERRY TREE

Type: hardy, evergreen tree
Soil & situation: fertile, humus-rich, well-drained soil/full sun
North American hardiness zone: 7–9
Height: 2m (6½ft)
Spread: 1.5m (5ft)
Grow for: ornamental bark; glossy foliage; clusters of flowers; strawberry-like, red fruit

A most unusual tree and a favourite of mine. The fruit is remarkably like a strawberry and is edible. A translation of *unedo* is 'I eat only one' and this is probably true, since they are vile tasting.

Even as a young plant *Arbutus unedo* 'Elfin King' flowers and fruits well. It forms a gnarled, compact, bushy tree with coarse, shredding, red-brown bark and 10cm (4in) long, glossy, mid-green, slightly toothed leaves. The urn-shaped, lily-of-the-valley-like flowers are white with a hint of pink. They hang in clusters during autumn at the same time as the fruit of the previous year's flowers ripen. The 'strawberries' are red with warty, rough skin.

A. unedo is the hardiest of the species and will tolerate most conditions but needs protection from cold winds. It grows well in coastal areas, being native to Southwest Ireland and the Mediterranean coast.

Although ericaceous it will tolerate an alkaline soil. As it dislikes being transplanted when large, plant in its permanent position as a young plant with shelter from frost for the first season. Pruning is best carried out in late winter but is seldom necessary. Propagation is by seed sown in autumn and over-wintered in a cold frame. Pot the seedlings as soon as they are large enough. Semi-ripe cuttings are easy to root in late summer with bottom heat. **JC**

Arisaema sikokianum
Plant of the Week (see page 185)

Arisarum proboscideum
MOUSE PLANT

Type: hardy, herbaceous perennial
Soil & situation: moist, organic soil/dappled shade
North American hardiness zone: 7–9
Height: 15cm (6in)
Spread: 30cm (12in) or more
Grow for: novelty flowers from early to late spring

Excuses for buying plants. Number one, 'I've bought this for the children!' As you can imagine, it just didn't work. OK, so I bought this for me and the children are interested – honest! Roy Lancaster first introduced me to this fun-packed plant – rummage among the mats of arrow-shaped leaves and you'll find lots of long thin 'tails' often with a twist at the end! Dig further and you'll see they're attached to the pretty dark brown 'mice' with pure white and chocolate stripes at the base. It looks just as if hundreds of tiny rodents have dived into the foliage to take cover! I've just been into the garden and dissected a flower. At the top of the spadix is a lump of tissue that looks exactly like a fungus. It's there to attract fungus gnats that live in moist, organic-rich soil, where the plant likes to grow. They see the 'fungus', lay their eggs on it and it's pollinated! Fantastic!

In the wild it is found in moist, shaded woodland, particularly in marshy areas under cork oaks in southwest Spain and central and southern Italy. It is ideal for the woodland or rock garden where it establishes large colonies. Plant 8cm (3½in) deep in organic-rich, moist soil in partial shade. If necessary, dig in plenty of well-rotted organic matter before planting; mulch in autumn to protect over winter. Sow seed from the greenish berries in spring; divide from autumn to spring. **MB**

Arisarum proboscideum

Aronia x *prunifolia* 'Viking'
CHOKEBERRY

Type: hardy, deciduous shrub
Soil & situation: any soil/full sun or part shade/moist site but not waterlogged
North American hardiness zone: 5–9
Height & spread: 2m (6½ft)
Grow for: easy, problem-free vitamin-C-rich alternative to blackcurrants; masses of white flowers in spring; fantastic autumn colour

Chokeberry is one of the great unknowns that ought to be in every garden. It is problem free and easy to multiply; the flowers are much loved by insects; and the fruits make a delicious blackcurrant/myrtle-type conserve with a hint of pine. The autumn leaf colours are among the best of all plants. Indeed, it is more often grown for this leaf colour than for the fruit.

Originally grouped with pears, this native of North America has, as the name suggests, a styptic puckering quality, but once made into conserve it is a great source of vitamins, many times richer than oranges or blackcurrants. *Aronia* comes from the Greek name for sorbus, which has similar fruits.

It does not like dry, limy soils and prefers full sun, but will survive in shade, although the autumn colouring will be less impressive. Protect fruits from birds! The species can be grown from seed but varieties grown for their fruit, such as 'Viking', must be propagated by layers, hardwood cuttings or division. No real problems with this easy subject. **BF**

Aronia x *prunifolia* 'Viking'

Artemisia abrotanum

Artemisia abrotanum
LAD'S LOVE, SOUTHERNWOOD

Type: hardy, deciduous shrub
Soil & situation: dry, sandy soil/full sun to light shade
North American hardiness zone: 5–8
Height & spread: to about 1–1.2m (3–4ft)
Grow for: very good edging plant for large borders or specimen for difficult dry sites with poor soils; aromatic smell; gorgeous grey-green appearance even in droughts; AGM

This plant smells so sweetly of lemon-pine toilet cleaner that it is always worth having it near a door or gate where you can brush past it. Although it rarely flowers, when it does it can be covered with small yellow buttons. *Artemisia absinthium* 'Lambrook Silver' flowers more easily and has more silvery leaves. Easily multiplied, it makes a good informal hedge up to a metre or so high, or it can be trimmed tight back and kept quite compact and low more easily than lavender, which is a much laxer shrub.

Southernwood has been widely used for medicine since ancient times. A native of Europe, it has also been loved in gardens, and put to good use in homes where its stems were placed among clothes as its smell is reputed to keep away moths. Also used for strewing and for pot pourris, and a handful stuffed into your pillow is supposed to help you fall asleep if it doesn't poke your eye out!

In dry sandy soil lad's love is long lived, but in damp shady places it dies away. To keep it compact cut back hard in spring just before growth commences. The seed is rarely offered but cuttings in spring take easily, or divide an old clump if it's multi-stemmed. No real problems with this plant. **BF**

Artemisia dracunculus
FRENCH TARRAGON

Type: hardy, perennial herbaceous herb
Soil & situation: poor dry sandy soil/full sun
North American hardiness zone: 3–7
Height & spread: 30cm (12in); may reach 50cm (20in) in a good spot
Grow for: pleasing foliage from late spring to mid-summer with a superb, unique flavour

'French' tarragon is the herb to make a wonderful vinegar for use with fish; the commoner 'Russian' is miserable and coarse, but far more widely available as it endures so much longer and is easier to propagate.

Natives of Europe, other artemisias, such as *A. absinthium*, have long been used medicinally and are not so useful as edible herbs. However, they were once included in absinthe, an addictive alcoholic liqueur. Weirdly it is named after the Greek god of chastity.

Tarragon must be grown in dryish sandy soil in full sun or it will be very short lived. It dies back in autumn so needs tidying; protect the crown with sharp sand or grit. If offered seed, refuse as it will be the 'Russian' form. To ensure a true variety propagate by root division in early spring. Tarragon must be divided and replanted every third year, or it dies away! **BF**

Artemisia dracunculus

Arum italicum 'Marmoratum' *growing with snowdrops.*

Arum italicum 'Marmoratum'
LORDS AND LADIES

Type: hardy tuberous perennial
Soil & situation: well-drained, moisture-retentive soil/sun or shade
North American hardiness zone: 6–9
Height & spread: 30cm (12in)
Grow for: broad, spear-shaped leaves exquisitely marbled in grey-green in late autumn; an excellent foliage plant, ideal for Christmas decorations; bright red berries in summer when the foliage has died down; AGM

The beautifully marked leaves of this plant look as though they have been deftly hand-painted. They look perfect and pristine through many of the winter months – what could be more endearing? If they do get a little affected by the frosts in extremely cold sites, new growth quickly appears to replace them. (This has not happened yet to mine.) They are hardy to about –10°C (14°F), and will survive lower temperatures still with the insulation of a protective mulch. I grow them intermingled with a range of ferns, and they are extremely complimentary neighbours, with the arums stealing the scene in the late autumn as the ferns start to look a little tired. The roles are reversed in late spring as the lush, emerald foliage of the ferns hides the slowly shrivelling arums.

This plant comes pretty true from seed, though do not become disenchanted if young plants look plain, the markings take a couple of years to develop. It is worth selecting out the particularly stunningly marked plants. **BG**

Asparagus officinalis
ASPARAGUS

Type: half-hardy, herbaceous, perennial vegetable
Soil & situation: rich, well-drained, moist soil/full sun
North American hardiness zone: 4–8
Height: fern may reach 1.2–1.5m (4–5ft)
Spread: crown may grow to 1m (3ft) across, when the roots will extend by ten times as far
Grow for: simply the finest of all vegetable crops, which happily comes when few others are ready; the fern is also attractive in ornamental areas

Any gourmet gardener has to have a bed of this luxury as it is so much better when fresh cut, although patience is required to build up the crown's strength for three years before cutting – it is worth the wait. Also, only six weeks or so of cutting is possible each year as the remaining shoots must be left to form fern to replenish reserves for the following year.

The attractive fern and the pretty, red berries on the female make it easy to fit it into the ornamental border. Do not get all male versions, as I reckon females give bigger buds and they give free plants everywhere as they self-seed fiendishly.

A wild seashore plant from the Mediterranean, asparagus has been grown since Roman times and is little changed in form or even name; indeed, ours appears identical to theirs in every way. It is said to be an aphrodisiac, which is possible, but it certainly gives the consumer's urine its own

Asparagus officinalis

distinctive aroma. In the markets asparagus is commonly referred to as sparrow grass.

Asparagus needs a well-prepared site as it may last for 20 years or more. Tidy up dead fern once it's died down and keep the bed scrupulously weed free, but do not thickly mulch as this makes for a late, light crop. Best sown *in situ*, or transplanted as one-year-old crowns but no older. Take care not to damage buds on the crown or the fleshy roots, which need spreading out just under the soil surface. Asparagus beetle is best controlled by hygiene and strong, soft soap sprays when the 'grubs' are seen eating the fern. **BF**

Asparagus officinalis

Asphodeline lutea
KING'S SPEAR, YELLOW ASPHODEL

Type: hardy, evergreen perennial
Soil & situation: any moderately fertile soil/sun
or dappled shade
North American hardiness zone: 6–9
Height: 70cm (27½in) although often taller
Spread: 30cm (12in)
Grow for: dense racemes of fragrant, yellow
flowers with conspicuous buff/reddish-brown
bracts from late spring into summer; stout, leafy
stems above the evergreen whorls of interesting,
rather thin, grassy, grey-green foliage

This is a fine plant which is rapidly increasing in
popularity as it associates well with grasses and
large-scale perennial planting. It will naturalize
well in these sort of situations – it occurs naturally
in scrubby meadows and on rocky slopes. It is also
highly suitable for mixed or herbaceous borders.
Its individual, star-like flowers are up to 3cm (1in)
across. They open after midday at uneven
intervals up the spike for several weeks, giving the
plant an unusual, rather outlandish look.

These plants are not so successful in rich soils but
otherwise tolerate a range of conditions. They
can be increased by seed or division but the latter
needs care, making sure that the fleshy rhizomes
have two or three growing points on each piece.
This is best carried out in late summer or early
autumn. It benefits from an autumnal mulch in
colder areas. **BG**

Asphodeline lutea

Asplenium scolopendrium

Asplenium scolopendrium
HART'S TONGUE FERN

Type: hardy, evergreen fern
Soil & situation: happier in alkaline soils/will
tolerate neutral or more acid conditions/prefer
well-drained soils/full or partial shade/less than 3
hours sunshine a day, otherwise they get a yellow
discoloration of their leaves or brown lesions can
be burnt into their fronds
North American hardiness zone: 6–8
Height: to 70cm (27½in)
Spread: to 60cm (24in)
Grow for: simple but highly attractive foliage,
which contrasts well with the heavily divided
fronds of most ferns; AGM

The hart's tongue is a highly adaptable fern. I
have seen it many times growing out of shady
free-standing walls, reasonably high above
ground. In natural woodlands it forms beautiful
evergreen carpets studded with the occasional
foxglove. This idyllic scene is easy to recreate in
a garden situation by breaking up the clumps of
strappy fronds, to a greater or lesser extent,
with wild-looking colour from white epilobiums,
comfrey, camassias and such like.

Their leaves are ever-present and highly attractive
throughout the winter but start to shrivel as the
young fronds start to unfurl in spring. It has many
different cultivars with crinkled leaves in a variety
of shades of green, for those who find the
common form too common. But I think you can't
beat it and I hope my garden is never without it,
no doubt exploiting new cracks and crevices all
the while.

Care for this plant as for *Dryopteris filix-mas* (see
page 154). **BG**

Astelia chathamica

Astelia chathamica

Type: half-hardy, herbaceous perennial
Soil & situation: moist, humus-rich soil/dappled shade
North American hardiness zone: 8–9
Height: 1.2m (4ft)
Spread: 2m (6½ft)
Grow for: striking, silvery, sword-shaped leaves; AGM

Now here's a rarity: a bold architectural plant with silvery foliage that thrives in dappled shade! It forms a large clump of sword-like leaves, each terminating in a sharp point, which are silvery above and completely white below. Wow! The colour, shape and form lend themselves to contemporary planting schemes. Try it with the silver bramble *Rubus cockburnianus*, the black-leaved ground cover of *Ophiopogon planiscapus* 'Nigrescens', or the large bronze leaves of *Ajuga reptans* 'Catlin's Giant' or *A. r.* 'Pink Surprise', which have the bonus of blue and pink flowers respectively. It also looks wonderful as a feature plant in a black or blue container with crushed glass mulch! Think minimalist; concrete, glass, stainless steel and ceramics – a complete contrast to its home among the leafy forest margins of the Chatham Islands off the Pacific Coast of New Zealand! *A. nervosa* forms a denser clump of narrower, even more metallic leaves.

It needs dappled shade in constantly moist, humus-rich, acid soil; incorporate leafmould or peat substitute if necessary. Do not plant in frost pockets, as they cannot withstand long periods of sub-zero temperatures but have survived snow and are probably more cold tolerant than is supposed. Propagate by detaching rosettes from a parent plant in spring. The problem is that astelias hate disturbance and the only way to divide is to lift the whole plant and detach a rosette complete with its own roots; it is less risky to buy new micro-propagated plants. Pests: queues of people asking for divisions! **MB**

Aster x *frikartii* 'Mönch'

Type: hardy, herbaceous perennial
Soil & situation: well-drained, neutral to slightly alkaline soil/sun
North American hardiness zone: 5–8
Height: 90cm (36in)
Spread: 40cm (16in)
Grow for: gorgeous lavender-blue flowers from mid-summer to mid-autumn; AGM

Although spring has a joy and vibrancy of its own I'm a great fan of late summer and early autumn, particularly those days when the humidity has gone and it's still, warm and sunny without being unbearably hot and sticky. It's the time of year when asters come to the fore, enriching the garden with their bold splashes of colour. They come in a range of colours and sizes from the cerise pink *Aster novae-angliae* 'Andenken an Alma Pötschke' to the tiny-flowered, *A. ericoides* 'Golden Spray' with its bold centres and *A. amellus* 'King George', a reliable old rich purple cultivar. One of the best, however, is *A.* x *frikartii* 'Mönch'. It begins its display much earlier, in mid-summer producing masses of soothing, cool lavender-blue flowers up to 8cm (3½in) across, which cover the plant; it is utterly beautiful. Christopher Lloyd, that great garden writer, enthuses about it as an 'essential' plant for every garden. It is also America's favourite aster. It's good to know I'm not alone!

They need a sunny position in neutral to slightly alkaline, well-drained soil. Incorporate well-rotted organic matter, horticultural grit or sharp sand if necessary; grow in raised beds on clay. Feed with general fertilizer and mulch in spring. Although the stems are thin, they rarely need staking and are drought resistant, but they must be watered over long periods without rain. Divide every two to three years in autumn or spring, or take softwood cuttings from mid to late spring. They are mildew resistant. **MB**

Aster x *frikartii* 'Mönch'

Astilbe 'Fanal'

Type: hardy, herbaceous perennial
Soil & situation: moist, fertile, humus-rich
soil/full sun or light shade
North American hardiness zone: 4–9
Height: 60cm (24in)
Spread: 90cm (36in)
Grow for: a dazzling display of crimson flowers
making a feathery spire; easy to grow

Given the right soil conditions this perennial will
perform well with little or no imput from the
gardener. It needs no special treatment and is
easy to grow. It will flower profusely for up to four
years without being in serious need of dividing.
The glossy, dark green leaves are toothed along
their margins. They make a contrasting backdrop
for the dense panicles of small, dark crimson
flowers, which form a feathery spire. Long-lasting,
they flower for weeks in early summer.

Astilbe 'Fanal' prefers a moist soil in full sun. If it
is planted in a soil that dries out it will do better
if it is shaded for the hottest part of the day.
Where the ground is clay based and prone to
drying out in summer it will not thrive. It is a
good plant for the bog garden or at the edge of a
pond with its feet close to water.

Propagation is by division in winter or early
spring. Small rooted pieces should be potted up
in a free-draining compost and kept under glass
for the winter, or planted out in the border
straight away. Flowers that have not been dead-
headed will over-winter on the plant, gradually
turning an attractive deep brown. **JC**

Astilbe 'Fanal'

Astilboides tabularis

Astilboides tabularis

Type: hardy, herbaceous perennial
Soil & situation: soil should be fairly rich/should
drain but not dry out/enjoys moisture, so bog
gardens, pond margins or damp borders are the
order of the day/part shade
North American hardiness zone: 5–7
Height: up to 1.5m (5ft)
Spread: 1.2m (4ft)
Grow for: stunning architectural plant; bold
foliage; attractive flowers in mid-summer

Although this plant is fairly unusual, it is
definitely worth finding a spot for if you have
suitably moist conditions. A piece of moist and
lightly shaded woodland is ideal. If not, it may be
well worth considering making a bog garden to
accommodate it, together with several other
exciting moisture-loving plants. Do not make the
bog garden too small – the leaves are huge and
may be up to 90cm (36in) long. The colour is a
good, bright green, and the leaves have long
stalks and are sharply lobed. It flowers in early to
mid-summer, with spectacular panicles of tiny
white flowers on tall flowering stems that reach to
1.5m (5ft) high.

It is as well to mulch the plants annually in spring
to conserve water, and further watering maybe
necessary in dry periods. Propagation is by
division in spring. **BG**

Astrantia major 'Hadspen Blood'

Astrantia major 'Hadspen Blood'
MASTERWORT

Type: hardy, herbaceous perennial
Soil & situation: fertile, moist soils/sun or part shade
North American hardiness zone: 4–9
Height: up to 90cm (36in)
Spread: 45cm (18in)
Grow for: fabulous dark red flowers surrounded by co-ordinating dark red bracts from late spring to summer.

These striking, papery-looking flowers are shaped like mini-pincushions and have a charming simplicity about them. The stems are wiry and

Astrantia major

hold the colourful flowers above the mounded, deeply cut leaves. The flowering period is fairly prolonged so you can be generous and plant extravagant drifts of them, allowing them to hold the fort for well over a month, if not two. If you can bear to cut them, they dry extremely well for winter decoration. I also like *Astrantia major*, which has white flowers. It is more vigorous than the red forms, but less dramatic.

Unless you have rich, moist soil to maintain these plants in tip-top condition they will need frequent division and re-planting into a good, nourishing soil. Propagate by division in spring. **BG**

Athyrium niponicum var. *pictum*
JAPANESE PAINTED FERN

Type: hardy, herbaceous perennial
Soil & situation: moist, humus-rich soil/dappled shade
North American hardiness zone: 5–8
Height: 38cm (15in)
Spread: 35cm (14in) plus
Grow for: beautifully marked leaves; AGM

This is an exquisite fern, arguably the most beautiful you'll ever see; it's elegant, stylish and has a delicious colour scheme, even by the exalted standards of the plant world. It has soft, metallic grey-green leaves with mauve-purple midribs, the mauve diffusing into the leaf blade. It is worthy of a prominent place at the edge of a border; plant it in the spotlight where it cannot be missed, then go and view it regularly for a contented life! Plant with arisaemas (see page 185) and other woodlanders or combine with arisaemas and black bamboo for a display of contemporary class!

Selected forms include *Athyrium niponicum* var. *pictum* 'Cristatoflabellatum' which has 'crests' at the frond tips and ends of the leaflets; the fronds are slightly narrower. 'Kokage Nishiki' has larger, broadly triangular green fronds flecked with cream.

They tolerate full sun (with sufficient moisture) to deep shade but prefer dappled shade and winter shelter. Those in good light develop the richest colours. They flourish in moist, humus-rich soil; dig in plenty of well-rotted organic matter, preferably leafmould, before planting. Ideal for planting by ponds and in bogs. Propagate by division in spring.

Here are several other colourful ferns that are worth growing. *A. otophorum* (eared lady fern) has lance-shaped, pale green fronds with a burgundy midrib and veins. It is deciduous but holds its leaves into the autumn. *A. vidallii* has green leaves with a dark red midrib and veins. *Adiantum aleuticum* 'Japonicum' (Japanese maidenhair fern) has beautiful rose-pink foliage with contrasting black stems. It needs shelter. *Dryopteris erythrosora* has brick-red new fronds, fading to bronze, then becoming green. Its evergreen leaves turn yellow in winter. Wonderful! See also *Asplenium sclopendrium* on page 50 and other recommended *Dryopteris* on page 154. **MB**

Azara microphylla
Plant of the Week (see page 55)

Athyrium niponicum var. *pictum*

Azara microphylla

Type: hardy evergreen shrub to small tree
Soil & situation: any well-drained, preferably humus-rich soil/full sun to light shade. Needs warmth in cold areas.
Hardiness zone: 8–10
Height: can reach 12m (40ft) in a perfect site, smaller in UK
Spread: 3m (10ft)
Grow for: evergreen, box- or cotoneaster-like leaves year round; highly perfumed flowers which emerge before most others, at the end of winter; occasional orange berries; AGM

Azara microphylla (below) is not unpleasing as a foliage shrub but rarely catches the eye. However, in late winter until early spring it produces the most amazingly powerful scent of vanilla and chocolate from tiny, yellow, powder puff flowers on the underside of the leaflets. The scent is almost addictive and I have completely defoliated my specimen as high as I can reach snipping bits off to take indoors.

A native of South America, its generic name comes from a Spanish patron and the species name from its small leaves. It is one of a dozen species, most of which are too tender for Britain except in warm coastal areas – I can't grow the gorgeous *A. lanceolata*, pictured left, but it's fine against a warm wall in milder parts of the country. *A. microphylla* is tough enough to endure winters in my Norfolk garden, even without a warm wall. Some other species flower in autumn.

Apart from its tenderness, *Azara* is obligingly easy. The only real problem is biting cold winds. It can get drawn up and leggy so needs pruning back every few years to keep it compact and also to remove dieback after searing winds or frosts. It's not easy to obtain, or to grow, the seed, and other methods of propagation are not easy either; the best method is to use mature sideshoot cuttings in autumn or by layering – oh go on, buy a plant! **BF**

Begonia sutherlandii

Type: half-hardy tuberous perennial
Soil & situation: moist, organic-rich
compost/dappled shade
North American hardiness zone: tender in most
areas; normally grown as an annual
Height & spread: 45cm (18in)
Grow for: form and foliage from spring to
autumn; flower in summer; AGM

When you put out houseplants for their 'summer
holiday' they are usually left randomly on the
patio or dispersed to hide in the garden; however,
they look much better incorporated into an exotic
plant display. Place larger foliage plants together
for a 'jungly' effect and smaller plants in groups
with other summer-flowering containers.

Begonia sutherlandii, a native of southern Africa
where it grows among rocks by humid forest
streams is a demure little plant and a study in
elegance and form. It has slender trailing stems,
bright green, red-veined leaves and hanging clusters

Begonia sutherlandii

of pale orange flowers; it is perfect for shady patios
or resting in a bed of ferns or among terracotta
pots where its earthy tones combine. Its trailing
habit makes it ideal for a plinth, a hanging basket,
or anywhere you need a soothing summer display.

Although it is of borderline hardiness, unless you
live in a mild area, it is safer to dry it off over
winter and store in peat substitute. Repot in multi-
purpose compost in spring, gradually increase
watering as the stems appear; use tepid, never cold
water. Feed every two weeks with general fertilizer,
changing to high-potash fertilizer at flowering.

During the first year remove developing flowers;
start into growth in mid- to late winter under cover,
then harden off before moving outdoors once there
is no danger of frost. It produces
small bulbils in the leaf axils in late summer –
collect and store over winter, and sow the following
spring. It can also be propagated by stem cuttings in
summer. It is susceptible to mildew, so keep the
compost moist and avoid stagnant air. **MB**

Berberidopsis corallina

Berberidopsis corallina
CORAL PLANT

Type: half-hardy, evergreen, twining climber
Soil & situation: moist, acid to neutral
soil/shade/shelter
North American hardiness zone: 8–9
Height & spread: 6m (20ft) or more
Grow for: flowers from mid-summer to early
autumn

This treasure was first discovered in February 1860
by Richard Pearce, one of 22 collectors employed by
the great nurserymen Veitch & Co., who found it in
a forested ravine in the province of Arauco in Chile
where the Mapuche Indians still use the stems to
make baskets. The species was described by Joseph
Hooker in 1862, later to become a director of Kew,
who wrote 'it is not a little remarkable that so
striking a plant should hitherto have escaped the
notice of all botanists and collectors who have
explored a region now so well known as Chile'. The
limited natural distribution has been badly affected
by forest clearance for commercial timber
production and it is now an endangered species.
Many of the populations have been reduced or
destroyed and even though it's available in nurseries,
there is little genetic variation among the plants.
The dark green leaves are heart shaped, leathery
with spiny margins; the flowers on long stems from
the upper leaf joints are rounded with overlapping
petals and deep coral-red flowers like bunches of
luscious cherries. Have you room for one in your
garden? It is a priceless opportunity to grow a
beautiful plant and to conserve it in cultivation, even
if it is threatened in the wild.

It needs a sheltered, shady wall in well-drained,
moist, light, neutral or acid soil; it tolerates some
alkalinity. Make sure it gets protection from frost; it
flourishes in parts of the UK influenced by the
North Atlantic Drift and in sheltered gardens. Plant
in early spring, mulch annually to protect the roots
and tie in new shoots as required. Prune in spring
to remove damaged growths or to tidy up the plant.
Propagate by semi-ripe cuttings from mid-summer
to early autumn, or by layering in early spring. **MB**

Berberis darwinii

Berberis darwinii
BARBERRY

Type: hardy, evergreen shrub
Soil & situation: moist soil; tolerates chalk/sun or partial shade/shelter
North American hardiness zone: 7–9
Height & spread: 3m (10ft) or more
Grow for: glossy foliage; orange flowers in mid- and late spring; AGM

This robust, attractive Chilean native was discovered by Charles Darwin in 1835 when he was naturalist on the *Beagle*, but not introduced to the UK until 1849 by William Lobb who was collecting for Veitch's Nursery on the island of Chiloe.

It is a joyful sight in spring festooned with hanging clusters up to 5cm (2in) long of as many as 30 flowers. The massed, glossy, holly-like, evergreen leaves with three spines at the tip are the perfect backcloth for the flowers, which are a spectacular striking tone of orange with reddish stems. Like all berberis and mahonias, the stamens are touch-sensitive, springing inwards on contact and coating the head of visiting insects with pollen. In common with many plants, they often stage another smaller flowering display in autumn and are followed by plum-coloured fruits. I planted many of these in the miry Leicestershire clay and undeterred, they still glowed radiantly year after year. It is one of my favourite shrubs, good for creating barriers and as a border specimen. The cultivar *B. d.* 'Flame' has broader leaves with rich orange-red flowers.

Although tolerant of most conditions, except regular drought, it prefers moist soils in a sheltered position, protected from strong wind. It even grows well on chalky soils – how accommodating! Trim in late winter to keep within its allotted space, rejuvenate by removing older stems and encouraging those growing up from the base. Grow from seed in late winter to early spring, or heeled nodal cuttings. Berberis sawfly may be a problem. **MB**

Berberis linearifolia 'Orange King'
BARBERRY

Type: hardy, evergreen, upright shrub
Soil & situation: any moist, well-drained, fertile soil/full sun or light shade
North American hardiness zone: 6–9
Height & spread: 2m (6½ft) each way
Grow for: an excellent, evergreen, spring-flowering shrub

There are superb berberis and then there are the common types much used in local authority landscape plantings throughout Europe to deter vandals and hold, trapped in public gaze, every bit of litter in the vicinity. *B. linearifolia* 'Orange King' is a true aristocrat, flowering royally with the minimum of attention. It is a vigorous plant with lengthy, arching shoots and 5cm (2in) long, thin, glossy, dark green leaves. The clusters of orange-apricot flowers appear in late spring weighing down the stems. Early visiting bees go mad for the blossom. Small blue-black fruits appear in early autumn.

After planting, clip the plant, removing 30 per cent of the growth, to encourage it to form sideshoots. If allowed to grow unchecked, the base of all the branches will become bare of foliage. As it is a surface-rooting shrub, a deep mulch of composted bark will help retain moisture and prevent the ground drying out.

This is a shrub that seldom requires pruning. Remove individual branches that are spoiling the shape in early summer after flowering. When grown as a hedge, trim lightly every year after the flower has faded. Propagate by semi-ripe cuttings in mid-summer in a gritty compost. **JC**

Berberis linearifolia 'Orange King'

Berberis temolaica
BARBERRY

Type: hardy, deciduous shrub
Soil & situation: most soils/sun or partial shade
North American hardiness zone: 6–9
Height & spread: 3m (10ft)
Grow for: uncommon deciduous shrub with red fruits and good autumn colour

I bought this at a county show at Hever Castle in Kent, simply because I'd never heard of the species and the name sounded unusual. It's rather like buying a car because you like the colour; how serendipity has triumphed! The small plant I carefully carried home has now settled into my heavy clay and is showing glimpses of its full glory, and will be wonderful when it reaches its full height. The arching stems are an unusual whitish-grey at first, later becoming purple and shiny brown. There are few spines and the pale yellow flowers in late spring are followed by red, egg-shaped fruits covered with a delicate bloom; I must have missed them last year, but not the fiery orange and yellow autumn colour, which would not look out of place on 5 November. It was first discovered by Frank Kingdon-Ward on the Temo La in Tibet in 1924. I wonder if my plant came from that area or from seed collected by Ludlow, Sherrif and Taylor from the nearby Tsari district in 1938. I don't know, but whatever its origin, in one corner of my garden there's a piece of that Hallowed Kingdom.

Berberis temolaica thrives on most soils including those that are dry and shallow, but dislikes waterlogging. A sunny site encourages fruiting. Regular pruning is not required, just trim it in late winter to keep it within its allotted space and regenerate by removing older stems and encouraging those growing up from the base. Grow from seed from late winter to early spring or take semi-ripe cuttings with a heel. **MB**

Berberis temolaica

Berberis valdiviana

Berberis valdiviana
BARBERRY

Type: hardy, evergreen shrub
Soil & situation: most soils/sun or partial shade
North American hardiness zone: 6–9
Height & spread: 4m (13ft)
Grow for: robust, handsome evergreen; flowers in late spring

See a specimen at maturity and you can only admire its bulk standing there nobly and defiant like Goliath, daring anyone to challenge it! Three-pronged spines, almost hidden by the elegant glossy leaves, sprout from the stems, waiting to trap the unwary. How strange, then, that this plant should produce such fine orange-yellow or saffron flowers in clusters of 20–30 that hang like pendent earrings, up to 5cm (2in) long. Is it having an identity crisis or just a laugh? I've yet to decide, but what is certain is that it is a fine plant in leaf and flower, as the one by Victoria Gate at the Royal Botanic Garden Kew amply demonstrates. I'm sure it would be planted more often if it were freely available. It was discovered in the Valdivia province of southern Chile in 1856 and could easily be mistaken for a holly (see *Desfontainia spinosa* on page 142 and *Osmanthus heterophyllus* on page 283).

It thrives on a sheltered, sunny site on most soils including dry and shallow, but dislikes waterlogging. Good as a wall shrub or in a sheltered corner. Regular pruning is not required, just trim in late winter to keep it within its allotted space and regenerate by removing older stems and encouraging those growing up from the base.

Grow from seed from late winter to early spring or take semi-ripe cuttings with a heel. Be warned – it is extremely difficult to propagate from cuttings. It can suffer from leaf spot with purple-black spots on the leaves, which is disfiguring rather than debilitating. Beware of berberis sawfly. **MB**

Bergenia 'Beethoven'
ELEPHANT EARS

Type: hardy, evergreen perennial
Soil & situation: moist, well-drained soil/sun or partial shade
North American hardiness zone: 3–8
Height: 45cm (18in)
Spread: 60cm (24in) or more
Grow for: architectural foliage and early spring flowers

I've never worried about my 'elephant ears', they suit me rather well. Some people pass comment, others laugh, but I think they're very nice; OK, they may go red in cold weather but so does my nose – to me that is part of their charm!

I don't know why bergenias aren't planted more often. They can look untidy (so tidy them up!), but make excellent evergreen ground cover with their bold, green, glossy leaves; even when the older leaves die they turn yellow and scarlet.

There's character in the thick creeping rhizomes, and the early flowers and stems are beautiful. If you have an 'elephant's ear' for music, *Bergenia* 'Beethoven' is beautiful with dark green leaves and spikes of bell-shaped, pure white flowers with

Bergenia 'Beethoven'

a red to greenish-pink flush on the reverse and red or purple stems; you may well find yourself in harmony. 'Bach' has rounded, deep green leaves and pink-flushed flowers – 'Brahms', 'Bizet', 'Bartok', 'Britten', 'Mozart', they all know the score. There's plenty to choose from, and I'm relieved that 'Eroica' has missed her 't'!

The foliage and flowers last well in indoor displays. They need moist, well-drained soil in sun or partial shade. An open site on poorer soil improves their winter colour. Frost may damage early flowers. Divide every three to four years; root young rhizome sections with one or more leaf rosettes after flowering or in autumn in open ground. They are susceptible to slugs, and snails; leaf spot may be a problem. Dry brown rot may affect the rhizomes; remove infected parts and dust with fungicide. **MB**

Beta vulgaris esculenta 'Burpee's Golden'
BEETROOT

Type: hardy, herbaceous, biennial root vegetable
Soil & situation: rich, moist soil/full sun or very light shade
North American hardiness zone: normally grown as an annual
Height & spread: to 30–45cm (12–18in) each way; when flowering can reach almost 2m (6½ft) x 60cm (24in)
Grow for: unusual, golden, turnip-shaped root with attractive yellowy-green foliage; if left to bolt when fully grown it produces a magnificent flower spike of small flowers with a sweet, mawkish scent

Most beetroot are red and grown purely for the table, but this old variety has a different appearance in root and leaf so can be used in the

Beta vulgaris esculenta 'Burpee's Golden'

Beta vulgaris esculenta 'Crosby's Egyptian'

ornamental garden to good effect. It is sweeter than many red cultivars and makes an excellent preserve in vinegar or as pieces in piccalilli. The leaves are more palatable than those of the red sorts and can be eaten as a spinach.

Almost unknown to the early Romans, beet were developed as a fodder crop in the Dark Ages in Europe, probably from the native maritime plant, and seem to have come from Germany. Originally they were cooked in ashes or fried but now they are invariably boiled or pickled.

The soil must be rich and moist or beet may bolt; they enjoy the addition of seaweed products and wood ashes. To further avoid bolting space widely and do not let them dry out. Sow seed from early spring to early summer. Beet seed is in a 'pellet' of several, so single them out in rows at least 12–15cm (5–6in) apart. Birds eat young leaves unless protected. **BF**

Beta vulgaris esculenta 'Crosby's Egyptian'
BEETROOT

Type: hardy, herbaceous, biennial root vegetable
Soil & situation: rich, moist soil/full sun or very light shade
North American hardiness zone: normally grown as an annual

Height & spread: as for *Beta vulgaris esculenta* 'Burpee's Golden' (see previous entry)
Grow for: the best beetroot for pickling; if left to bolt produces a flower spike similar to that of 'Burpee's Golden' but more red than yellow.

This old variety may bolt more readily than some newer sorts, but in my trials it performed well when grown, and when pickled in vinegar it kept its colour, taste and texture the longest. It can be used in the ornamental garden to good effect, and the leaves can be eaten like spinach, but they are less palatable than those of 'Burpee's Golden' or white sorts, such as 'Albina Vereduna'.

As an old variety 'Crosby's Egyptian' has a flattish bottom and is not as globular or cylindrical as modern sorts. Beet is very valuable nutritionally as it is rich in minerals but this makes the demand on the soil far heavier than most crops, so it must be rotated each year.

The soil must be rich and moist or the beet may bolt. Give wide spacing to avoid bolting. The same problem can occur if sown in a cold period, so wait until no more than a fortnight before the last frost is expected. Beet can be sown from early spring until early summer; seed is in a 'pellet' of several so either give very wide spacing, 30cm (12in) each way, and leave in natural clumps of three or five, or thin to singletons in a more closely packed row at say 10cm (4in) apart. Protect young leaves to deter birds from eating them. **BF**

Betula utilis var. jacquemontii

HIMALAYAN BIRCH

Type: hardy, deciduous tree
Soil & situation: moist, well-drained soil/full sun or partial shade/tolerates exposure
Hardiness zone: 5–7
Height: 18m (60ft)
Spread: 10m (33ft)
Grow for: an elegant, fast-growing tree with striking white bark, shown to best advantage in wintry gloom.

I love all birch, but this is my favourite. The pure white bark heading into the uppermost limbs creates a ghostly effect on a dull afternoon in mid-winter. The 12cm (5in) long, oblong, dark green, double-toothed leaves turn to buttery-yellow in late autumn. In early spring pale brown, male catkins the same length as the leaves appear. In the slightest breeze they dispense clouds of bright yellow pollen.

It is fast growing with the bark colouring early. Sited correctly, it is an ideal specimen tree for drawing your eye and highlighting one part of the garden. It will grow and thrive in damp ground but isn't partial to waterlogged soil. They dislike being moved, but asmall, bare root tree up to 1.8m (6ft) high will transplant without too much fuss, providing it is planted as soon as it loses its leaves. It may also be planted just as it is about to come into leaf in the spring. Plant at the same depth as before and water frequently for the first season. I admit to washing the bark every winter to remove the older, peeling bark and green algae and as I pass by the main trunk I usually give it a pat.

Other varieties worth growing are *Betula utilis* var. *jacquemontii* 'Doorenbos' with white bark peeling to reveal pale orange new bark. *B. utilis. var. jacquemontii.* 'Jermyns' has 17cm (6⅝in) long male catkins. The variety 'Silver Shadow' is, if anything, whiter than *jacquemontii* but I think my plant is brilliant. **JC**

Beta vulgaris 'Ruby Chard'

Beta vulgaris 'Ruby Chard'

Type: hardy, biennial vegetable
Soil & situation: good, deep, fertile but well-drained soil
North American hardiness zone: normally grown as an annual
Height & spread: 45cm (18in)
Grow for: ornamental foliage; culinary purposes lasting right through the winter till late spring the following year; highly productive, easy to grow and very resistant to bolting

The foliage on this plant is highly decorative: it has dark purple-green, puckered leaves with intense, almost florescent red stems and veins. Admittedly, I value it far more for its appearance than its taste. The midribs and stalks can be steamed and taste like a watery asparagus, while the young leaves can be treated as spinach but are not so good. The best culinary use, I think, is to pick the leaves young and use them to add splashes of colour and some bite (a mild, peppery, spinach flavour) to a salad. It is a strong enough plant, visually and culturally, to be used as a container plant. Indeed a winter window box full of these would certainly outdo the Jones' jaded pansies next door. There are excellent different types available. *Beta vulgaris* 'Bull's Blood' has exceptionally deep red-purple, glossy leaves and the young leaves can be used as a cut-and-come-again, though the purple colour intensifies as the plant matures and autumn approaches. 'Bright Lights' is so bright it looks unreal with its yellow, cream, orange or red midribs and veins amongst the leaves – an exceptional plant. Leaves of this in a Christmas salad are very festive.

These cut-and-come-again vegetables have the edge for busy (and forgetful) gardeners – you cut them to 2.5cm (1in) above the soil and in a few days they produce new leaves. You can do this at least four or five times before you exhaust them. To prolong their life you can 'pick them round' which means instead of stripping all the leaves off you leave half the leaves around the plant. Make two sowings a year, one in mid-spring and one in mid- to late summer and you will have leaves almost throughout the year. Thin the plants to about 23cm (9in) apart when they are large enough to handle. **BG**

Betula pendula 'Youngii'
YOUNG'S WEEPING BIRCH

Type: hardy, deciduous tree
Soil & situation: fertile, moist, well-drained soil/full sun or light shade
North American hardiness zone: 2–7
Height: 8m (25ft)
Spread: 4m (13ft)
Grow for: a beautifully shaped weeping tree with smooth, silver-grey bark when young

When the poet Samuel Taylor Coleridge referred to the birch as 'the lady of the woods' he was not

Betula pendula 'Youngii'

thinking of 'Youngii'. A better description for this highly desirable tree would be 'the little old lady of the garden'. When mature, it forms a mushroom-shaped head. Quite often a vigorous branch will grow out at right angles to the trunk before deciding to weep. Its side branches may do the same, giving the tree a lopsided appearance. Densely twiggy, its weeping outline is apparent all year round. The silver-grey bark eventually turns a dark brown with deep cracks. The diamond-shaped leaves are mid-green turning buttery-yellow in autumn.

If you want to attract leprechauns to your garden and space allows, plant a group of three *Betula pendula* 'Youngii' 4m (13ft) apart and underplant with the hardy *Cyclamen hederifolium* (see page 136). This is exactly the quiet, calming environment they love to hide in. If they don't settle no matter, you will enjoy it!

Pruning may be necessary to maintain a tidy weeping shape. Branches should be cut in early winter before the sap starts to rise otherwise wounds will 'bleed' for days, soaking the ground. Propagation is by grafting in winter. **JC**

Betula utilis var. *jacquemontii*
Plant of the Week (see page 61)

Billbergia nutans

Billbergia nutans
FRIENDSHIP PLANT

Type: tender, evergreen perennial
Soil & situation: warm, moist, rich compost/full sun/under cover
North American hardiness zone: 10–11
Height & spread: clump-forming, can reach 45cm (18in)
Grow for: a very tough bromeliad house or conservatory plant with attractive multi-coloured, though not large flowers coming out of evergreen, wide, rush-like foliage

This is a real survivor, hard to kill with neglect or even with over-watering and a good plant to start off a child's interest. The long, narrow leaves strongly resemble the well-known (unvariegated) spider plant without the little 'spiders'. Once pot bound and a big enough clump, billbergia throws out flower spikes of green, blue and yellow blooms from bright pink shoots at any time of year. It can go out on the patio in summer. Big clumps make excellent conservatory subjects.

Named after a Swedish botanist, this plant is almost hardy and may grow outdoors in very sheltered, warm gardens near the coast. It has survived for several years in my Norfolk garden at the base of a hedge in a dry, sunny spot but it does not flower very well there – probably because it is too dry, but any wetter and it would rot in winter.

A perfect houseplant, it can live for many years despite bad treatment. It flowers better when a little pot bound; remove dead flowers, though, as they're unsightly. Seed is not widely available, so use division as the simplest method of propagation, which can be done at almost any time. Otherwise remarkably problem free. **BF**

Brachyglottis monroi
(syn. *Senecio monroi*)

Type: hardy, evergrey shrub
Soil & situation: sharp draining soil/hardy to about −10°C (14°F), maybe more/needs a little protection in a cold, first winter/tolerates windy conditions/thrives in seaside locations/sunny position enhances the grey of their foliage/leaf colour becomes more green than grey in dappled shade
North American hardiness zone: 9–10
Height and spread: 1m (3ft)
Grow for: exquisite foliage, neater and more compact than the better known *B*. Dunedin hybrids; leaf has an attractive wavy edge; yellow flowers in summer but very much secondary to the foliage effects; AGM

This plant has a good dense habit, forming a well-mounded dome of foliage. The tops of the leaves are a green-grey, and because the wavy edges of the foliage, which look as if they have been cut with blunt crimping scissors, turn upwards slightly, it pleasingly accentuates the contrasting silver-white undersides of the leaves. The young shoots and flower stalks are also silver-white. The main problem with this plant is that having lived with it you tend to turn up your nose at the commoner *B*. Dunedin hybrids or *Senecio greyi*, as it used to be called. This is larger, generally coarser, with a tendency to sprawl, and seems to be mobbed by the rather vicious yellow-coloured, daisy flowers for too long in the summer. And to think I used to think it a not unattractive, good-tempered plant.

I prefer this plant without the flowers and with a good tight habit, so I cut it hard back in spring, shortening the shoots by about a third. If you like the flowers, then do this procedure after flowering. It is easy to propagate from cuttings, and semi-ripe ones in summer work well, but you could probably succeed at most times of the year. It is that obliging. **BG**

Brachyglottis monroi

Brassica oleracea var. *italica*

Brassica oleracea var. *italica* (syn. *B. o. botrytis cymosa*)
BROCCOLI ROMANESCO

Type: near-hardy, herbaceous, semi-woody, biennial vegetable
Soil & situation: very fertile, moist, lime-rich soil/full sun
North American hardiness zone: normally grown as an annual
Height & spread: up to 60cm (24in)
Grow for: totally unique appearance, somewhat like a cauliflower but lime-green and pointy with an exquisite flavour

The sprouting and heading forms of broccoli and the true cauliflowers are two very similar types of brassica. The former are hardier and will usually over-winter, whereas true cauliflowers are more tender and rarely make it through the winter.

Despite being called a broccoli, romanesco more closely resembles a cauliflower, as it is grown from a spring sowing to crop in late summer/early autumn, and once the main head is taken it rarely produces many sideshoot heads. Although a little tricky to grow, this native of Italy is a gourmet vegetable with a wonderful flavour and a fine melting texture, making it nearly as luscious as asparagus and almost certainly more nutritious. The head warrants close examination with a hand lens, as its form of tight, pointed spirals is aesthetically pleasing and quite unique.

The soil must be rich and moist or romanesco will bolt and give minute heads that are of little use. Break and bend over big leaves to protect the ripening curd from the sun. Sow only in spring, preferably *in situ*, or move on at a very early stage from individual pots or cells. Transplanting from a seedbed is often unsuccessful as plants may then bolt. For good heads give them at least 60cm (24in) each way.

Romanesco suffers all the usual brassica pests and diseases: white moths/flies and various caterpillars are kept off by growing plants under horticultural fleece; slugs are best thinned out with slug pubs of fermenting beer; sowing *in situ*, under plastic bottle cloches also keeps away many of the pests otherwise attracted by the smell given off by seedlings bruised when transplanted. **BF**

Brassica oleracea 'Noisette' (syn. *B. bullata* var. *gemmifera* 'Noisette')
BRUSSELS SPROUT

Type: hardy, herbaceous, semi-woody, biennial vegetable
Soil & situation: rich, moist, firm soil/full sun or light shade
North American hardiness zone: normally grown as an annual
Height: 1m (3ft)
Spread: 30–60cm (12–24in)
Grow for: when in England, you have to have sprouts for Christmas and this is one of the best

'Noisette' is a small, firm hazelnut-sized sprout that rarely gets big and blowsy like some sorts, and it does not have the same rank taste as many unless it's grossly overfed with manure. There are other sprouts bred to have a sweeter, less mustardy flavour but this old variety is still best to my taste, although the red Brussels sprout, *B. oleracea* 'Rubine', is a good alternative.

From the name and lack of reference to it by the ancients, it is commonly believed to have been bred from a Savoy-type cabbage in Belgium in the late Middle Ages. Some say it is derived from the same ancestor as the Jersey tree cabbage, which is much like a very tall (2m/6½ft plus) kale. Indeed, if a cabbage of almost any sort has its head removed then small sprouts may form on the stem and, likewise, the head of a Brussels sprout can be eaten just like a loose cabbage or kale.

A rich, moist soil is essential but most important is to plant the seedling quite deep and to ensure the soil is firmed down hard. Removing the head will cause the sprouts to form sooner; they are said to taste better after a frost has hit them. Sow in early spring in several batches and transplant the best seedlings by late spring/early summer, spacing them at least 60cm (24in) apart each way. Sprouts suffer all the usual brassica pests and diseases (see previous entry), although slugs and caterpillars are less of a problem than with most of the others in the family. Sprouts tend to be loose and blowsy if grown shallow or in uncompacted soil. Keeping the soil moist will deter the flea beetle, which can be a problem when prolific. **BF**

Brassica oleracea 'Noisette'

Brassica oleracea var. *capitata* 'Grand Prize'
SUMMER CABBAGE

Type: half-hardy, herbaceous, semi-woody, biennial vegetable
Soil & situation: rich, moist, limy soil/full sun to light shade
North American hardiness zone: normally grown as an annual
Height & spread: 60cm (24in)
Grow for: it grows big easily, and is significantly sweeter and better flavoured than all the other summer cabbages I've tried

Although I have chosen several cabbages as my favourite plants you may find it surprising to know that I am not very fond of cabbage as a vegetable. However, I do like it in coleslaw and my choices all depend on their suitability for this purpose. This cabbage is really superior in flavour, and I strongly suggest any 'cabbage-phobes', like me, try this one for its almost nutty taste. I even quite like it steamed!

There are many different sorts of cabbage and summer cultivars are distinctly different to the spring and winter varieties, most obviously in that they are far less hardy so are probably related to the old Roman varieties. The Romans believed the cabbage was created from the divine perspiration of Jupiter when he was trying to solve contra-dictory oracles, and they attributed great healing powers to cabbage, as well as thinking it prevented drunkenness. However, they probably only had loose-leaf cabbages as it is still hard to get them to form hard heads in warmer climates. The art of growing a hard head was most likely not developed until the times of the Norman conquest, as the first references appear after 1066.

Summer cabbages need to be grown quickly and smoothly so they need a rich, moist, limy soil or they may bolt. They are not very hardy and must be gathered before the frosts return. If the cabbage head is removed and a cross cut made across the stem several smaller, looser heads will form, which can be used in succession. Also it is not necessary to take the whole head at once; half can be removed and the remaining half covered with foil or plastic wrap, as it will stay fresher on the stem than if cut and stored in a refrigerator.

Summer cabbage can be started off in pots or cells under cover and planted out after the frosts, sown *in situ* or transplanted out from a seedbed, or use all three methods to give a spread of ripe heads from early summer until the frosts. It suffers from all the usual brassica pests, but is hit harder than other cabbages as it grows when pests are at their most prevalent. However, the crop rarely fails entirely but it can be messy to clean plants. Growing under horticultural fleece prevents a lot of problems and slugs can be thinned by using slug pubs; flea beetles are best kept off the seedlings by maintaining a moist soil.   **BF**

Brassica oleracea var. *capitata* 'Spring Hero'
SPRING CABBAGE

Type: hardy, herbaceous, semi-woody, biennial vegetable
Soil & situation: rich, moist soil/full sun or light shade
North American hardiness zone: normally grown as an annual
Height & spread: not much more than 30cm (12in)
Grow for: a significantly better (harder, more densely packed) spring cabbage than older, more pointed sorts

Spring cabbages have to be really tough and hardy to over-winter. Most of them have pointed, fairly loose conical heads, but 'Spring Hero' has a round-shaped head, which is hard enough to use for coleslaw and comes in many weeks before the summer cabbages are ready for the same use. It is a significant improvement and worth the eating. The pointed-headed conical spring cabbages are thought to have some Chinese cabbage blood in them, although others suggest they may derive from the Savoy group of loose-headed cabbages – either way they are much tougher than but not as good to eat as the summer sorts. 'Spring Hero' is a new hybrid with the toughness of the old sorts but with almost the eating quality of the summer ones.

A rich, moist soil in full sun is essential. In winter if it is really cold protect young plants with cloches; in spring give water and shade if there is a sudden hot, dry spell while the plants head up to prevent splitting and bolting. A dose of nitrogen-rich liquid feed in early spring as the soil warms up will help promote an earlier crop. Sow mid- to late summer, preferably *in situ* or transplant out from individual cells or pots in early autumn, or over-winter in a cold frame and plant out in early spring. They can be squeezed in together more than summer or winter cabbages as they are usually more compact and they form a microclimate, helping each other to keep out the cold wind.

It suffers all the usual brassica pests and diseases (see *Brassica oleracea* var. *italica*, page 64). Slugs may be an especial menace as they climb up inside in winter and do their damage unseen. Luckily these cabbages often escape the summer caterpillar and whitefly attacks as they are cropped and gone by the time the pests are in force. They will need extra protection and care when first sown, but this is easy as they are still small.   **BF**

Brassica oleracea var. *capitata* 'Spring Hero'

Daphne odora 'Aureomarginata'

Type: frost-hardy, variegated, evergreen shrub
Soil & situation: rich, moist, well-drained soil/full sun to light shade
Hardiness zone: 7–9
Height & spread: 1m (3ft), but maybe more
Grow for: similiar leaves to *Daphne tangutica* (see page 141), but with a silvery-gold narrow margin; gorgeously scented clusters of reddish-purple (outside) and white (inside) flowers opening for a long period. Like many daphnes, it brightens the late winter garden with its scent; AGM.

Daphne odora 'Aureomarginata' has the best perfume in this sweet-scented family. Of all the daphnes it is the toughest, one of the most attractive and even nearly the longest lived, though that is still only about as long as a good-quality automobile! The scent is amazing, in that it often projects itself across the garden and can be smelt strongly upon approach, only to disappear and reappear as you get closer to the small flowers.

D. odora, a neat and very attractive Chinese and Japanese evergreen shrub, was introduced to the UK in 1771 but always proved miffy and not hardy unless given some protection. This superior form, unusual for a variegated plant, is tougher and more vigorous than the plain and survives longer in much less comfortable conditions.

It is the least demanding of a difficult family and does best in rich, moist, humus-rich, limy soil in light sun. Do not prune and do not move once established. You may get 10 or 15 years, but even if it only makes five it will be worth it. It can be layered and is among the easiest of this family to root from cuttings taken in early summer. All daphnes get virus infected and die away, so never prune them. If aphids become a problem, spray with soft soap. **BF**

Daphne mezereum

MEZEREON

Type: hardy deciduous shrub
Soil & situation: moist, preferably slightly chalky soil, partial shade
Hardiness zone: 5–6
Height & spread: to 1m (3ft)
Grow for: early flowering with purple-red scented flowers from February, attractive foliage, red fruits in autumn (which are poisonous). Like *D. odora* 'Aureomarginata' (see page 67), its scented flowers are a late-winter joy.

Although the mezereon is notoriously short-lived and prone to virus infections that make it just fade away, it is still a very good garden plant. The flowers are delightful, come very early in the year and have a sweet orange-flower-like perfume that is most pleasing. There are improved selections such as 'Rosea', 'Grandiflora' and the white-flowered form 'Alba' (top right), which gives yellow berries, but the common mezereon is quite good enough for most people.

A native of Europe and the Middle East, this daphne's name comes from the Persian Arabic *mazarjun*. The plant used to be used as a 'cure' for alcoholism: enough poisonous berries were forced on the miscreant to only make him rather sick; but if he then also drank alcohol he would become really sick – do not try this at home…

Daphne mezereum likes a moist soil in partial shade on a woodland's edge with some chalk in it and it will then last up to a decade or so. Never ever prune it or it will die back. It is best grown from seed; those sown fresh, *in situ* so that they are never moved, do best of all. It may get the occasional aphid attack, but generally no curable problems other than being short-lived; the cure for that is to buy or sow another. **BF**

Brassica oleracea var. *capitata* 'Dutch White'

Brassica oleracea var. *capitata* 'Holland Late'/'Dutch White'
WINTER CABBAGE

Type: frost-hardy, herbaceous, semi-woody, biennial vegetable
Soil & situation: rich, moist, limy soil/full sun or light shade
North American hardiness zone: normally grown as an annual
Height & spread: 60cm (24in) each way
Grow for: the best cabbage to store for winter use

There are many different cabbage varieties that can be available in the coldest months of the year: some summer cabbages can be stored for early winter use and the curly-leafed Savoy Group are hardiest and will stand outside most winters. The latter are not hard headed, really not much better eating than kales and they are useless for coleslaw, whereas 'Holland Late' is perfect and will keep for months. Taken up by the roots it can be hung upside-down in a shed or garage for winter use, though I find it best stored in a dead refrigerator (with the door shut to keep out air and rodents) after liberally dusting it with salt to prevent the slugs moving around and causing further damage. The cabbages go horrible on the outside in the store but clean up nicely.

'Holland Late' or 'Dutch White' is one of the longest developed varieties and has been selected by cabbage growers for several centuries to grow late into the autumn; it will stay in good condition for some months after lifting. Traditionally it would have been stored in a clamp under a layer of straw and soil, likewise it can be kept fresh in the garden by covering it with a large plastic bag stuffed full of straw to keep out the frost. Red cabbage is closely related and grown and stored in much the same way, but is most often used for pickling in vinegar.

Like the majority of brassicas these varieties need full sun and moist, rich, limy soil to be able to grow big, hard heads. As the stumps often come through a winter if left after the head is cut then it is worth cutting a cross in the top of the stem and removing diseased leaves but leaving the healthy ones, in the hope of getting bonus heads in spring. Sow in spring in pots, cells or a seedbed and transplant out in late spring/early summer. Make sure the soil is firm, as uncompacted soil produces loose heads which do not store so well.

As with all brassicas there are many pests and diseases – rotation and hygiene cope with lots of these, and growing under horticultural fleece deters several pests, such as white moths/flies and various caterpillars, while moist soils prevent heavy flea beetle damage. **BF**

Brassica oleracea var. *gongyloides* 'Superschmelz'
KOHL RABI

Type: half-hardy, herbaceous, biennial vegetable
Soil & situation: rich, moist soil/full sun to light shade
North American hardiness zone: normally grown as an annual
Height & spread: 45cm (18in)
Grow for: amazingly versatile; huge variety; easier to grow than turnips in adverse conditions

In light soil or in hot, dry weather it is easier to succeed with kohl rabi than it is with turnips. It can be used either cooked as turnips or raw as a crudité or in a salad. But I am no fan of most kohl rabis, as the majority of varieties attain only tennis-ball size before, like turnips, they become hot and woody.

'Superschmelz' is the exception. It is of Dutch origin and attains an astronomic size; I have grown it to bigger than a football and yet inside the flesh was as sweet and crisp as many a supermarket apple. Moreover this variety can be taken up in autumn and stored for several months without deteriorating as rapidly as some sorts of cabbage, especially if kept in cool conditions such as in a dead refrigerator. It is then available for making kohl slaw all winter.

Kohl rabi is an odd vegetable that has been developed to have a huge swollen stem and is probably derived from the old marrow cabbage. It first appeared in the 16th century in Italy, though the name suggests a more central European origin, and it is claimed to be from the Italian cavoli rape, meaning cabbage turnip. In France there are ornamental varieties with cut and frizzled leaves, and another with artichoke-like leaves apparently once favoured by confectioners for decoration!

It will grow in poor, dry conditions but does best in rich, moist, limy soil. Kohl rabi is not very hardy, so is best sown after the last frost and lifted before the first frost in autumn. Sow ideally *in situ* or in pots or cells from late spring into early summer. Space the plants 45cm (18in) apart when transplanting or thinning out, or more if going for big roots. Although closely related to the other brassicas, kohl rabi – once established – is remarkably unaffected by most of their problems. However, flea beetles can almost destroy small plants, so keep the soil moist. **BF**

Brassica rapa chinensis
PAK CHOI

Type: half-hardy, herbaceous, biennial vegetable
Soil & situation: rich, very moist soil/full sun/under cover in winter and light shade outdoors in summer
North American hardiness zone: normally grown as an annual
Height & spread: may reach 30cm (12in), or more when flowering
Grow for: one of the few vegetables to be available for 52 weeks of the year, and especially useful under cover in winter

Pak choi is like a cross between celery and a loose-leaf cabbage and is incredibly fast growing – even in winter if kept under cover. It is full of valuable minerals and vitamins and easy to use as a spinach, for braising like celery and in stir fries. The closely related *Pe-tsai* has less celery-like stems and more cabbage-like leaves and is probably the most slug-attractive plant in the garden.

It was not known to Europeans until the Victorian period. The Chinese have a whole series of brassicas, many of them closely resembling our

Brassica rapa chinensis

European ones, but whereas ours come mostly from the wild coleworts, such as found on the chalk cliffs of Dover, the Chinese developed theirs from the very similar and closely related mustards; indeed, the seed can be ground into a mustard condiment.

Pak choi needs rich, moist soil with plentiful lime. It is prone to bolting if crowded, too hot or too dry – keeping the soil moist is crucial. It can be successively sown in situ all year round under cover and outside from mid-spring until late summer. It is possible to cut back or pull off leaves to get renewal growth and also to detach and transplant small offshoots. Pak choi can be started off in pots and planted out with care – space plants at least 30cm (12in) apart each way.

It is very prone to slug damage and suffers the same pests and diseases as most other brassicas, many of which can be kept off by growing it under cover or under horticultural fleece. Flea beetle attacks this less than other brassicas, as the soil is always kept so moist. **BF**

Briza maxima
QUAKING GRASS

Type: hardy, annual grass
Soil & situation: any free-draining soil/sun
North American hardiness zone: annual
Height: 30cm (12in)
Spread: 25cm (10in)
Grow for: dainty flowers from late spring to mid-summer

This is such a pretty plant and dainty in every way. From late spring to late summer it forms dense, tufted clumps of narrow, pale green leaves only 20cm (8in) long that dry to become straw-coloured later in the season. However, the finest feature are the loose, open flower clusters that hang from arching, hair-fine stems. The tiny, heart-shaped 'spikelets' like pearlescent lockets, 1cm (½in) long, dance enthusiastically to the sound of the leaves rustling in the wind; they start light green, become mid-green and turn pale straw-yellow, like the leaves, as they mature.

It is possibly one of the earliest grasses grown for any use, other than edible purposes. *Briza minor* and *B. maxima* will self-seed and in good conditions can become weeds, but they are excellent for drying and should be picked immediately once they are fully developed, which sorts out the 'weed' problem too.

Briza maxima

There are other quaking grasses worth considering:

B. media is taller and perennial, the flower stems developing from a thick tuft of 'grass' from early to late summer. In Yorkshire, it is known as 'Trimmling Jockies' or 'Doddering Dickies' and it is used in pest control. It's said 'A trimmling jock i' t' house and you weeant hev a mouse'. Precisely!

B. minor is a short, dainty annual only 20cm (8in) tall, with tiny spikelets 5mm (¼in) long. It flowers from early summer to early autumn. All need a sunny position on free-draining soil. Sow seed outdoors in spring or autumn in the position where it is to flower. **MB**

Brugmansia aurea

Type: evergreen shrub or small tree
Soil & situation: good, but well-drained
soil/sunny position/minimum temperature of
7°C (45°F) in winter/fair amount of moisture
when in growth
North American hardiness zone: 10–11
Height: 5–10m (16–33ft)
Spread: 2–4m (6½–13ft)
Grow for: copious quantities of huge, yellow to
apricot hanging trumpets from summer to
autumn; large, ovate leaves add a tropical feel to
the garden

You can guarantee that the sight of these in full
bloom will cause a stir among gardeners and non-
gardeners alike. Those who do not grow them will
think that you are really clever to grow such
exotic-looking plants and to get them to flower so
prolifically. But they are dead easy. The only
possible stumbling block is whether you are able
to lug them into a frost-free greenhouse, if you
have one. They can be grown outside in a warm
garden in the milder areas of the country, and in
areas which receive little or no frost they will
bloom for most of the year. They do get huge very
fast – too huge – but it does not cause a problem
as in spring you can cut them down to within
15cm (6in) of the ground or to any convenient
height, and they burst back forming a grand

Brugmansia aurea

multi-stemmed flowering shrub. I usually maintain
mine at a height of 3m (10ft) at which size they
look stately and impressive. The exotic flowers are
scented at night and I have been told that if you
inhale the fragrance it triggers hallucinogenic
dreams – not surprising then that *Brugmansia* spp.
are cultivated for their narcotic properties! I play
safe though and stick to a glass of wine and have
never dared let it give me a whirl.

Assuming you do not have the luxury of frost-free
conditions outside, grow it in a large pot, or, for
better results, plant it directly into the open
border in late spring. If pot-grown, re-pot – or at
least top dress – each spring, and water and liquid
feed during growth. Slugs and snails will decimate
the foliage, so in this respect pot growing is
superior as you can easily control them. But in
other respects, apparently, they do better in the
border. At the end of autumn I drag it in (if
grown in the border then pot it up), and because
my temperatures are low, the leaves yellow and
drop. This is to be expected unless you have bags
of warmth. I keep it on the dry side over winter
but as soon as everything starts to move in spring,
I increase the food and water as it extends its
growth. **BG**

Brugmansia suaveolens
(syn. *Datura suaveolens*)
ANGELS' TRUMPETS

Type: tender, perennial, semi-woody shrub
Soil & situation: rich, moist compost/full
sun/under cover in winter, outdoors in summer
North American hardiness zone: 10–11
Height & spread: best as a 'small tree' in a tub at
1.5–1.8m (5–6ft) each way, but can get twice as
big
Grow for: a profusion of very big, scented,
funnel-shaped flowers; AGM

A native of Brazil, the group's name was changed
from the closely related *Datura* to *Brugmansia*
when Queen Victoria was a virgin. We haven't
taken to it yet. Nomenclaturial botanists, a plague
on them and their dirty habits!

Angels' trumpets is a relatively reliable and
impressive specimen for your patio or conservatory, which looks a million dollars but grows as
easily as a fuchsia. Indeed, daturas can be thrown
under frost-free cover and forgotten about until
spring and will nearly always recover. The pure
white forms of the soft, funnel-shaped, hanging
flowers have the strongest most sweet perfume;

Brugmansia suaveolens

other colours have been selected, but these are
not as sweet. *Datura metel* and *D. meteloides* are
more tender, and therefore better suited to the
greenhouse or conservatory rather than the patio;
both have upright funnels. Similar but smaller is
D. stramonium, the thornapple, and it is a weed!

Best confined in a tub, put out for summer and
returned under cover all winter. Water heavily
during the growing season. Plants can go on
many years, but they are easy to replace anyway.
Prune back hard to form a standard with a small
head when it's taken in at the end of the growing
season or in spring before growth commences.
Over the winter keep it almost bone dry and frost
free. It can be grown from seed but cuttings are
easy any time of year, indeed too easy as these
plants multiply on you. Daturas seem to get a host
of aphids, whiteflies, red spider mites et al but
this never seems to stop them. Don't eat any parts
as they are all toxic. **BF**

Buddleja fallowiana var. *alba*

Type: frost-hardy, deciduous shrub
Soil & situation: well-drained soil/will often grow in thin, stony, poor soils/if they are being pruned back annually, they do better in a fertile soil/sun/warm, sheltered environment/hardy to −10°C (14°F)
North American hardiness zone: 8–9
Height & spread: 3m (10ft)
Grow for: handsome white-felted foliage; secondary bonus – creamy-white, fragrant flowers from late summer to early autumn; AGM

This buddleja has elegant, white-felted shoots and very long, lanceolate, silver-green leaves, which are covered in white felt below. The flowers are usually the main reason for growing these shrubs, their fat, densely packed, flowering panicles being produced in large quantities, often heavily fragrant and stuffed with nectar. This one has more slender flowers on long, arching wands so they do make less impact than the flowers on many buddlejas. The eye is orange, creating an unusual, almost quaint appearance. But then, most things about this buddleja are different from the run-of-the-mill purple-flowered job that you more frequently see. But that is why I like it!

The pruning is best carried out in early spring as the buds begin to swell. Simply cut back all the wood to within 5cm (2in) of a low, permanent framework which you make in the first two to three years after planting, or cut back harder to ground level. It is a good idea to give it a thick, protective mulch in the winter. Propagation is very easy – you simply take hardwood cuttings in autumn. **BG**

Buddleja fallowiana var. *alba*

Buddleja 'Lochinch'

Buddleja globosa
Plant of the Week (see page 145)

Buddleja lindleyana

Type: half-hardy, deciduous shrub
Soil & situation: free-draining soil/sun/shelter
North American hardiness zone: 8–9
Height: 3m (10ft), or higher against a wall
Spread: 2.5m (8ft), sometimes taller
Grow for: elegant flower spikes in mid- and late summer

This plant with ecclesiastical connections reminds me of three splendid gentlemen: the Rev. Adam Buddle, an English botanist and vicar; John Lindley, a great horticulturist, administrator and writer; and a great friend of mine, Father Hugh Flower, a Kew-trained horticulturist turned parish priest who gave me the plant. What a wonderful gift! It's a plant with immense finesse; the sleek, gracefully arching stems are tipped with slender flower-spikes, up to 20cm (8in) long, of rich deep purple-violet to lilac flowers; each curved flower is covered on the outside with fine hairs, creating a velvety lavender sheen. In flower there's a cascade of blooms, like an exploding firework. Even the leaves, an attractive dark green, are narrow, tapered and elegant with a simple network of impressed veins; they are the perfect foil to the cinnamon-coloured older stems. Butterflies (and hummingbirds) love it!

In milder climates, grow against a sheltered, sunny wall, or in a cool greenhouse where weather conditions are more extreme. It thrives in moist, fertile, well-drained soil; feed and mulch in spring. It will become chlorotic if under-fed. As a shrub, cut back the previous year's shoots in early or mid-spring to one or two pairs of buds at the base. It can be fan trained against a wall, but the stems are rather stiff. Cut them back to within one or two pairs of buds of the framework of old wood; remove the oldest stems at the base and replace with new growth. Propagate by semi-ripe cuttings. **MB**

Buddleja 'Lochinch'

Type: hardy, deciduous shrub
Soil & situation: well-drained fertile soil/full sun
North American hardiness zone: 6–9
Height: 2.5m (8ft)
Spread: 3m (10ft)
Grow for: superb pewtery, green-grey foliage greening with age; beautiful lavender-blue 20cm (8in) long panicles, which arrive at the end of the summer, staying for many weeks; AGM

This is my favourite buddleja and a really stunning hybrid. It is, in fact, a cross between *B. davidii* and *B. fallowiana*. The flowers are produced in substantial numbers and the strong, but subtle, blue of the flower (it has an orange eye) tones well with the grey-green of the foliage and they have a sweetly scented fragrance too. It has a good bushy form and the structure of the bare plant in the winter is an asset too – not that common in deciduous shrubs.

Prune it back hard each year to keep growth compact and encourage better flowering. It is well worthwhile cutting back the flowerheads to a pair of leaves as they go over – this prevents them seeding around and can, if you are lucky, result in a second flowering. **BG**

Buddleja lindleyana

Buddleja x *weyeriana* 'Sungold'

Type: hardy, deciduous shrub
Soil & situation: fertile, well-drained soil/full sun
North American hardiness zone: 6–8
Height: 4m (13ft)
Spread: 3m (10ft)
Grow for: fragrant orange-yellow flowers in summer and early autumn; AGM

I have to admit I, as well as butterflies, love the large, solid flower panicles of *Buddleja davidii* and its cultivars. The rounded flower clusters of *B. globosa* 'Orange Ball' are also appealing.

B. x *weyeriana* is a cross between the two and the result is an improvement on both parents. *B.* x *w.* 'Sungold' has long arching branches and 20cm (8in) long, lance-shaped, mid-green leaves. The rounded clusters of fragrant, dark orange-yellow flowers are spaced along a grey-white stem to form a loose 30cm (12in) terminal panicle. The flowers are produced in summer and the plant will often still be in flower in late autumn.

Pruning should be carried out in spring, removing all last year's flowering shoots to within several centimetres of the older wood. Enormous growth of up to 2m (6½ft) will be made before summer, when it will produce flowers. Old, neglected shrubs can be rejuvenated by cutting into the old wood. Water and feed with a general fertilizer in late spring and the stumps will send out new growths. Propagate by softwood cuttings in early summer or hardwood cuttings inserted in the ground outside in late autumn. **JC**

Buddleja x *weyeriana* 'Sungold'

Buxus sempervirens
BOX

Type: hardy, evergreen shrub
Soil & situation: wide range of soils, providing it is well-drained/will tolerate a pH range from about 5.5–7.5/sun or light shade
North American hardiness zone: 6–8
Height: up to 8m (25ft) but usually grown as a multi-stemmed shrub to 1m (3ft) or less
Spread: to 8m (25ft)
Grow for: evergreen with small neat, shiny leaves; excellent for clipping and topiary work; AGM

Box has come back into vogue big time in the last 20 years or so. It is much used for giving some formality and structure to gardens whether with clipped forms, hedges, parterres or topiary, in classic or contemporary styles. Since the end of the 20th century, it has suffered from box blight, a disease which has affected several notable gardens including Sir Roy Strong's, The Laskett, but there are certain factors which reduce this risk. For low hedges, *B. sempervirens* can be used – it is less susceptible than the 'edging box', *B.* 'Suffruticosa'. I prefer the larger form anyway as it forms a plumper hedge but admittedly may need a second trim later on in summer due to its vigour. In the moister, more westerly parts of the country it is far more likely to be susceptible to blight than in the drier east. Apparently in Victorian times they used to rip it up and re-plant it at 12-yearly or so intervals – I think possibly because it grew to be too dense and so disease became more of a problem.

If the drainage is not good, do put this right before you plant. If I am planting a low hedge of this, I plant at 6 or 7 per metre (3 feet) run. This will form a recognizable, bushy hedge in three years or so (assuming you put in bushy liners), providing you trim the sides and top to get it to bush out. The best time to trim it used to be Derby Day in early summer, but with the milder winters if I waited this long I would have a scruffy looking hedge for longer than I want, so I tend to do mine in late spring, and if a heavy frost looms, I bring out the fleece or pray. I usually give it a secondary cut in late summer/early autumn to neaten it up before winter. Try not to water it overhead, this is thought to be one of the main factors that encourages the dreaded box blight. **BG**

Buxus sempervirens 'Handsworthiensis'
BOX

Type: fully hardy, evergreen shrub
Soil & situation: fertile, well-drained soil/sun or partial shade
North American hardiness zone: 6–8
Height & spread: 5m (16ft)
Grow for: the dense habit provides an excellent background for more colourful plants, and makes it ideal for hedging or screening

When the specification calls for a tall, dense, evergreen hedge for maximum privacy, use this plant. Kept clipped, not even an x-ray machine could see through it.

The dark, sage-green, cupped leaves are 4cm (1½in) long on stiff, upright stems. Box will withstand regular, close clipping to keep it in shape. It is tolerant of deep shade, making it ideal undercover in woodland. Left unclipped it will eventually form a large, straggly, multi-stemmed tree or shrub. In spring the foliage on the new growth is pale yellow turning to yellowish-green before it is due its next short back and sides. Terminal shoots are orange-tinted in autumn. The tiny, yellow-green spring flowers are insignificant.

The foliage exudes an unusual aroma, not unpleasant but immediately recognizable for what it is – box hedging. Rabbits, while catholic in taste, invariably leave box unnibbled. Snails, on the other hand, consider it their personal hotel. Within the branches there are likely to be hundreds, complete with their mobile homes – a point worth considering before you plant box hedges round fancy vegetable plots.

It is not a deep-rooted plant – most of its fibrous roots lie close to the soil surface. A combination of dry soil and full sun stunts growth causing sickly foliage. This is a common occurrence with pot-grown box. An annual mulch of bark or rotted farmyard manure applied to the base of the hedge in spring will prevent the soil drying out. Propagation is by softwood or hardwood cuttings.

It will be noticed I avoided mentioning its use for my pet hate, topiary. If you must and bearing in mind its stiff, upright nature, 'Handsworthiensis' will allow you to clip a full-size giraffe! **JC**

Buxus sempervirens 'Handsworthiensis'

Caiophora lateritia

Type: tender, annual or perennial climber
Soil & situation: free-draining soil/hot sunshine
North American hardiness zone: normally grown as an annual
Height & spread: 3m (10ft)
Grow for: weird flowers from mid-summer to early autumn; weirder seedpods

I first saw this in the garden at Red Gables, a house just outside Evesham, southwest England, where Derek and Rowlatt Cook, a brother and sister with an infinite enthusiasm for plants, were growing this through the spiny stems of a berberis in a potential 'double whammy' of pain! It was probably the only way to 'cage' their caiophora and deter passers-by from touching this fascinating plant! The grey-green leaves are covered in soft, bristly hairs; stroke them and you'll recoil in pain as hidden among them are sharp, stinging spines!

The brick-red, apricot or white flowers, with unusual keeled petals and tufts of anthers projecting along the centre, hang like hovering flying saucers waiting to land. It looks wonderful scrambling through silver-foliage shrubs like cotton lavender, but avoid planting it through sage, though I have seen it done, as you might need the leaves for flavouring! The seedpods look like screws with an irregular wing and a spike at the end, but having seen the flowers it's no surprise that they're strange!

Treat as a tender annual or biennial. Sow under glass in early spring and plant out before it starts to twine, after the danger of frost has passed. The stinging hairs are usually (!) ineffective on young plants at transplanting time. It needs a warm, dry, sunny position and free-draining soil; incorporate grit before planting if necessary. Grow in mild, sheltered climates as a short-lived perennial, mulching with straw or bracken over winter. Alternatively, grow it in a container and over-winter in a conservatory. **MB**

Caiophora lateritia

Calendula officinalis

Calendula officinalis
POT MARIGOLD

Type: hardy, herbaceous, semi-evergreen annual/biennial
Soil & situation: any soil/preferably full sun to light shade
North American hardiness zone: normally grown as an annual
Height & spread: 30cm (12in) each way in good soil
Grow for: attractive year-round-foliage; striking orange flowers; easy, reliable and edible

This multiple-value plant is fast and easy to grow; it retains its foliage in all but the hardest winters; it isn't prone to pests or diseases; and its pungently scented flowers add flavour to stews and salads, and can be dried for winter use. The leaves have the same flavour as the flowers and can be used when none are available, but they do have an even more pungent taste. Indeed, it is a classic 'children's plant'.

A native of Europe and North Africa, calendula has been known for millennia and is so named because it was always to be found in flower on the *Kalends*, the first day of each month, which it can do in warmer countries than Britain. In the Middle Ages it was called Mary-buds and

dedicated to the Virgin, as it was allegedly always in flower on her holy days. In the past marigold petals were used for turning grey hair yellow and the leaves for treating wounds.

They can be almost left to themselves as they self-sow happily, but for a guaranteed year-round supply sow some under cover where they will flower constantly. They are reputed good companions as they attract beneficial insects. Dead-heading promotes more flowers and is worth doing to prevent excessive self-seeding. Sow, preferably *in situ*, from early spring onwards and they will start flowering within 10 to 12 weeks, making them among the fastest annuals to bloom. They suffer no problems at all apart from self-sowing everywhere. **BF**

John adds:
The flowers may be single or double and up to 10cm (4in) across, flowering from early summer to autumn. Colours include cream, orange, yellow and gold. There are many varieties including bicolours such as 'Fiesta Gitana'. 'Indian Prince' is excellent for flower arrangements and grows to 80cm (32in) with dark orange-brown tinted flowers.

Calendula officinalis 'Indian Prince'

Callicarpa bodinieri var. *giraldii* 'Profusion'

Callicarpa bodinieri var. *giraldii* 'Profusion'
BEAUTY BERRY

Type: hardy, deciduous shrub
Soil & situation: fertile, well-drained soil/full sun or light shade
North American hardiness zone: 6–8
Height: 3m (10ft)
Spread: 2m (6½ft)
Grow for: small, astonishingly coloured, deep violet fruits that resemble beads sprayed with metallic paint; AGM

If this shrub likes you and your garden it will out-perform most other berrying plants. It may, however, sulk, in which case give it a ride in the wheelbarrow to a different site. Even as a big plant it transplants well. The bead-like fruit are a special treat in winter.

The 15cm (6in) long, young leaves are bronze, turning dark green as they age. Clusters of pale pink flowers appear in summer from the leaf axils and are followed by groups of small, metallic-looking, deep violet fruit. The colour is so non-gardening they look artificial. They will fruit better after a long, hot summer. Provide shelter from cold, drying winds.

Prune in early spring, cutting back the older stems to the main framework. Old, neglected plants may be hard pruned to within 45cm (18in)

of the ground. Feed with a high-nitrogen fertilizer and water well all summer after a hard pruning. New, strong flowering shoots will grow to replace the old branches. Propagation is by softwood cuttings in late spring or semi-ripe cuttings pulled off with a heel and rooted in a heated propagator during summer. **JC**

Matt adds:
This is an unusual plant mainly because its ideas of colour co-ordination, based on violet-purple and tawny, could have come straight from the 1970s. It's fascinating how nature combines the most unusual colours and they are still visually acceptable; if they were artificially reproduced in paints or plastics it would look hideous! That's probably because the 'tones' and 'shades' are always perfect.

What's in a name? In this case, plenty! The Greek *kallos*, meaning beauty and *karpos*, fruit, and two missionaries Emile Marie Bodinieri from France and Guiseppe Giraldi from Italy, who were both avid plant collectors. And 'Profusion'? Just grow it and wait until you see the mass of berries! This plant was especially selected for this feature and its bronze-purple young leaves. The insignificant, pale pink flowers appear in mid-summer in evenly spaced dense clusters wrapped round the stem. They are followed from mid- to late autumn onwards by clusters of dark violet fruits spaced along the tawny-coloured branches. The berries look remarkable, particularly when you add the deep rose-purple autumn colour of the leaves.

Callistemon citrinus 'Austraflora Firebrand'
BOTTLEBRUSH

Type: half-hardy, evergreen shrub
Soil & situation: moist, well-drained, fertile, neutral to acid soil/full sun
North American hardiness zone: 9–11
Height: 2m (6½ ft)
Spread: 4m (13ft)
Grow for: crimson flower spikes that make an excellent focal point

The bottlebrushes are so wonderfully exotic in flower, they grab the attention and hold it over a long period. The silvery flower buds form like a string of pearls, opening to the familiar 'brushes' and finally there is a decorative cylinder of hard, woody seedpods. The habit of growth is low and spreading, forming a wide, medium height, bushy plant. The 10cm (4in) long, lance-shaped, dark green leaves open from young, silvery-pink shoots. Bright, crimson flower spikes are 10–15cm (4–6in) long and freely produced during late spring and early summer.

Pruning is necessary only where branches are spoiling the shape. The shrub continues to grow beyond the flower spike. Eventually each branch has a series of 10–15cm (4–6in) lengths of dead, woody, seed cases strung along the stem. Bottlebrushes tolerate hard pruning to rejuvenate old plants. Propagation is easy by semi-ripe cuttings in late summer. Sow the fine seed on the surface of a moist, loam-based compost in late spring. Keep the temperature at 18°C (64°F). **JC**

Callistemon citrinus 'Austraflora Firebrand'

Helleborus orientalis

LENTEN ROSE

Type: hardy evergreen perennial
Soil & situation: limestone or chalky soils/light or moderate shade in damp woodland/tolerates sun, though dislikes exposed conditions
Hardiness zone: 4–9
Height: to about 50cm (20in)
Spread: 45cm (18in)
Grow for: exquisite, usually white or greenish flowers from late winter to spring; various cultivars in a range of colours from black-purple, through purple to pink, from yellow-white to white and green; evergreen foliage, except in exceptionally cold winters. Called the Lenten rose because its blooms are usually at their best just before Easter.

Many people, understandably, become enchanted by the hellebore flowers and there are numerous cultivars, which have been selected and named, with stunning flowers, such as 'Phillip Ballard', which is a dark purple, and 'Cosmos', which is pale pink with attractive purple spots. The plants exhibit their flowers rather discreetly – you have to make a special visit to the plants to admire them properly, but it is definitely worth it.

The flowers apart, hellebores are good for their foliage, too. The deep, glossy, green basal leaves are handsome and look very presentable even in late winter after a regular battering of snow, frost, winds and wet. They self-sow freely, a big asset, and it is exciting to see what amazing colour flowers the new seedlings will produce, as they are a promiscuous bunch. Take care that the seedlings do not submerge the parent plant, especially if it is a special named cultivar. It is worth trying a choice plant like this in different places, for instance in a meadow setting – in light shade where the grass is not too dense a sward – or in a window box where the plants can be admired regularly at close quarters. Hellebores do not take too kindly to being moved. If you do need to divide up an old plant, it is best done in winter or spring when it is in flower and while the roots are fairly dormant. Then cosset it until it re-establishes itself. **BG**

Callistephus chinensis 'Ostrich Plume'
ANNUAL ASTER, CHINA ASTER

Type: hardy annual
Soil & situation: fertile, moist, neutral to alkaline soil/full sun
North American hardiness zone: annual
Height: 60cm (24in)
Spread: 30cm (12in)
Grow for: summer bedding in a range of bright colours

As a boy I used to sell these as cut flowers to earn money to buy my first greenhouse. The only problem was they lasted for more than a week in water and I only did my selling on a Saturday morning. I still think they are hard to beat.

Callistephus chinensis 'Ostrich Plume'

The mid-green leaves are 8cm (3½in) long and toothed. The daisy-like flowers are held on long, branched stems well clear of the foliage during late summer and all autumn. They are mainly in shades of pink and crimson with feathery, reflexed, double flowerheads. The Milady Series are more compact, growing to 30cm (12in) in a wider range of colours including white, blue, scarlet, pink, rose and red. The double, daisy-like flowerheads are rounded.

Dead heading extends the flowering season. They prefer a moist soil and shelter from cold winds. Water regularly in summer to prevent the soil drying out and the plant's growth slowing down. Propagation is by seed sown in early spring in a cool greenhouse or in late spring *in situ*. China asters are more resistant than most other asters to aster wilt but are very prone to aphid attacks in the young foliage. **JC**

Caltha palustris

Caltha palustris
KINGCUP, MARSH MARIGOLD, MEADOW BRIGHT, MAY-BLOB

Type: hardy perennial
Soil & situation: shallow water to a depth of 15cm (6in)/bog gardens/prefers a sunny site/will grow happily in part shade
North American hardiness zone: 3–7
Height: to 40cm (16in)
Spread: 45cm (18in)
Grow for: golden-yellow, large, long-lasting, waxy, cup-shaped flowers on long stems in spring; after flowering, glossy green leaves carry on growing, providing particularly good foliage effects for waterside areas; AGM

This is a stunning native plant, with its giant, buttercup-like flowers and large, shiny leaves. As it is a native, it is pretty easy to please, so decent groups quite quickly establish to form a good display along the water margins, both in water and in boggy patches. It will also survive being planted in border situations if the soil is moisture retentive and the situation is shady. *Caltha palustris* var. *palustris* is different in habit: its stems are creeping and it roots as it goes. As such it is useful for spreading over damp banks, marshy areas and in shallow water. The leaves are smaller, but the flowers are large initially and then reduce in size later on. The often grown *C. palustris* 'Flore Pleno' (see next entry) has double, yellow flowers and is often admired, but I prefer the native, single-flowered kingcup.

Depending on where it is positioned, this plant may be established in large aquatic baskets or straight into the the ground or planted on the pool base in spring or autumn. It likes a good rich organic soil and so mulching in spring, when grown in land situations, pays dividends. If grown in baskets, it is best divided and re-potted with additional fertilizer and organic matter as soon as it looks confined. It is easily propagated by division in spring, but can also be grown from seed, sown in summer under cover. Apparently American forms of *C. palustris* will self-sow in suitable conditions. Mine, alas, have not done so. **BG**

Caltha palustris 'Flore Pleno'

Caltha palustris 'Flore Pleno'
KINGCUP, DOUBLE-FLOWERED
MARSH MARIGOLD

Type: hardy, aquatic, deciduous perennial
Soil & situation: rich, boggy soil/full sun
North American hardiness zone: 3–7
Height & spread: 30cm (12in)
Grow for: interesting shaped leaves; cheerful
double yellow flowers in spring; perfect for damp,
boggy ground; AGM

I saw a remarkable planting of the double-flowered
marsh marigold many years ago in the
Netherlands. The owner had planted it on both
sides of a narrow dyke in front of his house. It was
in full flower. There was a blue sky and when I
looked along the length of the dyke the picture on
the still water was of two solid lines of gold with a
narrow reflected strip of blue sky in between.

The kidney-shaped, toothed, dark green leaves
appear in early spring and can be up to 10cm
(4in) long. *Caltha palustris* 'Flore Pleno' produces
waxy, double, buttercup-yellow flowers in spring
on 25cm (10in) bare stems. Before the flowers
fully open the centre of each bloom has a
greenish tinge. A second flush of flowers may
appear in the early autumn. The variety *C. p.* var.
alba is more compact, flowering in early spring
before the leaves appear. It produces solitary,
single white flowers with bright yellow stamens.

C. p. 'Flore Pleno' tolerates growing in water for
short periods but prefers to be in boggy,
constantly wet soil at the side of a stream or
pond. Propagation is by division of the large
clumps in late summer or, in cold areas, in early
spring before flowering. **JC**

Camassia quamash
QUAMASH

Type: frost-hardy, bulbous perennial
Soil & situation: rich, deep, moisture-retentive
soils/sun or part shade
North American hardiness zone: 4–9
Height: to 90cm (36in)
Spread: 5cm (2in)
Grow for: deep blue starry flowers produced in
racemes in late spring

This plant is a vigorous clump former, with linear,
green leaves about 40cm (16in) long and 1cm
(½in) wide. In late spring it produces bright blue
flowers which are shown off to their best
advantage in slightly wild or natural-looking
areas. This particular camassia is a strong grower
and is often highly successfully naturalized in
grass. I often also use it in open woodland areas
where it will get sun for part of the day. *Camassia
leichtlinii* subsp. *leichtlinii* (AGM) is also a useful
plant but is slightly taller and has white flowers.
The flowering period is short though, and it is
not so able to compete with grasses in a meadow
situation.

This plant does not give of its best in drier,
poorer soils – the flowering period will be
reduced (or even non-existent). It produces seed
freely, which usually ripens by mid-summer. It is
ideal to propagate by this method or you can take
offsets in summer. **BG**

Camassia quamash

Camellia 'Cornish Snow'

Camellia 'Cornish Snow'

Type: hardy, evergreen shrub
Soil & situation: neutral to slightly acid soil
(between pH 5–7), moist but well-drained and
humus-rich/sheltered site either shaded, partially
shaded or sunny/hates exposed, cold, windy
sites/avoid east-facing walls unless shaded
North American hardiness zone: 7–9
Height: 3m (10ft)
Spread: 1.5m (5ft)
Grow for: superb evergreen foliage; small, single,
white flowers from mid-winter to late spring; AGM

This plant is a hybrid between *C. cuspidata* and
C. saluenensis and is an excellent, hardy, faster-
growing camellia. It has slightly pendent branches
and 5cm (2in) long, lance-shaped, bold, glossy
leaves which are bronze-purple when young, later
turning dark green. It is free-flowering, producing
multitudes of the petite, white flowers which are
pink-tinged on opening, along the stems. These
smaller flowers are far less susceptible to frost and
wind damage than the very large-flowered forms.
Camellias are often thought to be successful in
more shady sites but when grown on a south or
west wall they do flower more readily – as long as
they still get the necessary moisture and their
roots are cool, they will not suffer from bud drop.
They are ideal for growing in containers.

These are fantastically long-lived plants, so it is
important to find the right position where they will
always be appreciated. Dense shade will inhibit bud
formation; early morning sun, late frost and
sunshine on frosted flowers will damage them. We
did use a digger to move a mature specimen
some two years ago and it re-established
afterwards with no apparent ill effects. Camellias
are best purchased as larger plants, about
60–90cm (24–36in) high and planted with lots of
rotted organic matter. They need little pruning,
just trimming lightly to shape the plant, only if
needed, and the removal of dead and damaged
young growth in spring before growth starts.
Neglected plants will take hard pruning back into
old wood. **BG**

Camellia japonica 'Bob Hope'

Camellia japonica 'Bob Hope'

Type: hardy, evergreen shrub
Soil & situation: moist, acid soil/sun or dappled shade/sheltered position
North American hardiness zone: 7–9
Height: 3m (10ft)
Spread: 2m (6½ft)
Grow for: glossy foliage and deep red flowers; AGM

I was visiting a camellia nursery when a glorious specimen at the far end of the greenhouse caught my eye. I ran down the path, picked up the plant and claimed it as my own, imagining a romantic name that conjured up images of the orient and vast hillsides clothed with camellias. Then I saw the label – 'Bob Hope'. I've nothing against him, but how could such a wonderful camellia be called 'Bob Hope'? So now Bob, a chance seedling from a nursery in California, stands in a large pot by my back door, displaying his spectacular, deep red, semi-double flowers and a boss of golden stamens. One day he'll be allowed into the garden; I hope he doesn't leave divots in the lawn!

It needs a sheltered position away from cold wind, and in bright light or dappled shade; avoid sites that get the early morning sun as it can damage the blooms. Grow in acid soil, dig in plenty of well-rotted organic matter if necessary before planting, do not plant too deeply, and mulch in spring with well-rotted compost, forest bark, pine needles or similar. Keep the soil moist, particularly from mid-summer to mid-autumn when next year's flower buds are being formed; use rainwater during dry periods.

It can be grown in a container during its early years; use multi-purpose or ericaceous compost, and feed with liquid fertilizer every three weeks. Prune if necessary immediately after flowering. Propagate by leaf bud, or by semi-ripe cuttings from late summer onwards. It is susceptible to aphids, scale and sooty mould – check plants regularly. **MB**

Camellia x *williamsii* 'Anticipation'

Camellia x *williamsii* 'Anticipation'

Type: hardy, evergreen shrub
Soil & situation: moist, well-drained, humus-rich, acid soil/partial shade/shelter from morning sun
North American hardiness zone: 7–9
Height: 4m (13ft)
Spread: 2m (6½ft)
Grow for: glossy, evergreen foliage and lovely double flowers in spring; AGM

It is difficult to set one camellia on a pedestal when there are so many excellent varieties.

However *Camellia* x *williamsii* 'Anticipation' was my first camellia, a present from a great nurseryman, Leslie Slinger of Slieve Donard nursery, at the foot of the Mourne Mountains, Northern Ireland. It is still my favourite. It forms a tight, upright shrub with glossy, bright evergreen leaves. The large, deep rose-pink, double flowers, appearing in late winter and early spring, resemble those of a peony.

While the plant is totally hardy, its flowers are easily damaged in spring after a frost. If the morning sun thaws out the frozen flowers quickly they turn brown. The secret is not to plant spring-flowering camellias where they would be hit by the early sun. In the right site it makes a great wall plant and is equally at home in the shrub border or in a woodland situation.

C. x *williamsii* is one of the best hybrid shrubs. All its cultivars, including 'Anticipation', are free flowering, ranging from the single, white-flowered 'Francis Hanger' and the single pink flowers of 'Saint Ewe' to the double-flowered 'Water Lily' (bright pink) and 'Bow Bells' (deep rose).

Incorporate as much humus, in the form of leafmould, rotted farmyard manure or home-made compost, into the soil as possible. Plant at the same depth as in the pot with the rootball close to the surface. Mulch with composted bark every spring to retain moisture in the soil. Water during dry spells, especially in the autumn. If, at this time, the soil dries out, the camellia will drop its unopened flower buds. **JC**

Campanula persicifolia 'Telham Beauty'
WILLOW BELL, PEACH BELLS,
PEACH-LEAVED BELLFLOWER

Type: hardy perennial
Soil & situation: moderately, fertile and well-drained soil/sun or light shade
North American hardiness zone: 3–8
Height: 90cm (36in)
Spread: 30cm (12in)
Grow for: a strong and vigorous plant, a mainstay of the herbaceous border; single, very large, good blue flowers in summer, which repeat again in autumn; attractive to bees and butterflies; foliage of evergreen leaves; an excellent cut flower

Lovely, graceful flowers are produced which fit into various parts of the garden. They are highly effective when inter-planted with shrub roses, as they all flower together and are two good ingredients of those much sought-after, classic, colourful mixed borders. They thrive equally well in light woodland and in bold groups looking relaxed and informal with lace-cap hydrangeas, ferns and the like. They work well, too, when mingled with other perennials in large sweeps of planting with their tolerance to light shade and sun, making them come into their own. They look almost animated in full flower in dappled sunlight. The white form, *C. persicifolia alba* is equally good.

There are many other good cultivated and wild campanulas, such as *C. latiflora*, which is available in different varieties, colours and heights; they tend to seed and have similar evergreen foliage. I also have the native harebell, *C. rotundifolia*, which is a really beautiful wild flower, growing in the meadow.

If your soil is thin and light this plant will not produce the goods so, if this is the case, it may be worth bulking up your soil. It does not require staking unless it is grown in an extremely exposed position. Propagation can be from division, basal cuttings and seed. It will seed around fairly actively. **BG**

Campanula persicifolia 'Telham Beauty'

Campanula zoysii

Campanula zoysii
CRIMPED BELLFLOWER

Type: hardy, semi-evergreen perennial
Soil & situation: well-drained, gritty, alkaline soil/full sun
North American hardiness zone: 5–7
Height: 5cm (2in)
Spread: 10cm (4in)
Grow for: an unbeatable plant for the rockery – cushion forming with lavender-blue flowers

When it comes to plants suitable for a rockery scree bed this gem is the number-one contender. It will thrive in a soil which is almost totally composed of grit.

It forms a cushion with small, glossy, mid-green leaves. Flowers appear in summer on short, erect stems. Each carries several tubular, lavender-blue flowers, almost totally enclosed at the mouth as if they have been crimped. It will survive only in very well-drained soil and hates winter rain, needing a sheet of glass overhead to act as an umbrella. Alternatively it may be grown in a container and plunged into the rockery for the summer, then lifted and moved under cover for the winter.

Propagate by seed sown in autumn and over-wintered in a cold frame with lots of ventilation but protection from rain. Root softwood cuttings in early summer in a heated propagator, removing the growing tip to prevent it trying to produce flowers. **JC**

Campsis x *tagliabuana* 'Madame Galen'
TRUMPET CREEPER

Type: frost-hardy, deciduous climber
Soil & situation: fertile but moist well-drained soil/sunny and warm wall with support/requires a little time to 'settle in' and start flowering/needs protection in the first two years during cold periods
North American hardiness zone: 5–9
Height & spread: 10m (33ft)
Grow for: exotic-looking, highly vigorous climber; brilliant salmon-red trumpet flowers over a long period from late summer to autumn; AGM

I must admit I have not yet grown this plant but have admired it in a friend's garden. She has it clambering up the front of her London terrace house and the massive production of the extraordinary brilliant tuber-like flowers causes passersby to stop and gawp. With her it has survived some very cold periods and I have it on my list for the garden here, confident that the tropical appearance belies its hardiness. The foliage has pinnate, dark green leaves which are up to 30cm (12in) long, so it is not a delicate-looking plant in any way, but bold and quite headstrong both in appearance and growth. This fact makes it suitable for spreading over a roof of an outbuilding or up a dead tree. Campsis is also used as a free-standing bush or hedge but needs heavy pruning to keep it in shape.

This plant is one for a spring planting in a sharp-draining site. A couple of layers of fleece at the ready for those sharp frosty nights and a good mulching over the roots should get it through those first two winters. When the plant has grown to fill the allotted space, pruning should be carried out in late winter or early spring, and consists of cutting back the previous season's growth to two or three buds of the framework. It may well require a fair bit of tying in as it clings on by aerial roots. **BG**

Campsis x *tagliabuana* 'Madame Galen'

Canna 'Durban'

with a high-potash fertilizer. They need good, rich soil and a rich diet; it is impossible to over-feed! Dead-head regularly. In autumn, when frost blackens the foliage, lift the rhizome, cut stems back to 10cm (4in) from the base, store in slightly moist peat substitute or similar in frost-free conditions. Divide when necessary at replanting time, ensuring each division has at least one strong bud. Re-plant into pots in early spring and start them off in a greenhouse; water sparingly, increasing as more growth appears. Plant out when there is no danger of frost.

Slugs and snails bite through young foliage while it is 'scrolled'. One that was brought to *Gardeners' Question Time* looked as if 666 had been etched on the leaf – it provided plenty of laughs! Who says molluscs don't have a sense of humour?　**MB**

They need a warm, light spot, so are better in pots on staging than down in the cold border soil, unless it's a hot summer. They can live for several years if given the right conditions. Spread shoots and nip out tips to encourage bushier plants when small, as the fruits are borne at the joints. Over-winter to crop in the second or even third year, when they will produce fruit earlier than a seed-grown plant. Sow in early spring in individual pots in the warmth, and keep the soil moist but never let it get waterlogged. You may succeed with them outdoors in a very warm sheltered garden, but they are really only worth cropping under cover. Aphids are always a problem especially when the plants are young, but soft soap sprays will cure them. Slugs may damage ripening fruits.　**BF**

Canna 'Durban'
INDIAN SHOT PLANT

Type: tender perennial
Soil & situation: rich soil, plenty of moisture/sun
North American hardiness zone: 7–10
Height: 2m (6½ft)
Spread: 60cm (24in)
Grow for: fabulous foliage and flowers from early summer to autumn

Cannas are amazingly easy to grow in containers or sunny borders, look magnificent in big groups and are wonderful when lit by the evening sun; they are 'must have' plants for the 'tropical' garden. I visited one of the National Collection holders, Keith Hayward, and his small plot was packed with plants of all shapes, sizes and colours; there's an incredible choice. At the time of writing he has well over 200 cultivars; there must be one for you!

Canna 'Durban' has bronze foliage and pink stripes in a herringbone pattern; the leaves gradually turn green and yellow. The flower is big, bold and orange! Wow! *C.* 'Australia' has dark bronze foliage that deepens to almost black by summer with red flowers. I've just bought one and so has my mate Mike, in Florida. 'Fatamorgana' has spectacular dark pink flowers and 'Alaska' has cream-coloured flowers. Where space is limited, there are smaller cultivars for pots on the patio. 'Flameche' is about 30cm (12in) tall with green leaves and pale orange flowers; 'Gnom' has rich pale pink flowers.

They need a sheltered site, fertile soil and full sun. Dig in a generous amount of well-rotted organic matter, provide plenty of water and feed regularly

Canna iridiflora (syn. *Canna* x *ehemanii*)
Plant of the Week (see page 257)

Capsicum annuum
SWEET PEPPER

Type: tender, annual/semi-perennial crop
Soil & situation: rich, well-drained compost/full sun in warm position
North American hardiness zone: normally grown as an annual
Height: 1m (3ft) or more
Spread: at least 30cm (12in)
Grow for: attractive-looking crop of great value economically and nutritionally

Almost every gardener grows tomatoes but few grow sweet peppers. Yet given a greenhouse they are actually easier to grow as they require less nipping out, less support and less watering in smaller pots to produce a respectable crop, which is worth far more than tomatoes in cash value and in vitamins. Green peppers usually turn red as they ripen and become less indigestible – the green are reputed to cause wind. There are hundreds of varieties, including some that ripen from orange to purple, each with a slightly different flavour.

Capsicum comes from the Greek word *kaptos*, meaning to bite. Natives of tropical America, sweet peppers were ignored until recent times when they have become valued for their vitamin content and their colour, which is always welcome on a plate, especially in salads and on pizzas.

Capsicum annuum

Capsicum chinense (syn. *C. tetragonum*) Habanero Group
CHILI PEPPER

Type: tender, annual/semi-perennial crop
Soil & situation: very well-drained, rich compost/full sun in warmth – not for the open garden in Britain
North American hardiness zone: normally grown as an annual
Height & spread: 1m (3ft) each way in good conditions
Grow for: extremely expensive to buy, yet fairly easy to grow

All chili peppers, including *Capsicum frutescens*, which is used to make tabasco, are even better value to grow than tomatoes or sweet peppers as they are expensive to buy, yet not difficult to grow given a greenhouse or even a sunny windowsill.

This particular group is known as Habanero or Scotch/grannies bonnet peppers, well beloved by much of South America, the people of Jamaica and other Caribbean islands. They give a fierce heat but also an aromatic flavour, whereas most chilies give more heat than flavour. All chilies are much interbred and there are hundreds of sub-varieties, so you can find Red Habanero, Orange Habanero, Chocolate Habanero, Scotch Bonnet Red and Scotch Bonnet Yellow. The true Habaneros are best eaten raw, while the true Scotch Bonnets are better for cooking.

Most hot or chili peppers were introduced long before the sweet sorts, probably to substitute for the increasingly expensive black and white pepper brought from the East Indies, which was needed to spice up a bland diet of dubiously valid meat. (The modern *chinense* appellation is a misnomer, as it is definitely of South American origin.)

If grown in a well-drained compost in warm, light conditions the plant may live for two or three years but it usually dies after the first grim summer. Sow in early spring in individual pots and keep in a warm, very light place. Do not let the compost become waterlogged or allow it to stand wet in cool or cold weather. Aphids need spraying with soapy water. **BF**

Capsicum chinense

Cardiocrinum giganteum

Cardiocrinum giganteum
GIANT LILY

Type: hardy, bulbous perennial
Soil & situation: rich, moist, organic soil/dappled shade
North American hardiness zone: 7–9
Height: 4m (13ft)
Spread: indefinite
Grow for: flower spikes from mid- to late summer

The elegant spires of flowering cardiocrinums are one of the most glorious spectacles in gardening. Huge, heart-shaped, glossy leaves, up to 45cm (18in) across, diminish in size towards the apex of the stem as a fanfare of as many as 20, fragrant, white, trumpet-shaped flowers up to 15cm (6in) long with a reddish-purple staining in the throat sound their triumphal crescendo. In the dappled light of a woodland glade against a background of dark-leaved rhododendrons they look magnificent.

Tragically this majestic display is their final reveille. They die after flowering but produce up to six offsets that flower after two to three years; the secret is to plant bulbs of different sizes, or a new one each year for a display over several years.

Cardiocrinum giganteum var. *yunnanense* has slightly shorter black stems with bronze young leaves.

They need cool, moist growing conditions and shade to protect the roots; ideally they should be surrounded with small shrubs or mulched with straw in colder areas to protect them from spring frosts.

Dig in old growbags, multi-purpose compost, leafmould, well-rotted manure and anything organic to create a cool, moist soil at least 60cm (24in) deep. Plant the bulbs immediately, no less than 1m (3ft) apart when they arrive in autumn (do not let them dry out), position their tips level with the surface and cover with a thin layer of leafmould. Given space and time they naturalize. Alternatively, after they have flowered, dig up and replant the young bulbs in a new position or leave the sausage-like fruits to burst, then sow the seed; they take between six and eight years or more to flower. The old flower stems make an attractive feature in the garden and home. Slugs can damage young leaves. **MB**

Bob adds:
This is not an easy plant to keep happy but when/if you do it is formidable. Stately, magnificent, impressive, highly scented enormous flowers make it a tangible garden status symbol.

Aquilegia canadensis

COLUMBINE, GRANNY'S BONNET

Type: hardy, herbaceous perennial
Soil & situation: cool, moist, fertile, well-drained soil/sun or dappled shade
Hardiness zone: 3–8
Height: 90cm (36in)
Spread: 30cm (12in)
Grow for: dainty spring flowers and foliage; AGM

Tiptoe among the sun-dappled, silent woodlands and damp shady banks and you may see fairies. You may not see them or believe in them, but that doesn't mean to say that they don't exist! From east Canada heading south to New Mexico, the Canadian columbine is one of the ultimate fairy flowers. Like so many *Aquilegia* species, everything about it is delicate and ethereal. Its leaves, a filigree of the finest dark green 'maidenhair' float silently in the breeze. Hovering above them on dainty stems are clouds of fairies dressed in dainty bell-like skirts of lemon-yellow with deep red or scarlet wings.

Its relatives are just the same: *A. elegantula* swoops, its spurs follow like beams of pale red; *A. formosa* var. *formosa* has a pale orange-red trail, like a cluster of shooting stars. Fairies in the forest? You would almost believe it was true!

They need cool, moist, fertile, well-drained soil in sun or dappled shade; dig in plenty of well-rotted organic matter if necessary. They are perfect for woodland gardens, planted on banks for easier viewing or in borders, though their dainty flowers may be lost without equally delicate companions.

Sow seed in containers in a cold frame as soon as they are ripe or in spring; you can divide plants but they dislike disturbance and take a long time to re-establish. Cut back foliage in autumn or spring and mulch. Keep moist during dry weather. Susceptible to powdery mildew in dry conditions.   **MB**

Carex comans 'Frosted Curls'
SEDGE

Type: hardy, evergreen sedge
Soil & situation: prefers moist soil in sun or partial shade
North American hardiness zone: 7–9
Height & spread: 30cm (12in)
Grow for: swirling coloured leaves all year round

There are lots of super sedges for the garden and many of them come from New Zealand, the land of the 'Long White Cloud'. It's a wonderful country and I've visited it several times; my wife comes from there and the children have dual nationality, so I'm happy to promote the place and particularly its plants! *Carex comans* 'Frosted Curls' is a New Zealand introduction. I love the dense tufts of arching, pale silvery-green, hair-like leaves that twist and swirl. I've seen it hanging like Rapunzel's hair from a pot on a plinth and used to create swirling 'water' in a wonderful seaside garden. But it's not alone, there's plenty more!

C. comans has narrow, dark chocolate coloured leaves. *C. comans* bronze, the familiar form, has the habit of 'Frosted Curls' but is rusty-red. *C. c.* 'Kupferflamme' has copper-bronze flowers from mid-summer until autumn. *C. buchananii* is stiffly upright but arches with age and has narrow, rich reddish-brown leaves to 60cm (24in). It does best in sun. *C. flagellifera* is a real beauty, with greenish-chestnut leaves and light brown flower spikes which reach over 1m (3ft) as the seeds mature. Variants in cultivation often have red-brown foliage and grow to 72cm (28in) x 90cm (36in). *C. testacea* forms a tussock of narrow olive-green leaves tinted bronze and orange, particularly in winter. *C. t.* 'Old Gold' turns golden-yellow in winter.

They need sunshine or partial shade and are happy in most soils, but dislike extreme wet or dry conditions. Divide frommid-spring to early summer. Aphids sometimes infest the stem bases. **MB**

Carex comans 'Frosted Curls'

Carpinus betulus

Carpinus betulus
COMMON HORNBEAM

Type: hardy, deciduous tree
Soil & situation: most soils, including clay and chalk/withstands exposure/tolerates sun or part shade
North American hardiness zone: 4–8
Height & spread: to 20m (66ft), possibly more
Grow for: beautiful foliage especially when it first opens and has attractive clusters of fruit; fast growing; will tolerate poor soils; can be used as a specimen tree, a woodland tree, a supreme hedge and for pleaching and forming into bowers, arbours and the like; AGM

Hornbeam is a fine parkland specimen tree with a good broad head and a grey, fluted trunk. It is more often grown as a hedge and is frequently confused with beech, though hornbeam does not turn russet in autumn. It just drops its leaves. I think it far superior to beech but some would argue the toss. I frequently specify it for forming pleached screens. These are rather like hedges on stilts, and if you had one in Tudor times, it was a sign that you had 'arrived'.

Today, with problems of privacy from neighbours, hornbeams are unbeatable for forming higher-level screens in confined spaces. With modern hedgecutters, once trained they are simple to maintain. I have also used them for forming 'porches' to highlight a front door and arbours. With these I get a simple metal framework made up and plant the plants around the edge and clip them to it. Similarly I like 'green' garden houses and make a wooden, trellis structure and train the hornbeam around the edge. When the trellis rots, I have the living version.

Although hornbeam, unlike beech, does tolerate being planted at standard size, I always plant small, between 60cm–1.5m (24in–5ft), depending on what I am going to do with it. I have planted ready-made pleached trees on jobs for impatient clients, but they take ages to settle in and do not form a good leafy, thick screen for several years, whereas when I grow them from trees a metre (3 feet) or so tall, they settle in and soon get going. As always, keep all grass and weed competition away from the base and water in dry periods. **BG**

Caryopteris x *clandonensis* 'Arthur Simmonds'
BLUE SPIRAEA, BLUEBEARD

Type: hardy, deciduous shrub
Soil & situation: light, free-draining soil/sun
North American hardiness zone: 6–9
Height: 1m (3ft)
Spread: 1.2m (4ft)
Grow for: soft foliage and blue flowers from late
summer to early autumn; AGM

This valuable late summer-flowering shrub forms
a rounded mound of aromatic leaves which are
dull dark green above and silvery-grey below.
Clusters of soft blue flowers appear towards the
tips of the stems in the leaf axils from late
summer to early autumn, encircling one side of
the stalk, hence the common name Bluebeard.
They are excellent grouped together or
combined with santolina and rosemary, and are
attractive to butterflies; they can also be used as
cut flowers. Arthur Simmonds found this hybrid
in his garden in West Clandon, Surrey, southeast
England.

There are several cultivars of *Caryopteris* x *clandonensis*, most with minor differences, and it is not
unusual for 'Arthur Simmonds' to be sold as
'Heavenly Blue'. 'Ferndown' has darker leaves
and flowers than 'Arthur Simmonds'. 'Heavenly
Blue' is more erect and compact, with a slightly
deeper flower colour. 'Kew Blue' has slightly
darker flowers than 'Arthur Simmonds'.
'Worcester Gold' has yellow foliage and lavender-
blue flowers. 'First Choice' is dense and compact,
up to 1m (3ft) each way, with tiny, very dark
green leaves, tightly clothing the stems, making
the perfect foil for the lavender flowers.
Flowering starts in mid-summer.

It needs a hot, sunny position on moderately
fertile, free-draining soil, protected by a wall in
cooler climates. It thrives on chalk and tolerates
drought. From early to mid-spring, remove the
stems to a strong pair of buds just above ground
level. Propagate from greenwood or semi-ripe
cuttings. Growth tips and flower buds may be
attacked by capsid bugs.   **MB**

Caryopteris x *clandonensis* 'Kew Blue'

Caryopteris x *clandonensis* 'Arthur Simmonds'

Cassiope 'Edinburgh'

Cassiope 'Edinburgh'

Type: hardy, evergreen shrub
Soil & situation: well-drained, humus-rich, acid
soil/partial shade
North American hardiness zone: 2–6
Height & spread: 30cm (12in)
Grow for: pretty pendent flowers that bring
welcome cheer to a spring garden; AGM

Given the right conditions this little plant is the
best-behaved shrub in the garden. It is ideal in a
rock garden or as a dot plant among heathers.
A group of three or more in an open woodland
site will brighten the whole area. It forms an
upright shrub with whipcord-like stems closely
wrapped in small, lance-shaped, overlapping
leaves. The white, bell-shaped flowers have
contrasting red-brown calyces in late spring.
They are produced in the leaf axils at the tips
of the stems, nodding in the slightest breeze.

In full sun the plant seems to be less happy,
remaining 'sulky' and refusing to grow. A late
frost may damage the flowers, browning those
which are fully open. Mulching with leafmould
every autumn close to the plant will keep the soil
moist and encourage the stems to re-root – a
source of free, ready-rooted cuttings.

Propagation is by fresh seed sown in the autumn
and over-wintered in a cold frame. Semi-ripe
cuttings taken in summer root best in a mist
propagator. Pot the rooted plants in an
ericaceous compost. My plants never seem to
suffer from pests or diseases but the dreaded vine
weevil has been known to cause havoc to young
plants, destroying their root system.   **JC**

Catalpa bignonioides

Catalpa bignonioides
INDIAN BEAN TREE

Type: hardy, deciduous tree
Soil & situation: moist, well-drained soil/full sun
North American hardiness zone: 5–9
Height & spread: 10m (33ft)
Grow for: an impressive specimen tree; AGM

In this case, the common name of Indian refers to native Americans. *Catalpa* is Indian rather than Latin and means 'winged head', describing the flower shape. Whatever, it makes a magnificent specimen tree on a lawn.

The 25cm (10in) long, heart-shaped leaves unfurl purple turning to a rich mid-green with an unpleasant odour when crushed. Upright, pyramidal trusses of flowers appear on mature trees in summer. Each bell-shaped flower is white with purple and yellow spots and frilled edges. The flowers are followed in autumn by 40cm (16in) long, thin, green, bean-like seedpods which ripen to dark brown and hang long after the leaves have fallen. *Catalpa bignonioides* 'Aurea' has sulphur-yellow leaves and makes a smaller tree.

It prefers a well-drained site in full sun, sheltered from strong winds. The branches are pithy and brittle and subject to breaking in strong winds. Wind will also shred the large leaves. Although it makes a large tree it may, if it is pollarded, be grown in small gardens.

Every year the tree is cut to a stump in late winter. The shoots it will send up are thinned to one to three and allowed to grow. They will reach a height of 3m (10ft) in one season, with enormous leaves up to 45cm (18in) across. The operation is repeated in subsequent years. Alas there will be no flowers the year it is pruned.

Propagation is by fresh seed in autumn in a cold frame. Softwood cuttings root in a gritty compost in summer. Root cuttings can be propagated in early winter. **JC**

Ceanothus 'Concha'
CALIFORNIA LILAC

Type: frost-hardy, evergreen shrub
Soil & situation: fertile, well-drained, alkaline soi/full sun
North American hardiness zone: 9–10
Height & spread: 3m (10ft)
Grow for: a breathtaking vision of blue in early summer; AGM

There are white- and pink-flowering ceanothus but blue is the colour most commonly associated with this shrub. Of all the shades of blue, for me, 'Concha' stands out with its deep, non-fading, Oxford blue. It forms a dense, rounded shrub with arching branches and 5cm (2in) long, finely toothed, dark green leaves. In late spring and early summer deep red-purple buds open to dark blue flowers in tight, rounded terminal heads.

It is prone to damage from biting, cold winds in spring. Grown against a sheltered, sunny wall it will present a memorable sheet of blue. Little pruning is necessary but for training on a wall, prune after flowering, shortening the sideshoots by half.

Ceanothus are short-lived shrubs, especially in the wetter parts of the UK. Where necessary dig in lots of coarse grit and 13mm (½in) gravel to assist drainage. They dislike being transplanted and should be purchased as small plants with a good root system which isn't pot bound.

Propagate using semi-ripe cuttings with a heel in late summer in a propagator with bottom heat.
JC

Ceanothus 'Concha'

Cedrus libani

Cedrus libani
CEDAR OF LEBANON

Type: hardy, evergreen tree
Soil & situation: a wide range of pH/acid and alkaline soils/tolerates shade early on, then soon needs full sun and light to form a good specimen/space
North American hardiness zone: 7–9
Height & spread: 30m (100ft)
Grow for: a majestic tree with a sculptural form that few trees can rival, its initial conical outline spreading to form the characteristic, tiered-plate arrangement; AGM

It is thought that this tree was introduced to England around 1645, and it has been hardy here since 1740 when a frost to –30°C (–22°F) killed nearly every tree. Capability Brown did not approve of exotic trees in his landscapes, quite rightly, but he did, wise man, plant this one. It does grow faster than you would think, often 9–10m (30–33ft) in 20 years, 15m (50ft) in 30 years, and after 100 years it will take on its familiar, mature, characteristic appearance. Your children may well be able to appreciate it in its full glory, if you do not.

This is definitely a plant worth planting at a small size: 45–60cm (18–24in) is plenty big enough. Avoid the 'specimen' trees in large containers at 2m (6½ft) plus – they need so much more care in terms of irrigation and staking, and undoubtedly will take far longer to get away than the smaller specimens which will quickly overtake them. If it should happen to send up a double leader, remove the weaker shoot in autumn. It is equally important to keep the ground free of all vegetation around the trunk in a good 1m (3ft) diameter for four to five years after planting. This removes moisture competition from grass. It is definitely better planted without a stake, but if the leader grows away from the vertical, a temporary cane may be necessary. **BG**

Centaurea cyanus
CORNFLOWER

Type: hardy annual
Soil & situation: well-drained soil/sun
North American hardiness zone: annual
Height: 80cm (32in)
Spread: 15cm (6in)
Grow for: blue flowers from late spring to midsummer

This was long regarded as a pestilent weed. The poet and countryman John Clare wrote of 'the blue "cornbottle" crowding their splendid colours in large sheets over the land and troubling the cornfields with their destroying beauty'.

Considering the colour and the fact that it must have been growing with other plants like corn cockle and red field poppies, it must have made an impressive sight. It was last seen on a large scale between the First and Second World Wars, but by the end of the 1970s, with the widespread use of herbicides, it became scarce. Happily it has returned with the advent of the 'set-aside' policy for agriculture. The juice from the flower, mixed with alum is used by watercolourists; it is also the traditional flower of Harrow School.

It is upright with narrow, lance-shaped leaves and dark blue flowerheads with violet inner florets. It is attractive to bees. There are several cultivars, including 'Baby Blue', a dwarf with stems to 30cm (12in); 'Black Ball' grows to 1m (3ft) and its double, dark, rich chocolate-coloured flowers

Centaurea cyanus

Centaurea macrocephala

look almost black on cloudy days; 'Blue Diadem' has double flowers and stems to 1m (3ft); 'Frosty' (also known as 'Frosted Queen') reaches 50cm (20in) and is mixed, with some flowers having a white rim on the florets; 'Polka Dot' is also mixed; its stems are dwarf and bushy and grow to 40cm (16in). *C. moschata* 'Dairy Maid' is yellow, good for cutting and smells of chocolate.

They need well-drained soil in full sun. Sow from early to late spring for flowers from late spring to early autumn; in early autumn to flower from early to late summer the following year. Plants will self-seed, or collect seed and sow it *in situ*. Powdery mildew may be a problem. **MB**

Centaurea macrocephala
GLOBE CORNFLOWERS, HARD HEADS, KNAPWEED

Type: hardy perennial
Soil & situation: well-drained soil/will tolerate poor, limy soils/sun or partial shade
North American hardiness zone: 3–7
Height: 1.5m (5ft)
Spread: 60cm (2ft)
Grow for: distinctive yellow flowers in summer

This is a robust, charismatic perennial, with tall leafy stems supporting the firm thistle-type knobs. These knobs are topped with a mass of deep orange-yellow florets. One, or preferably several, clumps of these in a border will definitely add some punch. I wish it had a longer flowering season, but maybe that is partly why it makes so much impact. It is especially useful because it will thrive in poor conditions. If you have the space it is worth growing extra plants for cutting as they make a spectacular cut flower and are also great for drying.

This plant is easy, no staking, little feeding, just cut back the dead material in winter or spring. If it is over-vigorous – it tends to get a little carried away in good soils – split it up when necessary to keep it under control. Propagation is easy by division in spring or autumn. **BG**

Centranthus ruber 'Albus'
WHITE VALERIAN

Type: hardy perennial
Soil & situation: thrives in thin chalky soils/poor, free-draining soil/sun
North American hardiness zone: 5–8
Height & spread: up to 1m (3ft)
Grow for: large, dense cymes of white, fragrant flowers over an exceptionally long flowering season in summer; a plant which performs well and looks healthy even in extremely poor conditions

The attraction of this plant lies in the cottagey feel it conveys, perhaps because of its obvious similarity to the red valerian which can be seen all over country villages in England, perched on top of tall, stone walls or growing in invisible spaces at the edge of pavements displaying, as often as not, a profusion of rosy crimson flowers. The white form is more elite, with its eye-catching white flowers. But they both have the characteristic greeny, glaucous, almost fleshy, lance-shaped leaves. Writing this in late winter, I can see lush, thick, attractive foliage through the window even though we have had snow and hard frosts. I have seen it successfully used in borders, where the staying power of its flowers is particularly welcome, and it maintains a better, more compact habit than in an infertile, dry position. Perhaps though, the most fetching positions are the unexpected: growing out of walls, flowering from under large boulders, on a summer house roof, where you are astounded at its *joie de vivre*. It is highly useful, too, for covering steep, awkward banks where most other plants would protest.

To prevent this exuberant plant colonizing your entire garden, it is best to keep cutting it back after flowering. That way you will have flowers all summer long and it will be unable to seed it itself in its accustomed prolific manner. If you need to propagate it, then seed is the easiest, but division is perfectly feasible. Plants are short-lived and are best replaced every three or four years. **BG**

Centranthus ruber 'Albus'

Cephalaria gigantea

Cephalaria gigantea
GIANT SCABIOUS, YELLOW SCABIOUS

Type: hardy perennial
Soil & situation: wide range of soils/prefers a sunny site/will tolerate partial shade
North American hardiness zone: 3–7
Height: to 2m (6½ft)
Spread: 80cm (32in)
Grow for: giant of a plant, with magnificent soft-yellow flowers for a long period in mid-summer

This species of cephalaria is the one most frequently seen in cultivation. The yellow scabious is huge, but whereas traditionally it would be recommended for large herbaceous borders only, I think it can work superbly in smaller areas too.

Tall elements can look dramatic in little spaces, providing a mass of flowers and foliage at eye level and at fairly close quarters, making a huge impact. It helps create a more lax, burgeoning feel. It is also a good plant for naturalizing in wilder parts of the garden, coping with competition from grasses and other wilder-type planting. It does not need staking despite its thin, wiry and rather erect stems.

Another gem of a plant that is easy and flowers well, sometimes thoughout the summer. It can be propagated from seed, though apparently some strains are infertile. The fertile ones though are not aggressive self-seeders. It can also be propagated by division. Both seed and division are best done in spring. **BG**

Ceratostigma willmottianum
HARDY PLUMBAGO, CHINESE PLUMBAGO

Type: hardy, deciduous shrub
Soil & situation: well-drained soil/sun
North American hardiness zone: 6–9
Height & spread: 1m (3ft), sometimes 30cm (12in) taller
Grow for: stunning mid-blue flowers from mid-summer to late autumn; AGM

Miss Ellen Willmott was a formidable, intelligent woman who spent vast sums of money creating a magnificent garden at Warley Place near Brentwood in Essex. At its peak, she employed 104 uniformed gardeners and one nurseryman confided that from 1890 to 1900, she spent £1,500 a year at his nursery alone. Several beautiful plants are named for her, including this one – she raised two *Ceratostigma willmottianum* plants from seed sent to her by the great plant collector Ernest Wilson, who found it growing in the semi-arid Min Valley of Western Sichuan in China.

It produces lance- to diamond-shaped leaves on a mass of wiry stems, tipped with clusters of tightly packed, pale to mid-blue, plumbago-like flowers from mid-summer until mid- or late autumn, depending on the weather. In autumn the foliage develops bright red tints making a pleasing contrast with the flowers. *C. plumbaginoides* is herbaceous, spreading with rhizomes, with remarkable dark blue flowers and it reaches a height of 50cm (20in).

Ceratostigma willmottianum

It needs a sheltered, sunny position on light, moist, moderately fertile, free-draining soil. Grows well on chalk or against a wall. Mulch well over winter. From early to mid-spring, remove the stems to a strong pair of buds just above ground level. Propagate from soft tip cuttings in spring, or semi-ripe cuttings in summer or layers. **MB**

Bunny adds:
Although this is a shrub, in cold situations you can simply treat it as a herbaceous plant, cutting it down to ground level in the spring and away it goes again. It will flower later when treated this way, perhaps not until early autumn, so reducing its flowering period. Otherwise, when flowering on old wood, it will come into flower in midsummer.

Cercidiphyllum japonicum
KADSURA TREE

Type: hardy, deciduous tree
Soil & situation: prefers deep, moist, fertile soil; tolerates some lime/dappled shade
North American hardiness zone: 4–8
Height: 20m (66ft)
Spread: 15m (50ft)
Grow for: form, delicate foliage, autumn colour and fragrance; AGM

In autumn as the leaves change colour, it's the wonderful smell of burnt sugar that alerts you to the presence of this elegant tree long before it comes into view. The delicate, almost heart-shaped leaves with finely scalloped margins turn soft golden-yellow and fall to create a carpet of colour. It's very hardy but prefers a continental climate with long hot summers (don't we all!) and the climate in the UK makes a small- to medium-sized tree. Timber is light, highly valued and used for house interiors and furnishings in Japan. Because of its floral characteristics, scientists have long debated whether this plant is a relic of some primitive flowering plant that has ceased to exist. Inevitably, they still disagree!

Cercidiphyllum var. *magnificum* is a rare, medium-sized tree with smoother bark and larger, broader leaves with coarser serrations on the margins, and yellow autumn colour. *C. japonicum* f. *pendulum* has long hanging branches and has been cultivated in Japan for many years.

They need a sheltered position where the young leaves are protected from frost and cold winds. Soils should be deep, moist and humus-rich and although they tolerate some lime, autumn colour

Cercidiphyllum japonicum

is better on acid soils. Mulch in spring with plenty of well-rotted organic matter until they are well established. Prune when dormant just to remove dead, diseased, dying, crossing, rubbing, damaged or weak branches. They are often multi-stemmed but can be pruned to make a single stem. Propagate by sowing seed under glass as soon as possible after ripening or by taking basal cuttings in late spring/early summer. **MB**

Cercis siliquastrum
Plant of the Week (see page 153)

Euphorbia myrsinites

Type: frost-hardy, evergreen perennial
Soil & situation: very free-draining soil/sun
Hardiness zone: 5–8
Height: 10cm (4in) or more
Spread: 30cm (12in) or more
Grow for: sculptural form and long-lasting flowerheads from mid-spring to late summer and beyond. We've put it in March because that's when the flowers first appear, but like many of the plants in the this book it is at its best for several months; AGM.

My garden's being taken over by aliens! Every time I pass the euphorbias I hear robotic voices saying 'Take me to your leader'! I'm sure they arrived from Mars as stowaways on a passing spaceship! They're all utterly bizarre; this one is no exception! It's a seething mass of semi-prostrate stems to 30cm (12in) long, with spirally arranged almost lance-shaped, succulent blue-grey leaves.

As if to confirm my paranoia it produces 8cm (3½in) clusters of strange flowers, like glowing acid-green eyes that gradually become pink after staring into the sun for several weeks. I'm sure they're on the move too; they love to bask on sunny banks or by the edge of borders and in my garden one hanging over a low wall looks as if it is about to metamorphose into a snake and slither away. I have a love-hate relationship with these plants: I marvel at their surreal form and flower and see their strange beauty – but I'm sure they're out to get me!

It needs light, free-draining soil in hot, baking sunshine and dislikes shade. Add grit or sharp sand to the soil if necessary to improve the drainage. Mulch with gravel to prevent the leaves and stems from rotting in winter. The sap can be an irritant, so avoid contact with the skin and eyes. Wear gloves when handling. No regular pruning is necessary; cut back old or damaged stems to the base in spring. Divide in spring or grow from seed. **MB**

Cereus grandiflorus (syn. *Nyctocereus grandiflorus*)
QUEEN OF THE NIGHT

Type: tender, perennial, evergreen, trailing cactus
Soil & situation: well-drained, gritty, humus-rich compost with some lime/full sun or light shade/under cover in warm greenhouse or conservatory
North American hardiness zone: 9–10
Height & spread: flowers up to 30cm (12in) across. The plant can be confined to 1.2–1.5m (4–5ft) each way in a big pot or hanging basket, but reaches 3m (10ft) in nature
Grow for: staggering flowers, which are also the prettiest and the most sweetly scented of almost any houseplant. Angular, pliable (within reason) and tough stems, but without significant thorns, make this a pleasant house companion, unlike so many other cacti.

Cereus grandiflorus is a knock-you-over plant when in flower but, unfortunately, the immense flowers only open once, late at night and close again for ever in the morning. However, all through that one night, the white and gold flowers with a hint of pinky-chocolate on the outside, which resemble enormous exotic dahlias or water lilies, give off puffs of the most incredibly strong vanilla-like perfume. The other species are similar but not as imposing, and some of them carry spines. One of about half a dozen species from the

Cereus grandiflorus

Cerinthe major 'Purpurascens'

Caribbean and Central America and obviously suited to dense forests, these are trailing, scrambling plants, most often seen grown at ground level. I have found that this plant does supremely well in a hanging basket under cover.

Given a big pot or basket of well-drained compost, it can make an imposing plant, especially as even a small one can carry up to a dozen of the enormous flowers at one time, if well watered. It can live for many years. The compost needs to be kept nearly dry in winter, but water regularly and heavily once growth commences in spring, giving a weekly light feed in the water. It can be grown from seed but cuttings are easy to root in summer in a sandy compost. Mealy bug can be a problem, so wash it off with soapy water.   **BF**

Cerinthe major 'Purpurascens'
HONEYWORT, WAXFLOWER

Type: hardy annual
Soil & situation: wide range of soils/sun or partial shade
North American hardiness zone: annual
Height & spread: to 60cm (24in)
Grow for: early and long-flowering annual; dark smoky, purple-blue flowers; pewter-blue fleshy foliage; lasts through one winter in many areas

This annual has become increasingly admired as its undemanding nature and chic appearance has led to it being a deservedly populist plant. You will probably find that some over-winter so they flower even earlier the following year along with the irises in late spring. Spring-sown plants will come into bloom later on in mid-summer. This plant comes from the Mediterranean, enjoying hot sunny conditions particularly. Bees can be seen working the tubular, nodding flowers and are said to obtain wax from the flowers, hence its common name. It is one of the best flowers for cutting.

Cerinthe is usually sown *in situ* early on in the spring, depending on temperature. The soil should be 7°C (45°F), at least. They can be sown the previous autumn and in colder areas over-wintered as young plants in a cold frame. This gives them a head start in spring when planted in their final position. It is more than likely that these beauties will self-sow for you. If you want more control of what goes on you can gather your own seeds and will find that these can be collected from those flowers that have set seed at the base of the plant while the higher flowers are still performing. The seed is short-lived though, so it is best to sow it immediately.   **BG**

Chaenomeles japonica – fruit in this condition will be great for jam.

Chaenomeles japonica
JAPANESE QUINCE

Type: hardy, woody shrub
Soil & situation: any soil/sun to heavy shade
North American hardiness zone: 5–8
Height & spread: to 3m (10ft) in rich soil
Grow for: an abundance of very early cheerful flowers and edible (well, once cooked) fruits with pleasant aromatic odour and flavour

There are many different varieties of the Japanese quince, with flowers varying from cream to scarlet. My favourite is *Chaenomeles* x *superba* 'Boule de Feu' as it was given to me as a cutting by Cherry Hills, the wife of the founder of the Henry Doubleday Research Association, on the day I was admiring it on their house wall at Bocking, Essex. However, many other varieties are as good and some have large, more usable fruits, making them more of a crop than an ornamental.

Not introduced until 1815, but now one of the more common ornamental plantings where durability is required, it is said you can knock a nail in with the fruits, but they soften once cooked to make a delicious jelly. Strangely the name comes from the Greek *chaino*, to gape, and *melon*, for apple, as it was completely misunderstood (only by nomenclatural botanists no doubt) to be a fruit that split when it was ripe.

It is a robust, long-lived plant for almost any site, with little attention ever needed. It should be trimmed immediately after flowering. It can be grown from seed but propagate the best varieties only by layers, cuttings or suckers. There are no problems other than the unruly habit, which makes it difficult to train. **BF**

Chaenomeles speciosa 'Nivalis'
JAPANESE QUINCE, FLOWERING QUINCE, JAPONICA

Type: hardy, deciduous shrub
Soil & situation: moist, free-draining soil/sun or partial shade
North American hardiness zone: 5–8
Height: 3.5m (11ft)
Spread: 7m (23ft)
Grow for: pure white flowers from early to late spring, and fragrant fruit

The Latin *nivalis*, snowy or snow-like, is the perfect description for the pure white flowers. This plant's a rule breaker. It usually flowers from early to late spring but doesn't seem to care; it can be earlier – Christmas – or later – June – depending on the location and weather. As a shrub it's no beauty: the leaves are moderately attractive but the stems grow out at ungainly angles and it easily becomes an unkempt mass of interwoven, sparsely spiny stems. Even the fruits are awkward. They are round or pear shaped, glossy greenish-yellow when ripe, speckled and fragrant. When used for jellies or jams, just wash and cook the fruits; don't try to peel them. I did, they're rock hard and I came off worst! But all is forgiven when it flowers.

It grows in any aspect except in a cold, shady spot, but prefers sunshine. Good as a specimen shrub, in open borders, as an informal hedge or fan trained against a wall, it can also be trained as an espalier. It needs moist, fertile, free-draining soil.

For a wall shrub: prune the current year's growth to four to six leaves in early to mid-summer (unless it's needed to fill gaps); cut back secondary growth from these to two to three leaves in early autumn. When the framework becomes congested, cut back summer-pruned growth to two to three leaves in winter. For free-standing shrubs: cut back sideshoots to two to three buds at the base after flowering; remove some of the oldest growths at the base in winter. Propagate by semi-ripe cuttings, layering or removing suckers. Aphids can be a problem. **MB**

Chaenomeles speciosa 'Nivalis'

Chaenomeles x superba 'Crimson and Gold'
QUINCE, CYDONIA, JAPONICA

Type: hardy, deciduous, bushy shrub
Soil & situation: well-drained, fertile, neutral to acid soil but tolerant of a little lime/full sun or light shade
North American hardiness zone: 5–8
Height: 1m (3ft)
Spread: 2m (6½ft)
Grow for: attractive flowers in late winter; good for training against a wall; AGM

Growing this plant against a warm, sunny wall I can enjoy the flowers from late winter, long before the leaves emerge, until mid-summer. It forms a mass of spiny branches which can be thinned out after flowering. The clusters of five-petalled, dark red flowers show off their conspicuous golden anthers. Glossy, mid-green leaves appear after the first flush of flowers. Rock hard, green fruit turns yellow-green and aromatic in autumn, hanging long after leaf fall. It is too hard for garden birds to handle, and although the fruit is edible it is only palatable once cooked. While *Chaenomeles* x *superba* 'Crimson and Gold' is my favourite variety, there are many others in contention: 'Cameo' with fully double, peach-pink flowers, 'Rowallane' is scarlet and low growing, and 'Pink Lady' produces early, deep pink flowers. *C. speciosa* 'Moerloosei', sometimes labelled 'Apple Blossom', has large white flowers, flushed deep pink.

When trained against a wall the sideshoots should be shortened to two or three leaves. The quickest way to propagate is to layer a suitably low branch. It will be well rooted within one year. Chaenomeles is prone to canker, so prune out any dead or sickly branches and burn. **JC**

Left: Chaenomeles x *superba* 'Crimson and Gold'

Chamaecyparis pisifera 'Filifera Aurea'
GOLDEN THREAD-LEAF CYPRESS

Type: hardy, evergreen conifer
Soil & situation: moist, well-drained, neutral to acid soil/partial shade
North American hardiness zone: 4–8
Height: 8m (25ft)
Spread: 6m (20ft)
Grow for: year-round interest, especially its striking winter foliage; AGM

This beautiful, slow-growing conifer gives me pleasure every day of the year. The thin, bright yellow, pendulous, summer foliage deepens to a golden yellow in winter. In 16 years it has played host to more birds' nests than it has grown in feet. *Chamaecyparis pisifera* 'Filifera Aureovariegata Nana' is a variety with which it is sometimes confused but, as the name suggests, 'Nana' is quite dwarf.

The foliage will scorch if planted in full sun. A situation where there are evergreens positioned to block the afternoon sun is ideal. If planted in front of dark green conifers, holly or rhododendron, it will, during the dark days of winter, stand out like a golden beacon.

Clipping in late spring will keep young plants in shape. A mature tree can be pruned to prevent it from becoming straggly or too large for its position. Prune in late spring after all risk of frost is past. Propagation is by semi-ripe cuttings taken from the leading shoots. If taken from side branches they will, in their early years, grow into globose plants later reverting to type. These conifers are often erroneously labelled and sold as 'Filifera Aurea Nana' – be warned! **JC**

Chamaecyparis pisifera 'Filifera Aurea'

Cheiranthus cheiri

Cheiranthus cheiri (syn. *Erysimum cheiri*)
WALLFLOWER

Type: hardy, herbaceous biennial/perennial
Soil & situation: any soil with some lime/sun to light shade/moisture useful while young but will survive in dry cracks in a wall!
North American hardiness zone: usually grown as an annual
Height & spread: can make a bush up to 60cm (2ft) high by 1m (3ft) across, but usually half this size, or less if crowded
Grow for: very good value as it is cheap and easy to grow, and its red and yellow flowers are among the most powerfully scented in the garden

This is a must for every garden, useful as a short-term filler, as well as for the mixed border. Wallflowers give a lot of flower and scent for very little effort and have been bred to a vast number of varieties. I prefer the dark red colours as I reckon their scent is the sweetest, although some whites are close; and double-flowered forms the more so and their flowers are longer lasting. Native to Europe, the wallflower is closely related to the brassicas and has been very popular since Elizabethan times. It was so common in nosegays and posies that it was given the Latin name *cheiranthus*, which means hand-flower.

It needs a lime-rich soil, to be sown early, transplanted early and well established by the first frosts, if it is to make a good show of flowers the following spring. It is a short-lived perennial but in the UK is usually treated as a biennial. Dead-heading makes the plant flower for longer and, in most cases, live for another year. Usually grown from seed but propagate by layers and cuttings for the choicest varieties. Sow in mid-spring, transplant into a seedbed in early summer and to its final site by late summer, giving it masses of water. Wallflowers can suffer the same pests and diseases as the rest of the cabbage family (see page 64), but rarely do so badly. **BF**

Chimonanthus fragrans
(syn. C. praecox)
WINTERSWEET

Type: hardy, deciduous shrub
Soil & situation: any soil, especially limy/sun or
part shade
North American hardiness zone: 7–9
Height & spread: up to 3m (10ft) each way
Grow for: crimson and yellow waxy petals give off
a wonderful perfume all winter

The standard wintersweet may not be the most
attractive or impressive shrub in summer, but
through the depths of winter it produces flushes
of gorgeously scented flowers with the perfume of
violets. The leaves also have a slight smell. The
form *Chimonanthus praecox* 'Grandiflorus' has the
biggest flowers but is less fragrant, and *C. p.* var.
luteus flowers later with clear yellow blooms.

A native of China, wintersweet was introduced to
Britain in 1766. Three of the species are closely
related to the allspice, *Calycanthus floridus*, and
they are distantly related to the divine true lemon
verbena – now, an inter-genus hybrid of these
would really be something special.

Rather like a camellia it prefers a moist, rich soil
and shelter from cold winds, so is good sited on a
sunny wall where it should be long lived.
Removing the seedheads prevents the plant
wasting its energy and gives more flowers the

Chimonanthus fragrans

Chionodoxa forbesii

following year. Propagating from seed is very slow,
cuttings are not easy and the best option is to
layer in spring. Do not cut many stems of flowers
as these are borne on the back of old leaf axils
and will remove too much flowering wood; instead
pull off individual blooms and float them in a
saucer and their perfume will fill the room.   **BF**

Matt adds:
I find this needs a sheltered, sunny wall
(preferably by a window or door) on deep free-
draining soil; it thrives on chalk. It can take over
five years to flower, but the wait intensifies the
sense of anticipation! They open well in water, so
do cut some for indoors. The Chinese in their
wisdom use the flowers with linen the way we use
lavender.

Chionodoxa forbesii
GLORY OF SNOW

Type: hardy, bulbous perennial
Soil & situation: moist to moderately dry
soil/sunshine or dappled shade
North American hardiness zone: 3–9
Height: 10cm (4in)
Spread: 55cm (22in)
Grow for: bright flowers in late winter and early
spring

This is the bulb you'll often find wrongly named
in garden centres and catalogues as *Chionodoxa*

luciliae. In fact several species in commerce are
wrongly named and as it's a challenge trying to
unravel them, I'm going to leave it to the experts
and bury my head in the sand!

Tiny but tough, this little gem flowers early in the
year high on the mountains of the Greek island
of Crete, western Turkey and Cyprus, often
pushing itself through the snow to reveal its glory
against a glistening white background. An
impressive achievement when you consider it's
barely 10cm (4in) tall! The star-shaped, lilac-blue
flowers in compact clusters are only 2cm (^{3}/$_4$in)
across with white centres; they pop up from the
cold soil in early spring, accompanied by two
green leaves. It's a bright and beautiful reminder
that spring is on its way.

They look wonderful at the edge of borders or as
blue streams flowing under shrubs where they
spread and self-seed freely; plant them anywhere
that remains undisturbed. *C. forbesii* 'Pink Giant'
has an attractive spike of pretty, soft pink flowers
1.5cm (^{5}/$_8$in) across with white centres. It is 13cm
(5in) tall.

Plant them in sunshine or partial shade where
they will not dry out too much in summer. The
soil should be well drained; fork in leafmould
and sharp sand or grit in heavy conditions or
partial shade. Propagate by lifting and removing
offsets in summer and sowing seed in
containers.   **MB**

Choisya ternata
MEXICAN ORANGE BLOSSOM

Type: hardy, evergreen shrub
Soil & situation: fertile, well-drained soil/full sun
North American hardiness zone: 7–9
Height & spread: 3m (10ft)
Grow for: clusters of fragrant, white spring blossom and glossy foliage; AGM

I love this shrub. It has never annoyed me or let me down. It looks good all year with guaranteed flower and fragrance. The glossy, dark green leaflets are grouped in threes and when crushed they are strongly aromatic. The wonderfully fragrant clusters of white flowers are reminiscent of orange blossom and appear in late spring. Most years there will be a second flush of bloom in early autumn. *Choisya ternata* 'Sundance' has bright yellow, young leaves when grown in a sunny site. In light shade the leaves become pale green-yellow.

I have found *C. ternata* ideal for supporting summer-flowering clematis. It is happy for the visitor to scramble through its stems, close enough to the new growths for the flowers to poke their heads out through the foliage.

Pruning is seldom necessary. Where branches need to be removed to retain a good shape cut them in early summer after the main flowering period. Large, mature shrubs will form an outer shell of leaves with bare branches on the inside. Old plants respond well to a hard pruning and will quickly regrow. Remove one third of the stems each year.

Propagate by softwood cuttings in summer, rooting them in compost or in water. Large branches respond well to layering, being well rooted within 12 months. Snails love to hide within the plant and regular visits to remove them, shell and all, will reduce the population significantly. **JC**

Choisya ternata

Chrysanthemum chinensis

Chrysanthemum chinensis
SHUNGI-KU

Type: hardy, herbaceous annual
Soil & situation: any soil/sun or light shade
North American hardiness zone: annual
Height: to 1m (3ft)
Spread: 60cm (24in)
Grow for: easy to grow; bright yellow and white flowers and healthy, green, edible, ferny foliage

Also known as chop-suey greens, shungi-ku is little known to British gardeners but is rather valuable as it can be sown successionally to give young leaves for stir fries throughout most of the year. The flowers are cheerful, beneficial to insects and can be used for cutting, while the petals are also delicious in salads. This tough, easy-to-grow plant gives a lot of show from a spring sowing or three.

There are about 200 species in the chrysanthemum family, including ox-eye daisy, a native of Britain. Most have a less than pleasant scent, often resembling that of stale perspiration, but, fortunately, shungi-ku tastes better than those. In the East it is esteemed as a good companion to brassicas – its scent seems to help prevent many pests of that family locating them. *Chrysos* is the Greek for gold and *anthos* for flower, so chrysanthemums are gold-flowers.

Moist soil is necessary in the early stages but otherwise it is an easy plant to grow. It can be cut back hard to get renewal growths for stir fries but tastes best in the first six weeks from seed. Sow successionally from late winter under cover, through spring and summer outdoors and under cover again in autumn for a winter crop. Remarkably problem free. **BF**

Cirsium rivulare 'Atropurpureum'
PLUME THISTLE

Type: hardy perennial
Soil & situation: moist, fertile soil/sun or partial shade
North American hardiness zone: 4–8
Height: 1.2m (4ft)
Spread: 60cm (24in)
Grow for: elegant stems and flowers from late spring to autumn

This came to prominence after starring at the Chelsea Flower Show one year and briefly became a name that was on everyone's lips. It still has its admirers, including me. It is a striking, upright, 'architectural' plant and is wonderful for designs using a naturalistic style or in large borders where it needs plenty of space. It is a plant with poise.

The smooth, almost leafless stems are self-supporting and topped with flowers which are dense, soft tufts of burgundy appearing singly or in clusters. It has a rather vicious basal rosette of elegant but spiny leaves like the teeth of a swordfish – wear gloves if you're thinking of going near them! Flowering can be erratic – they are good some years and not others – but they bloom intermittently over a long period from late spring to mid-autumn, making them a valuable garden plant. Their colour combines well with blues, purples and silvers. The winter seedheads attract birds. It is incredible to think that these are related to thistles that can be such a problem in the garden.

The Latin *rivulare* means 'brook loving' and its natural habitat is in damp meadows, usually on acid soils. Ideal in rich, moist, well-drained soil in sun or partial shade. Clear the foliage in spring. Propagate by division from autumn to spring. Mildew can be a problem. **MB**

Cirsium rivulare 'Atropurpureum'

Cistus ladanifer

Cistus ladanifer
GUM CISTUS OR SUN ROSE

Type: hardy, evergreen shrub
Soil & situation: free-draining soil; tolerates chalk/sun/shelter
North American hardiness zone: 8–10
Height & spread: 1.5m (5ft)
Grow for: scented foliage and stems; flowers in early and mid-summer; AGM

I once worked in a garden where *Cistus ladanifer* flourished on a sunny bank. On scorching, cloudless summer days, I could smell their sweet fragrance long before I reached them. It was so

beguiling; it even made hoeing a joy! Perfumers have long valued the fragrance; the young branches are the main source of a sticky resin called 'labdanum' which is still used in cosmetics, aromatherapy and potpourri. In ancient times, it was combed from the beards of goats that browsed among the foliage and in the Middle Ages it was a major ingredient of pomanders.

Their fragrance is not their only attribute. In early and mid-summer the bush is smothered by a succession of simple, tissue-thin, white flowers, up to 10cm (4in) across, each delicately crumpled petal with a deep blood-red blotch at the base. They last only a short time and before long the

ground round the bush is covered with a layer of 'confetti'. The form *C. ladanifer* var. *albiflorus* lacks the coloured blotch.

Cistus flourish on chalk or poor, free-draining soil in hot, sunny conditions and are wind and maritime tolerant. Frost hardy to around –7°C (20°F), cistus need shelter in colder areas. They dislike being transplanted; buy small plants and avoid root disturbance. Prune from mid- to late spring to remove dead, diseased, dying or weak shoots and keep plants within their allotted space. Do not hard prune. Propagate from softwood, greenwood or semi-ripe cuttings from mid-summer until they are almost hard in autumn. **MB**

Omphalodes cappadocica 'Cherry Ingram'

NAVELWORT

Type: hardy, evergreen perennial
Soil & situation: best in moist, moderately fertile soil/light shade
Hardiness zone: 6–8
Height: about 25cm (10in)
Spread: about 40cm (16in)
Grow for: good evergreen ground cover with forget-me-not-like blue flowers in early spring; AGM

This is not only an extremely useful, woodland ground cover but also a bit of a show stopper in its own right in springtime. At this time of year it produces abundant, large, true-blue flowers on stems about 35cm (14in) tall. After this it may produce more flowers intermittently. It is a clump-forming plant and makes attractive leafy mounds that are present for 12 months of the year. I find it useful for enhancing the character of open woodland – it is particularly effective when used in decent-sized groups. It will tolerate quite heavy shade and also a fair amount of sunshine, so is versatile, although it does not appreciate dry situations. *Omphalodes verna* is much quicker to establish but does not flower for so long and I find is more deciduous than semi-evergreen.

These are plants that can be slow to settle down and get going as they do not like being moved, but once they do get going they are extremely good value, requiring little attention. They will form good, dense ground cover, ideal for interspersing with foxgloves, ferns, white epilobium and woodland grasses. Most of the omphalodes do appreciate moisture so, if your soil dries out in high summer, you will need to give them some moisture to prevent them looking sad and shrivelled. Propagate by division in early spring. **BG**

Citrullus lanatus

Citrullus lanatus (syn. *C. vulgaris*)
WATERMELON

Type: tender, herbaceous, scrambling, annual fruit
Soil & situation: moist but well-drained, sandy soil/full sun under cover
North American hardiness zone: annual
Height: 30cm (12in)
Spread: 3m (10ft)
Grow for: the challenge!

I am determined not to be defeated by what ought to be an easy subject, but growing watermelons in Britain is a lot more difficult than I ever imagined – if you live anywhere warmer it is easier. But when I have succeeded the quality and sweetness of the flesh have amazed me, even if I have raised fruits of only about 3.2–3.6kg (7–8lb), whereas they should be reaching up to 45kg (100lb)! A very healthy food, and if you eat the seeds it is more nutritious than spinach.

Natives of Africa, they seem not to have been known to the Romans and remained relatively unknown to Europeans until the New World was explored when the watermelon proved very happy in its new home. Now you can find them in every part of the warmer world and in many colours, inside and out!

It must be grown in warm, free-draining, yet moist soil and in full sun under cover. Pollinate the fruits by hand and limit each vine to one or two at most Stand fruits on a wooden board to prevent the underside rotting. Do not stop the vines as for other melons, but let them run. Sow from mid-spring under cover, pot on and grow in large pots of compost or in a warm border under cover; never overwater and do not feed heavily. It is very prone to red spider mite, so use the commercially available predators or lose the plants! Also be prepared to fail in cool, dim years.   **BF**

Citrus x *meyeri* 'Meyer'
LEMON

Type: tender, woody, evergreen shrub to small tree
Soil & situation: well-drained, lime-free soil/full sun/kept moist in summer, drier in winter when it needs to be under cover
North American hardiness zone: 9–10
Height & spread: 60cm (24in) in a tub
Grow for: striking green foliage year round; gorgeously scented white pink-stained flowers in several flushes; a continuous supply of fruit; AGM

All citrus make good conservatory or greenhouse subjects, especially for their divinely scented flowers and their edible fruit. *Citrus* x *meyeri* 'Meyer', or the Chinese lemon, is one of the most reliable, amazingly compact and highly productive of all the citrus and is rarely out of bloom or out of fruits. Its flavour is not so acid as some varieties. It is one of the easiest of the genus to root from cuttings and one of the hardiest. No wonder it's popular.

The lemon reached Egypt and Palestine in the 10th century and was cultivated in Genoa by the middle of the 15th century. The new fruits were soon spread around the warmer parts of Europe and they are now mainly grown in California, Florida, Israel, Spain and South Africa, though every warm to tropical area produces their own and more. Unripe lemons are often sold as limes, which are more spherical-shaped fruits.

It must be grown in well-drained, gritty, lime-free, humus-rich compost in a large tub. Given careful watering and feeding it may live for hundreds of years. To prevent the plant getting too big it can be pruned hard in early spring as growth commences. Once frosts are over it prefers to be outdoors. It can be grown from seed and may occasionally come true, but it will take a decade or two to fruit; cuttings in spring may take with bottom heat or ideally bud onto seedling stocks. Aphids, mealy bugs, scale insects and red spider mite all infest the plants, but a sojourn outdoors and soft soap sprays keep them under control.
Matt adds:

I find lemons need a lot of care. Here are some guidelines to add to what Bob has suggested. They prefer constant temperatures and humidity. Winter temperatures should be moderate; they dislike being too wet, dry or hungry. Low light, low temperatures or erratic watering prevents flowering. Mist with soft water early in the morning or stand on a tray of expanded clay aggregate filled with water to the bottom of the pot. Dry air and under-watering causes flowers to drop.

Feed with liquid or foliar feed all year round with citrus fertilizers or high-nitrogen fertilizer with trace elements in summer; general feed in late autumn to winter. Apply weekly to leaves and roots when the plant is growing strongly, otherwise fortnightly or not at all.

Outdoors: when there's no danger of frost or cold wind. Stand in partial shade, wrapped in horticultural fleece; bring indoors at night for 7-10 days. At the end of the summer reverse the process. Put them in a sunny spot; excessive heat bakes them.

Pinch out shoots to retain shape. Prune mature plants in late winter or early spring. Repot every two or three years; flowering is better when restricted, so do not over-pot.

Citrus x *meyeri* 'Meyer'

Citrus reticulata

Phew.

Of the many other varieties available, 'La Valette' is compact, prolific and has medium-sized fruit. 'Garey's Eureka' (aka 'Quatre Saisons') is heavy fruiting.

Citrus reticulata
TANGERINE ORANGE

Type: tender, woody, evergreen shrub to small tree
Soil & situation: well-drained, lime-free soil/full sun/kept moist in summer, drier in winter when it needs to be under cover
North American hardiness zone: 9–10
Height & spread: 3m (10ft) x 2m (6½ft), but smaller in a tub
Grow for: striking green foliage year round; gorgeously scented flowers in several flushes; a Christmas supply of fruit

Whatever you call this small, loose-skinned orange, it is among the best for eating as it is so easily peeled. It is highly productive and gives far more fruits than a sweet orange tree of the same size and about as many as a lemon. These delicious fruits also conveniently ripen for Christmas, which is also when they are most often found in the shops.

It comes from Cochin China, and is known by several names and sub-varieties such as mandarin, satsuma, tangerine or clementine, whatever you will. These names are frequently confused and interchanged for several small, sweet, easily peeled and segmented sorts of sweet orange.

For plant care and propagation, see previous entry. **BF**

Citrus sinensis 'Valencia'
SWEET ORANGE

Type: tender, woody, evergreen shrub to small tree
Soil & situation: well-drained, lime-free soil/full sun/kept moist in summer, drier in winter when it needs to be under cover
North American hardiness zone: 9–10
Height & spread: can reach 6m (20ft) x 3m (10ft), but not in a tub
Grow for: striking green foliage all year round; gorgeously scented pure white flowers in several flushes; delicious fruit

Citrus sinensis 'Valencia'

I love all citrus for their scented flowers, their aromatic foliage and their fruit. *Citrus sinensis* 'Valencia Late' is my favourite as it fruits for me at Christmas time and is to my mind the best, though others are good such as *C. s.* 'Jaffa', which is large, thick-skinned and seedless, and *C. s.* 'Washington Navel', which is nearly seedless. Blood oranges, such as 'Maltese', are sweet oranges with a red tint to their flesh.

Native to China and South East Asia, the citron was known to the Romans, but oranges did not reach Arabia until the ninth century. It is said that St Domine planted an orange in Rome in 1200 and a Spanish ship full of these fruits landed at Portsmouth, England, in 1290. However, all of these may have been bitter oranges as many think the sweet orange did not reach Europe until 1421 when it arrived at Versailles. Another planted in 1548 in Lisbon became the 'mother' of most European sweet orange trees and was still living in 1823.

For plant care and propagation please see *Citrus* x *meyeri* 'Meyer' on page 104. **BF**

Clarkia amoena

Clarkia amoena
(syn. *Godetia*)

Type: hardy annual
Soil & situation: fertile, moist, well-drained, acid soil/full sun or partial shade
North American hardiness zone: annual
Height: 75cm (30in)
Spread: 30cm (12in)
Grow for: excellent cut flowers

I have always been used to calling these flowers godetia. It sort of rolls off the tongue, so I will continue to do so. They are one of the easiest annuals to grow from seed, providing a continuous flower show all summer.

The 5cm (2in) long, lance-shaped, mid-green leaves are held on erect stems. The single or double fluted flowers are 5cm (2in) wide and available in shades of pink, lilac and a deep pink-red, all with paper-thin petals. They form clusters at the tips of the leafy shoots from early summer until mid-autumn. They are excellent as cut flowers lasting for at least a week in a vase. Strip the leaves off the portion of the stem which will be immersed in water.

The Grace Series of godetia have single flowers with contrasting centres growing to 45cm (18in) high.

Avoid dry soil and humid conditions. Excess nitrogen will result in leafy growth and fewer flowers. Propagation is by seed sown *in situ* in autumn or spring in open ground. They dislike being transplanted. If it is necessary to thin the seedlings, dump the thinnings. Seedlings from an autumn sowing will need to be over-wintered under a cloche and protected from winter frost.

JC

Claytonia perfoliata
(syn. *Montia perfoliata*)
MINER'S LETTUCE/WINTER PURSLANE

Type: hardy, herbaceous, annual salading
Soil & situation: any moist soil/light shade/preferably under cover
North American hardiness zone: 5–7
Height & spread: 30cm (12in)
Grow for: good winter ground cover and green manure, but mainly because it's a delicious, mid-winter salad vegetable

Few plants grow in the depths of winter but this one thrives in moist shade year round and is especially good for growing in the winter greenhouse border when little else will do there. Not only does it produce masses of tasty greens, which can be eaten raw or cooked as a spinach, but it is easy to pull up and eradicate. It makes a superb ground cover, excluding weeds, and provides quite a bulk of material for incorporating, composting or feeding to hens. Claytonia also has a unique shovel-shaped leaf with the flower stalk coming out of the middle and even when flowering the whole plant is still edible and not hot or fibrous – it is even liked by children!

Originally from North America, this one of half a dozen species was introduced to France in the 18th century, when it was known as Cuban spinach. The closely related species are also edible but not as palatable. Little known in the rest of world, miner's lettuce really ought to be grown everywhere. It is named after John Clayton, an Englishman who after 1705 became described as the greatest botanist in America.

Allow it to self-sow in your greenhouse border and it will be there for ever. If the soil is too dry it does poorly – it needs copious moisture and thrives in partial shade. Sow *in situ* from late autumn and leave some plants uncut to self-sow. Individual sporadic plants in open ground attract slugs underneath them – if they start looking miserable and pinkish, it's time to investigate. **BF**

Claytonia perfoliata

Clematis armandii

Clematis armandii

Type: frost-hardy, evergreen climber
Soil & situation: any aspect, as long as it is sheltered/wide range of soils, but dislikes poorly drained, heavy soils
North American hardiness zone: 7–9
Height: up to 6m (20ft)
Spread: 2–3m (6½–10ft)
Grow for: fast and strong-growing evergreen climber; highly fragrant, creamy-white flowers in early spring

This plant is far tougher and more vigorous than it is generally given credit for. It has thrived in my garden for many years and survived through cold periods below –10°C (14°F). I first saw it transforming a north-facing trellis in the Midlands in full flower, where it engulfed the whole courtyard garden with its powerful, almond-scented fragrance. The leaves are large, up to 15cm (6in) long, shiny, green and will cover sizeable stretches of wall. The downside is, I suppose, the rather gnarled appearance as it ages. But this can be dealt with using a bit of know how and secateurs.

Plant as for *C.* 'Warszawska Nike' (see page 108). A good annual mulch of compost or farmyard manure helps this vigorous climber keep in good health. This clematis is in pruning group 1, which means it is not essential to prune it at all but if you feel the urge a little snipping does help it keep looking trim. This simply involves removing any dead, dying or diseased stems after flowering and shortening any lengths that have outgrown their allotted space. However as it becomes gnarled with age, it becomes the plant to remove one or two thick stems right back to ground level after flowering. When new, reinvigorated shoots are well on their way, replacing the removed wood, tackle another stem or two. **BG**

Clematis x durandii

Type: hardy, deciduous climber/scrambler
Soil & situation: cool, moist, well-drained soil/sun
North American hardiness zone: 6–9
Height & spread: 3m (10ft)
Grow for: beautiful flowers from early summer to early autumn; AGM

Blue is my favourite colour, particularly at the end of the spectrum where shades of deep and grey-blue abound. It's no surprise, then, that these colours appear regularly in my plant selections or that *Clematis* x *durandii* is one of my favourite flowers. The four, broad sepals of dark indigo-violet with textured midribs, wavy margins and a central boss of yellow stamens are up to 10cm (4in) across. These sumptuous aristocratic blooms are big, but not blowsy and look even better resplendent on a bed of silvery foliage, notably *Brachyglottis compacta* x *monroi* 'Sunshine' (what a horrible, lumpy name!) or *Nepeta* x *faassenii* or draped over plants with dark purple leaves like *Cotinus* 'Grace'. Planted in the middle of a border it scrambles through surrounding plants, but can also be used as ground cover or tied into trellis as a climber with a backcloth of mid-green leaves. It has valuable cut flowers too.

It needs moist, cool, free-draining soil in sunshine. Dig in organic matter before planting and mulch well. It is fast growing and free flowering; ensure that there's a plentiful supply of moisture; feed with slow-release fertilizer in spring and mid-summer. Prune in late winter or early spring, cutting back the stems to at least 1m (3ft) from the ground. When planted in spring, water well in dry periods until established.

Propagate by internodal cuttings in spring. It is prone to mildew if grown against hot walls or fences and performs much better growing through other plants. Avoid mildew by keeping the soil moist and improving air circulation. **MB**

Clematis x *durandii*

Clematis heracleifolia 'Wyevale'

Clematis heracleifolia 'Wyevale'

Type: hardy, woody-based perennial
Soil & situation: well-drained fertile soil/sun or part shade
North American hardiness zone: 3–8
Height: 90cm (36in)
Spread: 1.2m (4ft)
Grow for: scented racemes of deep azure-blue flowers in late summer to autumn; AGM

At home I grow this plant in repeated clumps under my pleached hornbeams, where they get enough light to produce strong splashes of colour at the end of the summer. Their flowers are small, hyacinth-like, and in clusters on erect stalks. The foliage is bold and vine-like. The plant spreads, not rampantly but usefully, enabling you to divide it up to make more. I can only think that the reason it is not more popular is that people assume it is a climbing, twining clematis and are not sure what to do with it. It is a self-supporting ground cover, though not one that leans or romps through other plants. I use it regularly in a variety of schemes in various situations from formal borders to semi-wild areas – in fact anywhere that will benefit from this late-summer, rather natural-looking beauty.

Apparently some gardeners do stake this plant but I have certainly never had to. I can only assume that it may be necessary on extremely rich soil. The dead growth should be removed in late winter or spring (they flower on the current season's growth). This plant is easily propagated from layers and I have also grown *Clematis heracifolia* from seed. Herbaceous clematis do not suffer from wilt. **BG**

Clematis x *jouiniana* 'Praecox'

Clematis x *jouiniana* 'Praecox'

Type: hardy, deciduous climber/scrambler
Soil & situation: cool, moist, well-drained soil/sun
North American hardiness zone: 4–9
Height & spread: 3.5m (11ft)
Grow for: masses of beautiful flowers from mid-summer to autumn; AGM

Life is full of odd couples! It's remarkable that the handsome yet rather coarse UK native 'Old Man's Beard' should pair up with a gorgeous Oriental, *Clematis heracleifolia* var. *davidiana*. Thankfully, the offspring aren't as rampant as their father and have inherited both parents' good looks!

The stunningly beautiful mid-summer to autumn-flowering *C.* x *jouiniana* 'Praecox' and its relatives should be more widely grown. Scrambling rather than climbing, they cover low walls, mounds or tree-stumps and can be used as ground cover or tied into trellis. That great gardener, Christopher Lloyd, recommends it for herbaceous borders, rambling over perennial plants; the clouds of small, white, lavender-blue tinted, star-shaped flowers combining well with asters. Although the flowers are not scented, they are attractive to butterflies. The species flowers from early to mid-autumn, *C.* x *j.* 'Praecox' from July to October; other selections, like the azure-blue *C.* x *j.* 'Côte d'Azur' from August onwards.

It needs deep, moist, cool, free-draining soil in sunshine. Dig in organic matter before planting; mulch well. It is hungry, fast growing and free flowering; ensure that there's always plenty of moisture and feed with slow-release fertilizer in spring and mid-summer.

Prune in late winter or early spring, cutting back the stems to at least 1m (3ft) from the ground or prune to keep within its allotted space. Propagate from hardwood cuttings about 10cm (4in) long, in late winter. Take a slice of rind 3cm (1in) from the stem, then plant in pots of cutting compost in a cool greenhouse or cold frame.   **MB**

Clematis 'Warszawska Nike'

Type: hardy, woody, deciduous climber
Soil & situation: best on alkaline soils/will grow on sunny aspect but enjoys a cool, shady root run/needs some support be it shrub, fence or pergola
North American hardiness zone: 4–9
Height: 2–3m (6½–10ft)
Spread: 1m (3ft)
Grow for: exuberant, large, beautiful, dark purple-crimson, velvety flowers from mid-summer well into the autumn; free-flowering; AGM

There are several reasons I particularly like this clematis: the flower colour is a good intense wine which contrasts obligingly with the yellow anthers; the large flowers (10cm/4in across) seem to keep coming and coming; and in my experience it is a fairly robust, high-performance clematis. I grow it climbing into *Trachelospermum jasminoides* (see page 381), where it twines elegantly through this ideal support, the dark purple, white and racing green working well together earlier on, and the clematis

Clematis 'Warszawska Nike'

flowering on its own later on. It will also work well on any aspect, whereas many light-coloured, flowering clematis go a dirty grey on a south wall. These darker colours do lighten a bit but they are still good colours. It is also ideal for climbing over and through shrubs, bringing them to life.

Many failures with clematis are because gardeners find them difficult to establish but they are much easier when you know how. The successful growth of clematis depends a lot on planting. Firstly make sure you buy a plant in at least a 2-litre pot so you are starting off with a decent volume of roots. Ideally plant it in the autumn so it can get its rooting system started over the winter. Plant deeply, with the surface of the compost 8cm (3½in) below the soil level. Mulch it with gravel to retain the moisture and deter slugs and snails, possibly using a sunken plastic pot rim to contain the gravel. I never use stones as these attract snails which love clematis. Make sure you water well during the first summer in dry periods. Leave all the growth on it for the first winter and then cut back to about 30cm (12in) above ground level, just above a good, strong pair of buds. For subsequent pruning, as this plant is sometimes is listed as a group 2 and sometimes a group 3 clematis, I think it is best in late winter or early spring to cut the plant back to about 1m (3ft) from the ground, discarding the less healthy growth. When grown amongst a shrub you just cut it back to the top of the shrub – if you take it right back to the ground it wastes too much energy climbing back up and flowers less well.   **BG**

Cleome hassleriana

Cleome hassleriana (syn. *Capparis spinosa*)
AMERICAN SPIDER FLOWER

Type: half-hardy annual
Soil & situation: light, fertile soil/thrives in sandy, free-draining soils/warm, sheltered sunny position
North American hardiness zone: annual
Height: to 1.5m (5ft)
Spread: to 45cm (18in)
Grow for: exotic, colourful and decidedly different annual; spikes of spidery pink, mauve or, my favourite, white flowers perform for an amazing length of time; bold foliage

This is an annual I grow most years. You are pushed to find something that makes such a statement as this or can match its long period of colour (sometimes mine go on till late autumn) and before this arrives you have the added plus of the bright green leaves. There are three main cultivars, 'Cherry Queen', 'Violet Queen' and 'Helen Campbell'. I am not a fan of the mixed packets and have never grown 'Cherry Queen', which is not cherry pink at all but more of a knicker-pink – insipid and not my shade. 'Violet Queen', though, while again not really violet but more of a mauve which fades off to a blush-white, is quite a sight when mixed with deep purples. But the white 'Helen Campbell' is always spectacular and will keep a planting looking fresh even late in summer. The foliage, apart from being armed with spines, is sticky and is an unexpected asset before the flowers swipe your attention. These annuals look great in containers and are useful for cutting. Bees also appreciate them.

Sow the seeds under glass in single pots in mid-spring, ready for planting out about eight weeks later, once the risk of frosts has passed. Dead-head with care (as there are painfully sharp spines at the base of the leaves) to prolong flowering. These plants should not need staking. **BG**

Clerodendrum trichotomum var. *fargesii*

Type: hardy, deciduous shrub or small tree
Soil & situation: rich, well-drained soil/sunny, sheltered position
North American hardiness zone: 7–9
Height & spread: 6m (20ft)
Grow for: fragrant flowers from late summer to early autumn; unusual fruits; AGM

Clerodendrum trichotomum is an upright small tree or shrub, with bold oval leaves, to 20cm (8in) long that are larger on younger plants than older ones. The sweetly fragrant, waxy, star-like, white flowers, with long projecting stamens, five narrow petals and maroon calyces are produced in long-stalked clusters. They make an impressive sight but are overshadowed by the extraordinary bright turquoise metallic-blue fruits that are backed with a maroon, fleshy calyx. The leaves are malodorous when crushed and smell of cats. *C. t.* var. *fargesii* was introduced to France from China, it flowers more freely and is hardier than the species.

The Latin name *Clerodendrum* comes from the Greek *kleros*, which translates as chance, and *dendron*, meaning tree; it is supposed to be a reference to the variable medicinal qualities of the group.

The young shoots and leaves of the species are cooked and eaten! The leaves are used for many ailments including dermatitis, rheumatoid arthritis and joint pain. When used in a clinical trial, the blood pressure of 81 per cent of the group dropped significantly – the problem returned when treatment was stopped. The crushed seeds are used to kill lice.

It needs fertile, humus-rich, well-drained soil in sunshine, and protection from cold wind and frosts which can damage young growth. Feed with general fertilizer and mulch in early spring with well-rotted organic matter; water regularly during drought. Prune in late winter to remove dead, diseased, damaged, crossing, rubbing or weak branches and any spoiling the shape of the plant. Propagate by semi-ripe cuttings from mid-summer to early autumn, or root cuttings in autumn. **MB**

Clerodendrum trichotomum var. *fargesii*

Ulex europaeus 'Flore Pleno'

DOUBLE GORSE, WHIN, FURZE

Type: hardy, evergreen shrub
Soil & situation: well-drained, impoverished soil/full sun
Hardiness zone: 6–8
Height & spread: 2m (6¹/₂ft)
Grow for: masses of yellow flowers with a wonderful scent; perfect for a barrier hedge. Good all year round, but particularly lovely in early spring; AGM.

I love wild gorse. The first thing you see when you fly into Northern Ireland is mile upon mile of bright yellow hedges separating the fields. There is no difficulty finding plants in flower at any time of the year. Bob Flowerdew will tell you 'when gorse is out of flower, love is out of fashion'.

Ulex europaeus 'Flore Pleno' is double flowered and without seed. The freedom from nuisance seedlings elevates it to a class of its own. This evergreen shrub with sharp-tipped shoots and pointed, spiny leaves makes a wonderful barrier hedge. The bright, deep yellow, double, pea-like flowers are deliciously scented of coconut. There is more good news. It is happy to grow in the most miserable, impoverished soil you can find. It will do best in a well-drained, gravelly site in full sun.

Prune half of the branches hard after flowering every few years to encourage new growth. Propagate in summer using firm current year's growths in a free-draining, gritty compost. There are no pests or diseases that would dare to annoy it.

Warning: old bushy plants retain their dead, tinder-dry leaves, making them a fire risk close to property. **JC**

Clethra alnifolia
SWEET PEPPER BUSH, SUMMERSWEET

Type: hardy, deciduous, suckering shrub
Soil & situation: moist, acid soil/from full sun to deep shade
North American hardiness zone: 3–9; *C. arborea* 8–9
Height: 2m (6½ft)
Spread: variable
Grow for: fragrant, white flowers in late summer and early autumn when the leaves turn yellow and orange

My first introduction to this genus was the evergreen *Clethra arborea*, a native of Madeira where, heaven forbid, they use the foliage as cattle fodder! While visiting the Quinta do Palheiro, a magnificent garden near Funchal, I detected a spicy fragrance and followed it round the corner to find a young tree in full bloom. Sadly it's suitable only for sheltered gardens in mild areas of the UK so try *C. alnifolia* instead. It's a handsome, deciduous shrub covered in late summer with upright terminal spikes of fragrant, white flowers and in autumn with yellow and orange leaves. In good conditions it forms large colonies. *C. barbinervis*, a deciduous shrub or small tree up to 3m (10ft) high, is similar but does not sucker and is not as hardy.

There are several cultivars of *C. alnifolia*, including: 'Paniculata', which is considered to be the best of all the hardy clethras. 'Rosea' has very glossy leaves and pink tints to the buds and

Clethra alnifolia

flowers. 'Pink Spire' grows to 1.2m (4ft) and has rose-pink tinted flowers. 'Ruby Spice' has deep rose-pink flowers and will reach 1.5m (5ft). 'Hummingbird' is only 38–95cm (15–38in) tall with white flowers.

It is very adaptable, preferring moist, acid soil but tolerates wet or dry conditions. It is surface rooting so mulch in spring to preserve moisture. Remove older stems in winter to maintain the shape; rejuvenate by cutting back hard and feeding in spring. Propagate by seeds or detaching suckers in spring, layers in late autumn or early spring, or semi-ripe cuttings with a heel and bottom heat. **MB**

Clianthus puniceus 'Red Cardinal'
LOBSTER'S CLAW, PARROT'S BILL

Type: frost-hardy, evergreen shrub
Soil & situation: well-drained soil/full sun/shelter from cold winds
North American hardiness zone: 8–9
Height: 4m (13ft)
Spread: 3m (10ft)
Grow for: looks phenomenal in flower

With plants I can be very persistent and I can prove it. Over the past 30 years I have planted a total of six clianthus. All in my own garden with each one following the death of its predecessor. They are not frost hardy and every so often a hard frost teaches the plant and me a lesson. One reason I admit to my weakness is to encourage everyone to try growing this super plant. You may have to wrap it up every winter and it will eventually die but for a few, or more, seasons you will enjoy its full glory in flower.

Given support it will grow on trellis or against a wall, with 15cm (6in) long, dark green leaves and numerous narrow leaflets. The pendent racemes of brilliant scarlet flowers appear in late spring and early summer. When open, each 7.5cm (3in) flower resembles a lobster's claw or parrot's beak. These are followed by pea-like seedpods. Other good varieties include *Clianthus puniceus* 'Albus', white flushed green, and *C. p.* 'Roseus', deep rose-pink.

Planted in well-drained soil on a sunny wall and sheltered from cold winds it will quickly make a large shrub. Protect the base of the plant in winter with a deep mulch of straw or bracken. If cut back by frost it may well throw new growths

Clianthus puniceus 'Red Cardinal'

from the base in spring. Immediately after flowering prune the shoots back by one third. Old plants dislike hard pruning. Propagation is by seed sown in spring. Semi-ripe cuttings can be rooted in a free-draining compost with extra grit in summer. **JC**

Clivia miniata
KAFFIR LILY

Type: tender, evergreen perennial
Soil & situation: loam-based compost with added grit/frost tender/minimum temperature 10°C (50°F)/tolerates low light levels and dry atmospheres, making it a useful house plant/shady conditions outside/fairly high levels of water when in growth
North American hardiness zone: 10–11
Height: 45cm (18in)
Spread: 30cm (12in)
Grow for: strappy foliage in a good bright green; magnificent orange, fragrant blooms from spring to summer; AGM

This South African plant does look difficult to grow, with its huge, glamorous, scarlet-orange, funnel-shaped flowers and broad leaves, often up to 7cm (3in) wide. The foliage is distinctive enough to be grown for that alone, looking splendid if several plants are crammed together in a large pot. Because of its low requirements for humidity and light it copes well with central heating and indoor light levels so it is, in fact, a surprisingly undemanding plant that is well worth getting hold of to accommodate in the house in the cooler months and to use as a superb pot plant, adding an exotic flavour to the garden in the warmer months.

Although this plant dislikes root disturbance, periodically it will be necessary to divide it. This is best carried out in late winter or early spring. Only do this when they become very crowded as they do flower far better when they are more confined. They also look better when you see generous clumps of leaves. Feed the plant with a liquid feed when the flower buds appear, and then cut down the spent flowerheads after flowering. I put my pots outside in early summer in a fairly shaded spot and bring them in in autumn when the weather starts to turn. **BG**

Clivia miniata

Here's a few fascinating facts! The branched tendrils are tipped with tiny hooks that hang onto the branches and twist tightly to drag the stems towards the branches; the hooks are so effective they will hold onto your skin. The large, open-mouthed, solitary flowers at the end of stalks up to 25cm (10in) long are at first creamy-green with an unpleasant smell and are fly pollinated, ageing to deep violet with a honeyed scent and are bee pollinated. Finally, they darken further and are believed to be bat pollinated. The plant is always covered with flowers at different stages of maturity. Now there's something to tell your friends while you're cooking the barbecue!

Cobaea scandens f. *alba* has white flowers, ageing to creamy-white. *C. pringlei* from eastern Mexico has dainty, greenish-white cups on elegant flower stalks. I have seen it growing outside in a sheltered London garden where it looked magnificent.

Although this can be grown in conservatory borders or containers as a perennial, here it is treated as a half-hardy annual. Soak the seeds overnight in tepid water and sow from early to

Cobaea scandens

Cobaea scandens

mid-spring; plant out when there is no danger of frost in a sheltered, sunny position on moderately fertile, free-draining soil. Rich soils promote foliage at the expense of flowers. Pinch out the growing tips to encourage bushiness then trim to keep under control. It is excellent trained over a shed or trellis. **MB**

Cobaea scandens
CUP-AND-SAUCER VINE, CATHEDRAL BELLS

Type: half-hardy perennial, usually grown as an annual
Soil & situation: free-draining soil/hot sunshine
North American hardiness zone: annual
Height & spread: 4m (13ft) or more
Grow for: unusual flowers from mid-summer to mid-autumn

Codonopsis clematidea

Codonopsis clematidea
BONNET BELLFLOWER

Type: hardy, herbaceous climber
Soil & situation: moist, free-draining soil/full sun
North American hardiness zone: 7–9
Height & spread: 1.5m (5ft)
Grow for: pretty flowers from mid-summer to early autumn

Some plants like to tease and this is one of them! It's a delicate twining climber with brittle slender stems and grey-green leaves. Viewed from a distance, it seems so refined but when you get closer, there is a slight odour that gets much worse when the foliage is touched. Gently upturn the nodding pale blue flowers (taking care not to touch the foliage!) and its true beauty is revealed. There, as if painstakingly inked with golden-yellow, blue, purple and black are the most exquisite markings. There are many good reasons for growing this delicate, delectable plant – just remember not to touch the leaves!

Codonopsis convolvulacea has saucer-shaped, sky-blue flowers with circular purple markings inside. The bud expands like a small balloon, bursting open to reveal the flower. *C. lanceolata* is bell shaped, slate-mauve and greenish-lilac with violet spots, stripes and veins inside.

C. pilosula has large green bells with purple markings; its roots are used extensively in Chinese medicine.

They need light, moist, humus-rich, well-drained soil in sun or light shade, and shelter. Dig in plenty of well-rotted organic matter before planting, if needed. It grows best through shrubs, dark leaves providing an excellent background. Alternatively create brushwood supports using birch twigs, or similar, and allow them to scramble through. Plant near paths so they can be easily seen.

Pinch out shoot tips to encourage bushiness. Cut back to 30cm (12in) in autumn and to ground level in spring. Mulch in autumn. To propagate divide established plants in spring or sow seed. They are susceptible to slugs and snails.   **MB**

Coffea arabica
Plant of the Week (see page 25)

Colchicum speciosum 'Album'
NAKED LADIES, AUTUMN CROCUS

Type: hardy, cormous perennial
Soil & situation: deep, fertile, well-drained soil/full sun
North American hardiness zone: 4–9
Height: 20cm (8in)
Spread: 10cm (4in)

Colchicum speciosum 'Album'

Grow for: it is hard to beat the sight of dozens of autumn crocuses in flower; AGM

A border full of naked ladies, well I never! The way to appreciate autumn crocus is as a large drift in full bloom. Without their leaves, individual flowers do look a bit naked whereas, en masse, they make a spectacular display.

The 20–25cm (8–10in) long, lance-shaped, thick, dark green leaves of *Colchicum speciosum* 'Album' appear in late winter and last until mid-summer. The corm produces one to three goblet-shaped flowers on long stems (perianth tubes) in late autumn. The tepals are pure white with yellow anthers. Fortunately, they are unaffected by adverse weather.

C. 'Waterlily' produces up to five fully double, pinkish-lilac flowers in autumn on long stems. They are followed by erect, 20–25cm (8–10in) long leaves during winter and spring.

The corms should be planted 10cm (4in) deep in late summer or early autumn. Soils which tend to dry out in summer will need additional leafmould or well-rotted farmyard manure to help retain sufficient moisture. Propagation is by fresh seed sown as soon as it is ripe. Keep in a cold frame over the winter and early spring. Corms may be divided in summer when the foliage has died down. Replant them immediately.   **JC**

Colletia hystrix

Colletia hystrix (syn. *C. armata*)

Type: hardy, spiny shrub
Soil & situation: free-draining, preferably sandy soil/sun
North American hardiness zone: 7–10
Height & spread: 4m (13ft)
Grow for: sculptural form; curiosity value; fragrant flowers from early to late autumn

Roll up, roll up, see the weird and wonderful in a grotesque horticultural freak show full of fascination and fear! These bizarre botanical specimens, direct from the scrubby hillsides of temperate South America, have shed almost all their leaves, exposing a naked mass of flailing stems, covered with vicious spines. Grey-green *C. hystrix* has opted for tight clusters of short, rounded spikes. In sharp contrast to this ungainly mass of vegetative violence, tiny, white, sweetly scented flowers appear directly on the stems from late summer to autumn. There is even a pale pink form called 'Rosea'.

C. paradoxa (syn. *C. cruciata*) is similar, but the spines are even more intimidating with all the appeal of living razor wire! For defence and attack they have pairs of triangular, fin-like, flattened stems, each topped with a short sharp spine. Each pair is set alternately and at right angles to the previous one, right down the stem – there is no escape! Clusters of small, white, fragrant flowers dare to appear among this armoury, proving that there is beauty in these beasts; tangle with them at your peril!

I find them strangely beautiful and would love to plant either species in a stainless steel pot to be illuminated at night as living sculptures; it's the perfect piece of haughty culture! It needs shelter on well-drained, even poor soil in full sun. In cooler climates, grow in containers and protect from frost. Propagate by semi-ripe cuttings of sideshoots in late summer. **MB**

Convallaria majalis
LILY-OF-THE-VALLEY

Type: hardy, herbaceous perennial with creeping roots
Soil & situation: moist, humus-rich soil/light sun to light shade
North American hardiness zone: 2–7
Height: less than 30cm (12in)
Spread: indefinite
Grow for: even people who find many scented flowers too strong or overpowering love the pure white, scented spikes of lily-of-the-valley; AGM

Flowering in late spring and early summer there are few flowers more welcome – the little one-sided spikes of hanging white bells are attractive enough, but their scent is divine. The creeping roots can make this plant invasive where it is happy, but who cares as it is better than almost any alternative. It can also be made into a hanging-basket subject, as was popular in Victorian times. There is a rare double form and rarer still a pink form and I have even read there was a red variety, long since lost to us. A native of the northern temperate zone in England, it used

Convallaria majalis

to grow wild and in profusion on Hampstead Heath, London, and at Lee, Essex, but is now almost only found in gardens. The name is from the Latin *convallis*, a valley.

Given a moist, humus-rich soil in light shade this plant can become a weed and in such a site it will endure for centuries. Because of its creeping habit careful weeding is essential but it's not easy, so mulches really are of double benefit. It can be grown from seed, but lifting and dividing roots each with a bud before growth starts in spring is the best option. Lily-of-the-valley is not at all happy in dry conditions, especially in full sun. **BF**

John adds:
When it comes to ground cover that tolerates deep shade, most woodland plants smell a bit fusty or worse. Lily-of -the-valley is in a class if its own. The perfume of my favourite variety, *C. m.* 'Flore Pleno', is magnificent. Picking flowering stems for the house evokes pleasant memories of years gone by and they last well in water. *C. m.* 'Albostriata' is unusual, with bright leaves longitudinally striped in creamy white. The mauve-pink flowering *C. m.* var. 'Rosea' is not to my liking, but it is different.

Convolvulus cneorum

Type: hardy, evergreen shrub
Soil & situation: impoverished, gritty, well-drained soil/full sun
North American hardiness zone: 8–10
Height: 60cm (24in)
Spread: 90cm (36in)
Grow for: early summer colour in the heather bed; AGM

If you want a Mediterranean garden, this is a good plant with which to start. It loves it hot and dry, forming a compact, rounded, bushy shrub.

I delight in the foliage of this plant. The 5cm (2in) long, silvery-green, silky leaves shimmer like old silver in the afternoon sun feeling smooth and polished. They contrast beautifully with its ivory-white, funnel-shaped flowers which are 4cm (1½in) across. Flowering from late spring to mid-summer, each bloom, opening from a shell-pink bud, has a splash of bright yellow in its centre. A great plant for the rock garden or scree bed, it looks cool dotted through a mixed heather and dwarf conifer planting.

Convolvulus cneorum

In areas with cold, wet winters it should be grown in a container and given the protection of a cold greenhouse. To keep the plant in shape, shoots which have flowered may be trimmed back after flowering. It dislikes hard pruning. Propagation is easy in late spring with softwood cuttings or in summer using semi-ripe shoots. **JC**

Cordyline australis
TORQUAY/TORBAY PALM

Type: half-hardy, perennial, evergreen palm
Soil & situation: most soils/full sun/preferably moist
North American hardiness zone: 10–11
Height: 12m (40ft)
Spread: 2m (6½ft)
Grow for: unusual palm-like appearance; attractive, long, sword-like leaves; enormous foamy white panicles of highly scented flowers; AGM

There are few true palms hardy enough to survive in the UK and although this is not a true palm it closely resembles one. Famous along the southwest coast of England, it prefers mild coastal districts but can survive further inland; I have two in my

Cordyline australis

Norfolk garden and despite getting battered by the weather they survive, and a large one in a neighbouring garden thrives and flowers most years. It is a big plant when it reaches flowering size so often a set of steps is needed to smell the beautifully perfumed flowers.

A native of New Zealand where it is called the cabbage tree, it has been taken all over the world. The name is from the Greek *kordyle*, meaning a club, for which use it would be of no use as the wood is light and fibrous, not hard or even very rigid.

Although it likes moisture in the growing season, cordyline dislikes waterlogged soil in winter; given good conditions it can become quite big and then is much tougher than smaller specimens. Avoid searingly cold windy spots. If the growing point is destroyed it sometimes bifurcates but more often dies back and new stems come up from the base. Protect young small specimens from hard frosts, but be careful not to smother them.

Although it is possible to propagate from seed, offsets taken in spring are more sure – take big ones rather than small as the latter rarely survive.

Cats can cause immense damage to the stems as they use them as the most appealing scratching posts – wrapping with galvanized chicken netting stops them. **BF**

Coriandrum sativum 'Santo'

Coriandrum sativum 'Santo'
CORIANDER, CHINESE PARSLEY

Type: hardy, annual herb
Soil & situation: free-draining, warm soils which are not too rich/sunny position
North American hardiness zone: annual
Height: 1m (3ft), including flower
Spread: 20cm (8in)
Grow for: home-grown supply of this divine, distinctively flavoured leaf, an asset to any cook and many dishes

This plant can zap up a salad, barbecue or plain bit of fish or meat, transforming it to new heights. When grown commercially this herb tends to have lower levels of flavour, either because it is produced under polythene or fleece with reduction in sun and light or because it is irrigated to maximize yields. Home-grown is superior. People seem to have problems getting this plant to produce decent quantities of leaf before running to flower. The main factor I think is variety. For several years I have been growing 'Cilantro', a variety that is resistant to bolting but now it is no longer recognized as a distinct form.

My seed suppliers, Tozer Seeds Ltd, who supply many commercial growers and do variety trials, recommend that 'Santo' is the best variety for leaf production. They make the point that it is very early days in terms of selection of good varieties as this is a relatively new commercial crop over here. So keep on the look out for good new forms. Another form is 'Bilbo': commercial growers use this one for pot-grown supply to supermarkets as it is compact and does not flop over the pot (good news at point of sale). It quickly bolts, so is no good for leaf production. 'Moroccan' is the variety recommended for seed production. The RHS's AGM is also awarded for excellent varieties of vegetables and herbs but as yet they have not awarded one for coriander.

This plant germinates quickly and can be broadcast or sown *in situ* in drills from early spring onwards, at about three-weekly intervals, depending on weather. You can thin the plants to about 25cm (10in) which probably helps them resist bolting as there is less moisture stress when it is hot and dry. Commercially they cut the complete row, plough it in and start again, but for gardeners it far better to use it as cut-and-come-again picking, if possible, a few leaves of each plant rather than stressing it by shearing it to a couple of centimetres or an inch off the ground. If you are trying to grow for seeds though, watch carefully as the seeds drop as soon as they are ripe. For some dishes I also use the green seeds which are softer and full of flavour.   **BG**

Cornus alba 'Sibirica'
Plant of the Week (see page 17)

Cornus controversa 'Variegata'
WEDDING CAKE TREE

Type: hardy, deciduous tree
Soil & situation: fertile, moist, well-drained soil/full sun or light shade
North American hardiness zone: 6–9

Height & spread: 7m (23ft)
Grow for: an excellent specimen tree with a horizontal structure; AGM

A cornus with attitude. When mature and in leaf this tree will leave you speechless. It is a tree of rare beauty which refuses to conform to normal tree shape. The branches spread out horizontally, forming tiers, sufficiently far apart to allow light and shade to affect the lower foliage. Its tiers have resulted in the common name of wedding cake. It makes a marvellous specimen on a lawn underplanted with blue-flowered, spring bulbs such as grape hyacinth.

The 15cm (6in) long, oval leaves are shiny green, margined with creamy-white or yellow. In early summer a mature tree will produce flattened clusters of small, ivory-white flowers, followed by blue-black fruit.

Avoid planting in sites subjected to biting, cold winds as the young leaves are emerging in spring. It dislikes waterlogged soil. There is seldom any need for pruning but, when necessary, it should be undertaken in early winter before the sap commences to flow. When it is planted in grass it may be necessary to remove the lowest tier of branches to accommodate a lawn mower. If the tree is planted when it is small it will only require staking for one or two seasons. Propagation is by grafting in winter.   **JC**

Cornus controversa 'Variegata'

Lunaria annua

HONESTY, MOON PENNIES

Type: hardy biennial
Soil & situation: fertile, moist, well-drained soil/partial shade or sun
Hardiness zone: 3–8, but often grown as an annual in North America
Height: 90cm (36in)
Spread: 30cm (12in)
Grow for: flowers from mid- to late spring; seedheads through the winter. In most years April is the month when the flowers first appear.

The name honesty was apparently adopted in the 16th century because you can see right through the seedheads; I prefer moon pennies, which is a more romantic description of the ethereal, translucent seedheads. It is a robust plant with coarsely toothed leaves, upright stems and sweetly scented reddish-purple to white flowers from late spring to early summer. The seedheads start off deep lime-green, become tinted purple and then dry to form rounded 'moons' with three or more seeds like flattened currants that dry and rustle in the wind. Cut for decoration after a dry day, as soon as they mature; they look lovely in winter displays. In Guernsey it is believed to be good luck to hang a dried bunch in the wardrobe; in Yorkshire it is considered bad luck to have it in the house or garden! I think I'll go to Guernsey! They are excellent for naturalizing on banks, borders or in wildlife gardens.

Lunaria rediviva is similar but perennial with pale lavender flowers. *L. annua* var. *albiflora* has white flowers; *L. a.* var. *a.* 'Alba Variegata' has cream variegation and margins, and white flowers; and *L. a.* 'Munstead Purple' has deep reddish-purple flowers, and was selected by Gertrude Jekyll. The leaves of *L. a.* 'Variegata' are variegated and margined creamy white and the flowers are purple or red-purple.

They prefer fertile, moist, well-drained soil in partial shade or sun. Dig in plenty of well-rotted organic matter if necessary. Sow seed in a prepared seedbed from spring to early summer for planting out early the following year. Alternatively, sow *in situ* or allow it to self-seed. Any pests or diseases affecting the family Cruciferae, including clubroot, can be a problem. **MB**

Corydalis flexuosa
'Père David'

Type: hardy, herbaceous perennial
Soil & situation: moist, humus-rich soil/dappled shade
North American hardiness zone: 6–8
Height: 30cm (12in) or more
Spread: 20cm (8in) or more
Grow for: turquoise flowers from mid-spring to late summer

This glorious species was first introduced to the UK in 1986 from the Wolong Panda Reserve in China. Mixed forest shelters this society beauty and its classy companions *Cardiocrinum giganteum* var. *yunnanense* (see page 85) and *Paris polyphylla* (page 287). I like to believe that occasionally the flowering may overlap – can you imagine what that would be like? Botanical ecstasy!

The form 'Père David' is vigorous with grey-blue, oval leaves with blood-red markings. They appear in autumn, remain over winter (where conditions allow) and become dormant in summer. From early spring to early summer it is covered in slender, brilliant blue, 3.5cm (1¼in) long flowers gliding over the foliage like a shoal of exquisite tropical fish. For any blue addict, it's just bliss! At first they are densely packed, then gradually

Corydalis flexuosa 'Père David'

disperse until they finally swim away to oblivion. Rather than being beautiful and temperamental, this is beautiful and obliging; what a wonderful plant to grow!

Other cultivars of *Corydalis flexuosa* include: 'Balang Mist' whose flowers are pale with a blue flush; the leaves of 'Blue Panda' are pale blue-green and the flowers sky-blue; 'Purple Leaf' has reddish-purple leaves and stems, and deep blood-red markings at the base of the leaflets; and 'China Blue' has greenish to sky-blue flowers and brownish-green leaves with small red blotches at the base.

They need partial shade and moderately deep, fertile, humus-rich, moist, free-draining soil. Dig in plenty of well-rotted leafmould if necessary. They tolerate both alkaline soil and drier soils. Divide in late summer when autumn growth is about to begin. Slugs and snails can be a problem. **MB**

Corylus avellana/C. maxima
COBNUT, RED-SKINNED FILBERT

Type: hardy, deciduous, woody shrub
Soil & situation: well-drained, poor soil/full sun to light shade
North American hardiness zone: 3–9
Height: 7m (23ft)
Spread: 3m (10ft)
Grow for: catkins in late winter, delicious nuts in autumn and useful for pea sticks

All the hazel family are good shrubs for the wild garden, though most are not attractive enough for an ornamental planitng. In the orchard they are very valuable as the tasty nuts are generously produced almost every year without fail. The catkins are gorgeous in late winter and the wee red female flowers, like tiny crimson starfish, are a joy to behold on a bright late winter's day. I grow several varieties but the most flavoursome, and slightly more compact, red-skinned filbert is by far and away the tastiest. The husks and shells are also useful as I save these up and use them for smoking cheese.

The hazel is a native of the UK but foreign blood has been introduced to the cobs and filberts. Once an important crop in Kent, the plants were ruthlessly trained and pruned to a wheel-shaped base with a cylinder of fruiting stems rising from the rim – sadly this intensive method has now passed and most nuts for sale are imported.

Corylus avellana

Hazel is long lived in a dry, gravelly, poor soil which few other crop plants enjoy. Prune to remove congested internal growths and strong vertical shoots, which are always useful to have in the garden anyway. Plants can be bought impregnated with truffle fungus on the roots but so far I've not had any success with mine, nor heard of any one who has, and they were not cheap! Seed does not come true, cuttings are difficult, layering is not easy, so I find inarching onto seedlings the best option. Without doubt, the only major problem is the squirrels who steal most of my crop and they will get yours too. **BF**

Bunny adds:

I grow a lot of hazel – they are ornamental in themselves and of course you can cultivate carpets of other plants around them. I often use them for screening children's areas; they create useful cover for children to play in, too, and great dens can be made between and from the sticks. We have no squirrels, but the Jack Russell pinches the nuts, cracks them open and eats them!

Corylus maxima 'Purpurea'

Corylus avellana 'Contorta'

Corylus avellana 'Contorta'
CORKSCREW HAZEL, HARRY LAUDER'S
WALKING STICK

Type: hardy, deciduous shrub
Soil & situation: fertile, well-drained, alkaline
soil/sun or partial shade
North American hardiness zone: 3–9
Height & spread: 3m (10ft)
Grow for: mad twisted stems which are its main
claim to fame – I'm old enough to remember the
famous twisted walking stick

I include *Corylus avellana* 'Contorta' in lots of
planting plans. Perhaps it is because it looks so
ludicrous in winter with its bare stems contorted,
as though following the silvery trail left by a
drunken snail. An edging of blown snow to
highlight the shapes makes a chilly, winter garden
walk worthwhile. Bright yellow 5–8cm (2–3½in)
long catkins appear in winter and early spring,
ahead of the mid-green leaves which turn pale
yellow in autumn. Another hazel I wouldn't be
without is *C. maxima* 'Purpurea' (the purple-
leafed filbert), which makes a big shrub with
rounded, deep, deep purple leaves.

C. a. 'Contorta' is grafted onto *C. avellana*
rootstock. Suckers must be removed where they
join the main stem or root as soon as they appear
(and they will). Left to grow, the faster-growing
common hazel will overpower and smother
'Contorta'. I prefer to thin the branches in spring
to prevent them forming a tangled mass. This
also allows the contortions to be better admired.
The prunings are much sought after by flower
arrangers. The easiest form of propagation is by
layering a low branch. It will tolerate most soils
but dislikes waterlogged or acid conditions. **JC**

Cosmos atrosanguineus

Type: tender perennial
Soil & situation: well-drained but moisture-
retentive soil/full sun/protection over winter in
many areas
North American hardiness zone: 7–10
Height: 75cm (30in)
Spread: 45cm (18in)
Grow for: stunning, small, solitary, rich chocolate-
maroon flowers from summer to autumn; with a
strange, strong, dark chocolate fragrance

This wonderful plant is well worth the effort
involved with winter protection – the exquisite
flowers are velvety, and look like mini dahlias.
The leaves are green, sometimes with reddish-
brown midribs. The long stems are often reddish
too, topped with the individual flowers that are
produced for months from summer to autumn.
At the start of the season the growth is upright,
later spreading out. If your soil is too rich you
may find masses of vegetative growth is produced
at the expense of flowers.

These plants start into growth very late in spring,
so in warmer areas you can get away with leaving
the mature tubers to over-winter outside
providing the soil is well-drained and you add a
protective mulch. If the tubers are planted deeply,
about 15cm (6in) below the soil surface, they are
also in with a far better chance of survival.

Otherwise, either lift the plants in the autumn and
over-winter them under glass in frost-free
conditions or lift and store the small tubers as you
would for dahlias. The mature tubers are hardier,
so for the first year at least, even in warm, sheltered
areas, it is advisable not to chance it. If you want to
propagate them, take basal cuttings from the tubers
as for dahlias, but a hormone rooting powder is
worth it as they tend to be a little tricky. **BG**

Cosmos atrosanguineus

Cotinus coggygria

Cotinus coggygria
SMOKE TREE, VENETIAN SUMACH

Type: hardy, deciduous shrub
Soil & situation: well-drained soil/sunny or partially shaded position/generally an easy plant to please and grow.
North American hardiness zone: 5–8
Height & spread: to 5m (16ft)
Grow for: bushy shrub with wonderful translucent, bright green foliage; autumn tints a spectacular red; flowers form a smoke-like blur all over the shrub in summer; AGM

I inherited a magnificent specimen of this plant – more like a multi-stem tree, it must be 5m (16ft) going on 6m (20ft), with five large limbs spreading from a short leg about 30cm (12in) high and with a diameter of the same order. This and an elderly, but delicious, greengage were the only inhabitants of my small walled garden, even though the house dates back to the thirteenth century. My new design was superimposed around them, and the cotinus has risen to the occasion and become more spectacular each year. The winter profile of its fine, comely multi-stem habit is as good as its dramatic performance of flowering in summer, then its seasonal turn in autumn is a show-stopper and for the rest of the year its stature and foliage command centre stage. I would never have planted it for this position, not having the wit, patience or foresight to know that it would be such a specimen. Normally it makes up a mixed border as a large and decorative shrub. The purple-leafed form

C. coggygria 'Royal Purple' has dark purple leaves that can look heavy, but equally can be dramatically offset by brighter limes and vivid oranges.

Cotinus coggygria is fairly fast growing and so, with a little patience, could be positioned and planted as a specimen tree. On the other hand, if a more compact, smaller plant is desired, pruning it back to a permanent framework each spring, before growth begins, produces larger foliage and restricts the size. For a more laid-back approach, just remove the undesirables – dead, dying, crossing limbs and anything that is getting too big – in late winter or early spring. **BG**

Cotinus 'Flame'
SMOKE BUSH

Type: hardy, deciduous shrub
Soil & situation: moist, well-drained soil/full sun or light shade
North American hardiness zone: 5–8
Height: 6m (20ft)
Spread: 5m (16ft)
Grow for: a fine-looking shrub with amazing orange-red foliage in the autumn; AGM

To see this plant in late summer and then in early autumn is one of the wonders of a garden. The contrast in leaf colour inside a few days is magical.

It forms a tree-like, bushy shrub with 10cm (4in) long, light green leaves. In autumn the foliage

Cotinus 'Flame'

Cotoneaster bullatus

turns a brilliant orange-red. The 15cm (6in) long, fruiting panicles are pale purple in late summer. *Cotinus* 'Flame' can tolerate light shade but the autumn leaf colour will not be so spectacular. *C.* 'Grace' is similar with brilliant, translucent, bright red leaves in autumn. Powdery mildew can seriously mark the foliage of both varieties.

Shelter from strong winds is essential as its brittle stems will break off, spoiling the overall shape. Pruning in spring by reducing all the branches back to a few buds of the main framework will result in new growth with large leaves. Propagation is by softwood cuttings in summer. Where there are suitably low branches layering will result in large, rooted plants within 18 months. **JC**

Cotoneaster bullatus
HOLLY BERRY COTONEASTER

Type: hardy, deciduous shrub or small tree
Soil & situation: most soils/full sun or partial shade
North American hardiness zone: 6–8
Height: 5m (16ft)
Spread: 3m (10ft)
Grow for: flowers in early and mid-summer; autumn fruits and colour; AGM

I can't help admiring plants that combine the attributes of physical toughness and attractive features. Cotoneasters fall into this category, yet they are cursed by being regarded as 'municipal' and consequently undervalued as garden plants;

Cotoneaster 'Rothschildianus'

Crambe cordifolia
GREATER SEAKALE

Type: hardy perennial
Soil & situation: well-drained soil/will tolerate some shade and poor soil/sunny position
North American hardiness zone: 6–9
Height: up to 2m (6½ft)
Spread: 1.5m (5ft)
Grow for: dramatic, large, cabbage-like leaves followed by a vast froth of tiny, white, honey-scented flowers in late spring to early summer; AGM

This plant is a relative of the edible seakale and is a fun plant for borders providing you have the space. It will rapidly swallow up 1m (3ft) of ground, so is fairly imposing. The superb flowers, carried in branched panicles, are equally imposing in the vertical plane. If the plant sets seed, it remains attractive for a good long period and is a useful structure for encouraging another plant to weave itself into. If this is not the case, soon after the flowering is finished the leaves start to go yellow and die back as all the resources are taken back to the tap root. This leaves you with a large space to fill, which may be was just what you wanted, but more likely not. With their huge stature and relaxed feel they are easier and perhaps better suited to other situations – for instance in wilder spaces or in summer-flowering meadows, where the higher cut later on in the year will not harm them.

On a wet, poorly drained soil this plant tends to succumb to bacterial rots. Propagate these plants by root cuttings in winter, division in spring or by seed. **BG**

Crambe cordifolia

they make good hedges, ground cover and specimen plants. A particular favourite of mine is *Cotoneaster bullatus*, a large shrub with an open arching habit and big oval to oblong corrugated leaves which are soft bronze when young. The flat clusters of up to 30 rose-pink coloured flowers are followed by bunches of large, bright, glossy red berries, which often weigh down the branches, and magnificent autumn colour of orange or red.

Other recommended plants in this genus include *Cotoneaster microphyllus*, a low-growing evergreen with stiff stems and masses of tiny leaves, flowers and red berries; and *C. franchetii*, semi-evergreen with pale green leaves and small clusters of orange fruits. *C. horizontalis*, the deciduous 'herringbone cotoneaster', is magnificent when massed with white flowers, in red autumn colour and fruit, and when covered with frost in winter. I also love *C. salicifolius* 'Rothschildianus' (see next entry).

It needs sunshine to partial shade in moist, free-draining soil, however it tolerates anything except waterlogged soil; nurture until established in drier soils. Prune in summer, if necessary. Propagate by semi-ripe cuttings in early autumn. Sow seed outdoors when ripe in autumn or stratify in damp sand and sow under glass in spring. It is subject to many of the pests which afflict apples, including aphids, scale and silver leaf. Prune from the start of late summer and early autumn. **MB**

Cotoneaster salicifolius 'Rothschildianus'

Type: hardy, evergreen shrub
Soil & situation: fertile, well-drained soil/full sun or light shade
North American hardiness zone: 6–8
Height & spread: 5m (16ft)
Grow for: a mass of golden-yellow berries in autumn; AGM

You couldn't have too many big cotoneasters but it is nice to ring the changes and with golden-yellow berries this one is worth the money.

Tree-like, this vigorous, upright shrub has arching branches. The 10cm (4in) long, pale green leaves are narrow and lance-shaped. Clusters of small white flowers appear in summer and are followed in autumn by golden-yellow fruits, which last well into winter or until eaten by birds. If planted close to a path and allowed to grow over, it will resemble a covered walkway with clusters of pendent berries on arching stems.

It will grow well in light shade but dislikes cold, drying winds. Prune in early spring to keep it in shape. When necessary large branches may be cut hard to encourage new, strong shoots from low down on the plant. Propagation is by semi-ripe cuttings in late summer. Pot the rooted plants during the following summer and allow to grow for a season before planting out. **JC**

Crambe maritima

Type: hardy, herbaceous perennial
Soil & situation: light, free-draining soil/sun
North American hardiness zone: 6–9
Height: 75cm (30in)
Spread: 60cm (24in)
Grow for: tasty shoots; ornamental leaves and
white flowers in summer; AGM

Seakale was harvested from beaches in the UK
long before it came into cultivation; the shoots
were blanched by heaping sand around them,
then cut and carried to market. In the late 16th
century, John Gerard in his *Herball* described
seakale like this: 'It groweth naturally on the
bayches and brimmes of the sea where is no earth
to be seen, but sande and rolling pebble stones.'
By Victorian times it had swept by a tide of
enthusiasm into the garden and was regarded as
an aristocrat among vegetables. The young shoots,
blanched using terracotta forcers, burst from the
ground as if twisted and contorted by a supreme
effort. It was lightly boiled and served on folded
napkins or pieces of toast with a sauceboat of
lemon-flavoured melted butter or simply
drenched in white bechamel or hollandaise sauce.
Now there's an incentive to grow it!

Blanch by covering the crowns in late winter. It
needs sunshine and deep, rich, moisture-
retentive, light soil. Add plenty of well-rotted
organic matter or sharp sand if necessary the
winter before planting. Water regularly; feed with
general fertilizer in spring.

In the vegetable garden, seakale needs a
permanent bed, like asparagus. Plant crowns or
root cuttings or pencil thick 'thongs', 7.5–15cm
(3–6in) long, in late autumn or early winter;
make a horizontal cut at the top and a slanting
cut at the base so you don't plant them upside
down and store in sand in a cool shed until early
spring. Make a hole with a dibber and plant
cuttings 3cm (1in) below soil level, 38cm (15in)
apart each way. They need at least a year to
establish before harvesting. Beware of club root;
flea beetle damages the leaves.   **MB**

Bunny adds:
A great vegetable for the ornamental kitchen
garden, but I have to say I think it looks better
than it tastes, though I adore the hollandaise
sauce. Removing any flowering stems before they
develop helps it establish and become more
productive. In my garden I usually let it flower
though, as we do not eat that much and the
flowers are a real asset.

Crambe maritima

Crataegus spp.
HAWTHORN, QUICKTHORN

Type: hardy, deciduous woody shrub to small tree
Soil & situation: any soil/in full sun or shade
North American hardiness zone: 5–8
Height & spread: grows to a small tree but if
regularly clipped it can be kept to 1m (3ft) x
50cm (20in)
Grow for: the thorns and bushy habit make this a
stock- and people-proof hedge

The congested habit makes the appearance of a
well-clipped hawthorn hedge look like a piece of
coarse tweed, even when out of leaf. Hawthorn is
overlooked because of its presence everywhere – it
is one of the finest of hedges and if it ever gets
too big and unwieldy it can be laid, pleached and
worked up again, which is more than can be done
for many others.

A native of Europe it has been used since time
immemorial for hedging fields and has been and
still is used on a vast scale. The wood is hard and
it was known to the Greeks as *kratos*, from which
we derive our name.

It will do almost anywhere and has no special
needs but if total impenetrability is required
then plant two offset rows, each plant at less
than 30cm (12in) apart and start trimming early
on. Shear at least once a year, or twice if
exquisite neatness is required. The young plants
are not so tough as an established hedge so
protect them with guards or windbreak netting.
Quickthorn is easy to strike from cuttings but in
the UK because of its wholesale use by farmers
can be bought by the hundred or thousand very
cheaply indeed. Sometimes webber caterpillars
or similar may defoliate a piece but it usually
soon recovers.   **BF**

Crataegus hedge

Crataegus laevigata 'Paul's Scarlet'

Crataegus laevigata 'Paul's Scarlet'
HAWTHORN, PINK THORN, MAY HAYTHORN

Type: hardy, deciduous tree
Soil & situation: any soil other than waterlogged/full sun or partial shade
North American hardiness zone: 5–8
Height & spread: 8m (25ft)
Grow for: mass of flowers in spring whatever the weather; AGM

All the 'thorns' are highly desirable plants. They are tough, well able to withstand icy blasts, salt-laden winds, impoverished soil and still manage to look good while preventing livestock from trespassing. The species is sometimes known as *C. oxycantha*.

The tree forms a rounded, compact shape with many thorns on all branches. In windswept sites it will bend with the wind, appearing lobsided. The 5cm (2in) long, glossy, mid-green leaves have three to five shallow lobes. They don't colour much in autumn and differ from the dark green, deeply lobed English hawthorn, *C. monogyna*, which is commonly grown as a field hedge.

Irrespective of the weather, in late spring *C. laevigata* 'Paul's Scarlet' is covered in clusters of up to ten deep pink, double flowers. It seldom produces berries but I am prepared to overlook this one small fault to be able to sit under a mature, gnarled tree laden with birds' nests and covered in rich blossom. There are two schools of thought about the English saying 'Don't cast a clout until May is out.' Either don't remove any clothes before the end of the month of May or else wait until the hawthorn is in bloom. You can please yourself, but if you are cold put your coat back on.

Propagation is usually by bud grafting onto a crataegus rootstock. Plant with the graft union above soil level. Remove suckers as close to the root as possible when they are still small. **JC**

Crataegus monogyna 'Biflora'
GLASTONBURY THORN

Type: hardy, small, spreading, spiny, deciduous tree or shrub
Soil & situation: moisture-retentive, free-draining soil/sun or partial shade
North American hardiness zone: 5–7
Height: 10m (33ft)
Spread: 8m (25ft)
Grow for: white flowers in mid-winter and late spring; red fruits; autumn colour

This fascinating and mystical plant flowers not only in late spring, like the common hawthorn, but in mid-winter too! Tradition says that it flowers on Christmas Day; I've seen it blooming then and on 7th January, 'old' Christmas Day. Depending on the weather, it blooms any time from late autumn until mid-spring.

There are many variations on the legend that tells of Joseph of Arimathea preaching Christianity in England and here is one of them. He went to Glastonbury, then called the Isle of Avalon, which at that time was surrounded by water. Tired from travelling and his preaching being ignored he rested on 'Weary-all Hill', and prayed for a miracle to convince the doubters. His prayer was answered; the staff he was leaning on, being thrust into the ground, burst into leaf and flower; it was Christmas Day and the miracle is said to be repeated each Christmas. Sprays are sent to the Royal family as decoration for Christmas Day; Queen Elizabeth II is said to have hers on the breakfast table; the late Queen Mother placed hers on a writing desk. It flowers only moderately in late spring.

One of the hardiest and most adaptable trees, tolerating sun to moderate shade and waterlogged or dry soil once established. It thrives in industrial and windswept sites. Pruning after flowering in spring will be necessary to keep the plant within its allotted space. Rejuvenate it by cutting hard after flowering in spring. Propagate by grafting or cuttings. Remove stems affected by cotoneaster webber moth; in dry seasons it may suffer from powdery mildew. Keep the soil moist as a preventative measure. **MB**

Crataegus monogyna 'Biflora'

Paulownia tomentosa

EMPRESS TREE, FOXGLOVE TREE

Type: hardy, deciduous tree
Soil & situation: well-drained, fertile soil/full sun/shelter from cold winds
Hardiness zone: 5–8
Height: 12m (40ft)
Spread: 10m (33ft)
Grow for: stunning, foxglove-like flowers; massive leaves; a compact tree for any size garden. If you are lucky, the flowers burst into bloom at this time of year; AGM.

This is one of my all-time favourite flowering, deciduous trees. It isn't rare but, in my book, deserves to be planted in every garden. It comes in two sizes: big and, when managed, small enough.

The felted, tan-coloured buds appear in autumn. From mid- to late spring, if these have escaped frost damage, the tree is covered in showy, 5cm (2in) long, fragrant, pale violet, foxglove-like flowers, marked with purple and yellow on the inside. The soft, hairy, bright green leaves are up to 30cm (12in) long, unfurling as the tree flowers.

It produces stumpy, thick branches, quickly forming a compact, round-headed tree. In a small garden you may sacrifice the flowers for enormous 60cm (24in) leaves by pollarding (cutting) the main stem close to the ground every spring. Allow one or two shoots to grow and these will quickly reach 3m (10ft) with huge leaves – the result looks stunning and makes quite a talking point.

Paulownia tomentosa prefers a sunny site, sheltered from biting, cold winds. It is totally hardy, although frost may damage soft growths and flower buds. Sow fresh seed in autumn and over-winter in a cold frame or propagate by taking root cuttings in winter. Powdery mildew may cause early defoliation. **JC**

Crinodendron hookerianum

Crinodendron hookerianum
CHILEAN LANTERN TREE

Type: half-hardy evergreen shrub or small tree
Soil & situation: cool, moist, acid soil/partial shade/shelter
North American hardiness zone: 9–10
Height: 10m (33ft)
Spread: 6m (20ft), or more
Grow for: unusual, lantern-like flowers opening in late spring; AGM

One of two species of glossy, dark-leaved evergreens from the temperate rainforests of southern Chile, where there is over 250cm (100in) of rain a year and the locals probably have webbed feet! *Crino* (lily), *dendron* (tree) was named for Sir William Hooker, the first director of the Royal Botanic Gardens, Kew and was introduced in 1848 by a Cornishman, William Lobb (1809–63), who was the first plant collector to be employed by the famous nurserymen Veitch & Co. The best specimen I ever saw was in Dublin, where it made a wonderful sight, reaching about 10m (33ft) tall and festooned with masses of red 'lanterns'. It shares with *Stachyurus praecox* (see page 371) the habit of producing flower stalks in autumn which bloom the following year; the flowers open in late spring and last for about six weeks – tap them and they rain yellow pollen. Atchoo!

C. hookerianum 'Ada Hoffman' has pink flowers; *C. patagua* has white, bell-shaped flowers in late summer and is more tender than *C. hookerianum*.

Plant in a sheltered, partially shaded spot or the leaves will be scorched by cold, drying winds or sun in cool, moist, acid soil. Shelter is vital as they are susceptible to winter damage. Mulch in spring and keep them constantly moist. They flourish in mild, moist regions of the UK like Cornwall and the west coast of Scotland. Plants grown in pots in the greenhouse in ericaceous compost should be watered with rainwater and fed with fertilizer for acid-loving plants. Containerized plants flower when young. Trim after flowering to keep within its allotted space. Propagate by semi-ripe cuttings from late summer to early autumn. **MB**

Crinum x *powellii* 'Album'
WHITE CAPE LILY

Type: hardy, bulbous perennial
Soil & situation: deep, moisture-retentive but well-drained, fertile soils/full sun
North American hardiness zone: 7–10
Height: 1.2m (4ft)
Spread: 30cm (12in)
Grow for: heavy umbels of highly scented, white flowers from late summer till autumn; AGM

You often see these glamorous plants being grown in large pots, which does show them off extremely well and gives you the advantage of being able to move them to a highly visible position when they are at their peak. This way you do not necessarily have to view the rather gangly leaves for too long. They are also fairly dramatic in the border, especially when you see impressively large clumps in full bloom. It is a surprisingly versatile plant – it can also be grown as a marginal plant in shallow water where the leaves look better than in the border.

This hybrid is hardier than many people think. Plant in spring, not too deeply: the neck of the bulb should just be at soil level. It is then best to leave them uninterrupted as they take some time to become established and reach their full potential. Once settled, they will spread by offsets quite quickly, become more congested and it is this which really helps them to produce those much sought-after blooms. **BG**

John adds:
When I first started growing these magnificent bulbs it was a love-hate relationship. I loved the big funnel-shaped pink or white flowers but hated the enormous, strap-like leaves. They tumbled over, smothering all nearby plants. In late autumn the leaves were still green but quite tattered. The solution was an accident. One clump was overplanted with *Cotoneaster* 'Coral Beauty', by mistake. This evergreen shrub has small leaves and is mound-forming, holding the crinum leaves in place as they grow through the stiff stems.

Crinum x *powellii* 'Album'

Crocosmia x *crocosmiiflora* 'Emily McKenzie'

Crocosmia x *crocosmiiflora* 'Emily McKenzie'
MONTBRETIA

Type: hardy, cormous perennial
Soil & situation: damp conditions/well-drained but moisture-retentive soil/shelter from exposure/sun or dappled shade
North American hardiness zone: 6–9
Height: 60cm (24in)
Spread: 10cm (4in)
Grow for: strident, bright orange flowers with mahogany markings in the throats in late summer; mid-green leaves are also attractive, lance-shaped with pleats or ribs

If you visit Portmeirion Gardens in Wales in the late summer, you see montbretias in abundance – huge clumps of pleated foliage and masses of burnt-orange-red flowers. I think it must be *C*. x *crocosmiiflora*, which is a parent of this cultivar. It is too vigorous for most gardens. 'Emily McKenzie' has larger, downward-facing flowers and is not invasive. It has a definite exotic flavour and both leaves and flowers last well in water, making this an excellent plant for cut flowers.

The plant forms chains of corms as new corms are formed from old ones and stay attached. When they become too congested the clumps should be divided, but you should leave the old corms intact as they provide the initial food source. The best time to do this is in autumn, and they regularly do not flower in the first year after planting. Very dense colonies tend to flower less, so you will find it pays dividends to watch the congestion stakes and act accordingly. **BG**

Crocosmia 'Solfatare'

Type: hardy, cormous perennial
Soil & situation: moderately fertile, humus-rich, well-drained soil/sun or partial shade
North American hardiness zone: 6–9
Height: 75cm (30in)
Spread: 23cm (9in)
Grow for: elegant foliage; flowers from mid-summer to early autumn; AGM

As the long hazy days of summer roll seamlessly into autumn with its cooler mornings and warm, still days, plants like this gorgeous *Crocosmia* 'Solfatare' come to the fore. It provides the perfect link between the seasons, the hot colours of summer and rich yellows, oranges and reds that dominate autumn colour. It is an elegant plant; the streamlined, sword-shaped, bronze-tinted leaves stand stiffly to attention, among them pure pale apricot to yellow trumpets appear on arching, wiry stems that are delightful in bud, accentuating the herringbone pattern of the flowerhead. Those nearest the base open first creating the shape of a bird's beak and as the flowers fade and fall all that remains is an

Crocosmia 'Solfatare'

ordered row of peg-like seedheads. The flowers are good for cutting.

While thinking of crocosmias, it is impossible to ignore 'Lucifer': reaching 1.2m (4ft) x 30cm (12in) it makes a bold clump for the larger garden; its big spikes of brilliant red flowers look like a cluster of birds' beaks above the foliage. *C*. 'Bressingham Blaze' is better for the smaller garden. These and several others were raised by the great nurseryman Alan Bloom.

They need moderately fertile, light, free-draining soils in sun or partial shade; fork in sharp sand or organic matter where necessary. In cooler areas, *C*. 'Solfatare' should be protected over winter with a layer of dry mulch, like bracken or straw, or planted by a wall. Plant 8–10cm (3½–4in) deep in spring. Lift and divide congested clumps in spring just before growth starts. **MB**

John adds:
'Solfatare' is my favourite variety, but I prefer to grow it on its own to let it show off its particular colour combination of flower and foliage.

Crocus 'E.A. Bowles'

Crocus 'E.A. Bowles'

Type: hardy, spring-flowering, cormous perennial
Soil & situation: gritty, well-drained, reasonably fertile soil/full sun
North American hardiness zone: 3–8
Height: 7cm (3in)
Spread: 5cm (2in)
Grow for: rich yellow flowers with purple feathering; a cluster gives a cheerful display

I love all crocuses. They are dainty little flowers in a wide range of colours. They can be forced for early indoor flowers, grown in containers or in the rock garden and be naturalized even in good lawns. Then they quietly disappear without fuss for another year. When they are forced for early indoor display only bring them into the warmth when the flower buds are showing colour, otherwise the flowers may abort.

Of them all, *Crocus* 'E.A. Bowles' is my favourite. Flowering in spring it produces compact, bright lemon-yellow flowers. The outer tepals (petals) appear to be hand-painted with purple feathering on a bronze base. Belonging to the chrysanthus hybrids, each corm displays up to three flowers. The 15cm (6in) long, narrow, grey-green leaves appear at the same time as the flowers. Within six weeks they are yellowing and can be removed.

Plant corms in early autumn 5–8cm (2–3½in) deep. They will increase quickly and clumps can be lifted and divided in early autumn. **JC**

Crocus sativus
SAFFRON CROCUS

Type: hardy, cormous perennial
Soil & situation: very free-draining soil/warmth/sunshine
North American hardiness zone: 5–8
Height & spread: 5cm (2in)
Grow for: flowers and delicate stamens

The large, lilac-purple flowers with dark purple veins appear with the leaves in mid- to late autumn. Each bloom has three deep red stigmas, up to 3.5cm (1¼in) long sometimes hanging over the flower; they are the source of saffron. Spain provides 70 per cent of the world's saffron; it takes 250,000 flowers to produce 2.2kg (1lb) and they are all harvested by hand! No wonder it is such a precious commodity!

Arabs spread the plant throughout the Mediterranean; Phoenicians brought it to England and traded it for tin. From the 11th to the 14th century penalties, even death, were imposed on anyone who adulterated it. In the UK it was grown in Cornwall, the Cotswolds and of course Chipping Walden, later renamed Saffron Walden. It dyed the yellow robes of ancient Irish kings, it is still used in liqueurs, notably chartreuse, for colouring rice and in paella. As a medicine it is a mild sedative and was once used as a cure-all; this may have some basis, as it is a very rich source of vitamin B.

It needs a warm, sunny position in preferably alkaline, free-draining soil and plenty of moisture in autumn for flower production and spring for growth. In the UK the best chance of success is to plant it 12–18cm (5–7in) deep so it dries out in summer, and replant every three to four years from early to late summer on soil enriched with rotted farmyard manure well before planting. Feed with sulphate of potash in autumn and spring. Saffron is sterile; increase by division in spring. **MB**

Bob adds:
Saffron is one of the most expensive plant products yet is not difficult to grow, although as you collect and dry only the three minuscule stigmata the yields are necessarily small. It is wonderful to grow your own, and educational as well. In the ornamental garden the plant is rather small and needs a special raised bed where you can look at it closely. Please do not confuse this crocus with other autumn-flowering croci, especially the colchicums, which are very poisonous! In other words, buy the corms or seed from a reputable seller and do not collect from self-identified plants.

Crocus sativus

Cucumis melo 'Extra Early Nutmeg'

Cucumis melo 'Extra Early Nutmeg'
MELON

Type: tender, herbaceous annual
Soil & situation: rich, moist, limy soil/full sun/under cover
North American hardiness zone: annual
Height: 30cm (12in)
Spread: 2sq m (22sq ft)
Grow for: there is no melon as sweet nor so perfumed as one ripened on the vine

Nearly all fruits taste better when home-grown but with melons they're are not just better but vastly improved. Allow them to fully ripen on the vine until they drop into the net. Then chill and slowly warm up a bit immediately before serving so the perfume in the green flesh develops, but does not go over. Many newer melons are a little more reliable but most lack the flavour of this really old variety, which I have cropped without any real difficulty under glass and plastic. Failing this, 'Jenny Lind' is similar and if anything even sweeter and more perfumed, but it needs slightly better conditions.

Cucumis melo 'Extra Early Nutmeg' was known in the USA before 1835 and to the great French gardener Vilmorin-Andrieux as 'Melon Muscade des Etats Unis'. It is a very reliable variety with a distinct pear-like shape with barely more than a sort of splattering of netting. It requires a rich, moist, loamy soil with both plenty of humus and lime. Stop the vine after the third or fourth true leaf to form up to four sideshoots which bear sooner than an unstopped vine. Leave no more than two or three fruits per vine. Female flowers may need pollinating by hand. It can be started a couple of weeks before the last frost and grown on under glass or plastic, even in a cold frame as long as it is kept frost free, and it can be planted outdoors under a plastic sheet in early summer. It is prone to red spider mite and slug damage. **BF**

Cucumis sativus (syn. *C. pepo*) 'Petita'
CUCUMBER

Type: tender, herbaceous annual
Soil & situation: rich, moist, limy soil/full sun/under cover
North American hardiness zone: annual
Height: 30cm (12in)
Spread: 2sq m (22sq ft)
Grow for: mini-cucumber is now one of the quickest and easiest crops to grow in a warm greenhouse

Cucumbers used to require more heat and humidity, and were hard to grow well. They were prone to diseases and pests, and needed all males ruthlessly removing every day. Now they are easy to grow. There are many small-fruited, all female cucumbers and every one of them is good, but I especially like this one as in most years it gives me something fresh to eat way before anything else is ready for cropping.

Cucumbers were known to the ancients and seem to have come from India – certainly they have been cultivated for thousands of years. In the past, believe it or not, they were eaten when fully ripe and yellow; our taste for green cucumber is recent.

They need to be grown in a humus-rich, moist, loamy soil with plenty of lime, under cover in the warmth. Pick fruits before they ripen and swell, as they stop more forming. They can be started from the New Year if given extra heat and will crop within three months or so. Other varieties known as ridge and Japanese can be planted outdoors under a plastic sheet in early summer. Cucumbers are prone to red spider mite and slug damage. **BF**

Cucumis sativus 'Petita'

Cucurbita pepo

Cucurbita pepo
PUMPKIN

Type: tender, herbaceous annual
Soil & situation: rich, moist, limy soil/full sun
North American hardiness zone: annual
Height: 60cm (24in)
Spread: 1.8–6m (6–20ft)
Grow for: Halloween would not be the same without a pumpkin and it is a good plant to get children interested in gardening

I am not a great fan of pumpkin pie but I love making the lanterns. I also find that winter-storing pumpkins are really good value for little labour and the flesh is handy in soups, while the seeds are good roasted.

Seeded varieties with no hull can be grown just for the seeds and others such as the acorn squashes are for storing late into winter. Spaghetti squash has amazing vegetable spaghetti-like flesh and I always grow some, but I still prefer the real stuff. Other pumpkins for winter storage are the Hubbard sorts and these belong to *Cucurbita maxima*; my favourite is 'Gold Nugget', which is almost like a sweet potato.

It needs a rich, moist, loamy soil with plenty of humus. It can be started a couple of weeks before the last frost and grown on under plastic or in a cold frame until there is no risk of frost, then planted outdoors; or sow *in situ* under a plastic sheet in early summer. If you want champion-size fruits then fill a car-size hole with well-rotted manure and plant in that under a plastic sheet held up on sticks. Prone to slug damage. **BF**

Cucurbita pepo

Cucurbita pepo
COURGETTE MARROW

Type: tender, herbaceous annual
Soil & situation: rich, moist soil/full sun
North American hardiness zone: annual
Height: 60cm (24in)
Spread: 1 sq m (11 sq ft)
Grow for: no crop so productive so easily, that's such great value too

There is no crop so impressive as a row of courgette plants; they can give you a fruit or two apiece every day for weeks, if the soil is right for them and the sun is kind. Any surplus courgettes are easily frozen after frying in oil and they can be made into ratatouille with surplus tomatoes. A good plant for kids to grow.

Courgettes are really small marrows, and zucchini are exactly the same thing. Indeed, if accidentally left on the plant you get marrows, which are not as much use in the kitchen but do store for some weeks. Only a few years ago courgettes were all trailing sorts but now they are all more compact, bushy forms.

It needs a rich, moist, loamy soil with plenty of humus. Keep removing courgettes as fast as they form, daily is not too often – small ones are much better eating! It can be started a couple of weeks before the last frost and grown on under glass or plastic, even in a cold frame as long as it is kept frost free. Plant or sow directly outdoors in early summer. It is prone to slug damage and often suffers from cucumber mosaic virus in warm, damp years; destroy the plant if the fruits are blotchy and distorted. **BF**

x *Cupressocyparis leylandii*
LEYLAND CYPRESS

Type: hardy, evergreen conifer
Soil & situation: most well-drained soils (tolerant of some chalk)/full sun to light shade
North American hardiness zone: 6–9
Height & spread: if trimmed it can be kept to 2m (6½ft) x 60cm (24in); if left it will reach 50m (165ft)
Grow for: the fastest-growing hedge which is neat, tidy and a boon to over-wintering insects, particularly ladybirds who love its dry interior; tolerant of salt-laden winds; AGM

Although yew and holly make as good a hedge in time, they take years more to reach the same size. x *Cupressocyparis leylandii* is very quick and beats all others, even similar species such as *Chamaecyparis lawsoniana*. Once trimmed in mid-summer it is very neat and as perfect a backdrop for flowers as you can find. There is a yellower form, x *Cupressocyparis leylandii* 'Castlewellan' that is slightly less vigorous but of pleasing appearance. x *C. leylandii* was raised as a hybrid between *Chamaecyparis nootkatensis* and *Cupressus macrocarpa* at Leighton Hall in Montgomeryshire, Wales in 1888.

For a hedge space the plants 60cm (24in) apart and prune back fairly hard, but only to green wood, in the early years in mid-spring; later trim annually in mid-summer. To stop it from reaching 50m (165ft), which it can do in very little time, it must be trimmed back hard. Leylandii hedges suit most soils that are not bone dry or waterlogged but are unhappy on thin chalk soils or heavy clay. It is fairly shallow rooted so is not suited to very windy sites with thin soil. If well established and regularly trimmed it will have a long life. It cannot be grown from seed and is best propagated from cuttings in early spring. Sometimes the plants die back; there are attacks on hedges giving rise to dead brown patches thought to be spread by aphids. There is no cure, and they cannot be cut back hard into 'dead' wood as it never re-sprouts. **BF**

x *Cupressocyparis leylandii*

Cupressus cashmiriana

Cupressus cashmiriana
KASHMIR CYPRESS

Type: half-hardy, evergreen conifer
Soil & situation: most moisture-retentive, free-draining soils/sun
North American hardiness zone: 6–9
Height & spread: 30m (100ft) x 10m (33ft) in its native habitats; considerably smaller in the UK
Grow for: the most graceful of all conifers; AGM

Perhaps it's cheating to include a plant that is so tender it can be grown outdoors only by the privileged few, but I have done so because you may be one of them! Style, elegance, grace and every flattering superlative are packed into this one glorious conifer! In the UK it is small to medium sized and usually container grown in a conservatory in John Innes no. 3 compost. I have only ever seen one growing outdoors in this country, at the Hillier Arboretum in Hampshire in a very sheltered spot, and another in Christchurch Botanic Gardens, New Zealand that's worth seeing if you're passing that way!

Conical when young, it becomes broader with age with good-looking, fibrous, red-brown bark but it is the weeping, pale blue-grey foliage hanging in long, flat, lacy branchlets that makes it so irresistible. It was first discovered growing in Buddhist temples and has never been found in the wild in Kashmir, only in a single locality in Bhutan. If you can't grow this outdoors, the similar *C. torulosa* is marginally hardier but nothing compares to the Kashmir cypress.

It must be grown in deep, fertile soil in a very sheltered position in the south or southwest of England or areas affected by the North Atlantic Drift. It really needs longer hotter summers than we have in the UK and it cannot tolerate frost or cold. No pruning is necessary. Propagate by seed in spring or semi-ripe cuttings from mid-summer to early autumn. Plants grown in containers produce cones from a very early age. **MB**

Cycas revoluta
JAPANESE SAGO PALM

Type: tender cycad (tree with a palm-type appearance)
Soil & situation: moist but free-draining soil/prefers full sun/in really strong sun requires some shade/winter protection/sheltered position
North American hardiness zone: 9–11
Height: up to 2m (6½ft) or more
Spread: 1–2m (3–6½ft)
Grow for: highly dramatic evergreen foliage; long, glossy, pinnate leaves up to 1.5m (5ft) long.

This plant is usually grown in a pot and positioned outside to add an exotic, jungle-type feel to the garden. It will survive temperatures marginally below 0°C (32°F), but only for short periods and if the crown is well protected with straw and sacking. I imagine as it gets larger it also becomes hardier, but as it is extremely slow growing (and therefore expensive) I would be loath to risk years of cosseting just to lose one's investment to an unexpected, extreme frost. Mature plants (but none that I've seen) produce woolly, honey-brown flowers, the males smelling of pineapples, the females producing oval yellow fruit about 3cm (1in) long. Do not get too excited as they are rarely produced by plants in pots. But with or without these extras, it is a truly tremendous palm that looks great on a kitchen window sill in its early years. When it outgrows the creature comforts of home it can be housed in a greenhouse for the winter – I put mine outside from late spring to autumn.

Pot this on using a free-draining compost, part soil-based, part loamless and with added grit and charcoal. A slow-release fertilizer also speeds it on its way. Water infrequently in winter but in the summer give it a moderate amount. It suffers from mealy bug and scale insects so keep a watchful eye on this, ready to wipe off the early invaders with a detergent wash. **BG**

Cycas revoluta

Cyclamen coum

Cyclamen coum

Type: hardy, tuberous perennial
Soil & situation: moisture-retentive, free-draining soil/sun or partial shade
North American hardiness zone: 5–9
Height: 8cm (3½in)
Spread: 10cm (4in)
Grow for: flowers from early winter to early spring; beautifully marked foliage; AGM

Small but perfectly formed rounded leaves ease themselves above the soil in late autumn after the flower buds have appeared. Then, springing one of winter's fabulous floral surprises, the tiny flowers open towards the end of winter, brightening the days with jewel-encrusted cushions. The flower colour is variable but always with a dark stain around the mouth. They combine well with winter-flowering heathers, rhododendrons, snowdrops and aconites but don't let them become overpowered by their companions.

Among this species and its forms there's an incredible range of leaf marking and zoning in silvery grey; flowers range from deep carmine to pink and white; the leaves are striking until late spring when the rest period begins. Do not buy plants that have been collected from the wild. Pewter Group has leaves that are almost entirely silver and carmine flowers. Silver Group has silvery leaves with a dark rim and flowers in tones of pink. 'Maurice Dryden' has pewter leaves with a dark green midrib and edge and white flowers.

They need shelter in sun or partial shade and prefer neutral to alkaline, but tolerate all except waterlogged or dust dry soil; they should be kept moderately moist in summer. Improve drainage by adding plenty of grit and well-rotted leafmould to at least 15cm (6in) deep. Plant tubers in early autumn or late spring, cover with 4cm (1½in) of loose leafy soil. In autumn, mulch with well-rotted leafmould; in poor soils, apply bonemeal; and propagate the species from seed. **MB**

Fritillaria imperalis

CROWN IMPERIAL

Type: hardy, spring-flowering bulb
Soil & situation: fertile, well-drained, alkaline soil/full sun
Hardiness zone: 5–9
Height: 1.2m (4ft)
Spread: 25cm (10in)
Grow for: large, handsome, orange, bell-shaped flowers on tall stems; statuesque form. Just coming into flower at this time of year.

A spectacular late spring-flowering bulb made all the more interesting by a story that just might be true. The sultan wrongly accused his sultana of infidelity and had her executed. The crown imperial fritillary saw what happened and cried. It has been crying ever since. Look up inside the pendulous flowerhead and you will see a clear, liquid 'teardrop' at the base of each petal. Why don't they run down? Touch them and they flow!

The flowers are carried on strong, bare stems up to 1.2m (4ft) high and the glossy, light green, lance-shaped leaves are arranged in whorls. Umbels of three to six pendent, bell-shaped, orange flowers are topped with an odd-looking cluster of upright, strap-like bracts. There are several other good colours. *Fritillaria imperialis* 'Lutea' (right) is bright yellow and *F. i.* 'Aurora' has orange-red flowers. *F. i.* 'Aureomarginata' has variegated leaves.

The fragile, hollow-crowned bulbs have an unpleasant foxy odour. They are prone to rotting in poorly drained soil. Plant them at least four times their own depth with a 5cm (2in) layer of washed 13mm (¹/₂in) gravel in the base of the planting hole.

In a windy site it may be necessary to stake the flower stems. The cane or stake should be inserted before planting to avoid spearing the bulb. Where there is good drainage the bulbs can be left in the ground over winter. Otherwise, lift the bulbs as soon as the foliage turns yellow. Cover the soil surface with a mulch of composted bark. Water if necessary in spring to keep the soil moist and as the weather warms up watch out for slugs and the bright red lily beetle. **JC**

Bob adds:
Clearly a plant that attracts legends: another version says that they were blooming near the Crucifixion of Christ and have shed a tear every year since. Originally from the Himalayas, this was introduced to Europe by Clusius in 1576. Often seen haunting old gardens where the drainage is good, they persist long after most garden subjects have passed on.

Cyclamen europaeum (syn. *Cyclamen odoratum*)

Plant of the Week (see page 361)

Cyclamen hederifolium (syn. *Cyclamen neapolitanum*)

Type: hardy, tuberous perennial
Soil & situation: fertile, humus-rich, well-drained soil/partial shade
North American hardiness zone: 5–9
Height: 10cm (4in)
Spread: 15cm (6in)
Grow for: an ideal plant for a woodland garden, eventually forming a carpet of colour in autumn; AGM

This is a wonderful small plant for the woodland garden. It may look fragile, but it is as tough as old boots and well capable of ignoring bad weather.

The 5–15cm (2–6in) long, heart-shaped, mid- to dark green leaves are patterned in shades of green. Occasionally they are purplish-green on

Cyclamen hederifolium

the underside. Fragrant flowers are produced in various shades of pink with maroon marks at the mouth and appear during autumn, before or just as the leaves appear.

They dislike soils that dry out in summer and are best grown in an area shaded from full sun. Plant the tuber 5cm (2in) deep. Apply an annual mulch of leafmould after the leaves die down.

Propagation is by fresh seed sown in a peaty compost. It will self-seed in the immediate area of its leaves. Trouble comes from mice and squirrels who eat the tubers and vine weevil who go for the roots, causing the plant to collapse when in flower. **JC**

Cydonia oblonga 'Vranja'

Cydonia oblonga 'Vranja'

QUINCE

Type: hardy, deciduous fruit tree
Soil & situation: moist soil/full sun to light shade
North American hardiness zone: 5–9
Height: 6m (20ft)
Spread: 4.5m (15ft)
Grow for: attractive flowers; fragrant, pear-shaped fruit; eye-catching autumn colour; good small specimen tree; AGM

This true quince, unlike the *Chaenomeles* sort (see pages 97–98), blooms very late so usually misses all the frosts. The flowers are like little barber's poles or more accurately strawberry ripple ice-cream cones; all white with a pinky-red stripe. The quinces are large, yellow, fragrantly aromatic and as hard as stones; once cooked they keep some texture and add flavour to fruit pies and other

puddings. The leaves turn a lovely yellow-gold in autumn and the grey-black framework has a certain form and appeal in winter.

A native of Southern Europe and the Middle East, it may be the original Biblical apple and was probably first cultivated in Persia. *Cydonia* is from the Latin *kudonea*, meaning a small tree, and it was certainly known to the Romans, indeed it was well suited to their climate. It is likely that quince comes from Old French *coine* or *cooin*, derived from the Latin *cotoneum cydoneum*. Quinces often occur in gardens where an old pear tree has died, as they were and still are used for the rootstock which may outlive the graft.

Quince trees can be long lived in well-drained but moist soil in a sheltered spot, but they are not so happy in exposed positions. They tend to make congested, twisted growth so may need early pruning to form a well-shaped framework. Seed does not come true; a poor variety can be had by taking almost any pear rootstock sucker, but the best named varieties of quince must be grafted. Otherwise remarkably problem free. **BF**

Bunny adds:
I think this in my favourite tree – I have four in the courtyard outside my office window, and they are attractive for many months of the year. We use all the fruit they produce, mainly for quince jelly. They are growing in extremely poor soil, virtually hardcore as it is an old crew yard, but they seem happy enough. They are very easily propagated from the suckers they produce, and the young trees make highly prized presents. In recent years people have complained of quince leaf blight, which is a fungus that causes the leaves to turn first yellow, then brown, and fall prematurely. This can be treated by removing infected parts and spraying with a copper-based fungicide in early spring as the leaves break.

Cydonia oblonga 'Vranja'

Cymbopogon citratus

Cymbopogon citratus
LEMON GRASS

Type: tender, perennial, evergreen, herbaceous weed
Soil & situation: any soil/full sun to light shade/will stand drought and will stand in water
North American hardiness zone: 9–11
Height & spread: 60cm (24in) each way in preferred soil
Grow for: unusual bedding plant for summer; lemon-scented foliage; essential for Eastern cookery and expensive to buy

When I worked out how much each piece cost me at the supermarket and I realized it grew like a weed, I never bought it again. Lemon grass can be grown on any warm windowsill, almost anywhere by anyone. It is always handy to have a fresh supply. The base of each offset is the part used; trim off the leaves and roots and split it into quarters lengthwise before including it in the dish.

Lemon grass is a common weed of dry stony places and ditches in much of the Far East, where it is an essential part of the cuisine. It is used to give the flavour of lemon but its texture is also liked by some people who enjoy chewing tough food. I treat it like a bay leaf or herb sachet and retrieve it before serving. There are several other closely related lemon-scented 'grasses' commonly found in warm countries, but none of them with such a fine flavour as *Cymbopogon citratus*.

Lemon grass is not very long lived if you use it faster than it multiplies, so have several plants. One of the few houseplants that can stand waterlogging, even though it often grows wild in dry places; I have one clump in a pot floating in my indoor garden pool with sodden soil and it thrives. It can be grown from seed but supermarket bits will root in a glass of water. The edges of the leaves are razor sharp, so take care when handling the plant. **BF**

Cynara scolymus
GLOBE ARTICHOKE

Type: hardy, herbaceous, semi-evergreen, perennial vegetable
Soil & situation: rich, moist, well-drained soil/full sun or light shade
North American hardiness zone: 7–9
Height & spread: 2m (6½ft) each way in preferred soil
Grow for: highly ornamental, silver-green foliage; attractive purple flowerheads on some forms; huge azure-blue flowers; AGM

It is one of the few vegetable crops that can be decently and sensibly grown in an ornamental situation. The nearly evergreen leaves rise in autumn to fall again the next and the purple flower buds make delicious eating, but if left to go over and open are full of a sky–blue to azure fuzzy thistle which has a pleasing perfume redolent of the barley harvest. The flower is immensely attractive to solitary bees.

Cynara is native to the Mediterranean coast and was known to the Romans who ate the blanched stems and leaves, as the French still do today, but of the form grown as the cardoon. The globe artichoke was not developed from this until the 15th century, and the huge flower buds now formed would have been esteemed by the ancient gourmets. Sadly they are still only a little known nowadays as they make some of the finest eating in the world.

A moist, rich soil is needed to grow good specimens and the crowns will need dividing and replanting after five to ten years. Tidy up decaying stems in autumn and protect bases and new leaves against hard frost with loose straw or bracken covering. It can be grown from seed: de-flower in the first year, choose the best in the third year and from then on multiply by dividing off 'thongs' or part-rooted sideshoots in mid-spring. Hard frosts can knock back topgrowth, waterlogging quickly kills, and geese and slugs can do heavy damage to young shoots. **BF**

Cynara scolymus

Cytisus battandieri
BROOM

Type: hardy, semi-evergreen shrub
Soil & situation: most soils/full sun to light shade
North American hardiness zone: 7–9
Height: 4.5–5m (15–16ft)
Spread: 2.5m (8ft)
Grow for: attractive clover-like foliage nearly all year round; deliciously scented, pineapple-shaped, yellow flowers; AGM

One of nature's natural beauties, this stately wall shrub is hardier than we used to think and survives unaided in several nearby gardens. I have mine on a wall where it is near evergreen in mild winters. The flowers are outstanding, and look and smell like small pineapples. The stems, once dried, are as hard as bamboo and have some use in the garden as sticks.

Not introduced to Britain until 1922, this tall member of a native European family closely related to gorse comes from the Moroccan coast of North Africa and was thought, at first, to be a greenhouse subject, then a wall plant and it is now grown as a free-standing specimen in most areas. Even if the top is lost it can come again from lower down if planted as a stool.

Cytisus battandieri needs a sheltered position in well-drained soil in full sun, against a warm wall in colder areas. Remove dead flowerheads and prune after flowering if necessary. If grown on a wall tie in over the winter. Watch for rootstock suckers with laburnum leaves and prune these out as soon as identified. It can be grown from seed, but it is normally budded onto laburnum seedling. Cuttings are not easy and neither are layers. It may be killed by hard weather.   **BF**

Matt adds:
This plant fascinates me because plants from Morocco are rarely represented in gardens. It's found at an altitude of 1,500–2,000m (5,000–6,600ft) in the sun-scorched Atlas Mountains among venerable Atlas cedars and regal oaks. Is it the joker in such majestic company? Absolutely not. No other plant combines bright golden-yellow flower clusters 10cm (4in) long with an enticing pineapple fragrance or has laburnum-like tri-lobed leaves cloaked with a sheen of silky white hairs that are particularly prominent and tactile when young.

The variety 'Yellow Tail' has flower spikes 15cm (6in) long, sometimes more. Suckers form when it's pruned close to the ground; allow several branches to develop and prune back to them.

Bunny adds:
I used this favourite in my tree-house garden at the Chelsea Flower Show. We planted it in full flower against a Tuscan pink wall which we had adulterated with sponge painting, algal deposits and lime to convey that faded, been-around look.

The combination of the various muted pinks of the wall, the yellow of the flowers and the silvery green silky leaves was mouthwatering. This is a very special plant, though, that does look stunning in many situations. In one garden we grow it as a standard. It is a cold garden some way north of me, but the plant is in a sheltered nook and looks very dramatic like that.

Cytisus battandieri

Dahlia imperialis

Dahlia imperialis
TREE DAHLIA

Type: half-hardy, herbaceous perennial
Soil & situation: rich, moist soil/sun/shelter
North American hardiness zone: 9–10
Height: to 6m (20ft)
Spread: to 4m (13ft) or more
Grow for: giant foliage and spectacular stems

I'd read the garden guide before visiting the Quinta do Palheiro in Madeira for the first time and among the plants listed was *Dahlia imperialis*. Further research told of a dahlia with a sheaf of stems to 6m (20ft) tall and 7.5cm (3in) in diameter that looked like a giant bamboo with leaves up to 60cm (24in) long. I could hardly believe my eyes! Could a dahlia really be so huge? In my excitement I ran down the garden, and there to my left stood a dahlia on steroids, a pumped-up muscle bound giant, 4m (13ft) tall and topped with unmistakable, hanging, rose-purple flowers – what an awe-inspiring sight! The long stems were used by the Aztecs to pipe water from mountain streams and the direct translation of their word for 'dahlia' is 'water pipes'. Although unlikely to flower outdoors in the UK it is a worthy 'architectural' plant and your friends will never believe its identity!

It needs a sheltered, sunny position, on rich, well-drained soil. Dig in organic matter the autumn before planting. Plant once the danger of frost is over, mulch with organic matter, water and support the young stems. Protect from late frosts with straw or horticultural fleece. In autumn, cut the stems back to 15cm (6in), lift and store in a cool, frost-free place; the tuber eventually becomes massive too.

Ideally, start it off early in pots. In a frost-free polythene tunnel it may flower in late autumn or form buds for the following spring. Propagate in spring by division or stem cuttings.   **MB**

Dahlia 'Moor Place'

Type: half-hardy, tuberous perennial
Soil & situation: fertile, humus-rich, well-drained soil/full sun
North American hardiness zone: 8–9
Height: 1m (3ft)
Spread: 60cm (24in)
Grow for: rich red pompom flowers make this an impressive sight in the border

Dahlia flowers come in all shapes and sizes. When you see them at a flower show they range from tiny buttons to giant 'cactus' flowers up to 25cm (10in) across. Others are as big and as round as footballs in every colour with the exception of black, green and blue. As cut flowers they haven't lost their popularity in 100 years.

The 20cm (8in) mid-green leaves are pinnate with toothed-edged leaflets and rounded tips. The 5cm (2in) diameter, wine-red, pompom flowers are perfectly round with incurved florets. They enclose the stem completely, flowering from mid-summer until the first frosts. Each stem is branched, carrying two to five flowers. For larger blooms take off the two flower buds immediately below the top flower. Removing spent flowerheads will result in more flowers, which will continue to appear until the first frosts. Dahlias benefit from a weekly application of a high-nitrogen liquid fertilizer from early to mid-summer, switching to a high-potash feed from then until early autumn.

In mild areas they may be left in the ground over winter with a deep, dry mulch of straw or coarse bark mounded over the soil surface. In cold gardens or where the ground is wet and heavy it is necessary to lift the tubers and store them in a frost-proof shed until late spring. Check them regularly for signs of rot and dump those affected.

Propagation is by division of the fleshy tubers in spring, retaining a shoot on each piece. Basal shoot cuttings can be taken in late winter from the tubers and rooted in a propagator. Slugs are a serious pest of dahlias, devouring shoots overnight. **JC**

Dahlia 'Moor Place'

Daphne bholua 'Jacqueline Postill'

Daphne bholua 'Jacqueline Postill'

Type: hardy, upright, evergreen shrub
Soil & situation: moist, well-drained, preferably acid soil/sun or partial shade/shelter
North American hardiness zone: 7–8
Height: 4m (13ft)
Spread: 2.5m (8ft)
Grow for: tight clusters of sweetly fragrant flowers from early winter until early spring; AGM

For many years visitors and passersby alike were beguiled by *Daphne bholua* 'Jacqueline Postill' as she leaned seductively by a friend's front door. They would not fail to comment on her beauty and fragrance, then take note of her name so their love affair could begin; I too fell for her delectable charms. In winter she was at her most comely when to the surprise and delight of her admirers she would adorn her deep green robes with dense clusters of jewels with a rose-purple flush. Postman and plant lover alike adored from afar or pressed their nose to the flowers to inhale more deeply of the sweetly intoxicating fragrance. Alain Postill named me after the woman he loved, she whispered breathlessly, telling tales of her home high in the mountains of eastern Nepal where she lived under the protective shadow of giant rhododendrons.

Her brother *D. b.* var. *glacialis* 'Gurkha', a hardier soul, is stripped of his raiment in winter yet still wears similar heirloom jewels and those of *D. b.* 'Darjeeling' are smaller but appear even earlier, from late autumn to late winter. This is a plant to treasure!

It tolerates full sun or partial shade on cool, moist, well-drained soil. It flourishes in a sheltered position, protected from cold winds, but even then it may lose the leaves and possibly the flowers in severe conditions. It dislikes pruning but trim minimally, if necessary, after flowering to keep within its allotted space. It resents being moved so transplant when still young. Propagate by grafting in late winter to very early spring. It can suffer from leaf spot; remove affected leaves and dispose of them.   **MB**

Daphne blagayana

Type: hardy, dwarf, spreading, evergreen to semi-evergreen shrub
Soil & situation: humus-rich soil/partial shade
North American hardiness zone: 7–9
Height: 40cm (16in)
Spread: 1m (3ft), or more
Grow for: sweetly fragrant flowers in spring

Count Blagay originally discovered this gem in 1837 on his estate in Slovenia, growing alongside *Erica carnea*, a lime-tolerant heather. Planted in a border with the cultivar *E. carnea* 'Vivellii' it creates a glorious contrast of creamy white and deep carmine. The prostrate branches root as they spread, terminating in rafts of leaves bearing rounded clusters of 20–30 gorgeously scented, creamy white flowers in early and mid-spring. There are records of a plant at Glasnevin Botanic Gardens in Dublin, 6m (20ft) across and covered with flowers; alas it is no more! My first meeting with this glamorous ground cover was in a raised

Daphne blagayana

Daphne x *burkwoodii* 'Somerset Gold Edge'

bed outside the refectory at horticultural college. As I waited in line for my meals, its sweet, powerful fragrance was the perfect antidote to the assorted odours emanating from the kitchen!

Plant in acid or alkaline soil; in its native habitat *Daphne blagayana* ranges over layers of leafmould in limestone areas. Mimic this in the garden with a layer of leafmould in semi-shade on alkaline or acid soil, and make sure there is plenty of space for it to roam. Raised beds make the flowers easier to appreciate.

Prune to keep within its allotted space immediately after flowering. Propagate from seed sown when ripe, or by soft-wood or semi-ripe cuttings or layering. It layers naturally; weigh down the previous year's growth with a stone when the young shoots are a few centimetres long and detach after a year. Weighting the stems also encourages the plant to spread.   **MB**

Daphne x *burkwoodii* 'Somerset Gold Edge'

Type: hardy, semi-evergreen shrub
Soil & situation: rich, moist, well-drained soil/light shade
North American hardiness zone: 5–8
Height & spread: 1m (3ft) each way
Grow for: from late spring to early summer the golden-edged, neat, finger-shaped, nearly evergreen leaves are covered in masses of heavenly-scented, pink flowers – this is a masterpiece and among the best plants in the garden

This variegated hybrid is quicker growing than most daphnes, reaching full size in five years or so, and it gives the most impressive display in and out of flower. In flower it is a stunner, out of flower it is still attractive. A 'must have' when you see and smell it.

A cross between *D. caucasica* and *D. cneorum* by the famous Burkwood, it has two sisters, *D.* x *burkwoodii* and *D.* x *burkwoodii* 'Somerset', which lacks the stripe but is more vigorous and is the biggest, longest-lived plant of the three.

D. x *burkwoodii* 'Somerset Gold Edge' is one of the more demanding but faster-growing daphnes. It does best in rich, moist, humus-rich, limy soil in light shade. Do not prune and do not move once established. It will have a short life but a glorious one. It can be propagated by layers or half-ripe woody cuttings but it's not easy. Go on buy one! All daphnes get virus infected and die away so never prune them. If aphids are on the attack spray with soft soap. Nip out tips in early summer if it looks straggly. **BF**

Daphne mezereum
Plant of the Week (see page 69)

Daphne odora 'Aureomarginata'
Plant of the Week (see page 67)

Daphne tangutica

Daphne tangutica

Type: hardy, evergreen shrub
Soil & situation: rich, moist, well-drained soil/light shade
North American hardiness zone: 7–9
Height & spread: up to 1m (3ft) each way, but probably less
Grow for: healthy, diamond-shaped, neat, leathery leaves and heavenly scented clusters of purple (outside) and white (inside) flowers; AGM

Daphnes are short-lived, expensive to buy, hard to propagate and impossible to move. However, many are also incredibly neat, compact, attractive, evergreen shrubs with a range of similar scented flowers each with a different, and in some cases overwhelming, perfume. *D. tangutica* is among the toughest of the family and one of the sweetest smelling. It is very similar to *D. retusa* but quicker growing and it has slightly longer leaves.

This neat, tough (for a daphne) Chinese shrub was introduced to the UK at the end of the Victorian period by E. H. Wilson. You should consider getting a collection, as their perfumes are superb.

D. tangutica is one of the least demanding of a difficult bunch. It does best in moist, humus-rich soil in light shade. Do not prune and do not move once established. Give a dressing of leafmould in summer and water in droughts and you may get a decade of pleasure from this plant. Most daphnes are species and can be grown from seed – it took me five years to produce a good flowering plant. They may hybridize, which doesn't matter as they're all wonderful. Pest and disease care is as for *Daphne* x *burkwoodii* (page 140). **BF**

Daucus carota 'Panther'
CARROT

Type: biennial, semi-evergreen, root vegetable
Soil & situation: deep, moist, uniform soil/full sun to light shade
North American hardiness zone: usually grown as an annual
Height & spread: 30cm (12in) each way
Grow for: the foliage is surprisingly attractive if seen unbiasedly; the root is tasty and good for you – this one is the most tasty

Unlike many other vegetables, carrots are not much detested; moreover, they are very good for us. I have grown many varieties and although reliability is important, flavour is crucial, and to

Daucus carota 'Panther'

my mind 'Panther' is the best. It has the odd habit of tapering the wrong way occasionally – these ones are even tastier!

Carrots were known to the Romans and seem to have come from Afghanistan. It appears there used to be more interest in the white and violet forms which are now reappearing; the orange was first reported about AD500 and achieved almost total exclusivity between AD1500 and 2000. Gourmets are now trying some of the other colours again, but not often repeating the experiment.

The soil must be uniform with no big stones, lumps, voids, or raw manure so the tap roots can run straight down, and preferably moist but never waterlogged. If you cut the shoulder and crown off a root and trim back the leaves, then stand it in a saucer of water on a windowsill, fresh green leaves will appear – well, it's cheerful and much cheaper than a houseplant or a bunch of chrysanthemums. Sow thinly *in situ* in early spring, cover sparingly and firm down. Protect with horticultural fleece supported on sticks to stop root fly. Slugs can also be a problem. **BF**

Davidia involucrata
DOVE TREE, HANDKERCHIEF TREE OR
GHOST TREE

Type: hardy, deciduous tree
Soil & situation: fertile, moist, well-drained
soil/sun or light shade/shelter from cold winds
North American hardiness zone: 6–8
Height: 15m (50ft)
Spread: 9m (30ft)
Grow for: dramatic show of flowers in late spring;
AGM

This is not a tree to be rushed. It may take ten
years of growing before you see a dove, ghost or
hankerchief but if you have the space then plant
one for later.

It forms a conical head with 15cm (6in) red-stalked
leaves, light green above and softly hairy on the
underside. They are sharp pointed and toothed
with a heart-shaped base. In late spring large white
bracts appear, one on either side of the small male
flowers with their red-purple anthers. The bracts
are uneven in size. Seen fluttering in a breeze
against a blue sky it is easy to see how the tree gets
its various common names. Pendent, pale brown,
ridged fruit with a red stalk appear in autumn,
hanging long after leaf fall.

When E. H. Wilson went to China in search of
this tree in 1899 he was given a map of the region
in which it had been seen. The search area was

Davidia involucrata

Desfontainia spinosa

larger than England. When he did find the tree
there was only the stump remaining. It had been
cut down to build a house. Fortunately he found
other ghost trees close by.

It does best in a sheltered site in full sun. The
variety *D. i.* var. *vilmoriniana* is better suited to cold
areas. Its leaves are green-yellow on the upper
surface and dark green and hairless underneath.
Propagation from seed is slow. Sow the whole
fruit in autumn. It may take two years to
germinate, whereas hardwood cuttings will be
well rooted in less than 12 months. **JC**

Desfontainia spinosa

Type: half-hardy, evergreen shrub
Soil & situation: moist, peaty, acid soil/partial
shade
North American hardiness zone: 8–10
Height & spread: 2m (6½ft)
Grow for: holly-like leaves and drooping, scarlet and
yellow flowers, which are almost guaranteed; AGM

For me this is like a holly with airs and graces. It
loves a moist climate with lots of rain and that just
about includes the northern half of the British
Isles. I have a seven-year-old-plant and it has never
refused to flower.

Slow growing, it forms a dense, bushy shrub with
5cm (2in) long, glossy, spiny, dark green leaves.

The similar length, pendent, tubular flowers are
produced from mid-summer to late autumn. They
are a bright scarlet with a golden-yellow mouth.
Feeding high-potash liquid fertilizer in late spring
increases the quantity of flowers and seems to
heighten the flower colour.

When planted in gardens with a dry atmosphere it
is necessary to provide a sheltered site with no risk
of cold winds. A mulch of composted bark or
leafmould in late winter will help to conserve
moisture in the soil. Pruning is not normally
necessary. Propagation is by semi-ripe cuttings in
summer in a peaty compost. Cover the tray with
clear polythene and place out of direct sunlight.
Pot the rooted cuttings the following spring. **JC**

Matt adds:
D. spinosa is native to Central and South America,
from Costa Rica to Cape Horn where the climate is
moist and temperate. In the north, it's found in
cool mountain cloud forests, descending further
south to the fjords and islands of the Pacific coast.
The best conditions in the UK are in the west coast
of Scotland and Northern Ireland, where the
North Atlantic Drift influences the climate. In
central Chile it grows alongside *Drimys winteri* (see
page 151), *Fuchsia* (page 182), *Gaultheria* (page
188) and *Pseudopanax* – a fascinating combination,
and firecrown honeybirds pollinate the flowers.

The delightful form 'Harold Comber' has larger
flowers of rich vermilion, up to 5cm (2in) long.

Deutzia gracilis

Type: hardy, deciduous, bushy shrub
Soil & situation: fertile, moist, well-drained soil/full sun or light shade
North American hardiness zone: 5–8
Height & spread: 1m (3ft)
Grow for: an abundance of pretty, fragrant flowers

My earliest memory of this delightful shrub was armfuls of branches wreathed in fragrant, white flowers. They were being used for indoor decoration for an early spring wedding. The plants had been forced in large earthenware pots. It forms a bushy shrub with erect branches and bright green, 5cm (2in) long leaves. The sweet smelling, star-shaped, pure white flowers are produced on upright 5–10cm (2–4in) long racemes in spring and early summer. Plant it in a position sheltered from the morning sun to prevent the flowers being damaged by spring frosts. The flower colour will fade more quickly if exposed to full sun.

Prune out the shoots that have finished flowering, cutting them back to within 5cm (2in) of the previous year's wood. Give it a high-nitrogen feed after pruning. Apply a high-potash feed in early autumn to harden up the new growths. Propagation is by softwood cuttings in summer or hardwood cuttings outside during winter.

D. x *hybrida* 'Mont Rose' has dark green leaves and grows to 1.2m (4ft). Star-shaped, pink-purple flowers with wavy petals and yellow anthers are carried in panicles in early summer. *D. scabra* makes a large shrub at 3m (10ft) with upright panicles of honey-scented, single, white flowers in mid-summer. *D. scabra* 'Pride of Rochester' produces double white flowers tinged with pink. **JC**

Deutzia gracilis

Dianthus caryophyllus

Dianthus caryophyllus
CARNATION

Type: hardy, evergreen perennial
Soil & situation: well-drained, limy soil/full sun
North American hardiness zone: 7–10
Height: 60cm (24in)
Spread: 1.2m (4ft) if not tied up
Grow for: attractive flowers with glorious clove perfume

The sea-green foliage is unusual, the flowers are attractive and freely produced, but the perfume, oh the perfume, is so tangible you want to eat it. The scent of cloves does not describe its sweet lusciousness. There are indoor carnations but they are not as easy as the hardy border forms. The name carnation comes from coronation, as the flower was used for garlands. A native of the Mediterranean, where wild carnations grow in pockets of soil in broken limestone formations. Transferred to gardens early on in history, carnations have become widely grown around the world for the cut-flower trade. *Dianthus* 'Fenbow Nutmeg Clove' was rediscovered in 1960 in a garden where it was recorded as originally growing in 1652. It dates from the 14th century and was used to flavour wine; it is fragrant, crimson-maroon and double, though small.

Drainage is crucial, not just under the plant, but the soil must itself be open, and full sun is essential; even so the plants do not last long. As they are short lived, get into the habit of taking slips and rooting them every year. If you do not want to pick the broken stems up, then stake and tie the plants early. The varieties that can be sown from seed are nowhere near as good as the many selected forms, most of which are double. The latter are propagated by slip cuttings in spring or summer. The main problem is slugs! **BF**

Buddleja globosa

ORANGE GOLFBALL TREE

Type: perennial, semi-evergreen, woody shrub
Soil & situation: lime-rich, well-drained soil/full sun or light shade
North American hardiness zone: 7–9
Height & spread: 3.5m (11ft)
Grow for: striking orange golfball flowers with a pronounced honey scent, appearing up to two months earlier than other hardy varieties; AGM.

All buddlejas are good garden plants (see other recommendations on pages 73–74). Many are lumped together and called butterfly bushes as they are scented, full of nectar and attract countless insects to their flowers. Although really deciduous, most of them hold their leaves until the depths of winter and *B. globosa* is particularly hardy, losing its leaves only in the hardest winters. Its bright orange, uniquely spherical flowers make it the best of all.

B. globosa is one of 70 species from subtropical Asia and America named after the 18th-century English botanist and cleric Reverend Adam Buddle, all of them floriferous and scented, easy to keep compact and able to make a good windbreak. *B. globosa* was first introduced to Britain in 1774, well over a century before most of the others arrived, but has not naturalized in the same way.

Other than not liking waterlogged soils, buddlejas are really easy to grow in most garden soils and situations. If it must be pruned, do so in early spring when growth gets under way, as the hollow stem can fill with water, freeze and rot if autumn pruned. Other species can be pruned back very hard to a stool, if desired, but I find *B. globosa* resents really tough treatment. Although it is possible to grow buddlejas from seed, they do not always come true and hardwood cuttings in autumn are remarkably easy. It is best to strike a cutting *in situ* where the new plant is wanted, because although it is easy to move a small plant it is difficult to shift a large one. Buddlejas suffer from no problems worth mentioning.   **BF**

Dianthus gratianopolitanus

Dianthus gratianopolitanus
CHEDDAR PINK

Type: hardy perennial
Soil & situation: well-drained, neutral to alkaline soil/full sun
North American hardiness zone: 3–8
Height: 15cm (6in)
Spread: 45cm (18in)
Grow for: pretty, pink, fragrant flowers

You can see sheets of this little plant growing on the rock face of Cheddar Gorge in the Mendip Hills in Somerset, England. It is one of the prettiest wild flower scenes I have been privileged to see; AGM

It is mat forming with a dense layer of 5cm (2in) long, grey-green leaves. In flower during early summer, the solitary, deep pink, very fragrant, single flowers have attractively toothed petals and are carried on short, stiff stems.

When planting make sure the soil is well drained. This species is usually pot grown so plant anytime that the soil is suitable. Do not plant deeply, but keep the collar of the pink above the surface. Feed with a liquid tomato fertilizer in late spring. Dead-head to prolong flowering and help the plant retain a compact habit.

Propagation is by seed sown in autumn and over-wintered in a cold frame. Small, non-flowering shoots root well in summer. Reduce the length of the leaves of the cutting by half to lessen transpiration. Insert the cuttings around the rim of a pot of gritty, free-draining compost, then water in and cover with horticultural fleece. It is an excellent plant for the rockery, especially if the rocks are limestone as in its native Cheddar Gorge. **JC**

Dianthus 'Mrs Sinkins'
PINK

Type: hardy, evergreen perennial
Soil & situation: well-drained soil/particularly happy on thin, stony, alkaline or chalky soils/sun/protection from rabbits and pigeons
North American hardiness zone: 5–9
Height: 45cm (18in)
Spread: 30cm (12in)
Grow for: highly perfumed, white flowers over the whole summer

It is thought that this plant, a charming, traditional and old-fashioned pink, originated from a workhouse garden in Slough, Berkshire. However, no one I know seems to know who Mrs Sinkins was. There is a *Dianthus* 'Miss Sinkins' too, but not nearly as well-known, and only two or so nurseries in the RHS *Plant Finder* stock it.

Anyhow, whoever she was, I think the double, white flowers of this deservedly popular plant are rather endearingly shaggy-looking, which is why I like it better than many. Some of the more modern pinks look a bit too perfect and regular, but there are many superb ones to choose from, and they are an extremely useful cut flower.

If straggly shoots are produced, just tuck them in under the soil, firming them in well, and then it is likely that they will form a new, bushy plant. Regular dead-heading prolongs the flowering greatly. These plants are so easy from cuttings that it makes a lot of sense to renew your stock every two or three years. They do seem to flower themselves out. The cuttings are best taken from non-flowering shoots any time in summer. **BG**

Dianthus 'Mrs Sinkins'

Dianthus plumarius

Dianthus plumarius
PINK

Type: hardy, herbaceous, evergreen perennial
Soil & situation: well-drained, limy soil/full sun
North American hardiness zone: 4–7
Height: 15cm (6in)
Spread: 30cm (12in)
Grow for: neat hummock of grey-green leaves and good-looking flowers with glorious clove perfume

Slightly tougher than carnations, the grey-green foliage is neater, the flowers are as attractive, if smaller, and more freely produced and the perfume, oh the perfume, is so tangible you want to eat it, again. Pinks were brought over with William the Conqueror and all the early varieties that survive are single flowered and deliciously scented. There are dozens of pinks in many colours and forms and most have that wonderful clove perfume.

The name *dianthus* comes from the Greek *dianthos*, as it was the Flower of Jove. There is a native UK pink is *D. gratianopolitanus*, Cheddar pink (see left), but most of our garden sorts are natives of southern Europe and the Caucasus Mountains, where wild pinks grow in abundance.

Drainage is crucial, not just under the plant but the soil must itself be open, and full sun is essential, even so the plants do not last long. As they are short lived, though slightly tougher than carnations, take slips and root them every year. Those that can be sown from seed are nowhere near as good as the selected forms of which many exist, these are propagated by slip cuttings in spring or summer. As with carnations, the main problem is slugs. **BF**

Dicentra spectabilis 'Alba'
BLEEDING HEART, LADY'S LOCKET, LADY IN THE BATH, DUTCHMAN'S BREECHES

Type: hardy, herbaceous perennial
Soil & situation: cool, moist soils/shady conditions
North American hardiness zone: 3–8
Height: 1m (3ft)
Spread: 45cm (18in)
Grow for: excellent foliage and flowers: foliage is a cool, soft green and much divided, and flowers, from late spring to summer, are locket-shaped, hanging in lines from pendent stems; AGM

The unusual-looking flowers have given rise to the string of folksy epithets. The rather ornamental appearance of this plant makes it better suited to more cultivated woodland or shady borders – it is perhaps too showy-looking for wilder parts. It is also not that vigorous and so would not hold its own that well with the more hearty woodlanders. Having said that, this form is more robust and longer-lived than the species. You can prolong the flowering period by not letting the soil dry out.

This plant does not appreciate strong winds, and will perform better if tucked into a snug situation. Do not be deceived by its rather delicate form – it is tougher than it looks. The dicentras can be propagated by division: their rather fang-like, fleshy roots are brittle, as are the shoots, so a little care is needed. As they like moist soils, I find the splitting up is better done in autumn rather than spring. It can also be propagated from root cuttings. **BG**

Dicentra spectabilis 'Alba'

Dicksonia antarctica

Dicksonia antarctica

Type: tree fern
Soil & situation: prefers slightly acid conditions, with moist, peaty soil/sheltered, fairly humid conditions with lots of water during the growing season/will not tolerate temperatures below -5°C (23°F)/needs some winter protection if left outside
North American hardiness zone: 9–10
Height: 6m (20ft)
Spread: to 4m (13ft)
Grow for: one of the most majestic plants with magnificent fronds sometimes reaching up to 3m (10ft) long; AGM

This is not a plant I would like to be without, although my natural soil conditions and climate are not at all conducive to its well-being. When the plants are small and easily portable I grow them in pots and over-winter them in my greenhouse. When this becomes too much of a chore I find it simpler to plant them into the soil, heavily modified soil in my case, with lashings of leaf mould. I planted them in a sheltered spot against a north-facing wall. Tree ferns feature widely in television garden make-overs. This is not surprising really, as the moment you wheel in a few of these they will totally change the set – a sort of organic equivalent to mobile scenery. The problem is they are exacting in their requirements and if you can not meet these they will be wheeled out shortly afterwards – only in the direction of the bin this time! In the garden a shady position saves regular hosing down of the trunk. If you are not of the frame of mind to have heavily wrapped up plants in your winter garden, grow them in containers instead. They do not require huge volumes of soil and are adaptable as long as you give them lots of water in the summer. They will grow at a snail's pace admittedly, but robustly.

I am embarrassed to say that I forgot to wrap up my tree fern this winter. It has been growing in its position for a good year, protected by a wall, and in late winter it is still looking as pleased as punch. Whew! In their native habitat they are subject to snow and some clones are hardier than others, particularly those from Tasmania, so maybe I have just struck lucky. I should have packed the trunk and crown with insulating material such as straw, with polythene to hold it in place and keep out too much wet. This should, ideally, be removed in mild periods. Treated like this you can keep them happy to about −15°C (5°F). The fronds may die, but they are soon replaced in spring. The larger the plant, the hardier it is, so do not be in too much of a rush to plant it outside. **BG**

Dictamnus fraxinella (syn. *D. alba, D. albus*)
DITTANY, DITTANDER, BURNING BUSH

Type: hardy, herbaceous perennial
Soil & situation: well-drained soil/sun
North American hardiness zone: 3–8
Height: 1m (3ft)
Spread: 60cm (2ft)
Grow for: attractive lemon-scented foliage, followed by a spike of exotic, orchid-like, white flowers with purple veining; AGM

It's amazing how many otherwise knowledgeable plants-people don't know this old garden favourite. The foliage has a delicious aroma but dittany has one of the most distinctive, memorable and imposing flowers with a haunting orchid-like beauty, and if you don't yet know it, go out there, find one and grow this superb bloom for yourself.

The name is a corruption through French of the Greek *diktamnon* which was reputedly a great wound herb as apparently goats ate it to expel arrows! (This herb was probably an oregano, but that's beside the point.) This is also a genuine burning bush as on hot days an oil is generated which can be lit – I have often tried this in England but the great heat required to liberate the oil has been lacking.

Dittany likes a well-drained soil in full sun where it will slowly grow to a goodly clump. It can be divided in spring or root cuttings taken in early winter and grown on in a cold frame. Seed is slow to germinate unless it is fresh, and plants take quite a while to reach flowering size. The only problem is slugs eating the emerging shoots. **BF**

Dictamnus fraxinella

Dierama pulcherrimum 'Blackbird'

Dierama pulcherrimum 'Blackbird'
ANGEL'S FISHING ROD OR WANDFLOWER

Type: hardy, evergreen, cormous perennial
Soil & situation: humus-rich, well-drained soil/full sun
North American hardiness zone: 7–10
Height: 1.5m (5ft)
Spread: 1m (3ft)
Grow for: nodding, dainty flowers on wiry stems and grass-like leaves; a great addition to the border

In the summer of 1966 I saw a field of dierama at the Slieve Donard Nursery, Co. Down, Northern Ireland, where Leslie Slinger was producing new varieties. He gave them the names of birds, hence 'Blackbird'. It was an incredible sight and I presume every angel in Ireland was fishing in that field!

The 1m (3ft) long, thin, grass-like, grey-green, basal leaves remain erect for most of the year. In summer tall, arched 'wands' carry pendent spikes of bell-shaped, deep wine-purple, 5cm (2in) long flowers. They are followed by dangling strings of 'beads' with shiny brown seeds.

The corms resemble those of gladioli but each year the new corm grows on top of the previous one forming a chain of old corms. They should be planted 7.5cm (3in) deep in spring in free-draining soil. Water regularly during the first summer. Clumps may be divided in spring taking care to dig deeply to avoid breaking the brittle roots. Young plants are slow to become established after moving.

Seed should be sown fresh in the autumn and over-wintered in a cold frame. Dierama will

frequently self-seed in the area and may be mistaken for seedling grass weeds. Used as a dot plant in a mixed border, a clump of dierama immediately becomes the centrepiece. Please plant one close to the edge of the pond and make some little angel happy. **JC**

Digitalis ferruginea
RUSTY FOXGLOVE

Type: hardy perennial/biennial
Soil & situation: moisture-retentive soil/partial shade
North American hardiness zone: 4–7
Height: 90cm (36in)
Spread: 50cm (20in)
Grow for: flowers in early and mid-summer; architectural form; AGM

Compared to the romantic cottage garden foxglove which has been enjoyed by gardeners for centuries, *Digitalis ferruginea* has only recently found its way into the hearts and minds of gardeners. In a relatively short time it's become a favourite among those who favour the naturalistic style of perennial gardening. From the basal rosette, the leaves become narrower and hang gracefully as they climb the stiff, elegant spires, as if supporting them on thin air. Take a close look at the flowers: the colour and markings are fascinating, they're tightly packed in leafy spikes

Digitalis ferruginea

and a golden honey-brown with red-brown veins on the inside. It is the perfect horticultural exclamation mark. From flowering in early summer, they gradually decline and die, becoming deep brown. Over winter they slowly fall, projecting like angled iron spikes from among the surrounding foliage and look simply gorgeous when dusted with frost.

D. ferruginea 'Gelber Herold' is larger and has golden-yellow flowers. *D. f.* 'Gigantea' reaches 1.5m (5ft) and has stiff yellowish-brown spikes. I must not forget to mention *D. parviflora* with its wonderful, silvery-haired, narrow leaves and dark chocolate-brown flowers with a purple-brown lip. (I love anything that reminds me of chocolate!) It is sculptural, elegant and deliciously understated.

Very accommodating, *D. ferruginea* prefers moisture-retentive soils in partial shade but also grows in dry shade and full sun, if the soil is moist. It is a short-lived perennial that can be grown as a biennial. Sow from mid-spring to mid-summer *in situ* or in containers in a cold frame. It self-seeds freely. Its leaves are susceptible to leaf spot.   **MB**

Digitalis purpurea

Digitalis parviflora

Digitalis purpurea
COMMON FOXGLOVE

Type: herbaceous biennial
Soil & situation: light, humus-rich soil/sun or light shade
North American hardiness zone: 4–8
Height: first year rosette to 30cm (1ft), second year spike to 1.8m (6ft)
Spread: 50cm (20in)
Grow for: a most impressive native wild flower with a tall spike of orchid-like blooms

The common foxglove, especially the wild purple, is such a flower of childhood wonder – who has never slipped a bloom upon their finger? It is so much flower for so little effort, and if you sow them two years running and let them be they will self-seed like weeds and can come up everywhere, forever. There are more refined varieties, all-white travesties and dingy near relations, but nothing approaches the common foxglove for sheer exuberance. I once saw these advertised in a scurrilous limb of the Sunday press as 'Lakeland Orchids' at a price to match and no mention of their humble ancestry or more common name!

Named after the Latin *digitus*, a finger, for the thimble-shaped flower, foxgloves would often appear on the dirt spoil from a fox's lair in woodland, thus becoming associated with the predator. However, the English name was first applied to *Atropa belladonna* and not to *Digitalis purpurea* until the 14th century. The foxglove is, of course, infamous for being the source of one of the earliest powerful cardiac drugs. It is also said to be a good companion to many plants. It will grow almost anywhere, but needs a good site to do well; add plenty of leafmould and moisture. If the spike is removed before it has finished flowering, several smaller ones may follow it. Sow *in situ* any time or transplant when very small. Don't eat the leaves or any other part of the plant!   **BF**

Dipsacus spp.
TEASEL

Type: hardy, herbaceous, biennial weed
Soil & situation: any soil, preferably moist/sun or shade
North American hardiness zone: 5–8
Height & spread: first year rosette to 30cm (12in) each way, second year flowering stem 2m (6½ft)
Grow for: imposing stately plant in second year; educational; good for wildlife

The teasel is not staggeringly beautiful, but it is statuesque, and the flowerhead, with its violet-blue sheen of flowers, is intricate, delicately made and loved by bees and butterflies, who visit it all summer. The leaf joints trap pools of water for birds and insects, and mosquitos too if the climate warms up!

In autumn the seedheads attract small birds and the dried, hollow stems can be cut up to make good wildlife shelters or, if a bundle of them is rolled in a tube of paper, a wonderful hibernation home for even more insects.

Dipsacus spp.

The name comes from the Greek *dipsa*, for thirst, as the teasel leaf base holds water. The teasel was used by fullers and weavers to draw up the nap of a fabric well into the industrial times, as the spiky flowerheads have prickles with recurved tips that were difficult to replace by man-made substitutes.

Being a biennial it needs a rich, moist soil to make a good-sized root to flower the next year and die. It can be transplanted when small, but this is not recommended as it is hard to dig up the tap root as one piece. Ideally sow *in situ* in autumn or spring. Avoid handling plants as they're prickly all over.   **BF**

Doronicum pardalianches
LEOPARD'S BANE

Type: hardy, deciduous, perennial rhizome
Soil & situation: moist, humus-rich soil/part shade
North American hardiness zone: 4–8
Height: 90cm (36in)
Spread: 60cm (24in)
Grow for: ideal for a shady corner and quick to fill a gap in the border

Doronicum pardalianches

This is a great spring-flowering herbaceous perennial for a shady corner. It thrives on neglect, forming large clumps in open woodland. The 7–12cm (2¾–5in) long, heart-shaped, basal leaves are softly hairy and mid-green. The stem leaves are lance shaped. Large, pale yellow, daisy-like flowers are carried on stiff, branching stalks, above the foliage, from late spring through to early summer and are excellent for use in flower arrangements. It is one of the best perennials for filling gaps in shrub borders where it quickly forms a dense clump. *Doronicum* x *excelsum* 'Harpur Crewe' is slightly smaller with large, golden-yellow, daisy-like flowers on branched stems.

Propagation is by division of the clump in autumn or early spring. In a damp situation protect the emerging shoots from slugs and snails. Where exposed to wind support the stems as they come into flower.   **JC**

Dracunculus vulgaris
DRAGON ARUM

Type: hardy, tuberous perennial
Soil & situation: free-draining soil/sun
North American hardiness zone: 7–10
Height: 1.2m (4ft)
Spread: 30cm (12in)
Grow for: curious flowers in mid-summer

This fantastic plant is a typically strange member of the arum family. The dark purple blotched stems, up to 1m (3ft) tall, formed from flower stems and leaf stalks are topped by an elegant, mid-green, umbrella-like leaf with up to 15 segments. The fun starts in mid-summer when it produces a revolting, floppy, cowl-like spathe,

45cm (18in) long, in rich velvety-maroon with a shiny, erect, deep maroon spadix protruding suggestively from the centre. Their disgusting, pungent odour pervades the atmosphere, encouraging clouds of excited flies that buzz round the flower or wait, rubbing their forelegs with glee, for the slightest opportunity to sip nectar from the malodorous chalice. If they are successful, pollinated plants produce an oblong head of rounded fruits. It's the type of plant which is beloved by small boys of all ages! There is a white-spathed form found occasionally on Crete and one from the Canary Islands. I understand both are now in cultivation! Yippeee!

They flourish against a sheltered, sunny wall on free-draining soil or among low shrubs that provide protection in winter. In the wild cistus bushes are their companions. In colder areas they should be covered with a layer of bracken or straw for winter protection. Propagate by offsets, lifting and dividing clumps in late winter and replanting at 15cm (6in) deep. Where conditions are good, they are inclined to spread, particularly if they find their way into gravel paths. **MB**

Dracunculus vulgaris

Drimys winteri

Drimys winteri

Type: frost-hardy, evergreen shrub or small tree
Soil & situation: fertile, moist, well-drained soil; tolerates chalk/sun or partial shade
North American hardiness zone: 8–10
Height: 15m (50ft)
Spread: 10m (33ft)
Grow for: attractive leaves, stems and flowers; AGM

In late spring and early summer *Drimys winteri* produces rounded clusters of simple, ivory, jasmine-scented flowers at the tips of young growth backed by a ring of tough, glossy dark green leaves that are blue-grey below. I made the mistake of eating them once, they're ferociously peppery – a good deterrent to predators, but rich in vitamin C, like the bark. The genus commemorates Captain William Winter who travelled with Sir Frances Drake through the Magellan Straits on the southern tip of South America. It was 'very useful to his ship's crew instead of other spices, adding it to their meat and as a medicine, it was

very powerful against scurvy'. It's a symbol of peace to several South American tribes, as we use the olive branch.

D. winteri var. *andina* is compact and slow growing; it flowers when 30cm (12in) tall with a height and spread of 1m (3ft). *D. lanceolata* is a medium to large shrub with coppery young growth, beetroot-red stems, dark green leaves and small creamy-white flowers in mid- to late spring.

It flourishes in sun or partial shade in moist, mild, climates, usually sheltered by a wall or in a woodland garden among other trees and shrubs. It's not reliably hardy but tolerates some frost. It needs moist, fertile, free-draining soil and copes with chalk, but not with dry or shallow soils. Cut out dead or damaged wood in spring. Plants in this genus are resistant to honey fungus.

Propagate from semi-ripe cuttings or by layering; sow seed in autumn, over-wintering in a cold frame. **MB**

Cercis siliquastrum

JUDAS TREE

Type: hardy, deciduous tree
Soil & situation: moist, fertile, well-drained, loamy, alkaline soil/full sun or light shade
Hardiness zone: 6–9
Height & spread: 10m (33ft)
Grow for: a mass of colour in spring with its profusion of pink flowers

The story persists that this is the tree from which Judas Iscariot hanged himself but, in truth, in France the tree is called 'l'arbre de Judée' translating as 'the tree from Judaea'.

When mature it becomes a spreading, multi-stemmed tree. The new growths form a zigzag pattern, changing direction at each leaf joint. The heart-shaped leaves are bronze when they first appear, turning a glaucous blue-green in summer and finally becoming primrose-yellow in autumn.

There can be a variation in flower colour from pale pink to magenta or pink-purple, with the occasional plant producing white flowers. My plant has what I would call icing-sugar pink flowers and looks as good as any cake, flowering on my birthday. The clusters of small flowers cover the tree before, and at the same time as, the leaves. They have the unusual habit of appearing directly from the bark of old branches. The flowers are followed by clusters of pendulous, flat, deep purple seedpods.

Young plants and the new shoots of established plants are prone to damage from cold winds and late frosts. Feeding with a high-potash liquid feed in autumn will harden up the shoots before winter. Purchase small, container-grown plants. Large plants dislike being transplanted and may die in the first season. Propagate from fresh seed sown in autumn and over-winter the trays in a cold frame. Semi-ripe cuttings are supposed to root easily in summer but it has never worked for me. **JC**

Dryopteris filix-mas

Dryopteris filix-mas
MALE FERN

Type: hardy, deciduous fern
Soil & situation: a wide range of conditions – sun or shade/moist, humus-rich soil but will tolerate dry conditions once established
North American hardiness zone: 4–8
Height & spread: 1m (3ft)
Grow for: stunning looks as the fronds are unfurling in late spring; stays looking great into early winter; valuable for use in areas which are too dry, too alkaline or too sunny for other ferns to grow; AGM

This, together with bracken (*Pteridium aquilinum*), is the commonest British fern. In moist, semi-shaded conditions it will look amazing as the fronds, which form a circle around the crown of roots, stretch up to over a metre (3ft) in height and spread. Needless to say, in my dry-as-a-bone soil, where they furnish the woodland floor around the children's play area, they are about half this height – they still look good though. I have also used them to clothe the dry banks of a massive natural-looking waterfall which we made on a 6m (20ft) high south-facing bank, and again they convey that lush, damp feel even though it's

bone dry. They will self-seed freely once they get going, coming up in a beguiling fashion and transforming a space in a way you had not thought possible.

If you are establishing these ferns in less hospitable conditions, they will need extra moisture for maybe the first year or two until they get their roots down. Each spring, as the new foliage emerges, cut away the dead fronds.

Sparsholt College – the agricultural and horticultural college near Winchester where *Gardeners' Question Time* has a garden – showed me a really simple way to propagate ferns, which they developed and I can highly recommend it. Put a frond with spores (usually in mid-summer) on a tray of moist, gritty compost with the underside touching the compost; seal the whole tray in a polythene bag and leave in a cool greenhouse; check periodically that it has not dried out too much or not is rotting. After perhaps three months (but it can be up to nine months) you will eventually see the tiny prothallus start to grow on the compost. Leave the bag on and next you will see the first true leaf develop from the prothallus. As more proper leaves develop you can start to wean the plants off the bag. To get a true fern it usually takes about two months after the formation of the prothallus. Using this method you can get a good fifteen ferns or so from one tray. **BG**

Dryopteris wallichiana
BUCKLER FERN, WALLICH'S WOOD FERN

Type: hardy, deciduous fern
Soil & situation: humus-rich soil/dappled shade/shelter
North American hardiness zone: 5–8
Height : 90cm (36in) or more
Spread: 30cm (12in) or more
Grow for: attractive form and elegant fronds; AGM

Ferns are elegant, stylish and graceful and this is an example of them at their glorious, majestic best. A regal fern with a 'shuttlecock' of stiff, dark green fronds and regularly spaced opposite leaflets that are golden-green when young. It is the midribs with the dark, chocolate-brown scales that are so inviting and a wonderful contrasting colour. I have only ever seen them growing singly or in small clumps, but it would be wonderful to see a huge group of them flourishing together in the manner of the shuttlecock or ostrich fern (*Matteuccia struthiopteris*). Dream on!

D. wallichiana is named for Nathaniel Wallich (1786–1854), born Nathan Wolff, a Danish botanist who went to India as a surgeon to the Danish settlement at Serampore. He was briefly imprisoned by the British before becoming superintendent of the Calcutta Botanic Garden. He went on several expeditions and encouraged collectors in India, Nepal and Burma, including Edward Garner, a British resident of Kathmandu, who sent the seeds of the first Himalayan rhododendrons to Kew packed in tins of brown sugar. Wallich also introduced the magnificent *Amherstia nobils* into European cultivation – it was named for Lady Amherst, the Governor General's wife, and there is a beautiful pheasant named for her too. He returned to England with a collection of over 8,000 specimens.

This plant needs a sheltered spot and moisture-retentive, humus-rich, well-drained soil in dappled to deep shade. Divide in spring or autumn or sow spores. **MB**

Dryopteris wallichiana

Ecballium elaterium
SQUIRTING CUCUMBER

Type: half-hardy perennial usually grown as an annual
Soil & situation: very free-draining soil/sun
North American hardiness zone: 8–10
Height: 23cm (9in)
Spread: 2m (6½ft)
Grow for: explosive fruits

This is another fun plant for children of all ages! It is found throughout southern Europe and has escaped into Africa; I saw it growing by the city wall in Tangiers. Although it is a cucumber it cannot climb but makes a large patch of dense ground cover when flourishing. The triangular leaves with the texture of rough sandpaper are upright with wavy edges. Nodding, pale yellow flowers are found on separate short stems in the leaf joint, the females singly, the males in small clusters! The hairy fruits are about 5cm (2in) long and when ripe the slightest touch sends out a jet of seeds and 'goo' from the fruit. It squirts at an average angle of 50–55 degrees; mathematically the ideal angle for distance is 45 degrees but the extra accounts for the leaves that would obstruct the seeds if they flew too low. The pressure inside the fruits reaches six atmospheres (6kg/sq cm or 84lb/sq in) and the seeds are projected up to 12m (40ft) at 10m (33ft) per second! Now that's impressive!

Warning: the juice is a powerful purgative, do not eat the fruit and wash your hands after touching it. Take care too when triggering the explosive seedpods, you would not want to be hit by squirting seeds. Otherwise just have fun!

Ecballium elaterium

Echinacea purpurea

It prefers a sunny site and free-draining soil, but flourishes in most soils exept waterlogged ones. It is a perennial, treated as an annual, and can survive warmer winters outdoors; mulch with straw or bracken to protect the roots. Sow under glass and plant out in early summer when the soil is warm and there's no danger of frost. It self-seeds freely in your garden and next door's!   **MB**

Echinacea purpurea
CONE FLOWER

Type: hardy perennial
Soil & situation: occurs naturally in dry habitats, so is ideal for free-draining soils/deep, humus-rich soils/sun or partial shade
North American hardiness zone: 3–9
Height: 1m (3ft)
Spread: 45cm (18in)
Grow for: eye-catching daisy-like flowers in a luminous shade of purple-red, with prominently domed, dark orange-bronze centres; long flowering period during the summer; attracts bees and butterflies

Not only is this plant adaptable in terms of soil type and situation but it is also adaptable in terms of the effects you can achieve with it as it has a relaxed, casual feel, a good strident-coloured flower and a significant winter silhouette. The traditional use, ever popular, is in the herbaceous border, not staked but ready for action from mid-summer to early autumn. More recently it can be found sprinkled and threaded through prairie plantings mixing with coreopsis, monardas and the like. It is also in vogue now to mix it with ornamental grasses, especially *Calamagrostis*, *Molinia* (see page 267) and *Stipa* (page 372) and, along with umbellifers and other bold perennials. Truly not a plant I would be without, although it has not yet been awarded an AGM.

These plants need cutting down in early spring. They can be left alone for years, quite happily, but if you want to divide them, spring is the time. They can be propagated by seed, root cuttings in winter or division in spring or autumn. I did mine from seeds, as being greedy I wanted lots and lots. They are dead easy but the seedlings are variable, so you simply discard the less intense shades. The amount of reflex on the petals varies too. In natural-type plantings it is a bonus to get ones that come out at different times, are a range of shades and look subtly different – you do not always want a shipment of soldiers. If you are being extravagant and buying in, *E.* Bressingham hybrids are a strong colour with less variation of both colour and form.   **BG**

Echinops ritro

Echinops ritro
GLOBE THISTLE

Type: hardy perennial
Soil & situation: well-drained garden soil/sun or partial shade
North American hardiness zone: 3–9
Height: 60cm (24in)
Spread: 45cm (18in)
Grow for: eye-catching globes of blue flowers in late summer; AGM

This is an old favourite that I would not like to be without. The metallic blue balls look almost sculptural sitting on top of tall, pale silvery-green, rigid stems and last for a month or so. The leaves are extremely spiny, stiff and leathery, dark green on top and white underneath. It is definitely a plant with character that looks good in the wilder areas or, as I grow it, in a more formal courtyard garden. However, it needs clever siting as it does look a bit too informal when the flowers start to go over. Mine sits behind a low, but buxom, box hedge. As soon as the flowers start to go over, cut them back and you may get a second flush. This is an excellent plant for cutting and drying, but cut it before the tiny, starry flowers are open.

These plants will thrive on a poor, thin soil: on heavier soils it is worth adding grit to help drainage before planting. They do not need staking, and if you do not want to dead-head in the hope of a second flowering, you can leave the dead flowerheads intact until they start to look over-scruffy. Echinops are easily propagated by division in autumn or spring or by root cuttings in winter. **BG**

Matt adds:
Because of their shape, I always imagine banging kettle drums with a pair of these! The flowers are irresistible to bees, who arrive en masse to forage for nectar; moths take over at night. It forms a wonderful combination with *Stipa gigantea* (see page 372) and orange and yellow kniphofia (pages 228–229 and 345); it is also useful in flower arrangements.

Echinops ritro 'Veitch's Blue' is repeat flowering with darker blue flowerheads. *E. bannaticus* 'Blue Globe' has dark blue flowerheads to 6cm (2½in) across; it blooms for a second time if the stems are cut back after flowering. *E. b.* 'Taplow Blue' has rounded, powder-blue flowers on prominent silvery-white stems from mid-summer to early autumn.

John adds:
I much prefer to plant 'Veitch's Blue' in a large group of at least five. When it comes into flower the mass of 'globes' looks spectacular. Dead-head the spent flowers to prevent them self-seeding. Left alone they can become a nuisance weed. The species *Echinops giganteus* lives up to its name. The spherical, grey-blue flowerheads are up to 20cm (8in) across and it will reach a height of 5m (16ft).

Echinops ritro 'Veitch's Blue'

Echium vulgare 'Blue Bedder'

Echium vulgare 'Blue Bedder'

Type: annual or biennial
Soil & situation: wide variety of soils, not too fertile/especially suited to free-draining soils/sunny position
North American hardiness zone: 9–10
Height: to 40cm (16in)
Spread: to 30cm (12in)
Grow for: fast-growing, easy but most attractive infiller; large quantities of charming blue flowers

Try not to be put off this plant by the name 'Blue Bedder'. It may not conjure up a plant that is in any way inspirational or exciting, but this is a peak performer. It is an old variety that is not commonly grown but it will produce for you, for several weeks, a good, bushy, soft-looking plant with copious blue, bell-shaped flowers. It looks particularly good when mixed with other simple annuals such as flax and cornflowers, to form a more natural-looking, yet cohesive, planting.

This plant is best treated as an annual. Either sow the seeds *in situ* in spring or under glass. I find it far more successful to sow the seed in small 7cm (3in) pots inside and then to plant them out when they are ready. Although this is not in anyway essential for this plant, I find the results superior. Planted out at just under 10cm (4in) centres, you will get a good density of its foliage knitting together to from a colourful mass. If the soils are too fertile, too much foliage will be produced and fewer flowers. Once they are past their best and form a totally knitted tangle, clear the space – unless you wish to leave them to self-sow, which they frequently do. **BG**

Edgeworthia chrysantha
PAPER BUSH

Type: half-hardy, deciduous shrub
Soil & situation: rich, moisture-retentive, fertile soil/sun/shelter
North American hardiness zone: 7–10
Height & spread: 1.5m (5ft)
Grow for: scented, rich yellow flowers from late winter to mid-spring

I first came across this plant while looking for daphnes in a flower border at the Royal Botanic Garden, Kew; it's amazing how something that looks so fragile flowers early in the year. The dense, hanging clusters at the end of every twig are only 3–5cm (1–2in) wide, yet contain up to 50 fragrant, rich cowslip-yellow flowers, each clothed with a layer of white silky hairs. The young shoots are incredibly supple and can be tied into knots without breaking them, while the older branches are covered with papery bark that in Japan is carefully peeled off and used for making paper for currency. It's native to the forests and streamsides of the Himalayas, South Korea and southwest China and was named for Michael Pakenham Edgeworth (1812–81), an employee of the East India Company and keen amateur botanist.

A form with vivid red-orange flowers is known as *Edgeworthia chrysantha* 'Red Dragon' and is sometimes labelled f. *rubra*. There is also a selection *E. c.* 'Grandiflora' which is larger in growth and flowers.

E. chrysantha needs a warm, sheltered position among other shrubs in a sunny border protected from frost, on well-drained, moisture-retentive, loamy soil enriched with plenty of well-rotted organic matter; mulch in spring. In colder areas grow in a cool greenhouse in loam-based compost, watering freely and feeding monthly when in growth; reduce watering in winter. Prune if necessary after flowering. Propagate by seed or semi-ripe cuttings in summer. **MB**

Edgeworthia chrysantha

Elaeagnus pungens 'Maculata'

Elaeagnus pungens 'Maculata'

Type: hardy, evergreen, bushy shrub
Soil & situation: well-drained, moderately fertile, neutral to acid soil/full sun
North American hardiness zone: 7–9
Height: 4m (13ft)
Spread: 5m (16ft)
Grow for: variegated foliage with large splashes of golden yellow

This shrub is largely grown for its foliage. The shiny, dark green, oval leaves are generously splashed with golden yellow. Even on the darkest day of winter it seems to brighten the whole garden. During and immediately after rain each leaf collects and reflects light.

In autumn small, very fragrant, white flowers appear followed by shiny red, edible fruits. *Elaeagnus pungens* 'Maculata' is one of my favourite shrubs for seaside sites. It withstands sea spray, harsh winds and is very tolerant of a dry, gritty soil.

It is prone to reversion where vigorous branches with all green leaves appear. They should be cut out when young or they will take over the plant at the expense of the variegated growth. Do take care as it occasionally produces a few spines, not many, but it only takes one to cause injury. Plants are usually grafted so remove any emerging suckers as close to the main stem or root as possible. As a shrub it is indispensable but as a tough, variegated hedge it is memorable. Another excellent variegated relation is *E.* x *ebbingei* 'Gilt Edge' with leaves bright green in the centre and broad golden margins. **JC**

Embothrium coccineum
CHILEAN FIRE THORN OR FLAME FLOWER

Type: hardy, evergreen tree
Soil & situation: moist, well-drained, fertile, neutral to acid soil/full sun or partial shade
North American hardiness zone: 8–10
Height: 10m (33ft)
Spread: 5m (16ft)
Grow for: an unbeatable specimen tree for its scarlet flowers

In flower, this tree has no equal. Seen as a specimen tree on the lawn it seems to be on fire with its red flower.

It often forms a multi-stemmed tree with numerous suckers. If these are not removed they will eventually form a copse. The lance-shaped, mid- to dark green leaves are 12cm (5in) long. They almost disappear under a sheet of scarlet flowers carried in 10cm (4in) long racemes and produced in late spring and early summer. Occasionally they carry yellow flowers but I have never seen it happen.

Plant in a sheltered situation well protected from biting, cold winds. Pruning is not normally necessary but where branches have to be removed, in order to retain the shape of the tree, cut them out in winter before the sap starts to rise. Propagation is by seed sown in a heated propagator in spring. Softwood cuttings can be taken in early summer or semi-ripe cuttings in late summer with bottom heat in a propagator. Pieces of root can be used for propagation in winter. If you carefully dig around a sucker at a depth of 20–30cm (8–12in), you can remove it with a section of the main root complete with fine hair roots. Pot it up in a loam-based compost watering regularly.

Embothrium Lanceolatum Group 'Norquinco' has narrow leaves and is hardier in cold areas. **JC**

Embothrium coccineum

Enkianthus perulatus

Type: hardy, deciduous shrub
Soil & situation: humus-rich, well-drained, neutral or acid soil/full sun or light shade
North American hardiness zone: 6–8
Height & spread: 2m (6½ft)
Grow for: a mass of white, urn-shaped flowers and the most amazing autumn-leaf colour; AGM

I am delighted to be able to grow this shrub. The flowers are pretty in spring but wait until you see its autumn colour. Grown in very peaty soil the leaves turn to a brilliant bright red, every year without fail.

The stems of the young growths are red tinted. The 5cm (2in) long, mid-green leaves are toothed and are mainly at the ends of the branches, leaving bare stems beneath. The autumn colour can be breathtaking. In mid-spring umbels of up to ten small, urn-shaped, pure white flowers dangle like drop pearl earrings.

Pruning is seldom necessary unless there is a crossing branch spoiling the overall shape. If so, it can be removed in winter. This is a great shrub for planting in light shade in woodland or in a copse where there is acid soil and a deep mulch of leafmould. From a distance the autumn colour will resemble a fire. Propagation is by seed sown in heat in early spring or semi-ripe cuttings in summer rooted under clear polythene. Low branches layered in autumn will be rooted and ready for transplanting within 18 months. **JC**

Enkianthus perulatus

Epilobium angustifolium 'Album'

Epilobium angustifolium 'Album' (syn. *Chamerion angustifolium* 'Album')
WHITE ROSEBAY WILLOWHERB

Type: hardy perennial
Soil & situation: many different conditions/prefers sun or light shade/well-drained, moisture-retentive soil
North American hardiness zone: 3–6
Height: to 1.5m (5ft)
Spread: 1m (3ft)
Grow for: racemes of white flowers which can enhance more natural plantings or wild areas

This white form of rosebay willowherb is not as invasive as the native variety – it only spreads by its stolons and rarely by seed, as it sets very little, if any, viable seed. Occasionally people encounter forms that do set copious quantities of viable seed, but I have yet to. It is fabulous to use in wilder spaces and it can really lift those less tamed parts of the garden by imparting charm, colour and life. The common pink form used to be known as 'Fireweed' as, after the fires following the blitz in London, it swiftly colonized vast areas both by seed and its running white roots. It is too invasive for the garden though. Not so the white form. Gardeners have often asked how to bulk it up quickly, but unfortunately, there does not seem to be a speedy route. So do not be mean but buy several, if not many, plants initially. And do cut it back after flowering so you get maximum value for money. My mother says she finds it too leafy in richer soils – certainly not my problem though.

This plant can be cut back by half after flowering and it will produce lots of new flower spikes later in the season. It can be obstinate to propagation by division: I find it more successful carried out in spring and I give it fair bit of 'TLC' afterwards until it starts to grow. **BG**

Epimedium stellulatum 'Wudang Star'
BISHOP'S HAT

Type: hardy, herbaceous perennial
Soil & situation: humus-rich, moist soil/dappled shade
North American hardiness zone: 5–9
Height & spread: 35cm (14in) or more
Grow for: attractive young leaves and flowers in spring

In 1983, Roy Lancaster found this plant in the walls of the Purple Clouds Temple in the Wudang Mountains of central China. Professor William Stearn, a world authority on epimediums, identified it as *E. sagittatum* and Roy named his introduction 'Wudang Star'. However, after further communication, his discovery was found to be even more exciting – the plant was new to science! In 1993, Professor Stearn renamed the species to *E. stellulatum*, meaning 'flight of little stars'; it describes the flowers perfectly.

It's clump forming, with arrow-shaped leaflets, bright pink young growth flushed with crimson in spring and arching stems to 30cm (12in) long,

Epimedium stellulatum 'Wudang Star'

which explode in a star-burst of up to 40 white flowers with orange-brown sepals and prominent yellow stamens. They're exquisite – how can anything be so beautiful?

I met the late Professor Stearn, academic, polymath and raconteur. He was a kindly man with rosy cheeks, a shock of thick white hair, a bushy moustache and piercing blue eyes. He looked like everyone's favourite grandfather yet was one of the world's greatest taxonomists. He'd interrupt his work to share his knowledge with anyone, fellow academics, researchers – even grubby-handed gardening students like me. I asked about plants, listened to discourses about them (and the distribution of herons on the Thames!) and watched one day as the underground train left the station where he always disembarked. As a carriage passed, I spotted Professor Stearn and his wife still on board, they were so engrossed in their books they'd missed their stop! A wonderful character and a great man!

It needs moist, fertile, humus-rich, well-drained soil in a sheltered, partially shaded position but grows in any soil, sun or shade. Divide in autumn or after flowering. **MB**

Eranthis hyemalis

Eranthis hyemalis
WINTER ACONITE

Type: hardy, tuberous perennial
Soil & situation: moist, free-draining soil/sun or dappled shade
North American hardiness zone: 4–9
Height: 8cm (3½in)
Spread: 5cm (2in)
Grow for: cheerful flowers and foliage in mid- and late winter; AGM

If you need something to cure the winter blues, it's here! Don't just put in a few, think 'big' and plant huge swathes through borders, under trees and over lawns so their golden-yellow beams illuminate winter's dullest days; why not add a few snowdrops too? Individually, winter aconites are fascinating, with deeply cut leaves and yellow, balloon-like buds that burst open to form cup-shaped blooms sitting on top of a ruff of leaf-like bracts. There's a bold hybrid between two species, *E. cilicia* and *E. hyemalis*, called *E.* x *tubergenii* 'Guinea Gold' that I've seen with bronze-tinted foliage and flowers like golden bowls; it tolerates more sunshine than *E. hyemalis*. *E. cilicica* has bronze-tinged leaves, larger flowers and more lobes on the leaves.

Tubers are normally bought dry; soak them overnight in cool water before planting. They can also be bought and planted in full leaf immediately after flowering, this is known as 'in the green' and they establish more successfully. Several specialist nurseries sell them this way.

They like any soil providing it is not waterlogged, stagnant or dry; dig in plenty of organic matter then leave undisturbed to form colonies; they flourish in alkaline soil. Cool, moist soil below deciduous trees and shrubs is ideal. Plant the knobbly tubers about 5cm (2in) deep. Divide after flowering; sow seeds of the species in spring. Birds may damage the flowers; aphids disfigure and cause sooty mould.

Legend has it that in England they bloom only where Roman soldiers have shed their blood. **MB**

Smilacina racemosa

FALSE SPIKENARD, TREACLE BERRY

Type: hardy, herbaceous perennial
Soil & situation: any soil/sun or shade
Hardiness zone: 4–9
Height: 90cm (36in)
Spread: 30cm (12in)
Grow for: hosta-like leaves; foamy, feathery, fragrant, white flowers and occasional, apparently edible, sweet, aromatic, glossy red berries. The freshness of the flowers heralds the change from spring to summer; AGM.

I am always on the look out for edible 'wild' fruits that could be improved – after all, the modern strawberry is enormous compared to those before Victoria's reign. This delightful plant has a red berry that was eaten by the native North Americans and called the treacle berry for its sweet taste. These are not prolifically produced so a bigger berried, heavier cropping selection would be wonderful.

Especially as this lily relative has a neat habit, is not invasive and exudes a wonderful perfume from the flowerheads. A really good plant, and what's more it grows in shade…

This is a small genus of North American herbaceous plants that strongly resemble polygonatums (see page 302) in growth though not in flower. The name is because it allegedly, in some faint way, resembles smilax, which is itself rather dubiously named after a green briar.

Smilacina is not fast growing but is fairly tough and will endure many sites, preferring moist, leafmould-rich soils in light shade. It can be tidied once the stems wither. Sow seed in spring or divide the roots in autumn. It has no problems and is a good alternative to hostas, as slugs avoid it. **BF**

Eremurus stenophyllus subsp. *stenophyllus*
DESERT CANDLE, FOXTAIL LILY

Type: hardy perennial
Soil & situation: rich fertile, well-drained sandy soils/acid or alkaline/sharp, cold winter temperatures/sunny positions
North American hardiness zone: 6–9
Height: 1.2m (4ft)
Spread: 60cm (24in)
Grow for: amazing, tall, upright stems densely packed with bright yellow flowers in early summer

When I was working in northern Japan recently, I saw masses of different flowering eremurus, flowering far better than they do, even in the books, over here. This brought home to me how well these plants really respond to the cold winter (they will easily get –17°C/1°F there) and strong sun in the summer. The flowers are far bigger and better, and last longer too. Sheltered sites are definitely worth seeking out, as you can then get away without the need to stake them. The taller *Eremurus himalaicus* reaches 2m (6½ft) and is white, flowering in early May. Both this and *E. robustus*, which is taller still, towering to 2.4m (7½ft) and is pink, are equally brilliant plants.

On a sheltered site you may get away without staking the taller types. If you do need to stake, it is best to insert a stout peg into the ground at planting to avoid damaging the crown of fleshy starfish-like roots. To make sure you have good enough drainage, you may need to plant the crown on – and cover ot with – sharp sand or grit, or plant it in a raised bed or on a bank. The leaves have mostly shrivelled up by flowering time, so disguise them with other planting, bearing in mind they love the sun. Reduce congestion in crowded groups by lifting them in early autumn when they are dormant. This involves sorting out the knitted roots to separate the crowns and then replanting individually, just below the surface of the soil. Place some grit or sand on top to stop slugs, snails and stray forks damaging the plants. **BG**

Erica arborea 'Estrella Gold'
TREE HEATH

Type: hardy, evergreen shrub
Soil & situation: moist, free-draining, gravelly soil/full sun/shelter from cold winds
North American hardiness zone: 9–10
Height: 1.2m (4ft)
Spread: 1m (3ft)
Grow for: total reliability; scented, white flowers; very useful for the border; AGM

Erica arborea 'Estrella Gold'

Heathers have a place in every garden and among the best of them are the tree heaths. They add character and height to any border all year round. I have never known a tree heath to refuse to flower.

Erica arborea 'Estrella Gold' is slower growing than *E. arborea* with lime-green, needle-like foliage tipped bright yellow in spring. Later, in summer, it will darken to golden yellow. Early spring, white flowers are honey-scented, appearing in long, spiky racemes. It has an upright habit with stiff branches.

Usually, the only pruning required is to clip the plant over after flowering removing the dead flowerheads. Large, overgrown plants may be pruned hard in late spring when all risk of frost is past. In early summer feed with a general, balanced fertilizer and mulch the soil surface. Propagate by rooting semi-ripe cuttings in summer in a gritty compost. In late spring pinch out the tip of young plants to encourage them to branch low down, forming a bushy plant. **JC**

Eremurus stenophyllus subsp. *stenophyllus*

Erica carnea 'December Red'
WINTER HEATH OR HEATHER

Type: hardy, evergreen shrub
Soil & situation: well-drained, fertile, acid soil/full sun or light shade
North American hardiness zone: 5–6
Height: 20–25cm (8–10in)
Spread: 60cm (24in)
Grow for: deep green foliage which contrasts with the long-lasting, rose-red flower spikes, making a cheerful display from mid-winter until mid-spring; superb ground-covering plant

Flowering times of *Erica carnea* depend on the variety, starting in late autumn until mid-spring. Colours range from white through pink to purple. The flowers of *E. c.* 'December Red' open a pale pink gradually deepening to a warm rose-red colour. Totally hardy, it loves the wind in its hair and will sit under a blanket of snow, emerging in full bloom. It manages to cheer me up on a cold day when the rain is dripping down my neck.

It is at its best in an open, free-draining soil with added humus. It prefers acid conditions but, providing there is a good depth overlying chalk, it is tolerant of alkaline soil. Regular mulches will encourage surface roots, thus extending the life of the plant. A general clip over after the colour has faded to remove the dead flowers will keep the plant compact. Planted in groups and spaced 45cm (18in) apart, they will soon join up to form a weed-suppressing carpet. **JC**

Erica carnea 'December Red'

Erica x *darleyensis* 'Silberschmelze'

Erica x *darleyensis* 'Silberschmelze'
DARLEY DALE HEATH

Type: hardy, vigorous, busy, evergreen shrub
Soil & situation: moist, well-drained soil/tolerates alkaline conditions/full sun
North American hardiness zone: 7–8
Height: 38cm (15in)
Spread: 90cm (36in)
Grow for: very reliable winter- and spring-flowering heather with pure white flowers

I love its habit of growth where it not only spreads well but is taller and more dense than most of the other varieties of *Erica* x *darleyensis*. The tiny, lance-shaped leaves are tipped with pale-cream in spring, turning a deep green in summer and tinged a rusty-red in winter. The urn-shaped, fragrant, white flowers that cover the plant in the dead of winter are so white they make virgin snow look grey. It trades under two other names, 'Silver Beads' and 'Molten Silver', both of which are good descriptive terms for this plant.

E. x *d.* 'Silberschmelze' is a good companion plant for dwarf conifers and, planted 80cm (32in) apart, forms a dense ground-covering mat which smothers most annual weeds.

An annual mulch of compost worked or washed into the centre of the heather will encourage the stems to root. Clip the plant over removing the dead flower stems as soon as it has finished flowering. It is sufficiently hardy for the coldest areas of the UK and is happiest in an exposed, windy site. Propagation is by 5cm (2in) long semi-ripe cuttings in early summer. Pot the cuttings up in late summer the same year to allow them to establish fresh roots in the compost before winter. **JC**

Erigeron karvinskianus
MEXICAN DAISY

Type: evergreen perennial
Soil & situation: sharp-draining, moderately fertile soil/naturalizes in stone walls/sun or part shade
North American hardiness zone: 5–7
Height: 15–30cm (6–12in)
Spread: 1m (3ft) or more
Grow for: a plant rarely out of flower in the summer; colonizes in gaps in paving or stone walls as it seeds itself freely; AGM

This flower must be one of the longest-flowering plants around and will perform from late spring to late autumn which is a real feat. The flower looks very like that of a lawn daisy, except they are not always white with a yellow centre. They start white or pink (with a yellow centre) and then finally end up red-purple. It is a star plant in terms of performance and, if you too like simple charm, then I think it is also a star plant in terms of appearance. When it colonizes a gridwork of cracks in paving, a dry stone wall or a stone roof it creates something totally different, away from the norm, which really lifts your spirits.

This is one of those plants that either takes a real shine to you or looks the other way. One major factor is drainage – if you have heavy, wet soil then you must lighten it up a lot. Apart from this, if you want it in copious quantities, I think the secret is to grow it from seed in spring, in 7cm (3in) pots, and then plant it out in late spring. Once you have it well established, it benefits from a hard cut back in early spring. This keeps it looking smart and natty right through to the end of flowering in late autumn, when you can leave the heads on for maximum seed dispersal. **BG**

Erigeron karvinskianus

Eriobotrya japonica

Eriobotrya japonica
LOQUAT/JAPANESE MEDLAR

Type: frost-hardy evergreen shrub to small tree
Soil & situation: any soil/full sun to light shade
North American hardiness zone: 8–10
Height: 9m (30ft)
Spread: 6m (20ft)
Grow for: very large, firm, leathery, evergreen foliage; hawthorn-scented flowers; AGM

The loquat first came to my attention as a student abroad. I ate the delicious fruit but never saved the seed, thinking the plant would not be hardy. Then years later I saw an old specimen in a friend's garden in Norwich where I first mistook it for a rare rhododendron, because of its impressive leaves. I have since grown many myself as evergreen foliage plants; they are easy from seed, and I have found them surprisingly tough. The exotically perfumed (well, hawthorn-like) drooping clusters of flowers come, sporadically, throughout winter if it is mild following a hot summer. Just occasionally fellow growers have reported fruits setting – these are like chewy apricots.

A native of China and Japan, it was introduced in 1787. It is named after the Greek *erion*, for wool, and *botrys*, for grapes, describing the woolly clusters of flowers. Loquat, comes from the Cantonese name, *lu-kywit*, for its orange fruits.

Any well-drained soil in full sun will suit this plant and it will survive for many decades in a sheltered position. Nip out the growing tip to make it into a bushy shrub, because as a tree it gets too leggy and windswept unless on a wall. It can be grown from seed but then you will only get a species, not an improved fruiting variety – which is fine in Britain where it is grown only for its ornamental value. Or take cuttings in late summer. No problems other than occasional wind burn.   **BF**

Eruca vesicaria
WILD ROCKET

Type: annual herb
Soil & situation: rich, well-drained but moist soils/will grow satisfactorily on a range of soils, but bolting may be encouraged in lighter soils/shade protection or a shady position can prolong leaf production
North American hardiness zone: annual
Height & spread: to 1m (3ft), usually less
Grow for: an essential spicy leaf for salads; harvestable leaves six to eight weeks from sowing; one sowing will generate a good five cuttings if not more; sown in very early autumn it will have leaves for cutting from mid-autumn right through to spring, with a bit of luck

Wild rocket is different in appearance from salad rocket, having thinner, smaller and darker leaves and a stronger taste, but the big advantage is that it will produce leaves for about twice as long as other rockets. It is also slower growing. It has been used since at least the first century AD for medicinal purposes, but now is a hot favourite in salads. It is a constituent of mesclun, which is a very tasty mixed salad of small leaves which originates from around Nice in the South of France. You should cut the leaves before the flowering stem is produced, as they become overpoweringly strong after this point.

Sow from mid-spring. Thin to about 15cm (6in) apart to stop the plants bolting prematurely.

Eruca vesicaria

Continue sowing till mid-summer and cover with fleece, if necessary, to prevent flea beetle attack. If you sow in late summer or early autumn, flea beetle is not a problem, and there is often foliage for picking from mid-autumn to spring. Cut the leaves to about 2.5cm (1in) above the ground, and carry on doing this till they bolt. Plants in a sunny position have more pungent leaves than those growing in shady spots, as happens with most herbs.   **BF**

Eryngium agavifolium

Type: frost-hardy, evergreen perennial
Soil & situation: a wide range of soil types from poor gravelly to limy and rich loams/free-draining moderately fertile soils are optimum/full sun
North American hardiness zone: 6–9
Height: flowers to 1.3m (4ft), basal leaves to 45cm (18in)
Spread: 60cm (2ft)
Grow for: amazing looks through the winter months with its striking silhouette iced with frost; evergreen clumps of foliage through which protrude several tall spikes supporting many rounded, teasel-type heads about 1cm (½in) in diameter

Eryngium agavifolium

This rather exotic plant will fit into many places in the garden. Because of its year-round appeal, I grow it in my entrance courtyard where the beds are edged in box. The garden is a funny mix of traditional and contemporary and this plant is a bit like that too. The thin, strappy leaves can be up to 75cm (30in) long, are slightly fleshy-looking, edged in neat little spines on both sides and form bold, solid clumps that look good right through the grey, cold winter months. The greenish-white flowers appear in late summer. They are perfect plants to grow as specimens in gravel, mixed with ornamental grasses, in containers, as part of prairie schemes, or more traditionally, with a dark green hedge behind them. How versatile can you get? They are superb for drying to use in winter decorations.

These plants do not appreciate root disturbance and I have left mine untouched for many years. One day, when they get too large, I will split the clumps in spring, as opposed to autumn, as they might well tend to sit and rot through the winter months if done earlier. They will be slow to re-establish. Propagate by root cuttings in winter or by seed.   **BG**

Eryngium bourgatii 'Picos Blue'
SEA HOLLY

Type: hardy, herbaceous perennial
Soil & situation: moist, free-draining soil/full sun
North American hardiness zone: 5–9
Height: 45cm (18in)
Spread: 30cm (12in)
Grow for: sculptural form and foliage; flowers from mid-summer

Now here's a conundrum! The genus is commonly called 'sea hollies', you'd think they were thistles but what are they? Carrots! It just proves that appearances are deceiving. I'd like to include them all as they're such wonderful plants. *E. b.* 'Picos Blue' is one of several with blue flowers and stems, but it's arguably the bluest and best. It has a basal clump of deeply cut, dark green leaves and a stiff candelabra of flowerheads and stems of deep metallic blue. The flowers are nectar rich, beloved by bees and other insects; cut at their peak and hung upside down, they dry and retain their colour.

E. bourgatii has deeply cut, silvery-grey, white-veined leaves and silvery-green bracts. *E. bourgatii* 'Oxford Blue' has darker silvery-blue flowerheads. *E. alpinum* has attractive foliage and a mass of

Eryngium bourgatii 'Picos Blue'

large, feathery, blue bracts surrounding the flowerheads. *E.* 'Jos Eijking' is intense steel blue. *E. proteiflorum* is a challenge: a deep pot and frost-free conditions is the solution in most gardens. It is silvery-white with an amazing ruffle of bracts about 15cm (6in) in diameter.

Their best colour develops in full sun on cool, moderately fertile, slightly moist, light, well-drained soil; they grow well on poor alkaline soil. Remove dead leaves in winter and put a gravel mulch round the crown of the top plants; they are ideal for gravel gardens. Propagate by root cuttings in summer, disturbing the plant as little as possible. Some cultivars are protected by 'Plant Breeder's Rights'. They can suffer from powdery mildew and crown rot in wet soil.   **MB**

Eryngium maritimum
SEA HOLLY

Type: hardy, herbaceous perennial
Soil & situation: most light soils of good depth/full sun or light shade
North American hardiness zone: 5–8
Height & spread: 30–60cm (12–24in)
Grow for: startling, spiny, whitish glaucous foliage; spiky heads of pinkish-blue; edible parts

This is a beautiful plant – not large, quite compact, yet perfectly formed as if die cast in white metal. There are many other species often planted in the garden and most of these are more showy, but *Eryngium maritimum* has edible parts. The young shoots can be eaten as asparagus, before the spines of the holly-like leaves harden, and the roots may be candied – which I keep intending to do but I lose the plants too quickly. This is unusual as they are normally long lived. The flowerheads and stems if cut in their prime and dried carefully become everlasting, which makes them even more valuable.

A native maritime plant, the roots were thought to be an aphrodisiac when prepared by candying and were called eringoes. They are mentioned by Falstaff, 'let the sky rain potatoes…hail kissing comfits and snow eringoes'. *E. giganteum*, a close but larger relation, is known as Miss Willmott's Ghost as she had the appalling arrogance and inconsideration to surreptitiously sow seeds of this weed in every garden she visited.

E. maritimum prefers to be on a sandy shoreline, even washed by the sea! So give it a light; sandy, well-drained soil in full sun. Most of this family can be easily propagated by root cuttings, but this one is easiest from seed. Sow *in situ* or in small pots and transplant ASAP to its final site before the deep tap root forms. Slugs, or so it would seem, have made off with mine on several occasions – be warned! **BF**

Eryngium maritimum

Erysimum 'Bowles' Mauve'

Erysimum 'Bowles' Mauve'
PERENNIAL WALLFLOWER

Type: hardy, herbaceous perennial
Soil & situation: moderate to poor soil/sun
North American hardiness zone: 6–8
Height: 75cm (30in)
Spread: 60cm (24in)
Grow for: compact form and flowers from mid-spring to late autumn; AGM

Edward Augustus Bowles (1865–1954) lived at Myddleton House in Enfield, North London. He was an educated and enthusiastic gardener and plantsman with a kindly personality. Before gardening, he was interested in entomology and it was on a moth and caterpillar hunting expedition to Wicken Fen in Cambridgeshire that he noticed part of a clump of native *Carex elata* with bands of bright yellow which he removed and planted in his garden; it became *Carex elata* 'Bowles' Golden'.

Another plant named after him, *Vinca minor* 'Bowles Variety', was found in a French churchyard and *Milium effusum* 'Aureum' or 'Bowles Golden Grass' came from Birmingham Botanic Garden. Sadly, he almost certainly didn't grow *Erysimum* 'Bowles' Mauve', the reliable bushy wallflower with grey-blue foliage and masses of mauve flowers from mid-spring to late autumn. He never mentioned this fine plant in his books nor was it recognized by any of his gardeners who were later questioned about its origin. It is a really good performer and worthy of being one of the seventeen plants that bear his name. Given shelter, it flowers all year round.

While we're talking 'wallflowers' I'd like to sneak in a mention of another particular favourite of mine called *E.* 'Jacob's Jacket' with purple and bronze flowers, turning orange and finally lilac. It's wonderful!

Flourishing in poor to moderately fertile, well-drained, neutral to alkaline soil in full sun, in a sheltered position, these are ideal plants for those difficult dry sunny spots. Take nodal or heeled softwood cuttings in spring or summer. It is worth having a replacement plant standing by, as it dislikes cold, wet winters; protect from severe frost. **MB**

Erythrina crista-gallii
CORAL TREE, COCKSPUR CORAL TREE

Type: tender, deciduous perennial
Soil & situation: moderately fertile, well-drained soil/sun
North American hardiness zone: 8–10
Height & spread: 2.5m (8ft) x 1.5m (5ft), as a perennial
Grow for: extraordinary flowers from late summer onwards

Looking for an exotic? Then here's the real McCoy. Forget tree ferns and hardy tropical lookalikes, bring a touch of the Copacobana into your British back garden! This elegant beauty has spiny stems, trilobed leaves and waxy, deep coral-red flowers, each one about 6cm (2½in) long on flower spikes reaching a staggering 60cm (24in)

Erythrina crista-gallii

long. All the best gardens have one! The specimen at Oxford University Botanic Gardens has its roots in a greenhouse, escaping under the glass to flower outside; at the Royal Horticultural Gardens, Wisley, it is treated as a herbaceous plant; there's one at Sissinghurst Castle in Kent too. Mine is in a pot, it's growing well and is yet to flower…. There's a bottle of champagne waiting!

Plant outside against a sheltered, sunny wall in southern areas of the UK. It needs moderately fertile, well-drained soil and tolerates temperatures down to −10°C (14°F), providing the base is heavily mulched with leafmould or compost then covered with bracken. Cut back the stems from mid- to late spring once the danger of frost is over and the new shoots should flower by late summer. Alternatively, grow it in a pot, in a free-draining loam-based mix, like John Innes no. 3 with added sharp sand. Overwinter under glass and put it outside after the last frost. Reduce watering in winter and re-pot or top dress when growth begins in spring. Propagate by seed or 7.5–10cm (3–4in) cuttings of young shoots in spring. **MB**

Erythronium 'Pagoda'
TROUT LILY

Type: hardy, bulbous perennial
Soil & situation: moist but free-draining soil/ partial shade
North American hardiness zone: 4–9
Height & spread: 35cm (14in)
Grow for: both for its foliage and flowers; attractive leaves are mottled, glossy and dark green and appear in late winter to early spring; the flowers, borne in mid- to late spring are yellow and last for several weeks; strong growers and spread quickly; AGM

Easy, very vigorous and undemanding to grow *Erythronium* 'Pagoda' spreads quite quickly, even in my dry soil. Even though I have read several times that it likes moist, acid conditions, I know of several dry, alkaline gardens where it copes admirably. Never believe everything you read in books! The leaves are large, elliptical and mottled with bronze and make quite a show. The tall stems each carry up to ten, pale sulphur-yellow flowers which hang way above the leaves.

Although the stems seem delicate, the flowers, like the plant, are robust and are not perturbed by inclement spring weather. I grow it in large drifts under my hazel bushes, with primroses, ivies and ferns. It competes surprisingly well even with the ivy. I think it looks best growing in a

Erythronium 'Pagoda'

naturalized way rather than in clumps in the border, which then leaves you with a gap as the leaves die down in summer. Another way to grow them is around the base of trees where the empty space in summer does not register so much. I am going to try them naturalized in thin, woodland turf where apparently it also does well. It is another of those plants that makes you wonder why it is not grown more.

This plant establishes well from dry bulbs but do plant them promptly on arrival. They look like a large canine fang, hence one of its common names is dog's tooth violet. If the clumps become congested you can either split them when the foliage starts to die in summer or just as the flowers are going over. **BG**

Escallonia 'Pride of Donard'

Type: hardy, evergreen shrub
Soil & situation: fertile, well-drained soil/full sun
North American hardiness zone: 8–9
Height: 1.5m (5ft)
Spread: 2.5m (8ft)
Grow for: a dense, compact shrub with an abundance of flowers in summer: AGM

I have a particular liking for escallonia. As an informal hedge they are in flower over a long period. Of the many varieties available, *Escallonia* 'Pride of Donard' is my favourite.

In maturity it forms an upright, dense, compact shrub with 3cm (1in) long, glossy, dark evergreen leaves. The short terminal racemes of bright, pink-red, chalice-like flowers are carried in profusion during summer. It is an excellent seaside plant tolerating sea spray and coming into flower earlier than when planted inland. Another good choice is *E.* 'Iveyi' with conical panicles of pure white, highly fragrant flowers and growing to 4m (13ft) high.

As a hedge, clip immediately after flowering and apply a general fertilizer to encourage growth. When it continues to flower into early autumn it is necessary to clip it over before it has finished flowering. Lightly prune free-standing shrubs in spring when all risk of frost is over. Old, neglected plants may be hard pruned in late spring, cutting into the old branch system. They will soon recover sending up strong, new shoots from the base.

Propagation is by softwood cuttings in early summer, semi-ripe cuttings from late summer to autumn or as hardwood cuttings taken in early winter. **JC**

Eschscholzia californica
Plant of the Week (see page 281)

Escallonia 'Pride of Donard'

Eucalyptus pauciflora subsp. *niphophila*
SNOW GUM

Type: hardy, evergreen, spreading tree
Soil & situation: moist, fertile, well-drained, neutral to acid soil/prefers sun
North American hardiness zone: 8–10
Height & spread: 6m (20ft)
Grow for: something pleasing in all its stages – graceful when young and in old age, which seems to come early, it becomes dome-headed, open and gnarled; AGM

A native of Australia, it is one of the hardiest eucalypts. Seed from trees growing at high altitude in New South Wales appears to be immune to frost and cold winds.

The mature bark has been likened to a python's skin but in case, like me, you are happy never to have seen a python, I will describe the trunk. Cinnamon brown, flaking to reveal green, grey and yellow patches, the latter turning to a creamy white.

The young shoots are covered in a waxy, white bloom. Adult foliage is leathery, grey-green and lance-shaped with the characteristic pungent aroma when crushed. The umbels of creamy-white, petalless flowers appear from late spring through to summer in clusters of between three and seven. The flower buds resemble acorns – each a small urn with a lid. The stamens push the lid off and fully expand.

Eucalyptus pauciflora subsp. *niphophila*

Eucomis bicolor

Where space is restricted the snow gum can be coppiced annually by cutting the tree down to within 30cm (12in) of the ground in the late spring. The resultant seasonal growth can be as much as 2–3m (6½–10ft) with juvenile, pale green, rounded leaves. Propagation is by seed which germinates easily after an eight-week period of cold, winter weather. Plant the young tree in its permanent position as soon as possible. Larger than 1.2m (4ft) high, and it will always be unstable, its roots staying in a ball rather than spreading in search of nutrients. If left lying, dead eucalyptus leaves will mark a patio surface, leaving a brown stain. **JC**

Eucomis bicolor
PINEAPPLE LILY, PINEAPPLE FLOWER

Type: hardy bulbous perennial
Soil & situation: well-drained fertile soil/full sun
North American hardiness zone: 8–10
Height: 60cm (24in)
Spread: 20cm (8in)
Grow for: unusual and charismatic flowers on thick stalks, surrounded by a cylinder of starry blooms, topped with a spout of leafy bracts in late summer to early autumn and, as their name implies, looking a little like pineapples; AGM

I have seen these plants growing in a thick colony all the way along the base of a mature yew hedge. It was facing due south and obviously in a very dry position, but the plants looked rather handsome and exotic. They are supposedly a little tender, but mine have survived outside for several years. If you are in a colder area, they can be planted out each spring, but they look best when they are well and truly established in thick clumps or ribbons.

You plant these bulbs in autumn, about 15cm (6in) deep, and I have to admit I do not think I have ever done anything to these plants in my life after planting them, except admire them. If I was not so reckless, I would give them a mulch in winter to ensure protection against the frost, though mine are in a narrow border running along the house and are fairly snug against the stone walls. I could also water them in active growth, which no doubt would spur them on. A feed too, would also have this effect, and be appreciated when they become active quite late in spring. **BG**

Eucomis comosa
PINEAPPLE FLOWER

Type: hardy, bulbous perennial
Soil & situation: moist but free-draining soil/full sun
North American hardiness zone: 8–10
Height: 1m (3ft)
Spread: 60cm (24in) or more
Grow for: attractive form, flower, foliage and fruit

The first specimen described in England was in 1732 by Dillenius, Professor of Botany at Oxford University who named it *Corona regalis lilii folio crenato* meaning 'crown royal lily with crenate (scalloped) leaves'. And you thought the current

Eucomis comosa

Latin names were difficult! *Eucomis* is from the Greek *eu*, meaning good, and *kome*, hair or tuft, describes the 'good tuft' of leaf-like bracts that top the dense head of waxy, star-shaped flowers.

Although all the eucomis are impressive, this is perhaps the most dramatic, reaching 1m (3ft) tall in a range of flower colours from pale green to cream, pink and purple. The developing fruits glisten and are suffused with burgundy tints like tiny beetroot and the stem is flecked and striped! It makes a wonderful specimen on a patio, particularly when it flowers in late summer and early autumn.

The most common of the others is *Eucomis bicolor* (see previous entry). *E. pole-evansii* is a giant, reaching a staggering 2m (6½ft) tall in warmer climates (it's not quite as enthusiastic in ours!), while *E. zambesiaca* is comparatively small at 20–30cm (8–12in) with white, coconut-scented flowers fading to green. There are plenty to choose from!

They need a sheltered, sunny position, against a wall or fence on free-draining, moist soil; dig in plenty of well-rotted organic matter before planting, water well in summer. Mulch in autumn to protect from frost. In cooler parts of the UK they are better grown in containers and overwintered in a cool greenhouse or shed. Propagate by division or seed in spring. **MB**

Eucryphia x *intermedia* 'Rostrevor'
Plant of the Week (see page 305)

Euonymus europaeus 'Red Cascade'
Plant of the Week (see page 357)

Euonymus fortunei 'Emerald 'n' Gold'

Type: hardy, evergreen, bushy shrub
Soil & situation: moist, well-drained soil/full sun or light shade
North American hardiness zone: 5–9
Height & spread: 1m (3ft)
Grow for: attractive leaves; neat, low hedge; AGM

When you need to fill a gap this is a good and easy filler. It will grow in any soil providing it isn't

Euonymus fortunei 'Emerald 'n' Gold'

waterlogged. Its small, shiny green leaves are delightfully edged in bright yellow. The variegation is more pronounced in a sunny site and when the weather turns cold the whole plant takes on a pink tinge. It forms a compact plant when mature, throwing the odd long, sparsely-leafed stem.

Trim lightly in late spring to keep it in shape and remove any green stems that appear. Planted close together and clipped regularly it will form a tight, attractive, low hedge. Planted against a wall it will go vertical, making 2m (6½ft) without support. A good companion plant is the cream-and-green variegated *Euonymus* 'Emerald Gaiety' with a spread of 1.5m (5ft).

E. fortunei 'Emerald 'n' Gold' dislikes biting, cold winds, preferring a sheltered sunny situation. Propagation is easy with softwood or semi-hardwood cuttings in a gritty compost. Cuttings where the stems root themselves into the soil are a quick way to increase stock. **JC**

Euonymus fortunei 'Silver Queen'

Type: hardy, evergreen climbing shrub
Soil & situation: huge range of soils/useful on dry, shady sites/also grows well in full sun on poor dry soils
North American hardiness zone: 5–9
Height: up to 2.5m (8ft)
Spread: 1.5m (5ft)
Grow for: useful and decorative foliage, leaves have a broad cream margin and in prolonged cold periods take on 'bottle-nosed pinkish tints', as aptly described by Christopher Lloyd in his book *The Well-Tempered Garden*; excellent against

walls and fences; more usually grown as ground cover.

Although not a great fan of variegated plants, I do think of this as a really choice plant and accordingly use it on a regular basis. The natty, compact foliage is well-behaved and will do what you tell it, be it scrambling up trees or fences (albeit slowly), forming sheets of classic, smart green and white ground cover or, clipped and trained, forming huge, solid but vivid topiary balls. It adapts to look appropriate to its neighbours somehow. In one very special garden, we have used it in a green and white border mixed with white *Gladiolus callianthus* (see page 194), *Rosa* 'Gruss an Aachen' (page 334), *Choisya ternata* 'Aztec Pearl' and others, all grown in repeated groups. The effect is simple and refreshing. Another big plus in its favour – it grows pretty much anywhere you tell it, lightening up rather dark, dry shade, or baking on a sun-soaked terrace.

These plants need little care except if you would like them to climb, and then support will be necessary. Otherwise you just shape them if their growth is lopsided or whatever, but this is hardly likely to offend anyway. I think it would be difficult to kill or damage them, whatever time of year you cut them, except perhaps by cutting too early or late in the year and so encouraging new growth at a time when it could be frosted. It is ever so easy to propagate by cuttings taken any time between early summer and mid-autumn.

BG

Euonymus fortunei 'Silver Queen'

Exochorda x *macrantha* 'The Bride'

PEARL BUSH

Type: hardy, deciduous shrub
Soil & situation: moist, fertile, well-drained soil/full sun or light shade
Hardiness zone: 5–9
Height: 2m (6½ft)
Spread: 3m (10ft)
Grow for: an abundance of large, white flowers, at their best in mid-spring; AGM

A lovely woman and a great gardener, Jane Higginson of Comber, near my home in Northern Ireland, has a matching pair of these wonderful shrubs, one either side of a path. In flower they are spectacular.

It forms a compact mound of arching branches. The 7cm (2¾in) long, pale green leaves are produced early in spring. Racemes of up to ten, pure white, five-petalled flowers on short, leafy stems appear in late spring and early summer covering the branches. It makes a wonderful plant in a mixed shrub bed or grown as a specimen in an open situation where its arched branches will reach the ground.

Another species, *Exochorda racemosa*, is one of the parents of 'The Bride'. It is an equally classy shrub but is more fussy, needing an acid soil. It will succeed in all soils but will become chlorotic (yellow leaves) in shallow chalk soils.

Prune back the branches that have flowered to healthy buds. Neglected shrubs may be severely pruned in late spring, removing a quarter of the old branches close to the base each year. This will encourage new, strong shoots. Propagation is by softwood cuttings in summer. Take short cuttings and remove most of the leaves. **JC**

Eupatorium rugosum 'Chocolate'

Eupatorium rugosum 'Chocolate'

Type: hardy perennial
Soil & situation: moderately fertile soil/responds well to moist soil/sun or part shade
North American hardiness zone: 4–9
Height: to 1.2m (4ft)
Spread: 25cm (10in)
Grow for: deep green foliage heavily tinted with a burgundy-brown colour; AGM

This plant is a new and unusual perennial, a selection from the white snakeroot, *Eupatorium rugosum*. However the main difference is the distinctively-coloured foliage which happily, is also fairly bushy and maintains a good colour throughout the growing season. Corymbs of good-looking white flowers are produced in late summer and last for just about a month, if you are lucky. They are much appreciated by bees and butterflies.

Another favourite is *Eupatorium purpureum* subsp. *maculatum* 'Atropurpureum' (AGM). This is a grand plant, towering to over 2m (6½ft) high. It produces intense reddish-purple flowers which last into the autumn, and are often a hive of activity with bees and butterflies.

This plant responds well to good moisture levels, so if necessary add good volumes of organic matter prior to planting, and maybe water a little in dry periods until it really gets its roots well down. Cut down in late winter or spring. Propagate by division. **BG**

Euphorbia amygdaloides 'Purpurea'
WOOD SPURGE

Type: hardy, evergreen perennial
Soil & situation: ordinary garden loam/tolerates moist conditions/sun or shade
North American hardiness zone: 6–9
Height: up to 70cm (27½in)
Spread: 30cm (12in)
Grow for: year-round, purple foliage and stems; lime-green flowerheads in spring/summer

This plant is a real favourite of mine. I first became intimate with it when I included it in a ruby-coloured planting scheme for a Chelsea Flower Show garden, and managed to take it home afterwards for 'safe keeping'. It did me proud at Chelsea and has done my garden proud for the next two years to date. My major concern is that apparently it is short-lived but as it comes true from seed, hopefully I will have some offspring to remember it by when the fateful day eventually comes. The stems grow quite upright in their first year and usually flower in their second year. As I write about it in winter, following a period of snow and frost, the foliage is still in pristine condition and looks as showy as ever. It manages to thrive in a dry and shaded spot with me, although moist conditions are its preferred choice. I also grow *Euphorbia*

Euphorbia amygdaloides 'Purpurea'

amygdaloides var. *robbiae*, a useful evergreen plant for colonizing awkward dry shady places but not a show stopper like 'Purpurea'. One small downside to be aware of: all euphorbias have milky, white sap, which is toxic if eaten and an irritant to the skin and eyes.

It is a good idea to remove stems after flowering which provides space for new stems to grow. This plant is easiest propagated from seed but as the seeds are released explosively, remember to encase the flowerheads in paper or light fabric just before the seeds are released. If using stems for flower arranging, seal the ends with boiling water or a flame, to prevent the sap bleeding.
BG

Euphorbia griffithii 'Dixter'

Type: hardy, herbaceous perennial
Soil & situation: rich, moist soil/sun or partial shade
North American hardiness zone: 5–9
Height: 1m (3ft)
Spread: 60cm (24in) or more
Grow for: colourful stems; flowerheads from late spring to mid-autumn; AGM

Yet another euphorbia that is highly sought after by Martian landscapers! Continuing in the generic tradition, it seems to have forgotten that it is supposed to be a plant and has absent-mindedly transformed itself into a piece of outrageous surrealist art. It looks more like a coral than a vegetable; particularly those extravagant flowerheads and stems during the early stages of growth.

As it explodes out of the ground like angry asparagus, the narrow, dark green-purple leaves folding out from the stems are edged and veined with orange-red. The massed stems make a wonderful architectural plant as the leaves cluster like a starfish round the stem. Topping each stem, the flowerheads resembling masts packed with satellite dishes have obviously decided that traditional 'lime-green' isn't ostentatious enough and glow brick-red instead; in autumn, the rest of the plant joins in the fun and the colour on the leaves and stems is incredible.

It is a spectacular plant, displaying all the creative flamboyance of the legend that is Christopher Lloyd; he selected this from a group of seedlings at Washfield Nurseries in Kent, and named it after his garden and home.

Euphorbia griffithii 'Fireglow' is more invasive, has green leaves with a red tinge and brick- to tomato-red flowers. It makes an impressive bold statement anywhere!

They need deep, humus-rich, moist soil in sun or partial shade. Colour is better in rich soil and sunshine. They are good in woodland gardens; cut back and mulch in spring. They can cause dermatitis, so wear gloves when handling. Divide in spring, take basal cuttings in spring and early summer; dip the cuts in warm water or charcoal to prevent bleeding.   **MB**

Euphorbia myrsinites
Plant of the Week (see page 95)

Exochorda x *macrantha* 'The Bride'
Plant of the Week (see page 171)

Euphorbia griffithii 'Dixter'

Fabiana imbricata f. *violacea*

Fabiana imbricata f. *violacea*

Type: hardy, evergreen shrub
Soil & situation: well-drained, impoverished, neutral to acid soil/full sun
North American hardiness zone: 8–10
Height & spread: 2.5m (8ft)
Grow for: mauve-lavender flowers that cover the plant in early summer; AGM

This plant resembles a well-grown tree heather. Given a sheltered site in full sun or planted against a sunny wall it will thrive. The branches are stiff and upright with sideshoots emerging horizontally covered in small, needle-like, dark green leaves. The single, tubular, mauve-lavender flowers appear in early summer. While it will eventually become too large for a container, a young plant looks good in an earthenware pot. A matching pair at the front entrance can be impressive. *F. imbricata* 'Prostrata' is lower growing at a mature height of 1m (3ft). It produces white flowers in summer.

Prune in late spring, removing stems which spoil the overall shape. Propagation is by softwood cuttings in early summer or semi-ripe heel cuttings in late summer. Seed may be sown in autumn and over-wintered in a cold frame.   **JC**

Fagus sylvatica 'Purpurea Pendula'
PURPLE WEEPING BEECH

Type: hardy, deciduous tree
Soil & situation: well-drained soil/full sun
North American hardiness zone: 5–7
Height & spread: 3m (10ft)
Grow for: good looks all year round as a specimen tree or in a large border

I am a firm believer in the saying, 'Every garden should have at least one tree', and there are few gardens too small to accommodate this lovely weeping beech.

It manages to look good all year round. In winter its mushroom-shaped head weeps gracefully on thin stems with shiny, pointed buds. The glossy, deep purple-black leaves emerge in late spring with a hint of green. It holds the leaves until late autumn when they turn to a rich brown before leaf fall.

It is tolerant of most soil types including thin soil over chalk but dislikes waterlogged conditions. Plant in a position in full sun and sheltered from cold winds. When planted in light shade the leaf colour is less intense with more bottle-green visible.

It is a well behaved tree but being top grafted it may occasionally produce all green shoots down the stem below the grafted head. Rub these off when they are young or cut thicker shoots as close to the main trunk as possible to prevent regrowth. Pruning may be necessary in the early years to shape and balance the tree. The weeping stems may be shortened by one third of the previous year's growth. They will produce several sideshoots, thickening the canopy of branches. Where staking is necessary to hold the tree, use a short stake with 45cm (18in) above ground level. Remove it as soon as the tree can stand on its own feet.

Tip: when selecting a purple weeping beech choose the tallest one possible. It may look a bit skinny and top heavy but in future years you will have a taller weeping specimen.   **JC**

Fagus sylvatica 'Purpurea Pendula'

Fallopia baldschuanica
RUSSIAN VINE, MILE-A-MINUTE

Type: hardy, deciduous climber
Soil & situation: moderately fertile, moist, well-drained soil/full sun or partial shade
North American hardiness zone: 5–9
Height: 12m (40ft)
Spread: indefinite
Grow for: extremely fast growing; an abundance of small flowers covering long stems

Russian vine frequently gets a bad name and is laughed out of the garden when recommended as a climber. If the plan calls for a fast-growing climber to take over a miserable-looking tree and transform it for the summer, good old 'mile-a-minute' has the last laugh.

The 10cm (4in) long, heart-shaped leaves are dark green and from spring to autumn they camouflage the vigorous, woody, twining stems. The panicles of funnel-shaped, tiny, pink-tinged white flowers cover the plant in late summer and autumn. They appear on the new growth and seem to overflow the climber like froth or soapsuds. To see long stems covered in 'froth' trailing out of a big old tree is fairly dramatic. Small, pink-white fruits follow in late autumn.

It is no exaggeration to state that this climber is rampant. So much so I suggest you strengthen the supporting trellis before planting one. The tree it is going to climb and take over, and the

Fallopia baldschuanica

Fascicularia bicolor

support needs to be well anchored into the ground. The top growth high up in the tree will act as a sail, offering resistance to any wind. Pruning consists of teaching it who is boss. After flowering or in early spring, it can be hard pruned to stay within its allocated space. Allow for 3–4m (10–13ft) of growth in one season. Try to keep the stems clear of the ground as they will root where they touch the soil. Propagation is by seed in spring. Semi-ripe cuttings, taken in summer with a heel, root quickly. Hardwood cuttings in autumn will be well rooted by the following winter. Space the cuttings at least 30cm (12in) apart to prevent the new growth tangling. **JC**

Fascicularia bicolor

Type: half-hardy, evergreen perennial
Soil & situation: extremely poor, very free-draining soil/sun or shade
North American hardiness zone: 9–10
Height: 45cm (18in)
Spread: 60cm (24in)
Grow for: fascinating form and flower from summer to autumn

Bromeliads, those spiny structures inhabiting deserts and rainforests, are rarely grown in gardens but this, one of nature's fantastic living sculptures, makes a fabulous novelty plant. It looks so 'spidery', I always expect it to get up and walk away!

The rosette, an arching, multi-layered mass of spiny-toothed stems is green for much of the year. At flowering time the insignificant central cluster of pale blue flowers seemingly strains, shoulder to shoulder in a united valiant effort to shine but all it can do is raise itself slightly and smile wanly at passersby. The leaves take pity on their shy, retiring friends and decide to help by lining their lips with glossy red lipstick and glowing like giant beacons. 'Hey, fancy some pollination?' they cry out to passing insects. Over the years, more rosettes appear, collectively there's more 'lippy' than at a tart's convention! It may be bold and brassy, but you have to say it's a 'tart wiv an 'eart'!

Given poor, very free-draining soil in sun or shade, it withstands light frosts. Plants produce offsets and colonies soon develop. They are long lived and over the years the leaves just grow longer.

How tough is it? E. Charles Nelson and Jorg Zizka in *The Plantsman* describe how a rootless rosette was left on a dry dark office floor for three weeks without water. It was finally planted in peat and left outdoors with no further care or water. Within two months it was growing strongly! Divide in spring or summer. **MB**

Fatsia japonica
JAPANESE ARALIA

Type: hardy, evergreen shrub
Soil & situation: moist, well-drained soil/full sun or partial shade
North American hardiness zone: 7–10
Height & spread: 3–4m (10–13ft)
Grow for: an unbeatable shrub for its architectural qualities; AGM

It is old fashioned and smacks of 'Victoriana' but it is still one of the very best architectural shrubs for the garden. On top of that, it flowers in late autumn. It forms a rounded, open shrub which readily suckers within the overall clump.

The large, 20–45cm (8–18in) long, glossy, dark green leaves are hand-shaped with between seven and eleven 'fingers'. Each lobe is wavy edged giving the leaf a crinkled appearance. The tiny, creamy-white flowers appear in autumn and form long-stalked umbels which are part of a larger loose umbel. They are followed by small, rounded, jet black fruit.

Aralia dislikes cold, drying winds. A sheltered woodland site in light shade, where its evergreen foliage can brighten a dull corner, is ideal. There are several variegated varieties, all of which require a shaded site. *Fatsia japonica* 'Aurea' is slow growing with golden variegation. *F. j.* 'Marginata' has creamy-white margined, deeply lobed leaves.

Prune in late spring removing low and crossing branches. Remove heavy falls of snow from the leaves before the weight breaks branches. Propagation is by seed sown in a heated propagator in spring. Softwood cuttings taken in early summer root well providing the leaves are trimmed by half to reduce transpiration. Air layering of young stems in summer is good fun, resulting in a large-rooted plant. **JC**

Fatsia japonica

Feijoa sellowiana

Feijoa sellowiana
(syn. *Acca sellowiana*)
PINEAPPLE GUAVA/FRUIT SALAD TREE

Type: frost-hardy, perennial, evergreen shrub
Soil & situation: light, well-drained, moist soil/full sun to light shade, or under cover in winter in a tub like citrus
North American hardiness zone: 8–10
Height & spread: makes a wall shrub up to 5m (16ft) each way
Grow for: evergreen, well evergrey, foliage with white felt underneath; bright red, paintbrush-like, edible flowers; delicious, well interesting, fruits

Feijoa sellowiana is closely related to the guavas and is just hardy. Although it can be fruited easily under cover, it is tough enough for most sheltered gardens in the warmer parts of the UK where it is an attractive, healthy shrub. The flowers when they unfurl are amazing, with sticking out red and white petals (which are edible and taste of cinnamon, sort of), and exceptionally decorative. The egg-shaped and egg-sized fruit, which occasionally sets outdoors, has a taste somewhat redolent of pineapple if you are generous or a tin of macedoine, or mixed fruit salad, if cynical. It is never seen for sale, so if you want to try it you must grow it!

A native of Brazil, it was not introduced to the UK until 1898. Still rarely known in this country, there are improved fruiting varieties such as 'Coolidge', 'Nazemetz' and 'Edenvale Supreme' available in the USA. These, however, deserve to be under cover so they can fruit.

Without doubt this needs a warm wall where it might then fruit, but it also makes an excellent cool conservatory subject and does well in similar conditions to citrus (see pages 104–105). It may need hand pollinating if you want fruit. I have some fine specimens grown from seed, but improved types need taking from cuttings or by layering. If you grow from seed or have older types you must have at least a pair of plants to get fruits to set, though the latest cultivars from the USA are, as they put it, 'self-fruitful'. **BF**

Tulipa 'Magier'

Type: hardy, spring-flowering bulb
Soil & situation: good garden loam/sunny position
Hardiness zone: 4–7
Height: 60cm (24in)
Spread: 15cm (6in) as an individual plant
Grow for: beautiful white flowers edged with pinky-violet rims; an excellent border tulip. As a Single Late-Flowering type, it is at its loveliest at this time of year.

A superb tulip for leaving in from year to year, this is also a most attractive flower with its smart coloured rim and occasional flecks of pink or violet on the white. It was raised in 1951 and flowers in late spring; the flowers last exceptionally well. 'Shirley', also a Single Late-Flowering, which is white with narrow purple margins, has been bred more recently and although it is now more readily available than 'Magier', is neither as good nor as bold. I think it might be more popular on the lists because of its better performance for commercial cut-flower growers – but they are often after different criteria to gardeners. 'Magier' used to be called 'Magician', but is rarely listed as such now.

Another tulip I use a lot is *T.* 'Purissima' (AGM). It is a sturdy number, only 35cm (14in) high, and has long-lasting milky-white flowers in spring.

Care for this tulip as you would for *Tulipa* 'Queen of Night' (see page 385). **BG**

Festuca glauca

Festuca glauca
BLUE FESCUE, GREY FESCUE

Type: hardy, perennial grass
Soil & situation: prefers light, well-drained soil/easily grown in many soils except those with winter damp/sunny position
North American hardiness zone: 4–8
Height: up to 35cm (14in)
Spread: 25cm (10in)
Grow for: neat, strong, textural, grey-blue tussocks of ever-grey-blue foliage; small, open flowerheads in summer which later become pale tan or beige

This is one of those plants that looks presentable for 12 months of the year, and as such, has become extremely popular, possibly too popular. Probably its most common use is as a low edge to the front of a border. Frequently it is planted in gravel areas where it can also be used in generous clumps, which may well increase as it self-seeds around. But beware, many seedlings will not come true. There are many cultivars available; 'Elijah Blue' is one of the most intense blues of all the fescues. It is worth trying to use this grass in different ways to stop it becoming a cliché. It could be used for a small area of lawn – it will tolerate being mown with the blades set as high as they will go – but this would be more of an ornamental lawn rather than one for a game of

rounders. It would also require higher maintenance, with the clumps being divided every fourth year or so.

When the clump becomes overcrowded it will start to die out in the middle and then it is necessary to lift and divide. This will probably be every three or four years. To maintain the vivid, blue foliage, the plants should be clipped in spring and summer. Dead leaves should also be removed. Propagation is best by division; seed is feasible but as the species readily hybridizes, the results are not always predictable. **BG**

Ficus carica 'Brown Turkey'
FIG

Type: hardy, deciduous shrub or tree
Soil & situation: for good fruit a sunny, preferably south-facing wall in the warmer parts of the country and restricted root growth/any ordinary garden soil, not too rich and preferably more or less neutral (with a pH between 6 and 7.5)
North American hardiness zone: 7–10
Height: 3m (10ft)
Spread: 4m (13ft)
Grow for: stunning foliage and the well-established atmosphere it conveys to a garden; delicious fruit in late summer or autumn; AGM

'Brown Turkey' is a smaller growing variety of fig, so much so that some say it is not necessary to restrict its root growth on planting by confining it to a tub within the soil. This is frequently recommended with figs so that the plant produces less vegetative growth and is encouraged to fruit. Often, if grown in paving by a house wall it is hardly in clover anyway. Figs are easy to grow but less easy to site in order to get regular, good crops of fruit. It is also said that figs should just be grown in the south but I know of many happily fruiting figs, including mine, in the Midlands. With the climate changing as it is, it is worth chancing your arm in many more northern areas too. If some years you are figless, you still have an amazing plant. 'Brown Turkey' is usually reckoned to be the most reliable variety for outdoor culture. I think the taste takes a lot of beating and the smaller size makes it more manageable.

Figs bear ripe fruit on last year's ripened growth. Therefore, do not go and hack it back in winter to reduce the size or you will remove prospective fruiting wood. Instead cut the growing ends that are getting into places that they should not be in summer, leaving the parts bearing fruit

Ficus carica 'Brown Turkey'

untouched. You can just, very gradually, thin out the remaining growth to keep it in bounds, at any time – when the mood takes you is always best.

Watering in dry periods as the fruit is swelling does seem to help plump up the crop, and protecting the near-ripe fruit individually, with bags or gauze, is often recommended to stop squirrels, blackbirds and wasps consuming them first. Apparently you then check them every few days to see if they have gone that amazing dark brown-purple colour. I have never had to do this, I can only think the cats guard them for me. True fig aficionados often talk about the volume of work needed to produce great figs, but the best crops I have seen are in neglected, walled gardens, where they have been left untouched for years. Get the site and variety right and you are there. **BG**

Foeniculum vulgare 'Purpureum' (syn. *F. vulgare* 'Bronze')
BRONZE FENNEL

Type: hardy, perennial herb
Soil & situation: undemanding of soil type providing it is well drained/sunny position
North American hardiness zone: 4–9
Height: 1.8m (6ft)
Spread: 45cm (18in)
Grow for: flavoursome use in cooking; excellent foliage plant with its part smoky-purple and part green-grey foliage

Bronze fennel is a huge bonus to many plantings; it looks particularly beguiling in early summer with its foamy, subtly coloured, fluffy foliage produced in a comely, voluminous manner. It establishes quickly and forms a strong presence, contrasting well with fresh lime greens and bold foliage. The flowers are, I think, secondary to the foliage – they are mustard yellow and borne in umbels.

The ordinary green form, *Foeniculum vulgare*, is also attractive and looks exceptional in naturalized types of perennial plantings. In winter its silhouette is good but then you may well find the plant becomes too pernicious, seeding and spreading too much for the garden's good. It occurs naturally in southern Europe, particularly in sunny, seaside areas.

This plant is a prolific self-seeder and its young seedlings put down deep, penetrating roots with terrific speed. If this is going to cause you problems (be warned – it usually does), it is well worth cutting off the flowering stems to prevent them setting seed. You can shear the whole plant down to the ground at this point as new foliage will be reinstated before the end of the season, giving a fresh new look to that part of the planting. **BG**

Foeniculum vulgare 'Purpureum'

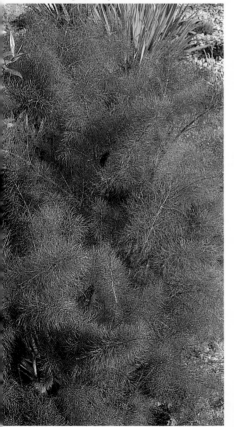

Forsythia x *intermedia* 'Karl Sax'

Forsythia x *intermedia* 'Karl Sax'
GOLDEN RAIN

Type: hardy, deciduous shrub
Soil & situation: moist, well-drained, fertile soil/sun or light shade
North American hardiness zone: 6–9
Height & spread: 2.5m (8ft)
Grow for: an abundance of yellow flowers from late winter to early spring

It has to be said forsythia is a common plant but only because it is easy to grow, flowers profusely every year and roots like a weed. I wish more plants were common! *Forsythia* x *intermedia* 'Karl Sax' in flower is slightly less well known. Its four-petalled flowers are a deep buttery yellow rather than a bright golden colour. They appear in late winter and continue making a show of themselves until mid-spring. The 10cm (4in) long, dull, mid-green leaves appear after the flowers and turn to shades of purple or red in autumn.

Forsythia is a surface-rooting shrub and benefits from an annual mulch in spring to retain moisture. I have seen mature plants wilt during a dry period but, being a professional performer, a drink soon revives them. Flowering on the previous year's growth it should be pruned immediately after flowering. Old plants can be rejuvenated by a severe pruning over two years, cutting half of the branches to within 30cm (12in) of the ground each spring. Propagation is by softwood cuttings in summer or hardwood during winter.

For early flowers for indoor arrangements cut branches as soon as the flower buds swell. Crush the base of the stem, place in water and they will open. **JC**

Forsythia x *intermedia* 'Lynwood'

Type: hardy, deciduous shrub
Soil & situation: fertile, well-drained soil/sun
North American hardiness zone: 6–9
Height & spread: 3m (10ft)
Grow for: bright yellow flowers in early and mid-spring; AGM

Tone down your forsythia, it's too loud! Start by planting the next one down the scale. *Forsythia* x *intermedia* 'Lynwood', a sport of *F.* x *i.* 'Spectabilis', is bold, but not as brash and slightly more refined; the large, rich yellow flowers are a vibrant, warming sight. It was discovered in a Miss Adair's cottage garden in Cookstown, Co. Tyrone, Northern Ireland in 1935 and I've seen it romantically described in French catalogues as 'Mimosa de Paris'. At the other end of the scale try *F. suspensa* or its form *atrocaulis,* with dark purple stems and pale yellow flowers. *F. giraldiana* has pale yellow flowers in late winter or early spring, while *F. ovata* reaches only 1.5m (5ft) tall.

Forsythia grows happily in most soils but prefers well-drained, fertile soil in full sun; flowering is reduced in shade, but it will flower on shady walls. Prune immediately after flowering, removing flowered stems to young, vigorous growth lower down the main stems and any thin or weak growth. If the plant is congested remove up to a third of the older stems at the base. Mulch in spring.

Propagate by semi-ripe cuttings in summer in a cold frame; or hardwood cuttings in winter, sealing the top and bottom of the stems with wax; plants layer naturally. Cut stems for the house for an earlier display will root in water and can be planted out by early summer. Forsythias suffer from galls and branches should be removed well below the gall. Spray if there is any sign of capsid bugs. If it is suffering from leaf spot, collect and dispose of leaves in autumn. **MB**

Forsythia x *intermedia* 'Lynwood'

Fragaria hybrids
Plant of the Week see page 233

Fragaria vesca
ALPINE STRAWBERRY

Type: hardy, herbaceous, semi-evergreen perennial
Soil & situation: any soil/sun or shade/moist or dry
North American hardiness zone: 5–9
Height & spread: 50cm (20in)
Grow for: cheerful foliage; small but pretty flowers; fruits all summer and autumn; good companion plant

Few plants flower for so long and, although these are only small plants with small flowers, they make very attractive, neat mounds of healthy foliage. *And* their delicious little fruits are produced for about half the year, without pause. Birds do not eat these fruits like they do the big ones, so they can be grown without nets or jars. I also love them as ground cover, for they are dense with bone dry centres much favoured by ground beetles and devil's coach-horses.

The alpine strawberry, unlike the wild strawberry of our woods, does not produce runners, but spreads everywhere by seed. This is not a problem as they are so useful and transplant easily. Natives of Europe, these have been improved by the French with varieties such as 'Baron Solemacher', but the standard sorts are wonderful enough anyway.

Fragaria vesca

They thrive in any soil, almost anywhere not bone dry and, besides, they only live for a few years. I pick the fruits over the entire season, freezing those I don't eat on the spot; once I have enough I shake the frozen berries to remove the seeds and then make them into the tastiest jam I know – try it! Sow in pots and plant out at any time; from then on move self-sown seedlings in early spring or autumn. Remove virus-infected, 'miffy'-looking plants to prevent the spread of disease and replace all old ones after a few years.   **BF**

Fraxinus ornus
MANNA ASH

Type: hardy, deciduous tree
Soil & situation: fertile, moist, well-drained, acid or alkaline soil/full sun
North American hardiness zone: 6–9
Height & spread: 15m (50ft)
Grow for: panicles of fragrant flowers; generally problem free; AGM

This tree is the source of manna sugar, a mild laxative obtained from the sap. It has no connection with the manna of the Old Testament which, incidentally, may have come from *Tamarix gallica*, a pink-flowering shrub that during the night exudes a honey-like nectar which solidifies on the ground.

A mature manna ash differs from other ash trees, forming a broad tree with a domed head. The grey bark is smooth and winter buds are fawn-brown rather than jet black. The pinnate, 20cm (8in)

Fraxinus ornus

long, glossy, dark green leaves are tulip-like as they unfurl. They are made up of five to nine leaflets turning an attractive, deep red-purple in early autumn. Large panicles of fragrant, creamy-white flowers are produced in late spring and early autumn. The flower also separates it from the common ash, *Fraxinus excelsior*, which, being wind pollinated, has no need for petals or scent.

In Europe, *F. ornus* is generally free of pests and diseases. Unfortunately in America it suffers from borers and oyster scale. The former may kill the tree but the scale is more troublesome than deadly. Propagate by bottom grafting onto common ash.   **JC**

Matt adds:
As there aren't many large trees with prominent flowers, it's a lovely surprise to see the abundance of blooms in late spring, appearing in large fragrant, creamy white clusters all over the tree. It's an amazing sight! Mulch young plants and water until established. Prune in late winter, particularly in the early years, so that only one leading stem develops. It can also be propagated from chilled seed in spring.

Fremontodendron californicum

Fremontodendron californicum
FLANNEL BUSH

Type: frost-hardy, evergreen shrub
Soil & situation: infertile, moist, well-drained, neutral to alkaline soil/full sun
North American hardiness zone: 8–10
Height: 6m (20ft)
Spread: 4m (13ft)
Grow for: excellent for a sunny wall; long flowering season

Given a warm wall, this is an easy shrub to grow and guaranteed to flower for longer than most of the opposition. Against a red brick wall it is as pretty as a picture. Fast growing, it forms an upright shrub.

The 5–10cm (2–4in) rounded, dark olive-green leaves have between three and seven lobes. The bright, buttercup-yellow, shallow, saucer-shaped flowers are 7.5cm (3in) across. The flower buds form immediately behind the newest growth and can be in flower within 10cm (4in) of the tip of the stems. Flowering kicks off in spring and goes on until late autumn. Its close neighbour from over the border, *Fremontodendron mexicanum*, is similar with slightly larger, deep golden-yellow flowers tinged an orange-red on the outside. As the flower dies it becomes a brick-yellow.

Plants which are growing very quickly will benefit from a liquid feed of high-potash fertilizer to harden up the growth before winter. Plant where there is protection from cold winds. Pruning is not usually necessary apart from training on wall wires or removing crossing branches and it should be carried out in winter before growth commences.

Propagation is by seed in spring. Softwood cuttings root readily in early summer. The young shoots and backs of the leaves are coated with a mealy grit which is a skin irritant. **JC**

Fritillaria imperialis
Plant of the Week (see page 135)

Fritillaria meleagris
SNAKE'S HEAD FRITILLARY

Type: hardy, perennial bulb
Soil & situation: moist, rich soil/sun or shade
North American hardiness zone: 3–8
Height: 30cm (12in)
Spread: 15cm (6in)
Grow for: unique claret-red to purple flowers with distinctive whitish-green variegation; the only bloom that has a chequer-board pattern

This is a beautiful flower, fragile and delicate with a most delightful patterning that makes you wonder why? It is easy in moist sites but not happy in dry, windswept spots so I have to go to great pains to keep them going in my Norfolk garden. Of course, although I found it hard to grow deliberately, one managed to self-sow and grow a bulb to flowering size beside a leaky water butt, which only seems to indicate its desired conditions.

A European native, it used to be common but is now found wild only in a few sites. The name obviously refers to the unique pattern, though it once was also known as the guinea hen flower for the same reason. The pattern is not actually truly square in most cases and there are also some plain white ones.

It needs a moist, rich soil, as in water meadows, and prefers really damp conditions during the growing season, plus lashings of leafmould as a mulch. It can be grown from seed in pots in a cold frame and planted out later, or plant bulbs in autumn. Voles steal flowers and eat them – I should know as I've had it happen. **BF**

Fritillaria meleagris

Fuchsia spp.

Fuchsia spp.

Type: frost-hardy to hardy, woody, perennial shrub
Soil & situation: any soil/sun or shade/loves moisture
North American hardiness zone: varies according to species, but roughly 7–10 (some more tender species 9–10)
Height & spread: depends on local climate, some may reach 1.8–2.2m (6–7ft) each way
Grow for: very good value as the cheerful white, scarlet, red and violet or purple flowers bloom from summer until the end of the year, plus the berries are edible

Most flowering shrubs are blooming in spring but far fewer are good from mid-summer through to the frosts, and there aren't many so easy to keep compact enough to grow in pots or even hanging baskets. In the mildest areas hardy fuchsias remain shrubs and are often used for a hedge. In such mild climates wet soil seems not to be a problem and the plant may become almost evergreen. They also remain evergreen under cover, when they often last in fair condition until growth starts again. Many sorts do not set very many berries but when they do these can be collected and used to make a good jelly. I wish someone would breed a sweet, big berried, hardy form – with scent!

Originally from South America, fuchsias took the early 19th-century gardeners by storm; the colours and robustness of the plants amazed

them and still does us. There are hundreds, if not thousands of indoor tender varieties and many of these will survive outdoors; even if cut down by frosts they will come back from their roots, if these are well protected.

Unless the soil is free draining fuchsias may rot while dormant. For over-wintering success choose a warm, sheltered spot. Trim back when the first frosts take off foliage and cover roots with loose straw or bracken in colder areas. The seed is minute and not easy to get to set or to germinate, and the young plants damp off easily; luckily each and every cutting is likely to take. Under cover the young plants are prone to aphids and whitefly, but when they go outdoors for summer these pests are no longer a problem. **BF**

Fuchsia magellanica 'Riccartonii'

Type: hardy, deciduous shrub
Soil & situation: fertile, moist, well-drained soil/full sun
North American hardiness zone: 7–10
Height: 2.5m (8ft)
Spread: 2m (6½ft)
Grow for: exquisite flowers and in a sheltered area may be grown as a hedge; AGM

The beauty of living on an island is the amount of coastline. As islands go the climate of Ireland is quite mild. When you combine these two facts you have a place where *F. magellanica* 'Riccartonii' grows like a weed. It forms high natural hedges and in Counties Down, Donegal and Mayo is accepted as part of the rural scene.

It forms an upright shrub with dark green, bronze-tinted leaves. The single flower is typically 'ballet dancer' shape with a scarlet tube and sepals. The 'under skirt' of the corollas is purple.

Fuchsia magellanica 'Riccartonii'

Fuchsia procumbens

Although it is deciduous, the mass of bare winter twigs provides considerable shelter by filtering the wind. Plants that have suffered from hard frosts may look dead but if they are left undisturbed until early summer they generally produce new shoots from the base. The dead branches can then be cut back and the new shoots allowed to take their place. A deep, dry mulch of coarse bark over the crown of the plant in winter will be sufficient protection in all but the coldest areas or where the soil is heavy and damp.

Propagation is by softwood cuttings in early summer. Semi-ripe cuttings can be rooted in autumn in a propagator with bottom heat. Autumn-rooted cuttings should be left undisturbed until the following spring after they have come into leaf. **JC**

Fuchsia procumbens

Type: half-hardy, deciduous scrambler
Soil & situation: fertile, free-draining soil/sun
North American hardiness zone: 9–10
Height: 15cm (6in)
Spread: 1.2m (4ft)
Grow for: pretty flowers and fruits in summer

This trailing or creeping fuchsia is worth growing for its novelty value and unusual coloured flowers, though you will need a magnifying glass to study them closely! It is a fine example of the diversity of fuchsias and the fascinating flora of New Zealand. You'd perhaps expect it to be a shrub, but it's a carpeting species that scrambles over the ground. Its tiny leaves are a rounded heart shape only 2cm (³/₄in) long. In summer it produces small flowers with greenish-yellow tubes that fade to banana-yellow then pale orange. Purple-tipped green sepals take the place of the petals. The stamens, when mature, release bright blue pollen and the flowers are followed by vivid red fruit, like tiny plums, with a glaucous 'bloom'. It's found on the North Island coastline in rocky, sandy places right on the shore above the high-tide mark, so it's no surprise that it is a good rockery and maritime plant.

Fuchsia excorticata, also from New Zealand, is a deciduous shrub with attractive papery bark, green and purple flower tubes and blue pollen.

Fuchsia procumbens needs a sheltered position in full sun or partial shade on moist, fertile, well-drained soil. Plant the base of the stem 5cm (2in) below the soil surface, mulch in winter. Shelter from cold, drying winds or grow in pots in cooler climate; it is frost tender and ideal for sheltered gardens. In pots, feed monthly when in growth with a liquid general fertilizer. Grow from seed and cuttings. Take cuttings annually in autumn in case plants are lost.   **MB**

Galactites tomentosa

Type: annual or biennial
Soil & situation: any free-draining soil, light or heavy, slightly acid or calcareous/self-seeds into waste ground, gravel cracks in pavements or wherever/sunny position/ tolerates some shade
North American hardiness zone: usually grown as an annual
Height & spread: up to 1m (3ft)
Grow for: exquisite evergreen foliage; fetching thistle-like pink-purple flowers in summer

Galactites tomentosa

This is possibly my favourite biennial and I haven't a clue why everybody does not have it.

The broad, thistle-like leaves are beautifully marked: the background is dark green and it has eccentric veining patterns picked out in pale verdigris. They form decent-sized rosettes, about 30cm (12in) across, sometimes more, often less. Beautifully evergreen, these rosettes crop up out of gaps in paving you did not think existed. They are surprisingly spiny. Then in mid-summer, or whenever it feels like it, it shoots up into flower with its perfect, thistle-like flowers. Another of its virtues is that it is not so prolific as to drive you mad, but I hope, prolific enough for you to keep and enjoy for ever. It was given to me by Molly Wheatley, a renowned local gardener with an interesting garden in Clipsham.

I suppose if it did ever get a little out of hand you could cut off the flowers as they were about to set seed, but I have never had to do this. I just leave it to do its own thing totally, and simply follow it around and see what new sites it has recently acquired. Its a useful plant for taking to friends as, no matter whether they are keen or indifferent gardeners, it is easy to grow and easy to appreciate. But do transplant it into a pot when it is very small as it has a long tap root.   **BG**

Galanthus reginae-olgae subsp. *reginae-olgae*

Type: hardy, bulbous perennial
Soil & situation: moist, free-draining soil/some sunshine
North American hardiness zone: 6–9
Height: 10cm (4in)
Spread: 5cm (2in)
Grow for: fragrant flowers in mid- and late autumn

This, the earliest flowering snowdrop, comes from southern Greece. At one time it was called 'Octobrensis' because it flowers so early, before the delicate leaves which are marked with a single silver stripe. It is dainty, delicate, absolutely beautiful and needs a warmer, sunnier, more sheltered position than most snowdrops. Plant with *Cyclamen hederifolium* (see page 136) and they will flower at the same time. Mix sharp sand and leafmould to improve the drainage if necessary. It should be kept quite dry during summer dormancy; at the front of a sunny border is ideal. Plant at 5cm (2in), but if the soil is very light go down to 8cm (3½in).

Galanthus reginae-olgae subsp. *reginae-olgae*

Divide and replant after flowering. Slugs and snails can damage petals and grey mould the foliage. Remove badly infected bulbs and dispose of them or drench them with fungicide and replant elsewhere.

Someone once said to me, 'All snowdrops look the same to me'. Wrong! Here's a few examples of different shapes, sizes and colours.

Galanthus reginae-olgae subsp. *vernalis* has a silver striped leaf; it appears early in the New Year and lasts for about four weeks. *G. plicatus* 'Wendy's Gold' has good size and vigour for a yellow snowdrop. The colour of its petals and ovary is acid yellow. *G.* 'Hippolyta' is double flowered and has more than one flower per stem. *G. nivalis* 'Lady Elphinstone' is double with a pale apricot ovary and markings. *G. n.* 'Viridapicis' has green markings on both its outer and inner petals. *G.* x *allenii* smells of bitter almonds.   **MB**

Arisaema sikokianum

COBRA LILY

Type: frost-hardy, tuberous perennial
Soil & situation: moist, humus-rich soil/dappled shade
Hardiness zone: 5–9
Height: 60cm (24in)
Spread: 15cm (6in)
Grow for: extraordinary leaves and flowers, at their weirdest in late spring

'Only blokes buy arisaemas,' the nurseryman told me. Perhaps he'd already spotted the distant look in my eyes and was moving in for the kill. I'd picked up several pots that day and only bought one, but now, the more I see, the more I weaken! My dream is to become rich enough to plant drifts of *A. sikokianum* through a woodland garden; it is a typical case of *Arisaema* addiction!

Look at the picture and you may understand why I'm vulnerable; if you do, then you are too! The hood is delicately marked and deep chocolate brown suffused with green, but the most extraordinary features are the thick, club-like spadix and throat, painted in pure, glossy, brilliant white. Aren't they amazing?

Here are a few of the many species. *A. candidissimum* is hardy and attractive with pale pink flowers with a white striped cowl, produced just before the leaves; it tolerates sun and shade; the leaves do not emerge until early summer. *A. consanguineum* has a dark purple spathe with white pinstripes and is up to 20cm (8in) long. It does best in semi-shade. *A. griffithii* is dark and sinister, deeply veined, has a broad hood and is positively reptilian!

Plant in dappled shade in humus-rich, well-drained soil. Add plenty of well-rotted leafmould or organic matter before planting about 15cm (6in) deep. They need protection from frost early in the year; mulch over winter with well-rotted organic matter. Propagate from seed in autumn or by detaching offsets, which may form on the tubers. **MB**

Galanthus 'S. Arnott'
SNOWDROP

Type: hardy, bulbous perennial
Soil & situation: moist, well-drained soil with added leafmould/partial shade
North American hardiness zone: 4–9
Height: 20cm (8in)
Spread: 8cm (3½in)
Grow for: early fragrant flowers that tolerate frost, snow, wind and rain; AGM

For me snowdrops are not so much harbingers of spring as a useful reminder that the worst of the winter is still to come. I love all snowdrops but 'Sam Arnott', as it is sometimes called, is a favourite. It exudes a strong honey fragrance which, on a calm winter's day, is a delight in any garden. This is one of the snowdrops much admired by galanthophiles.

The grey-green foliage appears in early winter growing to 15cm (6in) in height. The large, rounded, pure white flowers, 3–3.5cm (1–1¼in) long, are carried on 20cm (8in) stems. They have an inverted green 'v' mark on each of the inner tepals (petals). It manages to look delicate and frail yet it is as tough as old boots, tolerating extreme winter weather.

Avoid planting in soil which dries out in summer. Dig in leafmould and well-rotted farmyard manure to help retain moisture. Snowdrops self-seed and spread quickly but are often reluctant to grow from dry bulbs purchased in autumn. Lift and transplant the bulbs 'in the green' when they are still in leaf. **JC**

Galanthus 'S. Arnott'

Galega orientalis

Galega orientalis

Type: hardy, rhizomatous perennial
Soil & situation: prefers moist soils, but grows fairly well in drier, poorer soils/sun or part shade
North American hardiness zone: 5–8
Height: up to 1.2m (4ft) high
Spread: 60cm (24in)
Grow for: intense violet-blue flower spikes produced from mid- to late summer

This is an extremely rewarding plant to grow. It thrives (probably a bit too much) on moist soils and in these conditions may be considered invasive, spreading by creeping underground rhizomes. But otherwise, in a drier soil, it is a gentle, good-natured plant that performs well (Legumes are usually a good bet for poorer conditions). The flower spikes are held upright, making the beautiful, long-lasting (a good month or so) flowers more prominent. The foliage is deeply divided and forms a good substantial mass. My mother grows repeated clumps of it through a throng of apricot-flowered shrub roses and the colour combination works exceptionally well. She divides her galega every two years, to keep it at its best. Other gardeners just seem to leave it growing untouched for years, the excuse being that legumes are not that agreeable to being moved. But I think it is such a good doer that the check goes pretty well unnoticed.

This will need regular division if you want to keep it in check in richer soil conditions. Otherwise it really requires little looking after, except for cutting it down in winter or spring and dividing it up when the mood takes you. Propagation is by division but it does set seed and from my experience seems to come true from seed. Soaking the seed for 12 hours or so speeds up the process. **BG**

Galium odoratum
SWEET WOODRUFF

Type: hardy, rhizomatous perennial
Soil & situation: frequently occurs on alkaline soils but does tolerate a range of pH/cool, shady situation/tolerates dry conditions/becomes scorched in sunshine
North American hardiness zone: 5–8
Height: 45cm (18in)
Spread: indefinite
Grow for: superb native plant that will colonize the wilder parts of the garden with a thick carpet of attractive vegetation; clusters of small, starry, white flowers from late spring to mid-summer enjoyed by bees and butterflies

This is one of my favourite native wild flowers. It used to be called *Asperula odorata*, because it contains asperuloside – even if you do not recognize the name, you will the smell. It produces a compound which gives rise to one of the best smells in the world – that of new-mown hay – as the foliage dries. Try picking some and hanging it up to dry. It wafts out that wonderful fragrance, but only when dry, not just for one year but for several. Vita Sackville-West recommended making bags of it to hang in your cupboards to keep moths away or sleeping with it under your pillow. It certainly beats a well-used tissue.

The leaves are bright emerald green, lance-shaped and produced in whorls. The flowers are borne in large quantities, and while they are not showy, they are definitely appealing. It is the sort of plant to grow where not much else will grow: in the shade or under the drip of trees where it will colonize the space and stop weeds coming through.

If you require quantities of it, seed is ideal or else you can divide it and every bit of root will grow. **BG**

Galium odoratum

Gardenia augusta

Gardenia augusta (syn. G. florida, G. jasminoides)

CAPE JASMINE, FLORISTS' GARDENIA.

Type: tender, evergreen shrub
Soil & situation: loamy, lime-free compost/light shade/under cover
North American hardiness zone: 8–10
Height & spread: 2m (6½ft) each way, if you are patient and lucky
Grow for: gorgeous flowers with fantastic perfume on glossy evergreen foliage; AGM

Gardenia has one of the most opulently luscious perfumes, almost decadent in its undertones yet, somehow, retaining a sense of purity. The flowers are like miniature loose cabbage roses with layers of creamy-white petals, and the leaves behind them are so glossy and richly green. They make exquisite conservatory subjects along with citrus

(see pages 104–105), as they need similar conditions and their perfumes complement each other. I must admit, they are hard to grow on from the forced specimens you can buy, but once re-established in a new home they are immensely rewarding with flowers from summer until winter.

Named by Linnaeus after a Dr Garden of Charleston, it's a big genus with mostly tropical members which are nearly all evergreen trees and shrubs, although several are used as houseplants. It needs lime-free, leafmould-rich compost kept moist but never wet, in a humid atmosphere and light shade such as under citrus trees. Mist regularly and, if necessary, disbud to preserve the shape. Never move a gardenia!

The species can be grown from seed. Control red spider mite by misting and using commercially supplied predators. Bud drop is best prevented by misting and not moving the plant. **BF**

Garrya elliptica 'James Roof'

SILK TASSEL BUSH

Type: frost-hardy, evergreen shrub
Soil & situation: moderately fertile, well-drained soil/full sun or light shade
North American hardiness zone: 8–10
Height & spread: 4m (13ft)
Grow for: eye-catching clusters of catkins from winter to spring; AGM

This is one of a group of shrubs ignored by passersby for most of the year, but when they 'dress up' everyone takes notice. It has an upright habit, making it ideal as a free-standing shrub for planting in front of a wall. The leathery, dark sea-green leaves form a perfect backdrop for the pendent, dense clusters of silver-grey male catkins. These can be up to 20cm (8in) long, made up of hundreds of petalless flowers. They appear in mid-winter and last until early spring. Male and female catkins are on separate plants, the female being less noticeable but producing purple-brown berries in summer.

Garrya elliptica 'James Roof' is tolerant of poor, dry soil (usually to be found at the base of a wall) but dislikes cold, biting winds. When grown as a hedge it forms a great shelter for a seaside garden. Pruning is carried out after flowering and is only necessary to keep the plant in shape. Propagate by seed sown in autumn or by short, semi-ripe cuttings in a gritty compost in summer. *G. e.* 'Evie' is also a male variety with crinkly leaves and catkins 30cm (12in) long. **JC**

Garrya elliptica 'James Roof'

Gaultheria mucronata (syn. *Pernettya mucronata*)

Type: hardy, evergreen shrub
Soil & situation: peaty, moist, neutral to acid soil/partial shade
North American hardiness zone: 8–9
Height & spread: 1.2m (4ft)
Grow for: glossy foliage, pretty flowers and eye-catching fruit

A great plant which isn't afraid to show off its fruit in a range of colours set against dark green leaves which, in size, are no competition. It is necessary to grow male and female plants together to guarantee fruit.

It forms a bushy, compact, suckering plant with small, sharp-pointed, glossy, dark green leaves. Pendent, urn-shaped, white or pink-tinged flowers appear in late spring and early summer. They are followed, in autumn, by fruits which often persist through winter until the next season's flowers appear. Colours range from white, pink, red and crimson to deep purple-red. *Gaultheria mucronata* 'Wintertime' has pure white fruit and *G. m.* 'Edward Balls', which is male, has light green leaves.

Full sun is tolerated where the ground is constantly moist. It can be grown as an ornamental, informal hedge by lightly clipping the plants after they have finished flowering. Propagation is by semi-ripe cuttings in summer, though a quicker method is to dig up the rooted suckers in spring. Line them out in a moist shaded site for a year before planting in their permanent positions. **JC**

Gaultheria mucronata

Gaultheria procumbens

Gaultheria procumbens
CHEQUER BERRY, WINTERGREEN, TEA BERRY

Type: hardy, creeping ground cover
Soil & situation: moist, acid soil/shade to full sun
North American hardiness zone: 3–9
Height : 15cm (6in) or more
Spread: 90cm (36in) or more
Grow for: evergreen leaves; flowers in mid- and late summer; bright red winter berries; AGM

This is one of my favourite shrubs. For some reason it makes me smile, particularly when it's fruiting. Perhaps it's a response to the bright red berries; it must be a cheerful, happy plant so I should be happy too! The elliptic leaves sprout from creeping stems that spread to create a lush, deep textured carpet of dark, glossy green. In mid- and late summer it produces masses of lily-of-the-valley-like, urn-shaped, white or pale pink flowers followed by aromatic bright scarlet fruit to 1cm (½in) across, remaining until spring. Oil, extracted from the plant, possesses stimulating and tonic properties; the same oil is found in a birch, *Betula lenta*, and is used for Deep Heat, a muscle-relaxing cream, and other similar products. The crushed leaves smell strongly of Germoline, an antiseptic cream. Partridges like to eat the berries – they must be hungry; I can confirm that they taste as bad as they smell!

It is a native of eastern North America and makes excellent ground cover in moist, acid soil in shade and a container plant for winter displays with skimmias and heathers. It needs moist, acid soil, enriched with leafmould, peat substitute or well-rotted organic matter, in a sheltered, shady position. It tolerates full sun with extra moisture. Mulch in spring, water with rainwater and feed monthly with a fertilizer for acid-loving plants. Prune to remove dead wood and weak growths whenever they appear. Trim to keep it within its allotted space. Propagate by seed, division or semi-ripe cuttings from mid-summer. **MB**

Gazania Daybreak Series

Type: half-hardy, evergreen perennial
Soil & situation: light, sandy, well-drained soil/full sun
North American hardiness zone: normally grown as an annual
Height: 20cm (8in)
Spread: 30cm (12in)
Grow for: stunning flowers; a great plant for the patio

Unfortunately I have to grow this plant as an annual or else go to a lot of trouble molly-coddling it over the winter. It is well worth the expense of new seed each year with spectacular flower colour in summer and autumn. It is ideal in containers for patio use and it is one of the best plants for use in a coastal bedding display.

The 15cm (6in) long, glossy, dark green leaves are silky white on the underside. Flowering commences in early summer with short-stemmed, solitary flowerheads in a blaze of colours including white, yellow, orange, pink and bronze. Often they are zoned in contrasting colours such as white-pink and orange-bronze.

Although the Daybreak Series is my favourite, members of the Talent Series have a lot going for them too – they are vigorous with silvery leaves and a good range of colours. 'Talent Yellow' is a deep yellow, flowering at 25cm (10in) high.

Dead-head immediately after flowering to prolong the display. Propagation is by seed sown in a heated propagator in late winter. Take basal cuttings in autumn in a free-draining, gritty compost. Overwinter the rooted cuttings and do not pot on until spring. **JC**

Gazania Daybreak Series

Genista lydia

Genista lydia
BROOM

Type: hardy, deciduous shrub
Soil & situation: impoverished, light, well-drained soil/full sun
North American hardiness zone: 6–9
Height: 60cm (24in)
Spread: 90cm (36in)
Grow for: form and colour that will brighten up the border; AGM

Whether you want it to or not, *Genista lydia* always forms itself into a dense, compact mound. A single plant appears to have been clipped into shape. When planted as a group at 1m (3ft) spacing and in flower they resemble a lovely, large, bright, golden-yellow inkblot. The slender, grey-green, arching branches are pointed at the tip with thin, blue-green leaves. In late spring and early summer it produces masses of bright yellow, pea-like flowers which smother the plant.

Another excellent genista, which will spread to 1.5m (5ft), is *G. hispanica*, the Spanish gorse. It forms a dense mound of spiny stems, covered in golden-yellow flowers in early summer.

G. lydia performs best in a poor, undernourished, free-draining soil. It does not thrive in a heavy clay or badly drained soil. Avoid feeding or mulching. It tends to be a short-lived plant, but its useful life can be extended by annual pruning to remove the previous year's growth as soon as it has finished flowering. Don't cut into the older wood. Propagation is by semi-ripe cuttings in summer in a gritty compost. **JC**

Gentiana acaulis
TRUMPET GENTIAN

Type: hardy, evergreen perennial
Soil & situation: moist, humus-rich, well-drained, alkaline soil/sun or partial shade
North American hardiness zone: 5–8
Height: 8cm (3½in)
Spread: 30cm (12in)
Grow for: the most vivid blue flowers – a must; AGM

Anyone who dislikes gentians has got a problem. Even those unfortunates who find them difficult to grow keep on trying in the hope that gentians will come to like them. Quickly forming a dense mat of pointed, glossy, dark green rosettes of leaves, in late spring and early summer it produces single, 5cm (2in) long, trumpet-shaped flowers, a deep, vivid blue, spotted green on the inside. Flowering may be erratic, seemingly having an occasional 'off year'.

In areas lucky enough to have long periods of bright sun, site the plants in light shade, but in cool, damp climates they will need all the sunshine they can get. Propagate by fresh seed sown in autumn and overwintered in a cold frame or unheated greenhouse. Clumps may be divided in spring but it is essential they are planted firmly in reliably moist soil with added leafmould and grit. Watch out for attacks by slugs and snails. A collar of coarse grit around the plants will offer some protection. **JC**

Gentiana acaulis

Gentiana asclepiadea

Gentiana asclepiadea
WILLOW GENTIAN

Type: hardy perennial
Soil & situation: deep, moist, humus-rich soil/dappled to full shade
North American hardiness zone: 6–9
Height: 90cm (36in)
Spread: 60cm (24in)
Grow for: elegant arching stems of flowers from late summer to early autumn; AGM

This delightful gentian with elegant willow-like leaves has been grown in gardens in the UK since 1629. It's a small, bushy plant with graceful, arching stems and leaves in pairs. Clusters of two to three deep blue flowers, sometimes with a white throat, project from the leaf joints towards the top of the stems. It's perfect for borders, large rock gardens or naturalized in woodland. It is reliable, long lived and very, very beautiful.

Reginald Farrer, a writer, plant collector and tough-talking Yorkshireman, was also renowned for his lyrical prose and described it thus: '…flowers like a summer sky at dawn…its long, bending sheaves of graceful blossom make a famous loveliness in late summer…inclining this way and that beneath the burden of its beautiful sapphire trumpets'. He was obviously besotted!

The specific name comes from the Latinized form of the name of the Greek god of medicine, Aesculapius; he was usually portrayed with Hygieia, the goddess of wise living, and Panakeia, goddess of cure-alls. Gentian root has long been used as a tonic.

There are several forms of this lovely plant. *G. asclepiadea* var. *alba* has white flowers with greenish-cream throats. *G. a.* 'Knightshayes' has deeper blue flowers and a more upright habit. There are also pink, pale blue and yellow selections.

They flourish in dappled to full shade in cool, deep, moist, humus-rich soil and are lime tolerant. Water during dry periods, and cut back the stems and mulch with well-rotted organic matter in spring. Take basal cuttings in spring.
MB

Gentiana sino-ornata

Type: hardy perennial
Soil & situation: moist, acid soil/bright light
North American hardiness zone: 5–7
Height: 7cm (2³⁄₄in)or more
Spread: 30cm (12in) or more
Grow for: azure-blue flowers from early autumn to early winter; AGM

Gentiana sino-ornata

I'll never forget the first time I saw the magnificent display at Sheffield Park in Sussex, southeast England, where a green carpet of foliage was almost submerged in a sea of deep blue, white-striped, trumpet-shaped flowers. This delicate beauty comes from northwest Yunnan and Tibet where it grows in wet ground high in the mountains, where only the strong survive. The colour is mesmeric, life's not the same without them, and every time I see them I suffer another case of the blues!

It needs moist, acid soil and can be planted among paving slabs or in drifts at the front of borders. On alkaline soil, make your own compost using peat substitute or well-rotted leafmould and grit and grow them in shallow pans, pots, troughs, raised beds or 'acid' pockets in rock gardens; surely there's some space in your garden. It associates well with rhododendrons.

Grow in bright light and in humus-rich, moist, well-drained neutral to acid soil on an open site away from the 'drip line' of trees. Keep the compost moist using rainwater. Plant in spring, or autumn when it is in flower; handle it carefully as it resents root disturbance. Divide in early or mid-spring. It dies back in winter to fleshy 'crowns'.

Aphids, red spider mite, slugs and snails can be a problem. Gentian rust causes brown spotting on the leaves; remove infected stems immediately, spray with fungicide, destroy badly infected plants. Take off dead or damaged material in spring with a sharp knife to reduce problems with pests and diseases.   **MB**

Geranium himalayense 'Gravetye'

Type: hardy, evergreen perennial
Soil & situation: huge variety of soils, except ones that dry out or are waterlogged/sun or partial shade
North American hardiness zone: 4–7
Height: 30cm (12in)
Spread: 60cm (24in)
Grow for: highly useful, long-flowering geranium in summer; neat, attractive evergreen foliage; AGM

It is easy to be perplexed by the many hardy geraniums. Most of us include one or several different ones in our garden but I think this is one of the best. It has very divided leaves and it slowly spreads to form neat mats. The flowers are a good, clear blue fading to white at the centre

Geranium himalayense 'Gravetye'

and they attract bees and butterflies. Two reasons that this plant stands out are the length of the flowering period and the most agreeable-looking flowers.

After flowering it is best to cut the foliage right back, which will stimulate new, fresh-looking leaves, and most likely, another crop of flowers. It can be propagated by seed or division. **BG**

Geranium phaeum
MOURNING WIDOW

Type: herbaceous perennial
Soil & situation: any soil/sun or shade
North American hardiness zone: 4–8
Height & spread: rounded clumps to 50cm (20in)
Grow for: good ground cover and distinctive purple, almost black flowers over many weeks

Also called the dusky geranium or dusky cranesbill, this excellent and reliable plant has deeply toothed, lobed leaves which always look healthy. Some strains have an attractive blotch in the middle of the leaf. Above the neat foliage it displays a profusion of blackish-purple, flat, crinkley-edged flowers for many weeks. It will grow in almost any soil or site, and makes good ground cover in front of wall trees or for filling large areas that need a fairly low but neat and attractive plant. It combines well with *Alchemilla mollis* (see page 33), which it resembles in form and height and complements in colour. The genus gets its name from the Greek for cranes, *geranion,* for the resemblance its carpels bear to cranes' beaks.

It seems to do well anywhere – in both dry and moist spots, and in sun or shade, but prefers moist shade. It can be grown from seed, in pots or a seedbed, and it's easy to divide in spring or autumn. It suffers from no problems at all. **BF**

Geranium psilostemon
ARMENIAN CRANESBILL

Type: hardy, herbaceous perennial
Soil & situation: many types of soils/sun or shade
North American hardiness zone: 5–8
Height: 60–120cm (2–4ft)
Spread: 60cm (24in)
Grow for: vivid magenta flowers produced over a long period in summer; uninspiring but worthwhile delicately cut, bright green foliage, red in spring and colouring up again in autumn; AGM

There are many acceptable geraniums to choose from but I tend to use *G. psilostemon* far more than most. I think this is because many herbaceous geraniums tend to be background fillers that you stroll past, whereas this one will make you stop in your tracks. It is taller than many geraniums, too, which also makes it more noticeable. The flowers have a black centre and veins which enhances the strident colour of the petals. Because it has quite a bold presence it is a useful plant to grow in repeated clumps in a border as a cohesive element. It is also well adapted to growing in rough grassy areas, due to its height and vigour.

If the plant looks a little tatty after flowering, cut it down to the ground and then it will regenerate and possibly give you a good repeat flowering. It can be easily propagated by division, basal cuttings or seed. **BG**

Geranium phaeum

Geranium psilostemon

Geranium renardii

Type: hardy, herbaceous perennial
Soil & situation: most soils/ sun or shade
North American hardiness zone: 6–8
Height & spread: 30cm (12in)
Grow for: beautiful softly textured leaves in deep grey to olive green, with a prominent mosaic of veins; white or bluish flowers in early summer; AGM

I frequently use this plant having been inspired by it at Hidcote. There they use it in large drifts and the low grey-green olive mounds of foliage look simple but stunning. The flowers are a pleasant extra, also quite simple, but they do have conspicuous blue veins. There is apparently an excellent selection of this plant called *G. renardii* 'Whiteknights', the name commemorating the campus of the University of Reading, where it originated. This plant is said to have exceptional grey, felted foliage and impressive lilac-blue flowers. It is on my list. The other geranium I use predominantly for foliage is 'Ann Folkard'; this has lush, golden-green, young leaves followed by bright purple flowers which are freely produced. Cut away any tatty foliage in autumn or spring. It is easily propagated by division, basal cuttings or seed. **BG**

Geranium renardii

Agrostemma githago

June

CORN COCKLE

Type: hardy annual
Soil & situation: poor, dry soil/sun
Hardiness zone: annual
Height: 90cm (36in)
Spread: 30cm (12in)
Grow for: flowers from early to late summer

Is it right to try to rationalize the reasons why I adore this flower? As with many emotions, it's easier to accept that attraction in any form is indefinable, the same 'must have' desire that makes people fall for anything; art, gardens – even each other! In this case I'm beguiled by the sleek willowy elegance of the stems up to 90cm (36in) long that sway gracefully in the caressing breeze; seduced by the shape and colour of the delicately flecked, magenta-purple flowers balancing like saucers on top of stiff stems; and enchanted by the elegant narrow sepals. In other words, I go weak in the presence of beauty!

In times past it was persecuted as a cornfield weed because the bitter seeds tainted flour, but it is now very rare in the wild. It is a good nectar plant for insects and butterflies, the perfect plant for cottage gardens; the flowers are excellent for cutting and the seeds are short-lived. It was originally introduced to the UK with grain from the eastern Mediterranean.

There are several cultivars, including *Agrostemma githago* 'Milas,' with dark plum-pink flowers; 'Ocean Pearl', with white flowers flecked with black; and 'Pink Pearl', with soft, pale pink flowers.

Dead-head to prolong flowering, but allow a last seed crop to self-sow. It prefers poor, well-drained soil in full sun but survives in most moderate to light soils. Sow *in situ* in early spring, thinning to 23–30cm (9–12in) apart. For containers, sow in autumn, over-winter in a cold frame and plant out the following spring. The seeds are toxic.   **MB**

Gilia tricolor

Gilia tricolor
BIRD'S EYES

Type: annual
Soil & situation: any dryish soil/full sun
North American hardiness zone: annual
Height: may reach 60cm (24in), but often only half as much
Spread: 15–30cm (6–12in)
Grow for: excellent filler; very pretty; totally reliable; problem-free; and a funny scent

Bird's eyes is often given to children as it is so easy. A good filler for gaps seen in spring and an excellent bloomer, it bears masses of cheerful (yellow-inside, violet-purple-outside) flowers for weeks with almost no care or attention. I first grew this as it was alleged by a perfidious seedsman to have the scent of chocolate. In trials I conducted the commonest description given was of 'burning rubber' or by some as 'a mint chocolate dropped on a barbecue!' Do not let this put you off; it is a lovely little gem.

The genus was for some unknown reason named after an obscure 18th-century Italian astronomer. There are about 120 species, all natives of North America, and this sweet plant comes from California, where it carpets the wild hillsides with flowers all summer.

It is obliging and will grow almost anywhere, but does best on a loamy soil with plenty of space to each plant. Sow *in situ* in spring. It is easy and has no problems.   **BF**

Ginkgo biloba
MAIDENHAIR TREE

Type: hardy, deciduous conifer
Soil & situation: fertile, well-drained soil/sun
North American hardiness zone: 5–9
Height: 30m (100ft)
Spread: 8m (25ft)
Grow for: bright green leaves; long life; lovely autumn colour; AGM

Think about this fact. This tree was growing quite happily over 160 million years ago. The notched leaves with fan-shaped veins are found as rock fossils in many countries, including England (near Scarborough in Yorkshire), and are identical to the leaves produced today. The pale green 12cm (5in) wide leaves are pendulous on long stalks with deep notches that almost split the young leaves. In autumn they slowly turn to a beautiful butter-yellow, providing a variegated appearance until all the green fades.

Male plants produce 7.5cm (3in) long, yellow catkins at the same time as the new leaves appear. The female flowers are small and pale green. They are followed by plum-shaped, green-yellow fruits, which when ripe have a most unpleasant smell. The variety *G. biloba* 'Princeton Sentry' is more upright, with a height of 20m (66ft) and a spread of 5m (16ft). It is a male variety with no fruit and no bad smell.

It is quick growing in a moist, fertile, well-drained soil in full sun. It can tolerate an exposed, windy situation. Propagation is by seed sown as soon as it is ripe. Semi-ripe cuttings will root in summer.
                                                                    JC

Ginkgo biloba

Gladiolus callianthus

Gladiolus callianthus
(syn. *Acidanthera murieliae*)

Type: half-hardy, cormous perennial
Soil & situation: fertile, well-drained soil/full sun
North American hardiness zone: normally grown as an annual
Height: 60–90cm (24–36in)
Spread: 20cm (8in)
Grow for: a wonderful display of highly fragrant spikes of white flowers in late summer

I preferred it when it was called *Acidanthera*. It doesn't really look like gladioli as I think of them. It is deliciously delicate-looking with scented flowers that dance in the slightest breeze. It makes a great display in a container for a patio, or in a cool conservatory where its perfume fills the room.

The 30–45cm (12–18in) long, linear leaves are dark green. The flowers appear in late summer and autumn as loose spikes with up to ten flowers per stem. They are 5cm (2in) wide, pure white, with a deep, purple-crimson centre and have a wonderful fragrance. Funnel-shaped, they dangle on long, pale pink tubes.

Plant the corms 15cm (6in) deep on a bed of sand to aid drainage. After flowering remove the stem. When the foliage turns yellow dig the corms, dry them off and store in a frost-proof shed over winter. Propagation by seed is slow, taking up to five years to flower. Separate cormlets from the side of the corm when lifting and grow in containers until they are the size to flower, usually after three years.   **JC**

Gladiolus papilio

Type: hardy, stoloniferous perennial
Soil & situation: moist soil/sun
North American hardiness zone: normally grown as an annual
Height: 90cm (36in)
Spread: 8cm (3½in)
Grow for: subtle flowers from late summer to mid-autumn

Well possums! Dame Edna Everage and Morrissey from the rock band The Smiths love gladioli for their artistic exuberance, but they're not all gaudy and gauche; some, like this one have elegance and charm.

Its sword-shaped leaves to 45cm (18in) long have arching stems of up to ten hooded flowers of yellow-green, marked on the back with dusky purple and in the throat with dusky-purple and yellow. The first time I saw the colour combination I thought it was insipid rather than subtle – for some reason it reminded me of marzipan – but now I've grown to admire its poise and

Gladiolus papilio

understated beauty. *Gladiolus papilio* is difficult to place because of its colour, but plant it by a path for a closer view of the flowers or against a plain dark background to highlight colours that would be overwhelmed by brighter blooms.

Its home is in southern Africa, particularly in damp grassland around Transvaal and Natal. *Gladiolus* means sword shaped, referring to the leaves; the name *papilo* (butterfly) was given by Sir Joseph Hooker, one of the great directors of Kew Gardens. It's the perfect description. There are a few cultivars, one of which is 'David Hills'. At the time of writing, I've only seen photographs, but it has amazing red flowers. I hope this is a true representation!

G. papilio needs cool, moist, humus-rich soil in sunshine and is ideal for gaps in borders or rock gardens. It is hardy in most parts of the UK and unlike many gladioli, does not need lifting and replanting every year. In poorer soils it spreads but does not flower. It spreads by underground runners, which can be lifted and divided in autumn, and replanted in spring. Often damaged by slugs which eat new shoots underground. **MB**

Glaucium flavum

Glaucium flavum
YELLOW HORNED POPPY

Type: Hardy, biennial or short-lived perennial
Soil & situation: free-draining soil/thrives along sandy sea-shores but sometimes comes inland too/sunny position
North American hardiness zone: 6–9
Height: to 60cm (24in), sometimes taller
Spread: 45cm (18in)
Grow for: good foliage in the form of extremely glaucous rosettes; enchanting yellow flowers from late spring to late summer

Although this poppy is native to southern coastal Britain, it has been in gardens for centuries, usually popping up between cracks in paving or sowing itself serendipitously in a pebbly corner. It is one of those plants for which there is always a bit of space, however full your garden. The grey foliage, which has toothed lobes, is slightly rough and sends up grey stalks of the charming golden-yellow, papery poppies. These are produced in the first year when grown from seed. The seedpods are decorative too – long, curved and adorned with tiny warts. The down-side is their short lifespan. Some say they can be long lived, but I find that after three years they give up the ghost and this seems to be the norm.

G. flavum f. *fulvum* is a form of the species well worth obtaining. It produces bright orange flowers in summer and has the same attractive, glaucous, almost cabbage-like foliage of the species. It is also nicely robust.

Sow the seed for this plant in spring or autumn, either *in situ* or if you are more neurotic, like me, in small 7cm (3in) pots. It does not like being transplanted, so if it does self-sow it is not always possible to move it to your chosen position. **BG**

Gunnera magellanica

Type: frost-hardy, herbaceous perennial
Soil & situation: moist, humus-rich soil/open, sunny site
North American hardiness zone: 8–9
Height: 20cm (8in)
Spread: indefinite
Grow for: its pretty carpet of leaves from spring to autumn.

Life is enriched by contrasts. I just love the giant *Gunnera manicata* (see next entry) but what I find even more fascinating is that its relative is so tiny: the giant and the dwarf! Unlike its monster herbaceous cousin, it has rounded leaves only about 9cm (3³/₄in) across that are cupped and pleated when young and with wavy, toothed margins. They appear on 8–20cm (3¹/₂–8in) stalks that develop from stems that creep above and below the ground, rooting at leaf joints as they spread to form a dense leafy carpet; except in winter when frost kills the foliage!

Male and female flowers occur on different plants, most in the UK are males (females are rare in their native habitat too!), flowering just above the leaves in red-tinted clusters in spring. One of my ambitions is to visit Chile, the natural home of *G. magellanica*, for the plants, wine and scenery! Roy Lancaster has seen it in the wild from 1,200m (4,000ft) above a ski lodge in the Chilean Lake District down to the coastline by an iceberg-strewn sea in Patagonia – an impressive range of performance for such a little plant.

It prefers a moist, humus-rich, acid soil in an open position and could always be planted as ground cover around its larger cousin. It tolerates drier sites but tends to form mounds rather than sweeping carpets. I've seen it flourishing by garden ponds, in bog gardens and stream margins.

Gunnera magellanica

Gunnera manicata

Keep plants within their allotted space by reducing clumps in autumn or spring; simply dig them out with a spade – they are not deep rooted. Propagate from division any time of year. Keep new divisions well watered in summer. **MB**

Gunnera manicata

Type: hardy, deciduous perennial
Soil & situation: deep, permanently wet soil/sun or partial shade
North American hardiness zone: 7–10
Height: 3m (10ft)
Spread: 4m (13ft)
Grow for: huge, lush, jungle-like leaves; AGM

This is not a perennial for the herbaceous border. It is bold, dramatic, architectural and big enough to swamp its neighbours. I have a large clump close to a woodland path. In spring, as the leaves closest to the path grow, they are propped upright with long-handled brushes. The soft brush head prevents the stems being damaged. By summer they form a waterproof canopy overhead. The sun shines through the leaves and the rain is directed to the other side of the path.

Its dark green, lobed, kidney-shaped, heavily veined leaves can be 2m (6¹/₂ft) long and almost as broad. They are carried on 2.5m (8ft) long, prickly stalks. In summer 1m (3ft) long, vertical panicles of tiny red-green flowers appear in the centre of the clump and are followed by brown-green fruit. Since it is herbaceous, the absence of winter foliage causes a blank spot in the garden. Underplanting with yellow-flowered winter aconite (*Eranthis hyemalis*) and deep blue *Anemone blanda* 'Ingramii' will provide a carpet of colour in late winter and spring.

It won't tolerate a soil that dries out and is happy in boggy ground with its feet close to water. Planted at the edge of a stream or big pond it will quickly form a large clump. In cold areas the crown needs protection in winter but it provides its own cover. As the leaves die in autumn bend them over the centre of the plant. They certainly won't blow away!

Propagation is by seed sown fresh and over-wintered in a cold frame. Germination is slow. Large, basal buds can be removed in early spring. These are often well rooted on the underside. Pot up in a moisture-retaining compost and keep well watered for the first season. **JC**

Hacquetia epipactis

Type: hardy, herbaceous perennial
Soil & situation: moisture-retentive, humus-rich soil/dappled shade
North American hardiness zone: 5–7
Height: 15cm (6in)
Spread: 30cm (12in)
Grow for: unusual green 'flowers' in late winter and spring; AGM

I first saw this in the northeast of England in a rock garden that was mulched with grey gravel; it was the colour contrast that attracted my eye. It is a small plant with a mass of long-lasting blooms formed from a ruff of tiny green bracts, with a dense cluster of yellow flowers in the centre; both the flowerheads and ruff can be red-tinged in sunnier positions. It is a miniature version of the structure that is found in flowering dogwoods, *Davidia involucrata* (see page 114) and poinsettias.

It has pretty, shiny leaves divided into three segments with lobes at the toothed or rounded margins; the veining can be paler green. Looking at the colour I suppose that it's not surprising that it's in the celery family! It makes good ground cover under shrubs and a wonderful association

in the rock garden with *Gentiana acaulis* (see page 189) and other plants with early blue flowers such as *Hepatica nobilis* (page 206). It is long lived, slow growing and a true harbinger of spring. As you might expect from something so unusual, it stands alone; there are no other species in the genus.

It needs humus-rich, well-drained but moist, neutral to acid soil in dappled shade. Ideal for woodland or rock gardens. Mulch in autumn and water during drought. To propagate divide in spring, take root cuttings in winter and sow seed when fresh (it usually seeds prolifically); it takes about two years to flower. Slugs and snails can damage young growth. **MB**

Hamamelis x intermedia 'Jelena'
WITCH HAZEL

Type: hardy, deciduous shrub
Soil & situation: moist soil/sun
North American hardiness zone: 5–9
Height & spread: 4m (13ft), or more
Grow for: flowers in mid- and late winter; autumn colour; AGM

Hacquetia epipactis

Hamamelis x *intermedia* 'Jelena'

Witch hazel's spidery blooms are traditionally tones of yellow, but I like those with red and orange hues, particularly *H.* x *intermedia* 'Jelena', which was named for Jelena de Belder at Kalmthout Arboretum in Belgium. It has wonderful fiery autumn colour and petals with yellow tips diffusing down to red at the base. Look out too for these varieties of *H.* x *intermedia*: 'Orange Peel', with sharp orange petals; 'Orange Beauty', with orange flowers; 'Aphrodite', with large burnt-orange flowers; and 'Diane', red with good autumn colour.

They prefer a sunny position but tolerate dappled shade; excessive shade reduces flowering. Grow in any moist soil except thin soil over chalk; improve the drainage on clay; mulch and water in drought. Feed in spring with Growmore, chicken pellets or fish blood and bone at 40g/sq m (2oz/sq ft).

I read an article about witch hazels by Chris Lane, a *Hamamelis* enthusiast, that included new information about cultivation and pruning, and I'm sure that if what he said reached a wider audience it would encourage more people to grow these fabulous plants. Cut back the previous season's wood to two growth buds annually in winter unless they have only made a little growth. There is normally a cluster of flowers at the base of the growth and the growth buds are above these. Using this technique Chris had 14-year-old plants that were only 1.5m (5ft) x 1.5m (5ft). They lack the wide spreading habit but it allows them to be grown where there's minimal space. If space is not a problem, restrictive pruning is not necessary. It can be propagated by grafting, but it's easier to buy a plant from a nursery in late winter. **MB**

Hamamelis mollis 'Coombe Wood'
CHINESE WITCH HAZEL

Type: hardy, deciduous shrub
Soil & situation: neutral to acid, well-drained soil/full sun or partial shade
North American hardiness zone: 5–9
Height: 4m (13ft)
Spread: 5m (16ft)
Grow for: fragrant, unusually shaped, yellow flowers in winter; buttery-yellow autumn leaf colour

If you want a plant to brighten your day in the middle of winter this funnel-shaped shrub has a lot going for it, including a powerful, freely given fragrance. The individual flowers look like delicate, finely peeled lemon zest but are tough enough to withstand the worst of weather. Appearing before the leaves, the massed flowers resemble a yellow cloud against a washed-out wintery sky. Sited close to the house, its winter perfume will come looking for you through an open window.

There are other good species and varieties of witch hazel, but it is hard to beat *Hamamelis mollis* 'Coombe Wood' for fragrance and size of flower. Another favourite is *H.* x *intermedia* 'Jelena', but Matthew has chosen that one (see previous entry)! *H. virginiana*, from North America, flowers in late autumn and is the commercial source of witch hazel used in medicine.

Witch hazel is what I would call a 'kind' plant. It rarely suffers from pests or diseases, is fully hardy and requires minimal pruning. Cut out crossing branches in early winter to maintain a good shape. Plant in deeply dug, well-drained ground. It dislikes heavy clay soil. Layering is the easiest method of propagation, but leave the branch for two years to allow a good root system to form. **JC**

Hamamelis mollis 'Coombe Wood'

Hebe albicans

Hebe albicans

Type: frost-hardy, evergreen shrub
Soil & situation: range of free-draining soils, even very thin ones/coastal areas/sun or light shade/hates winter wet and very cold areas
North American hardiness zone: 9–10
Height: 60cm (24in)
Spread: 90cm (36in)
Grow for: dense, glaucous foliage; neat humpy habit; reasonably pretty white flowers, spotted with their chocolate-coloured anthers in early summer; AGM

Hebes are useful fillers in the garden. They root quickly from cuttings and rapidly establish into neat hummocks of foliage. This hebe has a particularly dense habit. The leaves are about 2cm (^{3}/4in) long and are a pale, soft grey-green – a fabulous foliage colour that works well with purples and mauves, oranges and whites. It does not seem to get all woody and open and leggy at the base like many hebes do if you do not cut them back regularly. Many people admire 'Red Edge', which is similar and the leaves have exactly what the name implies, but I do not like it half as much as this beauty.

You can, as with many hebes, clip them over annually in spring, but I find that the natural form is so dense, it is unnecessary. When the plant eventually does get leggy, it may well respond to a hard cutting back into old wood in spring but sometimes an aged specimen will give up the ghost. Generally I find they are so simple to propagate from cuttings, that this is the simplest method of rejuvenating the border. Semi-ripe cuttings can be taken in the summer. Beware if you are on a wet, heavy soil with lots of organic matter – hebes can suffer from Phytophthora, which is a rotting of the roots, so add lots of grit before planting to lighten things up a touch. **BG**

Hebe x *andersonii* 'Variegata'

Type: nearly hardy, evergreen shrub
Soil & situation: moist, well-drained, neutral or alkaline soil/full sun or partial shade
North American hardiness zone: 10–11
Height & spread: 2m (6½ft)
Grow for: bold, variegated, evergreen foliage and summer flowers

This hebe, while it needs mollycoddling, has a lot going for it. Larger-growing and less dense in habit than many others, it has beautiful, big, 10cm (4in) long, dark green leaves streaked grey-green in the centre and margined in creamy-white. It flowers all summer and into the autumn with 8cm (3½in) long spikes of pale violet which fade to blue-white as they age.

It needs a sheltered situation or a place against a warm, sunny wall. It makes a spectacular display facing a red brick wall. Avoid cold, windy sites. If it does get hit by cold leave it untouched until early summer. Prune it back to 30–45cm (12–18in) from ground level and it may reshoot from the base.

Propagation is by softwood cuttings taken in early summer. It roots easily and rooting a few every year as replacements means you will never be without one of the best varieties of hebe. **JC**

Hebe x *andersonii* 'Variegata'

Hedera helix 'Congesta'

Hedera helix 'Congesta'/ *H. h.* 'Erecta'/*H. h.* 'Conglomerata Erecta'

Type: hardy, perennial, evergreen shrub
Soil & situation: any soil/sun or shade
North American hardiness zone: 5–10
Height & spread: can slowly make a mound up to 1–1.5m (3–5ft)
Grow for: distinctive geometric form

Most ivies are clinging, creeping plants, but this one is an upright-growing shrub. Quite different to normal ivy, it is composed of vertical growing spikes covered with spirally formed leaves, giving a strange, somewhat alien look that is offset by the healthy dark green of the spade- to arrow-shaped leaves. On warm spring days this plant appears to be covered in small, bright red flowers, but on closer examination these turn out to be ladybirds just out of hibernation from inside the dry interior. As a uniquely sculptural plant it can be used in 'artistic' situations, such as combined with a large stone or old tree trunk.

Although given separate Latin varietal names these are very similar plants, differing in leaf shape but all with amazing architectural form.

Any soil or site suits this tough shrub which persists for many years, slowly increasing in size, though it is happiest in rich, moist, alkaline soil and partial shade. It is rather brittle so be careful when handling the shoots. It cannot be grown from seed, but cuttings taken in autumn and set in a cold frame are easy. In hot, dry sites it can suffer from red spider mite, so keep it misted. **BF**

Hedera helix 'Cristata' (syn. *H. h.* 'Parsley Crested')

Type: evergreen climber
Soil & situation: prefers shady conditions/does particularly well in limy soils
North American hardiness zone: 5–10
Height: 2m (6½ft)
Spread: indefinite
Grow for: a wonderful, rumpled green leaf, crumpled and twisted around the margins; a good climber; highly attractive plant.

This ivy stands out with its weird but rather wonderful leaf. The leaves do not look in any way poxed or diseased because they are fairly uniformly affected and the crimps look rather delicately applied. They are almost rounded, bright green and prominently veined. It will branch and trail as it grows and I have seen it sprawling neatly over a low wall in a fairly compact way, creating a bit of organic sculpture or green architecture. Ivies are multi-purpose, versatile tools suitable for topiary on wire frames, making solid, evergreen 'walls' from chain-link-type fences (which take up only a smidgen of space and form magnificent 'fedges') and of course for camouflaging monstrosities. On the whole I tend to use *Hedera helix* 'Conglomerata' or common or garden English ivy, *H. helix*. I am not a fan of those scores of bicoloured, brash-looking ivies, which you regularly see plastered against eyesores – obviously the intention was to conceal, not reveal, but their appearance is so artificial it works the other way.

This ivy is unlikely to become large and bulky and so cause problems to its support in the way that many vigorous ivies can in trees, roofs, fences and the like. If you want it to form a denser, flatter line then regular clipping of sideshoots helps create a more solid mass of vegetation. I saw a superb, arched 'porch' around a front door created entirely of ivy. This was regularly clipped over to give a flat, green surface. It not only transformed an otherwise unremarkable house, but was home to a robin and scores of insects too.

To propagate ivy, take cuttings of young shoots any time during the growing season. If you are forming and growing your ivy topiary in pots, do not forget to feed and water them. They are incredibly tolerant of neglect but really thrive with a bit of love and care. **BG**

Hedera helix 'Cristata'

Salvia sclarea var. *turkestanica* June

BIENNIAL CLARY

Type: hardy biennial or short-lived perennial
Soil & situation: free-draining light soils/copious
sunshine
Hardiness zone: 5–9
Height: 75cm (30in)
Spread: 30cm (12in)
Grow for: highly dramatic when in pink and white flower
from late spring to summer, and this drama is good and
prolonged; orderly, felted foliage is highly agreeable; will
usually seed itself around

A few, repeated clumps of this architectural, yet
colourful, perennial will pull any planting up a good
couple of notches in the summer. The flowers are white
and pink and have highly conspicuous, pale, red-purple
bracts. These, together with stout pink stems, form
hunky candelabras, which look sensational for a good
few weeks. The leaves are a good size (about 25 x
12cm/10 x 5in), ovate and a deep, sagey green.

The ordinary clary is also known as 'clear eye' and
'muscatel sage', though it is far less colourful than
S. sclarea var. *turkestanica*. It is in widespread cultivation
for medicinal and culinary uses and is reputedly an
aphrodisiac. Parts of it are used externally in eyewashes
and also to flavour Rhine wines with a muscatel bouquet,
hence the alternative common names.

I am not always prepared to make the assumption that
this plant is going to self-seed where I want it, and as it is
such a strong statement I think it is well worth
positioning where it gives maximum impact. It is a good
idea to sow a few seeds on the window sill in early spring
or *in situ* in late spring – it is so easy from seed. If it dies
out and I have forgotten to grow my own, I regret it so
much so that I have even been known to buy in some
replacements! After flowering, leave on some spent
heads for seed and cut down the remaining spikes so
that the plant recovers. This, with an annual spring

mulch, helps it to be more perennial in nature and boosts
performance. They are far shorter-lived and more
miserable in appearance when subject to winter wet. No
need to stake.   **BG**

Hedera helix 'Goldheart'

Type: hardy, perennial, evergreen climber
Soil & situation: any soil/sun or shade
North American hardiness zone: 6–10
Height & spread: will eventually cover any area
Grow for: the cheerful golden splash in each evergreen leaf makes this a useful wall or ground covering

Most ivies are somewhat funereal; yes, they are good covers for trellis, hiding tree stumps or clinging to unsightly walls, but they are undeniably grim, and more at home in the graveyard or the dark woods. However *H. h.* 'Goldheart' is cheerful, the yellow splash in the centre of each leaf redeems this plant so it can be used in narrow alleys or small courtyards without making them seem dungeon-like. It can even be grown as ground cover if the area is initially well weeded, but it does want to climb.

A native of Europe and the Near East, ivy has long been growing in gardens but has not necessarily been grown in gardens! *Hedera* is the Latin name for ivy, and the plant was held sacred to Bacchus, the god of wine.

Ivy is long lived and prefers a moist, alkaline soil in partial shade. It may be slow to start with but once it gets a hold it is in for good. It can be sheared back in spring to keep it flat against a wall. *H. h.* 'Goldheart' cannot be grown from seed but cuttings or layers are easy in autumn. It can get red spider mite on hot, dry walls and the answer is to spray with water on hot days.   **BF**

Hedera helix 'Goldheart'

Hedera helix f. *poetarum* 'Poetica Arborea'

Hedera helix f. *poetarum* 'Poetica Arborea'
POET'S IVY, ITALIAN IVY

Type: hardy, evergreen, climbing shrub
Soil & situation: moist, humus-rich, well-drained, alkaline soil/full sun or light shade
North American hardiness zone: 5–10
Height: 3m (10ft)
Spread: 1m (3ft)
Grow for: excellent bush ivy with orange fruit

Ivies have many attributes, being excellent evergreen coverers for horizontal and vertical situations. They have attractive juvenile foliage and late-season flowers which are beneficial to insects.

This variety is grown for its orange-coloured fruits. Usually sold as a bush or 'tree ivy', it is propagated by cuttings from adult arborescent growths. Pliny, in his *Natural History*, in the first century AD wrote 'One kind has black seed and another the colour of saffron, the latter is used by poets for their wreaths and its leaves are not so dark in colour'. I must admit my main interest is that it is unusual and makes a show in winter.

The 5–8cm (2–3½in) long, five-lobed leaves are pale green. The fruit are small, dull, deep orange and persist all winter. It is tolerant of most soils with the exception of waterlogged conditions but prefers alkaline soil. Pruning consists of clipping to keep the bush tidy and under control. Propagation is by softwood cuttings with a heel in a gritty compost under horticultural fleece. Trim the leaves of the cutting to reduce transpiration. Trailing stems may be layered in the open ground and should be well rooted within six months.

If you know a poet, don't risk buying him a plant in case he knows the original story of the use for 'poet's ivy'.   **JC**

Helianthemum apenninum
WHITE ROCK ROSE, SUN ROSE

Type: hardy, evergreen, spreading shrub
Soil & situation: well-drained, neutral to alkaline soil/full sun
North American hardiness zone: 6–8
Height: 45cm (18in)
Spread: 80cm (32in)
Grow for: excellent ground-covering plant with small, pure white flowers

Rock roses are dependable plants. They are guaranteed to flower no matter what, weather wise, has gone before. They are excellent for ground cover either in a rockery or tumbling down a steep bank. This species is native to the UK and can still be found in at least one part of Devon.

It forms a loose mat of branching stems with small, narrow, grey-green leaves. From late spring until mid-summer the plant is covered in small, five-petalled, saucer-shaped flowers. They are pure white with a centre of conspicuous, deep yellow anthers.

Pruning is essential every year to prevent the shrub becoming woody and leggy with little growth at the base of the plant. Clip it over after flowering to remove most of the young growth. Avoid cutting into the old wood of neglected plants as they may not produce new shoots. Propagation is by fresh seed sown thinly on the surface of the compost in autumn and over-wintered in a cold frame. Softwood cuttings root readily in early summer in a gritty, free-draining compost. Cover the cuttings with horticultural fleece rather than polythene.   **JC**

Helianthemum apenninum

Helianthus annuus 'Teddy Bear'

Helianthus annuus 'Teddy Bear'
SUNFLOWER

Type: half-hardy annual
Soil & situation: moist, well-drained, humus-rich, neutral to alkaline soil/full sun
North American hardiness zone: 5–7
Height: 45cm (18in)
Spread: 20–30cm (8–12in)
Grow for: a perfect size for children; adds colour, interest and height to the border

You don't have to be a child to appreciate growing your very own giant sunflower, but growing one with flowers at face level, such as *Helianthus annuus* 'Teddy Bear', must be satisfactory when you are small.

The hairy stems form a compact plant and carry 20cm- (8in-) long, heart-shaped, mid-green, hairy leaves. The fully double, golden-yellow flowers are 15cm (6in) in diameter and are produced during summer and autumn. *H. a.* 'Teddy Bear' is ideal as a dot plant in the centre of a container or en masse in a sunny border. It is useful for wildlife – bees love the nectar and the spent flowers can be left to produce seed which is much enjoyed by birds.

Sunflowers need a long, hot summer to flower well so plant a row along the base of a sheltered, sunny wall where they are in full sun. Propagation is by seed sown in late winter in a propagator. They may be sown outside where they are to flower when all risk of frost is over. Protect the young plants from slugs and snails, which can destroy a whole crop overnight.

If size matters, then grow the variety *H. a.* 'Russian Giant' with large, bright yellow, 25cm (10in) diameter flowers all summer. It grow to 3.5m (11ft) high and needs to be staked to prevent the wind felling it. **JC**

Helianthus tuberosus
JERUSALEM ARTICHOKE

Type: hardy, herbaceous perennial
Soil & situation: any soil/sun or shade
North American hardiness zone: 4–9
Height: up to 3m (10ft)
Spread: 25cm (10in)
Grow for: an instant windbreak with scented flowers and edible tubers

You have to learn to love Jerusalem artichokes, as once you've got them you can rarely get rid of them. This does not matter, as they can be relegated to an out-of-the-way place where they will look after themselves. Like a magic soup-pot, plant some tubers and walk away – there'll always be some there, giving you an ever-present source of food. The stems reach an amazing height in good sites and can quickly hide a garden eyesore or give privacy this summer, not in five years' time. The flowers are just like miniature sunflowers and have a warm vanilla-chocolate scent in some strains. (You can find the tubers in knobbly, very knobbly, white, pink and red colours.)

It is a native of North America and came to the UK in 1617, where it was thought to be a wonderful new crop to feed the poor but, unfortunately, it was not as palatable as the potato. (The dahlia was similarly introduced as a crop and only later became seen as a flowering plant for the garden.) The botanical name comes from the Greek *helios*, meaning sun, and *anthemon*, a flower. The English

Helianthus tuberosus

appellation Jerusalem is alleged to be a corruption of the Italian *girasole* (to turn with the sun) and artichoke, as it was thought to taste similar to the globe artichoke.

It will grow almost anywhere! For ever! Tidy up the dead stems in winter. Leave the crop in the ground until required as it stores badly once lifted. Plant tubers 10cm (4in) deep in moist, rich soil 30cm (12in) apart, and stand back. Tubers are quite tasty but cause dreadful wind, which is appropriate for a windbreak plant. **BF**

Helleborus foetidus
Wester Flisk Group
STINKING HELLEBORE

Type: hardy, evergreen perennial
Soil & situation: rich, well-drained soil/dappled shade
North American hardiness zone: 6–9
Height: 1.2m (4ft) in flower
Spread: 50cm (20in)
Grow for: sculptural form and colour; flowers from mid-winter to mid-spring

Mrs Mamie Walker discovered this plant with unusual reddish tints when she moved to the rectory at Wester Flisk on the Firth of Tay, Scotland, in the early 1970s. By a process of seedling selection she and others have produced plants with an even stronger, more widespread red stain. So where did this form come from? It is a scarce UK native, but does not grow around the Firth of Tay. However, from 1811 to 1832, the Reverend Dr John Fleming, a professor at both Aberdeen University and Queen's College, Edinburgh, lived at the rectory. An enthusiastic botanist, he may well have introduced the plant through the Botanic Gardens in Edinburgh or Aberdeen or had a special interest in the flora of Spain, where similar forms are found. There is also a double snowdrop growing in the woods nearby! I suspect that the professor did it!

It has narrow finger-like leaves and fascinating colouring. I find it a bit weird yet intriguing, like modern art! The crushed dark foliage is malodorous. Plant with snowdrops, bugle (*Ajuga reptans*), lungwort (*Pulmonaria officinalis*), silver-foliage plants or *Narcissus* 'February Gold'.

It flourishes in rich, well-drained soil, preferably alkaline, in dappled shade, but will also grow in dry shade or full sun. Mulch in spring; tall plants may need staking. Thin out older leaves and stems in winter to encourage new growth from the base and

Helleborus foetidus Wester Flisk Group

cut out the flower stems at ground level as they deteriorate. Sow seed in containers in a cold frame as soon as ripe. Divide after flowering, in early spring or late summer. It comes true from seed if isolated from other cultivars of *H. foetidus*. Prone to snails, aphids, leaf spot and black rot. **MB**

Helleborus niger
'Potter's Wheel'
CHRISTMAS ROSE

Type: hardy, evergreen, clump-forming perennial
Soil & situation: heavy, neutral to alkaline soil/light shade
North American hardiness zone: 4–8
Height: 30cm (12in)
Spread: 45cm (18in)
Grow for: beautiful, cup-shaped, white flowers in mid-winter

Miss Davenport-Jones, who named this plant, decided on 'Potter's Wheel' because every flower was perfectly round. What a lovely common name. It comes into flower with the minimum of fuss and, like the snowdrop, manages to flower in spite of adverse weather. When it was given the AGM in 1958 the flowers were described as follows: 'The immense flowers measure from 4–5 inches across with broad, glistening white, overlapping sepals, the bases of which, together with the nectaries, are a deep, clear green.'

The leaves are a glossy, dark green and the flowers are held on 23–30cm (9–12in) stems well clear of muddy rain splash. Unfortunately it seldom flowers for me on Christmas Day, but a few weeks later it is in bloom and continues to produce flowers until early spring. As a table decoration the simple flowers are exquisite. The secret to growing the 'Christmas rose' is choice of site and soil. It will love you if you provide it with moist, alkaline, humus-rich soil away from full sun. The base of a shady wall would get you brownie points. Whenever possible buy plants which are in flower. There are a lot of seed-raised plants on the market which, while white flowering, are inferior imposters. **JC**

Helleborus niger 'Potter's Wheel'

Helleborus odorus
FRAGRANT HELLEBORE, SWEET-SCENTED HELLEBORE

Type: hardy, herbaceous perennial
Soil & situation: rich, moist, loamy soil/light shade
North American hardiness zone: 6–9
Height & spread: clump of 30–60cm (12–24in) or so each way
Grow for: pleasant pale green, lightly striped foliage; large, similarly coloured flowers with strong sweet perfume

This is the only perfumed member of the genus. I notice that we have almost all chosen a hellebore as one of our favourite plants, yet they are not commonly grown. I think this is because they are not easy to establish as big plants and few amateurs want to grow them from seed or buy tiny plants, when big ones are available. Also many of them are a disappointment in comparison to their catalogue descriptions; for example, the typical label of 'red flowers' is misleading, because in fact the blooms

Helleborus odorus

are a pale wan red. Secondly the flowers droop, so you do not even get to see their beauty. It would be ideal if hellebores could live on top of a wall, so you could look up at them, but they can't.

A group of a dozen or so species, hellebores are among the oldest medicinal and garden plants. They were first recorded as early as 1500BC when they were used to cure the daughters of Proteus, King of Argos, of insanity. *Helleborus odorus* is a late arrival, introduced in the 19th century from Hungary, and still not common.

Hellebores are very long lived and if undisturbed in light shade may pass a century or more. Never ever try to move large or established plants; only small ones will take well. Grow from seed in individual pots in a cold frame or *in situ*. Particularly nice strains can be root divided after flowering but never make as good a plants as seedlings. Beware – poisonous plants! **BF**

Helleborus orientalis
Plant of the Week (see page 79)

Helleborus x *sternii*

Type: hardy, herbaceous perennial
Soil & situation: moist, free-draining soil/sun
North American hardiness zone: 6–9
Height: 35cm (14in)
Spread: 30cm (12in)
Grow for: fascinating form and winter flowers

This is a hybrid between *Helleborus argutifolius*, a hardy green-leaved and green-flowered species, and *H. lividus*, a tender species with short veiny leaves and unusual pink flowers. They combine to

produce a clump-forming perennial which looks sometimes like one parent, sometimes the other. Those that are more like *H. argutifolius* are less ornamental; those with more *H. lividus* are beautiful but not as hardy. It has smooth or spiny leaves with cream-coloured veins and strange pink-purple leaf stalks and main veins. If that isn't crazy enough the green flowers to 5cm (2in) across are also creamy-green with a pink-purple tinge. They appear in clusters from late winter until mid-spring.

There are several selected groups and cultivars. *H.* x *sternii* 'Boughton Beauty' has grey, strongly veined foliage with pink stems and leaf bracts. *H.* x *s.* Blackthorn Group are dwarf with purple stems, silver-grey leaves and green flowers with a pink tinge. Some are only 30cm (12in) tall and *H.* x *s.* dwarf is even smaller.

They tolerate most soils but prefer one that is neutral to alkaline and free-draining; incorporate leafmould or organic matter at planting time and add spent mushroom compost to acid soils. They prefer full sun but need to be protected from scorching sunshine; they tolerate dappled shade. Mulch in autumn. In colder climates grow strongly pink forms in containers and protect from hard frosts. Remove some of the leaves during autumn and early winter, particularly those showing signs of blackening. Just before they are in full flower, take off all the rest of the leaves. On windy sites, remove them entirely to prevent wind rock. Divide after flowering in late spring or early summer; self-seeds freely. They are susceptible to snails, aphids and black rot. **MB**

Helleborus x *sternii*

Hemerocallis flava
DAYLILY

Type: hardy, herbaceous perennial
Soil & situation: any soil/anywhere
North American hardiness zone: 3–9
Height: up to 60cm–1m (2–3ft)
Spread: a clump of 2–25cm (1–10in)
Grow for: pleasant, wide, flat, rush-like foliage; attractive, large, yellow flowers over many weeks with a warm sweet smell of honeysuckle

This is a marvellous plant for many reasons. Daylilies do best in moist, light shade, but they will succeed almost anywhere a weed will grow, making them very useful as a filler. The succession of blooms lasts right through the summer, and they need no dead-heading. Their scent is very pleasant and I have even taken to eating the petals in salads. They are also problem free with no serious pests or diseases, and if the leaves are left to wither down they naturally form a weed-suppressing mat. Yellow daylilies have perfume but *Hemerocallis fulva*, orange ones, do not; thus the hybrids, of which there are many, may have scent, especially if they are more yellow than orange.

Hemerocallis comes from the Greek *hemera*, meaning day, and *kallos*, beauty, and the plant was given this name as individual blooms last but a day, though they are continually produced for weeks on end.

Hemerocallis flava

Hemerocallis 'Prairie Blue Eyes'

The daylily can be long lived in a rich, moist, lightly shaded site. It can be grown from seed, preferably autumn sown, but root division is easier and quicker. Every bit of root with a bud can be divided off and will soon make another clump. These tough survivors suffer from no problems at all. None. **BF**

Hemerocallis 'Prairie Blue Eyes'
DAYLILY

Type: hardy, semi-evergreen perennial
Soil & situation: fertile, moist, well-drained soil/full sun
North American hardiness zone: 3–9
Height & spread: 75cm (30in)
Grow for: a continual show of flowers for a lengthy time in the summer

The good news is, however short-lived each flower may be, there are lots of them, making a show for between four and six weeks in mid-summer. Long, narrow, arching, strap-like leaves are mid-green and will over-winter on the plant in mild climates. The star-shaped, 13cm (5¼in) wide, maroon-purple flowers have a greenish-yellow throat. The unopened flower buds are edible, adding colour to salads. Daylilies are low-allergen plants, making them suitable for allergen-free gardens.

A mulch of bark on clumps which die down in late autumn will see them through the winter. Slugs and snails are a constant problem,

especially in spring when they devour the new shoots as fast as they grow. Weekly liquid tomato feeds from spring until the flower buds appear will strengthen the plant. If abnormally fat buds appear in late spring it will indicate an infection of gall midge. They should be picked off and burned, and the plant should be removed and destroyed in autumn.

Propagation is by division of the clump every two to three years in spring. Take care not to damage the fleshy roots. It can be grown from freshly sown seed in autumn but it will not come true. But, who knows, you may raise some good, new varieties. **JC**

Hepatica nobilis

Type: hardy, herbaceous perennial
Soil & situation: moist, organic-rich, free-draining soil/sun or dappled shade
North American hardiness zone: 5–8
Height: 10cm (4in)
Spread: 15cm (6in)
Grow for: pretty early spring flowers; AGM

In Japan the hepatica is known as *Yukiwariso*, which translated means 'herb of the snow', as they often emerge through snow cover in spring. It is found from Europe and Scandinavia east to Japan where it shows an incredible diversity of flower and form, not found anywhere else in its range. Capitalizing on this natural inclination, Japanese enthusiasts breed 'fancy' varieties and by 1995 almost 550 cultivars had been registered. Although they have been cultivated in Japan since 1730, it is only in the last 25 years that they've been developed for showing. Propagation is slow

Hepatica nobilis

and rare and unusual varieties are sold for huge sums of money; strangely for a member of the buttercup family, the rarest colour is yellow! There are doubles, triples and even 'thousand-layered' flowers and a range of pattern and colour classifications that includes nail-coloured and sprayed or wrinkled. A pot called *Tanba-Yaki* has been specifically designed for growing them.

The species is a simple, pretty little flower and ranges in colour from white to pink, blue and purple. It withstands low temperatures but not winter waterlogging and is ideal for scree and rock gardens; it flourishes in limy soil. Mulch in autumn and feed regularly, particularly in spring after flowering and in autumn when the flowers are formed. For perfect plants, grow in alpine houses in pots. Propagate from fresh seed; it may take 12 months to germinate. It is prone to slugs. **MB**

Hermodactylus tuberosus
WIDOW IRIS, SNAKE'S HEAD IRIS

Type: hardy, tuberous perennial
Soil & situation: very dry, free-draining soil/sun
North American hardiness zone: 7–9
Height & spread: 40cm (16in) or more
Grow for: unusual scented flowers from early to late spring

This bashful plant seems almost embarrassed by its own good looks! You could easily walk past the tussocks of leaves without realizing that hiding among the grey-green, grassy foliage are sombre, almost translucent greenish-yellow, iris-like flowers, about 5cm (2in) across with velvety black outer segments and an alluring perfume. They are so inconspicuous that some argue that, to appreciate them fully, they are better displayed in a vase! Perhaps they feel ashamed that they are not as bold as the iris, a group to which they once belonged, but there is no real reason to hide – this is a plant for those who appreciate subtle charms and the longer you look, the more you find.

John Gerard (1545–1612), the herbalist and gardener, described it thus: 'The lower leaves [petals] that turne downward, are of a perfect blacke colour, soft and smooth as is black velvet, the blackness is welted about with greenish yellow, or as we terme it, a goose turd greene, of which the uppermost leaves [petals] do consist'. Charming!

Hermodactylus tuberosus

Flowering is better after long, hot summers and it combines well with silver-foliaged shrubs or against a light-coloured wall. It comes from the dry slopes in rocky regions of southern Europe, North Africa, Israel and Turkey. Plant 6–10cm (2½–4in) deep in a hot, dry, sunny situation at the base of a wall in preferably alkaline soil. It must be very free draining and it's one of few plants that would be delighted if builders buried their rubble in your garden; if they haven't, throw in a few half bricks and gravel yourself! In areas where the soil is not regularly disturbed, it spreads happily.

Lift and divide in late summer and early autumn at the end of its summer dormancy. Slugs and snails can be a problem. **MB**

Hesperis matronalis
DAME'S VIOLET, SWEET ROCKET

Type: hardy perennial
Soil & situation: fertile, well-drained soil/sun or partial shade
North American hardiness zone: 4–9
Height: 90cm (36in)
Spread: 45cm (18in)
Grow for: flowers for about six weeks in late spring and early summer

This is a quintessential cottage-garden flower in shades ranging from purple to lavender and white. Robust, wholesome with a simple beauty and fragrance that pervades the garden in the evening, this pretty plant was introduced from Europe in the 16th century and is naturalized throughout the UK. Gertrude Jekyll in her book *Annuals and Biennials* writes that 'it looks best in a half-shady place, such as the edge of woodland or the beginning of a wood walk. The double kinds, of which the pure white is the best, should be treated as biennials'. William Robinson in *The English Flower Garden* notes that this is 'a popular old garden plant, and one of the most desirable of hardy flowers…the double kinds are much more valued'; an honest appraisal of a fabulous flower from two gardening 'greats'.

Hesperis matronalis var. *albiflora* is the best, with pure white flowers. It comes true from seed if isolated from other colours. *H. m.* var. *albiflora* 'Alba Plena' is a white, double-flowered form. *H. m.* 'Lilacina Flore Pleno' has dense spikes of fragrant, double, lilac-coloured flowers.

The single forms grow in any fertile, moist, well-drained soil in sun or partial shade; double forms need a little more pampering, preferring better drainage and additional well-rotted organic matter.

Treat as biennials or short-lived perennials; the first flush of flowers are nearly always the best. Divide every two years as flowering diminishes with age, and take basal cuttings in spring for planting out the following year. Slugs and snails can be a problem. **MB**

Hesperis matronalis

Meconopsis x *sheldonii* 'Slieve Donard'

BLUE POPPY

Type: hardy herbaceous perennial
Soil & situation: humus-rich, moist, well-drained, neutral to acid soil/partial shade
Hardiness zone: 7–8
Height: 1m (3ft)
Spread: 30cm (12in)
Grow for: beautifully shaped, long-lasting, rich blue flowers, which may appear earlier in the summer but are at their best now; AGM.

I love all the blue poppies, but this is truly the best blue. Also I met my wife in Newcastle, a seaside town at the foot of Slieve Donard 'where the mountains of Mourne sweep down to the sea'. As perennials go, this is a show stopper. A hybrid of *M. betonicifolia* and *M. grandis*, it is blessed with the best of its parents. In early summer flower stalks 1m (3ft) high carry large, bright, rich blue nodding flowers made up of four long, pointed petals. The drooping flower buds open slowly, allowing seemingly bright blue tissue paper to squeeze out. The lance-shaped, dark green, smooth-edged leaves have the decency to stay below flowering level.

Sometimes blue poppies tend to be monocarpic (they die after flowering). There is less risk of this if they are grown in a moist soil and are prevented from flowering for two years. Removing the flowerhead before it sets seed also helps to prolong the life of the plant. It prefers a deep, fertile, lime-free soil with good drainage. Add lots of leafmould to help retain a moist root area without waterlogging. Choose a sheltered site in partial shade such as a woodland glade. In cold areas protect the crown with bark mulch in winter. Propagation is by seed, preferably sown fresh in autumn. Use a soilless seed compost. Don't cover the seed as light is required for germination. Keep the seedlings under cover in a greenhouse or cold frame during winter and watch for any sign of damping off disease. **JC**

Bunny adds:
A fantastic plant, certainly, but difficult to grow unless you live in a moist part of the country.

Hesperis steveniana

Type: hardy, herbaceous annual/biennial/perennial
Soil & situation: moist soil/sun or light shade
North American hardiness zone: 4–9
Height & spread: first year rosette to 15cm (6in), second year spike to 60cm (24in)
Grow for: lots of beautiful violet blooms attracting masses of insects and smelling divine

Hesperis steveniana is very similar to the larger and better known dame's violet, *H. matronalis* (see previous entry), both resembling bluey-violet wallflowers. In the day it is magnificent with a mass of violet (or white, as there are always a few) blooms smelling of, well, violet. But in the evening return again and now the violet is augmented by a clove perfume, heavenly! It goes well with wallflowers as it comes into bloom with them and is not so huge as *H. matronalis*, but has a much longer flowering season.

A native of Europe, *Hesperis* has always been popular in gardens. The genus name is from the Greek for evening, when they are most highly perfumed.

H. steveniana does well in dryish soil in full sun, but is always short lived. Like wallflowers, some plants, especially if dead-headed, become short-lived perennials. Sown in early spring, they will flower, and probably die, like an annual; sown in a seedbed in late spring or early summer, many will become biennial and can be transplanted while dormant to flower the following year.   **BF**

Hesperis steveniana

Hibiscus sabdariffa var. *sabdariffa. The photograph was taken in Thailand – most of us would need a greenhouse to achieve this result.*

Hibiscus sabdariffa var. *sabdariffa*

Type: tender, annual crop
Soil & situation: rich, well-drained compost/full sun/under cover
North American hardiness zone: 10–11
Height: 1–1.5m (3–5ft)
Spread: 25cm–1m (10in–3ft)
Grow for: something completely different, and delicious

OK, this is an enthusiast's or gourmet's plant. Indian sorrel or roselle is grown in the tropics but in the UK it can be grown in a warm greenhouse. It is closely related to okra and needs similar bright light, heat and well-drained, fertile soil. The actual crop is the dark red calyces which surround the yellow flowers. These fleshy parts are dried, then in winter made into a tea, jelly, pudding or punch. Roselle has a wonderful taste of cloves, cinnamon and spices all. If that wasn't enough, you can also use the leaves as spinach or salad!

Hibiscus is a big genus with 300 members all in the warmer zones. Barely any have scented flowers as they are pollinated by hummingbirds, who find them by their bright colours. Roselle comes from India where it is used in a multitude of ways and it is very popular in the West Indies. Incidentally, the reason you so often see the large hibiscus flowers used in hotels and as decorations in the tropics is that they don't wilt for the whole of the day on which they are picked.

Not easy as it likes a hot, bright environment with a fairly low humidity. It takes many months to grow, won't flower readily without daylight-length manipulation, and will bolt while small if you're not careful. Don't stare in wonder at the ripe calyces when they arrive – use them before they rot. Sow in warmth in late winter and grow on in warmth, pot on into large pots or a greenhouse border and keep the air fairly dry once flowers set in autumn. To grow these you need to like a challenge!   **BF**

Hippophae rhamnoides
SEA BUCKTHORN

Type: hardy, deciduous shrub or small tree
Soil & situation: moist, well-drained, alkaline, sandy soil/full sun
North American hardiness zone: 3–8
Height & spread: 6m (20ft)
Grow for: excellent as a hedge; good for seaside areas; impressive fruit; AGM

Hippophae rhamnoides is one of the best shrubs for coastal planting and will grow in sand close to the hig- water line. It makes an efficient shelter belt and windbreak. When grown as a hedge the vicious thorns are a deterrent to animals.

The 5cm (2in) long, thin, grey-green leaves remain on the plant well into early winter. Male and female plants need to be close by for pollination. The small, insignificant, greenish-yellow flowers appear in spring. They are followed in autumn by masses of round, orange-yellow berries. The fruit is juicy but sufficiently acid to deter birds, thus allowing the shrub to hold its berries until early spring.

Older branches become brittle and have a habit of splitting. Hard prune in late summer, removing 50 per cent of the oldest branches. The following summer prune the remaining branches in the same way. This will encourage new shoots to grow from the base. Propagation is by seed sown as soon as it is ripe in autumn. Allow it to stratify in a cold frame. Examine the base of the parent plant for self-sown seedlings. Semi-ripe cuttings root in summer. Hardwood cuttings are rooted outside in the ground in autumn. Layering works well, forming large, rooted plants quickly.   **JC**

Hippophäe rhamnoides

Hoheria sexstylosa 'Stardust'

Hoheria sexstylosa 'Stardust'
LONG-LEAVED LACE BARK, NEW ZEALAND
LACE BARK

Type: hardy, evergreen tree or shrub
Soil & situation: tolerant of most soils except
heavy clay, prefers a well-drained
loam/sun/shelter
North American hardiness zone: 8–10
Height: 8m (25ft)
Spread: 6m (20ft)
Grow for: evergreen foliage; masses of white
flowers in mid- and late summer; AGM

My wife Gill planned a surprise party for my
fortieth birthday – what a treat! I arrived home
from work and was delighted – and shocked – to
find a host of friends had come to join the
celebrations. Among them were Roy Lancaster and
his wife Sue, who came bearing plants! Their trays
of treasures included *Hoheria sextylosa* 'Stardust', a
plant Roy had named. It's compact, columnar,
vigorous, appears to be hardier than the species
and flowers freely from an early age – mine has
already produced a few blooms, and I can't wait
until it matures when the great mass of mid-green
foliage will be star-spangled with dense clusters of
white flowers. They are so pretty that I'm growing
mine as a shrub for optimum flower power!

Other selections include the weeping form
H. sextylosa 'Pendula' and two related species
H. lyallii and *H. populnea*, not as robust but very
beautiful; there are plenty of spectacular New
Zealand plants, but these are among the best.

Although hardy throughout the UK, it flourishes
in damp, mild climates and is suitable for seaside
planting. Planted against a wall in a sunny
position with shelter from drying winds is ideal. In
cold winters it can lose its leaves but rapidly
recovers with the onset of spring. Prune to tidy up
in the spring after the last frosts. Propagate by
layering from late autumn to early spring, or by
semi-ripe cuttings in late summer.   **MB**

Hosta 'Gold Standard'
Plant of the Week (see page 241)

Humulus lupulus
HOP

Type: hardy, herbaceous, climbing crop
Soil & situation: rich, moist soil/full sun or light
shade
North American hardiness zone: 4–8
Height: 6m (20ft)
Spread: 3m (10ft)
Grow for: decorative, aromatic leaves; interesting,
scented flowers; and a useful crop

The hop is a strange plant, wreathed in mystery,
closely related to cannabis and used in beer
ostensibly as a flavouring and preservative. Just to
grow it is educational, but to use it to excess
detrimental. The young shoots, which can be
eaten like asparagus (in the manner of; they are
stringy and bitter) writhe from the ground like
snakes. They climb at an amazing speed, reaching

Humulus lupulus

over 6m (20ft) given the support, then they burst
into gorgeous cascades of golden-green panicles
of scented flowers surmounting the grapevine-
like, aromatic foliage. Glorious.

A UK and European native, hops were allegedly
known to the Romans but did not become widely
used for beer making until the 15th century. Our
name *Humulus* is a Latinized form of the old
European name *hummel*, while *lupulus* is Latin for
small wolf, from its habit of choking whatever it
comes upon. Male and female flowers are usually
borne on different plants and only the female
ones are of any use or value. Improved specialized
varieties are used for serious beer making.

It prefers a rich, moist old meadow, well-manured
soil, and plenty of sun and strong supports. To
use this plant to its potential you need tall
supports – and then a tall ladder! Leave only
three or so shoots per plant if you want crop
production and nip off rest. It can be grown from
seed but improved known female varieties only
from rooted offsets in spring. Hops can have
devastating attacks of aphids.   **BF**

Hyacinthus orientalis 'Lady Derby'

Hyacinthus orientalis 'Lady Derby'
HYACINTH

Type: hardy, spring-flowering bulb
Soil & situation: moist, well-drained, fertile soil/sun or partial shade
Height: 20–30cm (8–12in)
Spread: 8cm (3½in)
Grow for: pretty, rose-pink, fragrant, spring flowers

Spring wouldn't be the same without the bowls of bright, perfumed flowers and the huge areas of hyacinths bedded out in our parks. Then there are all the primary school windowsills filled with glasses, each holding a flowering bulb and showing a mass of white roots in murky water. *Hyacinthus orientalis* 'Lady Derby' is my favourite pink-flowering hyacinth. Neither too dark nor too pale, its single rose-pink flowers make up a 20cm (8in) raceme of up to 40 flowers. The lance-shaped, channelled, bright green leaves continue to grow after flowering to a height of 30cm (12in).

Specially prepared bulbs are available in late summer to force for early indoor flowering. Avoid waterlogged compost in containers or a heavy, clay border soil. They may be lifted immediately after flowering to clear the bed for other plants. Remove the dead flower and heel the bulb, complete with leaves, into damp sand or peat until the foliage has died. Always use gloves when handling hyacinths to reduce the risk of skin allergies. **JC**

Hydrangea anomala subsp. *petiolaris*
CLIMBING HYDRANGEA

Type: hardy, deciduous climber
Soil & situation: moist, fertile, well-drained soil/sun or shade
North American hardiness zone: 4–9
Height: 25m (80ft) if grown in suitable trees, usually much smaller
Grow for: attractive foliage, early summer flowers and peeling bark in winter

In the UK I'm often asked to recommend a climber for a north-facing wall; my answer is '*Hydrangea anomala* subsp. *petiolaris*' and the conversation goes something like this: 'Hang on, doesn't everyone plant that, it's a bit boring, isn't it?' to which I reply, 'Well yes, lots of people plant it, but I wouldn't say it's boring; dependable, more like with fresh green, serrated leaves in spring, beautiful lace-cap flowers in early summer and bronze peeling bark on the older stems in winter, year after year after year. Would you be able to retain such freshness and good humour after labouring at the coal-face for a life time? I doubt it'! There are few better plants for a shady wall, they are self-clinging but need some support until the roots 'get a grip' and can be trained as espaliers and free-standing shrubs too. The most impressive displays, however, are when they clamber up giant trees, holding on by their finger tips, then flaunt their lacy garments to be viewed from afar.

It thrives in fertile, moist, well-drained soil, high in organic matter. When planting, ensure that it is at least 60cm (24in) away from the base of the foundations. Tie the stems to a cane leaning

Hydrangea anomala subsp. *petiolaris*

against the wall during the early years and moisten the brickwork occasionally with a sprayer to encourage the roots to stick. Mulch and feed in spring with a balanced fertilizer. Prune in spring to encourage branching and to keep it within its allotted space. Propagate by layering or semi-ripe cuttings from mid-summer. **MB**

Bunny adds:
This is one of only a few self-clinging climbers, so it is highly useful to millions of more sporadic gardeners. Not only useful, it also has exquisite white lace-cap-like heads of sumptuous greenish-white flowers in summer. I do find that in certain gardens (mine for instance) where the dry conditions are not totally to its liking and the exposure levels are high, it is slow to get off the ground, but who can blame it? But in other conditions, it is up and away in no time. It clings adroitly, by its aerial roots. Hilliers catalogue mentions that it is picturesque when grown as a shrub, which had never occurred to me, but it seems like a great idea.

Hydrangea arborescens 'Annabelle'
Plant of the Week (see page 273)

Hydrangea aspera subsp. *sargentiana*

Type: hardy, deciduous shrub
Soil & situation: light, humus-rich, moist, fertile soil; tolerates chalk/bright, sheltered position
North American hardiness zone: 7–8
Height: 3m (10ft), or more
Spread: 2.5m (8ft)
Grow for: overall appearance; flowers in mid- and late summer

This sumptuously dressed, rather haughty, aristocratic shrub whose young stems are clothed in hairs and bristles and with leaves of the finest 'velvet' would not look out of place in a Victorian costume drama. Remarkable flat flowerheads up to 23cm (9in) across appear in mid- and late summer; the fertile flowers are lilac-rose, surrounded by guardian sterile florets, just over 3cm (1in) across, of pinkish-white. A well-grown, mature plant is magnificent, yet I find them slightly sinister. They combine elegance and serenity with an air of 'gothic' menace that's unmatched by any other; a compelling but unsettling plant!

This hydrangea is hardy but in need of shelter and protection, and although often grown in woodland gardens it is unhappy with competition from surrounding plants. It is reasonably tolerant of chalky soils and needs humus-rich, well-drained soil with plenty of well-rotted organic matter and an annual mulch in spring, when a top dressing of fertilizer is beneficial. Position in good light but protected from the scorching midday sun. Prune in spring to maintain the shape.

On established plants, young growth can be damaged by late frosts but it recovers very quickly producing a more resistant second flush, so the plant is often restored to health within four weeks. Younger plants are much more vulnerable and should be protected from frost. Propagate by layering in spring or semi-ripe cuttings in summer. **MB**

John adds:
If the flowerheads are allowed to remain they offer some frost protection to the new growths. The individual sterile flowers gradually deteriorate, becoming filament-like and see-through. Old plants may become leggy with all the leaf growth at the top of the plant. In late winter prune half the branches down to 45cm (18in) above ground level. Strong new shoots will appear from the stumps. The remaining branches can be cut the following year.

Hydrangea aspera subsp. *sargentiana*

Hypericum perforatum

Hydrangea aspera Villosa Group

Type: hardy deciduous shrub
Soil & situation: moist, but well-drained soil/fair amount of organic matter/part shade or sun/does not like windy conditions.
North American hardiness zone: 7–9
Height & spread: up to 4m (13ft)
Grow for: fantastic lilac-blue and whitish flowers in late summer; attractive, dark green leaves covered with soft down on their undersides and slightly downy on top; AGM

This hydrangea looks perfect in areas of light woodland or shady mixed borders. Although it grows exuberantly in the wetter and more acid areas of the country, *Hydrangea aspera*, together with *H. involucrata* 'Hortensis', are the most tolerant hydrangeas for growing on chalky soils. It is also a surprisingly strong-growing shrub which will settle in fairly rapidly and get on with life. Because hydrangeas come into growth early on, young shoots can get damaged by late frosts. After this initial setback, they quickly carry on producing their large, beautifully felted leaves. It is an ideal plant to grow in a prominent position against a shady wall: the protection from full sun is necessary to maintain the superb flower colour. If you are growing this plant on a thin, more impoverished soil, it is worthwhile adding lots of organic matter at planting and regularly applying a good mulch in autumn. Little pruning is required, the main task being to remove crossing shoots, diseased or unhealthy wood and anything that looks too eccentric. This is best done in late winter or early spring. **BG**

Hypericum perforatum
ST JOHN'S WORT

Type: herbaceous perennial
Soil & situation: moist soil/light shade
North American hardiness zone: 3–8
Height & spread: clump to 60cm (24in)
Grow for: good ground cover in shade, with dark green foliage and small yellow flowers

The most common member of this genus, *Hypericum calycinum*, the rose of Sharon, is everywhere; it fills supermarket and municipal car-park borders and even comes up as a weed. *H. perforatum* is much more civilized, and is effectively herbaceous, so can be cut back hard each winter and kept really neat. The flowers are yellow and small but welcome, and it is said the leaves taken internally under medical supervision relieve depression.

Hypericum is one of 160 species native to copses and woodlands in the UK and Europe. The Latin name is from the Greek *hyper*, meaning above, and *eikon*, picture, as the flowers were hung above icons to ward off evil on St John's day, June 24th, thus also giving it the common name of St John's wort. The *perforatum* part is from the tiny oil glands that appear as punctures through the leaf and can be seen if a piece of foliage is held up to the light. The French call it 'thousand punctures plant'. These oil cells make it an invaluable medicinal plant but not for home use, and have led to the breeding of varieties with a high oil content.

St John's wort copes quite well with a dry site, but will be long lived in moist, loamy soil in partial shade. Avoid handling because the oil gives this plant smelly leaves. It can be cut back like any herbaceous plant once the flowering stems wither. Sow in spring or divide established clumps. It suffers no problems. **BF**

Hyssopus officinalis

Hyssopus officinalis
HYSSOP

Type: small, tenderish shrub
Soil & situation: well-drained soil/full sun
North American hardiness zone: 6–9
Height: 60cm (24in)
Spread: 60cm (24in)
Grow for: a beautiful, semi-evergreen, bright blue flowered shrub

I find hyssop annoying as I keep losing it and having to replace it, but it is fairly easy to propagate and, occasionally, I even find odd seedlings self-sown. The azure-blue flowers are small but mass themselves over the entire bush, emitting a powerful fragrance on warm days, which attracts every bee in my garden. Some of the best honey too! Hyssop can be kept pretty tidy and is good for edging as long as it is not shaded or exposed. It has useful culinary properties – the petals have a sort of tangy minty-piney flavour and I use them in moderation in salads and stews.

The name hyssop stems from the Latin, which comes from the Greek *hussopos* and the Hebrew *esob* or *ezob*, holy herb, which is all very confusing because the hyssop of the Bible was probably

actually what we know as marjoram. Introduced in the Middle Ages, hyssop has never been much improved, though there are pink, and white, miffy forms.

Even in a well-drained, light, warm soil and position hyssop is not long lived as it soon succumbs to a bad winter. Trim to keep it neat and tidy as growth commences in spring. To propagate, sow seed in spring or divide the roots, or take summer cuttings. Hyssop can be lost in very cold weather so back up with half-ripe cuttings with a heel rooted in a cold frame in the summer. **BF**

Ilex aquifolium 'J.C. van Tol'
HOLLY

Type: hardy, evergreen tree
Soil & situation: moist, well-drained, humus-rich soil/full sun or partial shade
North American hardiness zone: 7–9
Height: 7m (23ft)
Spread: 4m (13ft)
Grow for: guaranteed clusters of bright red berries; AGM

With this holly there is no need to wonder if there will be a good crop of berries. Being hermaphrodite, it carries male and female flowers on the same plant ensuring pollination.

The 7.5cm (3in) long, glossy, dark green leaves are slightly puckered with few or no spines. The

Ilex aquifolium 'J.C. van Tol'

young shoots are dark purple. Small clusters of creamy-white flowers appear in early summer and are followed, in autumn, by bright red fruit.

Don't plant it in a site where the soil dries out in summer and avoid biting cold, drying winds. Once established, it dislikes being disturbed. Planting and transplanting should be carried out in late winter or early spring. Birds love the berries and to be sure of a supply for winter decoration you will have to secure them early by covering the clusters with muslin bags.

Prune in late winter to remove vigorous stems that are spoiling the shape. Where there are two erect branches, competing for leader and making a narrow angle, remove the weaker stem. A row of *I. aquifolium* 'J.C. van Tol' makes a wonderful hedge and it should be trimmed in early spring. Propagate by semi-ripe cuttings in late summer or early autumn in a heated propagator. **JC**

Ilex crenata 'Convexa' (syn. *I. c.* 'Bullata')
BOX-LEAVED HOLLY, JAPANESE HOLLY

Type: hardy, evergreen shrub to small tree
Soil & situation: most soils except waterlogged/ sun or shade
North American hardiness zone: 5–7
Height: up to 2.5m (8ft)
Spread: to 2m (6½ft)
Grow for: tiny, neat, evergreen leaves; useful for hedging and shaping; white flowers followed by glossy, black berries in the autumn; AGM

Ilex crenata 'Convexa'

The first time I was aware of this plant was when I saw a magnificent, cloud-pruned specimen that was about 1.5m (5ft) high. The leaves, being only about 1cm (less than 1/2in) long, make it an ideal plant to clip, shape and train. Because of the diminutive leaves, you would not necessarily know it was a holly – the leaves are elliptically shaped, curved and a mid-dark green colour. Several gardeners I know of, whose gardens have suffered from box blight disease, have replaced the dwarf hedges with this holly and it seems to work a treat. The downside is that it is more difficult to get hold of than box, but then it is not so much of a cliché. Hollies, as a rule, do not like being moved much, so they can take a little time to settle down and get into their stride.

The species *Ilex crenata* is also useful for low hedges, but the leaves are larger, about 2–3cm (1in) long, so not so neat-looking.

If shaping the plant, cut it in late summer so that you are cutting the shoots before they are fully ripened. If you cut before this, you may well get further new growth the same year, causing you to carry out a further cut to keep it looking pristine. Berries are formed on two-year-old wood and are black and glossy. When planting all hollies, reduce the stress as much as possible in the first few years. Although they tolerate exposure well, they hate it before they are established, so temporary shelter netting, adequate moisture in dry periods and no weed competition help dramatically to get this plant going. Propagate by cuttings in late summer. **BG**

Impatiens omeiana

Type: hardy, herbaceous perennial
Soil & situation: moist soil/dappled shade
North American hardiness zone: 7–8
Height: 50cm (20in)
Spread: indefinite
Grow for: beautiful foliage; unusual flowers from late summer to late autumn

American plantsman Don Jacobs found this treasure growing at 2,440m (8,000ft) among rhododendrons and tiarellas on Mt Omei in Sichuan, China in 1983. It was the first discovery of a plant that was previously only known as a lifeless two-dimensional specimen, pressed to a sheet of stiff paper in a herbarium (a scientific collection of pressed plants). To find it alive and flourishing must have been incredibly exciting! Now this delightful exotic is in cultivation; it is excellent ground cover for damp shade and perfect for a moist spot in a woodland garden, gradually spreading where conditions allow. Its crowning glory is the fabulous foliage that looks like that of a New Guinea impatiens. The leaves are long and narrow, purple to olive-green with yellowish-green ribs and a more prominent central vein and are arranged in circles around the stem. The apricot-yellow flowers appear in late summer or early autumn, hanging like elongated trumpets or plump goldfish – depending on your imagination! – from stems in the leaf axils. It looks good in a pot in a 'tropical' garden.

It needs full or part shade in moist, well-drained soil; mulch in spring. It is hardy – the weather in its natural habitat can be fairly chilly; cut back stems and protect with a layer of mulch over winter. Propagate by seed, division in spring or cuttings in spring or early summer. **MB**

Impatiens omeiana

Impatiens tinctoria

Impatiens tinctoria

Type: tender, tuberous perennial
Soil & situation: moist, free-draining soil/ sun/shelter
North American hardiness zone: 9–10
Height: 2.2m (7ft)
Spread: 1m (3ft)
Grow for: unusual flowers from late summer to mid-autumn

Impatiens tinctoria is not your average blowsy busy Lizzie (don't mention the name in its presence!). This spectacular species comes from mountainous forests, shady, shrub-filled gullies on damp banks and by streams from eastern Zaire and southern Sudan to Ethiopia and northern Uganda – exotic locations that conjure up an air of magic and mystery!

It's a lush, vigorous, upright plant that forms bold clumps of stout fleshy stems, each with large lance-shaped leaves to 20cm (8in) long, which look perfect in a 'tropical' garden. The remarkable, fragrant flowers hang on long upright stalks, like giant, pure white butterflies flitting above the foliage. The two lower petals are landing pads for visiting insects and the rounded throat is marked with a bold splash of colour ranging from violet to burgundy and magenta that trickles down onto the petals. It's a fabulous plant for the garden, with magnificent foliage but it's those amazing flowers that really make it a plant to savour.

It needs moist, humus-rich soil that is well drained in winter. Dig in plenty of well-rotted leafmould and grit in heavier soils. Ideal for a warm, sheltered corner by a wall or greenhouse in mild climates where it can be long lived. Cut back the stems in autumn and protect with dry mulch, like bracken or straw, until there's no danger of frost. In colder areas, treat it like a dahlia by lifting and over-wintering in a cool, frost-free place. Divide in spring, adding plenty of organic matter to the soil before planting. **MB**

Alcea rosea 'Nigra'

HOLLYHOCK

Type: hardy perennial
Soil & situation: sharply-drained soil/sunny position.
Hardiness zone: 3–9
Height: 2.4m (7$^{1}/_{2}$ft)
Spread: to 60cm (24in)
Grow for: the archetypal cottage garden plant; unusual, wine-coloured flowers, which give this well-loved flower a more extravagant air and last from early to late summer, sometimes longer

There is always room for these lofty beauties, which are easy and fun to grow. The single flowers are, of course, not black, but a rich, maroon-wine colour and have a yellow throat – quite a combination. The papery flowers are arranged all the way up the towering spires. I like them best growing against a building, preferably near a door, where you can get up close to them.

They will set seed in the most impenetrable-looking cracks that are rarely in intolerable positions. The far better known *A. rosea* comes in red, white, yellow and pink forms, and these too are fetching. They all form really striking cut flowers.

The problem with these beauties is, of course, rust. It is recommended that preventative measures are taken by spraying from late spring before the outbreak occurs. If it does occur, you get rid of the plant. However, in some areas rust is less prevalent. I do not spray routinely but remove them if they get attacked and plant new plants elsewhere the next year. As they are easy from seed this is no huge loss. They can be sown in summer and then planted out into their final position in autumn to flower the following summer. You can, of course, treat them as biennials and hopefully avoid a lot of the rust altogether. They may need staking, especially if your soil is fertile, but I tend to get away without having to do so.   **BG**

Imperata cylindrica 'Rubra'
JAPANESE BLOOD GRASS

Type: hardy, deciduous perennial
Soil & situation: moist, slightly acid, humus-rich soil/back-lit by sunshine
North American hardiness zone: 4–9
Height: 40cm (16in)
Spread: 30cm (12in)
Grow for: blood-red leaves

Take one bright green grass, dip the tips in blood red then watch it slowly diffuse down the stems until mid-summer and beyond. By autumn, it is completely crimson. It's incredible how so many unusual and beautiful plants come from Japan; *Salix gracistylis* 'Melanostachys', the willow with 'black' catkins (see page 347), 'fancy' hepaticas (page 206) and this spectacular grass. There have also been some complete duffers, like the horrendous *Salix integra* 'Hakuro-nishiki', which is weak, insipid and looks like a pile of vomit. This, however, is one of the best and most beautiful. Placed so that it is back-lit by the evening sun, it becomes bathed in a rich red glow and is a spectacular sight. This spreading, shallow-rooted plant emerges late and creates an excellent contrast between softer colours and arching grasses like *Stipa tenuissima*. I would place it in a pot on a plinth at eye level, rather than ground level, so that every centimetre could be savoured!

It needs moist, well-drained, fertile, slightly acid, humus-rich soil in full sun or light shade, though it tolerates some drought once established. It is also happy on clay. Not reliably frost hardy, grow in containers if your garden is exceptionally cold or in a frost pocket; over-winter in a cool, frost-free place. Cut back plants in spring and mulch with well-rotted organic matter. Divide in late autumn or spring. Aphids, slugs and snails can be a problem. **MB**

Imperata cylindrica 'Rubra'

Indocalamus tessellatus f. *hamadae*

Type: hardy evergreen perennial
Soil & situation: moist soil/partial shade
North American hardiness zone: 8–11
Height & spread: 3m (10ft), or more
Grow for: architectural form and leaves

There's always been an interest in bringing a tropical touch to the garden and anything with big bold leaves or unusual flowers is usually welcomed with open cheque book. It's inevitable that among the spiny cacti and hardy palms there are also some big bamboos and this is one of the best for its massive, delicately ridged leaves.

Formally known as *Indocalamus hamadae* but now classified as a form of *I. tessellatus*, this is a real beauty. The elegant stems, to 1.5cm (over ½in) thick, support noble leaves, usually about 40cm (16in) long, sometimes longer, and 8–60cm (3½–24in) wide. It's native to Kyushu in Japan, where the leaves were used for wrapping rice balls. *I. tessellatus* has long leaves too, consistently reaching 60cm (24in). It forms dense thickets of slender, bright green canes with a waxy bloom that simply collapse under the weight of the leaves to form a low mound. Both are stunning, just make sure that you have the space for them to grow.

They prefer partial shade on moist, humus-rich soils. They can be grown in pots but need regular division. Plant in a hole 90cm (36in) wide and 45cm (18in) deep. Dig in plenty of well-rotted manure or garden compost. Thoroughly soak the bamboo in a bucket before planting a little deeper than it was in the pot. Water well. It does not spread too far, but you can put in a plastic barrier about 10cm (4in) below the ground. Mulch annually in spring and keep the ground moist. Thin out the canes to keep them under control. Divide in spring. **MB**

Ipomoea batatas
SWEET POTATO

Type: tender, perennial, semi-evergreen climber
Soil & situation: rich, moist soil/full sun/under cover
North American hardiness zone: 9–11
Height: climbs to 3m (10ft)
Spread: 3m (10ft)
Grow for: attractive, ivy-like, edible foliage; very pretty flowers; edible roots

Ipomoea batatas

Sweet potatoes have slowly been improved and it is now possible, given a good summer, to grow them outdoors even in the UK. Young plants are actually being sold commercially. However they do much better under cover in a greenhouse or conservatory, though they can go out on the patio in the height of summer. The heart-shaped leaves have a healthy, vigorous, dark green luxuriousness which makes this a beautiful climber for a big tub. Many varieties flower with pretty bindweed-like blooms in pink, white and purple, and if they have done well at the end of the season you have a load of delicious sweet potatoes to eat as well!

A native of South America, sweet potatoes came to Europe even before the more common 'Irish' potato, which also came from the South America. The latter triumphed because the sweet is more frost tender and it is hard to over-winter the tubers. It has to be over-wintered as rooted layers or slips, which is not convenient. There are several strains; the yellow-fleshed and the white with pink, purple, red or orange skins. Don't confuse these with yams, which are another genus – *Dioscorea*.

It needs well-drained but moist, rich, limy soil preferably in a big tub or greenhouse border. Nip out tips and tie runners to a pole or strings to keep them off the ground – if they touch the soil they root everywhere and waste energy on making sweet potato spaghetti. Root tips as layers in early autumn and over-winter plantlets in the warmth. Alternatively force a supermarket tuber and detach shoots when a finger or so long, pot up and grow on in the warmth, potting up regularly, and as the new season gets underway move or plant outdoors a few weeks after the last frost. Tubers may get nibbled by rodents! **BF**

Iris 'Brown Lasso'

Iris 'Brown Lasso'

Type: hardy, perennial rhizome
Soil & situation: well-drained soil/sun
North American hardiness zone: 3–9
Height & spread: 55cm (22in) x 30 cm (12in), or more
Grow for: striking flowers in early summer; sword-shaped foliage; AGM

Beware of being seduced by the pictures in a magazine; they glamorize reality and the only limit is your imagination. The first time I saw this glamorous iris, it had made the front cover and everything I imagined about it was true! There are so many beautiful irises that it takes something extraordinary for one to stand out from the rest; here, the colours are irresistible – it seems that however unusual the colour combination, in nature, it seems to work. We are not worthy!

The three upright petals are deep butterscotch while those hanging downwards are light violet with caramel-brown margins and a yellow beard. The description is simple, the impact, stunning! 'Brown Lasso' is a border bearded iris, flowering in early summer and good for small gardens and windy sites. It is beautiful, robust and a good grower too. Some have everything; others, nothing. It's just not fair!

It needs free-draining soil and full sun, but tolerates partial shade. Dig in sharp sand or gravel on clay soils and grow in raised beds; add organic matter or leafmould to lighter soils. If possible plant so the cut end of the rhizome faces south and the fan north so the rhizome is not shaded. It needs a good baking in summer; don't let the rhizomes get weedy; remove dead leaves and spent flowers to save energy.

Divide every two to three years to keep plants vigorous; the top of the rhizome should be only 1cm (½in) below the surface. Feed with high-potash fertilizer at half rate when planting and in early spring to help flowering. It can be affected by aphids and rot in poorly drained soils.   **MB**

Iris danfordiae

Type: hardy bulb
Soil & situation: free-draining soil/sun
North American hardiness zone: 5–8
Height: 15cm (6in)
Spread: 7.5cm (3in)
Grow for: bright yellow flowers from late winter to early spring

This bulbous iris, a relative of the elegant *Iris reticulata* (see page 221), is a true harbinger of spring. It is always a pleasure to greet the small, bright yellow flowers about 5cm (2in) long that illuminate the winter border. Study it closely to enjoy the green tints and spots in the centre along a deep orange ridge; the upright petals or standards at the top of the flower have almost disappeared, all that remains are tiny bristles. It is found in the mountains of Turkey along the snowline and pushes its way through the snow to flower, as it sometimes does here in the UK. The glowing yellow flowers are a wonderful sight against the pure white background of snow and a sure reminder that springtime and sunshine are not far behind. It is good at the front of rockeries, in borders, containers or among silver-foliage plants. Combined with blue chionodoxas it is a thoroughly uplifting sight.

It is cheap and is better treated as an annual. According to Brian Mathew, an expert and connoisseur of bulbs, it has a habit of splitting into a tiny group of non-flowerings bulbs. He has been successful in establishing a group by planting them at least 10cm (4in) deep and feeding with high-potash fertilizer in early spring and autumn. Why not try it too?

It needs sunshine, ideally a good summer baking, and free-draining, preferably alkaline soil; dig in sharp sand or grit if necessary before planting. When growing as an annual don't worry about the soil, providing it is not waterlogged.   **MB**

Iris danfordiae

Iris foetidissima

Iris foetidissima
STINKING IRIS

Type: hardy, evergreen perennial rhizome
Soil & situation: moist, well-drained soil/partial shade
North American hardiness zone: 7–9
Height: 60–90cm (24–36in)
Spread: indefinite
Grow for: summer flowers; interesting seeds in autumn; AGM

It really isn't fair to call it stinking. It is not the flower but the leaf which has the unpleasant smell, and only when it is crushed. Most of us could go through life without crushing an iris leaf!

Vigorous growing, it has tufts of 80cm (32in) long, dark green leaves. The 5–8cm (2–3½in) wide, mat, purple-yellow flowers are produced in early summer on long branched stems each carrying up to five blooms. They are followed in autumn by large, club-shaped capsules, which split to reveal bright, orange-red seeds. Occasionally the seeds are yellow, scarlet or white. It is good for a woodland situation or on a shady bank close to a pond.

A deep surface mulch of composted bark in spring is beneficial. Propagation is by seed sown in autumn or spring without protection or by division of the fleshy rhizomes in early autumn and replanting immediately. The plant is poisonous to livestock, which is a very good reason for keeping cows out of your garden! **JC**

Bunny adds:
A useful plant for its leaves and the long-lasting and eye-catching seeds. It seeds freely all round my garden, and seems fairly happy in sunny situations too.

Iris germanica var. *florentina*
ORRIS ROOT

Type: hardy, herbaceous perennial rhizome
Soil & situation: dry, limy soil/full sun
North American hardiness zone: 3–9
Height: 50cm (20in)
Spread: indefinite
Grow for: attractive, sword-shaped, light green leaves; palest pastel decorated white flowers with heavenly scent; good for stuffing mummies and cleaning your teeth; AGM

Iris are often overlooked as 'common' and so they are, loads of them in all sorts of colours and sizes. They are adaptable and some variety or other will grow in every different place, usually putting on a good show. *Iris germanica* var. *florentina* is delicate, needing a warm, sheltered spot but then it is delightful. It is nice in leaf and the finely sculptured blooms are lightly scented of the finest soap, but it is the roots that captivate. Once dried they become orris root, which is used in potpourri, perfumes and toiletries and has been since ancient times. The smell of violets from the roots gets stronger as they dry and wither.

Iris is the Greek goddess of the rainbow. It was thought to come from Florence, and even though it is in fact from southern Europe, it was first known to be grown in gardens in 1500BC in Egypt, where it is shown distinctly on tomb walls at Karnak.

Iris germanica var. *florentina*

Iris pseudacorus 'Variegata'

In dismal weather it may not be very long lived and, anyway, it needs replanting every few years to keep up its vigour. Iris are hard to plant as their rhizome needs to be above the soil and the roots (few as there are) must not be buried deep or straight down, thus it is difficult to anchor with the green leaf on top; I use two bricks to temporarily hold down the roots under a thin layer of soil and pushed up to either side of the rhizome, thus still exposing it to the sun. The books say plant these rhizomes in mid-summer, but I have also split and replanted mine in spring just as they started into growth. It is not happy if shaded, cold or wet. **BF**

Iris pseudacorus 'Variegata'
FLAG IRIS

Type: hardy, perennial rhizome
Soil & situation: permanently moist, humus-rich, deep, acid soil/full sun or partial shade
North American hardiness zone: 5–8
Height: 75–90cm (30–36in)
Spread: 45cm (18in)
Grow for: bold, architectural leaves; perfect for waterside planting; AGM

I used to grow large quantities of this plant for sale. In spring the 1-litre black plastic pots of young, creamy-white striped, variegated, sword-like leaves were an instant buy. There were always a few plants with pure white variegation and they were highly sought after. I grew it because I liked it.

The variegation remains as the leaves lengthen and they continue to be rigid and upright. In mid- to late summer each branched stem produces between four and eight bright yellow flowers. Strong-growing, it spreads quickly by

Iris reticulata

There are many selections of the species, including 'Harmony', which is blue and yellow, 'Cantab', pale blue and yellow, 'J. S. Dijt', red-purple with orange markings, and 'Natascha', pure white with a butter-yellow strip. **JC**

Iris 'Superstition'

Type: hardy, perennial rhizome
Soil & situation: prefers very well-drained soil that is fairly neutral/will tolerate alkaline soil/hates acid soils and poor drainage/sun
North American hardiness zone: 3–9
Height: 90cm (36in)
Spread: 15cm (6in)
Grow for: beautiful dark wine-purple to black flowers during the early summer; foliage is grey-green and not unattractive; AGM

There are so many different irises to choose from it is not always easy to know which is the best for you. If you are keen on the exotic dark purple, almost black colour range, then you need look no further than Iris 'Superstition'. It is a difficult colour to find in plants generally, but bearded irises seem to come up trumps here. The whole plant is a good, strong, robust grower with the flowers carried on stout stems above the leaves. It is generally a good, healthy plant despite its truly exotic flower colour. My cousin, Claire Austin, who was an illustrator before starting her nursery where she now grows more than 400 different irises, describes this one far better than I could, 'in texture its falls are glossy as silk, and its standards are silkier still. The beard is dark purple, and the whole flower is ruffled and scented.' So you can see it is a difficult one to resist.

If your soil is wet it is worth considering growing irises in raised beds, or else digging a large hole and adding free-draining material, prior to planting. When you plant the rhizomes (assuming they have arrived bare rooted) the top of the rhizome should be just above the soil and the roots spread out to anchor it. If you have bought pot-grown plants, remove the potting compost before planting. Water the plant in gently with a sprinkling of water. Divide the irises once every three or four years: this is best done in late summer or autumn, discarding the older bits. Re-plant and cut the foliage back to about 15cm (6in), otherwise the routine care calls for removing any manky leaves in autumn to prevent the spread of disease. **BG**

thick rhizomes. This moisture-loving plant looks well positioned beside water and it can be grown in pots in shallow water but its growth is more restricted. Planted beside a strong-flowing garden waterfall it tolerates the water splash while providing camouflage for a change in levels.

Propagation is by lifting and dividing large, overgrown clumps. Re-plant straight away in their permanent sites. Healthy rhizomes can be cut into lengths retaining one shoot per length and rooted in trays of wet peat and grit mixed. Once rooted they are potted on for a season before planting out. The principal pests are slugs, which damage the young leaves and the flowers. **JC**

Iris reticulata

Type: hardy, spring-flowering bulb
Soil & situation: moist, free-draining, neutral to slightly alkaline soil/full sun or light shade
North American hardiness zone: 5–8
Height: in flower 5–10cm (2–4in); after flowering, foliage 30cm (12in)
Spread: 5cm (2in)
Grow for: bluey, fragrant flowers in winter; makes a fine show in a group; AGM

If you make it happy *Iris reticulata* can be in flower in mid-winter but more usually from late winter to early spring. The fragrant flowers come in various shades of blue, from Wedgewood through to deep velvety purple. The true wild form is a deep purple-blue with an orange-yellow raised stripe along the centre of each fall (petal). The thin, four-ribbed leaves appear to be square in section. After flowering they continue to grow to 30cm (12in).

Ideal in groups in a rockery, scree bed or container, they dislike being forced for early indoor show. Choose bulbs which are firm and packed in sawdust to prevent them drying out. Check the skin is creamy-white and free from the black blotches of ink spot disease, a fungus which first shows as yellowing foliage. The bulbs eventually turn black and rot. There is no control other than burning infected bulbs.

When grown on heavy, wet soil the bulbs often split after flowering and refuse to flower the following year. Planting in a raised bed in autumn in well-drained soil with extra grit prevents this problem. Lift and divide every few years when fully dormant, re-planting 10cm (4in) deep.

Itea illicifolia

Itea illicifolia

Type: hardy, dense evergreen shrub
Soil & situation: moist, fertile, free-draining soil/sun or partial shade
North American hardiness zone: 7–9
Height & spread: 5m (16ft)
Grow for: foliage and catkins of mellifluous flowers in late summer and early autumn; AGM

Yes, it's another holly 'doppelgänger'! You could easily be misled by *Itea illicifolia* until closer scrutiny reveals that the leaves are thinner and not as glossy or undulating and the young growth is coppery in colour. Long racemes of tiny, greenish-white flowers burst from the arching stem tips in late summer and early autumn, lengthening as the season passes until they hang like lamb's tails between 15–30cm (6–12in) long, barely moving in the passing breeze. At dusk and overnight, a heady, honey-sweet fragrance pervades the atmosphere around them, enticing moths in great numbers to come and sip of their nectar. Place a chair nearby and just sit and enjoy it too!

A related species, *I. yunnanensis*, is similar but the leaves are longer and not as spiny or rounded, the white flowers in hanging clusters up to 18cm (7in) long. *I. virginica* is a smaller, upright, deciduous shrub growing to 2.5m (8ft) with creamy-white, fragrant flowers in mid-summer. It often has good autumn colour, is hardier than the other two and needs good, constantly moist soil.

Prune at any time to keep within its allotted space. Propagate by softwood or semi-ripe cuttings from late summer to early autumn. It needs a warm, sunny position in fertile soil. In colder climates where it is not hardy, the shoots can be frosted and it even loses its leaves; it is best to train *I. illicifolia* along wires or grow it as a shrub against a sheltered, sunny wall. Protect and mulch plants in winter until they are established. **MB**

Jasminum nudiflorum
WINTER JASMINE

Type: hardy, deciduous shrub
Soil & situation: fertile, well-drained soil/full sun or light shade
North American hardiness zone: 6–9
Height & spread: 3m (10ft)
Grow for: colour in the winter garden; AGM

I have a soft spot for the winter jasmine. While it doesn't have the fragrance of other summer-flowering jasmines, its bright yellow flowers on leafless stems are a welcome sight in winter. Arching, dark green stems are coated with small lateral branches. The dark green leaves are divided into three, 3cm (1in) long leaflets. The solitary, six-petalled, bright yellow flowers appear in winter and early spring from the leaf axils. The tight flower buds are tipped red, making a contrast with the open flowers. They are immune to inclement weather. Left to its own devices it will scramble about forming a low, untidy mound of stems. Planted against a wall or trellis and given support it can display its winter charm.

Annual pruning after flowering will prevent stems becoming bare from the base upwards. Cut the flowered shoots to young growths lower down the stem. With small plants trim back to healthy buds. Mature, straggly plants should be hard pruned removing one third of the growths at ground level. Tie in the new shoots as they grow.

Propagate by semi-ripe cuttings in summer. Make the lower cut immediately below a pair of leaves. Stems layered in autumn will be well rooted and probably in flower by the following winter. **JC**

Jasminum nudiflorum

Jasminum revolutum

Jasminum revolutum (syn. J. humile 'Revolutum')

Type: frost-hardy, near-evergreen shrub
Soil & situation: any soil/sun to light shade
North American hardiness zone: 8–9
Height: 2m (6½ft)
Spread: 1m (3ft)
Grow for: unusual and very beautiful shrub with fragrant yellow flowers; AGM

Everyone knows the common jasmine, many know there are numerous other climbing jasmines, tender and hardy, but few gardeners know or grow any of the shrubby species. In fact, there are around 200 jasmines in all. *J. revolutum* is almost evergreen, although in severe weather it will drop its leaves. It has fragrant yellow flowers over a long season and is amenable to being neglected, but is more suited to the damper, milder west of England than in the east where I live. However, I had one for years until I foolishly moved it.

This jasmine is one of several shrubby species almost all of which have deciduous foliage and yellow flowers. *J. revolutum* was introduced to the UK from China in 1814 and is closely related to the more deciduous and inferior *J. humile*, but is not to be confused with the scentless *J. nudiflorum*, which flowers through winter. The name *revolutum* refers to the flowers having rolled-back edges.

It is happy in most soils and positions, but not in waterlogged or windy, exposed sites. Trim it in early spring if you need to remove wind-burnt leaves. It can be layered, otherwise try semi-ripe cuttings in summer with bottom heat. **BF**

Jasminum x stephanense

Type: perennial, deciduous climber
Soil & situation: most soils/full sun
North American hardiness zone: 8–10
Height: 8m (25ft)
Spread: 1–1.5m (3–5ft)
Grow for: young foliage in spring gives the striking effect of a ball of fire, then changes to yellow-green until the autumn; pink, scented flowers all summer

Common white jasmine, *Jasminum officinale*, is a well-known garden plant needing a sunny spot to thrive in evergreen glory and scented white flowers. It has dozens of relations, including *J. beesianum*, which has small carmine-coloured flowers. The cross between these two, *J. x stephanense*, was raised in France in the 1920s and is the only jasmine hybrid. The leaves are similar to both parents, less evergreen and more decidedly deciduous, and have fantastic colours when first unfurled, looking quite simply as if the foliage is on fire in red, yellow and cream. Later the foliage settles down to a pleasant lemon-green and the flowers take over. Masses of them for weeks; stupendous.

J. officinale has been grown from early times and is originally from the area between Persia and China, yet made it to England in time to be popular with the Tudors. The Arabic name was *yasamyn*, the Chinese *yeh-lse-ming*, and we made it sweet jessamine or jasmine and Latinization makes it *jasminum*.

Jasmines can be long lived in a sunny sheltered site with a well-drained soil and the addition of some lime. They may need shearing back one year in ten. I have sown seed of *J. beesianum* crossed with *J. officinale* and grown half a dozen plants all very similar to *J. x stephanense*; otherwise propagate by layers. It has no problems. **BF**

Jasminum x stephanense

Jeffersonia dubia

Jeffersonia dubia

Type: hardy, herbaceous perennial
Soil & situation: organic-rich, free-draining soil/dappled shade
North American hardiness zone: 5–7
Height: 20cm (8in)
Spread: 15cm (6in)
Grow for: flowers in late spring and early summer

If you're looking for delicate beauty, this is another 'must have'. This 'woodlander' from the forests of Manchuria has kidney-shaped or rounded, two-lobed leaves, blue-purple when first unfolding but gradually turning to green with deep purple tints. Appreciate the simple, dainty flowers of soft lavender-blue while you can, as they only remain open for two days, then gradually fade away – how transitory is beauty!

Its North American cousin *Jeffersonia diphylla* (rheumatism root or twinleaf) is found on limestone woodland near rivers and is very rare in the wild. It grows to 20cm (8in) plus x 15cm (6in) and has more petals than *J. dubia* and white flowers with a central boss. The leaves hover over the white like giant green butterflies protecting the tender flowers. It has been used extensively in herbal medicine as the name suggests, for anything from diarrhoea to cancer. The Shakers used it for several ailments including spasms and cramp.

This genus is named for Thomas Jefferson, third President of the USA, who was also a great gardener, landscape designer and agriculturist. In 1811 he wrote, 'No occupation is so delightful to me as the culture of the earth and no culture comparable to that of the garden'. Hear! Hear!

Grow in light to moderate, moist, well-drained soil in dappled shade. Add plenty of well-rotted organic matter, preferably leafmould, before planting if the soil is lacking it. Mulch around the plants in spring, if necessary. They are slow-growing in ideal conditions, where they make large clumps. They can be divided in early spring but resent disturbance. Sow seed as soon as possible in a cold frame. Prone to slug and snail damage. **MB**

Plectranthus argentatus

Type: tender, evergreen shrub
Soil & situation: medium fertile soil/sun or light shade/frost-free conditions in winter
North American hardiness zone: 9–10
Height & spread: 1m (3ft)
Grow for: a stunning foliage plant with silver, hairy leaves. Good at any frost-free time of year, but a perfect foil for summer flowers; AGM

Plectranthus argentatus is one of my most admired foliage plants. It has eye-catching (up to about 15cm/6in) grey-green leaves covered with silver hairs. These in turn are supported by downy, ascending, pinky-purple stems. The undersides of the ovate leaves are paler than the top. The flowers admittedly are less significant than the foliage. They are carried on 30cm (12in) racemes, are a not unattractive bluish-white and are shown off to their advantage against the pretty coloured stems. I use this put adjacent to plants like *Dahlia* 'Bishop of Llandaff', where the silvery leaves contrast with the purple, almost fern-like leaves. It is also a great plant for a summer container – something a bit different and rather good.

Although technically a shrub, it is usually treated as a tender perennial; small, rooted cuttings in spring will quickly form a presentable plant, whereas a larger shrub with its spreading habit will need annual cutting back to keep it in shape and take up too much precious greenhouse space during the winter. It is extremely easy to root from cuttings from new growth, which can be taken at any time of the year.   **BG**

Juglans regia 'Franquette'

Juglans regia 'Franquette'
WALNUT

Type: hardy, deciduous tree
Soil & situation: well-drained soil/sunny position
North American hardiness zone: 3–7
Height: 30m (100ft) or more
Spread: 15m (50ft)
Grow for: fragrant leaves, beautiful form, edible nuts

Walnuts make big trees and are only suited to large sites, although the variety 'Franquette' is, for a walnut, compact and early bearing. In fact it cropped for me after only a few years, possibly because I knew that to pollinate the female flowers with saved up male catkins, which also flower early, would aid cross-pollination. It is an old variety, probably French, with a long, large nut.

A native of southeastern Europe to China, the walnut was introduced to the Romans from Persia and allegedly did not arrive in the UK until the 15th century, when it was prized as much for its timber, which was used for veneers and gun stocks, as for its nuts. The nuts make a very good cooking and salad oil. The name in English comes via Old English from the Low German *walh-knutu* for foreign nut. The botanical is from *jovis* or Jupiter and *glans*, an acorn. They used to be planted near the outside privy, as the scent of the aromatic leaves was thought to keep the flies away. *Juglans nigra* is the American walnut and is similar but faster growing.

Walnuts are very long lived and although not fussy about the soil, they do prefer a heavy, moist one. They should not be planted in a frost pocket. Collect male catkins and keep dry and dust their pollen on female flowers which open a week or two later. Seedlings are easy enough to grow but may not crop for 20 years and could then produce inferior nuts. Grafted plants are necessary for true varieties. Their only real problem – squirrels! **BF**

Juniperus communis 'Compressa'
NOAH'S ARK JUNIPER

Type: hardy, evergreen conifer
Soil & situation: moist, well-drained soil/full sun/shelter from cold winds
North American hardiness zone: 2–6
Height: 80cm (32in)
Spread: 45cm (18in)
Grow for: dot plant in scree bed or stone trough; AGM

This little gem is the best conifer ever to have graced a rockery, sink or alpine scree bed. It is slow growing, forming a dense, compact column of light to mid-green. The needle-like leaves form an outer shell on a mature plant, camouflaging the brown interior of dead foliage.

Juniperus communis 'Compressa'

Keep the surrounding area weed free and prune back or transplant any other plant that may smother it. Plant a group of these miniatures 1–1.2m (3–4ft) apart on a gravel bed and watch them slowly mature, growing about 2cm (³/₄in) yearly. In autumn spiders swing like Tarzan from one to the other, leaving silver threads in their wake.

Juniperus communis 'Compressa' is tolerant of an alkaline soil but will suffer from dieback disease if planted in a heavy, wet soil or exposed to cold winds. Propagate using well-ripened current year's growth as small cuttings in autumn. Examine this conifer from mid-summer onwards for red spider mite. This pest, if not treated, will yellow the leaves and eventually defoliate the plant. **JC**

Kalmia latifolia 'Olympic Fire'

Kalmia latifolia 'Olympic Fire'
CALICO BUSH, MOUNTAIN LAUREL

Type: hardy, evergreen shrub
Soil & situation: moist, humus-rich, deep, acid soil/partial shade
North American hardiness zone: 5–9
Height: 3m (10ft)
Spread: 2m (6½ft)
Grow for: clusters of cup-shaped, pink flowers; AGM

As a child I loved hard icing (I still do). The unopened flower buds of kalmia are identical to the crimped design squeezed out of an icing bag and it is difficult to imagine them opening to cup-shaped flowers. A mature plant forms a dense, bushy shrub with 12cm (5in) long, lance-shaped, wavy-edged, glossy, dark evergreen leaves. Large 10cm (4in) clusters of pink flowers up to 3cm (1in) wide open from tight, dark red buds from late spring through until mid-summer.

Kalmia latifolia 'Dollar Spot' has large white flowers; *K. l.* 'Bullseye' is white with wide, red-purple banding on the outside; and *K. l.* 'Clementine Churchill' has deep pink buds which open to large, pink, waxy flowers.

Water newly planted shrubs regularly for the first season. Mulch with composted bark, leafmould or pine needles in spring before the soil surface dries out. Pruning should be kept to a minimum, only clipping off damaged or misshapen branches. Old specimen plants may be pruned hard in late spring, removing up to 50 per cent of the branches in the first year. Large shrubs will be slow to recover and may not flower for two years. Propagation is by softwood cuttings taken in late spring or semi-ripe shoots in mid-summer. Low-growing branches layered outdoors in late summer will root within 12 months. **JC**

Kerria japonica 'Pleniflora' (syn. *K. j.* 'Flore Pleno')
JEW'S MANTLE

Type: hardy, deciduous shrub
Soil & situation: well-drained, fertile soil/full sun or partial shade
North American hardiness zone: 4–9
Height & spread: 3m (10ft)
Grow for: an easy-to-grow, graceful shrub with golden-yellow flowers; AGM

It is surprising how many people don't know or grow this foolproof flowering shrub. Its suckers can be removed complete with roots, making it ideal for bulking up plant stalls at charity, church and school sales.

It is a vigorous plant, forming a tall, upright shrub. The mid-green, deciduous leaves are held

Kerria japonica 'Pleniflora'

Kirengeshoma palmata

on bright green stems which add interest to the garden in winter. The rich yellow, spring flowers are fully double like miniature chrysanthemum flowers. As they age the petals become paler. *Kerria japonica* 'Golden Guinea' has large 5cm (2in) single, bright buttercup-yellow flowers in early spring. *K. j.* 'Picta' has grey-green leaves edged with creamy white. It is more compact, growing to 1.5m (5ft) in height. I have struggled with this variegated form for three years and it is still only 60cm (24in) high, which may suggest it doesn't like me.

After flowering cut out the older branches as close to the base as possible. Younger stems may be pruned back to healthy buds lower down. Dieback will affect the thin tips of flowering stems in winter and early spring. The whitened twigs may be removed. Propagation is by softwood cuttings in summer. Suckers should be taken off in the autumn after leaf fall and planted out in the border or potted up. **JC**

Kirengeshoma palmata

Type: hardy, herbaceous perennial
Soil & situation: deep, moist soil/partial shade
North American hardiness zone: 5–8
Height: 1.2m (4ft)
Spread: 75cm (30in)
Grow for: foliage, form and soft yellow flowers in late summer and early autumn; AGM

Here's another plant that has stolen my heart, though I have to confess I succumbed willingly, and I know I'm not alone! It is a clump-forming perennial from the woodlands of Japan and Korea with flat, slightly lobed leaves, like those of an acer, which appear in opposite pairs along the stiff stems, diminishing in size towards the tips. Those near the flowerheads seem to clasp the dark stems with all their might, the leaf bases overlapping as if supporting each other, terrified that they might slide down the stems and disappear from view. The long, arching flowerheads look as though they are straining under the weight of the plump, rounded buds and soft butter-yellow flowers with thick, waxy petals. I have seen them described as 'loose, airy flights of ivory shuttlecocks…which pervade the entire plant'. Perfect!

The contrast between the pale yellow buds and flowers and the purple-maroon stems is delightful and its deportment, poise and grace, even without the flowers, are utterly enchanting. It is a privilege to grow it in your garden.

It needs deep, moist, fertile soil in shelter and dappled shade. Add plenty of well-rotted organic matter if necessary; it tolerates clay. Ideal in a shady border, woodland garden or a sheltered shady position. Divide in spring when growth starts, handle with care to avoid damaging the young shoots. Cut back the stems and mulch in winter with bracken or straw in colder areas. Slugs and snails attack shoots and leaves. **MB**

Knautia macedonica

Type: hardy perennial
Soil & situation: free draining soil/warm site
North American hardiness zone: 5–9
Height: up to 80cm (32in)
Spread: 45cm (18in)
Grow for: flowers of an extraordinary crimson colour over a long period

This plant has become extremely trendy over the last few years, mainly because of its very long flowering season and the bright, zany shade of its flowers. They are produced on thin, spindly, rather wiry stems, and in my garden reach about 40cm (16in) in height. The flowering season starts in early to mid-summer and will often carry on to late summer to early autumn. It looks far better as it establishes to form good-sized clumps as it can look too weedy and lacking in substance initially. If you are buying it in, it is worth buying well-established plants in 1-litre pots rather than in the smaller 9cm (3³⁄₄in) pots. They tend to get away more quickly. Some people recommend staking it, but I find it far more attractive to grow the plant between supporting neighbours where it tends to thread itself into them.

The field scabious, *K. arvensis*, grows in meadows, hedgerows and open woodland, often on calcareous soils, and is a charming native for wilder parts of the garden. It is easy to grow from seed and often flowers in the first year (unusual for perennials).

Knautia macedonica is a short-lived perennial, sometimes a biennial. Cut down the plant in late winter, early spring. To propagate, take basal cuttings in spring.   **BG**

Knautia macedonica

Kniphofia rooperi

Kniphofia spp.
TORCH LILY, RED-HOT POKER

Type: hardy, semi-evergreen, clump-forming, herbaceous perennial
Soil & situation: most soils/full sun/preferably moist in spring and summer, but dry in autumn and winter
North American hardiness zone: 6–9
Height: compact varieties under 50cm (20in), old-fashioned sorts may reach 1.5–1.8m (5–6ft) when flowering
Spread: 60cm–2m (2–6¹⁄₂ft)
Grow for: summer flowers with spectacular red, orange and yellow heads, and attractive long leaves for most of year

I rarely grow anything that is not either edible or scented, yet none of the kniphofias are known for these attributes. Then some years ago I noticed that the blue tits were feeding on the nectar, much like hummingbirds, so I thought I would have some in my garden just for them. However, I then noticed that if I placed a bowl under the flowerheads and shook them an amazing amount of green nectar fell out. I cannot recommend that you do the same but I have tried drinking this sweet fluid (ten heads can give a wineglass full) with no apparent ill effects. As they are originally from South Africa, it is surprising they survive in the UK at all, as they do not like dry summers and wet winters, preferring the converse.

The soil must be well drained in winter, so raised beds can be of help in heavy soils; do not plant in shade or they die away, and in colder regions position against a warm, sunny wall. Take off the dead flower stems and tidy up decaying leaves in autumn, but do not remove old leaves as these protect stem bases from hard weather. They can be grown from seed but offsets are much quicker, easier and come true; so split clumps in mid-spring as growth commences. They do tend to rot away if in shade, or if damp in winter. Otherwise problem free.   **BF**

Kniphofia caulescens
Plant of the Week (see page 345)

Kniphofia rooperi (syn. *K. 'C. M. Prichard')*
RED HOT POKER, TORCH LILY

Type: hardy, evergreen perennial
Soil & situation: deep, fertile, well-drained, sandy soil/full sun or light shade
North American hardiness zone: 7–9
Height: 1.2m (4ft)
Spread: 60cm (24in)
Grow for: a distinctive plant for the border with bright flowers on tall, vertical stems

Once an essential component in traditional cottage gardens, the red hot poker now shares its affections with modern planting designs. I love the bold clump of architectural leaves and its tall, bright, sturdy, late-flowering 'torches' of flower. The long, arching, dark green leaves are wide and pointed, managing to look tidy even in the dead of winter. The broad, stumpy, erect racemes of flowers are held well above the foliage on strong, mid-green stems. The pendent, 5cm (2in) long, tubular flowers are a bright orange-red, becoming orange-yellow and finally a clear yellow. Flowering commences in late summer and continues through to late autumn.

They are a good late source of nectar for bees. After flowering dead-head to prevent seed forming. The leaves form a hotel for snails and frequent examination during the year can reduce the population significantly. In the first winter after planting, protect from frost by covering with bracken foliage or straw, held in place with netting wire. Propagation is by division of established plants in spring. Large, woody clumps produce few rooted sideshoots. They can be taken as basal cuttings in early summer and rooted in a propagator in a gritty compost. **JC**

Koelreuteria paniculata
GOLDEN-RAIN TREE, PRIDE OF INDIA

Type: hardy, deciduous tree
Soil & situation: fertile, well-drained soil/full sun
North American hardiness zone: 5–9
Height: 10m (33ft)
Spread: 9m (30ft)
Grow for: flowers when most other trees have moved on to fruit or autumn foliage; AGM

It may well be the pride of India but this tree originated in China! I wouldn't be without it. It is in flower when most others are relying on fruit or autumn leaves for colour.

The 45cm (18in) long, pinnate leaves have scalloped leaflets. The young leaves open pink-red, turning to mid-green and finally buttery-yellow in autumn. Large – 30cm (12in) – loose panicles of small, golden-yellow flowers appear in early autumn, standing well clear of the foliage. The flowers are followed by bladder-like seedpods, bright pink at first, gradually becoming a rich brown colour.

It dislikes waterlogged ground and cold winds. Remove dead and damaged branches during winter before the sap starts to rise. Propagation is by seed sown thinly in autumn and over-wintered in a cold frame. Root cuttings taken in late winter and inserted upright in pots of soil-based compost will produce shoots the following spring and will be ready for repotting a year later. **JC**

Koelreuteria paniculata

Kolkwitzia amabilis
BEAUTY BUSH

Type: hardy, deciduous, suckering shrub
Soil & situation: fertile, well-drained soil; thrives on chalk/sun and tolerates some shade
North American hardiness zone: 5–9
Height: 3m (10ft)
Spread: 4m (13ft)
Grow for: gorgeous flowers in late spring and early summer

Kolkwitzia amabilis

This is an elegant, hardy, densely twiggy, medium-sized shrub. In late spring and early summer the drooping branches are massed with delightful, white, bell-shaped flowers, with the softest pink flush and a splash of deep golden-yellow in the throat. The broad, mat, dark green leaves are the perfect foil to this graceful display; in winter, the peeling bark is attractive too. It is hard to believe that something which looks so dainty and delicate could be so robust.

Its home is among the rocks along the Han and Yangtse rivers in China at a height of 3,000–3,300m (10,000–13,075ft). It is yet another gorgeous shrub introduced by Ernest Wilson, this time in 1901 when he was collecting for Veitch's Nursery; it first flowered in the UK in June 1910 – what a cause for celebration! I remember it as one of the outstanding plants from my days working on Leicester City Council's Parks Department.

Kolkwitzia amabilis 'Pink Cloud' is pink flowered. Foliage can be damaged by late frosts, so plant in a sheltered border or in dappled shade. Prune out old, damaged or weak shoots at the base immediately after flowering to younger stems lower down on the original branches. On older plants, remove weak growth and about one fifth to a quarter of the oldest stems after flowering in spring. Then feed with a slow-release general fertilizer and mulch. Propagate by semi-ripe cuttings from mid-summer or a sucker detached from mature plants in winter. **MB**

+ *Laburnocytisus* 'Adamii'

+ *Laburnocytisus* 'Adamii'

Type: hardy, deciduous tree
Soil & situation: moderately fertile, well-drained soil/sun
North American hardiness zone: 6–8
Height: 8m (25ft)
Spread: 6m (20ft)
Grow for: curiosity value and unusual flowers

This graft hybrid between *Cytisus purpureus* and *Laburnum anagyroides* occurred in 1825 when Jean Louis Adam accidentally grafted purple broom onto a laburnum at his nursery near Paris. The resulting plant had a core of laburnum wrapped in a layer of cytisus and where it breaks down branches of pure laburnum burst through. Amazingly it produces not only purple or yellow flowers but some that are coppery-pink, an intermediate between the two! It's also known as a chimaera; in Greek mythology this was a monster with a lion's head, a goat's body and a serpent's tail; when it comes to looks, Adam's plant is not far behind!

It is an uncommon occurrence, + *Crataegomespilus dardarii* 'Bronvaux' is a graft hybrid between hawthorn (*Crataegus monogyna*) and medlar (*Mespilus germanica*) with a central core of hawthorn and an outer sleeve of medlar. The leaves and fruits are like a medlar; the flower clusters and spiny branches are similar to the hawthorn but smaller. Another graft hybrid, 'Jules d'Asineres', occurred at the same time, but this has an outer layer of hawthorn. The leaves and flowers are hawthorn but the shoots and calyx are covered with greyish wool, like a medlar; even weirder was a branch of hawthorn that changed to 'Jules d'Asineres' near the tip!

It needs a moderately fertile, deep, well-drained soil in full sun. Buy a plant, as they are propagated by grafting. It may suffer from leaf spot, which is worse in some years than others. **MB**

Laburnum x *watereri* 'Vossii'
GOLDEN RAIN

Type: hardy, deciduous tree
Soil & situation: fertile, well-drained soil/full sun
North American hardiness zone: 6–8
Height & spread: 9m (30ft)
Grow for: long, fine racemes of golden-yellow flowers; AGM

This must be the best-known tree in the northern hemisphere. You don't have to be a gardener to recognize its chocolate-box appearance. Considered by some to be a common plant, I prefer to think of it as popular and much loved. Trained over an arch, it is a spectacular sight when in flower and viewed from underneath. Planted in such a situation, with blue-flowered wisteria (see page 398) scrambling through, it would be breath-taking.

The young shoots are hairy, as are the dark green, three-palmate leaves on the underside. In late spring and early summer 50cm (20in) long racemes of bright, golden flowers trail down like 'golden rain'. It is a well-known fact that its small, black, round seeds are toxic. If enough of them are eaten they could be fatal. This variety of laburnum produces very few seedpods and the seed is usually sterile.

Pruning is necessary only to shape the tree and should be undertaken in early winter when the tree is dormant and before the sap starts to flow. Propagation is by winter grafting or summer bud grafting. Unfortunately laburnum does suffer from diseases. Honey fungus and silver leaf disease will eventually kill even established trees. **JC**

Laburnum x *watereri* 'Vossii'

Lamium orvala

Lamium orvala
DEAD NETTLE

Type: hardy, herbaceous perennial
Soil & situation: moist soil/dappled or full shade
North American hardiness zone: 4–8
Height: 60cm (24in)
Spread: 30cm (12in)
Grow for: flowers from mid-spring to early summer; compact foliage

Not all nettles are nasty; some are civilized and make excellent ground cover, like the forms of *Lamium maculatum*, the dead nettle. *L. m.* 'Beacon Silver' is a real beauty with silvery leaves, narrow green margins and clear shell-pink flowers; *L. galeobdolon* 'Hermann's Pride' has silvery net-like venation on the leaves; but if you want a nettle with an aristocratic aura, look no further – *L. orvala* reigns supreme. It's not bright and bold, that would be soooo vulgar; its qualities are understated and discreet, just take the time to admire. *L. o.* f. *alba* has off-white flowers and the leaves of *L. o.* 'Silva' have a broad central stripe.

L. orvala is a fine, clump-forming foliage plant with square stems and oval to triangular, softly hairy leaves on opposite sides of the stem that combine to create a soft, textured look. The flowers are typical of nettles, but a subtle coppery-pink to rich purple with delicate markings in the throat that draw you down to view. Always walk round the garden with a magnifying glass in your pocket, there's great pleasure in the hidden details of every plant: stamens, petals, bark and bough wait patiently to be appreciated by those passing by. Few take the trouble to view but the reward is pure delight.

It makes good ground cover in borders or among large shrubs. Give it a moist but well-drained soil in deep or partial shade. It is more vigorous in moist, moderately fertile soil; poorer soil reduces its growth. Cut back to ground level and mulch in early spring. Divide in autumn or early spring. Slugs and snails may damage early growth. **MB**

Lathyrus odoratus

Lathyrus odoratus
SWEET PEA

Type: hardy, annual climber
Soil & situation: any moist soil/full sun or light shade
North American hardiness zone: annual
Height & spread: 2m (6½ft)
Grow for: the cut flower; the gorgeous scent and, because it is leguminous, providing nitrogen for other plants

I adore sweet peas – the scent is so edible I can stuff my head into a bunch and just inhale their intoxicating fragrance. I do not like cutting flowers and taking them indoors; they look best where nature placed them. However sweet peas must be cut, as if you leave just one to drop its petals then all is lost; you don't want to see the small green pods because as soon as the seed has ripened the plant will stop producing more blooms and die away. This wild strain is powerfully scented, the flowers are purple and violet and only two or three per stem, but what fragrance! I find that if you self-save seed of almost any mix of sweet peas, within a few years this original form reappears and eventually dominates.

First brought from Sicily at the end of the 17th century, the wild form was good enough to keep everyone happy until the late Victorian period, when they were suddenly widely grown and bred. The flowers became bigger and more fancy, and the process continued until the Second World War when interest waned. This was probably because the highly bred plants had lost their scent and become hard to look after, unlike their wild ancestors.

Rich, moist soil in full sun is essential for a continuity of blooms. Dead-heading is hardly the word, live-heading is more to the point. Do not shirk this! Sow in autumn and over-winter in a coldframe, or sow *in situ* in spring. Plant out early and train onto a support such as a wigwam or trellis. Sweet peas are prone to drought so add more water than you think necessary, unless it's raining. **BF**

John adds:
If, like me, you have a soil which tends to dry out if there is even a hint of summer you should invest a bit of your time digging a planting trench. The deeper the better as sweet peas have an extensive root system. Lay lots of wet newspaper in the base, mixing old farmyard manure and moisture-retentive compost into the soil as you back-fill the trench. Water the soil well a few days before planting.

Laurus nobilis
SWEET BAY TREE, BAY LAUREL

Type: frost-hardy, evergreen shrub or small tree
Soil & situation: well-drained soil/full sun
North American hardiness zone: 8–10
Height: 12m (40ft)
Spread: 10m (33ft)
Grow for: an excellent evergreen and essential for the kitchen; AGM

This is the laurel the ancients made into crowns of glory and that cooks still use today. Bay is often cut into a geometric shape – a pair stands outside every pretentious restaurant like a couple of barber's poles. I love the flavour the leaves give, particularly the aged ones, and use a lot in my cooking – they're expensive to buy. There are male and female trees and only the latter carry the black, inedible berries.

A native of Southern Europe, this was named in Roman times after *laus* or praise as it was used for the victor's laurel and was presumably then introduced to the UK about 2,000 years ago.

In a warm, sheltered spot and a well-drained soil bays can become old and venerable, but on a heavy wet soil and in a windy exposed site get something else, or put it in a tub up against a warm wall. Make sure young plants are given some form of shelter against cold winds, and protect roots in containers against frost. If top growth is seared by wind you can prune back hard in spring and it will come again, if well established. It can be clipped, or preferably pruned to different shapes, which is best done in several stages from spring to late summer.

It can be grown from seed sown in pots in a coldframe in spring, or by hardwood cuttings with a heel in a coldframe in late autumn or winter; layering also works, and occasional suckers can be detached and potted up. Scale insects are often a problem and these are nearly always farmed by ants, so dispose of those first. Honeydew on leaves is caused by scale or aphid infestation higher up; wash it off with a sponge of soapy water. **BF**

Laurus nobilis

Fragaria hybrids

STRAWBERRIES

Type: hardy herbaceous perennial
Soil & situation: rich, moist soil/full sun
North American hardiness zone: 5–9
Height: 30cm (12in)
Spread: 60cm (24in)
Grow for: do I have to tell you?

Whenever I give a talk on gardening I like to pose a few questions to my audience; one is 'How many of you like strawberries?' and another is 'How many of you grow strawberries?' It's odd because although this fruit is almost unanimously liked it is relatively rarely grown, which is crazy as it is one of the quickest and easiest, let alone tastiest crops! To grow it really well is not easy, but to grow and fruit it is fairly simple if you are not after commercial yields. And I know you are supposed to grow it a year before fruiting them, *but* you can crop half of your plants the first summer if you throw them away afterwards. Leave the alternately planted ones you properly de-runnered and de-flowered to grow on and they will make the bed productive for the next few years.

The huge, sweet strawberry available today is a relatively modern fruit. The ancients gathered tiny, wild strawberries, and in the Middle Ages these plants were brought into gardens where they remain almost unimproved. A Victorian hybrid between a North American Virginian strawberry, with flavour, and a South American Chilean sort, with some size, gave rise to the whole gamut of modern strawberries, which can fruit for most of the summer and autumn, but few match those ripening around the longest day, eaten in the warmth of a summer's evening.

Rich, moist soil with added bonemeal suits this hungry crop. Plant in full sun, or cool shade for a successional crop, and replace one-third of the bed every year, re-planting on a new site. Do not remove the leaves until the plants die down, then shear off the residue. In the growing season trim off runners regularly. De-flowering in the first summer will lead to bigger, stronger plants and huge crops later. Do not grow from seed but obtain the first runners of healthy plants, rooted into pots in late spring, and plant in a new bed by mid-summer. Weevils, slugs and miserable weather plague this delightful crop but hygiene, jam jars over the ripening trusses and eternal hope combat these – well, maybe not the last. **BF**

Lavandula angustifolia 'Twickel Purple'
LAVENDER

Type: hardy, evergreen shrub
Soil & situation: moderately fertile, well-drained soil/full sun
North American hardiness zone: 5–8
Height: 60cm (24in)
Spread: 90cm (36in)
Grow for: no garden is complete without it

I cannot imagine having a garden without at least one lavender plant. I can dream of a garden with hundreds of plants in many varieties. Reality is in the middle – I have between 30 and 35 plants in six varieties in my garden. Around 18 *Lavandula angustifolia* 'Twickel Purple' are planted round a weeping pear, *Pyrus salicifolia* 'Pendula' (see page 316), and they form a magic circle.

It makes a compact, rounded, bushy shrub with narrow, 5cm (2in) long, grey-green, aromatic leaves. In mid-summer it bears dense spikes of very fragrant, bright purple flowers on long stalks. The flowers are held above the foliage, providing a wonderful contrast in colour. The variety *L. a.* 'Hidcote' is compact with silver-grey foliage and deep purple flowers. *L. a.* 'Nana Alba' produces white flowers and grows to a height and spread of 30cm (12in).

Annual pruning to prevent the plant becoming leggy is carried out each spring. Cut last year's growth back to within 2.5cm (1in) of the older wood. Lavender tends to be a short-lived plant becoming woody and bare at the base after seven to eight years. This is more likely to occur in heavy soil and moist climates. The answer is simple: pull the old plant out and replace it with another or, if there is space, two more.

Propagation is by semi-ripe cuttings in summer. Insert them in a gritty, free-draining compost and cover the container with horticultural fleece. **JC**

Lavandula angustifolia 'Twickel Purple'

Lavandula pinnata

Lavandula pinnata
LAVENDER

Type: tender, evergreen shrub
Soil & situation: tolerant of many soil types except wet ones/sunny position
North American hardiness zone: 9–10
Height & spread: 1m (3ft)
Grow for: fragrant, strong blue flowers with a hint of purple, ever-present from late spring/early summer to early autumn

This tender lavender is probably one of my top 50 if not top ten plants. I treat it as a bedding plant, planting it into the border in late spring, where it quickly fills out to form an excellent small foliage plant. Come early summer, it starts to flower its heart out and continues till autumn. Then I leave it until it is killed by the frost and quickly discard it. Grown like this, from well-rooted liners taken towards the end of the previous summer, they do not reach 1m (3ft) high, perhaps only 60cm (24in), by the end of the year. But I plant them pretty close together, about eight or ten per square metre/yard so the plants knit together to form a sea of grey-green leaves within a few weeks.

The rather hairy, aromatic foliage supports tall, unbranched stalks topped with the ever-flowering, intensely coloured spikes. Because of their wonderful flowering capacity and their ability to withstand hot dry periods, they are also tailor-made for summer containers – looking

particularly good in faded terracotta or lead. I like them best massed together on their own. Simple, stunning and sweet-smelling.

Even though I could never get away with leaving this plant to over-winter outside, I still think it is worth propagating new stock every summer from softwood cuttings, to over-winter under cover before going out the following spring. They will root in a couple of weeks and it speeds up rooting if you keep pinching out the flowers. **BG**

Lavandula 'Sawyers'

Type: hardy, evergreen shrub
Soil & situation: according to Henry Head of Norfolk Lavender, there are three things that lavender needs – 'drainage, drainage and drainage'/sunny position
North American hardiness zone: 6–9
Height: 60cm (24in)
Spread: 80cm (32in)
Grow for: winter colour: exceptional foliage looks attractive throughout the winter with its large leaf and excellent silver colour; attractive two-tone flowers; AGM

Lavandula 'Sawyers'

Henry Head recommended this lavender to me and I have to agree it is a star. Looking at my collection of lavender plants, now in late winter, this lavender is head and shoulders above most of them. The large leaves, often 4cm (1½in) long and 5mm (¼in) wide, are a positive presence in the garden rather than looking like tired hedgehogs as most other lavenders do at this time of year. Most people grow lavender not for the foliage but for those summer months when the plant is covered with its captivating flowers. This one has pale purple flowerheads, which are a deeper blue in the centre and flowers from mid- to late summer. *L.* 'Richard Gray' is very similar but has large, rich purple flowers.

Given that drainage is the key to success, if you do not have sharp drainage it is worth digging a large hole and incorporating masses of free-draining material before attempting to plant on top. On poorly drained soil, lavender will probably look good for a mere six years or so and then need replacing, otherwise it will go on for a good 15 years.

Pruning is important in keeping it looking dapper. As soon as it has finished flowering cut back all this year's growth, and if necessary, a little into the hardwood too. Many people recommend pruning in late spring, but the problem here is that they tend to wait too long for fear of new growth being frosted, and so also remove incipient flowerheads, reducing flowering performance. Propagate from cuttings, which will root virtually at any time of year, but early summer is best. **BG**

Lavandula stoechas
FRENCH LAVENDER

Type: hardy, semi-evergreen shrub
Soil & situation: well-drained soil/full sun
North American hardiness zone: 8–9
Height & spread: can make clumps 30–50cm (12–20ft) round
Grow for: neat, whitish-greyish-green evergreen with purple flowers, excellent for edging; AGM

Any lavender is good, but this is the best. It is superbly scented in a spicier way than the old English and although less hardy, it has survived in my Norfolk garden through many a cold winter and has even self-sown. It may lose its verdure in winter but if you rub the greyish foliage or a flowerhead there is that pungent warmth and sweet comfort reminding you of summer. It makes a neater, more compact edging than most lavenders.

Lavandula stoechas

French lavender originates from the tiny island of Stoechas, off the coast of Marseilles, and was introduced into the UK in the 16th century. The name *Lavandula* comes from the Latin word for washing or soap, *lavo*, as the lavender scent extracted even back then was used as a perfume.

The soil must be well drained, ideally with some chalk, and full sun is essential or it just moulds away…. Trim if you must in early spring before growth commences, but preferably just tidy off dead flower stems, and do keep other plants cut back so as not to shade this delicate beauty. In early spring sow in a very chalky, gritty compost in a cold frame, or take root cuttings. Plant out the next spring. This plant sulks in cold, dank springs and grey, damp summers! I feel much the same. **BF**

Lavatera thuringiaca 'Burgundy Wine'

Type: hardy, semi-evergreen subshrub
Soil & situation: light, well-drained soil/full sun
North American hardiness zone: 8–10
Height & spread: 1.2m (4ft)
Grow for: attractive foliage; a profusion of dark purple-red flowers in generous quantities through summer till early autumn

There are several forms of *L. thuringiaca*, perhaps the most widely grown are 'Barnsley', with its pale pink flowers, and *L.* x *clementii* 'Rosea', with bright pink flowers. These two are highly productive, quickly becoming established and bearing huge volumes of flowers in the first couple of years. These are for impatient gardeners. But the only one I grow is 'Burgundy Wine'. This has bags more charm, is more unusual and not as rampant and blowsy as the others. The habit is more compact, but the foliage is still an attractive grey-green and if grown in a sheltered warm spot the leaves will last throughout the year in a mild winter. The flowers are a rich, pink colour, but unfortunately not that of wine. What is more, they are produced for well over a month. They are perhaps not as beautifully textured as the commoner ones and are slightly smaller, but they just hit the right spot for me.

All the subshrub mallows or tree lavateras are fast-growers and with most plants that indicates they are short-lived; these are no exception. If the term 'flowered themselves to death' applied to any plants, it certainly would to these. As they root extremely easily from softwood cuttings in spring and early summer, it is no bother to propagate a new batch every three or four years. Do not be tempted to over-feed them – on a rich soil you will get all foliage and far fewer flowers – but do be tempted to give them a protective autumn mulch and a bit of shelter from cold winds. **BG**

Lavatera thuringiaca 'Burgundy Wine'

Ledum groenlandicum

Ledum groenlandicum
LABRADOR TEA

Type: hardy, evergreen, bushy shrub
Soil & situation: moist, well-drained, humus-rich, neutral to acid soil/full sun or partial shade
North American hardiness zone: 2–6
Height: 1m (3ft)
Spread: 1.2m (4ft)
Grow for: survives terrible weather conditions; small, white flowers

I admire this tough little plant. It is at home in Alaska and Greenland so is quite capable of dealing with the worst of any weather. It is now included in the family *Rhododendron* and its shape resembles a dwarf form. When mature it makes a bushy, open, rounded shrub with pale brown, woolly shoots and 5cm (2in) long, dark green leaves, fawn-felted on the underside. The oblong leaves are recurved along the margins. Small, white flowers with prominent stamens form terminal clusters up to 5cm (2in) across in late spring and early summer.

It is a good companion plant with heathers, pieris and dwarf conifers. I have a 12-year-old-plant and have never had to prune it. I do, however, deadhead it after flowering to prevent seed forming. Propagation is by semi-ripe, short cuttings in late summer or by layering *in situ.* **JC**

Lespedeza thunbergii
BUSH CLOVER

Type: hardy, deciduous subshrub
Soil & situation: fertile, well-drained soil/full sun
North American hardiness zone: 6–8
Height: 2m (6½ft)
Spread: 3m (10ft)
Grow for: a good show of colour in late autumn; AGM

I have this plant in a mixed border and I always forget about it. Suddenly, in late autumn, it reminds me, yet again, how good a plant it is by making a show of itself. Delicate, arching stems carry three palmate, blue-green leaflets, each 5cm (2in) long. The 15cm (6in) long, pendent racemes of small, pea-like, purple-pink flowers appear in autumn. *Lespedeza bicolor* is similar in size, but more upright with dark green leaves. Its purple-pink flowers are produced in mid-summer.

With me, each winter, the stems are cut to the ground by frost. In late spring new shoots appear and by early summer they are quietly draping low-growing plants. Propagation is by seed sown in spring without heat. Softwood cuttings can be rooted in summer under polythene. Mist the foliage over daily to prevent them wilting. Large clumps may be divided in spring taking care not to damage the fine roots. **JC**

Lespedeza thunbergii

Leucojum autumnale

Leucojum autumnale
AUTUMN SNOW FLAKE

Type: hardy, bulbous perennial
Soil & situation: sandy, free-draining soil/sun
North American hardiness zone: 5–9
Height: 15cm (6in)
Spread: 10cm (4cm)
Grow for: dainty white flowers for the whole of autumn; AGM

This is one of the daintiest plants you'll ever see. The flowers, appearing just before the leaves in early autumn, hang like tiny white bells from slender grassy stems only 10–15cm (4–6in) tall. Everything in their world is so tiny I would not be surprised if fairies crept out unseen at night to dance around them and ring their pretty bells!

These delicate relatives of the snowdrop grow in rocky, stony woodland scrub and grassy places in the western Mediterranean. They need careful positioning to ensure that they are visible and you don't stand on them by mistake! Ideally they should be raised up in planting pockets on rock gardens where they are easier to view; dark stone or evergreen shrubs highlight the white flowers and protect them from cold wind too. Alternatively, grow them by dry hedge bases, as edging plants or against a sunny wall and remember that they need a good baking to develop flower buds for the following year; don't shade them with shrubs. *Leucojum autumnale* 'Cobbs Variety' has larger flowers from late summer to mid-autumn.

It needs a sunny position on sandy, free-draining soil. Dig in plenty of sharp sand before planting about 5cm (2in) deep in mid- to late summer. Propagate by division in spring or autumn after flowering. Sow seed when ripe in autumn, in gritty compost. It takes up to three years to produce a flowering bulb. It will also grow in containers of gritty sand. **MB**

Levisticum officinale
LOVAGE

Type: hardy, perennial herb
Soil & situation: naturalized in meadows throughout Britain and Europe/will grow pretty well anywhere in pretty much anything
North American hardiness zone: 4–7
Height: up to 2m (6½ft)
Spread: 1m (3ft)
Grow for: a herb indispensable in cooking; yeasty, celery-like flavour; it can be shredded finely and added to salads; one plant gives ample leaves for the entire growing season; said to have widespread medicinal properties

I grow about five plants of this magic herb in my kitchen garden. It sits in a square of dwarf box, part of a pattern of herb squares that form 'stops' on the corners of all my vegetable beds. This makes the vegetable garden look the business even in mid-winter. More importantly, it stops rushing children and chasing dogs cutting corners over my beds. I need not grow five plants – with this quantity I could supply our local hotel too – but that way the plants are a continual presentable mass. They are not unattractive: their flowers are borne in umbels which look good with the greenish-yellow flowers. I always cut them off, before they look their finest, to favour leaf production. But you can use the seeds for flavouring, as well as the roots and shoots for a vegetable or in a salad, grated, raw or cooked. The dried root has a strange, almost nutty flavour and was once used as a condiment. It is one of those useful plants that the longer you grow it, the more uses you find for its wide-ranging facets. If you grow this herb in shade the flavour will be less intense but as it is pretty, if not extremely punchy, I do not think this is a problem. It is easily propagated from seed or from division in early spring. **BG**

Levisticum officinale

Lewisia tweedyi

Lewisia tweedyi

Type: hardy, evergreen perennial
Soil & situation: humus-rich, well-drained, neutral to acid soil/light shade
North American hardiness zone: 4–7
Height: 20cm (8in)
Spread: 30cm (12in)
Grow for: brightening up the rockery in early summer; AGM

I have to admit that this plant is a bit fussy but then so was my grannie and I loved her. The 10cm (4in) long, fleshy, mid-green leaves form a tight rosette and are often tinted purple. Fully open, the star-shaped flowers can be 5cm (2in) across. They appear from spring to early summer either singly or in clusters of up to four; they are a clean pink-white or a deeper apricot shade. The variety *Lewisia tweedyi* f. *alba* has pure white flowers but is not as readily available. *Lewisia* Cotyledon Hybrids produce panicles of flowers in a range of bright colours including pink, yellow and apricot.

L. tweedyi dislikes being planted in full sun. A site on the shady side of a large rock where it is in the open but out of the sun is ideal. It suffers from winter wet and will rot if not protected. A roof made from a sheet of glass secured on either side of the clump between two bricks will be sufficient protection. Alternatively it can be grown outside during summer in a shallow pot of gritty compost and moved under cover in a greenhouse in winter. Seed can be sown in a cold frame in autumn or offsets may be removed in early summer and rooted in pots. **JC**

Leycesteria formosa

Leycesteria formosa
HIMALAYAN HONEYSUCKLE

Type: hardy, deciduous shrub
Soil & situation: moist, well-drained soil/full sun to light shade
North American hardiness zone: 8–10
Height & spread: 2m (6½ft)
Grow for: provides pendent flowers in summer and autumn followed by purple berries; AGM

I love the bare, bamboo-like stems in winter. The unusual flower resembles something a girl would dangle from her ear.

Of upright habit, this shrub will form a thicket. Its 15cm (6in) long, dark green leaves are held on sea-green, hollow stems. The 10cm (4in) long, pendent spikes of flowers are produced in summer and early autumn. They are white and just visible among the dark claret-red bracts. The flowers are followed by red-purple berries which are loved by birds.

Don't plant in heavy, wet soil or where there are cold, drying winds. A deep mulch in autumn is beneficial, especially if there are likely to be prolonged frosts. It loves the shelter of a woodland garden, providing it is not too shaded in summer.

Pruning is necessary to prevent the plant becoming bulky with non-flowering stems. After flowering, cut the two-year-old stems, which are a dark green, back to a strong sideshoot or low down close to ground level. Propagation is by sowing fresh seed in autumn and over-wintering in a cold frame. Softwood cuttings taken in summer root quickly and may be potted up in a soil-based compost in the autumn. **JC**

Libertia formosa

Type: hardy, rhizomatous, evergreen perennial
Soil & situation: medium loam soil, preferably slightly acid/sun or light shade
North American hardiness zone: 8–10
Height: leaves up to 45cm (18in), flowers to 1.2cm (4ft)
Spread: 1m (3ft)
Grow for: year-round foliage; white flowers in small umbels in spring

This is one of those charming, low-key plants that never knock you out, but you are always pleased to have around. I grow it in a large drift in my orchard where it mingles with masses of ferns. The tough, thick, grassy leaves are evergreen and a good evergreen at that, not tatty but nicely strappy, even in late winter, then at the end of spring a mass of small white flowers appears. I remember featuring it widely in a woodland garden I designed for the Chelsea Flower Show (always at the end of May). It was fun arranging it in wide drifts, and it was a dream to use as it looks at its best then so needed no forcing and little titivating or 'dressing up'. It does look right in light woodland, although is possibly happier in full sun; either way, it will self-seed around.

After a few years the old leaves tend to get congested and the plant responds to being cut back to just above ground level. Alternatively you can start afresh with new seedlings. Propagation can either be by division in spring or seed. **BG**

Libertia formosa

Ligularia dentata 'Desdemona'

Ligularia dentata 'Desdemona'

Type: hardy, herbaceous perennial
Soil & situation: rich, deep, moisture-retentive soil/dappled shade
North American hardiness zone: 4–8
Height: 1.2m (4ft)
Spread: 1m (3ft)
Grow for: bold purple foliage in spring; pale orange daisies in summer; AGM

This is an amazing plant with excellent foliage and flowers. The foliage comes in the form of basal leaves up to 30 x 40cm (12 x 16in), rounded and toothed, which are purple above and below initially and then become a deep green on the top. Because I am on free-draining soil I have positioned them in the shadow of a north-facing wall, having added lots of organic matter, and in dry periods I water. Little sacrifice to grow this spectacular plant. This is the only one I grow, though if I had more favourable conditions I would grow others in wild areas. One other would be *L. tangutica* 'The Rocket', which has coarse, toothed leaves, often blackish stems and flower stems that launch up to a height of 2m (6½ft).

If you have dry conditions, grow this plant in a man-made bog garden and it will thrive. Other suitable places are beside streams, lakes or in naturally marshy places. It does not need staking except in exceptionally exposed conditions.

Beware if you are an allergic gardener – it can cause reactions. My main grouse with this plant is slugs: ligularias are the McDonalds of the plant world, feeding millions at every sitting. Unfortunately they do not produce new leaves quickly when you remove their manky ones but just look ravaged for weeks. Propagate by division or the species by seed. **BG**

Ligularia dentata 'Othello'
GOLDEN GROUNDSEL

Type: hardy, herbaceous perennial
Soil & situation: deep, fertile, moist soil/full sun
North American hardiness zone: 4–8
Height: 90cm (36in)
Spread: 80cm (32in)
Grow for: a particularly handsome perennial plant with a good combination of flower and leaf colour

This is a wonderfully dramatic perennial for the front of a border. The leaf and flower colours contrast beautifully. Unfortunately there is a constant battle against slugs, which seem to prefer the leaves even to those of a hosta. But if you win the war you will have a sight worth fighting for.

Ligularia dentata 'Othello'

Clump-forming, the rounded, 25cm (10in) wide, deep purple-green leaves are purple-red on the underside. The 10cm- (4in-) wide corymbs of deep orange, daisy-like flowers are produced from mid-summer to early autumn on long stiff stems above the foliage.

Ligularias need to be protected from the midday sun. The leaves will droop if there is a shortage of water but soon recover after a shower of rain. They are totally hardy but the foliage is easily shredded in strong winds. Propagation is by division after flowering or in spring. The seed of *Ligularia dentata* 'Othello' will not come true, but the plants will be very similar in appearance.

Whoever named these two varieties was fond of Shakespeare but 'Desdemona' (see previous entry) is more likely to be murdered by slugs! **JC**

Hosta 'Gold Standard'

July

PLANTAIN LILY

Type: hardy, herbaceous perennial
Soil & situation: fertile, moist, well-drained soil/
light shade
North American hardiness zone: 5–8
Height: 70cm (27¹/₂in)
Spread: 90cm (36in)
Grow for: a mass of heart-shaped leaves; excellent for
beds and borders in dappled shade. The leaves are lovely
throughout the growing season, but the flowers are an
added dimension at this time of year.

This hosta produces leaves that improve with age. It is
happy growing in the border or in a container where its
foliage is better protected from slugs. It is clump-forming
with large, 18cm (7in) heart-shaped leaves. When they
first open they are splashed green-yellow. As they age they
become a brighter yellow, edged with a narrow margin of
dark green, then cream before fading to a beige-green. In
mid-summer, the long stems carry funnel-shaped,
lavender-blue flowers above the leaves. Plant hostas in a
situation where they won't suffer from strong, biting, cold
winds. Mulch annually in spring using composted bark or
leafmould. The new emerging shoots are prone to slug
and snail attack, so lay poisons and traps to lessen the
numbers in the area. Select a site away from full sun,
which will scorch the leaves. Too much shade will cause
the leaves to become green.

Propagation is by division in late spring or early autumn.
The clumps are dug up and divided into small plants each
with their roots attached. With large clumps it is difficult
to tease out these small rooted pieces. Where necessary,
chop the clumps apart with an axe or sharp spade.
Discard the old, woody centre section. Pot them into a
moisture-retentive compost in the containers and leave
them on a sheltered side of the garden.   **JC**

Ligustrum delavayanum (syn. *L. ionandrum*)

Type: hardy, evergreen shrub
Soil & situation: any reasonable soil/sun or part shade
North American hardiness zone: 7–10
Height: just over 2m (6½ft)
Spread: 3m (10ft)
Grow for: a relatively fast-growing, evergreen plant used for topiary and hedging

This useful plant has smallish, elliptical leaves up to 3cm (1in) long, but more usually 1.5cm (⅝in). It does not produce topiary of the calibre of box and yew as the foliage is not so tight, and because of its faster growth rate. This is good in that you get the final result more speedily, but not so good for the guy with the clippers who will need to have them at the ready three times a year (at least) to keep them in trim!

I have often used this plant in gardens, though, because you can get instant topiary specimens in *L. delavayanum* for half or even a third of the price of their slower-growing counterparts and they look pretty good, making bags of immediate impact. I have seen them in Italian nurseries shaped as helicopters, elephants, swans and other bizarre shapes. A lot of preformed topiary shapes are

Ligustrum delavayanum

imported into the UK from Italy and Holland. Most frequent are the mop-head standards. Some say they are not so hardy and in a cold winter become more semi-evergreen. I think the answer is that they are variable, but looking at some I planted recently in the Midlands, they are definitely evergreen, even after some very cold winter conditions.

As these plants are not so tall, the mop-head standards often look far superior in a large pot, so the 'mop' can be brought up to eye level. To stop them blowing over and to avoid them being dependent on being watered, I cut the base out of cheap terracotta pots (I usually do a coloured wash over them so they look expensive) with an angle grinder, and put good soil beneath the pot, allowing the plant to root through. This works well in gravel or in soft areas with a 'plinth' of planting around the base. In exposed areas I drive a bar through the pot and into the ground, for initial stabilization. I water for the first year, and then slowly wean them. Clip from late spring to mid-summer.   **BG**

Ligustrum lucidum
CHINESE PRIVET, WHITE WAX TREE

Type: hardy, evergreen tree or shrub
Soil & situation: well-drained soil; excellent on chalk/sun
North American hardiness zone: 8–10
Height & spread: 10m (33ft)
Grow for: attractive form, glossy leaves and small white flowers; AGM

I first saw this neat, compact tree with gorgeous glossy leaves in a garden in Fulham. I selected some shoots, carefully took them home and discovered to my enduring surprise that in this part of west London even the privets are posh! Someone with a cultured eye must have selected this plant, not for them the humdrum drudgery of a dull privet hedge but something far more impressive – an elegant, regal tree that bathed in the sunshine and luxuriated in the warmth of London's microclimate. It was a fine specimen standing serenely in the middle of the lawn with long, glossy leaves, attractive bark and bouquets of white flowers in late summer and early autumn. The rest of the year it stands, statuesque and looking divine; it's such a charming plant, my dear, you simply must have one!

Those dressed in contemporary 'haute couture' include *Ligustrum lucidum* 'Excelsum Superbum', which has bright green leaves marked with pale

Ligustrum lucidum

green and edged with yellow and greenish-yellow. It is not as hardy, needing protection from cold winds. The narrow, deep green leaves of *L. l.* 'Tricolor' are prominently marked with grey-green and edged with creamy-yellow, tinged pink when young.

Hardy but unsuitable for cold or exposed areas. It needs a warm, sheltered position, flourishing in warmer parts of the UK, in sunshine or part shade on well-drained soil; it's excellent on chalk. Mulch in spring and water young trees during drought. Prune to tidy in spring. Propagate by semi-ripe cuttings in winter.   **MB**

Ligustrum vulgare
COMMON PRIVET

Type: hardy, semi-evergreen shrub
Soil & situation: any soil, poor soils too/sun or part shade
North American hardiness zone: 5–8
Height: to 5m (16ft)
Spread: 3m (10ft)
Grow for: highly useful plant when mixed into native thicket and hedgerow plantings, adding a fast-growing, semi-evergreen element

This is a native hedgerow and woodland plant that is most frequently seen on limestone and chalky soils. I frequently use this invaluable plant for planting on boundaries with the countryside, mixed in with other appropriate natives, for shelter belts, hedges and natural plantings. Its leaves are much smaller than those of the common hedging privet (*L. ovalifolium*), which I rarely use. It has a darker green leaf and in autumn produces conspicuous shining black fruit in long clusters. It

Ligustrum vulgare

rapidly establishes in even quite inhospitable soils where it is windy and cold, and keeps a respectable covering of leaves on to the end of winter in most areas. It is ideal for providing shelter both for us and for the wildlife.

I invariably plant this as a bare-rooted plant, at usually a fraction of the cost of container-grown ones, and strangely enough, it establishes better. It is essential to keep the soil clean at the base of the plant for a good metre (3ft) if possible, as then there is no competition for moisture from grass or weeds and it will grow up to 70 per cent faster. On planting for use in a native hedge, I usually reduce all growth back to 15cm (6in) from the ground and a better, bushier, more vigorous plant is the result. For the next two or three years I reduce the new side growth back to half in spring. Then, when it is the size I want, I just clip over the sides and top it again in spring or when all the berries have been had by the birds and before nesting. **BG**

Lilium candidum
MADONNA LILY

Type: hardy, bulbous perennial
Soil & situation: well-drained, humus-rich, neutral to alkaline soil/full sun
North American hardiness zone: 6–9
Height: 1–1.8m (3–6ft)
Spread: 30cm (12in)
Grow for: the most lovely, fragrant, pure white flowers; AGM

When I see this lily, whether as a single plant, a clump or as cut flowers I can't help but think, WOW. It is perfection in flower.

Broad, lance-shaped, 20cm (8in) long, bright, shiny green basal leaves appear in autumn. Stiff flower stems emerge in spring and carry small, 7cm (3in) long, twisted lance-shaped leaves. Racemes of up to 20 wonderfully fragrant, pure white flowers appear in mid-summer. Each 5–7cm (2–2³/₄in) long flower is trumpet-shaped with a yellowish base and golden-yellow anthers. They are ideal for growing in mixed borders or as clumps among shrubs or herbaceous plants.

Plant on top of a small mound of coarse grit in the base of the planting hole to encourage good drainage. The tip of the bulb should be level with the top of the surrounding soil. Insert a marker cane or label before planting to avoid spearing the soft, scale-like bulb. Space the bulbs 20cm (8in) apart. They flower better when they are crowded and clumps should only be replanted when they are congested.

Seed will germinate more easily when sown fresh. The first stage of germination is the formation of the root. The seed appears to be dormant until the leaves appear in the following season. Keep the seed trays moist and shaded for at least two years after sowing. **JC**

Lilium candidum

Lilium 'Casa Blanca'

Lilium 'Casa Blanca'

Type: hardy, bulbous perennial
Soil & situation: more tolerant of alkaline conditions/moist, but free-draining soil when growing/sun or part shade/needs less mollycoddling than many people think
North American hardiness zone: 5–8
Height: 1m (3ft)
Spread: 30cm (12in)
Grow for: flamboyant, fragrant, white flowers from mid-summer to early autumn; can be grown in pots or in the ground; AGM

This is a very flashy lily which has an extraordinarily powerful, sweet fragrance and flowers for a good five or six weeks. The exotic, rather flat white flowers have reddish anthers which contrast well with the whitest of flowers. It is ideal for growing in pots where you can give it the exact conditions it demands and position it exactly where you want it when it starts to look its finest. This also helps deal with the slug problem.

It is worth taking a little extra time and trouble with the ground preparation for these lilies. Add a lot of well-rotted, organic matter – ideally leaf-mould and extra grit if your soil is on the heavy side. They hate wind, heavy, poorly drained soils and also over-dry conditions during growth. If you have problems with mice, squirrels and slugs eating them over winter, you can prevent this by planting them individually in 2-litre pots when they arrive in autumn. Keep them in a dryish spot, such as by a wall where winter rains will not drench them, and cover the pots with netting to fend off the rodents. Pop them in the ground (without their pots) in early spring and they will get off to a good start in an ideal compost. You can then leave them in the ground from then on and if the numbers start to dwindle you can bulk them up with new. If the spot is well sheltered those in the border probably will not need staking; those in pots do tend to as the ideal conditions make them taller and floppier. If you want to grow them permanently in pots, lift and divide them in late winter/early spring at least every other year. As long as you top dress and feed well in the year you do not re-pot every year. Dead-heading after flowering is also important to help as much energy as possible to go to the bulb. Remove the flower as soon as it has withered with just the top two or three leaves, no more. **BG**

Lilium regale
REGAL LILY

Type: hardy, bulbous perennial
Soil & situation: well-drained soil/full sun to very light shade
North American hardiness zone: 4–7
Height: 2m (6½ft)
Spread: 20cm (8in)
Grow for: staggering flowers, staggering perfume; AGM

Lilium regale

Limnanthes douglasii

I love this flower and have been fortunate to see one grow to more than 1.8m (6ft) tall with over a dozen flowers. Each bloom is an enormous funnel of pure white, golden within the throat and occasionally flushed with a whiff of burgundy on the outside. The sweet perfume is overwhelming and you wander around with a yellow nose from the golden anthers having given you a good dusting. This is one of the easiest and most obliging of lilies and can flower in only a couple of years from seed.

Although we have had many wonderful lilies since before Biblical times, *Lilium regale* was not found until 1903, when it was stumbled upon by the great plant hunter E. H. Wilson, in a high mountain valley on the border of Tibet and China.

This lily is not particular as to soil, or even planting depth, as long as it is well drained. It likes full sun, but can be planted under or between very low shrubs to keep off early frost damage. Remove stamens and the flowers last for longer. Take off dead flowers to prevent seed forming and weakening the plant. It is remarkably easy to grow from seed, especially self-saved as it is fresh, and no matter how hard you try it seems to resist hybridization and apparently always comes true; or divide bulbs in early spring. Late frosts may twist or damage new growths. **BF**

Limnanthes douglasii
POACHED-EGG PLANT

Type: hardy annual
Soil & situation: any soil/full sun to light shade
North American hardiness zone: annual
Height & spread: mound to 30cm (12in)

Grow for: good ground cover; ferny foliage; cheerful yellow and white scented flowers; attracts beneficial insects; AGM

The poached-egg plant or meadow foam was first recommended to me by Lawrence Hills, the founder of the Henry Doubleday Research Association, who suggested it as a companion plant for attracting hoverflies. I noticed that it was not just a good self-seeder but also seemed to suppress almost all other weeds over winter and yet could be easily stripped off itself. If left it is a mass of flowers for weeks but never gets very tall, so it could even be used under gooseberries.

Their sweet scent fills the air and attracts butterflies and bees by the thousand. It is marvellous value and a sprinkling of the seed can be thrown in every neglected area to advantage – the ferny foliage and pretty yellow and white flowers of this 'cultivated weed' are nicer to look at than real weeds. I now even use it as a green manure to incorporate under a sheet.

Limnanthes douglasii is one of about a dozen species related to geraniums which come from North America, and it hails from California where it gained its sunny disposition. Its name is Latin for marsh flower – *limne* (marsh) and *anthos* (flower) – but meadow foam or poached-egg plant sounds much better. And why a poached egg, when truly a fried egg would be a more accurate a description?

It will grow on any soil, but prefers moist ones. Sow in autumn *in situ* initially, then let it self-sow. It is easy to weed out if unwanted. Sow self-saved seed in spring and early summer for a later flowering crop of blooms. However invasive it may be, it is too beautiful to weed out when you know you should. **BF**

Lippia dulcis

Type: tender, perennial, evergreen, sprawling sub-shrub
Soil & situation: moist soil/full sun or light shade/under cover
North American hardiness zone: 9–11
Height: 30cm (1ft)
Spread: 1.8m (6ft)
Grow for: unique ground cover under cover; interesting scent; weird flowers; super-sweet foliage

I first grew this plant to find out about its super-sweet leaves, which if chewed are really quite impressive and can be used to make a tea. I then noticed that, although tender, it was quite tough and made a good subject for a hanging basket; however, it self-seeded onto the floor, where it made a dense, aromatic carpet. It was full of whitefly initially, but when I introduced the predators the pest almost disappeared, and now the plant remains a source of both the whitefly and the predator, but I rarely see any large outbreaks of the former.

Very closely related to the true lemon verbena, *Aloysia triphylla* (see page 36), they are both native to South America. Named after Lippi, an Italian botanist killed in Abyssinia, the species name *dulcis* (Latin for sweet) is because of the sweetness of the leaves.

Any soil or compost suits this obliging plant; it even works well filling a hanging basket for the summer. It can be sheared back as growth commences in spring. Very easy from seed, layers and cuttings. Whitefly bother it no end, so use commercially available predators, *Encarsia formosa*.
BF

Liquidambar styraciflua 'Worplesdon'
SWEET GUM

Type: hardy, deciduous tree
Soil & situation: reliably moist, well-drained, acid soil/full sun
North American hardiness zone: 6–9

Lippia dulcis

Height: 20m (66ft)
Spread: 10m (33ft)
Grow for: maple-leaf-shaped foliage and autumn colour; AGM

In North America it is called sweet gum. In the UK it is simply known as liquidambar. As common names go, neither are very descriptive. Glowing torch, flame tree or autumn glory would all suit it better. Perhaps it is a case of once seen, never forgotten.

The bark on the young shoots is often winged and corky. Older bark remains raised and corky. The deeply lobed, glossy, mid-green leaves turn purple in early autumn and then orange-yellow in winter, often persisting until Christmas time. They could easily be mistaken for those of a maple but they are alternate on the stem, while those of maple are opposite each other. Tiny, green-yellow flowers of male and female are carried on the same tree, the males being in groups of three. Small spiky fruits appear in autumn.

L. styraciflua 'Moonbeam' is slow growing, maturing at 10m (33ft) high with a spread of 6m (20ft). The creamy-yellow leaves turn to shades of yellow, red and purple in autumn.
Liquidambar requires a soil which is constantly wet but not waterlogged. Leaf colour will be better when it is planted in full sun. It has brittle, fleshy roots and dislikes being transplanted. Ignore large, containerized trees for sale. Buy small and plant in its permanent position.

Basal suckers may be a problem. Remove them as close to the root as possible. Cutting at ground level will result in even more shoots. Pruning, when necessary, should be carried out in early winter before the sap starts to rise. Propagation is by seed sown and over-wintered in a cold frame. Softwood cuttings will root in summer with bottom heat. **JC**

Liquidambar styraciflua 'Worplesdon'

Lithodora diffusa 'Heavenly Blue'

Type: hardy, evergreen shrub
Soil & situation: well-drained, humus-rich, acid soil/full sun
North American hardiness zone: 6–8
Height: 15cm (6in)
Spread: 60cm (24in)
Grow for: trailing stems covered in deep blue flowers from the end of spring until late summer; perfect for growing over a low wall; AGM

This gem used to be called *Lithospermum diffusum* 'Heavenly Blue'. Then it was a great plant for tumbling over a rock or dwarf wall and it still is. If it is happy with the soil conditions it will flower without fail every year.

It has a prostrate habit, forming a dense carpet and shaping itself to whatever it grows over. The narrow, deep green leaves are noticeably hairy. From late spring until late summer the plant is covered in small, azure-blue flowers. In full sun the effect is quite startling, with the leaves, where they show through the sheet of blue, acting as a metallic backdrop.

Lightly trim with hedge clippers after flowering and feed with a high-potash, liquid fertilizer.

Lithodora diffusa 'Heavenly Blue'

Mulch the crown of the plant in autumn with peat, washing it down around the inner bare stems. This will encourage the plant to re-root. Propagation is by semi-ripe cuttings in summer. Root them in an ericaceous compost, otherwise the leaves will become yellow and rooting will be slow.

Lithodora oleifolia produces sky-blue flowers from pink tinted buds in early summer. It is not as dense with upright stems 20cm (8in) high. Propagation is easy since it readily sends up rooted suckers which should be removed. It requires a neutral to alkaline soil. **JC**

Lobelia cardinalis

Lobelia cardinalis
CARDINAL FLOWER

Type: hardy, perennial rhizome
Soil & situation: fertile, deep, constantly moist soil/full sun or light shade
North American hardiness zone: 3–9
Height: 90cm (36in)
Spread: 30cm (12in)
Grow for: the vibrant spikes of red flowers make a great show; AGM

I think my main interest in this plant is the way it surprises me every year. It is always bigger and brighter than I remember from the previous year. It also gets Brownie points for enjoying a soil which is always moist. The red-purple stems bear 15cm (6in) long, lance-shaped, glossy, bright green leaves with more than a hint of bronzing. In summer and early autumn it produces upright racemes, 38cm (15in) in length, made up of many bright, scarlet-red flowers. Tubular in shape, each flower has two lips with purple-red bracts.

Constant moisture is essential in summer and autumn but, although fully hardy, it can't tolerate heavy, wet ground in winter. Where drainage is poor in winter, lift and containerize the clump, replanting the following spring. My favourite position for the cardinal flower is at the edge of a pond where its reflection resembles the glow from an electric fire.

Propagation is by seed sown fresh in autumn and potted up in a peaty compost when small. Bud cuttings root well in summer. Over-winter in a cold frame and repot in the spring. **JC**

Lobelia 'Hadspen Purple'

Type: hardy, perennial rhizome
Soil & situation: moist, fertile soil/sun or part shade
North American hardiness zone: 5–8
Height: up to 80cm (32in)
Spread: 25cm (10in)
Grow for: a hardy lobelia that will flower from mid-summer well into the autumn; extremely floriferous with striking plum-purple flowers

This plant has only been very recently released, and I have grown it for only a few months. My mother though, sniffed it out at the very early stages, and has been well and truly smitten by it. I am beginning to see why. The flowering spikes

Lobelia 'Hadspen Purple'

are densely covered with masses of an almost luminous colour, and despite the fact that mine were battered with extreme wet and cold weather conditions, they looked perfect for well over a month, almost incongruous amongst the grey, autumnal weather. Although the plant has an upright habit with very leafy stems, there is no need to stake it. It holds its own against the autumn gales.

These plants enjoy moist, fertile soils, so it is worth adding fertile organic matter prior to planting if your soil is on the thin side. Dead growth can be removed during early winter or spring. This plant would also grow as a marginal plant, but apparently would not live so long if submerged. Propagate by division in spring.   **BG**

Lobelia tupa
DEVIL'S TOBACCO

Type: half-hardy perennial
Soil & situation: deep, moist, fertile soil/sun or partial shade
North American hardiness zone: 8–10
Height: 2m (6½ft)
Spread: 1m (3ft)
Grow for: foliage and flowers from late summer to mid-autumn

This, another extraordinary Chilean plant was introduced to the UK in 1824. It's difficult to believe that this is a relative of the plant with little blue flowers that decorates your hanging basket and there are giant lobelias over 2.7m (9ft) tall

Lobelia tupa

Lonicera etrusca

that grow on Mt Kenya; it's such a diverse group, that anything can happen. It is in the family Campanulaceae, so is related to campanula too. It has earned its common name from the Mapuche Indians who smoked the leaves and used a juice pressed from the foliage to treat toothache.

This is a real gem. I first saw it at Kew Gardens growing against a hot, sunny wall and couldn't believe my eyes – or the label! It's a robust, upright plant with red-purple stems and tactile, oval- to lance-shaped, grey-green, felty leaves. The narrow, tubular, brick-red to orange flowers appear on upright spikes up to 45cm (18in) long from mid- or late summer through till autumn, and a well-grown specimen in flower looks amazing.

It needs a sheltered position in full sun to partial shade, on deep, fertile, constantly moist soil. Hardy in mild climates like the south and west of Britain, it needs to be protected from frost by mulching with bracken or straw. In colder climates, lift in autumn and over-winter in pots or grow as a container plant. It grows tall and usually needs supporting. It may be attacked by slugs; in mild, moist winters the crown is susceptible to rot. Propagate by fresh seed in the autumn, sown as soon as it is ripe; divide in spring.   **MB**

Lonicera etrusca
ETRUSCAN HONEYSUCKLE OR GREEK HONEYSUCKLE

Type: hardy, perennial, semi-evergreen climber
Soil & situation: any soil/full sun to part shade
North American hardiness zone: 7–9
Height: 10m (33ft)
Spread: 4–5m (about 16ft)
Grow for: soft, semi-evergreen foliage; purple shoots; glorious blooms with stunning fragrance

I love walking round my garden on a warm summer's eve sniffing the various fragrant delights; I often start and end with this vigorous climber which has engulfed one end of my cottage. I'm loath to cut it back and lose a year or two's flowers, so it continues to rampage. It is so gorgeous in flower with each large bloom opening cream flushed with red and deepening to a golden-yellow, and their scent permeates the whole garden. The foliage is healthy, attractive, pleasant and actually soft to touch as it is downy, while the youngest shoots carry a purple hue – wonderful.

Lonicera is a genus consisting of 80 or more mostly fragrant plants named after Lonitzer, a 16th-century German botanist. The species name, *etrusca*, suggests it comes from Tuscany – Etruria – in Italy and it is in fact a Mediterranean plant, often referred to as the Greek honeysuckle.

It will grow in almost any site or soil, in sun or light shade but preferring some shelter. It is quite rampant so needs good supports; only prune when overgrown. It is slow to come into bloom but once established is very free flowering. As a true species it can be grown from seed but is quicker to flower from summer softwood or autumn hardwood cuttings. It may get aphids but does not suffer as badly as the commoner *L. periclymenum*.   **BF**

247

Thymus spp.

THYME

Type: hardy or nearly hardy evergreen shrub
Soil & situation: well-drained soil/sun
North American hardiness zone: varies from species to species, but roughly 4–9
Height: 20cm (8in)
Spread: 50cm (20in)
Grow for: neat compact plants to fill areas with a magic carpet of white, pink, purple or red scented flowers. They flourish in the warmth of mid-summer.

There are many dozens of thyme species and varieties easily available, all similar, but with different coloured flowers or foliage or scent. The ones illustrated are (left) *T. hirsutus* 'Doerfleri' and (right) garden, golden and silver thyme (*T. vulgaris, T. v.* 'Aureus' and *T. v.* 'Silver Posie'). Each is delightful in itself, but even better if many are massed together to fill one bed as a patchwork quilt. Because they are so flat they can be used where most plants would be too intrusive, such as down the middle of a driveway or in front of a basement window. Sadly the finest varieties for flavour tend to be fairly upright, but still make low shrubby hummocks; others are so prostrate as to cling to the contours of the ground, flowing over large stones like water. Grand, go on, get yourself some.

Most thymes are natives of warmer parts of Europe and Asia and were well known to the ancients. We get our name from the Latin *thymum,* which came from the Greek. Thyme has strong bactericidal properties and has long been used in home remedies; it is also much loved by bees. It needs a well-drained soil, sandy is good but most species need chalk too. Give it full sun. Plants are short lived, so propagate them every year. The species can be grown from spring- or summer-sown seed, or propagated by cuttings most of the year if taken with a heel, and root division is easy in spring or autumn. No real problems other than fiddly weeding. **BF**

Bunny adds:
I find that if you give them sharp drainage and one cutback after flowering, they will look good for several years.

Lonicera fragrantissima

Lonicera fragrantissima

Type: hardy, perennial, semi-evergreen shrub
Soil & situation: any soil/sun or shade
North American hardiness zone: 5–8
Height & spread: to 5m (16ft) if not supported
Grow for: small, fragrant, cream flowers all winter; red berries in summer

This is one of the longest flowering shrubs; the first flower may open before Christmas and the last after Easter. As each flower is small, only the size of a fingernail, and creamy, pale yellow in colour, they seem insignificant but are powerfully fragrant. They also allure bees, who flock to them on sunny days. The flowers are borne along twiggy shoots so it is easy to pick stems to take indoors to perfume a room though, sadly, they do not last long in a vase. Although partially evergreen, it is not a particularly attractive shrub as such and is best hidden at the back of a border.

Lonicera fragrantissima was introduced to the UK from China by Robert Fortune in 1845. Do not be deceived into getting *L.* x *purpusii* (a cross between *L. fragrantissima* and *L. standishii*), the similar but rather disappointing hybrid.

The shrubby honeysuckles are very long lived and vigorous on almost any soil or site. This is a shrub not a climber, but as it is not totally rigid it will need something to lend it support, such as a post or old tree against which it can be tied. It can be grown from seed but summer softwood or autumn hardwood cuttings are quicker to flower. *L. fragrantissima* is not so prone to aphids as the climbing honeysuckles.
BF

Lonicera periclymenum 'Graham Thomas'
COMMON HONEYSUCKLE, WOODBINE

Type: hardy, deciduous, twining shrub
Soil & situation: moist, well-drained, humus-rich soil/full sun or partial shade
North American hardiness zone: 5–9
Height: 4m (13ft)
Spread: 1.8m (6ft)
Grow for: it speaks for itself; AGM

Summer wouldn't be the same without honeysuckles. A walk down a country lane with the heavenly scent of the woodbine scrambling through the hedges with its nectar-filled flowers is a memorable experience. Did you suck the nectar from the unopened tube? Didn't we all? In autumn the bright, glistening, red berries outshone the red hips and haws of the dog rose and the hawthorn.

Lonicera periclymenum 'Graham Thomas' is a much-improved form of that wild woodbine. The 7.5cm (3in) long, mid-green leaves are glaucous on the underside and carried in pairs on the vigorous, twining branches. From early summer to autumn the plant is covered in whorls of two-lipped, very fragrant, tubular, white flowers, which gradually fade to yellow with a hint of copper, giving the

Lonicera periclymenum 'Graham Thomas'

plant a bicoloured appearance. They flower on the previous year's shoots and are best pruned back, after flowering, to some strong, young shoots.
L. p. 'Belgica' is more vigorous with white flowers that turn yellow with bright red streaks.

Propagate by inserting hardwood cuttings into open ground in early winter and they will be well rooted by the following autumn. Aphids can be a serious problem. When chemicals fail to control them the only solution is to hard prune in summer and allow new clean foliage to regrow. **JC**

Matt adds:
I smoked Woodbines years ago, they never smelt as sweet as this! This variety is named after the late Graham Stewart-Thomas, the garden writer and former Chief Gardens Advisor to the National Trust, who found it in a Warwickshire hedgerow in 1960; it's very free-flowering and typically vigorous. Derrick Cook found just a single seedling under a holly tree in his garden near Evesham and decided to nurture it. It matured to a dark reddish-green leaved plant with dark red flowers that are honey-coloured on the inside; this delightful plant is named after his home, 'Red Gables'. Roy Lancaster was walking along a beach in Sweden when he spotted one with cream and yellow flowers growing in a mound of brambles; Roy named it after his wife, 'Sweet Sue'. Where will you find yours?

Lonicera syringantha

Lonicera syringantha

Type: hardy, perennial, deciduous shrub
Soil & situation: any soil/full sun to light shade
North American hardiness zone: 5–8
Height & spread: makes a lax shrub 1–2m (3–6½ft) each way, or possibly wider
Grow for: arching sprays of stems and neat, grey-green foliage; wonderful, pink, scented flowers; occasional red berries

This is a plant to fool your friends. The grey-green foliage is small, neat and almost geometrical; the lilac-like flowers come in clusters in the axils of the leaves and can coat the stems with a multitude of blooms, each with a daphne-like perfume. Your friends will never guess this is a honeysuckle!

Introduced from China at the end of the 19th century, this beautiful plant was named for the resemblance its flowers bore to those of lilac (*Syringa*).

It will grow in most soils and situations but flowers best in sun. Although shrubby, it is very lax and makes an arching shrub given the space or can be trained to supports. As a species it can be grown from seed but cuttings in summer or autumn are quicker to flower. It has brittle wood, which is easily snapped.   **BF**

Lonicera x tellmanniana

Type: hardy, deciduous climber
Soil & situation: moist, well-drained soil/sun or light shade
North American hardiness zone: 7–9
Height: 5m (16ft)
Spread: 45–60cm (18–24in)
Grow for: twining climber; copious clusters of soft coppery-orange flowers in late spring to early summer; AGM

Although this honeysuckle has no fragrance, it is one of my favourites. The tubular flowers are up to 5cm (2in) long, very bold but not brassy and definitely eye-catching. When the plant is grown in light shade it produces its best, but will grow fairly well in full shade too. You can appreciate the vibrant hue of the flowers better in the softer light, they become more intense and fiery. I have not seen it scrambling up a tree but it would be highly suited to that type of situation, and being a fast mover, you would not have to wait too long for the startling results. I grow it twining up and over a dark blue, metal swing-seat with gold leaf finials, and love the strong colour combination of blue, gold and orange – rather exotic.

These are easy plants to grow although they do need a supportive framework of some sort, be it trellis, wires, a fence or the like. They will do better with an annual mulch of organic matter. Too much nitrogen will result in much leaf and little flowering, in which case potash will help redress the balance. Pruning is straightforward: you can just remove the shoots that have flowered immediately they are over; no other attention is necessary. They can be propagated from semi-ripe cuttings in summer or hardwood cuttings in late autumn.   **BG**

Lonicera x tellmanniana

Lotus hirsutus

Lotus hirsutus
HAIRY CANARY CLOVER

Type: hardy, evergreen perennial or subshrub
Soil & situation: free-draining, moderately fertile soils/sunny position
North American hardiness zone: 6–9
Height: up to 60cm (24in)
Spread: about 1m (3ft)
Grow for: extremely useful foliage plant with silver grey-green, tiny, hairy leaves; AGM

This is a close-textured, rather natty foliage plant that will form an attractive low hedge or edge to the front of the border; it can also be used as a specimen or group grown in gravel. It is a fairly unusual plant but is easy to grow, easy to propagate and extremely well-mannered. Because it has such fine leaves it is useful for contrasting with more informal, or larger-leaved types. It flowers in summer with not very conspicuous, but typical pea-type flowers that are cream flushed with shell pink. They are just an also ran, not unattractive though, but the prime reason for growing this is definitely the silvery foliage.

Leave on the growth throughout winter (it looks quite presentable) and then cut it down in spring if more bushy growth is required. It is worth growing replacement cuttings every three or four years so you can rejuvenate your stock period-ically. Propagation from softwood cuttings is straightforward in summer. It can, apparently, also be propagated from seed but the offspring is variable.   **BG**

Lunaria annua
Plant of the Week (see page 119)

Lupinus arboreus
TREE LUPIN

Type: semi-woody, usually evergreen, perennial shrub
Soil & situation: dry or at least well-drained soil/sun
North American hardiness zone: 8–9
Height: 1.8–2.2m (6–7ft)
Spread: 1m (3ft)
Grow for: effectively evergreen; fast-growing, scented, yellow flowers all summer; AGM

I like the usual run-of-the-mill lupins; they are easy and obliging plants that have the biggest aphids I've ever seen and they put on a gaudy show. But the tree lupins are different. This shrubby form is more refined, with greyer more spidery foliage and pale creamy-yellow blooms with a wonderful sweet scent. I like this delicate form, and the fact that it keeps its evergreen, silvery leaves in mild winters is an added bonus. It is a bit like a tree peony, but much quicker growing, positively frenetic by comparison. It is very useful for dry sunny banks and although short lived, it does self-seed.

The name comes from the Latin for wolf, *lupus*, as lupins produce 'peas' fit for a wolf/dog – we refer to unpalatable plants as dog(berry) or horse (…mint). Lupins were well known to the Romans as many of the genus are natives of the Mediterranean, but this one was brought from California in 1793.

Lupinus arboreus

It needs a dry sandy soil and apparently does well by the sea, but I've never seen it growing there. Dead-heading helps to keep them flowering and living a bit longer. As it is semi-shrubby you can try cuttings, but it is easier and quicker to make a spring or autumn sowing. Aphids can be a problem, but nothing like as much as they are with the more herbaceous species. **BF**

Lupinus 'The Governor'

Lupinus 'The Governor'
LUPIN

Type: hardy, clump-forming perennial
Soil & situation: fertile, well-drained, light, slightly acid soil/full sun or light shade
North American hardiness zone: 5–8
Height: 90cm (36in)
Spread: 75cm (30in)
Grow for: the coloured spikes of flowers in early and late summer

When I think of cottage and farm gardens they conjure up images of tall, multi-coloured spikes of lupin flowers standing above dense clumps of palmate leaves, each with a bead of dew at the base above the leaf stalk.

The softly hairy, mid-green leaves are made up of lance-shaped leaflets held on strong, thick, pale green stems. Flowering in early summer, the bicoloured racemes of royal blue and white pea-

like flowers are up to 45cm (18in) long. Removing the spike after flowering prevents the plant using its energy to produce seeds. These are contained in numerous small, pea-like pods. Early removal will encourage the plant to send out another flower spike in late summer.

Propagation is by seed sown in autumn or spring. Autumn seedlings need to be over-wintered in a cold frame. Soaking the round, black or brown seed in water for 24 hours before sowing will soften the outer seed coat and speed up germination. Basal cuttings can be rooted in a gritty, free-draining compost in spring. New young shoots are prone to slug damage. **JC**

Luzula nivea
SNOWY WOODRUSH

Type: hardy, evergreen grass
Soil & situation: will tolerate a wide range of soils/best in moist, humus-rich but free-draining soils/sun or shade
North American hardiness zone: 4–9
Height: 60cm (24in)
Spread: 45cm (18in)
Grow for: a useful grass for shady areas such as woodland; low-key but graceful year-round foliage; attractive, fairly long-lasting white flowers in late spring

I was pleased when I first fell upon this plant – 'fell' in the literal sense too! We were in the exhausting period of pulling to bits and removing one of our Chelsea gardens, when I saw a nice clump of *Luzula* in the bottom of the skip, exactly where I was about to dump a huge barrow of hardcore. You can guess the rest. Suffice to say they now are thriving in my woodland garden in bold drifts, jostling next to ferns, arums and primroses. They have a natural-looking habit with loose tufts of thin, strap-like dark green leaves which contrast with the snowy-white flowers borne in relaxed panicles. They have now established well and are tolerant of my dry conditions (which is not what the books would have you believe), though I must admit they are not spreading like wildfire.

The other one I grow, also purloined from a skip, is *Luzula sylvatica*, the greater woodrush. Its leaves are broader and it is a coarser plant generally but grows and spreads in a pleasingly compact fashion. The chestnut flowers are not a patch on the snowy woodrush, but it is a plant I like.

This plant, once established, needs next to no looking after. Because it is a plant often used in

Luzula nivea

rather large, natural-looking drifts, it is a useful one to propagate in quantity. This can be done by division or seed. Division is best done between mid-spring and early summer. Seed can be sown in spring or autumn.   **BG**

Lychnis coronaria
DUSTY MILLER, ROSE CAMPION

Type: hardy biennial or short-lived perennial
Soil & situation: prefers free-draining soil but will grow in any moderately fertile soil/sun or partial shade
North American hardiness zone: 4–8
Height: up to 80cm (32in)
Spread: 45cm (18in)
Grow for: incredible, intensely bright magenta flowers in mid-summer lasting over a month; basal rosettes of ever-grey, felted foliage; AGM

This is an old cottage-garden plant, but none the less is highly versatile because the vibrant hue of the flowers can be used to give a high-voltage effect to many a colour scheme. It is tolerant of extremely poor soil conditions too, and sets seed freely all around the edges of my gravel courtyard – it is growing in lines against north- and south-facing walls. It is also fine in borders and if it sets seed next to an unsympathetic neighbour and the colour combination sets your teeth on edge, it is simple to whip out. In truth I never notice whether my plants are biennial or perennial because they are not over-invasive but always there, a much appreciated presence. There is a white form, *L. c.* 'Alba', for those who find the magenta too much or too common.

To prolong flowering you can dead-head these adaptable plants. After flowering, they look a bit seedy. They are simple to remove and I either cut them down to leave the basal rosettes or just pull out the whole plant if I want to put in some later, temporary colour. The seedlings are adaptable and if I would rather they were elsewhere they can be moved with little setback. Propagation is easy with fresh seed sown immediately after flowering or in spring.   **BG**

Lycopersicon esculentum 'Aromata'
TOMATO

Type: tender, annual scrambler
Soil & situation: rich, moist compost/sun/under cover
North American hardiness zone: annual
Height & spread: up to 3m (10ft)
Grow for: delicious good-looking fruit packed full of vitamins; an easy and highly reliable greenhouse plant

In the UK we have one of the highest levels of amateur greenhouse ownership in the world and in most tomatoes are grown. There is an unbelievable number of tomato varieties, each with its own characteristics and virtues. However I am recommending 'Aromata', and in second and

Lychnis coronaria

third places 'Moravi' and 'Merlot', as the most outstandingly reliable croppers of round red tomatoes throughout the year. Not only do these grow well, crop well and not show any tendency to problems such as greenback, they have proved resistant to the majority of diseases that plague greenhouse-grown tomatoes.

The original tomatoes were ribbed and somewhat flattened in shape and the spherical tomato was not noticed or bred until about 1700. This is not surprising, as in Europe we only really started showing much interest in the tomato as a food at about that time and indeed, a century later most people were still unfamiliar with this new fruit.

Indoor tomatoes should be grown in an enriched border soil rather than in pots or bags of compost as they do better and require less attention with a big root run. At the end of the growing season if you do not heat your greenhouse through winter or when the light levels fall, the plant will wither and mould; at this point carefully take off the ripening and green fruits and put them in a warm place to ripen. Sow in individual pots in the warmth in late winter, pot on and plant out in the greenhouse border as soon as it can be kept frost free. Remove excess sideshoots; these can be rooted to make more plants. 'Aromata' avoids many of the diseases suffered by other tomatoes but may come under attack from aphids and whitefly; soft soap sprays prove effective.   **BF**

Lycopersicon esculentum 'Dombito'

Lycopersicon esculentum 'Dombito'
TOMATO

Type: tender, annual scrambler
Soil & situation: rich, moist compost/sun/under cover
North American hardiness zone: annual
Height & spread: up to 3m (10ft)
Grow for: an excellent large salad tomato

Having suggested indoor tomatoes for reliability I now want to recommend two for using as salad, beefsteak or slicing tomatoes. There are bigger beefsteaks – the old 'Marmande' is very good but really does better outdoors in a warm climate – but 'Dombito' was bred to be a modern, large, greenhouse tomato. Fairly reliable and on the whole disease resistant, and although it isn't early it does give a lovely crop of huge, round, sweet fruits. These peel like a peach, which is very handy, and do not get the corky, greeny-white, tough ring of poor flesh called greenback, which so many greenhouse tomatoes suffer from if exposed to heat stress. Of course if you want an old-fashioned, hard to peel and unreliable beefsteak with an incomparable flavour, grow 'Pink Brandywine', but be prepared for disappointing plants and crops in cool damp years.

Our larger tomatoes, such as 'Marmande' and 'Pink Brandywine' often revert to the ribbed and slightly flattened shape of older varieties. 'Dombito' is a significant improvement and the nice-looking fruits still have a good flavour.

Indoor beefsteak tomatoes are better off in an enriched border soil than in pots or bags of compost, as they do better and require less attention with a big root run. These big tomatoes need more care than others: add more wood ash to the soil, water diligently and foliar feed with seaweed sprays. Remove all excess shoots and reduce each truss to only a few fruits. At the end of their growing season carefully take off the ripening and green fruits and take these into a warm place to ripen. Sow in individual pots in the warmth in late winter, pot on and plant out in greenhouse border as soon as it can be kept frost free. 'Dombito' avoids many of the diseases but may still suffer from aphids and whitefly; soft soap sprays prove effective. **BF**

Lycopersicon esculentum 'Gardener's Delight'
TOMATO

Type: tender, annual scrambler
Soil & situation: rich, moist soil/sun/shelter
North American hardiness zone: annual
Height: 2m (6½ft)
Spread: 30cm (12in)
Grow for: I defy you to find a better flavoured tom!

In almost every taste trial of outdoor tomatoes that has taken place over the last few decades 'Gardener's Delight' has come out a clear winner. It can be grown indoors but tastes the best when grown outdoors. Being a cherry-sized fruit, it is quick and easy to crop and not very prone to pests or disease, except blight. The small, bite-sized fruits have a delicious flavour with a pronounced acidity that makes them thirst quenching.

The cherry varieties, like 'Gardener's Delight', seem to have as old a lineage as the original ribbed tomatoes and were probably grown in South America alongside the larger sorts.

Outdoor tomatoes are better off in an enriched border soil than in pots or bags of compost as they do better and require less attention with a big root run. Take off all sideshoots and remove the tip once six trusses of fruit form. At the end of the growing season, before the frosts come, carefully lift the vines and hang them upside down under cover somewhere frost free to let green fruits ripen on the plants. Sow in individual pots in the warmth in early spring, pot on and plant out in a sheltered border once the last frost is over. Outdoor tomatoes avoid many diseases and pests but are plagued by potato blight in damp years; I protect them by keeping them dry under a polythene flysheet. **BF**

Lycopersicon esculentum 'Gardener's Delight'

Lycopersicon esculentum 'Sakura'
TOMATO

Type: tender, annual scrambler
Soil & situation: rich, moist compost/sun/under cover
North American hardiness zone: annual
Height & spread: up to 3m (10ft)
Grow for: a fast, tasty, reliable crop – and not just tasty but TASTY!

I have already recommended an indoor tomato, 'Aromata' (see page 253), for reliable cropping, but it is not the tastiest. One of the tastiest for years was 'Gardener's Delight' (see previous entry); however it never has such a good flavour grown inside as out. This new variety is even better than the old champ when grown indoors, which amazes me as it is also fairly problem free and remarkably quick to crop – a superb, bite-sized cherry tomato.

Cherry tomatoes have been grown nearly as long as the larger ribbed sorts but appear to be of different lineage. They are usually better flavoured, prolific and often early croppers, and some resist diseases better than the larger, more conventional tomatoes. Of course this may be due to more breeding in the big ones, making them miffy.

Indoor cherry tomatoes are better off in an enriched border soil than in pots or bags of compost, as they do better and require less attention with a big root run. However if you are after an extra early crop, then keep them in pots on the staging and do not feed heavily. Sow in individual pots in the warmth in mid-winter, pot on and plant out in the greenhouse border as soon as it can be kept frost free. If you have space it can be left unpruned to ramble, otherwise remove excess sideshoots. 'Sakura' avoids many diseases but may still suffer from aphids and whitefly; soft soap sprays prove effective. **BF**

Lycopersicon esculentum 'San Marzano'
TOMATO

Type: tender, annual scrambler
Soil & situation: rich, moist soil/sun/shelter
North American hardiness zone: annual
Height: 2m (6½ft)
Spread: 30cm (12in)
Grow for: plum tomatoes are the best for cooking and hard to buy fresh

It is impossible to find good, fresh, ripe plum tomatoes so you have to grow them. They are the only tomato to cook alongside bacon and eggs

Lycopersicon esculentum 'San Marzano'

and are invaluable for almost all Italian or Spanish recipes. If you haven't tried fried plum tomatoes, please do – the flavour changes completely as they cook and becomes divine, and is especially good if eaten with some organic smoked back bacon. They are less runny than most tomatoes with a more solid flesh.

Plum-shaped tomatoes were developed mostly in Italy where they were originally called, and were more, pear shaped. For planting and aftercare please see *L. e.* 'Gardener's Delight', opposite. **BF**

Lysichiton americanus
YELLOW SKUNK CABBAGE

Type: hardy, aquatic, deciduous perennial
Soil & situation: fertile, humus-rich, deep, moist soil/full sun or partial shade
North American hardiness zone: 7–9
Height: 1m (3ft)
Spread: 1.2m (4ft)
Grow for: fine-looking, bright yellow spathes in spring; ideal for a waterside planting or in a bog garden; AGM

Not so long ago I was admiring hundreds of plants growing in a sheltered, low-lying, water garden in the West of Scotland. The sun was shining and all was well with the world until two passersby came along and proceeded to moan about the problems of the 'imaginary', nearby compost heap. The musky smell of yellow skunk cabbage is only noticeable when there are lots of flowers or when your attention is drawn to it.

The leaves, which appear at the same time as the flower is fully open, are leathery, shiny, dark green and grow to 50–100cm (20–39in) long. Appearing in early spring, each 'flower' comprises a large, bright yellow spathe up to 40cm (16in) long, with a central yellow spadix made up of hundreds of tiny, bisexual, green flowers turning yellow. It is a striking plant for the edge of a pool or stream where its reflection doubles the display. It is also a 'talking point' for those who have never seen it before.

When planting allow adequate room for the leaves to grow, spacing the plants about 1.5m (5ft) apart. Propagation is by seed in wet peat as soon as it is ripe or by pulling offsets from the base of the plant in early summer and potting into a peaty compost.

JC

Canna iridiflora/C. x ehemanii July

Type: tender rhizomatous perennial
Soil & situation: moisture-retentive soil/full sun/winter protection
North American hardiness zone: 7–10
Height: up to 3m (10ft)
Spread: 50cm (20in)
Grow for: highly exotic-looking, dramatic foliage; superb rose-coloured flowers, which appear later than other cannas and are glorious in the bright mid-summer light; AGM

This plant is a real knock-out and will stop you in your tracks. It is a huge plant growing frequently to above 1.5m (5ft) with massive, purple-edged, green leaves and pendulous, relatively small and delicate-looking, yet punchy flowers. Cannas are easy to grow generally. I have tried them in different areas and they invariably just get on with life even in excessively free-draining areas, though I do shovel in the odd wheelbarrow load of compost. Some years odd plants are overlooked and left out; they survive to tell the tale but bloom much later, so I would not do it on purpose. This one is hardier than many and is also grown far less, perhaps because of its size, but in a small garden it would fill the space with zing – very exciting. Another possible reason for its low profile is that it comes into flower relatively late and is worth growing on under glass for a bit longer to bring it forward. The most likely reason though is just that it is difficult to come by, but I do not know why. The more common *Canna indica* and its many cultivars are more widely grown. They are all great assets to the garden, transforming it with their lush structure and vibrant colour.

Do not be put off by the following routine. It is simple and the results are inevitably stunning. I always pop a few extra into pots as they can plug gaps or just stand alone. All cannas need lifting as soon as the frost has blackened their foliage, then their top growth should be cut off. Over-winter them in a cellar, greenhouse or shed, keeping them just slightly damp and frost-free. Do not let them dry out. Plant them back out in late spring or early summer. If the weather is hot and dry give them a good drink to maintain that lush feel and pull off dead flowerheads to encourage more. Slugs and snails are fairly keen on them but I find a thick mulch of cocoa shells adds to the tropical effect, deters pests and retains the moisture. **BG**

Macleaya microcarpa 'Coral Plume'

PLUME POPPY, TREE CELANDINE

Type: hardy, rhizomatous perennial
Soil & situation: wide range of soils/prefers moist conditions/tolerates light shade
North American hardiness zone: 4–9
Height: to 2.5m (8ft)
Spread: 1m (3ft)
Grow for: fabulous bold foliage; beautiful plumed racemes of long-lasting, rich coral flowers in summer; AGM

I grew this plant in my previous garden in deep, rich soil and it thrived, producing increasing quantities of wonderful juicy stems each spring, followed by softly stunning flowers. People are wary of its over-enthusiastic nature. It is on the keen side, so hem it in with sturdy neighbours or just spade through its outer limits each spring and show it who is boss. When I moved to my current free-draining, light soil, I thought its exuberant nature would be over-subdued, but it has come up trumps again. Try to seek out 'Coral Plume', as this clone has warmer hues to its foamy flowers.

Macleaya cordata (AGM) has creamy-white flowers and is another favourite of mine. The foliage has an architectural feel with bold leaves that are up to 20cm (8in) wide, lobed, with a soft olive green colour above but downy white below. I have a big clump of them beside my front door and the

Macleaya microcarpa 'Coral Plume'

Magnolia liliiflora 'Nigra'

architectural leaves complement the chunky stone carving of the quoins around the doorway. Not a plant I would be without.

I do next to nothing to this plant – I don't stake it, nor divide it up unless a friend wants a bit – all I do is admire it and cut it down in autumn. Slugs are supposed to go for it, and I have more than my fair share, but they never make it unsightly.   **BG**

Magnolia liliiflora 'Nigra'

Type: hardy, deciduous shrub
Soil & situation: moist, humus-rich, well-drained, neutral to acid soil/sun or partial shade
North American hardiness zone: 6–9
Height: 3m (10ft)
Spread: 2.5m (8ft)
Grow for: continuous display of dark purple flowers from late spring and through the summer; AGM

This delightful variety is regarded by many as having the longest flowering period of all magnolias. Plants flower early in life, often the year after planting.

It is a vigorous variety with glossy, dark green leaves up to 20cm (8in) in length. The large, chalice-shaped flowers appear in late spring and it can still be in flower in the autumn. Externally they are a dark purple and an ivory-white with purple staining on the inside. As the flowers age, they resemble an untidy tulip with some of the petals peeling back to reveal their inner colouring.

Pruning is not normally necessary with this compact-growing variety. Branches which are crossing or spoiling the shape may be removed in winter when the shrub is dormant. *M. l.* 'Nigra' dislikes being transplanted when large. Check the roots of container-grown plants and if they are congested tease them apart before spreading out in the planting hole. Avoid a site exposed to cold winds or late spring frosts which will blacken the early flowers.

Propagation is by semi-ripe cuttings in late summer. Use small cuttings and cut the leaves in half to reduce transpiration which causes wilting. Layering in early spring is guaranteed to work but can be slow, taking up to 18 months to root well.   **JC**

Mahonia japonica
Plant of the Week (see page 33)

Mahonia x *media* 'Charity'

Type: hardy, evergreen shrub
Soil & situation: well-drained, fertile soil/shade or partial shade
North American hardiness zone: 7–8
Height: 4m (13ft)
Spread: 3–4m (10–13ft)
Grow for: fragrant, deep yellow flowers in winter; spiny, architectural, evergreen foliage; blue-black fruits in summer

Its shiny, dark green, spiny-toothed, pinnate leaves ensure this plant creates interest all year round. From late autumn until late winter it carries long, prominent racemes of small, scented, deep yellow flowers followed by berries. Even the stems and roots are interesting: cut them and you will find the wood is bright yellow.

Mahonias can be divided into two groups: the taller Asian species such as *M. lomarifolia* and the more compact Americans, including *M. aquifolium*. Those from North America can tolerate a more sunny situation. Both parents of 'Charity' are Asian, *M. lomarifolia* and *M. japonica*, resulting in a plant with 45cm (18in) long leaves made up of between 17 and 21 leaflets. *M.* x *m.* 'Charity' has, over many years, proved to be totally reliable.

Mahonias dislike being transplanted, so buy small plants which are not pot bound to avoid disturbing the roots. Dig a generous-sized

Mahonia x media 'Charity'

planting hole and add lots of rotted farmyard manure. Plant firmly and water regularly during the first season. In exposed, windy sites the tips of the young leaves may be scorched. Occasionally it will throw up a long flowering shoot devoid of lower leaves. After flowering remove the shoot close to the ground to encourage new growth.

It is seldom troubled by pests or diseases, so for me 'Charity' begins at home.   **JC**

Mahonia x *media* 'Lionel Fortescue'

Type: hardy, evergreen shrub
Soil & situation: any soil/partial shade
North American hardiness zone: 7–8
Height & spread: 4m (13ft)
Grow for: architectural form and winter flowers; AGM

There are several excellent hybrids between *Mahonia japonica* and *M. lomariifolia*, collectively known as *M.* x *media*. They have terminal flower clusters surrounded by an umbrella of stiff, glossy, spiny leaves topping upright jointed stems.

Lionel Fortescue at the Garden House in Buckland Monachorum in Devon, southwest England, produced 200 seedlings; five were retained. *M.* x *media* 'Lionel Fortescue' produces masses of branched, bright yellow, fragrant flower spikes up to 40cm (16in) long. From the same batch came M. x m. 'Buckland' with up to 14 upright, branched, arching, spreading flower spikes to 45cm (18in) long. *M.* x *m.* 'Charity' (see previous entry) is another favourite – it was selected by Sir Eric Savill from seedlings raised in Ireland around 1950.

They were busy in America too! *M.* x *m.* 'Arthur Menzies', up to 4m (13ft) x 4m (13ft), is similar, with yellow flowers on upright spreading spikes up to 25cm (10in) long. The leaves can be as long as 45cm (18in). This was selected at the University of Washington Arboretum.

They need moist, slightly acid to neutral soil with plenty of well-rotted organic matter and prefer partial shade. Protect plants from cold winds. When they become spindly and bare at the base, cut the stems back to within 30–60cm (12–24in) of the base after flowering in spring; feed with general fertilizer and mulch. They regenerate with denser growth. Propagate by leaf bud cuttings in late winter.   **MB**

Mahonia x *media* 'Lionel Fortescue'

Malus coronaria 'Charlottae'

Type: hardy, deciduous tree
Soil & situation: moisture-retentive, free-draining soil/sun
North American hardiness zone: 5–8
Height & spread: 9m (30ft)
Grow for: delicate, fragrant flowers in late spring and early summer

It took a journey to New Zealand to discover this magnificent *Malus* growing in the pretty garden in Taranaki created by Gwyn Masters. Among all her treasures was a young specimen of *Malus coronaria* 'Charlottae', resplendent in light and shell-pink blooms, perfectly placed by a path so I could press my nose to the fragile, semi-double flowers and inhale a draught of the delicate violet perfume. It's a good 'value for money' tree. The branches are at first upright, then spread with age (I know the feeling!) and the flowers not opening until the end of spring are quite late for a crab apple. The large, lobed leaves often colour brilliantly in autumn to a rich orange-red; the tree also fruits prolifically after long, hot summers. It was found as a chance seedling in the wild in 1902 near Waukegan, Illinois, by Mrs Charlotte de Wolf. Sir Harold Hillier, the great English nurseryman, once remarked, 'In my opinion this is the best of the semi-double American crabs for English gardens with a strong constitution'. What more can I say?

It prefers a sunny position, where autumn colour is better, and moisture-retentive, fertile but not waterlogged soil; it tolerates some shade. Water young trees well to help them establish and mulch in spring. Feed with slow-release fertilizer in spring until mature. Prune in winter to remove dead, diseased or damaged wood. Propagate in winter by grafting or budding. It can be attacked by any pests and diseases that affect apples like powdery mildew, scab and woolly aphid. **MB**

Malus coronaria 'Charlottae'

Malus domestica
RUSSET APPLE

Type: hardy, long-lived, deciduous tree
Soil & situation: any well-drained soil/sun
North American hardiness zone: 5–8
Height & spread: 30cm–18m (12in–60ft), depending on rootstock
Grow for: prolific, pink, scented flowers in late spring; green- or reddy-brown, aromatically flavoured apples in early autumn

There are many apple varieties – over 2,000 different sorts are known – and it is fairly easy to buy several hundred different ones if you want a collection. There is every size, quality and keeping ability, but one group remains unique and that is the russets. While every other apple is glossy and shiny, these have a corky matt skin overall or in large areas. The fruits are usually reddy-brown or even greeny-brown and the skin is tough. The flesh is often more substantial than other apples. It is also drier, which is why they store well, and their sweet, strong, aromatic, even nutty flavour makes them a good choice for the gourmet. The skin is usually scentless, but resists scab well. Indeed, a great many of the best apples have some russet patches, if only as flecks on the skin. 'Brownlee's Russet' was introduced in 1848; it is an upright tree

with very prolific pink blossom which is a feature in itself, and the fruits are juicier than most russets and aromatic. They store well, being good all winter up until spring when they come into bloom again. 'Rosemary Russet' is even older (1831), not strong growing but upright and productive. The apples are best from mid-winter till spring.

Ideally any apple wants a rich, moist but well-drained, loamy soil in a warm, sheltered spot but it will thrive almost anywhere not totally barren and windswept. Most russets are not tip bearers and thus can be pruned, or trained; they are best on very dwarfing rootstocks as cordons or espaliers. 'Brownlee's Russet' needs a pollinator and 'Greensleeves' suits it. Plant bare-rooted trees in autumn, preferably as soon as their leaves have fallen. Russets suffer less than many apples from pests and diseases, and crop well regardless. **BF**

Malus domestica 'Court Pendu Plat'
WISE APPLE, WALLATON PIPPIN

Type: hardy, upright, deciduous tree
Soil & situation: all except waterlogged soil/sun
North American hardiness zone: 5–8
Height & spread: depends on growing conditions and rootstock
Grow for: history; flavour; fruit from early winter to late spring

This apple, believed to have originated in Roman times, is still used in breeding programmes because it keeps well and flowers at the end of spring, escaping the frost, hence the name 'Wise Apple'. 'Court Pendu' means 'suspended short', as the stalk is so short the fruit appears to sit upon the branch. Around Herefordshire, it is called garnons because the Cotterell family from Garnons near Hereford grew it without knowing the name; for the same reason it is often known as the 'Wallaton Pippin' because Lord Middleton in Wallaton, Nottinghamshire, lost the label too! It was among the top ten Victorian apples, prized for its looks and fine flavour and its use as a decorative tree for borders or pots when grown as bushes or espaliers.

The small, flat, rounded fruit is dull yellow with a vermilion flush and slight russetting. In the UK leave on the tree until late October if possible; it will then ripen from December to January and store until April/May.

It is full flavoured and fruity with a pineapple-like taste, but mellows to become scented and

intensively flavoured. Delicious! Pollination group 3. It needs moist, loamy soil in a sheltered sunny site; mulch in spring and don't let the soil dry out. Grow as cordons or espaliers in small gardens. As it is spur fruiting, prune in winter and mid-summer. It is very hardy, prolific and scab resistant, but suffers from pests and diseases common to apples, including mildew, codling moth and woolly aphid. **MB**

Malus domestica 'Discovery'

Type: hardy, long-lived, deciduous tree
Soil & situation: any well-drained soil/sun
North American hardiness zone: 5–8
Height & spread: 30cm–18m (12in–60ft), depending on rootstock
Grow for: prolific white and pink, barely scented flowers in late spring; brightly coloured red apples in late summer; an early cropper; AGM

Early apples are so delicious; they are such a delight to eat straight from the tree and warmed by the sun on a bright, late summer's afternoon. Of course being early means most of them won't keep, and some go woolly within hours of picking.

Malus domestica 'Russet'

'Discovery' is, however, an early that stays fresh a little longer (that's why it is so common in the shops) and despite this is still a very, very good apple. The sweet crunchiness makes for really excellent eating. I love to stand with a large scarlet 'Discovery' in one hand being heartily munched and to alternate it with fistfuls of Japanese wineberries (*Rubus phoenicolasius*, see page 342) which I collect with the other – yummy!

There are several dozen wild *Malus* species, but most of our domestic tree's ancestry comes from *M. pumila*, a wild crab common all over Europe. Domestic trees were known to the early Romans but not as our modern fruit – they were much closer to the crab; however by late Roman times they had selected over three dozen improved varieties! 'Discovery' was introduced in 1962 and makes an upright tree with healthy foliage, it is fairly resistant to scab and tolerant of late frosts. It is now the most popular early apple.

Ideally an early apple wants a rich, moist but well-drained, loamy soil in a warm, sheltered spot but it will thrive almost anywhere not totally barren and windswept. Most early apples are tip bearers and thus should not be pruned or trained, so are best on very dwarfing rootstocks as small bush trees. 'Discovery' does form spurs as well so can be trained, just. It needs a pollinator; 'Greensleeves' suits it and is a good apple, ripening after 'Discovery'. Plant bare-rooted trees in autumn, preferably as soon as their leaves have fallen. **BF**

Malus domestica 'Winston'

Type: hardy, long-lived, deciduous tree
Soil & situation: any well-drained soil/sun
North American hardiness zone: 5–8
Height & spread: 30cm–18m (12in–60ft), depending on rootstock
Grow for: prolific, pale pink and white, lightly scented flowers in late spring; yellowish-green flushed red apples in late autumn; a long keeper; AGM

I want to be able to eat my own apples all year, but even more importantly I want good apples for coleslaw almost all year round. Although 'Winston' is one of the longest keepers of all, I find it also stays as a high-quality apple until well into the early summer of the following year, unlike some others I could name. It is resistant to scab, can be trained and has vigorous growth which overcrops if you are not careful – a first-class choice. There are many late keepers, 'Granny Smith' being one example, but few of them make

as good eating as late as 'Winston'. Long-keeping apples were very popular in previous times as they could be taken as ship's stores. However, those that kept for longest (some were claimed to keep two years) were hardly fit for eating, being more akin to hard green crab apples. 'Winston', originally called 'Winter King', was raised in Berkshire in 1920 as a cross between a 'Cox' and a 'Worcester Pearmain'; fortunately it gets its flavour from the former and its habits from the latter – good job it wasn't the other way round.

Ideally it wants a well-drained, loamy soil in a sheltered spot so that the apples can hang on the tree as late as possible. It can be trained but also does well on any dwarfing rootstock as a small bush or medium-sized, freely grown tree. Thin the crop or they will be prolific and small. 'Winston' needs a pollinator and goes well with 'Jupiter' or 'Ellison's Orange', which ripen well before it. Plant bare-rooted trees in autumn, preferably as soon as their leaves have fallen. **BF**

Malus 'John Downie'
CRAB APPLE

Type: hardy, deciduous tree
Soil & situation: fertile, moist, well-drained soil/full sun or light shade
North American hardiness zone: 5–8
Height: 9m (30ft)
Spread: 5m (16ft)
Grow for: cup-shaped flowers, colourful fruits and good autumn colour; AGM

This is one of the best crab apple varieties for fruit. It is a regular and heavy cropper. Even better news is that you can eat the fruit from the tree without it bringing a tear to your eye.

Malus domestica 'Winston'

Malus 'John Downie'

Young trees have narrow heads with upright branches. Eventually it forms a broad-headed tree. The glossy, bright green leaves appear before the clusters of pure white flowers, which open from pink buds in late spring and are followed by 5cm-(1in-) diameter apples. The fruit hangs in bunches on long stalks and their shiny skin colour starts off yellow, ripening through orange to red or deep scarlet. This is the variety with fruit capable of prize-winning crab apple jelly. It dislikes heavy, wet soil where it is prone to apple canker disease. On light, very free-draining soils the crop will be reduced. Avoid sites exposed to cold, drying winds. Low areas prone to spring frosts will damage the blossom.

Pruning is necessary to keep the centre of the tree open for light. Diseased and crossing branches should be removed in winter. Suckers at the base of the tree and up the stem will be from the rootstock and should be removed. Propagation is by budding in summer or grafting in winter. **JC**

Matt adds:

This is a fine tree for small gardens, and its fruits look wonderful in the autumn sunlight. It increases its value by being an excellent pollinator in orchards, it's self-fertile, producing fruit when planted alone and the fruits are good for jellies and winemaking. Some nurseries offer 'family trees' with three or more different varieties all grafted on to the same tree, including other legends like *M.* 'Golden Hornet' with masses of white flowers in mid-spring and golden-yellow fruit, and *M.* 'Red Sentinel' with its pink flowers in late spring and glossy fruits lasting until early in the New Year.

Matthiola bicornis
NIGHT-SCENTED STOCK

Type: hardy annual
Soil & situation: any soil/sun
North American hardiness zone: annual
Height & spread: 50cm (20in), spindly
Grow for: staggering fragrance; pastel, bluey-violet, purple, white evening blooms, usually two-tone

This is a knock-you-down scent, sort of a sensual cruise missile, and if you have not enjoyed the pleasure of this night-flowering bloom you have not lived. It is often overlooked as it is too easy to grow and so given to kids – who are sent to bed before it comes out. This is a hardy plant that can be sown in almost any bare soil and will then flower throughout summer, giving you untold nights of delight. The perfume is so delicious that when I make a clear fruit jelly, such as white currant, I drop petals of *Matthiola bicornis* into it as it cools, capturing that memory of a summer evening. You would hardly call the plant attractive, the grey foliage is scrappy and the flowers only open at night, remaining closed and limp looking all day, so it should be mixed with *M.* Virginian stock, which has no scent but brightly coloured flowers all day. (Virginian stock is another wonderful misnomer, as it comes from the Mediterranean islands!)

A native of southern Europe, night-scented stock is a hardy biennial, but we treat it as an annual more successfully. The genus is named after a 16th-century botanist Mattiola.

Happy on any soil in the sun, it will over-winter for an earlier show of flowers but is often lost to the vagaries of the weather and slugs. It does really quite well in pots. In an outdoor spot it can be sown fairly densely from early spring. Keep weeded and watered, and remember to visit at dusk. This plant suffers no problems. **BF**

Matthiola incana
WILD STOCK

Type: very hardy, short-lived, evergreen, perennial subshrub
Soil & situation: well-drained soil, especially chalky/sun/shelter
North American hardiness zone: 7–8, though may be grown as an annual
Height: 50cm (20in), top heavy
Spread: 30cm (12in)
Grow for: masses of white, highly fragrant flowers through summer and ever-grey foliage

Matthiola bicornis

There are many sorts of stocks and this is the mother of most of them. There are refined garden forms, but this wild original from the Atlas Mountains of Morocco is my favourite. There is no compromise with the scent, which is a heady clove, and given some winter shelter the plant may live long enough to make a fairly big mass of flowers. The grey foliage gets a bit battered in winter but soon revives in spring. They love the same conditions as pinks and carnations (*Dianthus* spp., see pages 143 and 146), lavender (*Lavandula* spp., pages 234–235) and so many other grey-leaved plants that it is worth having a border just for them.

A native of southern Europe and possibly even the UK, as it is apparently wild on the Sussex cliffs in the southeast. It was well known in early gardens and is the parent form from which we get our Brompton, Ten-Week, East Lothian and other series of fragrant bedding stocks, which between them fill the entire year with perfumed blooms.

It must have a sheltered, sunny spot on a free-draining, preferably chalky soil. Dead-heading is worthwhile as the plants may live a few years if they don't seed. It may be cut back to keep it bushy, in theory, but in practice it dies. Sow the seed in pots in late spring under cover, grow on and plant out in early summer. Give it some windbreak protection for the first, and then during the coldest, winters. **BF**

Meconopsis x sheldonii
'Slieve Donard'
Plant of the Week (see page 209)

Melissa officinalis
LEMON BALM

Type: hardy, herbaceous, perennial weed
Soil & situation: any soil/sun or shade/moist or dry
North American hardiness zone: 3–7
Height & spread: forms a 60cm (24in) dome
Grow for: lovely, healthy, bright, scented foliage in an attractive form

I like the smell of lemon balm's scented foliage enough to rub myself with it on a hot day. I also use the leaves in long, cool drinks and I plant this lovely weed in many different places just for its cheerfulness. The variegated form is splashed with bright yellow and gives a spot of colour in many a drab area; it is also quick and easy to chop into chunks and multiply in late winter. Balm is often accused of spreading rampantly by runners like mint, however I have never found this to be so; true, the clump grows, but it is the self-seeding that makes this a lovely weed.

A native of Europe and possibly of the southwest of the UK, this was allegedly introduced in the Middle Ages, but I reckon it was by the Romans for their bees. The name comes for the Greek for

Matthiola incana

bee, as this plant is loved by these insects for its flowers and their nectar, but also for the sweet lemon fragrance. Indeed it has long been held that the beekeeper should grow this plant to keep his bees from straying and also to rub over himself before approaching the hive. I do it and it's true, they seem to like the smell.

This is a remarkably useful plant as it will grow on any site, soil or situation given half a chance. Cut out any reverted all-green shoots and remove seedlings. Dead-heading is worthwhile to prevent self-seeding everywhere. The variegated form is propagated by root division in late winter or early spring; the plain green by seed sown anytime. One particular problem – this is invasive by seed! **BF**

Melissa officinalis

Melittis melissophyllum
BASTARD BALM

Type: hardy, herbaceous perennial
Soil & situation: moist soil/dappled shade
North American hardiness zone: 6–9
Height: 72cm (28in)
Spread: 50cm (20in)
Grow for: attractive flowers in late spring and early summer

This, the largest-flowered native of the mint family and a relative of the deadnettle, is rare in the UK and was first discovered in a wood near Totnes in south Devon. It is found in southwest England and southwest Wales, throughout Europe and east as far as Russia in hedges, scrub and mountain woods.

Melittis melissophyllum

The flowers, appearing towards the top of the stems have pink or purple-mauve lips or spots; there is also a white form. Their fragrance is described by some as 'honey', but others disagree, detecting a more pungent aroma, hence the French name *melisse de punaisse* or bug balm. When dried, it retains its fragrance (or odour) for a long time. This pretty, undemanding plant is ideal for mixed or herbaceous borders or woodland gardens; the flowers are attractive to bees.

When I look at the flowers I always think that they are like opera singers in flowing robes with their mouths open, ready to sing – it's as near as I'll ever get to an opera! The name *Melittis* is a variant of the Greek for honey bee; *melissophyllum* means honey sweet. Considering the Latin name, it is a shame that this pretty little plant isn't called something more flattering like the honey balm.

Plant in organic-rich, moisture-retentive soil in dappled shade. Incorporate plenty of well-rotted organic matter before planting; cut down stems and mulch in spring. Divide in spring. **MB**

Mentha rotundifolia
BOWLES' APPLE MINT

Type: hardy, herbaceous, perennial weed
Soil & situation: any soil/partial sun to heavy shade/loves moisture
North American hardiness zone: 6–9
Height: 1–1.2m (3–4ft)
Spread: 9m (30ft)
Grow for: delicious flavour; good ground cover; pale green, roundish leaves

Mint is a cheap way of covering a lot of shady ground with something other than nettles, and the flowers in autumn are really good for insects. But I grow it because I love mint sauce. I rarely have lamb but often have the sauce with carrots and peas, and especially with new potatoes. I make a delicious sauce by shredding the fresh leaves into a white currant and apple jelly made with vinegar – it is just so gooood! Anyway Bowles' apple mint is the best of all the mints for flavour and it is not so prone to rust as most other sorts.

There are many mints, the majority of them occurring naturally in damp places, and they have been used since time immemorial both in cooking and for strewing on floors. They are mentioned in St Matthew's Gospel. The name is *minthe* in Greek and then, as now, mint was much used for eating with suspicious lamb. (You have to be crazy to buy pre-minted lamb, didn't you see the television programme?)

Mint does not thrive in full sun unless the soil is very moist; it prefers a rich, damp soil and does not like wood ashes or dry chalky soils. Traditionally mint is planted in the ground in a bottomless bucket so the runners are confined. Many mints can be grown from seed but any bit roots and spreads like water. Plant the new roots in autumn or spring; they can also be taken inside in pots for an out-of-season forced crop. If you get rust then cut off all the foliage, burn it and cover the roots with a sterile mulch. **BF**

Mentha rotundifolia

Mirabilis jalapa

MARVEL OF PERU

Type: tender, tuberous-rooted perennial or half-hardy annual
Soil & situation: any well-drained soil/sun
North American hardiness zone: 8–11
Height & spread: to 1m (3ft)
Grow for: amazing striated flowers with strong perfume, One of the many joys of mid-summer.

The Marvel of Peru is not fashionable now but was immensely popular a century ago. I first came across it on clearing an abandoned Victorian conservatory. Among a few surviving plants and a lot of rubbish was a brick-sized tuber of some sort. I took it home and nurtured it back into life, got it to flower and was staggered by the orange, red-striped flowers with such a powerful orange blossom scent. A couple of hand grenade-like seeds were formed and I was able to multiply this old relic. The flowers open at tea time and last a mere day, but what flowers! They really are unique as the striping is not symmetrical or sensible but it is pleasing.

Introduced to the UK in the 16th century from South America, the generic name is the Latin for wonderful and *jalapa* is a distortion of the Mexican place name Xalapan. It is also known as the four o'clock plant, as that is the time when the flowers open.

It needs a free-draining compost or soil and a site in full sun. It can be treated like a dahlia or even a potato, as the large tuber can be dug up in autumn and over-wintered somewhere frost free to be replanted in early summer. Alternatively it can be kept under cover in a pot and allowed to die down over winter to be started again in spring, much like a datura or fuchsia. Or it can be sown under cover in warmth in early spring to be planted out in early summer; it will then flower soon after. A remarkably tough plant, but it sometimes gets aphids – and it is poisonous!   **BF**

Mespilus germanica
MEDLAR

Type: shrub or small tree
Soil & situation: most soils apart from boggy or very dry/needs sun
North American hardiness zone: 6–9
Height: to 6m (20ft)
Spread: to 8m (25ft)
Grow for: compact form, attractive flowers and autumn colour; unusual fruits

This robust, no-nonsense fruit tree has been cultivated in British gardens for centuries. It needs an open, sunny site on most soils and makes a small, spiny shrub or small tree. The dark green leaves, which turn yellow in autumn, highlight simple white or pink blush flowers in late spring or early summer. They are followed by small brown fruits with persistent calyces that are 'bletted' (left to rot) until they become edible. It is found in the wild in Asia Minor, was cultivated by the ancient Assyrians and is believed to have been taken to the United States by French Jesuits.

The earliest reference to it in England was in 1270, when the gardener of Westminster Abbey was instructed to provide the monastery with medlars and other fruits. A German book records the wood being used for making the spokes of wheels and the twigs turned into for horsewhips for carters.

Of the several varieties around, *Mespilus germanica* 'Nottingham' has brown fruit 4cm (1½in) across, *M. g.* 'Dutch' crops heavily, ripens in mid-autumn and is ready for Christmas. They are an acquired taste, but is it worth acquiring? Give it a try and find out! **MB**

Mespilus germanica

Metasequoia glyptostroboides

Metasequoia glyptostroboides
DAWN REDWOOD

Type: hardy, deciduous conifer
Soil & situation: open position in moist soil
North American hardiness zone: 5–10
Height: 40m (130ft) or more
Spread: 5m (15ft) or more
Grow for: its elegant form; foliage in summer and autumn; winter silhouette; AGM

This is one of botany's and horticulture's most exciting stories, proving that there are still plants waiting to be discovered. Keep looking! In 1941 this species was described from fossils unearthed in Japan, then the same year living specimens were found by Mr T. Kan in a village in central China but were not collected until 1944, when further trees were discovered. They were not scientifically described until 1948. It is a native of western Huphe and northeast Sichuan on streamsides and ravines and although it was new to science, it had long been cultivated in its native region where it was used to stabilize river banks and paddy fields. The first seeds, collected in 1947, were sent to the Arnold Arboretum in the USA and distributed to gardens in America and Europe, and some of these original seedlings are still flourishing in gardens within the UK.

It is an outstandingly beautiful tree, conical habit when young, with shaggy, fibrous, cinnamon-brown bark, and bright green feathery leaves, that turn pink and gold in autumn in good conditions. It grows rapidly, almost as fast as its popularity! There are several selections available in nurseries, including some that are variegated.

It needs a sheltered position, protection from frost, which can damage young growth, and deep, moist soil; it is slow growing on poor soils like chalk or sand. It flourishes in warm summers and pefers a Continental climate. Propagate by seed, semi-ripe cuttings from mid-summer and hardwood cuttings in winter. **MB**

Mirabilis jalapa
Plant of the Week (see page 265)

Miscanthus sinensis 'Variegatus'

Type: hardy, perennial grass
Soil & situation: moist soil when young/sun or light shade
North American hardiness zone: 4–9
Height: to 1.7m (5½ft)
Spread: indefinite
Grow for: striking, variegated foliage; pink blossom in a warm summer; AGM

This plant, like many of the variegated miscanthus, forms fantastic, dense tussocks of bright, variegated foliage. The leaves will often arch over so the tips touch the ground and it makes an intriguing rustling sound as breezes move through its leaves. Towards the end of a hot summer it will usually send up arching panicles of silky spikelets. These look dramatic and should be left through most of the winter in their bleached, pale straw-coloured form. The flowerheads can be used for cutting, if you can bear to do it.

Miscanthus are also good screens and effective filters for the wind as they can establish fairly fast to form a tallish, attractive barrier that is economical in terms of space. Another use is for aquatic planting: they enjoy a waterside position as long as they are not crowded out by more vigorous neighbours. There are many good ones to choose from; others I like particularly are *M. sinensis* 'Kleine Fontane', which has early and abundant flowers, and *M.*

Miscanthus sinensis 'Variegatus'

sinensis 'Flamingo', with pink flowers and great autumn colour. They tolerate many soil conditions but do particularly well in a more moist soil. A sunny situation is required and they look most effective situated so as to catch the low evening sunlight on their flowerheads. Miscanthus are generally trouble-free. If you leave the stems on for winter effect, cut them to the ground in spring. To propagate, divide in early spring. **BG**

Molinia caerulea subsp. *arundinacea*
TALL MOOR GRASS

Type: hardy, deciduous perennial
Soil & situation: acid soil/dry, sunny position
North American hardiness zone: 5–9
Height: 1.2m (4ft)
Spread: 2.4m (7½ft)
Grow for: elegant stems and seedheads from early summer

These wonderful plants have come to the fore with the introduction of the naturalistic style of perennial planting promoted and developed by Piet Oudolf, Jaques Wirtz and others. They have a graceful habit, attractive foliage and dense to open flowerheads held high above the foliage,

Molinia caerulea subsp. *arundinacea*

and they are bold enough to provide structure, yet 'transparent' enough to make good screens. The flower stems and seedheads move with the slightest breath of air and look wonderful in the low autumn light. They are all magnificent; never malign a molinia!

Molinia caerulea subsp. *arundinacea* forms a low, rounded mound; the flower spikes develop in early summer. Varieties worth seeking out include 'Fontane', which has dense heads of dark grey flowers that weigh down the tips of the stems like a fountain, as its name suggests. It grows to 1.5m (5ft) tall, the same height as 'Karl Foerster' which has large dark heads of bronze flowers on stiff upright or arching stems. 'Transparent' is deliciously beautiful. It is 1.8m (6ft) tall and creates the lightest haze of tiny dark flowerheads that catch raindrops and dew. My favourite! 'Windspiel' moves elegantly in the breeze. The stems are upright in flower but arch like a fountain when it's wet. It also reaches 1.8m (6ft).

All need moist, well-drained, preferably acid to neutral soil, in full sun or partial shade. Unlike most grasses, the leaves and stems detach easily from the rootstock in winter. They are slow to establish; buy moderate to large plants rather than smaller ones. Divide in spring and pot up until established. Trouble free of pests and diseases. **MB**

Monarda didyma
BERGAMOT

Type: hardy, herbaceous perennial
Soil & situation: any soil, ideally moist/sun or shade
North American hardiness zone: 4–9
Height & spread: forms a 1m (3ft) dome
Grow for: lovely, healthy, bright coloured scented foliage in an attractive form, with attractive purplish-red scented flowers

This is another plant (see *Melissa officinalis*, page 262) with whose leafy aromatic smell I like to rub myself on a hot day, and I use the leaves and petals in long, cool drinks. I grow this lovely plant in many different places just for its petals, which I put in salads. There is a pineapple-scented form and some with improved flower colours, but I prefer the original as it is a good doer and a useful plant for adding colour to the border all through summer and into autumn.

A genus of half a dozen species native to North America, this was named after a Spanish botanist and was used by the natives for a beverage. I remember my grandmother's shop having packets of Oswego tea made from this very plant. The name bergamot is supposed to be from the bergamot orange, which annoyingly has a totally dissimilar perfume. Oswego is after the town on Lake Ontario where it was noted by a botanist named Bartram who sent seed to the UK in 1745.

This is a remarkably useful plant as it will grow on most soils and situations given half a chance and thrives in damper soils. Deadheading is worthwhile to prevent seeding. The choicest forms are propagated by root division in late winter or early spring, the natural by seed sown any time. It does benefit from splitting and replanting every few years and needs tidying in late autumn. Bergamot has no problems other than being unhappy in drought. **BF**

Monstera deliciosa
Plant of the Week (see page 41)

Monarda didyma

Morina longifolia

Morina longifolia
WHORL FLOWER

Type: hardy, herbaceous perennial
Soil & situation: well-drained, preferably sandy soil/full sun
North American hardiness zone: 6–9
Height: 90cm (36in)
Spread: 30cm (12in)
Grow for: sculptural form; flowers from mid-summer to early autumn

The fact that this handsome evergreen is not bone hardy must be the only reason why it's not more familiar. It is absolutely beautiful; elegant, refined, colourful, charming – we have absolutely nothing in common!

There is a basal rosette of narrow, glossy, lemon-scented, thistle-like leaves diminishing in size and number towards the top of the stem, which provide a perch for tiers of thorny candelabras. The flowers with narrow, arching tubes about 3cm (1in) long and beautifully rounded petals explode from these in a glorious starburst of white, rich rose-pink and crimson. I dislike most shades of pink but here the tones and contrasts are refined, not sickly, the white is pure and the arching flowers and sculptural stems create a wonderful sense of dynamism. In winter, they dry to deep brown, making great decorations for the home; in the garden, they look gorgeous when dusted with frost and delicately embroidered with spider webs.

The plant is used to make incense. The flowers are moth pollinated, but if they haven't been visited by morning the pistil curves over, effects self-pollination and the flower changes colour!

It needs humus-rich, fertile, well-drained, moist, sandy or gritty soil in sun. It is not difficult to grow but is short lived, hates waterlogging and rots if cold and wet. It does better in milder climates. It hates disturbance! Propagate by root cuttings in late autumn; sow fresh seed in gritty compost and over-winter young plants in a well-ventilated cold frame. In waterlogged, cold conditions it may be attacked by slugs and rot. **MB**

Morus nigra
Plant of the Week (see page 353)

Musa chinensis
CHINESE/DWARF CAVENDISH BANANAS
Type: tender, herbaceous perennial
Soil & situation: rich, moist soil/full sun/under cover
North American hardiness zone: 9–10
Height & spread: 3m (10ft)
Grow for: impressive subject, large leaves, amazing flowers and sweet edible fruits

If you've got it flaunt it, and you do need quite a lot of space to grow this to perfection. In the ground under cover these make trees – a strange, succulent, soft sort of tree, but really impressive, even more so when the gigantic corn cob of a flowering shoot pops out at the top and hangs down like a triffid, and flowers for weeks and weeks and weeks. The small flowers are stuck on the ends of the wee bananas and the inflorescence carries a smell of tropical rainforest. Months later the bananas start to ripen and then the old stem is cut down (the fruits are ripened on the detached stalk), and another stem grows up to replace the old. If in a pot the plant can go outdoors for summer, but will need a sheltered spot as wind shreds the leaves.

Musa chinensis

Musa basjoo

Originally from China, this small banana is a tough survivor and has become grown all over the world where quality is seen as more important than size, or where sheer size is inconvenient. As it was first grown for the European market in the Canaries it is also known as the Canary banana. Other larger bananas from India have followed and colonized most hot countries. However, it seems not to have been known to the Romans, though early Muslim texts indicate it had already arrived in Arabia. Our word banana comes from Arabic via Spanish or Portuguese.

You've got to have a frost-free light place about 3m (10ft) high, although if you cramp the plant, say in a plastic dustbin, it will stay smaller. Fill a big hole or enormous container with a humus-rich, well-drained compost, and water and feed regularly. Remove all new shoots from the base until the main shoot is nearly full grown, then allow only one to replace it. In the tropics the crown can last for 50 years or more, though each shoot is only there for a couple. Bananas can be grown from seed, but not the good ones such as this. Offsets need be taken in spring with as much root as possible. These do not suffer many problems other than cold and damp causing moulds. **BF**

Matt adds:
I was first introduced to *Musa basjoo* (zone 8–10) as a student when it was flowering in a frost-free greenhouse; observing its long, pendent flower stem, we gave it a nickname that was none too polite! It's since become popular as a patio or border plant for gardeners wishing to add a little 'exotica' to their lives. The narrow stem, made up of old leaf bases, supports several paddle-shaped leaves that emerge from the top of the stem like long cigars. In summer it needs a warm, sheltered spot and plenty of moisture, in winter, the protection of a frost-free shed or greenhouse.

Myosotidium hortensia
CHATHAM ISLAND FORGET-ME-NOT

Type: half-hardy, evergreen perennial
Soil & situation: humus-rich, gritty, moist, well-drained soil/light shade
North American hardiness zone: 8–9
Height: 60cm (24in)
Spread: 80cm (32in)
Grow for: clusters of forget-me-not-like blue flowers; glossy, bright green foliage

On its native Chatham Island, to the east of New Zealand it, while not the first, was one of the earliest plants to see the dawn of the new millennium – a well-deserved honour for one of earth's most beautiful perennials.

Clump forming, the large, 30cm (12in) long, fleshy, bright green leaves are so glossy they appear to have been varnished. They are heart-shaped with conspicuous veins and wavy edges. The dense clusters of small, bell-shaped flowers appear in early summer on strong stems. Pale to dark blue, they are occasionally white-margined.

Myosotidium is not the easiest plant to grow, doing best in damp, cool conditions. A sheltered coastal site would be ideal with an annual spring mulch of seaweed. In cold areas plant in dappled shade under a tree and cover in winter with bracken or straw for frost protection. In late spring remove the old deteriorating leaves at soil level.

If it likes you, it will self-seed in the immediate area. Leave the young seedlings *in situ* until they have produced at least three leaves. Saved seed should be sown fresh and over-wintered in a cold frame. Alternatively it may be propagated by dividing the clump in spring. Slugs and snails prefer this plant to hostas, so be warned and take preventative action. **JC**

Matt adds:
When John says this is not the easiest plant to grow, he isn't joking, at least as far as most British gardeners are concerned. They may march you to a single plant or pot and proudly announce, 'This is my Chatham Island forget-me-not.' The usual response (a combination of admiration and envy!), 'Did you really grow that?' 'But of course,' comes a self-satisfied reply. This plant should be your destination at the end of a red carpet, it should be enthroned, pampered, praised and every demand satisfied in order for it to flourish. I once visited a garden in New Zealand where it was rampant, scattered through a border without a care. Gardening can be so cruel!

Myosotidium hortensia

Myosotis sylvatica
FORGET-ME-NOT

Type: hardy biennial
Soil & situation: moist, well-drained soil/sun or partial shade
North American hardiness zone: 5–9
Height: 30cm (12in)
Spread: 15cm (6in)
Grow for: pretty spring flowers

Forget-me-not is quite a recent name. It is not mentioned in Shakespeare or in the *Oxford English Dictionary* between 1532, when it's mentioned in an old French translation as *une fleur de ne m'oubliez mye*, and 1817, quoting Samuel Taylor Coleridge's poem 'The Keepsake': 'Nor can I find, amid my lonely walk, By rivulet, or spring, or wet roadside, That blue and bright eyed flowerlet of the brook, Hope's gentle gem, the sweet Forget me not.' It was probably inspired by the tale of a German knight and his lady walking by a river: while picking 'water forget-me-nots' the knight slipped and fell in the water. Before he drowned, he threw the flowers to his lover crying, '*Vergisz mien nicht.*' So remember! Don't wear your armour while picking forget-me-nots.

The water forget-me-not, *Myosotis scorpioides*, may have been the earliest garden introduction; most now come from the wood forget-me-not,

M. sylvatica. There are ten species in the UK. Selections include 'Royal Blue' with rich royal blue flowers; mixed selections with pink, white and blue flowers; Victoria Series cultivars are dwarf, compact and have white, blue or pink flowers. 'Victoria Rose' with bright rose-pink flowers, grows to 10cm (4in).

They need moderately fertile to poor, moist, well-drained soil in sun or partial shade. Water in dry weather; after flowering allow to self-seed before lifting, or lift early to prevent self-seeding. Sow seed in seedbeds or *in situ* for planting out the following spring. Susceptible to powdery mildew, so as a preventative measure keep the soil moist. Slugs and snails may cause damage. **MB**

Myosotis sylvatica

Myrrhis odorata

Myrrhis odorata
SWEET CICELY

Type: hardy, herbaceous perennial
Soil & situation: rich, moist soil/full sun to heavy shade
North American hardiness zone: 3–7
Height & spread: 60cm (24in)
Grow for: healthy, green, ferny foliage from early in the year; foamy white flowers; decorative seedpods; edible salading

This is a multiple-use plant; first it is tough, reliable, and dense enough to be used as ground cover. Then it is early to shoot and looks good when little else does, moreover these shoots are edible along with the ferny soft leaves, which go well in soups and stews, and the foamy white flowers which can be used in salads. The roots are small but, once cooked, are interesting and could be improved by plant breeders. The seedpods add aniseed flavour to liqueurs.

The plant is a native to Europe and the Romans seem to have used it for a pot herb; it was known to the Greeks as *murrhis* in place of the true myrrh which comes from an African tree, and also as *seseli*, which was their name for a herbal umbelliferous plant.

Sweet cicely likes rich, moist soils in cool damp glades. It is not long lived individually but spreads around sufficiently. Dead-heading will stop this self-seeding, though do retain some seedpods as they are nice to use in cooking. Trim and tidy in autumn. Sow *in situ* in spring or in small pots and plant out as soon as possible. Sweet cicely can be troublesome as a self-seeding weed. **BF**

Myrtus communis
COMMON MYRTLE

Type: frost-hardy, evergreen shrub
Soil & situation: free-draining, moist fertile soil/sheltered, sunny position in cold areas
North American hardiness zone: 8–9
Height: up to 4.5m (15ft)
Spread: 3m (10ft)
Grow for: aromatic, polished, evergreen foliage; copious numbers of fragrant flowers in mid- to late summer, followed by black berries; AGM

Myrtle was and is considered a symbol of love, peace and a happy married life, and as such, makes the best wedding present of all. The fragrant foliage and flowers of this plant have long been used in bridal wreaths and garlands. It has been grown in England since the 16th century but not just for ornamental purposes. It has many herbal uses too: the oil is used in perfumery; the leaves can be added to pork and lamb dishes; the fruits are used in the Middle East as a spice, and apparently when ingested, the active compounds are quickly absorbed and give a violet-like aroma to urine within 15 minutes – certainly a fairly dynamic and useful plant! It is not difficult to grow, but flowers and fruits better in a sunny, sheltered site such as at the base of a warm wall, preferably somewhere where the rich and spicy fragrance will linger and not be wafted away. The thousands of flowers produced on the mature bush have a generous, central burst of long, yellow-white stamens.

For gardens in mild or coastal areas it forms a most magnificent, very special hedge that tolerates clipping well and it can be used to form exquisite and unusual mop-head standards or pyramids.

This plant will tolerate –10°C (14°F) given shelter and sharp drainage, so even if you need to give added protection such as fleece now and then, it is well worth finding the ideal spot for it and cosseting it in its early years.

It is best pruned in spring, but only when needed to maintain the size and shape and remove any frosted growth. It can also be grown as an espalier. I have never seen this, but it would be spectacular for enlivening a dull facade of a house, or for training along a discordant elevation to pull it together. It is easily propagated by semi-ripe cuttings taken in summer. A dwarf form, *M. c. tarentina*, makes a great dwarf hedge. **BG**

Bob adds:
I love myrtle, not for the attractive, neat foliage, nor for the strangely scented creamy-white paintbrush-like flowers that remind me for some bizarre reason of garlic sausage, but for the black berries that make an excellent jam and reputedly a good wine. However, for those of you looking for a neat shrub for a sunny patio or wall, do not be put off by the garlic-sausage smell as it is so faint; instead, rejoice in the healthy appearance of this lovely shrub. I find *M. c. tarentina* attractive but too small for any real use other than as a bonsai specimen; it has white berries. *M. ugni*, the Chilean guava, is similar with pinky bell-like flowers and sweeter purplish berries; it is slightly more tender than *M. communis* and best as a conservatory subject.

Myrtus communis

Narcissus poeticus var. *recurvus*

Narcissus poeticus var. *recurvus*
PHEASANT'S EYE

Type: clump-forming, hardy, bulbous perennial
Soil & situation: rich, moist soil/full sun to light shade
North American hardiness zone: 5–8
Height: 50cm (20in)
Spread: 30cm (12in)
Grow for: beautiful, highly perfumed flowers as spring becomes summer; AGM

I love these flowers as they are the last of the spring bulbs to bloom and their arrival heralds the warmest days a-coming in. Its scent is intoxicating yet fresh and clean, making it one of the few flowers I love to cut and take indoors in quantity. It is also a very personal favourite as when I moved to my garden 20 years ago there was just one small clump of pheasant's eyes and another of the old green and yellow, double daffodilly; I have multiplied and multiplied both of these, and now have long walks lined with these delightful gems.

The pheasant's eye narcissus grows wild around the shores of the Mediterranean, and although undoubtedly known to the Romans was apparently not introduced to the UK until some were brought back after the Battle of Waterloo. The story of Narcissus is alleged to be the name's derivation, and the *poeticus* – well, because poets write about it. The English name comes because, like its namesake, *Adonis annua*, it resembles a pheasant's a*** (oops, sorry, couldn't help myself).

Given a well-drained soil in an orchard or glade, these will naturalize, albeit slowly, as they seldom seed but do clump up and go on for ever. Deadheading will prevent seed being formed if you want more flowers. Digging and dividing as soon as the leaves die down helps to multiply these

more quickly and is especially useful for old congested clumps which cease to bloom. I've not seen the seed offered so plant the bulbs as soon as you can get them. No common problems bother this species very much. **BF**

Narcissus pseudonarcissus
LENT LILY, WILD DAFFODIL, TRUMPET NARCISSUS

Type: hardy, bulbous perennial
Soil & situation: almost any soil/spreads best in a moist well-drained soil/prefers sun or part shade/does not like heavy shade
North American hardiness zone: 4–9
Height: 15–35cm (6–14in)
Spread: 10cm (4in)
Grow for: subtle, beautiful, native daffodils which flower in early spring and naturalize well; AGM

This charming wild daffodil is well suited to naturalizing – it spreads well and looks thoroughly in keeping in wilder areas with its small, but exquisite, nodding, mid-yellow flowers in early spring. It looks so delicate compared to the relatively large, stronger-coloured, rather brash daffodils that you see in most front gardens in spring. Being native, it is a good, hearty plant and looks a dream in large drifts, in orchards, paddocks, meadows and in the more natural garden areas. I am not a fan of daffodils in borders – I would rather pot some up and have a few simple containers of them where I can admire them at close quarters, near a window or doorway.

Plant the bulbs about one and a half times to twice their depth or thereabouts, although you can go deeper in lighter soils. They will increase in quantity if you plant them shallowly, but the resultant bulbs are smaller. Conversely, if you plant deeper you will have bigger bulbs, but the increase is slower. Bigger bulbs generally equate to better, bigger flowers. I never divide bulbs in grass areas, life is too short and they manage perfectly well without my help. But I do not treat them mean! I try never to cut them till a good month or preferably six weeks after the flowering is well on the wane. In some lush springs though, it is difficult to resist. You can almost feel the mower twitch as you try to veer away from the rather sad mess of leaves. These smaller varieties do have less conspicuous, smaller leaves and once the time is up, cutting even green leaves does little harm. Wood ashes added in spring are a useful source of potassium which can help flowering. **BG**

Narcissus pseudonarcissus

Hydrangea arborescens 'Annabelle'

Type: hardy deciduous shrub
Soil & situation: ordinary garden loam/sun or shade
North American hardiness zone: 3–9
Height & spread: 1.2m (4ft)
Grow for: white, spherical flowerheads for a long period from early summer; attractive dried flowerheads in the autumn; AGM

I think hydrangeas are my favourite plants but on my dry soil many do not thrive. This one certainly does, however. I frequently use it in planting schemes in a wide variety of conditions and often the client will be bowled over by it, often after only the first year.

An individual flowerhead may be as much as 20cm (8in) across, though most of the flowers are sterile. The late summer flowering comes at a time when many shrubs have done their bit, and the white looks particularly fresh on a hot summer's day. I leave the dried flowerheads on the plant until they look battered, which may well be in spring when its time to prune it anyway. (It is well worth picking a few flowerheads in their prime and drying them by hanging them upside down somewhere airy.) Another great hydrangea, *H. aspera* (see page 212), tends to wilt on my soil, but if you have a good loam soil I recommend it strongly.

Hydrangea arborescens flowers at the tip of the current season's growth, and you can cut all this back to two or three pairs of buds in late winter or spring. Doing it this way you will get extra-large panicles of flowers. If you just leave it unpruned you will have a taller shrub and smaller flowers. Hydrangeas are hungry, so they respond to a good feed, but do not feed them in the summer as you might well encourage them into late growth, which is susceptible to frost. **BG**

Narcissus 'Yellow Cheerfulness'
DAFFODIL

Type: hardy, bulbous perennial
Soil & situation: moist, moderately fertile, well-drained soil/full sun or partial shade
North American hardiness zone: 4–9
Height: 45cm (18in)
Spread: 15cm (6in)
Grow for: stunning, gold-yellow, double flowers; AGM

The only thing nicer than a single-flowered daffodil is one with double flowers and fragrance. Performing in mid-spring, the strong stems carry clusters of three or four double, golden-yellow flowers. The corona (trumpet) is short, divided and doubled, making an attractive centre. The mid-green leaves are strap-shaped and narrow. In great demand as a cut flower, it is also recommended for growing in containers indoors for early, scented flowers. *N.* 'Cheerfulness' is white with a cream centre and has larger, double, fragrant flowers.

Plant bulbs in autumn at twice their own depth with the 'nose' pointing up. In light, sandy soil and when being naturalized in grass plant slightly deeper. When dividing, usually every three years, wait until the foliage has withered and turned yellow. Dead-head, removing the old flower to prevent the bulb's energy being used to form seed. When naturalized in grass, avoid cutting the foliage for at least six weeks after flowering. **JC**

Narcissus 'Yellow Cheerfulness'

Nemesia strumosa

Nemesia strumosa

Type: half-hardy annual
Soil & situation: moist soil/sun
North American hardiness zone: annual
Height: 30cm (12in)
Spread: 16cm (6¼in)
Grow for: colourful flowers from early summer onwards

It's always in the catalogues and is easy to grow, so why don't gardeners plant them more often? This is such a happy, gay little plant, with bright, cheerful blooms creating a chorus of colour in such pure distinctive tones. They are so mood enhancing; if you feel down, those eager little faces just lift you up; you simply have to smile. So pack them in pots, use them as edging plants for borders or draped like colourful curtains from a window box and take one look three times a day or as prescribed by your doctor.

Here are some of its varieties with intensely coloured flowers. 'Orange Prince' is a vibrant, warming orange; you can almost feel the heat. 'Fire King' is a wonderful rich, iridescent scarlet. 'Sundrops', an award winner, is compact with masses of large vivid yellow flowers and is perfect for containers.

The bicolours are really eye-catching and always provoke comment. 'KLM' reminds me of my visits to Brentford FC, in my student days when they were sponsored by KLM; the flowers are mid-blue and white, the colours of the Dutch National Airline. 'National Ensign' waves the flag of St George in bright red and a white 'lip' – your own 'barmy army'! Just to prove that they aren't all outrageously coloured there are soothing shades like 'Coconut Ice' with a soft fragrance and pink and lilac flowers and 'Pastel Mixed', a lovely selection of lilac, yellow and blue.

They need moist, well-drained, moderately fertile, slightly acid soil in full sun. Keep them well watered and feed with general fertilizer every two weeks until established; change to high-potash fertilizer to encourage flowering. Sow from early to late spring for flowers in early and mid-summer. Harden off before planting out when the danger of frost has passed. **MB**

Nemophila menziesii 'Penny Black'

Type: hardy annual
Soil & situation: fertile, moist, well-drained soil/sun or partial shade
North American hardiness zone: annual
Height: 20cm (8in)
Spread: 30cm (12in)
Grow for: pretty flowers in spring and summer

The name comes from the Greek *nemos*, meaning grove, and *philos*, loving, alluding to their habitat and offers an interesting slant if you have any friends with the surname Lovegrove. It is a delicate carpeting plant found in California from coastal sands to chaparral and redwood forest. In spring and summer it is covered with flowers that have a simple beauty, like those of a herbaceous geranium. There are many forms and selections. The species, commonly known as baby blue-eyes, has pale blue flowers with a white centre; there's a pure white form too. *Nemophila* subsp. *atomaria* is white with minute speckles and spots radiating from the centre that look as though they have been drawn with a fine drafting pen. I favour *N. menziesii* 'Penny Black' (sometimes sold as *N.* var. *discoidalis*) for its unusual colouration; it is predominantly black with a white centre and margins. Another species, *N. maculata*, has pretty violet blotches at the outer edge of each petal. They are ideal as a border edging or for tumbling over the side of a window box.

They need fertile, moist, well-drained soil in a sheltered position in full sun or partial shade; they will grow in an open shady position. Keep the compost moist during hot, dry weather, otherwise they stop flowering. Feed with high-potash fertilizer if necessary to encourage flowering. Sow seed *in situ* in late summer for spring flowering and mid-spring for summer flowering; they self-seed freely. Aphids may be troublesome. **MB**

Nemophila menziesii 'Penny Black'

Nepeta cataria

Nepeta cataria
CATNIP

Type: hardy, herbaceous perennial
Soil & situation: any soil/sun
North American hardiness zone: 3–7
Height & spread: 1m (3ft) to prostrate, well flattened
Grow for: grey-green aromatic foliage loved by cats

The catnips are named because they are attractive to cats. I love my cats and it is a pleasure to feed bits of this plant to them as they go all kittenish and frisky and then drowsy, often enjoying a good roll on *Nepeta cataria* before taking yet another nap. (What do cats dream of while they're sleeping? Of having a nice nap, of course.) *N. cataria* is a UK native often found wild in ditches. *N. mussinii* is quite different – more compact, more colourful and more floriferous, so more widely grown in the ornamental garden – and there are several other interesting species. However, if you love your cats, grow this.

Before our present tea, people drank catnip tea made with milk and sugar in much the same way and the herb was also thought good for a black eye. If you don't like cats then put catnip plants in parts of your garden you can't see easily and thus keep them out of sight. The botanical name is *Nepeta* for a mint-like plant, which in medieval Latin became *nepta*, then in Old English we get cat nepte, changing to catnep and it is now catnip, but should be cat-kip.

Catnip wants to be put in a warm sunny spot, say between paving slabs on a patio so the cats can roll on it comfortably. It will be short lived unless protected when young by an inverted wire hanging basket. Trim off foliage before it dies, then dry it to stuff cushions for cats. Catnip can be sown at almost any time, ideally in pots in a coldframe or you can divide the roots in spring. Its only problem is cats, who nibble and chew it. **BF**

Nepeta x *faassenii* 'Snowflake'
CATMINT

Type: hardy perennial
Soil & situation: enjoys well-drained soil/tolerant of poor soils/full sun
North American hardiness zone: 4–8
Height & spread: up to 30cm (12in)
Grow for: copious white flowers for about five weeks during the late spring and early summer

Nepetas are extremely common garden plants – highly popular as they are good, solid performers that are easy to grow. This one is definitely easy to grow but is quite unusual. The delightful little white flowers, which are produced on spikes, sometimes have a bluish tinge to them. They are frequently enhanced by the presence of a butterfly or two, hard at work around them. The foliage is beautifully compact, being low and spreading. The leaves, also an asset, are tinted grey. *Nepeta cataria* (see previous entry) is said to repel rats - presumably because if you bruise its leaves it releases essential oils that are extremely attractive to cats. But I, for one, do not partic-ularly want cats romping in my borders, so give me *N.* x *faassenii* 'Snowflake' any day. My mother's favourite form is *N.* x *faassenii* 'Walkers Low', which grows to 60cm (24in) and has dark blue-mauve flowers on dark stems. They appear earlier than ordinary catmint, and again the first flowering lasts for about five weeks.

In common with most forms of *N.* x *faassenii*, this plant will give a good flush of second flowers if it is cut back when the first flowers are going over. It is simple to propagate by division in spring or autumn or by softwood cuttings in spring or summer. **BG**

Nepeta x *faassenii* 'Snowflake'

Nerine bowdenii

Nerine bowdenii

Type: hardy, bulbous perennial
Soil & situation: well-drained soil/full sun
North American hardiness zone: 7–10
Height: 45cm (18in)
Spread: 20cm (8in)
Grow for: the most elegant pink blooms late in the season; AGM

Anywhere else this shade of pink would be sickening, but in the garden you can get away with it and what's more it looks and feels right.

Umbels of six or more funnel-shaped flowers on long stalks appear in autumn before the leaves. They are fragrant, icing-sugar pink and 8cm (3½in) across with wavy-edged outer tepals. The strap-like, broad, mid-green leaves are 30cm (12in) long. *Nerine bowdenii* f. *alba* has white flowers which may be flushed a pale pink shade.

They flower best when the bulbs are congested. Plant them in well-drained soil at the base of a warm wall in full sun. Nerines are well suited to growing in containers, making a show late in the season. Protect the bulbs in winter by wrapping the pot in hessian and moving it to a sheltered side of the house. The bulbs should be planted in spring with their noses at soil level. Cover them in winter with a dry mulch of chopped bark or straw for protection from frost.

Propagation is by seed sown as soon as it is ripe in a heated propagator or by division of crowded clumps after they have finished flowering. Nerines are prone to damage by slugs, especially when they are coming into leaf. **JC**

Nerium oleander
OLEANDER

Type: half-hardy, evergreen shrub
Soil & situation: rich compost/sun/under cover in winter
North American hardiness zone: 8–10
Height: 3m (10ft)
Spread: over 2m (close to 7ft)
Grow for: prolific, scented, pink, red or white flowers all summer on handsome evergreen plants

Despite this plant killing and sickening people every year it is such a beauty and so enduring that it is one of the commonest roadside plantings in the south of France. It is ironic that in many tropical holiday resorts there are warnings about this or that dangerous local tree, local plant or local local, but it is rare that this plant is so labelled although I've seen it in all the hotel gardens I've ever visited. I used to grow it myself for its perfume, but in a fit of desperation to make more space it was given a hardiness trial along with some citrus hybrids and other experimental plants, and it did not last. I would soon get several oleanders as they are impressive patio plants but my winter storage space is already overflowing.

Nerium is a genus of mostly tropical shrubs and trees that contains poisonous sap which has been the death of many cattle, and people foolish enough to use the enticingly straight stems for kebab sticks and barbecue skewers.

It can be treated much like citrus or patio fuchsias, being out all summer but going under cover in winter to escape the frosts, though it may survive on a warm wall with occasional covering in severe weather. It needs cutting back to encourage new shoots and this is best done before growth starts in spring, though I used to

Nerium oleander

do it in autumn to squeeze the plants into limited space. It can be grown from seed or take ripe cuttings in autumn to root in a glass of warm water. It can suffer from scale but soapy sponging will clear this up. **BF**

Nicandra physalodes 'Violacea'

Nicandra physalodes 'Violacea'
SHOO FLY, APPLE OF PERU

Type: hardy annual
Soil & situation: fertile, moist, well-drained soil/full sun or partial shade
North American hardiness zone: annual
Height: 90cm (36in)
Spread: 30cm (12in)
Grow for: a very attractive late-flowering annual

This plant is supposed to keep flies at bay, hence its common name. Whether it does or not, it is a fine, late, free-flowering annual for the garden. It is a vigorous, upright plant with 10cm (4in) long, wavy-edged and toothed, mid-green leaves. The 4cm (1½in) wide flowers open in the middle of the day and are in flower from summer to late autumn. They are a deep mauve with deep blue and white corollas. The small brown fruits which follow are enclosed in attractive, Chinese lantern-like, papery, deep purple calyces. Its branches can be dried, complete with the fruit and 'lanterns' for indoor winter decoration.

Propagation is by seed sown in a propagator in early spring or outside, *in situ*, in late spring. It will, if allowed, self-seed. **JC**

Nicotiana sylvestris
Plant of the Week (see page 327)

Nigella damascena 'Miss Jekyll'
LOVE-IN-A-MIST, DEVIL-IN-A-BUSH

Type: hardy annual
Soil & situation: most well-drained soils/sun or partial shade
North American hardiness zone: annual
Height: 50cm (20in)
Spread: 20cm (8in)
Grow for: irresistible, long-flowering (if deadheaded), captivating blue flowers, followed by fat seedpods with spidery bracts which are an additional bonus; fine filigree, fresh green leaves which over-winter well

This is an old cottage-garden favourite, coming to England about 1570, purportedly from Damascus. It has many common names including love-entangle and love-in-a-puzzle. It is named after Miss Gertrude Jekyll, the famous gardener, who thought it to be the best garden nigella. The flower starts off pale blue, but matures to a more intense bright, sky blue. Not only is it wonderful to have self-seeding around the garden, but it is a superb cut flower both fresh and dried. It is also ideal for using in wildflower (not native) mixes with grass, where it blends and contrasts handsomely with whites, reds, yellows and other hues of striking annuals and perennials.

Nigella damascena 'Miss Jekyll'

Nymphaea 'Fire Crest'

When sown in autumn the attractive rosettes of foliage can develop well, so the plants come into flower early. These can then be deadheaded, and the subsequent flowers will be larger. Continuation of flowering is ensured with subsequent sowings in early and late spring. Give these beautiful plants a free rein and let them self-seed. Seedlings will transplant, but they do suffer a check.   **BG**

Nymphaea 'Fire Crest'
WATER LILY

Type: hardy, aquatic perennial
Soil & situation: undisturbed water/full sun
North American hardiness zone: 4–11
Spread: 1.2m (4ft)
Grow for: a blaze of colour on the water

I have no time for pale, insipid, cheerless waterlily flowers. Bright, sparkling and even a little gaudy in colour contrasts well with still, often dull water. *Nymphaea* 'Fire Crest' is all I could wish for. The rounded, two-lobed, mid-green leaves are 20cm (8in) across. They are purple when they first unfurl. The 15cm (6in) star-like, deep pink flowers have pale pink, inner petals. The inner stamens are orange, and surrounded by a pink outer ring.

Water lilies dislike moving water and can't tolerate a fountain constantly raining water on the leaves. These large floating leaves serve a practical purpose. They shade the water, which is one method of controlling algae growth. Always read the plant label to find which varieties suit your depth of water. If a variety for shallow water is planted too deep, the leaves will struggle to reach the surface and the plant will become exhausted. The tall variety in shallow water will spread its leaves all over the surface of the pond.

Propagation is by division of the fleshy root in summer, keeping an eye on each piece of root. Pot up in an aquatic compost. Place in shallow water, lowering the pot as the leaves begin to extend.   **JC**

Ocimum basilicum
SMALL-LEAFED BUSH BASIL, GREEK BASIL

Type: half-hardy perennial to tender annual
Soil & situation: rich, moist soil/sun/under cover
North American hardiness zone: annual
Height & Sspread: up to 30cm (12in)
Grow for: handsome, compact, neat herb with a delicious flavour

I grow most of my own food as I want it fresh and flavoursome, and once I have had fresh basil leaves in a cheese and tomato sandwich I have enjoyed my meal. It is such an essential ingredient for salads and particularly for tomato dishes. In fact I grow the basil with my greenhouse tomatoes as the vines always get bare and leave a bit of space at their base. They are reckoned a good companion, attracting the aphids off the tomatoes – this depends on your point of view: it does work but it's easier to clean the aphids off the tomatoes!

There are over 150 basils and most of them come from Africa and the Far East; the first arrived in the UK in Elizabethan times or before. They are very mixed in habit and parentage and although this is called the Greek, my favourite for its fine flavour and neat habit, which has now been grown in Europe for centuries, it apparently comes from Chile! Basil is named in Greek *basilikon*, the kingly herb, for its strong flavour and medicinal uses.

Ideally grow basil in a greenhouse in a pot on staging but it can be grown in a warm border or even outdoors in summer if given a cloche at the start. Cut and use all the leaves before it flowers and it will regrow until the cold returns. Sow in spring in the warmth, pot on and plant out after the last frosts. Basil is bothered by aphids but these can be jetted off with a hose. **BF**

Ocimum basilicum

Oenothera biennis

Oenothera biennis
EVENING PRIMROSE

Type: hardy, herbaceous, biennial weed
Soil & situation: any soil/sun or light shade/likes moisture
North American hardiness zone: 4–8
Height & spread: first year a prostrate rosette, spreading up to 45cm (18in); second year to 2m (6½ft)
Grow for: prolific yellow flowers from early summer to late autumn

This is another weed – a delightful one I would not be without, but a weed none the less. Good this week, in fact good nearly every week of the summer. This has one of the longest flowering seasons of any plant. It is full of pollen for beneficial insects for although the flowers open at night they remain partly open, if flaccid, early the next day. It comes up for free everywhere, is immune to pests and diseases, and even has edible roots. What more could you want? Well tasty, tender, edible roots would be nice, rather than the strong, coarse fare that's on offer, still they could be improved – bigger, double, sterile flowers, so no self-seeding, and tastier roots

please! The seeds are the source of evening primrose oil, a trendy substitute for monkey gland therapy. This is a good plant for cheering up desolate areas.

One of nearly 100 species, mostly from North America, this reached Padua in 1619 and is described by Parkinson in 1629 as the tree primrose. The Latin name is stolen from the Greek for no apparent reason – it was apparently originally applied to a different flower of Greek origin. The common name is too obvious. There are some very nice alternative species with more luxurious flowers and scents such as *Oenothera odorata*, but none is as easy to grow as this thug.

The ideal site is just about anywhere initially; from then on just weed out the ones everywhere else. You have to be crazy not to deadhead this and it does make for more flower spikes. Sow in late spring or early summer *in situ* or in pots in a coldframe and plant out in early autumn. Because they are so deliciously scented in the evening you can't help sniffing them – so please wipe the yellow splodge of pollen off your nose before going anywhere in public. I've forgotten to do this many a time. **BF**

Olearia macrodonta

Olearia macrodonta
NEW ZEALAND HOLLY, DAISY BUSH

Type: hardy, evergreen shrub
Soil & situation: fertile, well-drained soil/full sun/shelter from cold winds
North American hardiness zone: 9–10
Height: 6m (20ft)
Spread: 5m (16ft)
Grow for: wonderfully fragrant flowers cover this shrub every summer; AGM

A neighbour has an enormous, overgrown, unpruned *Olearia macrodonta* in the front corner of her large garden. Every summer it is plastered with white flowers. Without fail, once a year the postman asks me its name and have I noticed its perfume!

The 8cm (3¹/₂in) long, leathery, sage-green, holly-like leaves are sharp pointed with a silvery-white underside. Enormous 20cm (8in) panicles of small, daisy-shaped, fragrant, white flowers with yellow centres are produced in summer. The warmer the summer the more flowers are formed.

This is one of the best evergreen plants to use as a windbreak or hedge for screening in exposed, coastal gardens. It thrives on a shallow chalk soil. Prune after flowering, reducing the stems by half their length. Old, neglected plants will tolerate hard pruning in spring and will send out new growths from the old stumps. Propagate by semi-ripe cuttings in summer. If they are not well rooted by autumn leave until spring before potting on.   **JC**

Omphalodes cappadocica 'Cherry Ingram'
Plant of the Week (see page 103)

Onopordum acanthium
SCOTCH THISTLE, COTTON THISTLE

Type: hardy, biennial/perennial herb
Soil & situation: free-draining, preferably alkaline soil/sun
North American hardiness zone: 6–9
Height: 3m (10ft)
Spread: 1m (3ft)
Grow for: architectural form; flowers from mid-summer to early autumn

This, one of the best architectural plants, is believed to be the plant chosen by James I as the emblem of Scotland; however, it is uncommon north of the border so we could be wrong! The Latin name *Onopordum* means 'ass's fart'. It's derived from the Greek *onos*, ass, and *porde*, fart, because of the effect it has on their digestive system. If they're growing in your field, don't stand downwind of the donkey!

It stands defiant and proud, with a distinct air of menace that's created by the wide, wavy-edged, spiny wings protecting the silver-grey candelabra. At the top of each stem a dense tuft of pale purple to white, nectar-rich flowers sits on a tight 5cm (2in) diameter globe of spiny projections, scowling threateningly from behind a white cobwebby covering. It is outstandingly beautiful and worthy of the utmost respect. Wear gloves when working nearby and site it away from paths in deep borders, against a dark background to highlight its sculptural form. In the past the down was used for stuffing cushions and pillows and the bracts were eaten like artichokes. I remember filming one for Channel 4's *Garden Club* while in Scotland; because we were recording I missed the only chance I have ever had of seeing an osprey. It appeared briefly over the top of a hill, then

disappeared for good! Every Scots thistle I see reminds me of that day!

Grow in fertile, well-drained, preferably alkaline soil in full sun; it tolerates heavier soils and light shade. This biennial or short-lived perennial resents root disturbance; sow *in situ* in summer or in pots to plant the following spring, and avoid knocking the taproot. It may become unstable and need staking. It can self-seed and become a nuisance, so dead-head or collect seed before dispersal. Slugs and snails are a problem.   **MB**

Bunny adds:
This is the only plant in my garden that the farmer next door has remarked upon – farmers are notably uninterested in the minuscule scale of gardening, but even he could not help but notice these huge beauties as he whizzed past on his tractor. In the first year they develop large basal rosettes of white-felted spiny leaves. The following year they reach for the sky, sending up a monstrously stout, spiny stem which is much branched. As the flowers begin to colour the plant looks a dream, but as it starts to go over the foliage looks as though you have put it in the wash with a blue towel, and comes out underwear grey. If you want it to self-seed you just have to grin and bear it.

Onopordum acanthium

Eschscholzia californica

August

CALIFORNIA POPPY

Type: hardy annual
Soil & situation: free-draining soil/sun
North American hardiness zone: annual
Height: 30cm (12in)
Spread: 15cm (6in)
Grow for: vibrant shades from early summer to autumn. Still stunning at this time of year, when many other flowers are fading; AGM.

Put on your 'shades', pour an ice-cold beer and crank up the Beach Boys; surf's up, the sun's out and the California poppies are in flower! This party's a riot, you can feel the good vibrations blasting from their blooms, with more tones than the finest Hawaiian shirt. You want colour? Baby, you got it!

The variety 'Ballerina' grows to 40cm (16in) tall and has frilled and fluted semi-double or double red, pink, yellow or orange flowers. Dazzling! 'Dali' is compact with scarlet flowers to 25cm (10in). It has the subtlety of Salvador himself! 'Monarch Art Shades' bears semi-double or double orange-yellow, apricot-yellow, creamy yellow or red flowers with fringed petals. Funky and free stylin'. 'Alba' has smaller flowers that start creamy and become white. Cool! 'Apricot Flambeau' has moderate-sized flowers, semi-double with fluted and ruffed orange petals streaked with red. Blowsy! In 'Cherry Ripe' the flowers are edged with crimson, fading to a pale centre. Sensational! 'Thai Silk Rose Chiffon' has pale pink, double flowers. Hang loose! 'Thai Lemon Silk' is pale lemon and about 20cm (8in) tall. Wicked! The Thai Silk Series has similar flowers at different shades from red and purple to white. Easy!

Buy a packet of each, mix them up and shake out a cacophony of colour. They look great when naturalized in a gravel garden; life's a beach! They need full sun in poor, free-draining soil. They self-seed freely and can become invasive if happy. The short-lived flowers only open in sunshine. Sow *in situ* from mid- to late spring for a continuous display through the summer. Pests and diseases? They wouldn't dare! **MB**

Opuntia ficus-indica

Opuntia ficus-indica
EDIBLE PRICKLY PEAR, INDIAN FIG

Type: just hardy, perennial cactus
Soil & situation: well-drained, dry, sandy soil/sun
North American hardiness zone: 6–10
Height & spread: may make 1m (3ft) in UK;
much bigger in warmer climes
Grow for: astounding foliage plant, pretty flowers,
edible fruits (you'll be lucky, matey)

This really is a conservatory or windowsill subject,
none the less it is hardy. I have grown one
outdoors for eight years here in Norfolk and at
Kew they have some that are yonks older. There is
a spineless form which I have not been fortunate
enough to find as these are prickly b******s. The
flowers are pretty and the fruits, which are rarely
borne even under cover, are sweet and juicy; it's
not something you should eat in the dark. I've
found the best way to handle cacti pads is with a
heavyweight newspaper wrapped around them.
This is really worth growing to plant outdoors just
to shock your friends – and anyone wandering
around in the dark....

Named after a Greek town renowned for its figs,
because of the resemblance the fruit bears to a
fig, this is a New World plant now so widespread
that it is mistaken for a native in many countries.
In Australia it was introduced as a cheap
stockproof hedge but it naturalized and took
over, making incredibly large tracts of land
ungrazeable, indeed impenetrable. The plague

was ended with the introduction of one of its
natural parasitic controls, a moth called
Cactoblastis cactorum, whose larvae demolished the
plants almost totally within a few years.

In either pot or ground, a well-drained, gritty,
sandy soil is essential, preferably dry as a bone in
winter, and it does best in a sheltered position
facing the sun in front of a wall or on a sunny
windowsill indoors. There is no need for any care
except possibly to keep heavy rain and really hard
frosts off with a temporary cloche. Propagate
from seed sown on top of a gritty compost
indoors in the warmth. Grow on under cover and
plant out in early summer when they are about
30cm (12in) or more tall. Then select for the
hardiest by waiting. Opuntia will root pads if
these are taken off in spring or summer.
Although the weather never got my opuntia the
slugs did! Under cover watch out for mealy bug
and dab them off with an cottonbud soaked in
strong alcohol. **BF**

Origanum laevigatum
'Herrenhausen'

Type: hardy, perennial herb
Soil & situation: well-drained soil/sunny position
North American hardiness zone: 7–10
Height: 60cm (24in)
Spread: 45cm (18in)
Grow for: maroon buds and mauve flowers from
mid- to late summer; ornamental leaves and
shoots, purplish in colour when young and in
winter; culinary purposes; aromatic; AGM

I started off growing this in my herb garden, but
what a waste! When I saw its beautiful purplish
foliage and long season of most appealing pale
lilac flowers in large clusters, I propagated it up

and now I grow this beauty in large mats under
my pleached hornbeams. Not many plants
luxuriate in those dry conditions, but this one
certainly does. Many gardeners are confused over
marjoram and oregano: both belong to the
Origanum genus, but they are different species.
Origanum majorana is marjoram, but just to
confuse the issue, *Origanum vulgare* (see next
entry) is called wild marjoram in the UK.

If you want to propagate this plant from seed,
bear in mind that it and many origanums can
damp off after germination. To prevent this I put
a layer of fine vermiculite, about 1cm (½in)
deep, over the potting compost and sprinkle the
seeds over it. Then I cover the tray or pots with a
sheet of polystyrene and put it/them by a radiator
to germinate. As soon as they emerge, I put them
on the kitchen window sill, without the
polystyrene. Then I water the tray from the
bottom to help prevent damping off. In the
garden they are pretty well trouble free. The
plants are best cut back after flowering as this will
stimulate the growth of new rosettes of leaves,
ensuring that they look good at the back end of
summer. **BG**

Origanum vulgare
GOLDEN MARJORAM

Type: hardy, herbaceous, perennial herb
Soil & situation: any well-drained soil/full sun to
light shade
North American hardiness zone: 5–9
Height: 30cm (12in)
Spread: 1m (3ft)
Grow for: wonderful warm yellow foliage from
early in the year; purple flowers loved by bees;
edible herb

Golden marjoram is hardy and, although pleasant
enough to use in many dishes, is really an
ornamental plant rather than a valuable herb.
However, adding a few leaves to a salad brightens it
up and it can be used with tomato dishes. I use it
for ground cover between more important plants
in the herb garden as it is easy to propagate by
cutting it into chunks in spring, quick to recover
and the flowers are really loved by bees. It looks its
best from spring until summer, after which it
becomes less tidy as it flowers, but these can be
trimmed off to keep the neat yellow mounds of
foliage for longer. There is a plain green form but
it's a cheerless soul by comparison.

Origanum laevigatum 'Herrenhausen' *growing with
Sedum* 'Autumn Joy'.

Origanum vulgare growing with creeping thyme.

The oregano of pizza fame is *Origanum majorana* or sweet marjoram which is a tender biennial. The Greek for marjoram was *origanum* made up of *oros*, mountain, and *ganos*, joy, for the natural habitat and habit of this wild plant.

This is long lived, growing almost anywhere but preferring well-drained spots in full sun; in shade the leaves stay green. Trim back the dead stems in autumn or earlier for a late show of foliage. Marjoram is easy to grow from seed sown in spring or summer and the clumps can be divided in spring. It suffers no particular problems but the golden form can be burnt by sudden fierce sun after weeks of grim damp dimness. **BF**

Osmanthus x *burkwoodii*

Type: hardy, evergreen shrub
Soil & situation: moist, fertile, well-drained soil/full sun or partial shade
North American hardiness zone: 7–9
Height & spread: 3m (10ft)
Grow for: incredible fragrance; AGM

I fully expect big, blowsy roses and magnolias to have a lot of scent to offer, but I am constantly

Osmanthus x *burkwoodii*

amazed when tiny flowers exude fragrance by the wheelbarrow full. From mid- to late spring *Osmanthus* x *burkwoodii* does just that. The small, tubular, fragrant, pure white flowers are carried in clusters at the tips of last year's growth. On a calm, spring evening the scent from an informal hedge of *burkwoodii* is magic.

It forms a dense shrub with 5cm (2in) long, glossy, leathery, dark evergreen leaves. No regular pruning is required. If necessary old plants may be rejuvenated by cutting half the main branches to within 30cm (12in) of the ground in the first spring and the remainder the following year. Clip hedges immediately after flowering.

The flowers are impervious to rain and frost, but plant in a site protected from biting, cold, spring winds. Propagation is by semi-ripe cuttings taken in summer, with bottom heat in a propagator. If there is a suitably low branch, you can layer it into the soil in spring or autumn allowing 12 months for it to root. **JC**

Osmanthus heterophyllus

Type: hardy, slow-growing, evergreen shrub or small tree
Soil & situation: fertile, neutral to acid, well-drained soil/sun or partial shade
North American hardiness zone: 7–9
Height & spread: 5m (16ft)
Grow for: attractive foliage and fragrant flowers in late summer to autumn

Yes, here's another holly lookalike with dark green, glossy, sometimes spiny leaves, and the only apparent difference is that the leaves are opposite whereas in holly they are alternate. The real give-away though, perhaps the most obvious, are the

Osmanthus heterophyllus

sweetly scented, tubular flowers that appear from late summer to autumn. It was introduced to the UK by Thomas Lobb from Japan in 1856. Like his brother William, he collected plants for Veitch & Co., the legendary Victorian nursery, and visited locations from northeast India to Java and its nearby islands.

Osmanthus heterophyllus has several cultivars. 'Purpureus' is the hardiest form and its young growths are deep black and glossy and look as though they've been dipped in bitumen, later turning green with a purple tinge. 'Aureo-marginatus' has bold, yellow leaf margins. 'Goshiki' has conspicuously yellow- and bronze-tinted leaves when young. Its name means five-coloured and you'll either love it or hate it! 'Gulftide' has white flowers and leaves that are twisted and spiny or lobed. 'Myrtifolius', the 'myrtle-leaved osmanthus' is neat and compact, with unarmed leaves except for a spine at the tip, just like the mature leaves on the upper part of *O. heterophyllus* and holly. They root easily and do not revert. 'Rotundifolius' is a slow-growing curiosity with round, occasionally twisted leathery leaves with wavy margins.

'Sasaba' is a remarkable form from Japan; its leaves are deeply cut into numerous spine-tipped lobes.

Prune to remove straggly or winter-damaged growth. Trim in autumn to maintain shape when grown as a hedge. Propagate in late summer by semi-ripe cuttings. Layer in autumn or spring. It is susceptible to scale. **MB**

Pachysandra terminalis 'Variegata'
MOUNTAIN SPURGE

Type: hardy, evergreen perennial
Soil & situation: any moisture-retentive soil/sun or partial shade
North American hardiness zone: 4–8
Height: 25cm (10in)
Spread: 60cm (24in)
Grow for: excellent year-round ground cover; AGM

When I'm asked for an interesting ground-covering evergreen, pachysandra is always on the list. In late winter the variegated foliage will add colour even to a deeply shaded garden. Coarsely toothed, shiny, dark green, 10cm (4in) long leaves are clustered at the ends of short, bare stems. Spikes of small, slightly fragrant, white flowers are produced in late spring and early summer.

The type of soil is irrelevant, providing it doesn't dry out, and the good news is that pachysandra is tolerant of chalky soils. It will, however, respond to being planted in a humus-rich, well-drained soil where it will romp away, quickly covering the ground. This plant, together with English ivy (*Hedera helix*), is widely used in the USA as ground cover under trees, speedily forming a dense mat and creating maintenance-free areas. Propagation is by semi-ripe cuttings in summer. Alternatively fork up a clump and remove the stems which have rooted into the soil. Pot them up in a soil-based compost for a season before planting out in their permanent position.   **JC**

Pachysandra terminalis 'Variegata'

Paeonia lactiflora 'Sarah Bernhardt'

Paeonia lactiflora 'Sarah Bernhardt'

Type: hardy, herbaceous perennial
Soil & situation: rich, moist soil/sun or light shade
North American hardiness zone: 3–7
Height & spread: 1m (3ft), if not tied
Grow for: attractive, richly coloured foliage with enormous pink fragrant blooms; AGM

Peonies are an old-fashioned plant perfect for old-fashioned gardens. A peony bed is a short-lived display and is not labour free, as the stems need tying up or they flop. However, it is a marvellous thing with massive, soft pink, fragrant blooms borne in profusion on top of good-looking foliage. They go well along the sides of a path. Position them where they are easy to reach, as half the pleasure is in cupping the blooms in your hands and inhaling the sweet perfume. *Paeonia lactiflora* 'Sarah Bernhardt' is one of the finest, a fairly upright grower (still needs tying up) and suitable as a cut flower.

The lactiflora peonies come from China where they were grown for millennia, not arriving in Europe until the 19th century; whereas from ancient times in the West we had *P. officinalis*, the old red-flowered species. The name comes from the Greek for the plant of Paion, the god's physician, as it was used medicinally.

Peonies can be very long lived, often remaining in derelict gardens. They prefer a richly manured, loamy, moist soil and will take full sun or even fairly heavy shade without succumbing. Do not move or divide clumps unless necessary; mulches help immensely as they conserve moisture. Trim dead stems in autumn, stake and tie up new stems early and deadhead. Sow the seed for variable results or divide the roots in late

Paeonia lutea var. *ludlowii*

autumn. Their roots are brittle and must be handled with care. They take several years to settle down before they start flowering.   **BF**

Paeonia lutea var. *ludlowii*
TREE PEONY, TIBETAN PEONY

Type: hardy, deciduous shrub
Soil & situation: deep, fertile, moist, well-drained soil/full sun or partial shade
North American hardiness zone: 5–8
Height: 2.5m (8ft)
Spread: 4m (13ft)
Grow for: eye-catching specimen plant – attractive leaves, wonderful flowers and large seedpods

This is the very best in tree peonies. It forms a handsome, open, spreading shrub with no inhibitions regarding growth or flowering. Grown as a specimen plant out on its own it is quite startling in flower.

Bright green, architectural leaves are trifoliate and the large, buttery-yellow, single flowers are up to 13cm (5in) across with four to a stem. They are borne in late spring. Each flower produces two carpels. The seedpods are 7.5cm (3in) long, pale green flushed pink and sausage-shaped, and the seed produced is the largest of all peonies.

Tree peonies are long lived plants so give them plenty of space and they will, over many years, repay you with an annual display. The variety 'Superba' is of similar habit with bronze leaves when young turning to green and yellow flowers flushed with pale pink. The anthers are orange.

It will need protection from cold, drying winds. In its native habitat of Tibet, it grows wild in forests of holly and oak in a gravelly soil at an altitude of 3,000m (10,000ft). Propagation is by semi-ripe cuttings in summer or saddle grafting in winter.   **JC**

Paeonia mlokosewitschii

Paeonia mlokosewitschii
MOLLY THE WITCH, CAUCASIAN PEONY

Type: hardy, herbaceous perennial
Soil & situation: rich, moist soil/sun
North American hardiness zone: 5–8
Height & spread: 1m (3ft)
Grow for: attractive buds, leaves and late spring flowers; AGM

This is a plant that everyone raves about but its name can be spelt by hardly anyone. I'll be short on the description and long on planting and aftercare, as you can see from the picture it's an absolute beauty and you'll want to ensure that it flourishes. The glorious bowl-shaped flowers, a full 12cm (5in) across, are cool lemon-yellow with a bold central boss of yellow and pale pink stamens. They're held on stout stems high above a mound of red-stemmed, silvery-green leaves. It's a native of the southeast Caucasus Mountains, growing on sunny slopes in hornbeam and oak forest. You'd never group those together in a garden!

It needs moist, fertile, well-drained soil, at least 30cm (12in) deep in sun or partial shade. Where late frosts occur, avoid positions which get the morning sun and mulch with well-rotted manure or compost around, not over, the crown; if buried too deep, it stops flowering. It is long-lived and a heavy feeder – prepare the ground thoroughly. Dig a planting hole ideally 1m (3ft) each way, incorporate plenty of well-rotted organic matter and wait two weeks to allow for settlement before planting. Plant the crown in early autumn, no more than 3cm (1in), or slightly less, below the surface. Feed with general fertilizer in spring and support with wire hoops or plant supports when foliage is half grown. If necessary, protect with dry mulch during winter. Keep the soil moist during drought.

Paeonia suffruticosa 'Rock's Variety'

Prevent peony grey mould with good hygiene, drainage and air circulation. Spray with fungicide as leaves emerge when problems occur. Check plants regularly. **MB**

John adds:
Some nursery-raised plants produce flowers with pink colouring, but the true flower has no discolorization. There also seem to be strains which flower earlier or later which can't be explained by location or climate.

Propagation by seed can be very satisfactory. Make sure the seed is ripe before harvesting. Sow it fresh. A root will form in the first autumn with a shoot appearing the following spring. Stored seed may take two or three years to germinate. Large clumps may be divided in autumn or spring, taking care not to damage the fleshy roots. Root cuttings are easily propagated in winter.

Paeonia suffruticosa 'Rock's Variety'
TREE PEONY

Type: hardy, deciduous shrub
Soil & situation: any well-drained soil/sun
North American hardiness zone: 5–8
Height & spread: up to 2m (6½ft) x 2.5–3m (8–10ft), but may be much less
Grow for: enormous lightly fragrant blooms

I have always loved flowers, more often for their scent than plain beauty but was nearly overwhelmed when I walked through Kew Gardens one day and beheld a tree peony in full bloom. Similar to a peony but shrubby, a bit more like a hydrangea, it was overladen with gorgeous blooms, each with satin-like petals. Then I started looking for these rare beauties, which wasn't easy as they are not much grown because they can be cut back by late-spring frosts, surviving but without flowering. However, a good large specimen in full bloom is wonderful, some are even well scented, but with such beauty that kind of seems irrelevant!

Worshipped in China for thousands of years, tree peonies were originally found in bamboo groves and were developed into double-flowering forms grafted onto other roots before the Norman conquest had even happened. They were introduced to Europe in the 18th century; in the UK we got hold of the first varieties from an American plant collector, Joseph Rock, who introduced many interesting plants (see his sorbus, page 369), and it's because of this that they are often referred to as Rock's tree peonies.

Tree peonies are not so demanding of rich soil as are their herbaceous relatives and are happy in a well-drained soil in full sun or shielded just from the early morning sun to protect the blooms from frost damage. They do better among other shrubs or on a wall than in a windswept site or frost hollow. The named varieties are often smaller more compact selections than seedlings! Tree peonies are long lived unless pruned, but dead-heading is worthwhile, as it saves the plant wasting energy on seed. The species can be started from seed as soon as acquired or it can be layered in spring; commercially the named varieties are grafted onto herbaceous rootstocks. The young shoots sprout early in the year so protect these with fleece or nets if harsh spring frosts or winds are predicted; do not worry about apparent dieback after flowering as it's normal, and do not prune. **BF**

Papaver orientale 'Patty's Plum'

Papaver orientale 'Patty's Plum'
MRS MARROW'S PLUM

Type: hardy perennial
Soil & situation: deep, fertile but well-drained soil/tend to stop flowering in dry conditions/sun or part shade
North American hardiness zone: 4–9
Height: 78–85cm (31–34in)
Spread: 70cm (27½in)
Grow for: beautiful, papery flowers over a period of about six weeks from late spring to mid-summer; attractive foliage is an asset, but dies down after flowering; reappears with a new crop of leaves in late summer which remain through the winter unaffected by frost

The extrovert flowers of this fabulous poppy are a most unusual shade of sumptuous mauve-plum. The flowers are single (single oriental poppies tend to be less invasive than double-flowered forms) and the stunning colour fades as they age. The stems are stiff and have no leaves immediately below the flowers. Oriental poppies are, understandably, a big favourite generally as they are easy to grow, colourful and with many good varieties in reds, white, salmon and pink to choose from. The individual blooms last for one, two or sometimes three days.

Generally oriental poppies are survivors – once they have established they will be with you for years to come. There are quite a few cultural methods that help maximize the flowering period of these ethereal blooms: it is best to cut the stalk off at the base as soon as it starts to go over, not letting it waste flower power on setting seed; keep them well watered if necessary as they do not appreciate it too hot and dry (contrary to popular belief) because in dry conditions the plants soon cease to produce flowers; the flowers of 'Patty's Plum' and other mauve and purple poppies will last about twice as long if they are grown in part shade so, surprisingly, they are far better in north-, west- or east-facing borders. Some poppies need staking and some do not, but as 'Patty's Plum' has long stems it does tend to need it. Sometimes, unfortunately, if the weather is wet, the flowers fail to open. Propagate by root cuttings; seed will produce mixed results.   **BG**

Papaver rhoeas
CORN POPPY, FIELD POPPY, FLANDER'S POPPY

Type: hardy annual
Soil & situation: fertile, well-drained, alkaline soil/full sun
North American hardiness zone: annual
Height: 80cm (32in)
Spread: 15cm (6in)
Grow for: bright red, simple flowers

I have always loved these simple red flowers. They were so common in arable fields when I was growing up but, sadly, today weedkillers have

Papaver rhoeas

Papaver rhoeas 'Cedric Morris'

significantly reduced their numbers. They still appear in profusion after cultivation or where the soil has been disturbed for road works or building. The buried seed can remain viable for decades until it is disturbed and heat, light and moisture allow it to germinate. An example of this ability was demonstrated on the churned up soil of the Somme battlefield in 1916. Since then this memorable little red poppy has been adopted by the British Legion and is worn with pride and poignancy.

When crushed, the bristly stems exude a white sap. The 15cm (6in) long, downy, light green leaves are deeply cut into toothed lobes. Single, flimsy, bowl-shaped, scarlet flowers appear from late spring to early autumn. Occasionally the base of each petal has a black blotch. The stamens are numerous and jet black.

The round seed capsule releases its ripe seed through a ring of open pores rather like a pepper pot. Allow seedheads to form and, when ripe, collect and store dry for next year's flowers. Seed can be sown in spring *in situ*. Sow thinly.

There are selections available including 'Mother of Pearl' in shades of pink. The Shirley Series produce single and double flowers in yellow, orange, pink and red without blotches on the petals.   **JC**

Matt adds:
Cedric Morris, a great friend of Lucien Freud and Beth Chatto, was an artist-plantsman who created a wonderful garden at Benton End in Suffolk. He regarded flowers as an extension of his palette and loved species plants; a list found after he died shows that at one time there were over 700 different kinds in his garden. It's no surprise, then, that he scoured the fields and hedgerows for variants of the enchanting field poppy. *Papaver rhoeas* 'Cedric Morris' is his selection of soft ethereal shades of pale pink, white and smoky grey; 'Fairy Wings', 'Angel's Wings' and 'Mother of Pearl' are almost identical but with darker colours, and 'Angels Choir' is a double selection.

Paris polyphylla

Type: hardy, herbaceous perennial
Soil & situation: cool, moist, free-draining soil/dappled shade
North American hardiness zone: 5–8
Height: 90cm (36in)
Spread: 30cm (12in)
Grow for: leaves; flowers from late spring to mid-summer; fascinating fruits

Paris polyphylla (formerly known as *Daiswa polyphylla*) is one of the wonders of the woodland garden. Fascinating and stylish rather than beautiful, if you're looking for a piece of natural contemporary art this is it! It's the perfect lesson in symmetry – look at it from above for maximum impact then go to the side to marvel at how it's stacked up in tiers. There's a ruff of up to 15 lance-shaped, mid-green leaves at the base. Above them at the top of the stem is a single spidery flower comprising narrow, green, arching outer sepals, the finest thread-like filaments that you'd never believe were petals and a boss of yellow to bronze stamens with a dark, almost purple ovary. Wow! As a bonus, it lasts for about three months.

The grand finale is even more bizarre when the capsules burst open grotesquely to reveal their bright red, shiny seeds. The fruits are said to shine out in their native forests in the Himalayas to western China, where they must be a hugely impressive sight. Sadly, because this plant grows

Paris polyphylla

Passiflora edulis

slowly, dislikes disturbance and is desirable, it is under threat from over-collection in the wild. If you can't resist, and I hope you can't, please buy yours from a reputable, cultivated source.

Very easy to grow, it needs moist, fertile, well-drained, humus-rich soil, ranging from neutral to acid, in partial shade. Plant 12cm (5in) deep. It hates being divided and produces little fertile seed, but left undivided it spreads naturally and soon makes a fine clump. Slugs may attack rhizomes and young growth.   **MB**

Passiflora edulis
EDIBLE PASSION FRUIT

Type: tender, perennial, semi-evergreen climber
Soil & situation: well-drained compost/full sun/under cover
North American hardiness zone: 7–9
Height & spread: 10m (33ft)
Grow for: glossy, lobed foliage; fantastic large flowers for months; edible fruits

I just love this plant. The ease with which it grows from seed, the lovely leaves, the flowers which are just out of this world, then the fruits. I've grown dozens of different passion flowers and they are all fascinating, almost all fantastically flowered – and yet each species is differently fantastically flowered – and nearly all of them have edible fruits. The fruits come in giant forms, miniature forms, different colours and shapes; there is one

that looks like a small banana. The fruits have a tough skin surrounding an edible pulp coating the many seeds and this pulp when sieved is delicious in squashes and sorbets. And best of all is the form *Passiflora edulis*, the purple granadilla. You don't need buy the seed – every fruit from the supermarket is full of them. By the way, they're best to eat when wrinkled up.

Passion flowers, and there are hundreds of them, come from the Americas (and Australia – *P. herbertiana* is an Aussie thug I had to machete to death in my polytunnel). The name comes from the allegedly divine signs – each part of the flower supposedly representing the Passion (betrayal, torture and death) of Christ. Unfortunately, it's a fit-up that doesn't work well – for example, the ten petals represent the twelve disciples by leaving out Judas and Peter….

Passion flowers are a bit vigorous for most greenhouses or conservatories unless grown in a tub; they may survive on a warm wall outdoors if well protected in winter. A tub under cover means they can go out in summer, which helps keep them pest free. They need a gritty, well-drained compost kept moist in summer, with a regular high-potash feed in their water, and to be drier in winter. They are easy from seed and can even be cropping the same autumn from an early-spring sowing, or take summer heel or nodal cuttings with bottom heat. Passion flowers are prone to the usual greenhouse pests and mostly pine away if cold and damp.   **BF**

Sedum spectabile

ICE PLANT

Type: hardy, herbaceous perennial
Soil & situation: prefers alkaline, free-draining soil/sun
North American hardiness zone: 4–9
Height & spread: 45cm (18in)
Grow for: sculptural form and late summer-autumn flowers; AGM

Butterflies love *Sedum spectabile* – it's a great place to sup in late summer and early autumn; when the sky is blue and the sun shines, it's drinks all round at the butterfly bar! Broad, dense flowerheads, up to 15cm (6in) across, mean easy access and copious nectar for all, the tables are packed with 'shots' and they drink until satisfied from its bountiful blooms. One of autumn's finest sights is a cloud of red admirals and tortoiseshell butterflies out for a drink and at play, dipping and sipping from the tiny chalk-pink flowers. When they have a chance, the bees love it too!

Like so many sedums it's rather surreal, with upright green stems and toothed, succulent, grey-green leaves. It's fascinating in leaf and bud; over winter when the bars close, the tables are bare and they're brown, dried and dusted with frost, it has a wonderful sculptural form. *S. spectabile* 'Iceberg' has bright lime-green foliage and tiny icy-white flowers that burst from striking green buds in late summer. There's a form called 'Stardust' that also has white flowers. *S. s.* 'Brilliant' (right) has flowers with bright pink petals, darker pink carpels and anthers.

They flourish in all garden soils, including clay, in sun or partial shade, but prefer moderately fertile, alkaline soil or sandy soil with added organic matter. Excellent for the front of borders; cultivars of *S. spectabile* are best for butterflies. They are prone to slugs and snails, and may be affected by fungal, bacterial, crown and root rot. **MB**

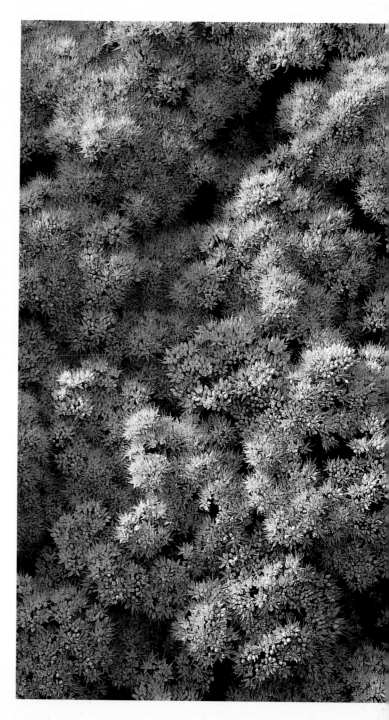

Paulownia tomentosa
Plant of the Week (see page 125)

Pelargonium 'Ardens'

Type: tender perennial
Soil & situation: free-draining compost/sun
North American hardiness zone: 8–10
Height: 30cm (12in)
Spread: 25cm (10in)
Grow for: striking flowers from mid-spring to mid-autumn

It is not difficult to fall in love with this plant – although it does not produce the bold display of so many pelargoniums, the flower colour is simply irresistible.

I first saw this several years ago and for some inexplicable reason didn't buy it. After that I couldn't stop thinking about it, then several months later I saw another at a flower show, I had butterflies in my stomach when I bought it! Is it normal to be so excited about buying a plant? I only have one, but it is beautiful and bright. Imagine a huge pot full outside on the patio, floating on their wand-like stems; here come those butterflies again!

Pelargonium 'Ardens' is my absolute favourite, it has clusters of intense ember-red flowers with darker teardrop markings on each petal topping long,

Pelargonium 'Ardens'

elegant flower stalks and grey-green foliage. It can be used as a cut flower, but you'd need a lot of stems – unless you go minimalist. Force into dormancy and divide in midsummer to create one of life's more difficult dilemmas, do you share them, or keep them all for yourself?

The species and 'primary' hybrids rarely get a mention; so here are a few more to whet your appetite.

Pelargonium sidoides has small, very deep purple flowers with orange pollen from late winter to late autumn, the grey-green leaves have a silvery sheen. There is a black form and a raspberry-coloured form with larger, bright, deep pink flowers. *P. tomentosum* (see page 291) looks great in a large pot. I'd also like to mention *P.* 'Splendide' which has fabulous flowers – the upper petals are red and the lower ones white. Delightful!

Grow pelargoniums in sunshine in John Innes No. 1 compost with added sharp sand. Water moderately and feed with a liquid general fertilizer every two weeks in spring, changing to high-potash fertilizer when flowering. In winter, water sparingly, keeping the compost almost dry. They are not frost hardy. Propagate from non-flowering shoots in spring and summer. Cut shoots just below a leaf joint, put them in warm, moist compost in bright light; do not cover. Beware of whitefly. **MB**

Pelargonium 'Lord Bute'

Pelargonium 'Lord Bute'

Type: tender perennial
Soil & situation: free-draining compost/sun
North American hardiness zone: 8–10, but often grown as an annual
Height: 45cm (18in)
Spread: 30cm (12in)
Grow for: handsome flowers from late spring to early summer; AGM

'Lord Bute' is a superb pelargonium for a summer patio display and it certainly lives up to its name as a Regal pelargonium. It's one of the oldest of this type and has a deep blackberry-coloured, velvety flower with fine cherry-red edges and orange pollen. It makes an excellent specimen for a decorative urn or with silver-foliaged plants. It has a distinct flowering period from mid-spring and is in full flourish by early summer; each flower cluster is about 10cm (4in) across. If you remove the spent flowers and feed with high-potash fertilizer like those used for roses or tomatoes, they will flower even longer.

Other dark-flowered Regal pelargoniums include *Pelargonium* 'Noir' with very dark, almost black flowers and mid-green leaves. 'Morwenna' has iridescent, floppy, black flowers. 'Springfield Black' is an almost black dark purple. The blooms of 'Black Velvet' are very dark velvety black with a fine purple margin. 'Marchioness of Bute' has flowers of deep maroon, almost black, with a light margin and exterior. 'Minstrel Boy' is deep mahogany. 'Australian Bute' has dark burgundy, wavy and lobed petals. Cultivate as for *Pelargonium ardens* (see previous entry). **MB**

Pelargonium tomentosum
PEPPERMINT-SCENTED GERANIUM

Type: tender, evergreen perennial
Soil & situation: potted in a free-draining, gritty medium and watered extremely sparsely during the winter months/sunny, sheltered position/needs over-wintering in frost-free conditions
North American hardiness zone: 9–10
Height: to 90cm (36in)
Spread: to 75cm (30in)
Grow for: divine foliage; heart-shaped, peppermint-scented, velvety leaves; AGM

This plant is not nearly as fussy or difficult as it sounds. I leave it out in a sheltered position through the winter, and when we get cold snaps, pull it in under our porch. (Normal people put it in a frost-free greenhouse, but mine is usually too full.) If you keep it on the bone side of dry, it survives. I rate it so highly because it forms a beautiful mound of touchy-feely foliage, spreading and flopping attractively over the pot with its softly hairy leaves, which you stroke it as you go past. Then, whenever you smell your fingers throughout the day, the strong, fresh, organic peppermint lingers on them. It does flower, with small white butterfly-shaped flowers in spring and summer – pleasant but not special. Feed and water this plant as it starts into growth. If you are lucky enough to be given a young, rooted cutting, pinch out the tips to develop a good, bushy shape. Avoid it becoming leggy as it ages – part of the beauty of the plant is a well-rounded form – so prune it back during the growing season to maximize this. It is very easy from cuttings, and a wonderful gift that will be appreciated even by non-gardening friends. **BG**

Pelargonium tomentosum

Penstemon 'Burgundy'

Penstemon 'Burgundy' (syn. *P.* 'Burford Seedling')

Type: hardy, semi-evergreen perennial
Soil & situation: infertile, well-drained soil/full sun or light shade
North American hardiness zone: 7–10
Height: 90cm (36in)
Spread: 60cm (24in)
Grow for: deep red flowers from summer to autumn

Burgundy by name and burgundy by nature. The wine-red flowers provide a long-term splash of colour in the mixed border. It has the decency to use up its allocated space yet not crowd its neighbours.

It quickly becomes a robust, bushy plant with 12cm- (5in-) long, light green leaves. The upright racemes of flowers appear in summer and go on until late autumn. They are bell shaped, 5cm (2in) long and deep red-purple with white stigmas and styles. The throat is white with pale red streaks. The upper lip of each flower consists of two lobes, while the lower lip has three. Dead-heading after flowering prolongs the display.

Avoid a fertile soil which will encourage growth at the expense of flowers and also make the growth lush and soft, prone to frost damage. Covering the base of the plant in late autumn with a dry mulch of coarse bark will help see it through a cold winter.

Propagation is by seed sown in heat in early spring. Take softwood cuttings in late spring or semi-ripe cuttings in summer. Cover with horticultural fleece. Large clumps can be carefully divided in spring discarding the old, woody centre of the clump. Penstemons have their share of problems. Slugs can be a real nuisance. Chrysanthemum eelworm distorts the foliage and infected plants should be dug up and burned. **JC**

Penstemon 'White Bedder'

Penstemon 'White Bedder' (syn. *P.* 'Snowstorm')

Type: frost-hardy perennial
Soil & situation: free-draining but not too fertile soil/sun or light shade
North American hardiness zone: 6–9
Height: 70cm (27½in)
Spread: 30cm (12in)
Grow for: a gloriously long flowering season from mid-summer to early autumn, provided it is dead-headed; freely produced, bell-shaped, pure white flowers; AGM

Not all the penstemons are reliably hardy, but with our milder winters, the range that will over-winter is increasing. For me, the ones that are reliably hardy are indispensable perennials. The foliage of these hardier types is generally evergreen and their free flowering over a period of several months is invaluable. *P.* 'White Bedder', despite its name, is reliably hardy in sharp-draining soil. It has bright green ovate leaves. But, of course, the main reason for including it is its handsome trumpet-like flowers, borne in racemes and of an eye-catchingly large size.

Another excellent new penstemon which I grew for the first time last year is *P.* 'Cassis Royale', a sumptuous dark wine-purple. It was quite hardy with me in its first winter and it is a far better, stronger colour than the widely grown *P.* 'Sour Grapes'.

It is worth tidying up penstemons in early spring with a bit of a cut back. They are generally short-lived perennials and ideally you replace your stock every few years to keep them looking their best. They root very readily from softwood cuttings which you can take from the new growth stimulated from being cut back. Ideally I think it is best to plant them out the following spring, giving them a full growing season to get their roots down before having to endure the frosts. Otherwise there is little more to be done, apart from dead-heading to keep them flowering and a light winter mulch to help them through the frosts. **BG**

Perovskia atriplicifolia 'Blue Spire'
RUSSIAN SAGE

Type: hardy, deciduous subshrub
Soil & situation: poorish, perfectly drained alkaline soils/tolerates slightly acid conditions/useful for coastal conditions/best in sun/will tolerate some shade though may need staking
North American hardiness zone: 6–9
Height: 1.2m (4ft)
Spread: 1m (3ft)
Grow for: excellent foliage and superb flowers; the former is aromatic, grey-green and finely cut; the latter are lavender-blue in late summer and autumn; AGM

This is an excellent, soft, see-through plant with many vertical but airy spires of flowers. It forms a delicate tracery of colour at a time in the year when you really appreciate it. The flowers are carried in effusive quantities and I like mixing it with dark black-purples and oranges, but it is a shade that mixes well in many colour themes. It is also adaptable to how you use it – it looks topical, current and trendy in widespread drifts of

Perovskia atriplicifolia 'Blue Spire'

perennial plantings; it works particularly well in gravels with expanses of other drought-loving plants and low mounds of grasses; and it is equally at home sunning itself against a house wall, or in a herbaceous or mixed border.

This plant is easy from cuttings, and they strike really easily if you remove very young shoots with a heel in late spring. These small, new shoots will only be about 3.5cm (1¼in) long, but they will rapidly root at that size. Although this is technically a subshrub, it is most usually grown as a herbaceous plant with the whole plant cut back to ground level when it becomes too ratty-looking in early spring. That way you leave the vertical white, leafless stems to add colour and structure to the winter scene. The new foliage in spring is also far better when treated like this. **BG**

Matt adds:
Perovskia atriplicifolia has a soothing effect when planted with lavender or white-flowered perennials, and contrasts well with late orange or yellow flowers such as *Solidago* 'Goldenmosa'. The branches are an attractive winter feature, particularly in clear, cold frosty weather.

There are several cultivars, possibly hybrids between Russian sage and *P. atriplicifolia* or *P. abrotanoides*, but who cares when they look so beautiful! *P. atriplicifolia* 'Little Spire' is slightly smaller than 'Blue Spire', with a height and spread of 1m (3ft); 'Filigran' has finely cut, almost fern-like leaves. But I agree with Bunny that 'Blue Spire' is the best of all with its deeply cut leaves and huge flower spikes.

Persicaria microcephala 'Red Dragon'

Type: hardy perennial
Soil & situation: moist but free-draining soil/full sun or part shade
North American hardiness zone: 5–8
Height: 60cm (24in)
Spread: 50cm (20in)
Grow for: dramatic foliage of various colours, the predominant being a burgundy maroon

The foliage of this plant is fairly extraordinary: the elongated heart-shaped leaves are stridently marked with a minty-white chevron; and the stems are bright red. The flowers are small, white and fairly insignificant and the foliage goes downhill when it puts its energy into flowering, so

Persicaria microcephala 'Red Dragon'

I think they are better removed. It does not spread fast and is in no way invasive as many of the bistorts tend to be. The most difficult thing I find with this plant is deciding where to fit it into the garden so it looks right. The habit and form imply that it is best in wilder parts, semi-naturalized, but the exotic colour does not lend itself to that treatment. I grow it adjacent to a grassy path in a narrowish border with some ferns, cyclamen and variegated euonymus. It seems to fit reasonably happily there. It is not as picky as to where it will grow as the colouring suggests and apparently is equally happy in raised beds, borders or containers. There are several other good persicarias. *P. bistorta* 'Superba' is one of my favourites: it is a handsome plant with mounds of large, soft-green leaves and long stems of abundant poker-like pink flowers produced all summer.

'Red Dragon' is a fairly recent introduction and I have only grown it for a couple of years. Up to now I have done nothing to it apart from removing the flowers and the usual initial watering to get it going. I think it is going to be one of those plants that generally does not need much doing anyway, just dividing if and when necessary. **BG**

Petroselinum sativum
CURLY-LEAFED PARSLEY

Type: hardy, short-lived perennial or biennial herb
Soil & situation: any soil/sun or shade/likes moisture
North American hardiness zone: 5–8
Height: first year to 30cm (12in), second year to 1m (3ft)
Spread: first year to 15cm (6in), second year to 60cm (24in)
Grow for: superb curly-leafed foliage plant; culinary herb

There is no herb more essential to a cook's garden. You can do without almost any other garnish, salading or flavour, but not parsley. Try a cold cooked leek in a parsley vinaigrette to see what I mean. It is also one of the first plants to produce fresh leaves in spring, which make a great tonic salad with curly kale. But then it is also such a lovely garnish to make your humble meal look more inviting; you can use the curly leaves as a soft cushioning bed for freshly picked strawberries in the punnet, too. This healthy-looking, verdant green plant is more than good enough to be a foliage plant in the flower garden.

The plant reached England in the Middle Ages and has been popular ever since. I reckon more parsley is used for garnishing (think butcher's display and restaurant food) than is actually eaten. The curly-leafed form was developed to prevent inadvertent poisoning by weeds such as fool's parsley, which resemble the flat-leafed form. The form Hamburg parsley is grown for its roots. In Italy a curly variety still exists as grown in Roman times and known to Pliny. We get both common and botanical names from the Greek *petros selinon*, rock celery, via Old French *perresil*.

Parsley is notoriously difficult to grow but does better if sown in summer not spring, in moist, warm soil. The plants do best when they're self-sown, usually choosing damp, partly shady sites. Dead-heading the plants and trimming them back encourages new growth and a longer life. Parsley needs sowing every mid-summer to ensure a continuous supply. It can suffer badly from carrot root fly and is then best grown under a horticultural fleece. **BF**

Petroselinum sativum

Peucedanum graveolens

Peucedanum graveolens (syn. *Anethum graveolens*)
DILL

Type: tender annual
Soil & situation: rich, moist soil/full sun to light shade
North American hardiness zone: annual
Height: 1m (3ft)
Spread: 15cm (6in)
Grow for: attractive ferny foliage; essential salad herb

I must have this plant as I need its sweet aniseed-like taste to go with my pickled gherkins, along with black peppercorns and a bay leaf; it's the flavour I crave. I also like dill in a mixed salad and as the herb to go with pickled fish, such as herring or gravadlax. And if the plant gets too big despite my depredations, I add the seed to my liqueurs as it is an old remedy for indigestion.

Very closely related to parsley and carrots, this is an ancient plant coming from North Africa and the Near East, which has long been cultivated. Our common name may come from the Norse *dilla*, to dull or soothe, as it was used in sedative mixtures. The botanical name comes from the Greek *peukedanon* because of its parsnip-like root. The Greeks called a different plant, *Pimpinella anisum*, anise, by the name *Anethum*, but now we apply it to dill instead. Don't you just love nomenclatural botanists???

Dill can be sown from early spring on well-drained soil in a sunny position. The early leaves are best in salads, the later in pickles and the seed needs saving by cutting the nearly ripe plants down and the ripening finished off under cover in a warm, dry place. Sow shallowly *in situ* in succession from early spring to mid-summer. In shade or damp dill moulds easily; it may hybridize with fennel so these two plants should be grown well apart if self-saving seed for sowing. The seeds as used in gripe water are harmless, but the sweet alcohol they are in is highly addictive and as strong as sherry. **BF**

Phaseolus 'Kingston Gold'
CLIMBING FRENCH BEAN

Type: half-hardy, annual vegetable
Soil & situation: sunny, sheltered site with free-draining soil; does not establish well in cold, wet soils
North American hardiness zone: annual
Height: 1.8m (6ft)
Spread: individual plants about 15cm (6in)
Grow for: tender, but tasty, ornamental variety that crops well, exceptionally early, and for a good period of time

This is a good-looking, good-tasting vegetable. The golden pods hang conspicuously, sometimes at eye level, for all the world to admire. The flowers are a creamy white. Margaret Robinson, from my favourite vegetable firm, W. Robinson and Son, recommends growing it with a dark purple flowering sweet pea on a hazel archway or some such structure. It must be a heady combination.

I am not a big fan of 'queer gear' vegetables that are extraordinary but taste pretty revolting, but these are extraordinarily good to look at and exceedingly good to eat. They will be cropping by mid-summer if you have them out by the end of spring, and what is more, you will still be picking a few in early autumn. The yields are heavy, and these beans are produced right from the bottom of the plant to the top. The pods are longer than normal French beans, you pick them when they are about 15–18cm (6–7in) long and you do not have to bend double to pick them either. They are tender – you only need to top and tail them – and they retain their gold colour when cooked, though

Phaseolus 'Kingston Gold'

if you pick them very small they go a pale green. Climbing French beans have a lot of advantages over bush types, especially in wet summers where the pods are less likely to be damaged by slugs and splashed by soil. Another very attractive climbing French bean, but without the copious yield, is 'Rob Splash'. The beans are yellow and beautifully marked with purple splashes.

I find with all my beans that I get far better results if I grow them singly in pots until two or three true leaves are produced, and then I plant them out. Otherwise germination can be a bit of a gamble. Slugs, mice, birds, cats and, last but not least, wet, all play a part in varying degrees preventing me from getting my apple-pie rows. Protecting them with fleece outside, at the vulnerable stage, is a quicker method and certainly increases the establishment percentage markedly. Popping a few extra beans at the ends of the row for gapping up failures makes this system fail-safe. **BG**

Phaseolus vulgaris
FRENCH BEANS

Type: tender, annual vegetable
Soil & situation: moist, warm soil/full sun
North American hardiness zone: annual
Height & spread: variable
Grow for: climbing varieties make ornamental vines with pretty flowers and coloured pods, otherwise for the crop value

I grow several sorts of French beans. I love the tiny, pencil-shaped, wax pod-type of dwarf green bean that is served small without slicing and squeaks as you eat it if it is fresh and quickly steamed. I love the climbing French beans which are like runner beans but smaller and with smoother, firmer flesh; these can be colourful with purple flowers and pods. I also adore the drying dwarf French beans as these are such value. You sow them and apart from weeding all you do is lift the plants and hang them up until you want a casserole. Then you pod the beans, soak them overnight, add the bacon, tomato, onion and so on, and simmer all day; food of the gods, and you sing their praises after….

We had none of these beans in the UK until an early explorer named de Soto saw them growing together with sweet corn and squashes in fields in Central America. These were long cultivated there and not long after de Soto's discovery were welcome in the Old World where their many uses were soon appreciated. Now there are countless

Phaseolus vulgaris

varieties for many purposes. The botanical name is from the Old Greek name for another almost totally unrelated bean!!!

French beans need a moist, humus-rich soil in a sunny, warm, sheltered spot. The climbing varieties must be given poles or supports. For fresh green beans keep picking regularly as the plants will go on producing more. For drying beans uproot the whole plant when the season ends and hang it to dry in a warm airy place. Sow only when the late spring frosts are over and the soil is warm, otherwise germination is poor. Apart from cold springs they are relatively problem free and being legumes enrich the soil. **BF**

Philadelphus spp.

Type: hardy, perennial shrub
Soil & situation: any soil/sun or shade
North American hardiness zone: 5–8
Height & spread: variable, from 1.2–3m (4–10ft)
Grow for: forget the blooms, it's their scent!

Philadelphus are too strongly scented for some people and not good in the house for many as the smell can be too much, ooh I love them. Gorgeous, heavy, orange-blossom fragrances: the original *P. coronarius* (mock orange) is the most powerful; *P.* 'Belle Etoile' has a peaches-and-cream lightness; *P.* 'Avalanche' is heavier, more fruit salad like; 'Virginal' more, well, virginal; and best of all, my own seedling, of course – to my mind anyway.

Native to southern Europe, there are a dozen species and the first, *P. coronarius*, was introduced to the UK in the 16th century and has often confusingly been called *Syringa*, the botanical name for lilac. They are also called the mock orange because their scent and appearance of smaller-flowered forms have been likened to those of the orange. *Philadelphus* is the Greek for brotherly love.

They survive almost anywhere on any soil and they like chalk, as long as it's not too dry. Once established they need no attention and can be pruned hard back after a few years to keep them compact, or the older shoots can be removed annually immediately after flowering. Seedlings are variable and worth growing; propagate the named varieties by autumn cuttings, which is on the whole easy. Apparently they can get devastating aphid attacks but thankfully these do little long-term harm. **BF**

John adds:
'Belle Etoile' is my favourite philadelphus. On a calm day the area surrounding a flowering shrub is heavy with its fragrance. It makes a fine display when planted in mixed, open woodland. Mulching in early spring will help to retain moisture close to the surface roots. It can be propagated by softwood cuttings in summer or hardwood cuttings outside in a sheltered site in late autumn or winter.

Like Bob, I also love *Philadelphus* 'Virginal', which will grow to a height and spread of 3m (10ft) with large, fully double, very fragrant, pure white flowers. Another favourite is 'Bouquet Blanc', with fragrant double or semi-double flowers in summer and a height of 2m (6½ft).

Phlomis fruticosa
JERUSALEM SAGE

Type: hardy, perennial, semi-evergreen, lax shrub
Soil & situation: well-drained soil/sun
North American hardiness zone: 8–9
Height: 1–1.2m (3–4ft)
Spread: 1.2–2m (4–6½ft)
Grow for: attractive ever-grey foliage and bright yellow flowers in summer; AGM

This is a lovely plant for a dry site with poor soil facing into a hot sun, where it will thrive. I've found it goes well with tree lupins (see page 252) and indeed any grey-leafed plants, which mostly love similar conditions. I'm fortunate in that I can smell the rich aromatic aroma of the leaves and

Philadelphus 'Belle Etoile'

flowers, but apparently many people are allergic to it. It is usually ever-grey with me as I have my current one in a sheltered spot, which makes a good winter home for ladybirds, and in the first sunny days of spring they come out to sit on it like orange flower buds.

A native of the Levant, this is one of several dozen species and was brought back after the crusades from the Mediterranean and recorded as growing in England in 1596. The botanical name comes from the Greek for another plant entirely!!!

Not a very long lived shrub, it survives best on a dryish sunny bank with some shelter. It can be lightly trimmed after flowering. Jerusalem sage may be deciduous in cold districts and cut back down to the ground in the coldest spots, but often returns if the soil is light, sandy and well drained.

It can be grown from seed or by softwood summer or hardwood autumn cuttings in a cold frame. It may be problem free but its scent causes severe allergic reactions in some people, so grow it away from paths and patios. **BF**

Solanum crispum

Type: hardy, evergreen climber
Soil & situation: moist, well-drained, neutral to alkaline soil/full sun
North American hardiness zone: 8–9
Height: 4m (13ft)
Spread: over 2m (7ft)
Grow for: the impressive sight of this scrambling climber in flower, which is all summer long and then a month or so longer

If I ever found a sport of this plant I would name it 'Disobedient'! It is a shrub that likes to pretend it is a climber, but unless you are constantly tying in the strong shoots they zoom off at all angles bursting with flower at the tips. My method of control is to train in the main stems to timber trellis and thereafter let it do its own thing. It does it beautifully. After flowering I take control once again.

The 12cm (5in) dark green leaves may become deciduous when growing in cold areas. From summer to autumn the fragrant, dark mauve-blue flowers appear in dense, terminal clusters. Each flower is 3cm (1in) across with bright golden-yellow stamens.

Avoid exposed sites subject to cold winds. Planted against a sheltered, sunny wall in well-drained, fertile soil, it will quickly cover its allocated space. Water regularly from spring onwards. Annual pruning is essential. Shorten back the long shoots immediately after flowering. In winter prune them back to 10–15cm (4–6in) of the old wood. Propagation is by semi-ripe cuttings in a free-draining compost in late summer in a heated propagator. **JC**

Phlomis fruticosa

Phlox paniculata 'White Admiral'

Type: hardy, herbaceous perennial
Soil & situation: moist, fertile soil/sun or half shade
North American hardiness zone: 4–8
Height & spread: 90cm (36in)
Grow for: an immensely useful, tall-growing perennial which produces white flowers from mid- to late summer; does not require staking; AGM

There are many phlox to choose from, but this strong white phlox is a reliably good performer. It invariably contributes good long-lasting flashes of white and loads the summer air with clouds of fragrance. There are many other colours available – every shade of pink, red, purple, lavender-blue and orange-scarlet, and many other great varieties. *P. maculata* 'Alpha' (AGM) has lilac-pink flowers and is another favourite of mine. However, the fresh white flowers of 'White Admiral' against the strong green foliage look so outstanding in a border that I invariably end up using this plant again and again.

Generally phlox prefer soil which provides them with a good supply of moisture throughout the growing season and are least happy on an alkaline clay. So if your soil is on the thin side, beef it up with copious organic matter prior to planting. Eelworms are a pest – to avoid them propagate from root cuttings, rather than division or stem cuttings, and you will not have a problem. To prolong the flowering period it is worth cutting off the dying flowerheads and then they will produce sideshoots with yet more flowers.

Vigorously growing plants are more likely to produce the goods. They respond to irrigation and should not be overcrowded, so divide them every three or four years, leaving decent-sized hunks to make sure they flower in the first year. **BG**

Phormium 'Sundowner'
NEW ZEALAND FLAX

Type: hardy, evergreen perennial
Soil & situation: fertile, moist, well-drained soil/full sun
North American hardiness zone: 9–10
Height & spread: 2m (6½ft)
Grow for: this versatile, broad-leafed plant is good in the border or as a hedge; AGM

This is a tried and tested plant for adding shape and texture to the garden. Grown in the mixed border or in a large container there is instant impact. Planted in a row it forms an effective, informal hedge or screen.

It is clump forming with 1.2m (4ft) broad, upright, sword-like leaves which, close to the base, are folded to form a 'v' shape. They are purple-green with dark pink-red margins and cream stripes. In summer, enormous 2m (6½ft) high flower stalks shoot up from the centre of the clump with tubular, bright, yellow-green flowers. The green seedpods that turn black form at right angles to the stem. When ripe they twist open to reveal the shiny, black seeds.

Where there is a risk of heavy frost they will benefit from a deep, dry mulch of composted bark in winter. When planting, allow sufficient space for the plant to grow and form a striking large clump. Pull off the old, dead outer leaves when they turn a grey-brown colour.

Propagation is by seed sown in spring in a heated propagator. When transplanting seedlings take care not to damage the brittle roots. Large clumps may be divided in late spring by teasing pieces out, complete with roots. Replant as soon as possible without allowing the roots to dry out. **JC**

Phlox paniculata 'White Admiral'

Phormium 'Sundowner'

Photinia x *fraseri* 'Red Robin'

Type: frost-hardy, evergreen shrub
Soil & situation: moist, fertile, well-drained soil/full sun or partial shade
North American hardiness zone: 8–9
Height: 4m (13ft)
Spread: 5m (16ft)
Grow for: brilliant red leaves; AGM

There is nothing fickle about *Photinia* x *fraseri* 'Red Robin'. The new young leaves and shoots emerge in spring a bright, shiny red and retain their colour well into the summer. An actively growing mature plant can appear to be totally red for most of the season. Even in winter some mahogany-red remains on the younger leaves. The American-raised variety *P.* x. *f.* 'Birmingham' has coppery-red young leaves.

The 15–20cm (6–8in) long, leathery, dark evergreen leaves form a dense, compact screen for privacy, shelter or protection. When grown as a hedge or trained as a standard with a shaped head, it is important to clip over the young growths in early summer to allow new sideshoots to form and be hardened sufficiently to withstand winter frosts. It is tempting but unwise to put off the job in order to take advantage of the coloured foliage. Plant shaped, standard plants far enough apart to allow for an increase in the size of the head. Regular clipping restricts growth, but it doesn't stop it.

Cold winds and hard frosts may damage soft growth, spoiling the following year's display.

Photinia x *fraseri* 'Red Robin'

Feeding the plants with a high-potash fertilizer, such as a liquid tomato feed, in late summer will firm up the growth. Propagation is by semi-ripe cuttings in summer in a propagator with bottom heat. All photinias are prone to fireblight disease. Avoid planting where shrubs such as pyracantha have suffered. **JC**

Bunny adds:
There is not a huge range of good, large, structural evergreen shrubs in the garden, but this is one that I have used a lot. It is ideal for decorative screening purposes, but I have to admit I have mainly used it for impatient clients and have brought in ready grown and shaped ones which have been good, plump 3.5m (11½ft) specimens, with a stem girth of up to 25cm (10in), grown in Italy. I think the Italians have selected larger, more vigorous clones than we generally get in the UK, and of course the hotter summers speed up the growth rate. The shrubs establish surprisingly well when planted at this large size, tolerate the climate change and certainly can be less expensive than an inorganic, structural screen. They are often grown clipped into wide columns or mop-head standards, ideal for blocking out troublesome neighbours at first-floor level, and no planning permission required either! They look magnificent and can change the whole appearance of a garden in an instant.

Phygelius x *rectus* 'Salmon Leap'

Type: hardy, evergreen shrub
Soil & situation: fertile, moist, well-drained soil/full sun
North American hardiness zone: 8–9
Height: 1.2m (4ft)
Spread: 1.5m (5ft)
Grow for: a spectacular summer display of bright orange, tubular flowers; AGM

A very sensible plant. It has the good sense to hold its flowering stems at an angle resembling a fishing rod when reeling in a fish. This allows the pendent, tubular flowers to hang at an angle rather than directly down the stem of the plant, thus making a better display. It forms an upright, suckering plant with 10cm (4in) long, dark green leaves.

The bright orange, deeply lobed, long, tubular flowers are slightly curved. They are loosely arranged along 45cm (18in) high panicles in summer and autumn. Pruning out panicles which have finished flowering encourages a succession of flowers through the autumn. *P.* x *rectus* 'African Queen' produces pale red flowers with orange lobes and a yellow mouth. *P.* x *r.* 'Moonraker' has creamy-yellow flowers.

Avoid sites exposed to biting, cold winds. In gardens where the temperature is below freezing for long periods it can be treated as a herbaceous perennial. A mulch of bark will see it through the winter. In spring remove the previous year's stems to ground level.

Propagation is by removing rooted suckers in spring. They can be planted out where they are to flower or potted up for a season. Softwood cuttings taken in early summer should be over-wintered in a cold frame for the first season. **JC**

Phygelius x *rectus* 'Salmon Leap'

Physalis peruviana

Physalis peruviana (syn. *P. edulis*)
CAPE GOOSEBERRY

Type: tender, perennial, evergreen climber
Soil & situation: any soil/sun or light shade/under cover
North American hardiness zone: 8–10
Height & spread: 2m (6½ft)
Grow for: attractive downy leaves; small yellow flowers; interesting paper lantern-shaped edible fruits

This delicious fruit, rich in vitamin C, is not widely grown, mainly because when it is started off from seed it does crop in the autumn but very late and so the berries are not really sweet and ripe. If you grow it on or make new plants from cuttings these flower and crop much sooner in the year with a sweeter, riper fruit. I've got it in the border under cover and in pots. The fruits are truly ripe when they drop, which is still late in the year, and then they keep pristine inside their wrappers, eventually turning into little raisin-like dried fruits. A marvellous crop. There is a smaller sweeter sister, *Physalis pruinosa*/*P. pubescens* (ground cherry) which is an annual and crops outdoors. Its big sister, *P. ixocarpa*/*P. philadelphica* has tomato-sized, tomato-like fruits used like tomatoes. Why grow them? Well, they do not get blight!

The Cape gooseberry is closely related to the aubergine and the Chinese lantern, *P. alkengi*, known to the ancients, which does have an edible fruit and even steals the common name for its red, papery, lantern-like calyx. The true Cape gooseberry has a translucent white calyx. The generic name comes from the bladder, *physa* in Greek, which surrounds the sweet berry, and the Cape name for *P. peruviana* from their being much grown at the Cape of Good Hope, though they originate in South America.

Cape gooseberries need to be under cover in winter but can go outside in summer. It is best as a short-lived perennial, as fruits are then formed earlier in the year and ripen sweeter. These can be left on the plant, or allowed to drop off, yet remain clean and ripe for weeks – the fruit inside its personal paper bag remains unsullied by the dirt and mud on which it rests. If necessary the plant can be cut back hard in winter, to tidy it up or to keep it within its allotted space. It can be grown from seed planted in spring, or rooted from cuttings or layered at any time of year. Cape gooseberries do get some common greenhouse problems but still crop heavily.   **BF**

Phytolacca americana
POKEWEED, RED INK PLANT

Type: hardy, herbaceous perennial
Soil & situation: fertile, moist soil/full sun or light shade
North American hardiness zone: 5–9
Height: 3m (10ft)
Spread: 1m (3ft)
Grow for: lovely flowers from mid-summer, followed by spectacular, 'corn-on-the-cob-like' berries

Phytolacca americana

My first plant arrived in the rockery about ten years ago as the result of a passing bird. Within weeks it was too large for the available space and was transferred to the herbaceous border. I have never been without a pokeweed since, rating it as good as most of its neighbours and better than some.

The erect, reddish stems carry large, lance-shaped, mid-green leaves which become tinged with purple in autumn. From mid-summer to mid-autumn the tiny pink or white flowers form 20–30cm (8–12in) long racemes, followed by a dense cylindrical mass of maroon-black berries.

Warning: the berries are toxic. Close up the plant exudes an unpleasant smell, but if planted at the back of the border this won't be obvious. Apparently native American Indians used to use the juice of the berry to write and draw. As it is deadly poisonous I hope they didn't lick their paint brush.

Pokeweed has thick, fleshy roots and dislikes being transplanted. Propagation is by seed sown in a propagator in early spring. Pot up the seedlings and keep containerized until planting out after all risk of frost is over.   **JC**

Picea pungens 'Koster'
KOSTER'S BLUE SPRUCE

Type: hardy, evergreen conifer
Soil & situation: deep, moist, well-drained, neutral to acid soil/full sun
North American hardiness zone: 3–7
Height: 10m (33ft)
Spread: 5m (16ft)
Grow for: attractive blue-green, needle-like leaves; graceful habit with a conical shape; AGM

This is one of the best of the blue spruces suitable for the average-sized garden. The trouble is, it needs to be loved. Not pampered, but if it is totally ignored you will end up with a miserable, baldy, misshapen conifer.

It has an open, loose habit, allowing a view of the trunk. New growths open from tight, yellow-brown buds. Its sharply pointed new leaves are glaucous blue-green, but as they age they settle down to an attractive blue-green.

A young plant may produce two leading shoots. It is essential one of these is removed to prevent the shape of the tree being spoilt. Prune out the weakest shoot 1cm (½in) up from the joint, leaving the strongest stem to grow and form a

Picea pungens 'Koster'

leader. The side branches often grow at different rates. In order to form a conical shape it may be necessary to trim back long shoots in spring. *Picea pungens* 'Hoopsii' is slower growing with beautiful blue-white foliage.

Propagation is by grafting in winter. Red spider mite does serious damage to the foliage, turning it yellow and eventually brown. It never recovers, leaving the centre of the tree spoilt and dead looking. It attacks from late spring through to early autumn. Spraying with a recommended insecticide every three to four weeks in summer is the only control.   **JC**

Pieris formosa var. *forrestii* 'Wakehurst'

Type: hardy, evergreen shrub
Soil & situation: moist, well-drained, humus-rich soil/full sun or light shade
North American hardiness zone: 7–9
Height: 5m (16ft)
Spread: 4m (13ft)
Grow for: an extremely handsome evergreen shrub with trusses of white flowers and vivid red leaves in spring; AGM

Even as a young plant this pieris earns its keep with masses of spring flowers and colourful young leaves. A mature plant can be tree-like, forming a mound of red and white in spring. The 10cm (4in) long, glossy, dark evergreen leaves are a brilliant red when young, gradually becoming bronze and finally green. Beautiful, 15cm (6in) long, pendent, terminal panicles of urn-shaped, white flowers appear at the same time as the red leaves.

An annual mulch of composted bark, leafmould or old compost will help retain moisture close to the surface where most of the fibrous roots remain. Mature plants may be successfully transplanted providing a large ball of soil contains the roots. After transplanting, water on a regular basis to prevent the roots drying out.

Avoid exposing the plant to cold, drying winds especially in late winter and early spring. There is no regular pruning needed, but if the shrub becomes too large or there are misshapen branches it can be cut in late spring. Try not to cause gaps in the outer covering of pieris as frost can penetrate and kill new growth.

Propagate using semi-ripe cuttings in late summer in a moist, peaty compost. Pinch out the growing tip of the rooted cutting to make it branch from the base of the plant. **JC**

Pieris formosa var. *forrestii* 'Wakehurst'

Pinus sylvestris 'Gold Coin'

Pinus sylvestris 'Gold Coin'
GOLDEN SCOTS PINE

Type: hardy, evergreen conifer
Soil & situation: well-drained soil/full sun
North American hardiness zone: 3–7
Height & spread: 5m (16ft)
Grow for: deep golden-yellow leaves in winter

There are those who think and say that the Scots pine is dull and drab. Don't listen to them, but if you have doubts then grow one of the yellow-leafed varieties. None of them make big trees, although labelling them dwarf is a bit risky.

Pinus sylvestris 'Gold Coin' starts off with good intentions to remain small, but in a fertile soil and a sheltered site it soon starts to put on 10–15cm (4–6in) of growth each year, in height and spread. In spring the needles are yellow-green, becoming grey-green in summer and in early winter they turn to a deep golden-yellow. The twisted leaves are in pairs. Seen at 100m (330ft) in a snow-carpeted garden with a leaden sky it seems to light up the surrounding area. Plant in a soil where there is a decent root run. They are prone to blowing out of the ground where the top soil is shallow overlying chalk. Pruning may be necessary to keep the tree in shape. Occasionally it will throw out a strong sideshoot which quickly grows beyond the rest of the branches. Cut it back immediately to prevent it spoiling the branches close to it – it may cause needle drop due to congestion and a lack of light. Where two leaders appear on the same plant the weaker one should be removed in spring. Propagation is by grafting in winter. **JC**

Piptanthus nepalensis (syn. *P. laburnifolius*)
EVERGREEN LABURNUM

Type: hardy, semi-evergreen shrub
Soil & situation: fertile, well-drained soil/sun or partial shade/shelter from cold winds
North American hardiness zone: 9–10
Height: 2.5m (8ft)
Spread: 2m (6½ft)
Grow for: cheerful, bright yellow flowers; easy to grow and maintain

By no means rare, this evergreen laburnum is seldom seen in gardens. It is a good-value plant with its three palmate, lance-shaped, dark bluish-green leaflets, green-white on the underside. Pea-like, bright yellow, terminal racemes of flowers appear in late spring and early summer, followed by bright green seedpods up to 20cm (8in) long, which hang well into winter before turning brown and curling open to disperse the seeds.

In frost-prone areas it will enjoy a sheltered situation. Grown and trained against a warm, sunny red brick wall it will quickly fill its allocated space, adding colour and interest. It is a trouble-free plant with no pests or diseases to worry about. Pruning consists of removing any crossing branches which clutter up the centre, making the plant look untidy.

Once established it dislikes being transplanted. Tease out any congested roots before planting. It germinates easily from sweet pea-like seed without the need for stratification and will be happy in an alkaline soil. Softwood cuttings taken with a heel in summer root within a few weeks. **JC**

Piptanthus nepalensis

Pisum sativum 'Rondo'

Pisum sativum 'Rondo'
PEA

Type: half-hardy, annual climbing crop
Soil & situation: most moist soils/full sun to light shade
North American hardiness zone: annual
Height: 1m (3ft)
Spread: 15cm (6in)
Grow for: the sweetest full-size peas

I have long grown green peas as they are a gourmet crop; the petit pois type are especially good but they are fiddly to pick and pod, as the pods and peas are minute. 'Rondo' is a normal-size pea plant with a long pod with up to a dozen full-size and very sweet peas. Its pods hang in pairs, which makes picking easy, and they also pod easily. In taste and appearance it's similar to a famous pea I used to grow called 'Onward', though 'Rondo' is by far the sweeter.

Green peas are relatively modern. The Romans ate peas but these were usually as dried ones used in soups and stews; indeed peas have been dated at sites of about 8,000BC! The green pea as we know it arrived in 17th century Europe and began a craze; in 1696 peas were being taken in a manner seeming like addiction! The pea in question is a wrinkled seeded type which is not very hardy and will not over-winter, and is known as a marrowfat pea.

Peas need a moist soil preferably in full sun; they'll just grow in shade but not be sweet. They like a bit of lime in the soil but do not need feeding as they're legumes. Do pick these clean as they will grow on and give a few more pods if none are left to fully ripen. Sow in rows, from mid-spring until mid-summer, under bird protection; do not pre-soak seed but thoroughly wet the drill if the soil is dry. Water heavily when you see the flowers. Pods may get a maggot in the peas but early crops usually miss this. **BF**

Plectranthus argentatus
Plant of the Week (see page 225)

Polianthes tuberosa

Type: tender, tuberous perennial
Soil & situation: well-drained compost/full sun/under cover
North American hardiness zone: 8–10
Height: 60cm (24in)
Spread: 15cm (6in)
Grow for: the most powerfully fragrant flower spike of white waxy blooms; AGM

This is not an easy plant, as it takes a little care to coax the tubers into growth without rotting them and it is difficult to propagate. But goodness what a flower: a tall spike of waxy creamy-white flowers

Polianthes tuberosa

with the most powerful fragrance emanating from them in waves. I find the perfume addictive, almost carnal; it fills my tropical house and some friends find it decadent in its call to indulgence. In the open garden it is still wonderful, but not as imposing. This is a genus originating from Mexico with just one species. The name is the Greek for whitish flower. It has been a much-loved flower ever since Shelley described it as the 'sweet tuberose, the sweetest flower for scent that blows'.

Tuberoses can be planted outdoors in sunny spots for the summer, but must be dried off and brought in for winter. They are very prone to cold and rotting off if damp in winter, but need copious moisture to get going in spring when they must be in the warm. They need a free-draining, gritty, leafmould-rich compost in big pots. They can go out for the summer but then the perfume is wasted and, anyway, they're better off in the conservatory, though some may find them overpowering. It is difficult to get hold of the seed and the small offsets rarely ripen well and take ages to reach flowering size, so go on, buy one – it's worth it. They are not pest prone but do suffer the odd attack. **BF**

Polygonatum multiflorum 'Striatum'
SOLOMON'S SEAL

Type: hardy, perennial rhizome
Soil & situation: fertile, humus-rich, well-drained soil/heavy or light shade
North American hardiness zone: 4–8
Height: 90cm (36in)
Spread: 45cm (18in)
Grow for: ideal for a shady position; arching stems; clusters of green-tipped, white flowers

A wonderfully, cheerful perennial for a woodland glade. The shoots push through the soil like the start of a crop of asparagus. They unfurl and continue to grow, sending out leaves. Once they decide to arch, the stems come into flower followed by fruit. Plant it close to the edge of a path where it can overhang and show off.

The lance-shaped, 5–10cm (2–4in) long, bright green leaves are striped and margined creamy-white and are arranged alternately along the stem. In late spring, clusters of two to six tubular, pendent, green-tipped, white flowers dangle from the leaf axils, followed by jet black spherical berries lined along the lower side of the arched stem.

Polygonatum multiflorum 'Striatum'

The common Solomon's seal, *Polygonatum* x *hybridum*, grows to 1.5m (5ft) in height with 20cm-(8in-) long, mid-green leaves and small, creamy-white flowers tipped green. The tubular flowers are waisted in the middle and are followed by blue-black berries.

Propagation is by ripe seed sown in autumn and over-wintered in a cold frame. Clumps can be divided in late spring. Lift the whole plant carefully to avoid damaging the emerging shoots. Tease out the rhizomes and pot up in a soil-based compost with added leafmould. Don't allow the rhizome to dry out. Greyish-white sawfly larvae have black heads and are a serious pest of Solomon's seal. They are capable of stripping the leaves, leaving bare stalks, but thankfully the plant will usually recover. The best control is to pick off the caterpillar-like pests. **JC**

Poncirus trifoliata
JAPANESE BITTER ORANGE

Type: hardy, deciduous shrub
Soil & situation: any well-drained soil/sun
North American hardiness zone: 5–9
Height & spread: 2m (6½ft)
Grow for: amazing green framework with enormous thorns; 5cm (2in) wide, white scented flowers and edible fruits

I first came across this plant in an old garden in winter; there was this peculiar shrubby mass of enormous thorns. I returned in spring to see the large orange-blossom flowers and smell their sweet scent; later the leaves came out but it failed to fruit. Sadly, so have both of mine which I have planted since; no matter, they are still fascinating plants. Apparently the American marines use this as a perimeter planting as it is said to keep out

intruders up to the size of a jeep. Believe me, if you want a weird front hedge that makes a statement this is the one for you.

Poncirus comes from China and Japan where it is grown for the fruits, which make a delicious conserve. It is often used for rootstocks for other citrus and occasionally suckers can be detached. The generic name comes from the French for a citron-like plant.

It does well on most soils, even chalk, and is hardy and tough enough to be used for hedges. Only prune or clip immediately after flowering. It can be grown from seed, or by layering in spring; I have rooted cuttings. It has no common problems. **BF**

Poncirus trifoliata

Primula florindae
TIBETAN COWSLIP, GIANT COWSLIP

Type: hardy perennial
Soil & situation: shade, or sun where conditions remain moist/moist, deep, humus-rich soil
North American hardiness zone: 3–8
Height: to 1.2m (4ft)
Spread: 90cm (36in)
Grow for: long-lasting umbels of eye-catching, soft yellow flowers; AGM

This is a foolproof, robust and charming plant. It is ideal for naturalizing as it is a prolific self-seeder and spreads itself freely with amazing vigour where conditions are suitably moist. Just be careful that it does not swamp more fragile neighbours. It has bold, ovate, almost heart-shaped leaves which are shiny and can be up to 20cm (8in) long. However, if the moisture levels

dry up these quickly become shrivelled and pathetic looking so, in dryer soils (and they will survive in normal garden soil), do make sure they get some shade. The large drooping clusters of funnel-shaped flowers are borne on stout stems in summer, and last for some time. Another great asset is the scent, which is bold and fruity. There are several other spring- and early summer-flowering primulas suitable for naturalizing in similar situations. *Primula japonica* 'Miller's Crimson' is smaller (60cm/24in), with strong crimson flowers. A good plant, too, and it can look effective mixed with *P. florindae*.

This is one of those welcome plants that, once you have planted it, you just let it do its own thing, particularly in a wild or naturalized part of the garden. Perhaps it may become over-dominant, which would entail removing clumps of self-sown seedlings, preferably when they are small and easy to deal with. If you want to propagate it, the simplest way is to get fresh seed from a friend and scatter it by hand. Alternatively transplant the seedlings as small as possible. **BG**

Primula florindae

Eucryphia x *intermedia* 'Rostrevor'

Type: hardy, evergreen tree
Soil & situation: moist, well-drained, acid soil/full sun or light shade
North American hardiness zone: 8–10
Height: 10m (33ft)
Spread: 6m (20ft)
Grow for: spectacular show of fragrant white flowers in summer and autumn. In August it is at its mid-season best, at least in my part of the world! AGM.

Rostrevor is a small village on the shores of Carlingford Lough in Co. Down, Northern Ireland. Squeezed between the sea and the Mourne Mountains it has a better than average climate for plant growth. Moist and mild is a wonderful combination for this tree. A mature tree has a broadly columnar habit and in full flower it is a spectacular sight.

The glossy, dark green leaves are pale green and glaucous on the underside with both simple and pinnate leaves carried on the same plant. In late summer and early autumn the pendulous, shallow, cup-shaped, single flowers cover the tree, bending the slender stems. They are fragrant, ivory-white and up to 5cm (2in) across.

It deserves shelter from cold winds, which scorch the foliage and brown the flower buds before they open. Ideally positioned, the root area should be in shade with the head of the tree in full sun. A deep mulch of bark will help keep the root area cool.

Pruning is seldom necessary apart from removing any branches that spoil the overall shape. Propagation is by fresh seed sown in late autumn and over-wintered in a cold frame. Root semi-ripe cuttings in a gritty compost in summer, and grow on under glass until the spring. **JC**

Matt adds:
Trust my mate Cushnie to display his national bias yet again by picking a plant that comes from Co. Down! There's not even a whisper that there might be a choice, like the magnificent *Eucryphia* x *nymansensis* 'Nymansay' (below), which is taller and smothered with even larger flowers. 'Nymansay' came from Nymans garden in Sussex when seeds were sown in the hope of producing a hardier form; John's favourite was a spontaneous hybrid found in a garden. No wonder he approves; none of the work, but all the glory!

Primula vulgaris

Primula vulgaris
PRIMROSE

Type: hardy, herbaceous perennial
Soil & situation: most moist soils/light sun to heavy shade
North American hardiness zone: 4–7
Height & spread: 20cm (8in)
Grow for: large attractive leaves; primrose-yellow fragrant flowers in spring; AGM

Quintessential flowers of spring and early summer, to quote John Clare (1793–1864): 'Aye, flowers! The very name of flowers,/That bloom in wood and glen,/Brings Spring to me in Winter's hours,/And childhood's dreams again./The Primrose on the Woodlands lee/Was more than gold and lands to me.'

Primroses are part of my childhood, little harbingers of better weather to come, flowering from Christmas in sheltered hollows protected by the skeletons of deciduous trees from the screaming winds of a Norfolk winter. I still warm to them, indeed as I write this on a cold, bleak day with a wind howling gusts of snow there is a clump I can see from my window, such plucky little heroes – it's strange that yellow should be the colour of cowards when primroses are so valiant.

Part of our myth, folklore and once eaten in salads, the primrose is one of over 500 species of the northern hemisphere generally originating in hills, valleys and open deciduous woodlands. The primrose name comes from the medieval Latin, *prima rosa*, for first flower of spring, though it was not applied solely to this bloom initially; it was the early English botanist Parkinson who divided *Primula vulgaris*, the primrose, from *P. veris*, the cowslip. Primroses live on the sides of ditches, on the lower part of banks and at the base of damp walls. Cowslips prefer it out in the open, even in the middle of a meadow.

P. vulgaris prefers a loamy, leafmould-enriched, heavy soil with plentiful moisture, though not waterlogged. The clumps self-seed, so in moist dappled shade they may live forever. They can be grown from seed, which is considerably better when fresh, so they are best sown in summer; their roots can be divided in winter. Vine weevil is now a serious pest; kill it with the commercially available parasitic nematode watered on to wet soil. **BF**

Prostanthera cuneata
ALPINE MINT BUSH

Type: hardy (in all but the coldest areas), evergreen shrub
Soil & situation: moist, fertile, well-drained soil/full sun
North American hardiness zone: 9–10
Height: 60cm (24in)
Spread: 90cm (36in)
Grow for: mint-scented foliage; white flowers; AGM

When crushed, its foliage smells more like mint than mint does, with none of the bad habits of the herb (*Mentha*). When visitors smell it for the first time it quickly becomes a talking point.

Prostranthera cuneata forms a bushy, compact shrub. The small, rounded, glossy, mid-green leaves have rolled margins and are strongly aromatic when handled. The tube-shaped, white flowers have yellow and purple markings on the inside and form 20cm- (8in-) long racemes in spring and early summer.

It makes an interesting, informal, low, aromatic, evergreen hedge which should be clipped immediately after flowering. Hard pruning of older plants may kill the plant. It is easily propagated by softwood cuttings in a gritty compost under polythene in summer and it germinates readily from spring-sown seed. It is short lived when planted in a heavy, wet, clay soil and does not favour exposed sites and biting, cold winds. **JC**

Prostanthera cuneata

Prunus 'Amanogawa'

Prunus 'Amanogawa'
FLOWERING CHERRY

Type: hardy, deciduous tree
Soil & situation: moist, fertile, well-drained soil/full sun
North American hardiness zone: 6–8
Height: 7m (23ft)
Spread: 3m (10ft)
Grow for: pretty spring blossom; lovely foliage colours in spring and autumn; AGm

I have a 30-year-old-plant at the front of my house and every year it is in flower on 23 April, my elder son's birthday. The coloured ballons tied to the branches tend to take away from the display of flower. It forms a small columnar tree with stiff, upright branches. The 12.5cm (5in) long leaves open bronzy-yellow and turn mid-green during summer. In autumn they change again to deep red, orange and yellow. In spring clusters of soft pink, fragrant, semi-double flowers cover the tree. The branches are stiff, which means they hardly sway in the wind, allowing the blossom to remain for a longer period than other cherry trees.

It will branch naturally in the second or third year. Where two branches fork leaving a narrow 'v'-shaped angle, remove one shoot to eliminate the risk of the branches splitting later in life. If any pruning is required it should be carried out in summer when the spores of silver leaf disease are dormant.

If you want to be one up on the neighbours and you have the time and money plant two *Prunus* 'Amanogawa' 2m (6½ft) apart to form an arch over a path or entrance. Bend and tie the branches over wire hoops. It will look a treat at any time of the year and on my son's birthday it will be spectacular! **JC**

Prunus armeniaca
APRICOT

Type: hardy, deciduous tree
Soil & situation: well-drained soil, ideally a calcareous loam/warm sheltered position/against a sunny wall/cold greenhouse/cold winters and early springs
North American hardiness zone: 6–8
Height: up to 10m (33ft)
Spread: 3m (10ft)
Grow for: delicious fruit in large quantities a few years after planting; well-trained fan looking superb against a wall

When I was 20, I planted my first apricot fan and two or three years later was eating the most delicious fruit. The tree looked beautiful too against a south-facing, mellow-red brick wall next to the front door. I wondered why everybody did not grow them in the West Midlands. Now, in the East Midlands, I also have a thriving, productive tree. But as you move further north late frosts scupper the blossoms or small fruitlets. As the climate seems to be warming up, I think more gardeners should chance their arm and have a go, helped with the use of fleece and especially if they have a warm wall – a large fan will spread about 3.5m (11ft). They are self-fertile but tend to flower early, often in late winter, so if no insects are around hand pollination is recommended (though I have never had to do this).

Plant in late autumn, about 30cm (12in) away from the wall if you are training it that way. Tie the branches to horizontal wires, about 15cm (6in) apart, fixed to vine eyes. It is simplest to buy a ready-trained fan. These consist of a short, 30cm (12in) stem, usually with 8 to 12 branches radiating out from it. The even spacing of these 'spokes' helps to ensure the fruit get enough sun and warmth. When pruning a fan, the aim is to build up a series of fruiting spurs about 15cm (6in) apart along the length of the branches, so pinch back the sideshoots from the main branches in early summer, leaving 7.5cm (3in) of growth. Carry on tying in the extension to the main branch to keep the 'fan' shape. Beds at the base of walls tend to be dry places, so copious water in dry periods while the fruit is swelling will help. The yield from a fan can be 9kg (20lb), probably half that from a free-standing tree, except it might be all frosted from the latter. One sad warning – my apricot has recently suddenly died. They have a habit of doing this for no apparent reason, and apparently have done so since the time of Henry VIII, when they were introduced. I am not deterred and have ordered another. **BG**

Bob adds:
You have not had a good apricot until you have had one ripened on a warm wall in England. The flavour is exquisite – true, they are good anyway, but believe me the best comes off a wall. Fortunately they are fairly obliging as they fruit on shoots on old wood and can be easily trained on a wall on a permanent fan-shaped framework. This also allows easy protection of the blossom from the frosts which prevent apricots ever being much use as free-standing trees. This is a shame, as I have had over half a dozen sorts doing, or rather not doing, exactly that for nearly 20 years; meanwhile those on walls fruit every year. Apricots can also be grown in tubs and moved under cover for flowering and until fruiting is over, going outside in summer and winter, but the flavour is not as good as those on walls.

Prunus armeniaca 'Moorpark' is an old fruiting variety that has dubious credentials as a pure bred and is thought to be a hybrid with some plum blood, but it doesn't matter as it's very good anyway; it was found as a seedling from the older 'Nancy' ('Pêche de Nancy' from France) in 1760.

Ideally enrich and lime the soil in front of a warm, sunny wall and plant a fan-trained *P. a.* 'Moorpark' there. Prune by the book – buy one specially. When the tree is in flower, hang a blanket in front of it on frosty nights but remove it during the day. Keep the soil moist and thin heavy crops. You can grow them from seed but with variable results and little fruit – I know, it's a shame. Apricots suffer from few diseases but dieback is symptomatic and needs pruning out in spring; sometimes scale insects may attack but they can be cleaned off in winter.

Prunus armeniaca

Prunus avium
SWEET CHERRY, WILD CHERRY, GEAN

Type: hardy, perennial, deciduous bird food
Soil & situation: any soil/sun
North American hardiness zone: 4–8
Height & spread: 10m (30ft), twice that height in the wild or as seedlings
Grow for: very floriferous tree; red and yellow delicious fruits stolen by birds; AGM

I have grown many cherries as free-standing trees only to stand helpless as the birds steal the crop. I love birds and the fruits are a small price for their songs, but I want some too. So now I grow them on dwarfing rootstocks in a fruit cage. Sure, they eventually get too big, but until then I get crops, which I never have from the trees in the open. I've also tried sweet cherries in tubs and this works, keeping them inside while flowering and fruiting but back outdoors the rest of the time. However the quality was not as good as from the outdoor crop and not really worth the effort. Most of the best varieties need a pollinating partner but that's no problem – two sorts are better than one!

Cherries are the first tree fruits to ripen in the open garden and have been popular since antiquity. Ironically the name *avium* means of the birds! (The bird cherry is *Prunus padus* and of no culinary value.) Wild sweet cherries are known as geans or mazzards and are found in woods throughout the UK, but the cultivated forms are much improved. Our name cherry comes from the Greek *kerasos*, though this was probably for the sour morello sorts, *P. cerasus*.

Prunus avium

Ideally cherries want to be on a chalky, loamy soil and kept moist during the growing season; they are poor choices to have by fine lawns or drives as their roots run under the surface and bulge it. Most need a pollinator. They are by far the best on super-dwarfing stocks in a fruit cage. Do not prune unless diseased or damaged. The seedlings come up variable – I have a delicious mini cherry, all stone with a sweet pasty covering! The main problem is birds, black aphids merely tip-prune for you as the tip withers after an attack, saving you the effort of summer-pruning them.   **BF**

Prunus cerasus

Prunus cerasus 'Morello'
MORELLO SOUR CHERRY

Type: hardy, perennial, deciduous bird food
Soil & situation: any soil/full sun or even shade
North American hardiness zone: 3–7
Height & spread: 5m (16ft)
Grow for: prolific white flowers in spring and gorgeous black fruits in summer; AGM

These are not sour; if they can be left on the bush long enough without the birds or damp getting them they are luscious and definitely sweet, well compared to a sloe – now that is sour! Sour cherries are not so watery sweet as sweet cherries and carry a much heavier, more aromatic flavour. This makes them perfect for cooked dishes where sweet cherries would be insipid. The bushes are also easier to keep small than sweet cherries, as they can be hard pruned more like blackcurrants; indeed this improves the crops.

Sour cherries were brought to us by the Romans, delighted us, and apparently were lost and re-introduced in the time of Henry VIII. They come from southwest Asia originally and, according to Pliny, the first was brought to Italy, thence to the town of Morello by Lucullus after his victory over Mithridates. They have been cross-bred with sweet cherries, and the epicure's choice, the Dukes, has such mixed blood.

Morellos like a chalky, rich, moist soil but can be grown in full sun or even in full shade; in the latter the fruits will be later and less sweet but there! As with sweet cherries a cage is essential. Morellos can and should be hard pruned, constantly replacing the old shoots by newer. I have had success growing this from seed but they are slow. The only problem is the birds.   **BF**

Prunus domestica 'Victoria', 'Czar' and 'Marjorie's Seedling'
Plant of the Week (see page 311)

Prunus domestica x *P. insititia* 'Reine Claude de Bavay'
GREENGAGE

Type: hardy, deciduous tree
Soil & situation: most soils, provided they are not waterlogged or do not dry out too much/thin chalky soils will need heavy feeding/shelter from cold winds/no late frosts
North American hardiness zone: 5–8
Height & spread: to 6m (20ft), depending on rootstock
Grow for: one of the tastiest fruits around; attractive garden tree, especially when not grown on dwarfing rootstocks such as Pixy

Greengages are a type of plum and were introduced to Britain about 250 years ago by Sir William Gage. When ripe, they are far tastier than a normal plum with their sweet, almost melting, translucent flesh. Forget the ghastly stewed greengages at school, eat them fresh and there is little to rival them. Unfortunately, their yields are not high. 'Cambridge Gage' is an excellent variety, similar to the old one simply called 'Greengage', but gives heavier crops and is more reliable although it is not ideal for colder areas.

When we moved to our present house there was a decrepit 'plum' tree that never fruited. One autumn I emptied the contents of the chicken-house on its roots and the next year it was hung with beautiful green-gold, tasty fruit. They do, as I

Prunus domestica x *P. insititia*
'Reine Claude de Bavay'

Prunus insititia
DAMSON

Type: hardy, deciduous tree
Soil & situation: any soil/sun
North American hardiness zone: 5–8
Height & spread: 3m (10ft)
Grow for: it's just about impossible to find a good or ripe damson in the shops

I know I'm being greedy, but I've just got to have a damson as well as all the plums and gages. They are never eaten raw as dessert as they are bitter, but this goes with their spicy flavour to make a wonderful preserve that can be used as a jam on bread or as an accompaniment to cold meat or cheese. They make a powerful wine but best of all is damson liqueur made in the same way as sloe gin but with damsons, brown sugar and rum – the perfect winter tipple.

Prunus insititia

The damsons originally came from Damascus, were known to the Romans and have changed very little since. There used to be many sub-varieties but now only a few commonly survive such as the 'Shropshire' and the 'Merryweather'.

Damsons do not need the warm sheltered spot required by plums or gages, in fact they are so tough as to make a good windbreak. They do like a rich, moist soil with plenty of lime but will thrive on almost any. Damsons, like plums and gages, resent pruning or training and are likewise best as orchard trees with a low bushy head, but they are smaller, more compact and twiggier, which helps. They are self-fertile. Seedlings come up and are fairly true but slow to bear. Damsons are budded onto a suitable rootstock so they are best bought in. They seem to escape almost all the problems that affect plums and gages. **BF**

found out, really appreciate rich, nitrogenous soils. When planting, avoid low-lying, frost-prone areas. Not all varieties are self-fertile so check this when you order. They can be shy to fruit because pollination can be disappointing – they tend to flower very early when few insects are about. Hand pollination can therefore be well worthwhile. Free-growing trees require little pruning: simply remove the dead wood and thin out the overcrowded growth. Do this in late spring or early summer. Although they can be trained as a fan against a wall, they need such hard, regular pruning that it is not that satisfactory. Brompton is a good rootstock, though quite vigorous up to 4m (13ft), and it resists suckering. With other rootstocks, the regular removal of suckers is necessary. **BG**

Bob adds:
The main reason for growing this plant is that you cannot find a good or ripe gage in the shops! I grow several: 'Golden Transparent Gage', 'Cambridge Gage' and 'Coe's Golden Drop'. They are all small green plums that turn yellow as they ripen and have a superb flavour, tart and yet almost honey-like. A flavour beyond the usual plum. They are candy when ripe off the tree, make delicious desserts and a divine conserve that is best with half ripe and half under-ripe gages. Gages need a warm sheltered spot and a rich, moist soil with plenty of lime. They are bushier than many plums but similarly resent pruning or training, and are best as orchard trees with a low, bushy head. *P. domestica* x *P. insititia* 'Reine Claude de Bavay' is self-fertile but does well with 'Victoria' as a pollinator. Seedlings come up but they are variable and slow to bear. These need to be budded onto a suitable rootstock, so the plant is best bought in. The major pest is wasp damage; other pests are minor by comparison, though silver leaf is a problem if they are pruned other than in summer.

Prunus domestica

PLUMS – 'VICTORIA', 'CZAR' AND 'MARJORIE'S SEEDLING'

Type: hardy deciduous tree
Soil & situation: any soil/sun
North American hardiness zone: 5–8
Height: 6m (20ft)
Spread: 60–80cm (2–2¹⁄₂ft)
Grow for: you cannot find a good or ripe plum in the shops! September is a great month for plums after a lot of the soft fruits have disappeared and before the real glut of apples and pears.

I know I'm being greedy but I've just got to have all three, as they are so tasty and I love each of them. They are good for cooking or even as dessert, and make delicious jam when just under-ripe. 'Victoria' (left and top right) is the best but easy to find everywhere; it is a pointy plum with a red and yellow skin and sweet, yellow flesh. 'Czar' has the edge for preserves and has a reddish-purple skin and yellow flesh. 'Marjorie's Seedling' (below right) is valuable as it hangs late into autumn; it has a purple skin and tart, yellow flesh.

'Victoria' was allegedly a seedling found in Alderton, Sussex, southeast England, and introduced in about 1840. 'Czar' was raised by Thomas Rivers and first fruited in 1874, when the Czar of Russia was making a visit to the UK. 'Marjorie's Seedling' was first sold in Staffordshire, central England, of apparently local origin.

Plums need a warm, sheltered spot on a rich, moist soil with plenty of lime. They resent pruning or training and are best as orchard trees with a low bushy head. These three are all self-fertile. Seedlings come up and are variable and slow to bear fruit; they need to be budded on to a suitable rootstock so the plant is best bought in. The major pest is wasp damage; other pests are minor by comparison, though silver leaf disease is a problem if the trees are pruned other than in summer.   **BF**

Prunus laurocerasus

Prunus laurocerasus
COMMON LAUREL, CHERRY LAUREL

Type: hardy, evergreen shrub
Soil & situation: any soil/sun or shade
North American hardiness zone: 6–8
Height & spread: 4m (13ft)
Grow for: prolific scented flowers in mid-spring; striking year-round foliage; a good screening plant; AGM

It is easy to overlook the good but commonplace. The common or cherry laurel is everywhere doing a fine job. As a hedge it makes a superb evergreen screen that is tough and hardy enough for most sites and will recover if cut back. In flower in spring it is a delight, with very strongly sweetly scented racemes of, admittedly, tiny, creamy-white blooms. It is even quite decorative in the autumn with its berries, which feed the birds and germinate about the garden. There are few shrubs so happy in shade or the drip from trees above them.

Introduced to the UK in 1576 this is not a native but an import from Asia Minor and Eastern Europe. It is such a useful plant with a dozen and a half different cultivars varying from the huge-leafed *Prunus laurocerasus* 'Magnoliifolia' to the sick-looking *P. l.* 'Variegata'. *P. l.* 'Otto Luyken' is reckoned to be the best form in leaf and flower but is a bit low growing for a hedge, for which *P. l.* 'Herbergii' is better, being erect and dense. It is probably rather obviously named as its leaves are like large *Laurus nobilis*, the classic laurel leaves, and it bears black, cherry-like fruits.

Laurels are long lived on well-drained soils but do not thrive on thin chalky soils. They will grow almost anywhere not completely dark or waterlogged. In mid-summer they ought to be trimmed with secateurs – if sheared the leaves on the cut branches brown and look miserable; mind you, I shear as they drop off soon enough. These can be grown from seed sown anytime, from layers they are easy and you can root autumn hardwood cuttings under a cloche. They suffer no usual problems but the leaves and fruits are poisonous, and they should not be burnt either.   **BF**

Prunus persica 'Rochester'
PEACH

Type: hardy deciduous tree
Soil & situation: rich, moist soil/sun
North American hardiness zone: 5–8
Height & spread: 4m (13ft)
Grow for: gorgeous pink flowers in late winter and early spring; attractive willow-like foliage; enormous sweet fruits; AGM

Oh I adore peaches, I curse the spraying and wait in trepidation as they flower. (The frosts can be kept off with fleeces but so often these don't work and the fruitlets fall off.) Then the wait for weeks as the small fruits that do survive slowly swell, and the hope of sunshine more for them to ripen. And then, in the good years, they are so large, so sweet, a bag full of syrup to melt in your mouth and down your front. In the bad years they are

Prunus persica 'Rochester'

jam. I also grow them in big tubs which is the surest way of getting a crop, but they are just not so tasty as the outdoor ones.

Peaches probably came from China as there are many varieties there. They were known to Theophrastus in 322BC, and he gave them the origin of Persia, whence they get their specific botanical name. They are as often grown for their beautiful flowering forms as for their fruits, but for me it's the latter!

Peaches are short-lived trees. I fruit them as bush trees in warm sheltered spots but this is not easy in many parts of the UK. They are hard work to train on a wall or under cover as they need careful replenishment pruning. They can be grown in a large tub to be brought inside in early to mid-winter, when the warmth kicks the plant off and it flowers safe from the frosts and the leaves safe from the curl brought on by wet weather; once the fruits have ripened it can go back outside. Seeds do come true for garden purposes but should be of a local variety! Otherwise peaches are usually budded. They are even more short lived if they do not get treated for leaf curl. This is stopped by keeping the tree dry, or by spraying with Bordeaux or similar fungicide in late winter just as the buds start moving.   **BF**

Prunus serrula
MAHOGANY-BARKED CHERRY

Type: hardy, round-headed, deciduous tree
Soil & situation: moist, well-drained, moderately fertile soil/full sun
North American hardiness zone: 6–8
Height & spread: 10m (33ft)
Grow for: shiny coppery-red bark in spring; AGM

This beautiful, ornamental Chinese cherry with its leaf colour, flower, fruit and amazing bark is good value for money. Imagine an old, highly polished, copper warming pan and you can just about conjure up the colour of mature bark on this tree. The outer bark is constantly peeling, or being pulled off by little fingers, to reveal the shiny, newly burnished, mahogany surface. The fawn circles of scars are lenticels contrasting with the bark.

The small, white flowers appear singly or in clusters of between two and four at the same time as the emerging 10cm- (4in-) long, tapered, dark green leaves. They are downy on the underside turning to a soft yellow in early autumn. The

Prunus serrula

small, red fruits are loved by blackbirds and disappear before they are fully coloured.

This cherry is not fussy as to soil type, succeeding on all but waterlogged ground. When purchasing the mahogany cherry make sure it has been bottom grafted. Top grafted trees won't have coloured bark on the main trunk. As with all cherries, prune in summer when the spores of silver leaf disease are dormant and can't enter the wound. **JC**

Prunus spinosa
BLACKTHORN, SLOE

Type: hardy, dense, deciduous, spiny, suckering shrub or small tree
Soil & situation: well-drained, moisture-retentive soil/sun or partial shade
North American hardiness zone: 5–9
Height & spread: 6m (20ft)
Grow for: white flowers in early or mid-spring; dark autumn fruits

In spring, the view from my office window is illuminated by blackthorn in bloom. Hedgerows forming billowing clouds of pure white flowers roll down the fields into the shallow valley below and punctuate roadsides dominated by hawthorn and holly. Its display matches any flowering cherry for impact and is a particularly welcome sight in dull early spring days. After the show, it merges with other foliage until autumn when it's decked with small dark fruits with an attractive blue 'bloom', which are harvested by keen-eyed collectors for winemaking or flavouring gin. It is widespread in UK hedgerows and

occasionally as a woodland tree reaching 6m (20ft); the wood is extremely hard and was valued for making hay-rake teeth and Irish shillelaghs, once described as 'ancient Hibernian tranquil-lizers'! English country lore observes that a period of cold weather coincides with blackthorn flowering; it is known as a 'blackthorn winter'. They are an important food for several caterpillars, they attract bees and they are good for nesting birds.

Prunus spinosa 'Plena' has pretty, pure white, double flowers. The dark stems increase their impact. *P. s.* 'Purpurea' grows to 2m (6½ft) and has deep purple leaves and white flowers. It makes an excellent purple-leafed shrub.

Robust and tolerant of variable conditions it prefers sunshine or partial shade in well-drained, moisture-retentive soil, but tolerates clay to sandy soils and some chalk. Many *Prunus* species suffer from several pests and diseases, but sloes are so robust that they are usually unaffected. Propagate by seed, semi-ripe cuttings or suckers. Suckers are easiest – detach them in late winter. **MB**

Prunus spinosa

Prunus x *subhirtella* 'Autumnalis'
WINTER-FLOWERING CHERRY, AUTUMN CHERRY

Type: hardy, deciduous, spreading tree
Soil & situation: well-drained, moisture-retentive soil; thrives on chalk/sun
North American hardiness zone: 6–8
Height & spread: 8m (25ft)
Grow for: buds and blossom from mid-autumn to early spring; autumn colour; AGM

This is such a pretty tree. The slender, wand-like branches are clothed in green through spring and summer, but when the autumn leaves fall in a blaze of rich red and bronze, it takes on an altogether more subtle hue. Dainty flowers appear like clouds of swirling snowflakes among the branches, capturing the mood of the darker seasons. From mid-autumn to early spring the display ebbs and flows, depending on the weather; during mild periods, the tree can be filled with bloom and it's difficult to resist the temptation to cut a few sprigs to bring into the house. Plant it in the back garden and keep the secret to yourself or in the front against a dark background to highlight the pale flowers. Those passing by can share their beauty and it will bring a little warmth to cheer the winter gloom.

There are several forms of *P. subhirtella*, including 'Autumnalis Rosea' with deep pink flowers; 'Fukubana' with rose-madder flowers; and 'Pendula' which is a slender weeping tree flowering later, from early to mid-spring.

It likes a well-drained, moisture-retentive loam and thrives on chalk. It dislikes waterlogged conditions. Keep pruning to a minimum, remove dead, diseased, dying, crossing and rubbing branches or stems from mid-summer to early autumn to avoid silver leaf. Propagate by semi-ripe cuttings from mid-summer onwards. It comes under attack from aphids plus dieback and leaf spots, which are worse in wet seasons or if the plant is under stress. **MB**

Prunus x *subhirtella* 'Autumnalis'

Psidium cattleianum
STRAWBERRY GUAVA

Type: tender, evergreen shrub
Soil & situation: well-drained compost/sun/
under cover in winter
North American hardiness zone: 10–11
Height & spread: 3m (10ft)
Grow for: scented if crushed, attractive, neat,
evergreen leaves; cute, creamy, fragrant,
paintbrush-like flowers; dark red strawberry-
flavoured fruits

This is a little-known fruit, yet is so much better in
many ways than the usual guava (see next entry).
I grow both and although guava is more exotically
perfumed, as a fruit I want to eat more of the
strawberry guava. The dark red, almost purple-
black skin hides a pure white flesh with annoying
seeds but worth it for the strawberry-like taste.
The jam is superb. It is surprising this is not more
widely grown as it makes a decorative conservatory plant and is happy to go out on the patio
in summer. A large tropical genus of 50 or so
species with whitish, fragrant flowers and
sometimes edible fruits.

The strawberry guava is almost hardy, indeed I
have only killed three or four out of eight so far
finding out. It likes a well-drained compost and is
quite thirsty. It tends to over-crop and needs
thinning if you want bigger fruits. It can be cut
back hard in late winter and will regrow. The
seeds can be sown any time in the warmth and
are easy to grow on under cover. It suffers from
few problems. **BF**

Psidium cattleianum

Psidium guajava

Psidium guajava
GUAVA

Type: tender, deciduous shrub
Soil & situation: well-drained
compost/sun/undercover in winter
North American hardiness zone: 10–11
Height & spread: 3m (10ft)
Grow for: large laurel-like leaves; cute, creamy,
fragrant, paintbrush-like flowers; very big,
incredibly scented, creamy coloured fruits

This little-known fruit is occasionally seen in
supermarkets or on ethnic stalls, where it is dry
and mealy. Grown under cover in the UK it is
more exotically perfumed than any other fruit
and the fragrance will fill a large lecture hall – I
know, I've done it. The yellow or red pulp inside
the creamy skin is full of annoying seeds and the
stringy texture could be improved, but the flavour
is delicious. The jam is also excellent. The rough
bark also sheds totally every year, leaving beautiful
new bark as growth sets in again.

It is surprising the guava is not more widely
grown as it makes a very decorative conservatory
plant and is happy to go out on the patio in
summer. It is quick and easy from seed, which is
in every fruit at the supermarket. There are two
main sorts of guava: the pear-shaped, which I
prefer, and the apple-shaped, which has a greener
skin and redder flesh but is otherwise similar.

Guava is almost hardy. It likes a well-drained
compost and is unbelievably thirsty – in fact I
reckon it's the thirstiest plant I grow. It tends to
need thinning if you want bigger fruits. It can be
cut back hard in late winter and will regrow. The
seeds can be sown any time in the warmth and
are easy to grow on under cover. It suffers from
few problems other than mealy bugs, which can
be controlled with sponging. **BF**

Ptelea trifoliata
HOP TREE, STINKING ASH, WATER ASH

Type: hardy, low, spreading, deciduous tree or
large shrub
Soil & situation: fertile, well-drained, moisture-
retentive soil/sun or partial shade
North American hardiness zone: 5–9
Height: 8m (25ft)
Spread: 4m (13ft)
Grow for: fragrance, foliage and unusual fruits

It's a signature of all members of the plant family
Rutaceae that they have a strong odour from the
essential oils found throughout the plant; rue,
Citrus, *Choisya*, x *Citrofortunella* and *Ptelia* are all in
this group. Look at a trilobed leaf against the
light and you can see that it's dotted with oil
glands that emit a fragrance, particularly if they
are crushed or it's a hot sunny day. I say
fragrance, you say odour; I say sweet, you say
stink; it's one of those smells that people tend to
feel strongly about! I like it, but then you should
smell my aftershave!

Ptelea trifoliata

Clusters of small, yellowish, fragrant flowers appearing in early summer are followed by bitter-tasting, pale green, disc-shaped, winged fruits with a seed in the middle, which hang on the branches long after leaf fall and have been used as a substitute for hops. The unusual shape reminds me of something from outer space like the planet Saturn or the sherbet spaceships I used to eat as a child! They are excellent trees for shrub borders or as specimens in the garden with their spreading 'crown' and attractive foliage. *Ptelea trifoliata* 'Aurea' has soft yellow leaves which make a fine contrast to purple or dark green shrubs.

It prefers fertile, well-drained, moisture-retentive soil in full sun or partial shade, but tolerates most, including waterlogged soils. Prune in spring if necessary. Sow seeds in autumn or spring; take greenwood cuttings in early summer. **MB**

Pyracantha atalantioides

Pulmonaria 'Sissinghurst White'

Type: semi-evergreen perennial
Soil & situation: deep, rich moisture-retentive soils/shady position/will tolerate full sun
North American hardiness zone: 6–8
Height: 30cm (12in)
Spread: 45cm (18in)
Grow for: ground-cover plant with attractive spotted foliage; pure white spring flowers; AGM

I love the harmony of green and white in woodland or shady situations. It is always such a fresh and stunning combination. With this plant, you have just that – throughout the year there are its heavily spotted green and white leaves, and in addition, in spring you have its enchanting white flowers. Admittedly, only small rosettes of leaves are retained throughout the winter, but they are

Pulmonaria 'Sissinghurst White'

still a bonus. Thick clumps of new, hairy leaves come on the scene, just after the funnel-shaped white flowers have started to appear, in early spring.

There are many other good lungworts; another favourite of mine is *Pulmonaria rubra*. It is also semi-evergreen, as is *P. saccharata*. *P. rubra* has lime-green new leaves that appear just after the salmon-red flowers make their appearance. They are unspotted but large, and look superb with the flowers in spring. This plant seems more tolerant of dry conditions than many other pulmonarias.

When the flowers are going over it is worth shearing the entire plant to the ground, then handsome new foliage returns which will be more resistant to powdery mildew and look fresh for the rest of the summer. Plants respond well to dividing and replanting every three years or so after flowering. It is easily propagated by division or root cuttings in winter. **BG**

Pyracantha atalantioides
FIRETHORN

Type: hardy, evergreen conifer
Soil & situation: fertile, well-drained soil/full sun or partial shade
North American hardiness zone: 6–9
Height: 6m (20ft)
Spread: 3m (10ft)
Grow for: a mass of flowers in spring; clusters of berries in the autumn; makes a good hedge

As a free-standing plant this species would almost qualify as a tree. It forms a large, dense shrub plastered with flowers and then with fruit. Trained on a wall it quickly fills its allocated space.

The 7.5cm (3in) long, lance-shaped leaves are glossy and deep green. The panicles of white flowers appear in spring in sufficient numbers to cover the plant. They are followed in autumn by large clusters of bright orange-red berries. The berries will last well into the spring and may be still evident when the new flowers appear. If the old fruit trusses are still hanging, remove them to encourage new growth. In my experience the birds aren't particularly fond of these berries, but your feathered friends may have different tastes. *Pyracantha atalantioides* 'Aurea' is similar but has bright golden-yellow fruit.

P. atalantioides makes a great, dense, evergreen hedge – spiny enough to deter trespassers. Clip hedges in mid-summer. Trim shrubs for shape in winter and prune trained wall plants in spring, removing unwanted shoots before the flowers appear. After flowering, shorten the sideshoots to two to three buds from the older branches. Propagate by seed sown in autumn and stratified in a cold frame. Protect the top of the container to deter vermin. Semi-ripe cuttings root easily in summer in a heated propagator. Pot the rooted plants before they grow large. They dislike transplanting, so plant in their permanent place when small. Pyracanthas are prone to scab, which turns the fruit brown. Fireblight is a killer disease and this species is liable to come under attack. **JC**

Pyrus communis 'Doyenne du Comice'
PEAR

Type: hardy, deciduous tree
Soil & situation: rich, moist soil/sun
North American hardiness zone: 5–9
Height: 2m (6½ft)
Spread: 4m (13ft) wide espalier
Grow for: prolific white flowers in spring; large luscious juicy pears – better than you ever dreamt; AGM

I have chosen several apples, several plums, several grapes, but one pear. But what a pear: it is undoubtedly the supreme pear. There is none better and few even approach the wonderful 'Doyenne du Comice'. Pears from the shops are

Pyrus communis 'Doyenne du Comice'

but street harlots to this courtesan of emperors, unforgettable for its flavour, perfume and the melting texture as the succulent flesh dissolves in your mouth to a lingering sweetness. Damn and they're all eaten until next autumn! You may have had a good pear from a shop and it will have been a 'Comice'. But I'll warrant you've never tasted home grown. They can get huge and really ripe.

So let them ripen late into the autumn keeping birds away with nets; wait until the first ripe ones fall, then gather them gently and keep them in a warm, humid place. Watch them carefully, as they yellow up and perfume, take them into the kitchen and don't delay eating them, as by the following day they will have gone over.

Pears are natives of Europe and were well known to the ancients; Pliny lists over 40 varieties! However for centuries the most popular way of enjoying pears was cooking them. It was not until the 17th century that improvement really started to happen and the modern luscious dessert pear was born. French and Belgian gardeners developed most of those we love today. 'Doyenne du Comice' was bred in 1849 in Angers, France.

Pears are long lived and have fibrous rootballs, which means you can take them with you as they can be moved even late in life. They require a warm spot with a moist soil. They do best as espalier-trained trees on a wall, with a summer and winter pruning. Pears need a pollinator – I grow a *P. c.* 'Beurre Hardy', but a 'Glou Morceau' or 'Docteur Jules Guyot' would do instead and they are all good. Pears are too variable, too vigorous, too big and too long before fruiting to try to grow them from seed, so why have I grown one? And it's fruited, a bit like a *P. c.* 'Conference'. Pears need working on dwarf stock so buy one ready worked. They are rarely troubled by pests and diseases, suffering far less than apples. **BF**

Pyrus salicifolia 'Pendula'
WEEPING WILLOW-LEAVED PEAR

Type: hardy, deciduous tree
Soil & situation: well-drained soil/sun
North American hardiness zone: 5–9
Height: 5m (16ft)
Spread: 4m (13ft)
Grow for: silvery foliage and attractive flowers in mid-spring; AGM

This is one of my favourite trees for the small garden, perhaps it is because the foliage always reminds me of After Eight mints. There is no other

Pyrus salicifolia 'Pendula'

tree with foliage that has a soft sheen of minty green, apart from *Pyrus salicifolia*, the more upright species. The flowers too are very pretty, in clusters of creamy-white, with prominent dark anthers and, although somewhat camouflaged among the emerging foliage, they are a wonderful, uplifting sight. They are followed by tiny, rounded pears which seem somewhat incongruous on an ornamental plant. A few weeks after emerging, the leaves undergo a subtle transformation, losing the silvery covering from their upper surface. They are still the perfect foil for pastel-flowered climbers, particularly clematis like the deep carmine 'Ville de Lyon' that fades to mauve, the blue tones of 'Perle d'Azur' or the rich deep blue of 'Lasurstern'. The purple-leaved vine, *Vitis vinifera* 'Purpurea' (see page 319), also looks wonderful growing through this weeping pear. Although I have often seen it planted in borders, it makes a fine specimen tree, with its curtain of leaves falling to the ground without the impediment of surrounding shrubs.

It needs an open, sunny positon and thrives in most soils except very dry or waterlogged ones. It is very robust, tolerating atmospheric pollution, drought and excessive moisture. Prune carefully to retain the weeping habit, thinning the 'crown' in winter to prevent it from becoming too dense and untidy. Propagate by grafting or budding in late winter. **MB**

Quercus ilex
EVERGREEN OAK, HOLM OAK,
HOLLY-LEAVED OAK

Type: large, frost-hardy, evergreen tree
Soil & situation: a wide range of free-draining
soils/useful for coastal or windy areas/dislikes
extremely cold, inland areas
North American hardiness zone: 7–9
Height: up to 27m (90ft) but frequently less
Spread: to 20m (66ft)
Grow for: one of the most magnificent evergreen
trees that grows in the UK; AGM

This is a highly useful, structural, evergreen plant
that I have used in many different ways in many
different gardens, including my own. The glossy,
dark green leaves are pale green-grey beneath,
some holly-like and some hardly toothed at all,
depending on the clone, the growing conditions
and the age. At its simplest, and if you have the
space, it is a wonderful specimen tree with a
lovely rounded head of branches which eventually
become slightly hanging as it matures. Do not be
too concerned about the height: it tolerates any
amount of clipping, pruning and shaping. In
smaller gardens they can be pruned to form
useful mop-head trees like majestic giant bay
trees, or as I have them, shaped into 4m (13ft)
high sculptural pyramids. They will form stout
architectural hedges, pleached screens (hedges

Quercus ilex

Quercus rubra

on stilts) or may be clipped to form vertical 'walls'
to blot out eyesores.

They are not so slow growing: plant them small,
keep them weed- and grass-free for a good metre
(3ft plus) radius around their base, water them in
dry summer periods, and you will be amazed at
the rapid new growth in response. Perhaps use
some proprietary shelter guard in the first few
years till the roots get down and they have
acclimatized to the wind. I think this system
would get them to establish in colder inland areas
too. The best time to clip them is mid- to late
summer, after the first flush of growth.   **BG**

Quercus rubra
RED OAK

Type: hardy, deciduous tree
Soil & situation: deep, fertile, well-drained, acid
soil/full sun or partial shade
North American hardiness zone: 5–9
Height: 25m (80ft)
Spread: 18m (60ft)
Grow for: spectacular autumn leaf colour; AGM

There are so many good, reliable species of
Quercus but with the red oak you have the bonus
of outstanding autumn colour. It can vary from
year to year, sometimes a lazy yellow-orange yet
the following season a brilliant red.

It is a fast-growing tree with a spreading head.
The 20cm (8in) long, dark green leaves have
deeply cut lobes. In early autumn they turn to
buttery-yellow, orange, red and pale brown. Small
quantities of hemispherical acorns ripen in late
autumn. The variety *Q. rubra* 'Aurea' is slower
growing with bright golden-yellow leaves in spring
which gradually revert to green in summer.

Pruning may be necessary in its early years to
ensure a good spread of branches. In winter
remove crossing stems and those creating a
narrow angle. Young, well-grown plants may make
up to 1.5m (5ft) of growth in a season.
Propagation is by seed sown as soon as it is ripe in
a cold frame. Plant up the seedlings during their
first year. Alternatively the seed may be sown
outside in a sheltered seedbed covered with fine
wire mesh to prevent damage from mice and
squirrels.   **JC**

Vitis vinifera 'Purpurea'

Type: hardy, deciduous vine
Soil & situation: well-drained, marginally alkaline soil/sun or part shade
North American hardiness zone: 6–9
Height & spread: 7m (23ft)
Grow for: luscious foliage of purple leaves, at their richest at this time of year; liberally hung with ornamental black grapes in autumn; AGM

The leaves of this vine start off as a very pale purple-white and downy, then as they increase in size the purple colour intensifies until they are a good claret-purple before they fall. This slow but ever-changing colour enhances its appearance. Some purple-leaved plants have a heavy, heavy, look – very monotone and dark. This is has a dynamic look with subtle and unusual combinations of warm, pale lilac-greys, reds and purples all mingling together. The small purple-black grapes complete the picture in autumn. However, do not be tempted to indulge! They are no culinary treat – a feast for the eyes only. This plant is not a vigorous grower and may not reach anything like 7m (23ft), added to which it often seems to be unusually slow at getting going. In order to help it on its way expeditiously, cosset it with a warm wall. Better autumn colour is produced on poorer soils.

This is a versatile vine, suitable for pergolas, trellis, training through large shrubs or trees and, of course, for walls. If the allocated space is restricted, it can be pruned back to a permanent framework in mid-winter as for *V. coignetiae* (see page 393), or else you can leave it pretty much to its own devices, just cutting away any weak or dying growth in mid-winter. In mid-summer it may be necessary to cut back the odd long shoot that is straying too far.   **BG**

Reseda odorata

Reseda odorata
MIGNONETTE

Type: nearly hardy annual
Soil & situation: any soil/sun
North American hardiness zone: annual
Height & spread: up to 30cm (12in)
Grow for: one of the sweetest pot or border plants

I love this old-fashioned, out-of-fashion plant. Sure it is about as unimpressive and as scruffy a thing as you could grow, with odd brownish-yellow flowers, but the perfume is something else – just too nice with no sickly overtones. Delightful. And you can be very cunning with it: if you grow a good specimen in a pot and keep deflowering it, meanwhile training the main stem to a stick, it will grow and become a shrubby little tree and the next year will be an amazing mass of fragrance that will literally fill the greenhouse or conservatory.

The botanical name comes from the Latin *resedo*, meaning to heal, as it was once used for bruises. It was first introduced to the UK in 1752 from France but it came from North Africa and was called Mignonette d'Egypte, 'little darling of Egypt', because Napoleon sent seed to Josephine from his Egyptian campaign. It is the only one of five dozen species from the Mediterranean region to have fragrance, but it more than makes up for the rest of them.

Sow any time from spring to late summer, in clean soil *in situ* in a warm, moist, sunny border. Thin the plants to about 20cm (8in) apart and they will flower from mid-summer until autumn. Sow in pots in autumn and over-winter under cover and they will flower in spring.

It suffers from no problems whatsoever, but do avoid the more highly bred cultivars with showy flowers and less scent.   **BF**

Rhamnus alaternus 'Argenteovariegata'
VARIEGATED ITALIAN BUCKTHORN

Type: frost-hardy, evergreen shrub
Soil & situation: just about any soil/sun or part shade
North American hardiness zone: 7–9
Height: 5m (16ft)
Spread: 4m (13ft)
Grow for: a fairly fast-growing evergreen shrub; variegated foliage. AGM

This was one of the first variegated plants to be grown for commercial production, and this particular form has been recognized since the 17th century – strange to think Charles I might have come across it, as it does not look like an historical plant. As variegated plants go, it is difficult to improve on.

The leaves are fairly small, about 3cm (1in) long and narrow. They are a polished grey-green colour with irregular creamy-white margins. It is not a brash variegated plant, but quite subtle, though lively, not dissimilar to a hunkier version of *Euonymus fortunei* 'Silver Queen'. Its speed of growth and year-round appearance make it a valuable addition to a range of planting schemes.

Rhamnus frangula is the native alder buckthorn. It may form a small tree but more often is used as a shrub in natural, thicket-type plantings. It is not evergreen but when in berry is a beauty. The berries start red then change to black and when the plant displays both colours it is a fine sight. Apparently its wood makes the finest charcoal for gunpowder.

This plant does not move well and will form quite a substantial shrub if you let it, so try to get it in the

Rhamnus alaternus 'Argenteovariegata'

right place first time. The only pruning required is the removal of unhealthy or overcrowded wood, to keep it within bounds. This can be carried out in late winter to early spring.   **BG**

Rheum palmatum 'Bowles' Crimson'
CHINESE RHUBARB

Type: hardy, rhizomatous perennial
Soil & situation: moist, deep, humus-rich soil/sun or light shade
North American hardiness zone: 5–9
Height: 2.5m (8ft)
Spread: 1.8m (6ft)
Grow for: unbelievably huge leaves; striking flower spike; eye-catching form

I love big, leafy plants, especially those that have the decency to die down in winter, reappearing in spring with new, unfurling, banner-like leaves. A mature rheum plant forms a massive, thick, fleshy rootstock supporting many large 1m (3ft) long, palmate leaves. Coarsely toothed, with between three and nine lobes, they are dark green on the upper surface. The crimson underside of each leaf is covered in soft hairs. In early summer the plant sends up an enormous 1.8m (6ft) high, leafless flower spike made up of hundreds of small, star-shaped, deep crimson flowers.

This is a great perennial for growing close to or beside water. It loves the moisture and will repay your kindness with a memorable display of leaf and flower spike reflected in the water. It is tolerant of light shade and is a welcome addition to the woodland garden where it will light up a dappled glade.

An annual mulch of old, rotted farmyard manure in spring will encourage strong growth. Lift and divide the roots in spring, making sure there are fat buds on each root. Watch out for slug and snail damage to young, emerging leaves in spring. **JC**

Rheum palmatum 'Bowles' Crimson'

Rheum rhaponticum 'Victoria'
RHUBARB

Type: hardy, rhizomatous perennial
Soil & situation: any soil/sun or shade
North American hardiness zone: 3–7
Height: 1.2m (4ft)
Spread: 2.4m (7½ft)
Grow for: enormous leaves; red stalks; foamy pink and white flowerhead

Rheum rhaponticum 'Victoria'

Rhubarb is the first fruit of spring and is so sharp to the taste, yet such a pleasure when made into a crumble served with custard. The plant is often treated badly, yet still gives plenty of stalks. However, for the best stalks, treat it well. Start with a virus-free clone as it makes all the difference. And do remember to pull the stalks with a twist rather than cutting them so that they bleed less. The leaves make handy mulch mats.

Originally grown for its medicinal qualities, rhubarb as we know it is very much an English crop, not much admired elsewhere. It may have been unpopular until cheaper sugar enabled its use as a 'fruit', but its value as a gentle laxative was much appreciated in the 17th and 18th centuries. However the earliness of the crop gives it an advantage over other fruits, coming as it does months before most fresh fare. It grows wild in Siberia and did not reach Europe until 1608 when it was hoped to be a substitute for the dried *Rheum officinalis* imported from China. There are several other edible species more used for medicinal purposes. The names come from the Greek name *rheon*, for the drug, and *rha barbaron* for foreign rhubarb.

Ideally grow rhubarb in a sunny spot in a well-drained, well-composted soil where it will do well

and be long lived. Give it a mulch of well-rotted muck every winter. Put a bottomless bin over it in late winter full of loose straw to force the shoots up. Remove the flowerhead spike before seed is set. Some rhubarbs such as 'Glaskin's Perpetual' can be grown from seed but usually the crowns and roots are split in late winter or early spring and sections with a good bud planted. Rhubarb suffers virtually no problems. **BF**

Rheum ribes
RHUBARB

Type: hardy, rhizomatous perennial
Soil & situation: moderately heavy soil/sun or partial shade
North American hardiness zone: 6–8
Height & spread: 1.5m (5ft)
Grow for: unusual leaves and flowers in late spring and early summer

This unusual plant is found in western Asia from Turkey to Iran in dry gorges and among rocks; it's a typically robust, rugged rhubarb with a tough woody rhizome. The leaves are large, grey-green, warty and ribbed up to 40cm (16in) across; they look like sandpaper poppadoms that dry and rustle in the wind. The flowers appearing through the centre of the leaves are green and red, while the stems to 30cm (12in) are eaten raw or cooked by the people of Turkey and Iraq.

Leonhardt Rauwolf left Austria in 1573 to search for some of the plants mentioned by classical writers; while examining the cedars of Lebanon he found *Rheum ribes*, the 'true *Ribes* of the Arabians' and made a specimen for his herbarium. He noted its presence in a market and saw several piles of the roots of this rhubarb, 'hairy, almost two feet long, waiting to be shipped in large quantities to the Turks, especially the Sultan'; it was one of many species that were valued as a cathartic. One herbarium specimen at Oxford University Botanic Garden was noted as having been brought back from Lebanon and had been growing in Eltham, south London, since 1724.

It prefers a deep, fertile, moderate to heavy, humus-rich, moisture-retentive, well-drained soil in sun or partial shade. It thrives in clay and can be long lived. Propagate in autumn or spring from seed sown in a cold frame. Divide in autumn or early spring with at least one growth bud in each division. Pot up smaller divisions and grow on before planting out; larger divisions can be planted out immediately. It is prone to crown rot and can be damaged by slugs. **MB**

Rhododendron 'Christmas Cheer'

Type: hardy, evergreen shrub
Soil & situation: moist, well-drained, acid soil/light shade
North American hardiness zone: 6–8
Height & spread: 2m (6½ft)
Grow for: in mid-winter the mass of pale pink flowers brings welcome colour

While this variety of rhododendron doesn't live up to its name, it produces its flowers very early in the New Year. In a sheltered situation it is a mass of colour in mid-winter and will continue to flower until mid-spring. Even when the early blooms are damaged by frost there is a succession of others to follow. When pot-grown in a cool greenhouse or conservatory it will flower in time to provide 'Christmas cheer'. It forms a dense, compact plant with medium-sized foliage and trusses of 5cm (2in) long, funnel-shaped, pale pink flowers. When planting dig in as much leafmould and well-rotted farmyard manure as possible. Lighten heavy soil by adding coarse grit. All rhododendrons have their roots close to the surface of the ground so they dislike deep planting. An annual mulch of leafmould in spring helps to keep the surface roots moist.

Dead-heading immediately after flowering, before the seedpods appear, will allow flower buds to form for the following year. Remove the whole truss by snapping it off above the top pair of leaves. Take care not to damage the new shoots which will be produced on either side of the old flower stem. **JC**

Rhododendron 'Christmas Cheer'

Rhododendron 'Praecox'

Rhododendron 'Praecox'

Type: hardy, evergreen shrub
Soil & situation: moist, acid soil/sun or dappled shade
North American hardiness zone: 6–8
Height & spread: 1.3m (4½ft)
Grow for: colourful early flowers in late winter and early spring; AGM

I was walking in a garden when I saw it! There in a distant border, a glow of rose-purple pierced the gloom of a winter's day. I rushed over and grabbed the label and the writing confirmed what my eyes disbelieved, there, etched in white lettering were the words *Rhododendron* 'Praecox'. A rhododendron flowering in winter? I couldn't believe it but it was true! The young plant was smothered in clusters of wide, funnel-shaped flowers in twos and threes at the tips of the shoots. They were a much deeper colour in bud and looked superb highlighted by the deep green leaves. What an uplifting sight on a cold grey day! From the same parents comes 'Emasculum', the pale lilac-purple flowers alone or in pairs up to 3cm (1in) wide. Have a look inside the flower, it is sterile and has no, or aborted stamens. Taller and wider – to 1.8m (6ft) each way – it flowers two to three weeks later than *R.* 'Praecox'.

It needs moist, free-draining, acid soil in sunshine or dappled shade and must be protected from frost which damages the flowers. Improve the soil with peat substitute, leafmould or well-rotted organic matter. Mulch annually in spring; dead-head (if practical) after flowering using the forefinger and thumb rather than secateurs; keep moist in drought using rainwater. The flowers are vulnerable to frost so plant under the protection of trees or on a slope where cold air drains away. Propagate by cuttings in late summer from young shoots. **MB**

Rhodotypos scandens

Type: hardy, deciduous shrub
Soil & situation: any soil/sun or shade
North American hardiness zone: 5–8
Height: 2m (6½ft)
Spread: 1m (3ft)
Grow for: delicate white flowers from late spring to late summer

Some plants are regarded as rather coarse yet are amply redeemed by their positive features; *Rubus* x *tridel* 'Benenden' is one and *Rhodotypos scandens* is another. *R. scandens* is a close relative of bachelor's buttons (*Kerria japonica* 'Pleniflora') and was once known as *Kerria japonica alba*. In dull, green leaf it is barely given a second glance but in flower, oh, in flower, its character is simply transformed by the cloud of white 'butterflies' that cover it. Admire their shape and simplicity, the elegant curve of the silky smooth petals; even the sharply toothed leaves become the perfect, textured foil.

Suddenly the peasant becomes prince and the whole plant rejoices in harmony in its moment of fleeting glory. Then as the flowers fade, it declines into anonymity again and all that remains of its moment of splendour are shiny black berries. Next time you see it dull, green and dowdy, don't complain about its lack of finesse, just recall those moments of incomparable, fleeting beauty.

It is one of those plants that cheerfully endures the worst conditions. It is very hardy, tolerates any soil, heavy shade and low temperatures; you will often find it hidden in the corner of a woodland garden. Please don't abuse its good nature: provide dappled shade in well-drained, moisture-retentive soil, if you can. Prune after flowering, removing flowering stems to a vigorous outward-growing shoot and taking off a quarter of the older stems to the base. Feed with a slow-release general fertilizer in spring until established. It is easily propagated by hardwood cuttings in late winter. **MB**

Rhodotypos scandens

Rhus typhina 'Dissecta'

Rhus typhina 'Dissecta'
STAG'S HORN SUMACH

Type: hardy, deciduous tree
Soil & situation: moist, well-drained soil/full sun
North American hardiness zone: 3–8
Height: 3m (10ft)
Spread: 3–4m (10–13ft)
Grow for: brilliant autumn leaf colour with deep red fruit; AGM

Those who claim it to be a common plant should remember that is because it is popular. So what if it suckers? There will be even more magnificent autumn leaf colour and spare plants for friends. Sometimes called *R. t.* 'Laciniata', it forms a large, open, multi-branched plant. The young, velvety-red shoots resemble a stag's horns.

The 60cm (24in) pinnate leaves are made up of deeply cut, dark green leaflets. In autumn they explode into a brilliant orange-red colour which in dry ground, deepens with age, to scarlet. The 20cm- (8in-) long, erect panicles of green-yellow female flowers appear in summer and are followed by dense clusters of small, round, dark crimson fruit. While it will tolerate light shade, a position in full sun will ensure better autumn leaf colour.

Pruning back to older wood in late spring will generate new growth. Old, neglected plants may be hard pruned close to the ground. Strong shoots will grow from the base and may be thinned to avoid overcrowding. Give rejuvenated plants a high-potash liquid fertilizer, such as tomato feed, in late summer to harden up the new growths before the winter frosts.

Remove suckers by digging down to remove all of the roots otherwise they will reappear. Propagation is by seed in autumn. Semi-ripe cuttings root well in summer. Root cuttings inserted in compost in winter root quickly. Removing rooted suckers is the quickest and simplest foolproof method. **JC**

Ribes divaricatum
WORCESTERBERRY

Type: hardy, deciduous shrub
Soil & situation: any soil/sun or shade
North American hardiness zone: 3–7
Height & spread: 1.5m (5ft) by too much
Grow for: good informal hedge for anti-social demarcation line

God gave us worcesterberries for where barbed wire won't grow. This mean brute of a plant is superficially like a gooseberry bush without the softer, gentler aspects. It has horrible curved spikes of thorns prolifically covering every woody surface. It is a lax shrub with arching branches layering and multiplying into a witches' nest of suckers wherever they touch. It makes a wonderful informal hedge to put across a burglar prone fence or unwanted entrance way. The small flowers are insignificant but valuable to insects and the red gooseberry fruits make a delicious conserve – if you can pick them, that is....

The worcesterberry was always believed to be a native UK species or a natural hybrid, but it is now thought to be an American species or hybrid. This is a tough, hardy plant that will grow almost anywhere, but does best in full sun with good air circulation. It will live too long and is too self-fertile. Prune in late winter if you can get to the branches. Seed gives variable, often very thorny results but autumn hardwood cuttings are easy and layers work at almost any time of year. Worcesterberries suffer from the sawfly caterpillar, but it is best ignored as there are far too many thorns to even attempt to get rid of it. Mildew is not a problem. If you fall into a bush you may ask to be shot rather than pulled out without complete anaesthesia. **BF**

Ribes divaricatum

Ribes x *gordonianum*

Type: hardy, deciduous shrub
Soil & situation: any soil/sun or shade
North American hardiness zone: 6–8
Height & spread: 1.5m (5ft)
Grow for: masses of fiery red and yellow blooms early in spring; good autumn colour

I like *Ribes sanguineum*, the well-known flowering redcurrant, which is a good reliable early bloomer and marvellous for the first beneficial insects. Unfortunately the whole plant does have an aroma of cat pee, which many find offensive. *R.* x *gordonianum* is a hybrid that is more sweet smelling without the feline overtones, which makes it much more useful near the patio or front door. It also has a laxer habit which does take more space but is not so stiffly formal as its parent, *R. sanguineum*; it is thought to get this from its other alleged parent *R. odoratum* (see page 328). However the main reason I grow this shrub is for the flowers; coming a little later than the others, they burst into a blaze of beauty, each drooping fat raceme made of blooms a rich coppery-red on the outside with a yellow burning colour from within – stunning.

Ribes is a family made up of about 60 members and widely represented in both flower and fruit gardens. The botanical name may come from the Arabic *ribus* for acid, as most of the edible berries are very acid. Gordon was a London nurseryman who died in 1791; this plant was noticed as a seedling and introduced in 1837.

A tough, hardy plant that will grow almost anywhere, it can be pruned hard and will usually recover. As it is a hybrid, seed is not available but autumn hardwood cuttings are easy, or layer it at almost any time of year. It suffers from hardly any problems. **BF**

Ribes x *gordonianum*

Ribes grossularia 'Langley Gage'

Ribes grossularia 'Langley Gage'
GOOSEBERRY

Type: hardy, deciduous shrub
Soil & situation: any soil/sun or shade
North American hardiness zone: 6–8
Height & spread: 1.2m (4ft)
Grow for: masses of incredibly sweet white berries

God gave us gooseberries for where grapes won't grow. This old adage is so true: I struggle with grapes but the goosegogs just do it all so reliably. I have tasted countless and grown more than a dozen sorts myself, and none have been like those hard green bullets sold in the shops. In fact most gooseberries are green bullets initially, when they can be used to make good jams and tart tarts; however, if they are left to ripen they make fantastic dessert fruits every bit as good as dessert grapes. Of all of them this is my favourite, for though the berries are small they are honey sweet when they turn ivory-white. When they are ripe the contents liquefy and I bite the end off, suck out the sweet pulp and discard the skin.

Gooseberries should be the national fruit of the UK as we grow them far more than any other country. They were first mentioned in our records as being supplied to King Edward I in 1276 but we surely gathered them from the wild before then. We used to have competitions, which are still carried on in some places, to grow the biggest berries. These caused a great surge in the fruit's development, especially in the northwest of the UK, but the improvements reached their peak when one variety, 'London', won for decades on end from 1829 until 1867.

This is a tough, hardy plant that will grow almost anywhere, but does best in full sun with good air circulation. Plant three different ones as,

although self-fertile, it does better with others. It will die after 15 years. Prune in late winter leaving an open framework which makes it easy to reach the fruit; i.e. leave branches at least a hand's breadth apart or you'll swear. Seed gives very variable, usually extremely thorny, results but autumn hardwood cuttings are easy or propagate by layers at almost any time of year. Remove lower buds from cuttings to give a bare leg.

Gooseberries suffer from a sawfly caterpillar best watched for and eliminated when small – look for leaves in late spring that have many tiny holes and squidge the tiny caterpillars before they split up. Mildew occurs but open pruning, watering, mulches and good air ventilation control this. **BF**

Ribes laurifolium

Type: hardy, spreading, evergreen shrub
Soil & situation: moist soil/sun or partial shade
North American hardiness zone: 7–9
Height: 1.2m (4ft)
Spread: 1.5m (5ft)
Grow for: pale green flowers in late winter

My first introduction to this unusual plant was in a newly planted winter border, outside the ancient Ice House at Kew. My attention was drawn to a low-growing, loosely branched shrub with leathery leaves, reddish-coloured young stems and greenish-white flowers. The colour would have rendered them inconspicuous if they had appeared at any other time of the year, but what was extraordinary was that the curious pendent racemes were disproportionately large and looked as though they had been squeezed out of the thin branches like thick globs of glue.

Ribes laurifolium

I believe this plant is at its best when young. The coarse foliage gives it character. Male and female flowers are on different plants and you need both sexes to produce the black berries. Male plants have larger flowers with longer racemes. I've discovered that it is enhanced when planted with *Skimmia japonica* 'Rubella' or plum-purple hellebores. It's not beautiful, just fascinating and certainly not a typical 'flowering currant'.

Give it an open or partially shaded site, away from scorching sunshine and sheltered from cold winds to prevent leaf damage. It needs moisture-retentive, well-drained soil. It is slow to moderate in speed of growth and can take several years to become established. Pruning is not necessary apart from the removal of old, bare stems to encourage new shoots from the base. Propagate from semi-ripe or hardwood cuttings with a heel.   **MB**

Ribes nidigrolaria
JOSTABERRY, JOSTA

Type: hardy, deciduous shrub
Soil & situation: any soil/sun or shade, even boggy shade
North American hardiness zone: 6–8
Height & spread: 2m (6½ft)
Grow for: masses of incredibly tasty large red/black currants

This hybrid plant takes up a lot of room; it crops heavily, often giving over 4.5kg (10lb) of fruit per plant; it is immune to all the problems that can attack gooseberries or blackcurrants; it is self-fertile, easy to propagate and totally thornless. If you don't know it, you are missing out on the easiest crop of all. The fruits are large, red to black in colour and, although they are much like gooseberries, they have a blackcurrant flavour and make great jams and tarts.

The jostaberry or josta is a hybrid between a gooseberry and a blackcurrant. It has a higher vitamin C content than gooseberries and is more vigorous than either parent. It was developed by the Dutch only recently and has not yet become widely known. The plants are like blackcurrants but even bigger and tougher, hardy shrubs that will grow almost anywhere, they do best in full sun and on a rich, moist soil. They need to be left to grow unpruned with plenty of space as they have a lax habit, but they can be trained with perseverance. Seed gives variable results, but autumn hardwood cuttings are easy and inadvertent layers set themselves all the time. Do not remove lower buds from cuttings and plant deep to get multiple shoots from below ground level. Jostas suffer no

problems other than bird losses – though this can, admittedly, lead to a wipe-out! Although the leaves look as if they have all had a disease it is their normal state.   **BF**

Ribes nigrum
BLACKCURRANT

Type: hardy, deciduous shrub
Soil & situation: any soil/sun or shade, even boggy shade
North American hardiness zone: 5–7
Height & spread: 1.5m (5ft)
Grow for: masses of incredibly tasty fruits and scented foliage

Just writing this has got me craving some; I love blackcurrant jam, and if you don't grow these currants you don't know how good it can be. I pick the very biggest, sweetest berries first, then I roughly pick the rest not worrying too much how many sprigs or bits of leaf go in with the currants. I juice this rough-picked crop and having sieved it, I add in the choicest berries and organic sugar to make my conserve. It is almost like black cherry jam in the depth of flavour, but of course different with that blackcurrant aroma. Blackcurrants are also wonderful if dropped into sugar and rum in a bottle and then left to stand for a few months; once strained off this is as delicious as the jam.

Although a European native and common enough in the wild to have been gathered in a time of

Ribes nigrum

famine, blackcurrants were never much admired. They were picked for medicinal use, particularly for sore throats and were probably effective as they have a high vitamin C content. With the advent – from about the 18th century onwards – of cheap, plentiful sugar from the West Indies to sweeten their acidity, suddenly blackcurrants became popular as a jam for which they are now grown as a commercial crop. There are many varieties with almost no difference between them other than size and season.

Blackcurrants are tough, hardy plants that grow almost anywhere, but do best in full sun on a rich, moist soil. Plant three different ones as although self-fertile it does better with others. They need to be hard pruned: remove one third of the whole plant each year, taking the oldest branches out right down to the ground.

Seed gives variable, small-fruited results but autumn hardwood cuttings are unbelievably easy and layers work at almost any time of year. Do not remove lower buds from cuttings and plant deep to get multiple shoots from below ground level.

Blackcurrants do get mildew though not often badly, aphids can be a problem on the tips but worst of all they get big bud disease. The big buds can be pulled off in winter but the pest inside carries a virus disease to which the plants inevitably succumb. Thus it will not be worth growing the same plants after ten years or so as they deteriorate and it is better to replace them with new ones.   **BF**

Nicotiana sylvestris

Type: half-hardy annual
Soil & situation: moist soil/dappled shade or sun
North American hardiness zone: annual
Height: 1.5m (5ft)
Spread: 60cm (24in)
Grow for: stately form and fragrant flowers from mid-summer to autumn. On those hot, still evenings of early autumn the scent is a particular treat. AGM.

If you only plant one annual, this should be it. A classic since its introduction in 1898, it is stately and stylish with the imposing presence and aura of a plant that feels it should carry a royal warrant. It has a lush rosette of mid-green, broad basal leaves and tall stout stems topped with curved, pure white, narrow, trumpet-shaped flowers 8cm (3^1/$_2$in) long. They are clustered in dense cascades that combine to create a wonderful display of floral fireworks.

Despite its height it rarely needs staking and is wonderful in bold ranks at the back of a border, against a dark background like a yew hedge that highlights its beauty. There should be a perfectly placed bench nearby, where you can sit with a gin and tonic, close your eyes, relax and luxuriate in the light and warmth of the setting sun and savour the flowers' evening fragrance. Bliss!

It needs a fertile, rich, moist, well-drained soil in full sun or partial shade. Dig in plenty of well-rotted organic matter before planting. Plant in a sheltered position to prevent the fragrance from being lost on the breeze, along the edge of a path or by a window or door. For further ideas, see above.

Sow indoors from late winter to mid-spring. Sow the seed over the compost surface and press in lightly with a board. Water from below, using tepid water. Harden off and plant out when any danger of frost is over. Protect from slugs. Aphids are a problem. You should also beware of tobacco mosaic virus and destroy affected plants immediately. **MB**

Ribes odoratum

Ribes odoratum
BUFFALO CURRANT

Type: very hardy, deciduous shrub
Soil & situation: any soil/sun or shade
North American hardiness zone: 5–8
Height & spread: 1.5m (5ft)
Grow for: delicate leaf; pretty, scented, yellow flowers; edible fruit

As I said before, I like *Ribes sanguineum*, which is a good reliable early bloomer but is not sweet to smell. *R. odoratum* is an alternative: flowering a little later, it has a more delicate leaf of a light green, and the yellow primrose-like flowers have a delicious clove scent. I first came across it when working in old kitchen gardens and, at first, did not know why it was there. The reason it appeared in odd places is because it was used as a rootstock for other *Ribes*, such as gooseberries, which died and then the buffalo currant would appear instead. The black berries that sometimes set are reckoned edible and much esteemed, but I've not found them very good; perhaps the selected varieties available in America produce better fruit.

R. odoratum comes from North America, whence its common name, and was introduced to the UK in 1812. There is allegedly another similar form *R. aureum*, also called buffalo currant, with more golden leaves and edible berries.

This is a tough, hardy plant that will grow almost anywhere. It can be pruned hard and will usually recover. Seed is available and should be sown in spring, autumn hardwood cuttings are easy, or propagate by layering at almost any time of year. It suffers from hardly any problems. **BF**

Ribes rubrum
REDCURRANT

Type: hardy, deciduous shrub
Soil & situation: any soil/sun or shade
North American hardiness zone: 6–8
Height & spread: 2m (6½ft)
Grow for: scarlet, edible bird food

This is glorious to look at when in full fruit with masses of the brightest red berries. These are very acid, though if you net the bush and keep the birds and wet off they will hang into autumn, becoming sweeter. They can be juiced and made into wine, and their tart flavour makes other juices such as strawberry more tasty, as well as adding good colour, and they do the same for jams. If you want cherry, raspberry or strawberry jelly or jam to set, add redcurrant juice, and it's magic. The fruits are also great garnishes.

Ribes rubrum is a common native plant of Europe but it was not cultivated until the 16th century. Even then it was taken medicinally or as an apéritif because of the acid fruit. The arrival of cheap sugar made it more widely usable, but it is still only a minor crop. All red varieties are very similar, but there are white ones as well and these are excellent for making a clear acid jelly for a mint sauce or for embalming scented petals in; I do this with night-scented stock petals and the jelly retains the perfume until the gloom of winter calls for it.

R. rubrum is a tough, hardy, self-fertile plant that will grow almost anywhere; it even thrives on a shady wall. It can be pruned hard and will always recover, indeed it is excellent to practise on as it is very forgiving. Seed can be sown in spring with similar results to commercial varieties, autumn hardwood cuttings are easy, or it can be layered at almost any time of year. It suffers from hardly any problems except birds. If you don't net or cage your redcurrants you'll never get a single currant. Be warned – these go as fast as cherries. **BF**

Ribes rubrum

Ribes sanguineum 'White Icicle'

Ribes sanguineum 'White Icicle'

Type: hardy, deciduous shrub
Soil & situation: an easy shrub to grow in any fairly decent soil; a moisture-retentive but free-draining loam is ideal/full sun or part shade
North American hardiness zone: 6–8
Height: up to 2.5m (8ft)
Spread: 2m (6½ft)
Grow for: attractive, rich, juicy, green leaves; conspicuous white flowers in spring; AGM

I am not a fan of *Ribes sanguineum* generally, as I think it is dull for much of the year and am not even keen on it when in flower. But 'White Icicle' does definitely earn its keep. It is easy to grow, tolerates dry soils and has lively foliage which is a bright, almost yellow, green. The leaves seem to glow in a rather dull, semi-shaded spot. The charming flowers are large and a good, bright white, added to which the racemes are usually generously proportioned too. In spring it really comes into its own, flowering for a good long period and livening up the spring scene in a non-brash fashion, unlike its commoner stablemates.

This plant is easy to look after. After flowering you can cut back the old, flowering shoots to a strong bud. Once the shrub becomes well established it is worth thinning out the old growth – remove about a fifth of the old shoots by cutting them right back down to ground level. It is an exceptionally easy plant to propagate from hardwood cuttings in winter, but this variety is protected by Plant Breeders' Rights, so you cannot sell them for commercial gain. **BG**

Ribes speciosum
FUCHSIA-FLOWERED CURRANT

Type: hardy, semi-evergreen, free-standing or wall shrub
Soil & situation: well-drained, moisture-retentive soil/sun/shelter
North American hardiness zone: 7–9
Height & spread: 2m (6½ft)
Grow for: attractive foliage and dainty flowers in mid- and late spring; AGM

I often wonder if Archibald Menzies, the great plant collector, was as excited as I was when I first saw *Ribes speciosum* – the frisson of excitement has reverberated until this day! He discovered it on his travels as naturalist with Captain George Vancouver when he circumnavigated the world from 1791 to 1795. It's among the most elegant plants you'll ever see; the slender arching shoots are covered with red, gland-tipped bristles when young and tufts of shiny, round, lobed leaves seem to hover, like a cloud formation, along the top of the stems. Below, rows of tiny, rich red, fuchsia-like flowers hang like dainty pendant earrings along the branches. They are simply gorgeous, particularly when viewed through a magnifying glass, as are the tiny, bristly fruits. It is elegant and refined, everything about it is classy, so it's a real surprise to discover, (and do whisper it quietly) that it's a posh relative of…the gooseberry!

In mild climates grow it as a shrub or informal hedge; elsewhere, fan train along wires against a sunny wall. It may still lose its leaves in cold winters but is one of the earliest to break into leaf in late winter. It needs moderately fertile, free-draining soil. Use young shoots growing from the base to replace older stems and keep the plant vigorous. Prune in late summer, tie in new growth and remove in-growing shoots or any growing in the wrong direction. It propagates easily by layering; less so from semi-ripe cuttings. **MB**

Ribes speciosum

Ricinus communis 'Carmencita'

Ricinus communis
CASTOR OIL PLANT

Type: best treated as a half-hardy annual
Soil & situation: moist, free-draining soil/sun
North American hardiness zone: annual
Height: 1.8m (6ft)
Spread: 1m (3ft)
Grow for: bold foliage

The oil from the seed of this plant kept the Victorians going and does the same for cars; it is an additive in the engine oil Castrol (hence the name). Ricin, found in the seed coat, is highly toxic and six times more powerful than cyanide; it is a potential weapon for terrorists, yet is useful in medicine and used to target cancerous cells. Why am I recommending this potentially damaging plant? Because you will not be daft enough to eat it, will take sensible precautions when using the plant and storing its seed; most importantly, you'll appreciate its fine architectural foliage and upright growth. The female flowers appearing at the tips of the flower spikes have a bold red stigma. Remember, the whole plant is toxic.

Here are some of its varieties. 'Carmencita Pink' has red stems, dark green leaves and bright, deep pink seedpods; 'Carmencita' has red stems, dark brown leaves, and red flowers and seedpods; and 'Gibsonii' has dark, red-veined leaves. The foliage of 'Impala' is bronze-green and it has dark red flowers and scarlet fruit. 'Zanzibarensis' has large, green-veined leaves.

In cooler climates, grow as an annual in fertile, humus-rich, well-drained soil in full sun. Plants on poor soils tend to produce smaller leaves. Soak seed for 24 hours before sowing in late spring and pot on before the plants become pot bound to prevent premature flower production. Plant out when danger of frost is passed. In mid- or late spring, remove any shoots to maintain the shape; dead-head regularly unless seeds are required. Red spider mite can be a problem. **MB**

Romneya coulteri

Romneya coulteri
CALIFORNIAN TREE POPPY, MATILIJA POPPY

Type: frost-hardy subshrub, usually grown as a perennial
Soil & situation: free-draining loam/sunshine/in colder areas an ideal position is by a sunny wall/will withstand temperatures down to −10°C (14°F)
North American hardiness zone: 7–8
Height: 1–2.5m (3–8ft)
Spread: indefinite
Grow for: beautiful, elegant, papery, white flowers with yolk-yellow centres over a long period from summer to early autumn; glaucous foliage is an attraction too; AGM

This plant established rapidly on my thin soil, and although grown as a free-standing plant, has survived several winters so far. In my experience it has been easy to get going, but many gardeners find it awkward. I think establishing it from good, well-rooted plants in good-sized containers, at least 1 litre if not 3 litres, is the key. Their down-side is undoubtedly that if they take to you, they can rather overdo things and end up taking you over. In large drifts of perennials they can do this fairly extensively in a desirable fashion. They can jostle amongst other similar beings and produce a successful, thriving mix. Their habit is such that they look tremendous in that informal setting too.

Plant these poppies into ground that has been well prepared: deep digging with the incorporation of humus seems to help. If you want to limit these plants to a specific area, either surround them by shrubby plants to hold them back or else spade round them in spring – they hate root disturbance so this does limit them. In the autumn or spring cut down the top growth (most of this will be cut back by frost anyway) and the new growth in spring will produce highly attractive foliage. It is recommended that they are propagated by root cuttings in late winter or, usually more successfully, by removing suckers which have developed a good root mass in spring, together with some rootball if possible. **BG**

Rosa banksiae 'Lutea'
YELLOW BANKSIAN ROSE

Type: hardy, evergreen, shrub rose
Soil & situation: moist, acid soil/sun or dappled shade/sheltered position
North American hardiness zone: 7–9
Height & spread: 8m (25ft)
Grow for: fragrant flowers in late spring to early summer; AGM

Introduced in 1824 from China via the Calcutta Botanic Garden this elegant rose is named for Lady Dorothea Banks, the wife of Sir Joseph Banks, one of my horticultural heroes, the first 'unoffficial' director of Kew. A stunning specimen climbed the walls of a Victorian museum at Kew, and every year the topmost stems would squeeze through the gap in a second- floor sash window and bloom well before the rest of the plant. The slender shoots produce few spines and delicate leaves of up to five leaflets. The tiny, double, soft buttery-yellow flowers barely 2cm (³/₄in) across with a slight fragrance of violets, appear in small clusters, creating a cloud of soft yellow in late spring to early summer.

All the cultivars given below are also fragrant. 'Alba Plena' has slightly larger, double, white flowers. It was introduced to Kew from a garden in Canton, China in 1807. 'Lutescens' has single, yellow flowers. 'Normalis' has single, creamy-white flowers. Ernest 'Chinese' Wilson discovered *R. b.* 'Lutea' in central and western China; it is common in glens and ravines, forming tangled scrambling masses over low trees and scrub. It requires a warm position against a sheltered, sunny wall on moist, free-draining soil. It dislikes shade and is damaged by cold winds, making it unsuitable for shady gardens. It needs training against wires or

Rosa banksiae 'Lutea'

Rosa 'Buff Beauty'

other supports. Thin out old wood after flowering, tie in new growths in mid-autumn, and cut back frost-damaged shoots in mid-spring. Propagate by hardwood cuttings in late autumn. **MB**

Rosa 'Buff Beauty'
BUSH ROSE

Type: hardy, deciduous, shrub rose
Soil & situation: most soils/sun or shade
North American hardiness zone: 6–9
Height: 1.5m (5ft)
Spread: to 3m (10ft)
Grow for: prolific, scented, apricot-buff coloured flowers all summer covering glossy dark foliage; reliable; AGM

This is the rose for those who want trouble-free gardening. It is incredibly healthy and makes all the others look miffy beside it. The foliage is glossy and dark. The plant is so floriferous that it covers its own foliage completely with masses of blooms. And it is repeat flowering with a main show in summer and another in autumn. The only drawback is somewhat brittle stems that are hard to train.

This is one of the hybrid musk roses now reclassified as a cluster-flowered shrub rose. I prefer the old grouping as it sounds better. These were developed after the First World War from *R. moschata* and with their shiny dark foliage and fragrance are good choices with members such as *R.* 'Moonlight' and the vigorous *R.* 'La Mortola'. Roses prefer a rich, heavy, moist soil that stays cool but never gets waterlogged. They will grow in shade but are rarely very long lived anywhere. This one does best as a free-standing shrub and can be fairly hard pruned. Deadheading is important, as is pruning out diseased wood. This is a hybrid and cannot be grown from seed, but autumn hardwood cuttings are easy. It does not get either blackspot or mildew attacks very often. **BF**

Rosa canina
COMMON BRIER, DOG ROSE

Type: deciduous, shrub or scrambling rose
Soil & situation: most soils/sunshine or dappled shade
North American hardiness zone: 3–7
Height: 4m (13ft)
Spread: 1.8m (6ft)
Grow for: attractive flowers and autumn/winter fruits

It may be the most common wild rose in the UK and a familiar sight in hedgerows and banks, but it is still charming and worthy of inclusion in wildlife areas or infomal hedging. I have planted some among a 'fruiting' hedge containing British natives like elder, hazel, honeysuckle, viburnum and sloe. I'm hoping that the local wildlife gives me a chance to share its bounty: hazelnuts, sloes for gin and elderberries for wine. Dog rose will clamber through nature's supporting cast presenting cascades of pale to blush-pink, sweetly scented flowers in early and mid-summer from arching thorny stems. They are followed in autumn by orange-red hips which are rich in vitamin C. The varied form of the sepals gave rise to a Latin riddle translated thus: 'Five brothers in one house are we, all in one little family, two have beards and two have none and only half a beard has one.' What am I? A dog rose!

Rosa canina hybridizes with all the other native species. 'Abbotswood', a chance hybrid (possibly with *R. gallica*), has scented, double pink flowers. 'Andersonii' is a deep pink, larger-flowered form with fewer thorns and bright red hips. 'Hibernica' (*R. pimpinellifolia* x *R. canina*) is massed with rose-pink flowers and long-lasting hips.

R. canina is tolerant of most soils and sites, but dislikes waterlogging and needs sunshine or dappled shade. Prune to keep under control; older stems can be cut hard back in spring if needed. Propagate by seed in spring or hardwood cuttings in late winter. **MB**

Rosa canina

Rosa 'Charles de Mills'

Rosa 'Charles de Mills'

Type: hardy, deciduous, shrub rose
Soil & situation: fertile, moist, well-drained, loamy soil/full sun or light shade
North American hardiness zone: 4–9
Height: 1.5m (5ft)
Spread: 1.2m (4ft)
Grow for: unforgettable flower colour and perfectly formed blooms; AGM

The flowers of this stunning rose are unusual in shape, colour and fragrance. It is long lived and well behaved – what more could you want? The origins of this Gallica rose are unknown.

It forms an upright, bushy shrub with arching stems, barely capable of holding the heavy heads of flowers. The mid-green leaves remain fresh and clean for most of the season. In mid-summer the pink buds open to 10cm- (4in-) wide, fully double flowers with wavy magenta petals with small pink and white blotches. The open flowers have a slightly flattened appearance and are quartered. The heady fragrance is a little spicy.

Pruning, in early spring, consists of getting rid of the old stems as close to the base as possible and removing crossing branches. Applying a high-potash liquid fertilizer or foliar feed in summer will strengthen the flowering stems. Feed with a rose fertilizer containing trace elements in spring. Propagation is by hardwood cuttings inserted in open ground in early winter. **JC**

Rosa 'Cooperi'

Rosa 'Cooperi'
COOPER'S BURMESE ROSE

Type: frost-hardy semi-evergreen, climbing rose
Soil & situation: moisture-retentive, free-draining soil/sun/shelter
North American hardiness zone: 5–9
Height & spread: 10m (33ft)
Grow for: beautiful, single, white flowers from late spring to early summer

This rose was introduced to the UK by Roland Cooper who was Superintendent of the Maymyo Botanic Garden in the Shan Hills of Burma from 1921 to 1927, and later became curator of the Royal Botanic Garden in Edinburgh. He sent seeds of Burmese plants to Lady Wheeler Cuffe in Ireland who, in October 1921, gave seeds of an unnamed rose to Glasnevin, Dublin's National Botanic Gardens, and some of these must have been sent to Kew where a plant flowered in the 1930s. Cooper could not remember from where they were gathered, though they were sent so soon after his arrival that they were probably collected from a plant in Maymyo known as *Rosa gigantea* and is regarded as a hybrid between this and *R.laevigata*. Whatever its origins, it's a beautiful white rose with large, 10cm (4in) across, scented flowers and pale brown stems and glossy foliage, which makes the perfect background for the flowers. It may flower from mid-summer, depending on the seasonal weather.

This definitely is a rose for a warm, sunny, sheltered wall in suitable microclimates and the southern counties of the UK as it is fairly tender. It needs moisture-retentive, free-draining soil. Prune in spring to keep within its allotted space and to remove winter-damaged stems. Propagate by sowing seed in spring or taking hardwood cuttings in late winter. **MB**

Rosa 'Dublin Bay'

Type: hardy, deciduous, climbing rose
Soil & situation: fertile, moist, well-drained, loamy soil/full sun
North American hardiness zone: 5–9
Height & spread: 2.5m (8ft)
Grow for: can't beat this rose for its wonderful flowers covering a wall or trellis; AGM

Of all the climbing roses this is my long time favourite. Introduced in 1976 it has stood the test of time and is still widely available in catalogues when other 'fantastic' varieties haven't lasted a decade.

Strong stems carry an abundance of glossy, dark green leaves. The rich, crimson, fragrant flowers are fully double and beautifully formed with each petal slightly down turned. The colour is consistent with no fading or blemishes on the outside petals. It is repeat flowering, carrying blooms from early summer through to autumn. Like most roses it is tolerant of a range of soil types, preferring a heavy clay or loamy soil to light, sandy ground or, at the other extreme, waterlogged conditions. Roses cannot be planted where there have previously been roses. A condition known as soil sickness will result in weak growth on plants which will never succeed.

Rosa 'Dublin Bay'

Pruning involves the removal of dead or old stems and crossing branches. This climber has a habit of growing as a bush instead of sending up strong shoots. When this occurs, hard prune the stems and train in the new growth. Arching the shoots over and tying them to wall wires or trellis will result in many more flowering sideshoots. Dead-head regularly, cutting two leaves below the old flower. Remove suckers as they appear, pulling them off where they join the stem or root. Cutting will encourage more suckers to grow from the stump. Apply a rose fertilizer containing trace elements in spring and surface mulch with composted bark or old, well-rotted farmyard manure to retain moisture. Propagate by hardwood cuttings inserted in open ground in early winter. **JC**

Rosa 'Etoile de Hollande'

Rosa 'Etoile de Hollande'
SCENTED ROSE

Type: frost-hardy, deciduous, shrub rose
Soil & situation: most soils/sun or shade
North American hardiness zone: 5–9
Height: 1.5m (5ft)
Spread: to 2m (6½ft)
Grow for: heavily fragrant, large, dark red flowers

This is a poor doer compared to some, but the colour of the summer flowers is magnificent and the fragrance heavy and intoxicating. I feel compelled to bury my face in a ripe bloom – the perfume is almost edible. I often tear a bloom to pieces and use it in salads and rice puddings.

The hybrid tea group, to which this belongs, is relatively recent and one of the largest with over

Rosa 'Ferdinand Pichard'

permanently covered with black spot, mildew and the like. Not so! What is more, it has a good bushy shape and the foliage is a fresh, light green. It repeat flowers, the only striped rose apart from the diminutive rose, 'Stars 'n' Stripes', to do so. The flowers produce a good, old rose fragrance which, as with all perfumes, lingers longer if it is sited in a sheltered spot.

Like all roses, it performs far better if grown in a good, fertile soil. On planting, generous quantities of well-rotted manure and compost are advisable on all but the best soils. A good mulching of well-rotted manure helps each winter, though the inevitable weeds that come along for the ride are a pain. I have switched to chicken manure and a mulch of organic matter, such as produce from my shredder, in a bid to rid my garden of weeds. We can live in hope!

Dead-heading helps produce further blooms and improves appearances. Planting amongst other plants, rather than in designated rose gardens, makes a huge difference in helping to reduce the incidence of many common rose pests and diseases. Prune as for *R.* 'Marie Pavie' (see page 335). **BG**

Rosa 'Golden Celebration'

Type: hardy, deciduous, shrub or climbing rose
Soil & situation: sun or light shade/ideally a humus-rich, well-draining but moist soil with a pH of around 6.5/grows satisfactorily in more acid or alkaline soils
North American hardiness zone: 4–9
Height & spread: 1.2m (4ft)
Grow for: rich golden-yellow flowers; repeat flowers throughout the summer; fantastic fragrance; a good 'full' shape – the sort you would not want for yourself but love in a rose; AGM

This rose is one of the most magnificent of the 'English roses' which have been bred by my uncle, David Austin. These shrub roses have many characteristics of the old roses, i.e. form, character and growth, but they have the repeat-flowering habit and the wider colour range of modern roses – a useful combination of characteristics – good-looking and hardworking. I think that this is one of his finest. Firstly, and for me most importantly as I am often working in gardens with less than perfect soil, it does well wherever you plant it. In addition it has healthy growth, with ample foliage, few thorns and a good rounded, but slightly arching, shape; the perfume is 'a combination of a sauterne wine and strawberry' – you want to drink it in

3,500 varieties! They were originally said to have the fragrance of tea, which is not a great compliment, and they are also criticized as being scentless. One survey found that indeed a quarter had no scent but nearly as many were highly scented, so you just have to choose carefully. This beauty was introduced in 1919.

Ideally roses prefer a rich, heavy, moist soil that stays cool but never gets waterlogged. It will grow in shade if it is open but is rarely very long lived anywhere. Dead-heading is important, as is pruning out diseased wood. It gives most flowers as a bedding rose. It is a hybrid and cannot be grown from seed, but autumn hardwood cuttings are easy. This rose suffers the usual problems and is to be honest a bit miffy, but the fragrance more than makes up for it. **BF**

Rosa 'Ferdinand Pichard'

Type: hardy, deciduous shrub rose
Soil & situation: good, moist but well-drained soil/full sun or part shade
North American hardiness zone: 5–9
Height: 1.5m (5ft)
Spread: 1.2m (4ft)
Grow for: the most beautiful, repeat-flowering striped rose: flowers have a pink background which is splashed and striped with crimson, the pink gradually fading to white while the crimson flashes intensify; AGM

This is my favourite rose. If you saw it on a chintz tablecloth you would assume the designer had had a flight of fancy then, when you discovered it was real, you would assume that it was a weedy, picky number that was awkward to grow and

Rosa 'Golden Wings'

deeply when you pass by; and the colour is a rich golden-yellow. As with many of the 'English roses', if planted against a wall or fence it will climb and can easily make 2.5m (8ft), especially in a warm position. It will form an excellent standard rose too.

As with all roses, regular dead-heading keeps them looking their best and also hastens the repeat flowering. If you wish to restrict the size of the plant you can cut back about 30cm (12in) of the plant at any time during the growing season. In countries with warmer, longer summers than the UK this works particularly well.

The pruning of this rose is simple, and best done in late winter. Firstly you remove all weak, dead, dying or diseased growth, then you reduce all the growth back by one-third to two-thirds its length. In colder climates than the UK this can be carried out just as the spring growth is starting.   **BG**

Rosa 'Golden Wings'

Type: hardy, deciduou, modern shrub rose
Soil & situation: as for *Rosa* 'Golden Celebration' (see previous entry)
North American hardiness zone: 4–9
Height & spread: 1.5m (5ft)
Grow for: large, almost single, sulphur-yellow flowers throughout the summer and into mid-autumn; longer in warmer climates than mine! AGM

These, simple, charming, scented roses are produced on a spreading bush with many prickly stems, and good, pale green leaves. The flowers, which fade as they age, are up to 13cm (5in) across with conspicuous brown stamens in the centre which stand out beautifully against the yellow. There are few good single-flowering roses, despite the fact that nature made them that way, and yet they are indispensable in the garden, particularly in more natural areas. This productive rose has something of the charms of a wild species and so is ideal for the wilder areas. It

will also make an excellent medium-height hedge, forming a pretty, impenetrable barrier, either mixed with other hedging plants or on its own.

Plant and mulch as for *R.* 'Ferdinand Pichard' (see page 333). This rose's habit does tend to be fairly open, rigid and poker-like. When you prune it, bear this in mind and try to encourage a more branching, bushier form by reducing the more stick-like growth. Dead-head as needed.   **BG**

Rosa 'Gruss an Aachen'

Rosa 'Gruss an Aachen'

Type: frost-hardy, deciduous, shrub rose
Soil & situation: as for *Rosa* 'Golden Celebration' (see page 333)
North American hardiness zone: 5–9
Height & spread: 1m (3ft)
Grow for: excellent, repeat-flowering, small shrub rose which will bloom from early summer to mid-autumn; large and lovely pale pink, fading to white flowers; good bushy foliage

These are the 'white' roses which are grown in the White Garden at Hidcote, chosen no doubt, even though they do not strictly conform in colour, for their magnificent flowering performance. The blooms start off a pearly pink and later fade to a creamy white. The individual flowers are up to 8cm (3½in) across and deeply cupped. The petals, having a silky texture, have bags of typical 'old rose' character. The plant itself is a robust grower with an erect, but bushy, habit and dark green foliage. It will grow well even in less than perfect rose soils.

Treat this rose as for *R.* 'Golden Celebration' (see page 333)   **BG**

Rosa longicuspis

Type: half-hardy, vigorous, semi-evergreen, rambling rose
Soil & situation: moist, free-draining soil/sun/shelter
North American hardiness zone: 5–9
Height: 10m (33ft)
Spread: 5m (16ft)
Grow for: attractive young shoots, leaves, flowers from mid-summer and fruits

The one in my garden is the true *Rosa longicuspis*, not *R. mulliganii* which is often sold under that name. This species, collected by Frank Kingdon-Ward in the Naga Hills of northeast India is also found in east Nepal and west China. It is very dense and vigorous; in spring you can almost see the stems growing, threatening to engulf anything in their path. I'm sure that somewhere in the middle of mine, Sleeping Beauty awaits her handsome prince! The stems, their hooked thorns (be warned, *longicuspis* means 'long pointed'!) and young leaves are an extraordinary reddish-brown when they first emerge with bronze-tinted young shoots, and look as though they have been dipped in lacquer. The leaves are made up of small, attractive, grey-green leaflets. The open clusters of as many as 15 single flowers, up to 5cm (2in) across, are cream in bud, opening to white, with yellow stamens and a banana fragrance. They are followed by orange-red fruits which decorate the plant through the winter.

It is slightly tender but flourishes in my Hertfordshire garden in a sheltered, east-facing location, on moisture-retentive, free-draining soil. Grown against a warmer, sunnier wall it would reach even greater heights. It enjoys clambering up trees or over buildings. Prune if necessary in spring to keep tidy. Beware of the thorns: use eye protection, wear gauntlets and a long-sleeved jacket! If possible, put the trimmings straight into a shredder before they can cause any harm. Propagate by seed in spring and hardwood cuttings in late winter.   **MB**

Rosa longicuspis

Rosa 'Mermaid'

Rosa 'Madame Alfred Carrière'

Rosa 'Madame Alfred Carrière'

Type: hardy, deciduous, climbing rose
Soil & situation: humus-rich, well-draining but moist soil/pH of around 6.5/grows best on a sunny wall, but performs well in any aspect
North American hardiness zone:
Height: 5m (16ft)
Spread: 3m (10ft)
Grow for: the best, reliable, repeat-flowering, hardy, white climber; AGM

This rose was bred in France by Schwartz and introduced in 1879. Sometimes the old ones are the best, and even today, most gardeners would agree that there is no rose as yet to rival its performance. The flowers, which are produced continually; are white flushed shell-pink, large and highly perfumed with a sweet, true rose scent. The foliage is bold and produced in copious amounts by this strong-growing climber, which will grow up to the eaves of a two-storey house on any aspect. It is also reliably free from disease. What more could you ask?

'Madame Alfred Carrière' does require fairly careful training. Her growth tends to be a little stiff and vertical so it may be necessary to encourage more horizontal growth. Although she is often seen growing against walls and is frequently at her finest in that position, she is also useful for growing over large pergolas, into an old tree or over an arbour. **BG**

Rosa 'Marie Pavie'

Type: hardy, dwarf polyantha rose
Soil & situation: will do better than many roses in less than favourable conditions/copes reasonably well on lighter, freer-draining soils/sunny position
North American hardiness zone: 5–9
Height & spread: 45cm (18in)
Grow for: non-stop, blush-white flowers in summer

The dwarf polyantha roses have *Rosa multiflora* in their parentage. *R. multiflora* is also the parent of many rambling roses and, as a result of this, their flowers are similar to those of a rambler. The dwarf polyanthas are very tough and hardy, as is *R. multiflora*, and as the parent name suggests they have an amazing capacity to produce copious blooms with continuous regularity. 'Marie Pavie' (sometimes also known as 'Marie Pavic') has tightly packed clusters of delicate, fresh, blush-white flowers which are one of the most appealing of this floriferous group – in both quality and quantity. The plant has an excellent bushy form so is highly useful for planting in groups to form good wedges of almost continuous summer colour in the front of borders.

Caring for this rose is generally as for *R.* 'Ferdinand Pichard' (see page 333). 'Marie Pavie', like most roses, benefits from annual pruning. For 'Marie Pavie' (and most repeat-flowering shrub roses), this is best carried out by initially removing any weak, dead or diseased growth. Remaining healthy growth can then be reduced by between one-third and two-thirds of its length. This is best done in winter or late winter, except in areas where very cold winters occur, when this should be carried out just as growth begins in spring. **BG**

Rosa 'Marie Pavie'

Rosa 'Mermaid'

Rosa 'Mermaid'

Type: half-hardy, semi-evergreen, climbing rose
Soil & situation: moist, free-draining soil/flourishes on sunny walls, tolerates shade
North American hardiness zone: 6–9
Height: 9m (30ft)
Spread: 6m (20ft)
Grow for: foliage and flowers from summer to autumn; AGM

This is often decribed as a classic, and rightly so. Choose its location carefully – it's a vigorous climber/rambler with long stems. The young wood is maroon coloured with large hooked thorns in pairs so it's a relief that regular heavy pruning isn't necessary. The foliage is rich glossy green, it is evergreen in shelter or warm climates but may lose its leaves in severe weather; this too should influence your choice of site. It flowers right through the summer into autumn, producing an almost constant stream of large, delicately fragrant, single flowers which can reach a massive 15cm (6in) across and are soft, rich lemon or sulphur-yellow with mahogany-coloured stamens. They seem to increase in quality and quantity as the season progresses, especially during warm summers. This really is a refined plant.

This is definitely a rose for a sheltered, sunny wall as it is slightly tender; however, it tolerates some shade with reduced performance. Do not plant in exposed positions where cold winds can cause dieback. Grow in moist, well-drained soil, and mulch in spring with well-rotted organic matter. Prune sparingly, to keep under control; remove old or frost-damaged wood in spring. Tie in shoots of wall-grown plants in autumn. Beware of the thorns: as with *R. longicuspsis*, wear eye protection, gauntlets and a long-sleeved jacket! If possible, put the trimmings straight into a shredder before they can do any harm. Propagate by hardwood cuttings in late autumn. Very disease resistant. **MB**

Rosa 'New Dawn'

Type: hardy climbing rose
Soil & situation: good moist, fertile but well-drained soil/ sun or part shade
North American hardiness zone: 5–9
Height & spread: 3m (10ft)
Grow for: excellent, repeat-flowering climber with pale pink, fragrant roses from summer to autumn; AGM

This was the first rose ever to receive a patent and nobody would go to all that trouble unless they had a gem. One of its outstanding assets is its repeat-flowering capacity. The pretty, pearly-pink flowers are produced in large clusters for a really long period. They smell good too, with a strong, sweet fragrance. The other asset is disease resistance. Its mass of shiny, mid-green leaves are produced in quantity and nearly always look in tip-top condition. Its habit is gently arching. Its use is not restricted to being trained up pillars, posts, walls, over low roofs and the like, as it can be grown as a hedge or pruned to form a free-standing shrub.

If you are training this climber up pillars, to avoid getting purely vertical growth, which can lead to flowers at the top only, it is recommended that the shoots are trained around the support in a spiral formation encouraging the roses to be produced along the stems.

A climbing rose is made up of the long main stems, which you train up and along the structure, and the short, sideshoots coming off the main stems which produce the flowers. As the main stems become crowded you remove the weakest, oldest ones, cutting them to about 30cm (12in) above ground, removing one or two main stems every one to three years. The sideshoots you just reduce back to about 7cm (2¾in). The best time to do this is late winter or early spring. For the first couple of years all you need to do (apart from watering in dry periods) is to remove dead and diseased growth and start tying it in to a support system. Otherwise dead-heading, annual mulching and regular feeding all help.   **BG**

Rosa 'New Dawn'
plant of the week (see page 337)

Rosa 'Phyllis Bide'

Type: hardy, semi-evergreen, rambling rose
Soil & situation: good moist, fertile but well-drained soil/in sun or part shade
North American hardiness zone: 6–9
Height & spread: 2.5m (8ft)
Grow for: clusters of small flowers, repeat flowering; fragrant apricot-yellow flowers tinged with pink; AGM

This is a charming, dainty rambler that is ideal for growing up 2–3m (6½–10ft) supports such as pergolas, fences, tripods and similar structures. This rose will reach the top but will not go rampaging on to towering heights, getting out of hand; with a bit of help, it will flower from top to bottom. It is a vigorous grower with fairly lax, mid-green but shiny leaves. The sprays of small (5cm/2in) double flowers are produced in summer and will carry on flowering well into autumn.

It is worth enriching the soil with lots of well-rotted organic matter prior to planting. Watering in dry periods during the first couple of years after planting really helps get it going, especially if it is planted at the base of a house wall. Regular mulching and feeding always pay big dividends.

Rosa 'Phyllis Bide'

Generally you just leave rambling roses without pruning them, only removing old wood when it becomes too dense to encourage renewal. Otherwise just give them their head and let them go; the less you do, the better they are. If you do need to constrain their growth they can be pruned as you would a climber (see *R.* 'Golden Celebration, page 333). Dead-heading is also worthwhile.   **BG**

Rosa rubiginosa

Rosa rubiginosa (syn. *R. eglanteria*)
SWEET BRIAR

Type: hardy, vigorous, climbing/rambling rose
Soil & situation: most soils/sun
North American hardiness zone: 4–9
Height: 3.5m (11ft)
Spread: 2.5m (8ft)
Grow for: fragrant foliage and delicate flowers

Few plants are grown specifically for the fragrance of their foliage but this is one of them. The upright, prickly stems are covered in dainty leaves composed of five to nine rounded leaflets deliciously scented of apples. Clusters of simple, clear pink flowers about 4cm (1½in) across punctuate the arching branches in mid-summer and are followed by bright red, oval fruits that last well into the winter. The fragrance is most intense after a shower of rain and whenever the atmosphere has been refreshed. If trained up trellising or grown near a window it can scent the whole house. It can be left free to scramble through a hedgerow or be the hedge itself growing up to 2.5m (8ft) tall, though it is usually kept smaller. It is better clipped each spring before growth begins to encourage young growth that exudes the strongest scent. It also makes a strong-growing shrub.

It has been cultivated for centuries and there were many varieties listed in 19th-century catalogues. Double-flowered hybrids have been cultivated since the 17th century, two raised before 1800 are still available and nurseries stock many varieties. It is one of the parents of the 'Penzance Briars' raised from 1884 onwards by Lord Penzance, who crossed this with other species and garden varieties.

Rosa rubiginosa can grow in a range of soils but prefers one that is moisture retentive and free draining; avoid waterlogged conditions. It flourishes in full sun but tolerates some shade. Propagate by seed in spring, hardwood cuttings in late winter.   **MB**

Rosa rugosa 'Alba'
RAMANAS ROSE, HEDGEHOG ROSE

Type: hardy, deciduous, shrub rose
Soil & situation: moist, well-drained soil/full sun or partial shade
North American hardiness zone: 2–9
Height: 2–2.5m (6–8ft)
Spread: 2.5m (8ft)
Grow for: it makes the most perfect hedge

Grown as a hedge this plant is not only sturdy and dense but, in flower, is spectacular. This is a vigorous-growing rose with prickly stems. The dark green, leathery leaves are heavily wrinkled and made up of seven to nine leaflets, each 5cm (2in) long. The 10cm (4in) wide flowers are pure white opening from pink buds. Single, cupped, fragrant flowers with golden stamens appear from early summer to autumn. These are followed by large, tomato-shaped, orange-red hips.

Rosa rugosa 'Alba'

Rosa rugosa is not a fussy plant and will enjoy most soils except those which are waterlogged. Never plant in soil which has previously grown roses. Prune by cutting out the older stems as close to the ground as possible. Flowers are produced on new growths and two-year-old stems. Avoid the temptation to trim the plant lightly, as this causes the new growths to form higher up, close to where it was cut. Old, neglected hedges and individual plants can be rejuvenated by cutting the whole plant in winter or early spring to within 20cm (8in) of the ground. Water and feed with a high-nitrogen liquid fertilizer to get the plants going again. In late summer apply high-potash fertilizer to harden up the growth before winter.

Propagation is by seed, stratified over-winter and sown in spring. Some of the resulting plants will be white flowering but most will be mauve and shades of pink. Hardwood cuttings taken with a heel in winter will root outside in the open ground. **JC**

Rosa sericea subsp. *omeiensis* f. *pteracantha*
WINGED THORNED ROSE

Type: hardy, vigorous, upright, deciduous shrub rose
Soil & situation: moisture-retentive, free-draining soil/sun
North American hardiness zone: 6–9
Height: 3m (10ft)
Spread: 2.2m (7ft)
Grow for: attractive thorns and hips; flowers late spring to early summer

Rosa sericea subsp. *omeiensis* f. *pteracantha*, one of the longest names in plant taxonomy, is one of few plants grown for gorgeous thorns. They are flat, thin, wedge-shaped to 3cm (1in) or more long, and 2cm ($^3/_4$in) tall, forming 'wings' down the stems, which are covered with fine, soft bristles. This treasure should be carefully placed in the garden so that the morning or preferably the evening sun shines through the gorgeous translucent thorns when the effect lasts longer and they glow like rubies as the sun goes down. It is shade tolerant and suitable for planting in woodland glades, but should always be placed where it is spot-lit by the sun; the narrow, vase-shape of the plant makes it an excellent specimen shrub for lawns or borders too. One day I'd like to visit Mount Omei in China, home to some incredible plants, so I could see this glorious plant growing in its native habitat. Bliss!

Rosa sericea subsp. *omeiensis* f. *pteracantha*

The thorns are accompanied by delicate, pale grey, ferny foliage and small, single, white, four-petalled flowers with crimson and yellow edible hips. In late spring white flowers 5cm (2in) in diameter appear in loose clusters.

It prefers free-draining, moisture-retentive soils but is tolerant of poorer conditions. The thorns are especially conspicuous on young, vigorous basal shoots; by the second year they are grey and woody. In spring, prune hard annually or biennially back to the base to encourage young growth and lots of thorns. Propagate by seed in spring or hardwood cuttings in late winter. **MB**

Rosa 'Sharifa Asma'

Type: hardy, deciduous, shrub rose
Soil & situation: As for *R.* 'Golden Celebration' (see page 333)
Height: 1m (3 ft)
Spread: 75cm (30in)
Grow for: almost continuous flowers, a beautiful

delicate blush-pink that fades to near white on the outer petals as they age

This is an excellent 'English' rose. It copes very well in less-than-perfect rose-growing soils i.e. in the thinner, lighter types like mine. I like the continuity of flowering and the vigour of the plant, yet it has the good qualities of the old roses: the beauty and charm of the flower and the strong, fruity but sweet fragrance which is 'reminiscent of white grapes and mulberry'.

The flowers are shallow cups which relax into rosettes as they age. The growth is rather upright, and to make more of a bushy group it is worth planting three or five (if not more) in a tight group at about 50cm (20in) centres. As long as they have good food and moisture, close planting will not affect their performance. The blooms can occasionally be damaged by hot sun but this is rarely a problem in Britain.

Care for it as you would for *R.* 'Golden Celebration' (see page 333) **BG**

Rosa 'Sharifa Asma'

Rosa 'William Lobb'

Rosa 'William Lobb'

Type: hardy, deciduous, shrub rose
Soil & situation: most soils/sun or shade
North American hardiness zone: 4–9
Height & spread: 2.5m (8ft)
Grow for: prolific, heavily scented, dark crimson flowers in summer following scented mossy buds; AGM

Many roses have scented flowers but only a few are mossy. This rose produces a moss-like formation on the buds and tops of the flowering stems that has an incense-like perfume. I love to rub it on my fingers and sniff the delicious aroma as I walk the garden. Later the blooms are just as delightful. I have trained it along wires but it threatens to grow too heavy. Still I expect it to recover from a massacre of a pruning once every five or ten years.

This interesting group is descended from *Rosa centifolia*, which was the old Rose of Provence. These mossy types were first grown in the 18th century in England but every other country also claims them. They have lost the great popularity they enjoyed a hundred years ago when masses of varieties were grown. *R.* 'Nuits de Young' is one of the varieties available today.

Ideally roses prefer a rich, heavy, moist soil that stays cool but never gets waterlogged. It will grow in open shade, such as on an exposed wall. It is relatively long lived and flowers most easily as a free-standing shrub. Dead-heading is important, as is pruning out diseased wood. It is a hybrid and cannot be grown from seed, but autumn hardwood cuttings are easy.

This rose does get pests and diseases, but you don't notice them, and its only real problem is that it gets too big for small gardens. **BF**

Matt adds:
I think that the 'old' roses are best, though there are exceptions, but I prefer species and older cultivars overall. I first saw this one at Chelsea Flower Show, its beautiful blooms against a buttermilk wall and the memory is still etched in my mind; it was a wonderful contrast I'd love to recreate. *R.* 'William Lobb' is vigorous and robust, like a tall shrub, and the flower clusters are so heavy that it arches to the ground, so it needs support of wires, trellis or placing at the back of a border where the long stems bend forward and mingle with other shrubs. It is a moss rose, the stems and buds covered with a bristly beard and there's something magical about the flower colour. It starts off purple, turns to magenta, then fades to violet-grey. As with all the best roses, there is a rich 'old-fashioned' perfume. This one is sometimes called 'Old Velvet'.

Rosa 'Zéphirine Drouhin'
CLIMBING ROSE

Type: hardy, deciduous, climbing rose
Soil & situation: most soils/sun or shade
North American hardiness zone: 6–9
Height: 3m (10ft)
Spread: unlimited, but probably 2m (6½ft)
Grow for: prolific, scented, silver-pink flowers in flushes from early summer to late autumn on thornless stems

Many roses are available in the pinky-red, semi-double format, but few have such a good fragrance and none are thornless. This alone makes 'Zéphirine Drouhin' a valuable rose, but add in the repeat flowering, the ease with which it can be trained to a shrubby or climbing habit and its ease of propagation and this is a real winner. I have many of these planted in my garden all from the same plant; those with a more moist site and good air flow get far fewer problems and a lot more flowers than those growing on dry walls.

This is one of the Bourbon roses, which all originated in the early 19th century from a cross between a Damask and a China rose. These were the first roses to be bred that flower several times in a year and this, combined with gorgeous fragrance, has made the whole group favourites, such as the superb 'Madame Isaac Pereire', 'Boule de Neige' and 'Souvenir de la Malmaison'. 'Kathleen Harrop' is a sport and definitely worth growing.

Ideally roses prefer a rich, heavy, moist soil that stays cool but never gets waterlogged. They will grow in shade but are rarely very long lived anywhere. Deadheading is important, as is pruning out diseased wood, but otherwise this rose gives most flowers if just trained up a pillar or tree and lightly pruned as the leaves fall; it can also be grown as a free-standing shrub. It is a hybrid and cannot be grown from seed, but autumn hardwood cuttings are easy. It suffers from aphid attacks, blackspot and mildew but who cares, it's thornless and scented. **BF**

Rosa 'Zéphirine Drouhin'

Rosmarinus officinalis
ROSEMARY

Type: frost-hardy, evergreen shrub
Soil & situation: well-drained, light soil/sun
North American hardiness zone: 7–10
Height & spread: 1m (3ft), possibly twice as much
Grow for: good neat evergreen for small informal hedge; gorgeous blue and white flowers in profusion and, of course, a useful culinary herb

There are few plants with such beauty all year round, with such amazing, if small, orchid-like flowers and such culinary appeal. (Mind you, I had a woman once ask me what was wrong with her rosemary as it was causing complaints when used with the lamb roasts – it turned out to be lavender!) Lavender is very similar, but rosemary is more upright and evergreen not ever-grey.

Rosemary is for remembrance – and for Romans, as they revered its culinary and medicinal uses. It is believed to have been brought to England by Edward III's wife. *Ros marinus* means dew of the sea, as it is found wild on sea cliffs of southern Europe

Rosmarinus officinalis 'Miss Jessopp's Upright'

Rosemary needs a well-drained, light soil in a sheltered spot otherwise it is short lived. It does not like the wind and in cold wet areas does best against a warm wall. It can be trimmed after flowering and will usually re-grow. The seed can be sown in spring or cuttings taken in spring or autumn. It does get cut back by hard frosts and recently has started to suffer from a form of dieback. **BF**

Rosmarinus officinalis 'Miss Jessopp's Upright'

Type: frost-hardy, evergreen shrub
Soil & situation: a range of soils/best in sharp draining, slightly limy soils/sun but tolerates part shade/dislikes winter wet/thrives in hot, dry conditions.
North American hardiness zone: 7–10
Height & spread: 2m (6½ft)
Grow for: multi-purpose plant: useful herb for culinary and other purposes; worth growing for foliage; using for topiary, hedging and in pots; pale blue flowers in mid-spring in large quantities; AGM

My rosemary is covered with masses of lovely blue flowers, today on St Valentine's Day, and has had a profusion for two or three weeks. It is in a pot outside my front door and everything in the courtyard is covered with a thick white frost. It is trained into a pyramid which, thanks to its natural upright habit, it was quick to achieve. As I am often away, it is an ideal pot plant. You can neglect it for a good two weeks, even in the height of summer, and it will hardly have noticed it is parched (though I always use huge pots and soak before I go). It is thought that rosemary was the original Christmas tree, being used long before the Norway spruce. Apparently if you bring a plant into the house on Christmas Eve, you have luck for the rest of the year. It does look charming in the house, especially when clipped to the romantic pyramid for 'Christmas card trees'. You can dress it up and even gild some of its leaves and the pot (as was often done in Victorian times). Cut off the gilded leaves later and then move it back outdoors to enjoy it in the garden till next Christmas.

Prune this plant after flowering to maintain a compact, bushy habit. Cuttings strike extremely easily, and can be taken as softwood or semi-ripe cuttings in the growing season. **BG**

Rubus fruticosus 'Bedford Giant'
BLACKBERRY

Type: hardy, deciduous, lax-stemmed shrub
Soil & situation: any soil/sun or shade
North American hardiness zone: 6–8
Height: 2m (6½ft)
Spread: to 10m (33ft)
Grow for: excellent fencing plant and delicious fruits

This is the plant for training on wires to keep out undesirables. It throws 10m (33ft) canes in a rich soil and these are prone to root and start new plants for free. There are more vigorous types still, such as *Rubus fruticosus* 'Himalayan Giant', but its canes are more brittle and harder to train onto wires. It not only makes an effective protective shield but is also good for wildlife who love the flowers and dry, safe centre. The fruits come early; they have a good flavour and are quite large and make excellent blackberry and apple jam, jelly and pie.

Although there are, theoretically, more than 250 species in the *Rubus* family there is no such thing as a pure-bred blackberry as they are all hybrids. This is one of the cultivated varieties. These were known to the Romans, who called them *Rubus*, but gathered them from the wild rather than growing them. Blackberry canes are very different to those of raspberry as the former are pliable, root at the tips easily and may live more than one year, while raspberry canes are stiff, do not root easily and usually die after fruiting.

Long lived, especially as it throws stems which root and grow almost anywhere on almost any soil. Prune out all the dead and old stems and tie the new onto wires after fruiting. The wires need to be strong with sturdy supports. The seedlings come up everywhere with variable results. The tips are layered in autumn and soon root to be planted out in spring. There are rarely any problems other than the vigour making it too big for small gardens. **BF**

Rubus fruticosus 'Bedford Giant'

Rubus hybrid
TAYBERRY

Type: perennial, deciduous, lax-stemmed shrub
Soil & situation: any soil/sun or shade
North American hardiness zone: 4–8
Height & spread: to 7m (23ft)
Grow for: huge delicious fruits

Although related to the blackberries this is not as vigorous and is more like a raspberry, except the stems are covered in very sharp prickles and thorns. I have grown almost every sort of berry and there are few that are this luscious; it is better eaten ripe and raw than any of the others. The berry can get as big as my thumb and is dark wine-purple in colour, aromatic and sweet, and once ripe it pulls off its plug like a raspberry. It is a significant improvement on all the other berries, and a good plant for cool, shady walls rather than needing the sunniest sites.

The tayberry was developed in Scotland and is like a much-improved loganberry. There are many hybrid berries, such as the loganberry, the veitchberry, the sunberry and the boysenberry, all of which are in between blackberries and raspberries in fruit and habit.

In the UK the tayberry is happiest in cool northern or western areas; I find it gets parched in full sun and wind here in East Anglia and my best berries are produced on the north side of a wooden panel fence. Prune out all the dead and old stems and tie the new onto wires after the old finish fruiting. The wires need to be strong with good supports. The seedlings come up everywhere with variable results. The tips are layered in autumn and soon root to be planted out in spring.

There are rarely any problems other than bird losses, which are heavy, so it needs be netted or caged. **BF**

Rubus hybrid

Rubus idaeus

Rubus idaeus
RASPBERRY

Type: hardy, perennial, deciduous, clump-forming thicket
Soil & situation: any soil/sun or shade
North American hardiness zone: 3–8
Height & spread: 3m (10ft) high clump
Grow for: most delicious fruits

Although related to the blackberries, raspberries are different. Their stiff canes support themselves and do not root easily at the tips, and they nearly always die after fruiting. Ripe raspberries usually leave their plug behind, making them more delectable than blackberries and the hybrids, which mostly pull off with the plug inside, and are more chewy. Raspberries can be eaten in quantity without the dire results of most fruits – I can testify to this. They also make the most brilliant jam, refreshing drinks and superb sorbets. They can be in fruit from early summer to well into late autumn if you have several varieties.

The name comes from the earlier *raspise*, which is possibly from the name for an old type of French red wine. Raspberries are common in the wild in northern European countries, where they are normally gathered rather than cultivated. In the USA they have their own series raised from their native raspberries rather than from our stocks.

In the UK raspberries are happiest in cool northern or western areas; they do not like hot, dry, thin or chalky soils and revel in a rich, moist loam. They are not long lived and deteriorate after eight years. Prune out all the dead old stems and tie the new onto wires after the old finish fruiting; for autumn fruiters remove all canes in mid-winter. Thinning new canes to a hand's breadth apart improves the quality of the crop. Supporting wires do not have to be very strong as they are only there to restrain the canes and stop them falling over. Raspberry seedlings come up everywhere with variable but usually acceptable results and any bit of root with a bud can be planted out in spring. Maggots are best avoided by growing autumn fruiters. Raspberry mosaic virus will creep in sooner or later, so eradicate any plants with mottled leaves. **BF**

Rubus phoenicolasius
JAPANESE WINEBERRY

Type: hardy, deciduous, arching shrub
Soil & situation: any soil/sun or shade
North American hardiness zone: 5–9
Height & spread: 4.5m (15ft)
Grow for: decorative russet stems; nice leaves; delicious, red, edible berry; pretty star-shaped calyces left after fruits

This is a rarity but should be common. It has a fruit you can just eat and eat and eat – good for parking children in front of to keep them occupied. Once the fruit has been picked, the white star-shaped calyces make the plant look in flower again. The stems are bristly rather than thorny and a colourful russet ruddy-brown; the leaves are decorative and a lovely lime-juice green. It is a shame the berries are not much use either as jam or juice, and I would love to cross this with a tayberry, but so far it has always come true from seed. The birds do not strip these berries as fast as many others – I think the birds reckon they are unripe blackberries.

Rubus phoenicolasius

The weird bit of the name is the Latin for purple hairs, which I suppose is close enough to its ruddy-brown hairs. It comes from Japan as the common name, for once correctly, indicates, though it is also found in China. It was brought to the UK in the 19th century and was more popular as an ornamental shrub than for its fruit, which is of little value other than as a fresh-picked delight.

The Japanese wineberry does well on almost any soil or site but looks best trained against a whitewashed wall. Prune out all the dead and old stems and tie the new onto wires after the old finish fruiting. The wires need be strong with good supports. The seedlings come true and the tips can be layered in autumn. There are rarely any problems other than it does self-seed rather abundantly.   **BF**

Rudbeckia fulgida var. *sullivantii* 'Goldsturm'

Type: hardy, herbaceous perennial
Soil & situation: moist soil; tolerates clay/sun or partial shade
North American hardiness zone: 4–9
Height: 60cm (24in)
Spread: 45cm (18in)
Grow for: golden-yellow 'daisies' from late summer to autumn

This genus is named after Olof Rudbeck (1630–1702), who has been described as 'one of

Rudbeckia fulgida var. *sullivantii* 'Goldsturm'

the greatest Swedes of all time', founder of Uppsala Botanic Garden in Sweden, and his son Olof the Younger, a friend of Linnaeus. Rudbeckias are among the most delightful and reliable of all late summer-flowering 'daisies'; when they are in flower, the sun shines every day. Like many other midsummer-flowering herbaceous plants, will tolerate clay and are high on the list of favourites to be planted in a new herbaceous border that I am planning for my garden.

Rudbeckia fulgida var. *sullivantii* 'Goldsturm' has a clump of hairy leaves and stems that are usually branched in the upper part. Each plant carries masses of bright yellow flowers with a small dark purple-brown (looks black) central cone. It makes a striking and desirable contrast that is further enhanced when they are planted with blue sea hollies, red hot pokers in orange and green, or crocosmias like the fiery red 'Lucifer' and apricot 'Star of the East'. *R. fulgida* var. *deamii* is similar but with smaller flowers. *R. occidentalis* 'Green Wizard' lacks the ray florets; the single dark cone is a novelty but has all the sex appeal of a bald woman. It is beloved by flower arrangers.

It does best on heavier, moisture-retentive soils, and where necessary dig in plenty of organic matter before planting. Mulch heavily with well-rotted organic matter and water if necessary during drought. Divide in spring every four to five years; sow seed in late spring to early summer to flower the following year.   **MB**

Ruta graveolens

Ruta graveolens
COMMON RUE

Type: hardy, deciduous shrub
Soil & situation: well-drained soil/sun
North American hardiness zone: 5–9
Height & spread: 1m (3ft)
Grow for: prolific, though small, scented yellow flowers in summer on beautifully aromatic, fern-like, blue foliage

True blue foliage is rare, yet rue has a lovely leaf that is almost blue in varieties such as *Rue graveolens* 'Jackman's Blue' (see next entry). The soft ferny leaves have a delicious citrus-like scent, which is so strong that the leaves have often been used to keep pests away. Although it is poisonous and sometimes used as a medicinal herb, I came across it being eaten in France where it was used as a flavouring for cheese. I have often done the same since with no apparent harm but for the woes of the litigious I must insist you do not try it, especially if you are pregnant as rue is undoubtedly dangerous.

The botanical name is for bitterness, as is the common name. Rue was officially introduced in 1652 but was probably brought by the Romans as this herb, a native of southern Europe, has long been cultivated for its medicinal qualities. Rue has a big family; there are over five dozen other species, most of which are tender and carry the distinctive citrus-like scent in foliage and flower. There are another 600 in the family of Rutaceae, often similarly scented, such as choisya.

Rue is not long lived and less so if the soil is damp in winter or it is in shade. It can be trimmed back lightly in spring before the growth resumes and it is worth shearing off the flowerheads before they set seed. It can be grown from seed sown in pots in spring or rooted by summer cuttings in a coldframe. Rue suffers few problems but is strongly irritant to the skin and care should be taken with the foliage, especially in hot weather. It may self-seed.   **BF**

Kniphofia caulescens

RED-HOT POKER

Type: hardy evergreen perennial
Soil & situation: fertile deep loam/sun or partial shade/young plants need protection with a mulch for their first winter
North American hardiness zone: 7–9
Height: up to 1.2m (4ft)
Spread: to 60cm (24in)
Grow for: striking, year-round, broad, grass-like, glaucous foliage; long-lasting stately spikes of cool coral and yellow flowers at any time in summer or autumn; AGM

For the most part I strongly favour hard-working plants. This, for sure, is one of those and I have never worked out why it is not more common. Perhaps because when you mention red-hot pokers a wide group of gardeners turn up their noses haughtily. But this one is streets ahead of your average red-hot poker. Apart from its dramatic, stately, long-lasting flowers – a subtle coral colour initially before fading up the spike to an unbrassy yellow as they age – their foliage is to die for. It is a good blue-green, does not look tatty even in late winter, spreads in generous basal rosettes with arching leaves and would be worth growing for that alone. I initially veered away from it, having been wrongly informed that it was tender. It certainly looks exotic but it thrives in my East Midlands patch, and I have never even given it so much as a protective mulch in winter.

To keep the foliage at its best, division of the plant every two to four years may be necessary. You do this in spring by breaking off pieces and replanting them with the foliage cut well back, but with some woody stem.   **BG**

Ruta graveolens 'Jackman's Blue'

Ruta graveolens 'Jackman's Blue'

Type: hardy, evergreen herb/shrub
Soil & situation: well-drained soils in full sun/tolerates partial shade quite successfully/ requires gloves when handling – the sap contains feranocoumarins and blistering can be triggered by contact with skin
North American hardiness zone: 5–9
Height: 60cm (24in)
Spread: 50cm (20in)
Grow for: intense blue-grey foliage; divided, fern-like leaves; an excellent year-round plant; AGM

Ruta graveolens (see page 343) has been cultivated for hundreds of years for its intense flavour, which has been used in sausage – though probably not served with egg, chips and ketchup! A tea made from infusing the leaves has long been used as a stimulant. This herb is also believed to have magical properties, especially when acquired by theft. Tantalizing to think how this was most likely discovered by desperate sorcerers shinning up monastic walls by moonlight.

Thudding back to reality, though, I grow it simply for its magical appearance. It is supreme as a low hedge or edging plant, especially in parterres with an unusual twist, mixed with dwarf myrtles, germanders, Japanese hollies and other plants with fascinating backgrounds. It is most commonly used in mixed borders too, where it quickly establishes to form a good-looking presence in its first year.

If grown as a low hedge this plant will need cutting back once, possibly twice, during the growing season. Grown as a shrub, one good cut back will do the job. The main time to cut back is early spring and the existing growth should be cut back by half to two thirds. A second cut later on, to tidy up the first flush of growth, will help to form a really compact habit. This will probably be at the expense of the uninspiring flowers – no bad thing as the mustard-yellow colour with the blue of the foliage is not an asset anyway. Old shrubs that look past it can be renewed by hard cutting back to 15cm (6in) from the ground. If this fails, cuttings in late summer are a sure winner. **BG**

Salix alba subsp. *vitellina*
GOLDEN WILLOW

Type: hardy, deciduous tree, often maintained as a shrub
Soil & situation: grow best in deep, moist but well-drained soils/will tolerate a vast range of conditions, including impoverished ones/sun or partial shade
North American hardiness zone: 2–9
Height: 25m (80ft) as a tree, 1–2m (3–6½ft) as a shrub
Spread: 10m (33ft) as a tree
Grow for: spectacular fiery new growth with young stems a bright yellow-orange; will grow in extremely inhospitable conditions, wet or dry, so is highly useful for reclamation work; AGM

This is a stunning willow which comes into its own at the end of autumn when the dramatic-coloured stems, devoid of leaves, brighten up the

Salix alba subsp. *vitellina* 'Britzensis'

winter landscape. I regularly use it in bold groups mixed with other willows of the same ilk, such as *S. alba* 'Chermesina', the scarlet willow, which has bright orange-scarlet young stems and *S. daphnoides*, the violet willow, whose purple-violet new stems are overlaid with a whitish bloom.

This is more sober than the previous two but attractive, nonetheless. Although all their maximum heights are tall, they are usually coppiced every other year to make sure the vigorous new stems are produced and so the height is kept at only 1–2m (3–6½ft). I think they look best in wilder parts of the garden, although you do see them in mixed borders, but they seem to me to be out of context when they jostle next to more refined neighbours. They are fabulous in marshy situations or on banks by water. They are also superb for creating living play areas around other play equipment as they form green den-making domains, which can be heavily trampled by hyperactive feet, but will always grow back providing they have established.

Assuming you want shrubs, not trees, coppice these plants a couple of years following planting and then about every other year. This simply entails cutting them back to about 10cm (4in) from ground level in spring. They are easy to grow from cuttings and these will take in open ground at pretty well any time of year, but hardwood cuttings in the dormant season are the norm. Willows have invasive roots, so do not plant them close to buildings or drains if you are going to let them form anything other than small shrubs. **BG**

Salix alba subsp. *vitellina* 'Britzensis'
RED-STEMMED WILLOW

Type: hardy, deciduous tree
Soil & situation: moist, well-drained, fertile soil/full sun
North American hardiness zone: 4–9
Height: 20m (66ft)
Spread: 10m (33ft)
Grow for: bright orange-red bark on new growths; yellow male catkins in spring; AGM

I think this variety is different enough from Bunny's choice (above) to merit a separate entry.

Viewed from a distance, against a dull wintery sky, the overall effect is of a stationary orange cloud. Up close the bark is as striking as that of dogwood (*Cornus alba*, see page 16).

Yellow male catkins, 5cm (2in) long, appear in spring together with the mid-green leaves, which are blue-green on the underside. It is, however, the bright orange-red bark which lifts this willow above most of the other species. As the tree grows the older bark becomes brown. With that in mind it is the fashion to prune (coppice) the branches hard every second year. They are cut close to the ground to encourage young, highly coloured growths. Every spring prune back hard and then feed with a high nitrogen fertilizer in early summer to help the growth. Left unpruned it will form an elegant tree with dyed hair.

A word of caution: avoid planting willows close to buildings or underground services, such as sewage pipes or drains. They have a vigorous root system capable of causing damage.

The simplest method of propagation is by hardwood cuttings. Large cuttings are easily rooted. It is not unusual to find large willows either side of a field entrance, where the farmer used willow branches as gate posts. They rooted and, in time, became matching trees. Like most willows, 'Britzensis' will tolerate wet ground and is happy with its roots close to the water's edge. It dislikes waterlogged soil, where it will be more prone to willow anthracnose disease. **JC**

Salix elaeagnos
HOARY WILLOW, ROSEMARY WILLOW

Type: hardy, deciduous shrub
Soil & situation: as for *Salix alba* subsp.*vitellina* (see page 346)
North American hardiness zone: 4–9
Height: 3–6m (10–20ft)
Spread: 5m (16ft)
Grow for: wonderful foliage, similar to an enlarged rosemary leaf; highly ornamental, yet tough plant very useful for 'lifting' native plantings in wilder parts of the garden or countryside

The leaf of this willow is about 10cm (4in) long by 5mm (¼in) wide, the new growth is silver and hoary i.e. covered with short white hairs (like an old man with a soft stubble). Later on, the leaves become dark olive-green on top and silver-felted below. They are densely produced covering much of the rust-coloured stems. Small catkins are produced with or just before the leaves.

This really choice willow is less vigorous than many. I often use it for screening with other native plants (*Viburnum opulus, V. lantana, Ligustrum vulgare*) to form attractive thickets

around compost heaps, play areas, children's gardens and the like. It can be maintained at a metre (3ft) high without wearing out or over-taxing your arm muscles, and yet will quickly achieve that height. It is a superb waterside shrub too.

Although these willows can be left to form a large shrub or small tree, they are often kept as busy shrubs so you can enjoy the foliage near to eye level. They can be maintained by cutting back to prevent them becoming too large. The best time to do this is early spring, and then you can really appreciate the new silvery foliage as it rapidly extends in the growing season. They are asy to propagate, the simplest method being putting hardwood cuttings, 15-30cm (6-12in) long or so, into open ground in the late autumn or winter. **BG**

Salix elaeagnos

Salix gracilistyla 'Melanostachys'

Type: hardy, spreading, deciduous shrub
Soil & situation: moist, heavy soil/sun
North American hardiness zone: 5–8
Height: 3m (10ft)
Spread: 4m (13ft)
Grow for: 'black' catkins and brick-red anthers

Oh those catkins! How could you resist a willow with 'black' catkins and brick-red anthers? Just think about it, black and brick-red and appearing before the leaves too! Look at the picture – aren't you tempted? OK the anthers later turn yellow but it is still magnificent. This has to be one of the most stunning colour combinations in the plant world. I can't seem to find out much about its origins, apart from that it's also known as Kureneko, Kurome and Kuroyanagi, the leaves are thicker than the species and strongly veined, there is only a male clone in existence and it was introduced into Europe via Holland in 1950. Perhaps it appeared as a 'sport' somewhere in Japan, Korea or China where *Salix gracilistyla* has

Salix gracilistyla 'Melanostachys'

its home, or was spirited from Japan by an entrepreneurial Dutch nurseryman. The dearth of information adds to the magic of this mysterious, seductive plant so I will search no more and continue to wonder because one thing is certain – ignorance is bliss!

Prune after flowering to keep within its allotted space. Propagate by 30cm (12in) hardwood cuttings of one-year-old wood in spring. It is prone to anthracnose. Brown spots occur on the leaves, which fall early, and cankers appear on the shoots. Affected parts must be cut out, and don't forget to sterilize your secateurs by wiping with a cloth impregnated with methylated spirits after use. Regular sprays with Bordeaux mixture or copper fungicide starting when the leaves unfold should give some control; rake up and dispose of fallen leaves. It is worse in wet seasons. **MB**

Salix viminalis
COMMON OSIER, HEMP WILLOW

Type: hardy, deciduous shrub or small tree
Soil & situation: as for *Salix alba* subsp.*vitellina* (see page 346)
North American hardiness zone: 4–9
Height: 6m (20ft) or more, but often maintained as a shrub
Spread: 5m (16ft)
Grow for: best willow for weaving into living or dead willow structures: arbours, dens, arches, fences

This willow was traditionally grown for basket-making and so has extremely pliable shoots. It is a large, vigorous willow with long, narrow, typical willow leaves. They are a flat green above and covered with fine hairs below. It is not especially ornamental as a shrub, so if you are growing it to produce cuttings, site it somewhere natural where it will fit it agreeably. Once woven into something it is obviously transformed.

I have used this willow for weaving all sorts of structures, including a crocodile which was a key element in my children's play area when they were small. For growing willow fences it is a gem. You can form a wide assortment of different lattice shapes or weaving styles with it, introducing an element of originality. One of my favourites was a living woven serpentine fence, on the same lines as those amazing crinkle-crankle walls.

To grow this plant commercially for cutting production, they are grown on a short leg, about 30cm (12in) high, and then cut back to that every year, rather like a mini-pollarded willow. They produce lots of wands or cuttings which grow from the top of the leg, ready for cutting and using at leaf fall, usually at the end of autumn. For good cutting production a moist, fertile soil obviously produces good long cuttings, well over 1m (3ft) long if not 2m (6½ft). When making growing structures, which can be done any time in the dormant season I insert the long (up to 3m/10ft) cuttings in their final position, just deep enough in the ground to make them stable, maybe 15cm (6in). Having woven the structure I want, I water the new cuttings in during dry periods and maintain bare earth, as opposed to vegetation around the base, to facilitate establishment. The new growth on the structures needs frequent cutting back, often three times in the growing season, to prevent it becoming a mass of verdant willow shoots. **BG**

Salix viminalis

Salvia glutinosa

Salvia glutinosa
JUPITER'S DISTAFF

Type: hardy, herbaceous perennial
Soil & situation: not demanding, but does appreciate a moister soil than many sages/some shade/will grow in full sun
North American hardiness zone: 5–8
Height: 90cm (36in)
Spread: 60cm (24in)
Grow for: attractive, yellow flowers from summer to late autumn; a good plant for naturalizing in semi-shaded, wilder areas; good, bushy foliage, with yellow-green heart-shaped leaves

I am ashamed to say that I grew this plant for a couple of years before I realized what a quiet star it is – the flowers in no way jump out at you. They are carried in tall spikes and are a soft, pale yellow with red-brown spots on the hooded top lip and red-brown stripes on the lower lip. They attract many species of bumble-bees and you do notice early on that the large, branched flower spikes are very sticky indeed. I grow it in a dry, sunny position, not the ideal position, but this was done out of total ignorance – I just gave it what I thought most sages liked – but it does well, flowering on and on. Now I am going to try some in a more natural setting, letting it naturalize in spangled clumps amongst ferns, luzulas, liberties and foxgloves in light shade and moister conditions. I think I will like it even better there. I cut this plant back in the early winter, and otherwise do very little to it. It can be propagated from softwood cuttings in early summer, which root very quickly, or from seed sown in spring. **BG**

Salvia indica
'Indigo Spires'

Type: tender perennial
Soil & situation: frost-free conditions during winter/good drainage/full sun
North American hardiness zone: 5–9
Height: up to 1.5m (5ft)
Spread: 50cm (20in)
Grow for: a see-through, floriferous plant with deep indigo-blue flowers from early summer till late autumn

I adore many of the more subtle, tender sages, but 'Indigo Spires' is my all-time favourite. It was raised in 1979, at the Huntingdon Botanic Garden in California. I plant generous quantities of them in my Cambridgeshire courtyard garden, dangerously early in late spring (standing by with fleece in the event of a late frost) and they flower pretty much from late spring to late autumn. The plant has a gentle, lax air about it; the pretty blue flowers are studded at intervals up the long, lean stems, giving a soft, gentle colour – none of this brash, bold and in-your-face stuff. I grow them threaded through lower clumps of perennials, and they waft around on their own with no staking. It is possible that this may not be the case if you are the lucky owner of deep, fertile loam as opposed to my poor, thin offering.

Salvia indica 'Indigo Spires'

Being a tender perennial, this plant does necessitate higher levels of care but gives real value in return. I lift them just before the first frosts and pot them up, keeping them in a frost-free greenhouse over winter. I keep them on the dry side and check them over every so often, removing any mouldy stems. In addition I take cuttings from the parent plants in late summer, to ensure I have a good supply of young plants too. Cuttings will root quickly and easily at any time in the growing season. Apparently excess nitrogen results in sparse flowering. **BG**

Salvia involucrata 'Bethellii'

Salvia involucrata 'Bethellii'

Type: tender perennial
Soil & situation: well-drained loam/sun/ preferably winter protection
North American hardiness zone: 7–10
Height: up to 1.5m (5ft)
Spread: to 1m (3ft)
Grow for: pinky-magenta flowers from late spring till autumn; AGM

This plant is a bit of an exhibitionist. It is a showy but stately plant with attractive, almost glabrous leaves, vaguely purplish on the underside. The non-stop flowers come in unbranched racemes and are curious in that they produce a large, fat, terminal bud which sits at the end of the flower spike on top of lots of densely-packed flowers.

One year I grew them in semi-shade under a line of pleached trees, in soil that is packed with dense tree roots. They still surprised me with a fair quantity of flowers although they did take a few weeks longer to get into their stride. Another year I left some out over winter and they survived to tell

the tale. However, I will not repeat the experiment as they took a long time to come into growth and it was late summer before they flowered.

Most of the time I give them what they like best – sun and free-draining soil – and they never succumb to disease, never need staking and are definitely star performers that I would not want to be without.

Before the frosts these salvias need lifting, potting up and then keeping in a frost-free greenhouse over winter. Alternatively, new cuttings can be taken any time in the summer, kept in frost-free conditions over winter and planted out the following spring after the frosts. **BG**

Salvia officinalis
SAGE

Type: hardy, semi-evergreen shrub
Soil & situation: well-drained soil/sun
North American hardiness zone: 5–8
Height & spread: 1m (3ft)
Grow for: attractive, aromatic, grey foliage; scented purple flowers; culinary herb

I could not be without sage, both for its delicious scent and pleasing appearance when young and tidy, and for its use in the kitchen. I must have a sage and onion stuffing with my home-grown roast chicken, indeed I like it more than the meat. I always put a little fresh sage in my salads and the flowers are an essential part of one of the best of my liqueurs. It's also much visited by all sorts of insects when in flower.

Salvia is the Latin for safe and well, or good health, as this plant was thought to keep you healthy, and the name became corrupted into the

Salvia officinalis

modern equivalent. It is an enormous genus with over 500 species, many native to southern Europe. It is reputed to be the herb to eat for a long life, though it was used originally to hide the flavour of over-ripe meat.

Sage is quite long lived in a well-drained, sunny site but gets rather leggy and scrappy, and if you cut it back it rarely regrows satisfactorily. In fact the best way to treat it is to replace it every few years with another. Sage can be grown from seed in spring but named varieties must be rooted or layered, which is easier; indeed, the whole plant can be earthed up in spring and then divided the next year. Sage rarely suffers any problems. **BF**

Salvia officinalis 'Purpurascens'

Salvia officinalis 'Purpurascens'
PURPLE SAGE

Type: hardy, evergreen subshrub
Soil & situation: sunny, well-drained soil/will tolerate a lightly shaded position/will not cope with heavy, cold soils.
Height: up to 80cm (32in)
Spread: 1m (3ft)
North American hardiness zone: 5–8
Grow for: rich, purple-mauve toned foliage which brings it into a class of its own; useful aromatic herb; spikes of blue-mauve flowers in early summer; AGM

This is a first-rate foliage plant when grown well and looking in the peak of condition. The young leaves are purple and as they age they turn green-grey, maintaining the purple veining and edging. The undersides have distinctive purple veining, which stands out against a grey backdrop. To keep these plants looking good they must be clipped lightly in spring to encourage new, well-coloured growth and to neaten them up. Also, being fast growers they are not in their prime of life for long and I think they are best replaced with new plants every four or five years, depending on your soil. They are easy to grow from cuttings and grow fast, making quite a statement after just one year of growth. The golden form, *S. officinalis* 'Icterina' (AGM), is superb too, but *S. officinalis* 'Tricolor' (AGM), with its colourful white, pink and purple foliage is tender, and really needs planting out each year. These plants are not good in cold, damp conditions, and suffer with wet periods followed by sharp cold nights. Cuttings root quickly and should be taken in the growing season, providing a stock of replacement plants as necessary. Regular replacement of plants, combined with an annual haircut in spring, will ensure they do their best. **BG**

Salvia patens

Type: frost-hardy to tender perennial
Soil & situation: moist but well-drained soil/sun or half shade
North American hardiness zone: 8–9
Height: generally 75cm (30in) but up to 1m (3ft)
Spread: 60cm (24in)
Grow for: strong Oxford-blue flowers from mid-summer to mid-autumn; AGM

Salvia patens

I love the depth of blue of these flowers, though because you do not often get more than one or two blooms flowering on each flower spike at a time, the overall effect is not overpowering. In order to create real impact I like to use several plants together, preferably in repeated groups. They will flower from mid-summer to mid-autumn, enabling you to see out the growing season with a bang. Their ovate to triangular leaves are mid-green, hairy top and bottom and are a good, relaxed foil to the flowers. I cannot quite fathom their degree of hardiness – they have been known to withstand temperatures of –7°C (19°F) in the wet, but die in –6°C (21°F) in drier conditions.

These plants do not flower well in baking hot summers, so do not be discouraged if one year its performance dips – it might be the temperature. Trim in late summer to neaten them up and encourage them to flower more profusely. If you do not want to take a chance and leave them out well-mulched over winter, you can treat them as you would a dahlia, as these too form tubers, albeit small ones, which you can lift and store over winter. Alternatively they are simple to grow from seed or from cuttings taken in mid-summer, allowing time for the tuberous roots to become established before the winter. **BG**

Salvia rutilans (syn. S. elegans 'Scarlet Pineapple')
PINEAPPLE SAGE

Type: tender, semi-evergreen shrub
Soil & situation: well-drained compost/full sun/undercover
North American hardiness zone: 8–10
Height: 60cm (24in)
Spread: 1.2m (4ft)
Grow for: pineapple-scented foliage and brilliant crimson-scarlet flowers

This stunner is too tender for most gardens though it may survive like a fuchsia, coming again from its roots. However it really is worth growing, and as it roots easily it can be propagated in the autumn and the small plants over-wintered undercover to be put out for the next summer. The scent of the heart-shaped leaves is amazing and they are sensually soft to the touch; the exquisite crimson flowers are fantastic set against the verdant green of the foliage. *Rutilans* means reddish, because of the flowers. The plant's origins are unknown but it appeared in the UK during the Victorian age and became very popular. We still grow other salvias as tender bedding plants.

Pineapple sage must have a warm, well-drained site or it will die promptly the first winter; on a wall with some protection it may come from the roots again. It can be grown as a conservatory specimen easily, though gets big and straggly so really needs constant replacement with newer stock. This is a species so can be grown from spring-sown seed but cuttings and layers are not difficult in summer in a coldframe. Under cover it does act as a magnet for whitefly! **BF**

Salvia rutilans

Salvia sclarea var. turkestanica
Plant of the Week (see page 201)

Sambucus nigra 'Aurea'
GOLDEN ELDER

Type: hardy, deciduous shrub
Soil & situation: any soil/anywhere
North American hardiness zone: 6–8
Height: 6m (20ft)
Spread: 5m (16ft)
Grow for: prolific, scented, white foamy flowers in late spring; striking yellow foliage; AGM

I have seen black elder growing as a weed from the tea plantations of Sri Lanka to the wild bush of Jamaica, it is a real survivor. In my garden it comes up everywhere as the birds spread the seeds and it is infuriatingly vigorous! The black berries of the standard form are excellent for jelly, though often giving me stomach ache as a kid when I ate them raw. I love the smell of the flowers and often cook them in batter, but they must be fresh or they taste fishy. I've selected the 'Aurea' form as a garden plant as this is one of the toughest of golden-foliage plants, and it is not so prolifically fruited as the wild form so you get fewer seedlings everywhere.

Related to the honeysuckles, there are 40 other species around the world. It was known to the ancients and used for both medicine and magic. The hollow stems were used as pipes, and by little boys to make pop-guns, the hollow trunks to make bigger instruments – *Sambucus* comes from the Greek *sambuca*, a harp.

Elders will grow almost anywhere but thrive on a moist site and even in quite dense shade; they do well on chalky soils. This yellow-leafed form does best in light shade as it may scorch in full sun. It needs pruning to keep it small and can be cut back hard each year, removing all the old wood. The wild form comes from seed, the variegated and yellow forms are unbelievably easy from autumn cuttings. Prone to aphid attacks, this is otherwise no problem save the self-seeding everywhere. **BF**

John adds:

The variety *Sambucus nigra* 'Guincho Purple' is spectacular with its dark green leaves turning to blackish-purple and then red in autumn. The pink-tinged panicles of flowers appear to have been stained with red wine and are carried on purple stalks. A striking plant for the large border.

Sambucus nigra 'Aurea'

Sanguinaria canadensis

Sanguinaria canadensis
CANADIAN BLOODROOT

Type: hardy, rhizomatous perennial
Soil & situation: moist, humus-rich soil/dappled shade
North American hardiness zone: 3–8
Height: 10cm (4in)
Spread: 30cm (12in) or more
Grow for: delicate white flowers from mid- to late spring; attractive leaves

This delicate-looking gem is very hardy. The heart- to kidney-shaped, blue-green leaves with scalloped margins and prominent red veins on the underside emerge folded, then open up to 30cm (12in) across. Before they do, the very short-lived white flowers have already opened. Just a breath of wind and the petals are quickly lost; if not, they remain on the plant for a month.

The orange-red sap, thought to be natural anti-freeze, is visible in the red leaf stems. It contains the active ingredient sanguinarine. Indians living by Lake Superior used it for cancer treatment. In the 1950s Dr J. W. Fell developed a paste based on bloodroot extract to treat cancers; it was placed on the tumour daily and when it became encrusted he made incisions, packed it with paste and within 2–4 weeks it was destroyed, falling out after 7–14 days, leaving a sore that rapidly healed. His results, mainly on breast cancer, detailed remissions if not cures. A revival of the technique was being used in 1977 – I'm not sure if it still is today.

Sanguinaria canadensis f. *multiplex* is a mass of petals. Each time I have seen it there is always a cluster around the plant and it has plenty to spare! *S. c.* 'Early Form' flowers in early to mid-spring. 'Jerry Flintoff' has semi-double flowers. *S. c.* f. *multiplex* 'Plena' (double bloodroot) has short-lived, double, white flowers. Check the plant regularly when flowering is anticipated.

It is ideal for a sheltered woodland garden and needs humus-rich soil in dappled shade or even full sun with adequate moisture. It spreads very slowly but can be naturalized in grass or under deciduous trees. Divide in late summer just after the leaves fully mature. **MB**

Morus nigra

BLACK MULBERRY

Type: hardy deciduous tree
Soil & situation: sheltered and sunny position/fertile soil
North American hardiness zone: 5–9
Height: 12m (40ft)
Spread: 15m (50ft)
Grow for: architectural form; attractive, bold, heart-shaped leaves; edible, bitter-sweet (but more sweet than bitter) raspberry-like fruits maturing in late summer. Like many plants in this book, it could have been allocated to almost any month, but the fruits are luscious at this time of year – and for weeks before and after; AGM

A mature mulberry tree conveys an almost magical feel to a garden. It gives it an ancient, old-established feel with its gnarled bark and often eccentric outline. Mulberries are fairly fast-growing trees and their characteristic habit does make them look prematurely aged, so maybe the next generation will relish them too. The leaves appear in late spring/early summer and are often not fully out till summer. They cast heavy shade, but even so grass thrives relatively well underneath the canopy and they fall early, most having gone by late autumn.

Paving under the canopy does not look good, as the small fruits will start to drop in summer and carry on ceaselessly until autumn, applying their intense colour to the hard surface below.

If you are keen on the fruit, which can be delicious when mature (about the size of a large loganberry) and fully ripe (when black), order a named selection that produces fine, juicy fruits as opposed to small, seedy, ones. An excellent form is 'Large Black', another is 'King James'. They are vegetatively propagated and will fruit when about six or seven years old.

When the leaves fall, the tree's other qualities come to the fore – the beautiful, warm, rough-textured bark and the architectural form.

Propagate by hardwood cuttings 18cm (7in) long in autumn, with a heel of two-year-old wood, in open ground in a shady spot. Larger cuttings are also successful. Train the tree with a clear stem of about 1.5m (5ft). It may take three or four years before the tree develops feathers, or sideshoots, which then can then be cut back. Once you have this clear stem, you simply let the tree mature. The naturally weeping habit may involve removing some lower limbs – cut these back when the tree is fully dormant to avoid the bleeding sap. Other pendent branches can be propped, and these props can add to the old, gnarled feel of the tree. **BG**

Santolina chaemaecyparissus

Santolina chaemaecyparissus (syn. *S. incana*)
COTTON LAVENDER, LAVENDER COTTON

Type: hardy, evergreen shrub
Soil & situation: well-drained, sandy soil/sun
North American hardiness zone: 6–9
Height & spread: 60cm (24in)
Grow for: delicate, finely divided, ever-grey, aromatic foliage and pretty yellow flowers in mid-summer; AGM

This is one of the best edging plants as it makes a change from the lavender and box you see everywhere doing the same job. The silvery, lacy foliage has a delightful perfume and as I hate to throw away the prunings I use them underfoot as a strewing herb in my sheds and stores. The French call it *garde-robe*, for it is supposed to be good at keeping out clothes moths, but it certainly did not keep them out of my attic where I hung it with some old clothes which are now only fit for making dapper scarecrows.

Introduced to the UK in the 16th century from the Mediterranean, this has about a dozen closely related and similar species. It was given its common name of cotton lavender or lavender cotton from its habit of growth and white woolly appearance. It was considered a good herb for feeding children to cleanse them of worms. The botanical name comes from the Old Latin *sanctum linum*, meaning holy flax.

Santolina needs a well-drained soil in full sun. It is not long lived and some spares should be kept at all times, as it may be lost in a wet or hard winter. Shear back lightly in early spring just before growth starts. It is easy to propagate from cuttings taken with a heel in mid-summer or autumn and can be grown from spring-sown seed. **BF**

Santolina rosmarinifolia subs. *rosmarinifolia* 'Primrose Gem'
COTTON LAVENDER

Type: frost-hardy, evergreen shrub
Soil & situation: thin, well-drained soil (often alkaline)/sunny position
North American hardiness zone: 6–9
Height: 60cm (24in)
Spread: 1m (3ft)
Grow for: aromatic, finely divided evergreen foliage; responds well to regular shearing so is an often-used component of knot gardens; beautiful pale lemon-yellow flowers in massive quantities in mid-summer; AGM

Santolina rosmarinifolia subsp. *rosmarinifolia* 'Primrose Gem'

The feathery foliage of this santolina is a refreshing, bright green that seems to have a lot of life about it. Somehow I find that some of the very silver-white forms can look rather flat by comparison. The knobbles of pale flowers are formed at the end of long stalks. This is a useful, rapid-impact plant and one well worth propagating up and then having at the ready to plug gaps in early spring. It will quickly fill out in one summer providing you plant at quite close intervals, about 20cm (8in). The only disadvantage with close planting (assuming you have propagated your own plants) is that they can suffer in dry periods. But as this plant relishes those conditions, it is not often a problem.

The foliage of this plant looks good throughout the year, except of course, when you have just cut it back in spring. It can seem a shame to lay into a fine-looking plant when others around it are looking far less bouncy, but it must be done otherwise it will start to flop and sprawl, exposing bare, leggy stems. Cut it back hard to 15–20cm (6–8in) from the ground. If you have an old specimen, cutting back into the old wood can be fatal, so take cuttings first. Young specimens will spring back to life and in about eight weeks time will look better than new. After flowering, the faded flower shoots must be removed and any long shoots shortened to neaten the plant. To propagate take semi-ripe cuttings in summer; they are quick, easy and successful. **BG**

Saponaria officinalis

Saponaria officinalis
BOUNCING BET, SOAPWORT

Type: hardy, herbaceous perennial
Soil & situation: any soil/sun or shade/preferably moist
North American hardiness zone: 3–9
Height: 60cm (24in)
Spread: 2m (6½ft)
Grow for: sprawling, straggly, cottage-garden delight with scented pink or white flowers; useful for wild, damp areas

Traditionally the leaves were boiled to extract the soapy sap. I've tried it and it worked, but be warned it is very irritant to the skin although quite effective on clothes. The books say this plant grows erect – don't believe them it flops everywhere. However it is an endearing troublemaker: the floppiness is bad enough but it runs underground when happy, popping up everywhere. The flowers are deliciously scented though, the double forms the more so and it is a delightful thing to put in difficult spots, but not if you like neatness and order.

Saponaria officinalis is a native wild flower and its name comes from the Latin for soap. There are 30 more species, mostly native to Europe. It was not used so much for washing people as wool, though it was a treatment for skin infections and the root extracts were used in medicines.

In a damp garden you'll never get rid of soapwort regardless of the soil; it even survives in my dry garden under a Leylandii hedge. Basically it is a tough plant; it can be trimmed but never trained so is better for the informal or wild garden. The wild forms come from seed sown any time and the roots can be divided whenever if kept moist. The only problem is this is a thug in tart's clothing! **BF**

Sarcococca confusa
Plant of the Week (see page 403)

Satureja hortensis
SUMMER SAVORY

Type: hardy, annual herb
Soil & situation: any soil/sun to light shade
North American hardiness zone: annual
Height: 30cm (12in)
Spread: 20cm (8in)
Grow for: brilliant flavour; good dwarf edger

This is not unattractive and makes a good, heather-like edging plant for low beds, but it is as a culinary herb that it shines. Summer savory, and don't be fooled by the coarse and rough perennial winter form, is the herb for savoury dishes. I put it in almost everything that is not actually sweet and I think it goes especially well with dried bean casseroles. It is easy to dry and retains its flavour well. Grow plenty, as once you've tried it you'll want more.

Well known and well loved by all the ancient Mediterranean people for its culinary uses, it retains its ancient name of *Satureia* or *Satyreia* as it was reputed to have aphrodisiacal properties; well maybe it does, I use a lot in my cooking and I certainly need a muzzle….

Although summer savory can be grown as temporary edging in the ornamental or herb garden, it deserves a place in the vegetable plot. A poor soil will do but moist and in full sun is preferable. Harvest just before flowering; if cut back hard, a second flush of growth can be induced with a good watering. Sow, preferably *in situ*, in mid-spring. I have never known it suffer any problem other than poor germination in cold years, so use a cloche at first. **BF**

Satureja hortensis

Saxifraga 'Ruth Draper'

Saxifraga 'Ruth Draper'
SAXIFRAGE

Type: hardy, evergreen perennial
Soil & situation: moist, humus-rich, very well-drained, neutral to alkaline soil/light shade
North American hardiness zone: 2–6
Height: 3cm (1in)
Spread: 20cm (8in)
Grow for: an attractive ground-coverer for summer show in crevices

Previously known as *Saxifraga oppositifolia* 'Ruth Draper', it is not very big, but in this case size doesn't matter. Accustomed to Arctic conditions, it will flower readily in well-drained soil .

Mat forming, with rosettes of tiny, stiff, dark green leaves on branching stems. The single, cup-shaped, rose-pink flowers appear in early summer on very short stems and may flower spasmodically until the autumn. This cheerful little saxifrage is ideal for growing in crevices in a rockery or scree bed where the drainage is good. It is not a rampant grower, making it a good choice for a stone trough or shallow pan.

Top dress with a surface mulch of riddled leaf mould in spring and water the plants in summer to prevent the soil drying out. If grown in the open, the afternoon, summer sun will scorch the foliage. Propagation is by fresh seed sown in the autumn and over-wintered in a cold frame. Individual rosettes can be rooted as cuttings in late spring and early summer. Remove the lower leaves and insert the cuttings in a peat-based compost with additional well-washed, coarse grit. **JC**

Euonymus europeaus 'Red Cascade'

SPINDLE BUSH

Type: hardy, deciduous shrub or small tree
Soil & situation: any soil, but flourishes on chalk/full sun or light shade
North American hardiness zone: 4–7
Height: 3m (10ft)
Spread: 2.5m (8ft)
Grow for: brilliant autumn colour and unusual fruits; AGM

You may well have passed this green-stemmed shrub with arching branches and narrowly oval, mid-green leaves without even realizing it. For much of the year the spindle bush crouches in the hedgerows playing its annual game of hide-and-seek, then suddenly in autumn it erupts into life. First there's an explosion of bright red leaves, then in a quick-fire burst of momentum it stuns a gasping crowd with one of nature's more psychedelic moments. 'Bravo,' they cry as masses of unusual pink fruits split to reveal bright orange seeds that are attractive to birds. 'More,' they plead, and pendulous, bronzed and red *Euonymus europeaus* 'Thornhayes' takes to the stage, accompanied by a pallid-fruited *E. e.* f. *albus*. Finally, *E. e.* 'Aucubifolius' with mottled yellow and white leaves saunters forward, 'He looks so ill,' some whisper. 'Don't worry,' comes the reply, 'he'll be in the pink by autumn.' 'It's true,' they all agree, 'when it comes to it the euonymus is really far from anonymous'!

It needs full sun or partial shade, and in the former it must have more moisture. It thrives in almost any well-drained soil, particularly on chalk. The easiest way to propagate is from nodal cuttings, which root well. It can suffer from mildew and is a host to the black bean aphid, which attacks broad beans, nasturtiums, philadelphus and dahlias.

The wood was once used for making skewers and toothpicks; the fruits were strongly purgative and sometimes baked, powdered and rubbed into the hair as a remedy for head-lice. **MB**

Scabiosa 'Chile Black'
PINCUSHION FLOWER

Type: hardy, herbaceous perennial
Soil & situation: well-drained soil/preferably
alkaline or neutral with moderate fertility/
sun/tolerates part shade
North American hardiness zone: 3–9
Height & spread: 60cm (24in)
Grow for: near-black to dark wine-coloured
flowers speckled with cream anthers in the
summer; an uncommon but extremely useful
colour shade; a vigorous and easy plant to grow,
except on heavy soils

It is always interesting to grow something a little
out of the ordinary and this curious colour is
different. I use it particularly with other wine and
purple plants but it looks great with strong
orange tones too. This is a fairly vigorous plant,
though it has a sparse habit, so it is more
successful to plant several plants close together to
achieve more impact. The flowers never come in
huge volumes, so the effect is subtle.

It is well worth dead-heading this plant, then the
succession of flowers will last for over a month if
not two. It is not long lived, and to maintain good
healthy plants it is best to divide them every three
or four years. To propagate it you can take basal
cuttings or divide. **BG**

Scabiosa 'Chile Black'

Schisandra rubriflora

Schisandra rubriflora
MAGNOLIA VINE

Type: hardy, deciduous climber
Soil & situation: well-drained, fertile soil/sun or
dappled shade
North American hardiness zone: 7–9
Height & spread: 10m (33ft)
Grow for: attractive buds, flowers in mid- and late
spring, and fruit

This twining, woody climber with aromatic bark,
slender red shoots and lance-shaped leaves, which
turn yellow in autumn, is believed to be a relative
of the magnolia. Look at the fragrant flowers,
appearing in late spring, and there are some
similarities. The buds, resembling ripe cherries,
open to dark crimson flowers, to 3cm (1in)
across. To obtain fruit, male and female plants
must be grown; several nurseries have been
sexing their schisandras and now stock both male
and female plants. The scarlet, fleshy fruits
ripening by early autumn hang in clusters up to
15cm (6in) long. In their native habitat, they are
eaten fresh or dried. No please, I insist, after you!

Schisandra grandiflora has aromatic bark, leathery
leaves with conspicuous veins and white to pale
pink flowers in late spring and early summer. The
shiny, edible, red fruits packed together in a tight,
bright, cluster are very ornamental.

They need fertile, well-drained, moisture-retentive
loam in sun or dappled shade, preferring slightly
acid soils but tolerating some alkalinity. Dig in plenty
of well-rotted organic matter before planting, mulch
in spring and water in dry spells. Prune in late winter
to remove dead wood and keep to their allocated
space. Grow as a wall plant twining up wires, up a
post or through trees or large shrubs. Propagate by
semi-ripe cuttings in summer, layers in autumn,
suckers or seed. They are susceptible to aphids. **MB**

Schizanthus x *wisetonensis*
POOR MAN'S ORCHID

Type: half-hardy or tender annual
Soil & situation: most soils/sun or under cover
North American hardiness zone: annual
Height & spread: 50cm (20in)
Grow for: attractive ferny foliage; unbelievable
mass of amazing flowers; good for diligent kids

Who could not fall in love with this beauty, as
even if badly grown she still produces the most
beautifully exotic flowers just not in such great
profusion? A well-grown, good specimen is a
magnificent sight. The common name is so apt as
there really is no other plant that can give such a
display, yet is so cheap and easy. The only
downside is that it's neither scented nor edible.
The botanical name is from the Greek *schizo*,
meaning to divide, and *anthos*, flower, as the
corolla is deeply cut. There are several related
species, mostly from South America, but the
modern selected hybrids are far superior.

Schizanthus needs a sunny spot on a warm bed to
be used for summer bedding, or grow it in a pot
or planter and have it on the patio. It should be
started off under cover in mid-spring and planted
out in early summer, or grown on and kept in
pots, ideally sowing the best selection for
whichever purpose. With careful culture in a
heated greenhouse, sown late with much nipping
out, the very dwarf, squat plants can be produced
with a mass of flowers for Christmas. It suffers no
problem other than it seems almost surreal in
bloom. **BF**

Schizanthus x *wisetonensis*

Scilla peruviana

Scilla peruviana
SQUILL

Type: Frost-hardy bulbous perennial
Soil & situation: very free-draining soil/sun
North American hardiness zone: 8–9
Height: 30cm (12in)
Spread: 30cm (12in) or more
Grow for: dramatic buds and flowers in late spring and early summer

It's comforting to know that Carl Linnaeus, the Father of Botanical Latin, had occasional bad days at the office. He named this plant *Scilla peruviana* when it's actually from the Mediterranean!

The rounded flowerhead on a mid-green stem elongates into a dense cone of up to a hundred violet-blue, starry flowers punctuated with yellow anthers, then dries to become a florist's dream! The rosette of waxy, long, green leaves becomes rather untidy by the time they flower but is easy to ignore. When my bulbs come into bloom I'm

reminded of the wonderful flower market in Funchal, Madeira, the 'island of flowers', where I bought them. The market is a buzzy, bustling place where 'Belladonna' lilies, strelitzias and orchids abound and it's overflowing with clamouring customers all eager to buy plants. Arrive early and visit the fruit market upstairs which is packed with exotics, such as balloon-sized avocados, then go to the fish market and see the scary-looking espada fish that is hauled up from the deep. My *Scilla peruviana* is packed full of happy memories! Look out also for the white-flowered *S. peruviana* 'Alba'.

Plant in autumn at the base of a sunny wall or fence with the tips just below the soil surface or grow in pots of well-drained compost in cooler climates. In needs a sunny position on very free-draining, moderate to poor soil; richer conditions bring more leaf rather than flower. Where necessary, encourage flowering with sulphate of potash in autumn or early spring. Divide and re-plant congested clumps in spring.   **MB**

Scrophularia auriculata 'Variegata'
VARIEGATED FIGWORT

Type: hardy, herbaceous perennial
Soil & situation: moist or wet soil/sun or part shade
North American hardiness zone: 5–9
Height: up to 75cm (30in)
Spread: 60cm (24in)
Grow for: an attractive foliage plant which quickly makes an impact

When I gardened on moisture-retentive, heavy loam, this plant was a firm favourite. It has ovate leaves with wavy margins which are picked out in broad irregularly creamy-white variegations. This striking foliage grows rapidly from basal evergreen or semi-evergreen rosettes. It will easily make 75cm (30in) of growth in a season, forming a good bushy clump and as such is a highly useful filler. It flowers in mid- to late summer; the yellowish-green flowers are insignificant. In favourable conditions where there is no shortage of water, this plant will stay looking in its prime until well into early autumn. In dryer conditions its charms, sadly, will be well over a month or two before this. Another way to enjoy this plant is as cut foliage – the stems last for a long time in water and are an unusual but showy and versatile favourite of florists.

To keep this plant looking good, remove the flowers as soon as they start to appear, otherwise the foliage goes downhill fast. Its leaves are also very attractive to slugs, capsid bugs and the mullein shark caterpillar, unfortunately, but they will quickly recover if you have to cut them down to size once in a while.   **BG**

Scrophularia auriculata 'Variegata'

Cyclamen europaeum (syn. *C. odoratum*)

CYCLAMEN

Type: hardy, evergreen corm
Soil & situation: well-drained, moist soil/light sun to shade
North American hardiness zone: 5–9
Height & spread: 15cm (6in)
Grow for: gorgeous evergreen leaves, gorgeous flowers, gorgeous scent! The best choice if you want cyclamens in autumn; AGM

Cyclamens are wonderful for their resistance to pests and diseases; their beautiful, marbled, heart-shaped leaves each with the most exquisite, finely executed pattern; the delicately sculptured flowers (up to a hundred of them per plant in a long flowering season); and the fantastic scent – this plant has it all. Shame it is not ten times bigger!

The name comes from the Greek word for circular. Cyclamens are native to Europe and were once so common that they were used as pig fodder – well, I guess the pigs dug them up, in fact – thus its old name of sowbread. It has an odd, spherical seed capsule held near the crown by a 'spring' made of old flower stalk.

It needs a moist, rich, limy, friable soil in dappled shade under a deciduous tree. Plant *C. europaeum* deeper than for other cyclamen at 10cm (4in), and dress with bonemeal in spring. I grow them from seed taken from my most scented plants; they take several years to reach flowering size. Small seedlings can be found around older plants and moved when tiny. Plant corms smooth side down. Unlike most other cyclamen, plant this one in spring. And presumably avoid having pigs visit. **BF**

Sedum telephium subsp. *maximum* 'Atropurpureum'

Sedum spectabile
Plant of the Week (see page 289)

Sedum telephium subsp. maximum 'Atropurpureum'

Type: hardy, herbaceous perennial
Soil & situation: light free-draining soils/neutral to slightly alkaline soils are more suitable than acid ones/full sun
North American hardiness zone: 4–9
Height: 45cm (18in)
Spread: 25cm (10in)
Grow for: superb, dark purple stems and glaucous, dark purple leaves; flowers in late summer to early autumn; AGM

I highly rate this fleshy plant for its decidedly useful, dark purple foliage, the leaves being succulent, oval, but slightly scalloped too. It has quite an open-spreading habit, which lends itself to being grown in an area of gravel, or mulched with a chipping, with other unusual-looking plants such as *Euphorbia myrsinites* (see page 95). It is also good in borders, contrasting especially well with strong, juicy limes. The purple leaves are good in border situations but best when growing out of a sea of low ground cover. The flowers are a pinky-red, with orange-red centres and are small, star-shaped and carried in sprays.

It needs little attention apart from cutting back at the end of the year. Dividing it up when it becomes congested, every three or four years, helps to promote its flowering capacity. Propagation is simple from cuttings.   **BG**

Sempervivum arachnoideum
HOUSELEEK

Type: hardy, evergreen perennial
Soil & situation: barely any soil/sun
North American hardiness zone: 5–8
Height: 3cm (1in)
Spread: 5cm (2in)
Grow for: weird cactus or dahlia flower-like plant for dry spots with little or no soil; occasional odd red flowers in clusters on stalks; rosettes of leaves and a strange cobweb of white hairs at the leaf tips; AGM

I like all the houseleeks, from the standard ones found on roofs to the coloured ones such as *Sempervivum* 'Rubine', but most of all this delightful beauty which makes its own spider's web joining together the tips of the pointed leaves, amazing. I love their low-maintenance requirements and have them not on my roof where I cannot see them, but growing in lumps of timber and rock as garden ornaments.

Native to southern Europe, it was known to the ancients – *semper vivum* is the Latin for 'always alive'. The usual form, *S. tectorum*, grows naturally on roofs, and was believed to protect the abode from lightning. Strangely this is now shown to be valid as points do discharge the accumulating electrical force, diffusing the risk – the same principle as for the modern lightning rod.

Houseleeks require almost no soil, or water, or attention; once old and congested they will flower and die rosette by rosette, slowly, and the dead ones can be removed and the others will fill in the gap. It can be grown from seed but is much quicker from offsets. Birds can devastate an old clump, ruining it in their search for worms; tie it down with black plastic netting or grow under wire cloches.   **BF**

Sempervivum arachnoideum

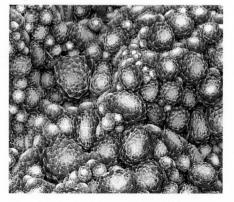

Skimmia japonica subsp. *reevesiana growing with snowdrops*

Skimmia japonica subsp. reevesiana

Type: hardy, evergreen shrub
Soil & situation: moist, humus-rich, well-drained soil/light or deep shade
North American hardiness zone: 9–10
Height & spread: 1m (3ft)
Grow for: clusters of red berries; aromatic foliage; tiny white flowers

Sexually this plant is confused. It's a hermaphrodite, with male and female flowers on the same plant, so doesn't require a partner for the production of berries. It forms a low, compact mound with narrow, 7cm (2³⁄₄in) long, mid-green leaves with a pale margin. The terminal panicles of white flowers appear in late spring and are followed by egg-shaped, mat, bright crimson-red berries. They will remain on the shrub through the winter and are often still looking good when the next season's flowers appear.

It will not succeed in ground which dries out or in an alkaline soil, but it thrives in city gardens and industrial pollution. Pruning is not usually necessary. Propagation is by semi-ripe cuttings in mid-summer. Rooting is speeded up with bottom heat in a propagator. Occasionally the base of the cutting will callus over, forming a large growth rather than roots. Scrape this off and start again. It will root the second time. Take care not to damage the brittle, white roots when potting.   **JC**

Skimmia japonica 'Veitchii'

Skimmia japonica 'Veitchii'

Type: hardy, evergreen shrub
Soil & situation: good, fertile soil/grows particularly well in light shade/will cope with a sunny position. This is a female clone and in order to produce the fruiting berries, it is necessary to plant a male clone with it, such as *Skimmia japonica* 'Rubella'
North American hardiness zone: 7–9
Height & spread: 70cm (27½in)
Grow for: superb, large bunches of vivid red fruit from late summer and still looks good until early summer the following year; eye-catching panicles of fragrant white flowers in spring; evergreen foliage which looks smart throughout the year

Skimmias, in common with many evergreens, are not the fastest growers, but this is a vigorous female clone. The leaves are particularly broadly ovate, and the habit of growth is fairly upright. Although the flowers are scented, the male forms tend to have a stronger fragrance (the equivalent of men's feet in the plant world but in a desirable form!). So when choosing your male clone to accompany this berrying stunner, go for *S. japonica* 'Rubella': the pretty flower buds stand up proudly and are a deep chintz pink, as are the margins of the leaf. If you are pushed for space, settle for *S. japonica* 'Robert Fortune', as this has both male and female flowers on the same plant.

In sunny positions you get more flowers, but the leaves can become rather yellow and scorched. Ideally plant in light shade or plant some big bruiser nearby to shade it for you. You can propagate it from cuttings in early summer or from seed sown in spring, but of course, the resulting plant will be different from the parent. **BG**

Smilacina racemosa
Plant of the Week (see page 161)

Solanum crispum
Plant of the Week (see page 297)

Solanum laxum 'Album' (syn. *S. jasminoides* 'Album')
WHITE-FLOWERED POTATO VINE

Type: half-hardy, semi-evergreen, climbing shrub
Soil & situation: reasonably well-drained but moist fertile soil/sun or part shade/may need some protection in colder areas until well established/flowers most profusely on a warm, sunny wall
North American hardiness zone: 8–9
Height: 6m (20ft)
Spread: 2m (6½ft)
Grow for: vigorous, climber with long climbing stems; flowers from summer to autumn/highly fragrant, beautiful, white flowers; AGM

Do not be put off by this elegant beauty's common name – it is the same family, of course, but not so down-to-earth. It is one of my favourite climbers, mainly because of the profusion of elegant, star-shaped flowers and obvious anthers borne over an incredibly long period. These are then followed by black fruit. In the East Midlands I find the foliage is pretty much evergreen as opposed to semi-evergreen. Despite a series of heavy frosts, gales and snow, it is still hanging on thickly now, at the end of winter, with its glossy, dark green, oval leaves. It is 3–4m (10–13ft) high now, and it is about five years old. It is a fast grower too and, to please impatient clients, I need a few of these up my sleeve.

Solanum laxum 'Album'

You do need to support this climber with a trellis, system of wires or whatever. As far as pruning goes you cut back the sideshoots to within three or four buds of the established, permanent framework, and thin out any overcrowded shoots as necessary. This is best done after flowering. **BG**

Solanum tuberosum 'Dunluce'
POTATO, EARLY CROP

Type: half-hardy, herbaceous vegetable
Soil & situation: most soils/sun
North American hardiness zone: annual
Height: 60cm (24in)
Spread: 30cm (12in)
Grow for: there are no potatoes like new potatoes; your own are the freshest and taste the best, and this is the finest variety

I love my new potatoes and grow them for more than half the year round, enjoying them forced from early to mid-spring until the outdoor lot crop in early summer and go on until late summer, when the main crop potatoes arrive (they make better chips). If you want the maximum crop of earlies, go for 'Rocket' instead, but if you want supreme flavour, grow 'Dunluce'.

Members of a wide family with many edible and many poisonous members, potatoes would not be allowed by governmental edict if found today; they would be classed as an illegal poisonous drug. Greened potatoes, the seedpods and the foliage actually are all potentially deadly! Coming from South America these originated in the high mountain valleys of Peru and have been much bred and selected to give the modern forms. 'Dunluce' is an 'early' and is very different to a 'main' crop (see *Solanum tuberosum* 'King Edward', next entry). Earlies crop early so miss the dreaded blight most years; many can be stored but they give light yields.

Although earlies can be grown outdoors at about 30cm (12in) apart they are much better grown under cloches, in a cold frame or in a greenhouse in pots, as then they give really early crops. Put the sets into pots at fortnightly intervals from early winter to early spring, also under cloches from late winter, and plant outdoors for summer crops from early to late spring. Ideally chit the later plantings beforehand by standing them in an egg tray in a frost-free, light place until they are used. Leave all the sprouts on the sets and plant them rose end (more eyes or sprouts on it and not the little bit of old stem) up. The only real problem is frost! **BF**

Solanum tuberosum 'King Edward'

Solanum tuberosum 'King Edward'
POTATO, MAIN CROP

Type: half-hardy, herbaceous vegetable
Soil & situation: most soils/sun
North American hardiness zone: annual
Height: 1m (3ft)
Spread: 60cm (24in)
Grow for: there are no potatoes like home-grown potatoes and this is finest of the main crop varieties

I love my potatoes and grow more than a couple of dozen varieties every year. There are more reliable and heavier-cropping sorts such as 'Remarka', some with better texture for salads such as 'Charlotte', but few match 'King Edward' for flavour and all-round kitchen use.

Main crops are very different to earlies and the two lines diverged years ago. Earlies are bred to be quick and many especially to grow under cover; main crops are bred to give the maximum yield of good storing potatoes. Thus, they

necessarily take a longer season to finish and need to be growing into autumn for the biggest crops. But they still need planting early, though they do not need chitting (see previous entry). However, the shoots are reduced to three at planting so as to get fewer but bigger tubers. This variety was originally a chance seedling of unknown parentage found in Northumberland and called 'Fellside Hero' for some years until re-introduced as 'King Edward' in 1902.

Main crops need a richer soil than earlies so include plenty of well-rotted manure, give them full sun. Plant the sets rose end up (see previous entry), removing all the shoots bar three, and further apart than earlies. Water generously when you see the flowers. Remove the flowers. Earth up the plants to prevent the swelling tubers seeing the light and greening. Dig on a drying day when the haulms have died down, dry the tubers for an hour or so before packing in paper sacks and storing in a cool, dark, frost-free place. Slugs are always a problem; baiting them with old potatoes cut into chips works well. Blight is a problem in many areas and few sprays work well – try prayer.

BF

Solidago 'Goldenmosa'
GOLDEN ROD, AARON'S ROD

Type: hardy, woody perennial
Soil & situation: moderately fertile, sandy, well-drained soil/full sun
North American hardiness zone: 5–9
Height: 90cm (36in)
Spread: 45cm (18in)
Grow for: bright yellow summer and autumn colour in the herbaceous border; AGM

I have fond memories of this plant. It was one of the first perennials I grew when I was a boy. Powdery mildew was a problem then and, while there is an improvement in the varieties, the mildew hasn't gone away.

It forms a vigorous, bushy plant with stiff, upright stems. The 10cm- (4in-) long, wrinkled, yellow-green leaves become sparse further up the stem. The conical panicles of tiny, bright yellow, mimosa-like flowers appear in late summer and early autumn. They are in great demand as a golden backdrop in flower arrangements. *Solidago* 'Loddon Gold' has a similar habit of growth with deep yellow, autumn flowers.

Remove the flowerheads after flowering to prevent self-sown seedlings appearing as weeds all over the garden. Clumps should be divided in spring every two to three years. The oldest centre portion becomes woody with few shoots and should be discarded. The outer growths can be teased apart, complete with roots, and planted out in the border or potted up. **JC**

Solidago 'Goldenmosa'

Sophora japonica

Sophora japonica
JAPANESE PAGODA TREE

Type: hardy, deciduous tree
Soil & situation: open sunny site with well-drained soil/will tolerate fairly thin soils
North American hardiness zone: 5–9
Height: up to 30m (100ft)
Spread: to 20m (66ft)
Grow for: a very elegant tree with several assets: attractive foliage; large panicles of creamy-white flowers in late summer till early autumn on mature trees; AGM

This tree is too rarely grown. It is similar to *Robinia pseudoacacia*, but I think far more useful: partly because it does not grow to such a massive size, and partly because it doesn't suddenly drop huge branches without warning; it does not sucker either; and because its leaves remain green and fresh on the tree, a good month after the robinias have lost theirs. So if you are looking for a tree that is fast-growing with very handsome divided leaves that look translucent with the sun through them and has a shapely, rounded head, then go for this. I did not add its flowering qualities: these are amazing too – huge fragrant flowers in the late autumn – but these are not produced on young trees. Be magnanimous and someone else will be able to enjoy these.

Establish the tree as for *Acer capillipes* (see page 22). Otherwise there is little care apart from removing dead, damaged and diseased wood. **BG**

Sorbus cashmiriana

Type: hardy, deciduous tree
Soil & situation: an open position in moist, well-drained, fertile soil/sun or partial shade
North American hardiness zone: 5–7
Height: 8m (25ft)
Spread: 7m (23ft)
Grow for: spring flowers; autumn and winter fruits; AGM

This is one of the prettiest trees for the small garden. It has a neat, open habit with leaves comprising 17–19 small serrated leaflets. In late spring, it's decked with flat clusters of soft pink flowers 18cm (7in) across, which are replaced by loose, hanging, pale green fruits made prominent in autumn when they become shiny and white. White fruits have the advantage of being ignored by birds and remain well into winter long after leaf fall and slowly moulder away.

Sorbus cashmiriana

It was introduced to the UK in the 1930s and is a native of the sub-alpine zones of the western Himalayas, including the area known as Baltistan, which you would have never heard of a few years ago but which is now famous for its Balti curries. Next time you have one, share it with your sorbus and give it a pungent reminder of home in what is now northern Pakistan. Other white-flowered sorbus include *S. hupehensis* and *S. prattii*, another fine small tree.

It prefers a good, moist soil and makes an ideal specimen tree for lawns. Plant a small group, if you have the space. Prune in winter to maintain the shape or remove dead, diseased, dying, crossing, weak and rubbing branches. Grow from seed chilled over winter and sown in spring. Sadly, it is susceptible to fire blight, but this should not deter you from planting this fabulous tree in areas where the disease does not occur. **MB**

Sorbus sargentiana

ROWAN TREE

Type: hardy, deciduous tree.
Soil & situation: deep, moist, fertile, well-drained soil/full sun
North American hardiness zone: 5–7
Height & spread: 10m (33ft)
Grow for: year-round interest – autumn leaf colour, flowers, berries and buds. I plumped for October because the autumn leaf colour is perhaps its greatest attribute, but it was a close-run thing. AGM.

This is my favourite sorbus and I am not likely to change my mind. It has the ability to show off for 12 months of the year.

The 35cm (14in) long, dark green, pinnate leaves turn orange-red and then a brilliant crimson in autumn. Even after leaf fall they lay out the red carpet. Large 20cm (8in) wide clusters of white flowers are produced in early summer followed by bunches of bright red berries. If left alone by the birds they will last well into winter. Finally, to complete the year, the short, stout shoots carry large, sticky, deep red buds like those of the horse chestnut. These open in spring as young, red-tinted leaves.

It is not fussy as to location but dislikes alkaline or waterlogged soil. When grown in light shade the autumn leaf colour is less intense. Occasionally it will send up erect branches forming a narrow angle where they join. Remove the weaker branch before it becomes large. If left to grow, the branches may split apart when mature, spoiling the shape of the tree.

Propagation is by budding on to *Sorbus aucuparia* rootstock in summer or grafting in winter. It is possible to root softwood cuttings in summer, but there is a low success rate. It will not come true from seed. **JC**

Sorbus 'Joseph Rock'

Type: hardy, upright, deciduous tree
Soil & situation: well-drained, fertile soil; short-lived on chalk/prefers sun or partial shade
North American hardiness zone: 7–8
Height & spread: 10m (33ft) x 7m (23ft), occasionally more
Grow for: attractive form, flowers, autumn colour, fruits. Another plant that is special over several seasons of the year, but again autumn colour and fruit carried the day.

Words can't express how much I adore this plant. If I had the chance, I'd cover the country with *Sorbus* 'Joseph Rock' then you could love it too! I remember the first one I ever planted outside a bank in Leicester and ever since then it's been my favourite tree! Sorbus are real 'value for money' plants with four seasons of interest, which makes them invaluable for the garden. There are flowers in spring, foliage in summer, fruits and colour in autumn, and sculptural shape and form in winter; S. 'Joseph Rock' is the best! It's a rowan of unknown parentage and is probably a natural hybrid that came from seed collected by Joseph Rock in China 1932. Thank you Dr Rock!

It is upright with a compact 'crown' and leaves composed of 15–19 narrowly oblong, sharply toothed leaflets. They are the perfect backcloth for the white flowers up to 10cm (4in) across that appear in late spring. In summer, it's decorated with fresh green foliage and clusters of up to 50 fruits, which start off pale green, become creamy-yellow, and turn primrose-yellow as they mature. The fruits remain on the tree, untouched by birds until long after leaf fall. They mingle with the rich autumn colour of the tree when ablaze with orange-red and purple, then re-emerge to illuminate winter with a soft buttery glow.

Sow seed in spring. Prune in winter to retain shape. Unfortunately it is highly susceptible to fire blight, but should be planted widely in areas where this does not occur. **MB**

Sorbus 'Joseph Rock'
Plant of the Week (see page 369)

Sorbus reducta
DWARF ROWAN

Type: hardy, deciduous shrub
Soil & situation: humus-rich, well-drained, neutral to acid soil/full sun or partial shade
North American hardiness zone: 5–8
Height: 1–1.2m (3–4ft)
Spread: 2m (6½ft)
Grow for: glossy leaves; clusters of white flowers; red berries turning to white; AGM

Size matters, and it is size that stops this sorbus being a tree. It has all the attributes of a good rowan, including brilliant autumn leaf colour, flowers and fruit in early winter.

A free-suckering shrub with stiff, upright branches, it will quickly colonize large areas. The 10cm (4in) long, pinnate, glossy, dark green leaves turn to red and finally purple before leaf fall. Clusters of small white flowers appear in late spring and are followed by spherical, deep red berries which turn white in early winter. A super shrub for the larger rockery where it can be contained within bounds.

It is totally hardy, well capable of withstanding cold winds and prolonged frost. Propagation is by transplanting suckers. There seems to be a strain in circulation which doesn't produce many berries. It would be a pity to plant it as the berries help to make this a special shrub. The birds leave mine alone until well into the New Year but that is no guarantee your feathered friends won't be really greedy or hungry. **JC**

Sorbus reducta

Spartium junceum

Sorbus sargentiana
Plant of the Week (see page 367)

Spartium junceum
SPANISH BROOM

Type: frost-hardy, deciduous shrub
Soil & situation: well-drained, alkaline soil/full sun
North American hardiness zone: 8–10
Height & spread: 3m (10ft)
Grow for: a mass of yellow in summer; AGM

Rabbits love this plant even more than I do, I stop short of eating it. The first three plants were devoured, so the fourth was better protected than Fort Knox and is a mass of colour every year. It seems to be trying to flower for the others as well. It forms an upright shrub with slender, dark green stems. Small quantities of tiny, dark green leaves, silky on the underside, furnish the stems. From early summer to mid-autumn the plant smothers itself in 45cm (18in) long terminal racemes of flower. Pea-like, golden-yellow flowers are sweetly scented. They are followed by 8cm (3½in) long, flat, brown seedpods. Trained on wires, against a red or brown brick wall, close to an opening window provides two of the senses, sight and smell, with a treat. It thrives in coastal gardens and on thin soils overlying chalk.

Pruning consists of removing straggly branches in spring. Old plants can be cut down close to the ground and will grow away flowering within two years. Propagation is by seed in spring or sown fresh and over-wintered in a cold frame. They dislike being moved so thin out seedlings when they are small and transplant before they become large. **JC**

Spiraea japonica 'Goldflame'

Type: hardy, deciduous shrub
Soil & situation: moist, fertile, well-drained soil/full sun
North American hardiness zone: 4–9
Height & spread: 1m (3ft)
Grow for: wonderful foliage colour; brings structure to the garden

There are spiraea that inspire and this, for me, is one of them. It lies dormant all winter with no hint of its beauty. Then, in spring, it bursts into life with a collection of leaf colours to make a painter's overalls look jaded. It seems to grow in two stages. Firstly it quickly forms a compact mound and stays about the same size for a season or two. Then it takes off, forming a dense, twiggy clump 1m (3ft) high.

The leaves emerge bronze-red, turning to a bright, buttery-yellow, while the next batch of new leaves provides a contrast in colour. In summer they become mid-green with occasional splashes of yellow. Dark pink flowers appear in summer at the tips of that year's growth. A similar variety, *Spiraea japonica* 'Golden Princess', retains its golden foliage through the summer, turning red in autumn.

I manage to fit *S. j.* 'Goldflame' into almost all of my landscape designs and love to plant it in groups of five or six spaced about 1m (3ft) apart. When pruning a group of them I cheat, clipping 50 per cent of them hard to within 10cm (4in) of the base of the plant. These produce maximum leaf colour. The remainder are lightly pruned resulting in early leaves with less colour on bigger plants. The following year I hard prune the other half.

Propagation is easy. Take small, softwood cuttings in early summer and root them around the edge of a pot of gritty compost. Cover with a clear plastic bag. They will root within weeks ready for potting on before autumn and their leaf fall. **JC**

Spiraea japonica 'Goldflame'

Stachys byzantina 'Big Ears'

Stachys byzantina 'Big Ears'
LAMB'S TONGUE, LAMB'S TAIL, LAMB'S EARS, WOOLLY BETONY

Type: hardy perennial
Soil & situation: well-drained, reasonably fertile soil/prefers sunshine
North American hardiness zone: 4–8
Height: 1m (3ft)
Spread: 60cm (24in)
Grow for: one of the most good-natured and tolerant of the silver-leaved plants with bold, attractive leaves and little tendency to flower

I think the common form of this plant was my favourite as a child, as like many children, I adored the furry leaves. But as a professional gardener, I quickly became disenchanted with it as after flowering it disintegrates into a messy mixture of spent flower stalks and miserable leaves. Then my mother gave me a clump of 'Big

Ears' and my affection was reawakened. This form has larger, cleanly-shaped, silvery, felted leaves that form a very decorative carpet. It does flower, but much less so than the ordinary form, and so the foliage keeps looking neat for most of the growing season. In the coldest winter months it does not totally disappear, but keeps some almost respectable-looking leaves. *S. b.* 'Silver Carpet' is a better-known form which only occasionally flowers, and as such is neater and better than the common form, but the foliage does not compare with 'Big Ears'.

This plant needs little looking after apart from dividing up old clumps every so often – this is also one of the best ways to propagate it. It is worthwhile removing any flower spikes as soon as they start to rise as it helps to keep the plant at its best. Some forms, particularly 'Silver Carpet', are prone to mildew, but dividing the clumps more frequently can help to prevent this.   **BG**

Stachyurus praecox

Type: hardy, medium to large, deciduous shrub
Soil & situation: moist, humus-rich soil/sun or partial shade/shelter
North American hardiness zone: 7–9
Height: 2m (6½ft)
Spread: 3m (10ft)
Grow for: yellow flowers in late winter and early spring; occasional autumn colour; AGM

Nature possesses an array of unusual colour combinations. Take the flowers of *Stachyurus praecox* for instance: they are an unfamiliar tone of yellow with a slight limy tint and unless my eyes are deceiving me, the purity of colour makes them almost iridescent. They hang in ranks of stiff, gravity-defying flower spikes to 7cm (2³/₄in) long from reddish-brown, leafless stems. The two colours may not be a combination for your lounge, but it's perfect to brighten up a dull grey winter's day!

Tiny, bell-shaped flowers are formed the previous year, maturing in autumn before leaf fall but not opening until late winter or early spring, depending on the weather. The species is hermaphrodite but there is a selection *S. p.* 'Gracilis' with female flowers. *S. p.* var. *matsuzakii* has thicker, pale green stems and larger leaves. The yellow flowers open later too, in mid-spring and it's only suitable for mild climates.

S. praecox needs sun or partial shade and shelter, particularly in cold areas where it can be trained against a wall as the flowers can be damaged by frost. Any soil will do, but cool, humus-rich, acid soil is favoured and it is also lime tolerant. Prune after flowering, remove dead, diseased, dying, crossing, rubbing or weak wood at the base; it soon regenerates. Thin out congested specimens. Tie in the strongest growth of wall shrubs after flowering, replacing the framework regularly using young growth at the base. Propagate by layering or semi-ripe cuttings with a heel from mid-summer to early autumn.   **MB**

Stachyurus praecox

Sternbergia lutea

Sternbergia lutea
AUTUMN DAFFODIL

Type: hardy, bulbous perennial
Soil & situation: free-draining, alkaline soil/sun
North American hardiness zone: 7–9
Height: 20cm (8in)
Spread: 30cm (12in)
Grow for: bright yellow, goblet-shaped flowers at the start of autumn

It's found in the Mediterranean on or near cultivated land in dry scrub and rocky grassy slopes. The cheerful golden-yellow, goblet-shaped flowers that appear in early autumn, accompanied by contrasting narrow, glossy green, strap-like leaves, look like crocuses but are members of the Amaryllis family. Lift a slab from the patio or plant them among grey foliage plants like sage or lavender, but make sure the bushes don't overshadow the bulbs; they need a good baking in summer.

Sternbergia sicula is a smaller version, with flower stems only 5–7cm (2–2³⁄₄in) tall. The narrow dark green leaves have a pale central stripe. *S. clusiana* has large flowers with greenish-yellow goblets appearing from early to late autumn before the strap-shaped, grey-green leaves. It is not totally reliable but worth trying at the base of a sunny wall.

It needs very free-draining, neutral to alkaline soil and full sunshine; the base of a sunny wall is ideal. Plant in autumn immediately after buying about 10cm (4in) deep and the same apart, watered in if the soil is dry. They may take a year or two to settle before flowering. Once established, they are better left undisturbed to grow into clumps for the most effective display. Lift and divide clumps after a few years in late summer or late spring while the leaves are green or they will become shy of flowering; a light feed of sulphate of potash in autumn and spring helps this too. **MB**

Stipa gigantea
SPANISH OAT GRASS

Type: hardy, evergreen or semi-evergreen perennial
Soil & situation: any reasonable, well-drained soil/sun
North American hardiness zone: 7–10
Height: up to 2.5m (8ft), leaves 75cm (30in)
Spread: 1m (3ft)
Grow for: an essential flowering grass, with strong form and a lasting presence; straw-yellow flowers for most of the winter; evergreen leaves; sends up its bold panicles in late spring; AGM

All the stipas are natives of the expansive grasslands of the world, particularly meadows, prairies and steppes. So consider this when choosing your site, giving them sun and reasonable drainage. This giant is one of the most spectacular as a specimen plant, with its huge, airy, oat-like, bristly spikelets soaring above the lower foliage. Yet it is quite delicate and see-through, so is equally useful for threading through lower plants to create a tracery effect. It will slowly form spreading, grey-green leafy clumps, which are a year-round asset. It is fairly drought resistant and will soak up any amount of sun. Unfortunately it tends not to seed around, more is the shame, as home-grown seed does not tend to be fertile.

The old flowering spikelets usually tend to start falling to bits at the onset of the harder winter weather, and at this point, usually after Christmas, they can be snipped off to tidy them up. They look fantastic covered in frost and in some years can be left on a good while. The easiest way to propagate this plant is from imported seed, as when it is propagated by division the plants seem slow to establish. Seed is best sown in autumn and left to be exposed to frost. **BG**

Stipa gigantea

Styrax japonicus

Styrax japonicus
SNOWBELL, JAPANESE SNOWBELL

Type: hardy, deciduous, large shrub or small tree
Soil & situation: moist, well-drained, acid soil/sheltered position in full sun to partial shade
North American hardiness zone: 6–8
Height: 10m (33ft)
Spread: 8m (25ft)
Grow for: dainty and delicate flowers in early summer; good winter form; AGM

The snowbell, an elegant, graceful tree, has spreading fan-like branches covered with clusters of fragrant, pure white, bell-shaped, pendent flowers in June (often earlier). It is better planted where their exquisite beauty can be appreciated from below. A bank is ideal, overhanging a path or simply lie on the ground below with a glass of chilled Chablis, and look up – then you can enjoy two of life's greatest pleasures! Once the oval to elliptic leaves turn yellow or red and fall in autumn, the stems provide winter interest. The bark is marked with fissures revealing orange-brown inner layers and the branches, forming a dense mound, look spectacular when covered with frost.

Styrax japonicus Benibana Group 'Pink Chimes' with pale pink flowers, is better than the similar *S. japonicus* 'Roseus'. *S. j.* 'Fargesii' is more tree-like with slightly larger leaves and flowers. 'Emerald Pagoda' (or 'Sohuksan') has larger flowers than the species, thicker petals and the leaves are leathery and deeper green. 'Carillon' is one of the prettiest weeping trees; to 5m (16ft) x 2.5m (8ft). Train the leading shoot vertically for extra height.

It needs a sheltered position, in sun or partial shade (ideally protected from morning sun; young shoots can be damaged by late-spring frosts), on moist, free-draining, acid soil. Add leafmould or peat substitute to the ground before planting. The bark may split if planted in cold or exposed locations. Remove dead, diseased, dying and damaged wood in winter. Propagate from seed or layering. **MB**

Symphytum 'Hidcote Blue'

Type: hardy, evergreen perennial
Soil & situation: pretty well any soil/easy and undemanding/full sun or deep shade
North American hardiness zone: 3–9
Height: 45cm (18in)
Spread: indefinite
Grow for: a neat mound of lush, evergreen leaves; pretty red buds open to mid-blue flowers which later fade to white; nearly unbeatable plant for rapidly colonizing difficult areas

I use sheets of this plant all around my cesspit – most exciting – but the point of the story is that the pit has four large concrete covers, each one a good one and a half square metres (five square feet) in size, and I had planted the comfrey immediately after one visit from the emptying lorry, however, the next time the man came to empty it he could not find the covers as the comfrey had totally camouflaged it! I do admit I leave the emptying interval longer than I should, a good 12 months, but even so it is magic. The plants have obviously not rooted into the slabs but spread out over them. I also use this same comfrey to form neat circles around the base of my old fruit trees in the orchard' where the solid rings of dark green look almost sculptural. It is a superb plant with great uses. Apart from this gem there are several other comfreys I am keen on too. One is *Symphytum* x *uplandicum* 'Variegatum' which is no thug but very striking with its handsome green leaves, edged with white. 'Hidcote Blue' will spread but if you grow it surrounded by grass, then there is no problem in containing it as the mower does it for you. Otherwise, you can simply spade round it. When I want it to spread in a new area, I just divide it up into small clumps and re-plant at virtually any time of year. **BG**

Symphytum 'Hidcote Blue'

Symphytum officinale

Symphytum officinale
COMFREY

Type: hardy, herbaceous perennial
Soil & situation: damp soil/sun or shade
North American hardiness zone: 3–9
Height: 1.5m (5ft)
Spread: 1.2m (4ft)
Grow for: good-looking leaves; tall stems with many small purple flowers; excellent for making liquid feed; attracts bees

Although it is very useful to me as I rot down the leaves and stalks to make a liquid feed, I would grow comfrey anyway as I like its rugged enthusiasm and the buzz of bees about its flowers. It is also an exceptionally useful plant for filling shady banks, the edges of ditches and many other damp spots with little sun.

This is a native European plant often eaten in times of famine and by those seeking relief from arthritis, but this is now discouraged as apparently if you feed rats almost nothing else they get sick on it, surprise surprise. *Symphytum* is the ancient Greek name for this plant, even then known as a wound healer. The common name may come from the Latin *conferva*, for grow together, as it has always been used to make poultices to help knit bones and heal flesh. The infamous comfrey tea is simply comfrey leaves rotted under water and diluted down to tea colour before using as a feed; it is similar to commercial tomato feed in constituents and ideal for most plants in pots.

It prefers a damp, rich soil and will grow on the sides of rank ditches in sun or shade. Once you have it you've got it for good! The species can be grown from seed but any bit of root takes almost any time. No problems other than tenaciousness if it's no longer wanted. **BF**

Syringa velutina (syn. *S. palibiniana*)
KOREAN LILAC

Type: hardy, deciduous shrub
Soil & situation: most soils/full sun or very light shade
North American hardiness zone: 4–7
Height & spread: 2.5m (8ft) x 2m (6½ft), eventually
Grow for: neat compact shrub with velvety leaves and a profusion of pinky-purple panicles of scented flowers in early summer

Many of the lilacs are lovely plants but they are no longer popular despite their gorgeous flowers and heavy scents. This pretty little shrub remains compact and yet is covered with flowers, even when young. These are pinky-lilac in colour and sweetly scented, but not as cloying as say the old double white. It makes a nice combination with the Persian lilac, *Syringa* x *persica*, and the small-leafed *S. microphylla*, giving you three shades of flower all on compact shrubs, but *S. velutina* is the best of them.

Syringa comes from the Greek for pipe as it has hollow stems. Botanists once grouped *Syringa* with *Philadelphus* (see page 295), but the two are now considered separate genera. The name lilac comes from the Arabic or Persian for bluish flower and *velutina* describes the somewhat velvety leaves.

Syringa velutina

Most lilacs like a moist, leafmould-rich soil but they will grow almost anywhere, even on chalky soils; they revel in sun, but can cope with shade although will flower less. It is worth removing seedheads as the flowers wither. This variety is compact and should not need pruning. It cannot be easily grown from seed but spring-softwood cuttings taken with a heel may take under mist, eventually. It suffers no common problems.   **BF**

Syringa vulgaris 'Katherine Havemeyer'

Syringa vulgaris 'Katherine Havemeyer'
LILAC

Type: hardy, deciduous shrub or small tree
Soil & situation: fertile, well-drained, neutral to alkaline soil/full sun
North American hardiness zone: 4–7
Height: 7m (23ft)
Spread: 6m (20ft)
Grow for: early summer fragrance for alkaline soil; AGM

Of all the plants that can and can't be grown on different soils I really do feel sorry for people who are unable to grow lilac. It dislikes acid conditions and while those same gardeners revel in a whole range of ericaceous plants, including rhododendrons, pieris and camellias, the absence of lilac leaves a gaping hole, metaphorically.

It has an upright habit with 10cm (4in) long, heart-shaped, mid-green leaves. In late spring and early

summer it produces dense, compact, panicles of very fragrant, double, lavender-blue flowers fading to light pink. In bud they are deep purple. In fact, the term 'very fragrant' is hardly adequate. Some flowers go beyond that and, for me, lilac is off the scale. Perhaps 'not heavy but heavenly' is more apt.

Prune in late winter to remove crossing branches. Old, neglected plants may be pruned hard into the old wood and will respond well with new growth. Dead head after flowering, especially in the first few years after planting. Where the plant produces extra-strong summer growth the stems should be cut back to half their length. When planted in shade it will struggle to reach the light, becoming straggly with all its flowers at the top of the plant. Lilac loves a humus-rich soil and a deep, annual winter mulch will be beneficial. For me the easiest method of propagation is by layering in early summer.   **JC**

Syringa vulgaris 'Madame Lemoine'

Type: hardy, deciduous shrub
Soil & situation: well-drained, fertile soil/ preferably neutral or alkaline/needs full sun to flower well
North American hardiness zone: 4–7
Height & spread: 7m (23ft)
Grow for: wonderful, fragrant, large, double, white flowers from late spring to early summer; AGM

Syringa vulgaris 'Madame Lemoine'

I used to be indifferent to lilacs, I think because I had seen so many grown as specimen trees in front gardens looking dull, almost oppressive, for most of the year. My interest in them was awakened when one day I was searching for a picture for the jacket of my first book. We came upon a neglected glade lined with lilacs in full glory and the long grass under the canopy was strewn with wild flowers. This was it! The decision was unanimous, the owners agreed and we arranged to return in a few days with the photographer. But it was not to be. The thoughtful owners (unbeknown to us) had cut all the grass and the idyllic illusion was shattered. Lilacs do look wonderful in more natural settings, and the compact, but very large white flowers of 'Madame Lemoine' look especially well against the multitude of fresh greens in spring gardens. I recommend using white clematis to extend the flowering period. They are ideal for intertwining amongst the mid-green, heart-shaped leaves, bringing the canopy to life a second time.

It is not necessary to prune lilacs every year, though it is worth removing the dead flowerheads as they look brown and well past it, as they go over. It is also generally agreed that dead-heading newly planted lilac prevents fruit forming, so helps them establish. Otherwise prune the shrubs after flowering when they become too crowded, to thin out the dead and older wood. Old plants can be renovated by cutting hard back as they respond favourably. This lilac is one of those that roots easily from cuttings. These are best taken with a heel, just as the wood is just starting to ripen. When purchased they are sometimes grafted which can lead to suckering. These need removing. **BG**

Tagetes patula
FRENCH MARIGOLD

Type: half-hardy annual
Soil & situation: any soil/sun or light shade
North American hardiness zone: annual
Height & spread: 30cm (12in)
Grow for: neat compact plant with verdant, fern-like foliage, a pungent smell that keeps pests away and ghastly orange flowers which clash with most colour schemes

The organic gardener has to grow these as they are so useful. I have them by the greenhouse doors and at the gates of my vegetable plot. I mix them with tomatoes and valuable crops and am convinced they deter many pests. And their roots have exudates that depress levels of pestilential soil nematodes. And they look really good all summer, it's just a shame about their colour.

Tagetes patula

They are not French at all, nor is the bigger African marigold from Africa. In fact 20-odd species of *Tagetes* marigold are from Central America, mostly Mexico. They are named after Tages, a god of the earth.

French marigolds are good as bedding in most soils and sites, but not heavy shade or cold. They do well in pots and containers. As a half-hardy annual they are best started off in the warmth early in spring and planted out as soon as the frosts are over. **BF**

Tamarix tetrandra
TAMARISK

Type: hardy, deciduous shrub
Soil & situation: well-drained soil/moist if not coastal/full sun

Tamarix tetrandra

North American hardiness zone: 5–9
Height & spread: 3m (10ft)
Grow for: a mass of blooms; AGM

When you first grow this shrub there is a temptation to treat it as less than hardy. The foliage and flower suggests a fragile plant, but it is tough enough to enjoy seaside conditions. I have an eight-year-old-plant which has flowered, without fail, every year since it went in.

The pale green, needle-like, ferny foliage appears in late spring on thin, arching, purple-brown shoots. In mid- to late spring lateral racemes of four-petalled, light pink flowers appear on the previous year's wood before the leaves. When grown on light soils at the coast it can withstand strong winds, making a first-class and attractive windbreak. On inland sites protect it from cold winds and choose a moist, free-draining soil. *Tamarix ramosissima* is another excellent species for seaside conditions, flowering on the new growth in late summer and autumn.

Prune immediately after flowering, cutting back to healthy buds. Old, neglected plants may be rejuvinated by a severe cutting into the old, gnarled wood, which will re-sprout by the following summer. Remove half of the branches in the first year. Feed with a balanced fertilizer during summer and cut the remaining branches the following season. Propagate by semi-ripe cuttings in summer or hardwood cuttings outside in winter. **JC**

Rhus glabra 'Laciniata' November

SMOOTH SUMACH

Type: hardy, deciduous shrub or small tree
Soil & situation: moist, well-drained soil/sun
North American hardiness zone: 2–8
Height: 3m (10ft)
Spread: indefinite
Grow for: flamboyant autumn colour; plume-like seedheads in winter, but the autumn colour wins out to make it a choice for November

This plant is a rough diamond. Rough – it has toxic sap and the suckers can take over your garden; diamond – it radiates warmth from spring to autumn in gratitude to the gardener for overlooking its shortcomings and allowing it space to shine. In leaf, the dainty, fern-like fronds projecting at a sharp angle from the smooth, spreading stems create an exotic, tropical ambience – the picture below shows it in a mixed planting with *Ricinus communis*, *Eucalyptus gunnii* and *Phormium* 'Sundowner'.

Autumn brings a transformation as it responds to the needs of gardeners when the weather becomes damp and chilling. Stand in its warming glow and you can almost hear the twigs crackling and feel the heat from the glorious shimmering leaves that fall around the plant like a pool of fire, before finally fading away.

It prefers moist, well-drained, moderately fertile soil in full sun. Control suckers by creating a barrier of paving slabs or thick polythene around the plant and grow in containers; or allow it to exert its right to roam; the impact is magnificent!

Prune in winter to keep within its allotted space. If you prune last year's growths to within 3–5cm (1–2in) of a framework of older wood or back to the base like a dogwood (see *Cornus alba*, page 17) and thin to leave the strongest growths, it produces fewer, broader leaves, up to 1m (3ft) long. Remove suckers by clearing the soil and pulling them from the roots. Propagate from suckers cut from the roots in winter.

Warning: the sap can cause dermatitis, so avoid skin contact. Wear gloves, a long-sleeved top and long trousers when pruning; do not burn the wood. **MB**

Taxus baccata
COMMON YEW, ENGLISH YEW

Type: hardy, evergreen tree
Soil & situation: wide range of conditions/acid and alkaline soils/grows more successfully in well-drained soils than in heavy, water-retentive ones, where it becomes susceptible to fungal root rots/shade/sun
North American hardiness zone: 7–8
Height: up to 15m (50ft), rarely to 27m (90ft), but can be maintained at just 30cm (12in)
Spread: to 10m (33ft)
Grow for: the best evergreen hedge, with its fine, dense texture; is not so slow growing if it is given the correct care; highly useful for topiary, arches, arbours and the like; with patience, forms a magnificent tree; AGM

I plant yew to form the garden structure more than any other plant as it conveys an air of permanence, forming magnificent boundaries which look like dark green walls. I have found that it will grow as fast as many deciduous rivals but the secret is to water it copiously in dry periods during the summer months. This is something that people rarely do, as its hatred of badly drained, heavy soil is legendary. I first found this out in my own garden. On one side of

Taxus baccata

my garden I have three sections of yew hedging backing onto my vegetable garden, on the other side the three sections are mirror images, backing onto my nuttery. The yew plants in with the vegetables are irrigated regularly, inadvertently along with the runner beans, courgettes and lettuces. This section formed a dense, above eye-level screen in less than eight years, while the other one grew at the speed generally expected, that of a boy from birth onwards. So do not be fobbed off with faster-growing alternatives – if this is what you really crave, go for it. It does not have to form a high hedge. My uncle, David Austin, uses it as a low 30cm (12in) hedge to edge around the front of his rose garden where it looks extremely smart and makes a change from box. Surprisingly he cuts it once a year. A word of warning: yew is toxic so watch nearby grazing animals and warn children about berries.

If planted as a hedge I plant a double staggered row unless I need a really wide hedge, in which case I use a triple staggered row. I plant far closer than many people recommend – at 50cm (20in) centres with 50cm (20in) between the rows. If your drainage is poor, it is essential to get this right before you plant, or opt for something else. I do not add copious amounts of muck into the trench but tend to add a mulch in successive springs, as this helps reduce the moisture loss. Feed is then washed down to the roots rather than away from the roots, which happens if you put muck in the base of the trench. Keep any grass a good 60cm (24in) from the base of the plant as grass roots steal precious moisture. Clip once a year in summer (at Hidcote they do it virtually 12 months a year due to the sheer volume) and just clip the sides till you have the height you want and then do the tops – such a great feeling when you do this for the first time. Your garden seems suddenly to come of age! **BG**

Taxus baccata 'Fastigiata Aurea'
Plant of the Week (see page 389)

Tecophilaea cyanocrocus
CHILEAN BLUE CROCUS

Type: hardy, bulbous corm
Soil & situation: rich, sandy, free-draining soil/sun
North American hardiness zone: 7–9
Height: 10cm (4in)
Spread: 25cm (10in)
Grow for: blue flowers from early to mid-spring

Tecophilaea cyanocrocus

What a magnificent name! It commemorates Tecophilaea Villotti, an Italian botanical artist, and I wonder if her beauty equalled this glorious vision in deep gentian-blue. Yet beauty has its perils: this priceless treasure is now thought to be extinct in the wild because of over-grazing and over-collecting; when you're so irresistibly beautiful, everyone wants a piece of the action! Conservationists from the Royal Botanic Gardens, Kew, are managing ongoing projects with their colleagues in Chile to re-establish plants at selected sites, yet I suspect their beauty will always be their downfall.

They are only worth risking outdoors in mild parts of the UK where they combine well with silver-foliaged plants. Plant corms about 5cm (2in) deep in rich, sandy, well-drained soil in sunshine; dig in grit or sharp sand if necessary and cover the surface with coarse gravel for protection. After flowering they become dormant; allow them to dry out but not 'bake' or the corms will desiccate. The safer alternative is to grow them in pots of gritty compost in a cool greenhouse; always keep the label with the pot! *Tecophilaea cyanocrocus* 'Leichtlinii' has paler, clear blue flowers with large white centres and *T. cyanocrocus* 'Violacea' has deep purplish flowers.

Pollinate the flowers with a soft brush and sow the seed in autumn when it is ripe. After germination, keep seedlings in a pot in a cold frame until they are large enough to plant out. They too will die back in summer but take care to not let them dry out completely. They produce some offsets; lift and replant when they are dormant. **MB**

Teucrium fruticans
TREE GERMANDER, SHRUBBY GERMANDER

Type: first-hardy, evergreen shrub
Soil & situation: well-drained soils/prefers neutral or slightly alkaline soil/needs a warm, sunny position
North American hardiness zone: 8–9
Height: up to 2m (6½ft)
Spread: up to 4m (13ft)
Grow for: aromatic foliage; attractive silver-grey green and felted leaves; pale blue flowers throughout the summer

This is a stunning small shrub which looks very Mediterranean. It is good towards or at the front of the border, where if you want to reform its naturally rather lax habit you can shape it up as required to produce a more rounded, compact dome. The leaves have great appeal all through the year, a neat, ovate- to lance-shape about 2cm (³/₄in) long and are woolly-white underneath with square-shaped stems to match. The pretty, pale blue flowers are borne in loose racemes. The form *Teucrium fruticans* 'Azureum' has darker blue flowers which look really special against the grey. Unfortunately it is slightly more tender but is worth growing on in a large pot till it is a more robust size for coping with cold, and then planting out in spring.

Prune this plant in spring as growth begins, removing any dead or weak growth and trimming it to produce more compact growth. It will cope well with hard pruning if required to renovate older, leggy plants. Propagation is by seed or is easy from softwood or semi-ripe cuttings. **BG**

Teucrium fruticans

Thalictrum delavayi

Thalictrum delavayi 'Hewitt's Double'
MEADOW RUE

Type: hardy, herbaceous perennial
Soil & situation: moist soil, sun or dappled shade
North American hardiness zone: 5–9
Height: 1.2m (4ft)
Spread: 60cm (24in)
Grow for: foliage and delicate flowers from early to late summer; AGM

This wonderfully light and airy plant has mounds of delicate, frothy, grey-green foliage and shimmering clouds of tiny, double, lilac flowers with pale yellow, petal-like stamens, resembling minute pompoms. It looks so pretty and fragile, you'd think that a strong gust of wind would shatter the plant and blow the fragments away. *Thalictrum delavayi* has graceful clusters of purple flowers with long creamy-yellow stamens. There is a white-flowered form called 'Album' which was introduced from China but has become naturalized in the UK.

To ensure that the more exotic species don't take all of the glory, I'm delighted that there are some 'garden worthy' species native to the UK. *T. minus* has delicate fresh green leaves and tiny heads of creamy-green flowers with prominent hanging stamens. It is found in chalky places on cliffs and banks throughout the UK and prefers limy soil. There is a selection called *T. m.* 'Adiantifolium' with delicate, tiny leaves like a maidenhair fern and small, creamy-green flowers. *T. alpinum* has green-flushed, purple flowers, with long yellow anthers. As its name suggests, it comes from mountainous areas. *T. flavum* subsp. *glaucum* has sulphur-yellow flowers and blue-green finely cut leaves and stems. This is a subspecies of the native meadow rue.

Grow in moist, humus-rich soil in sun to partial shade. Before planting dig in plenty of well-rotted organic matter if necessary; cut back stems and mulch in autumn; water during drought. Divide when new growth starts in spring. Susceptible to powdery mildew in dry conditions; slugs can be a problem. **MB**

Thuja occidentalis 'Rheingold'

Type: hardy, evergreen conifer
Soil & situation: moist, well-drained soil/full sun
North American hardiness zone: 3–7
Height: 3m (10ft)
Spread: 2.5m (8ft)
Grow for: golden-yellow foliage in summer, coppery-orange in winter; AGM

This is one of my favourite conifers for year-round colour. In summer it is golden-yellow but in winter the foliage turns to a warm coppery-orange. When grown in an exposed site its winter cloak can be deep bronze.

The foliage often causes arguments and confusion. There are two distinct forms: juvenile leaves, which are soft and ferny and usually to be found at the base of a young plant, and the rest of the plant, which is made up of normal adult foliage. As the plant matures it becomes conical or pyramidal in shape, losing the juvenile growth. Avoid soil contaminated with perennial weeds, which will smother the plant, causing the foliage to brown. Plant in a well-prepared hole with rotted farmyard manure worked into the soil. Tease out the rootball and spread the roots. Water as necessary during the first year after planting. A surface mulch of composted bark will help retain moisture in summer. **JC**

Thuja occidentalis 'Rheingold'

Thymus spp.
Plant of the Week (see page 249)

Thymus serpyllum 'Minimus'
MINIMUS THYME

Type: hardy, evergreen perennial
Soil & situation: free-draining soil, preferably calcareous/sun
North American hardiness zone: 4–9
Height: 5mm (¼in)
Spread: to 20cm (8in)
Grow for: a ground-hugging, aromatic plant that keeps healthy-looking foliage throughout the year; smothered in pinky-mauve flowers for several weeks in the summer

This is a hard-working, highly desirable, completely prostrate thyme with tiny leaves. It is ideal for using in paving areas, perhaps in large squares to form a chequerboard pattern or perhaps in bold stripes. It quickly forms dense mats of green, which will tolerate a certain amount of walking on, providing living paving for 12 months of the year. When it comes into flower in early summer, it transforms into a mass of enchanting pink flowers, which, due to their abundant production of nectar, will be alive with bees. Of course there are many different types of *Thymus serpyllum* (the wild thyme), such as 'Goldstream' with variegated leaves, and 'Snowdrift' with white flowers, both which are excellent too, but I find the minimus thyme the most useful creeping one.

Thymus serpyllum 'Minimus' *in Bunny's Herbalist Garden for the 1998 Chelsea Flower Show.*

Tiarella wherryi

This plant thrives in conditions with really sharp drainage, otherwise it will die out in wet winters. So do make sure you lighten the soil if necessary. It also prefers calcareous soils. If you want to establish respectably sized areas of it, I find it useful to plant it into completely weed-free substrate (such as sterilized compost) to avoid intensive weeding before it has completely covered the ground. After flowering, trimming back is advisable, which rejuvenates the plant. Propagation is very simple and cuttings can be taken in spring or summer. **BG**

Tiarella wherryi
FOAMFLOWER

Type: hardy, herbaceous perennial
Soil & situation: moist, humus-rich soil/dappled shade
North American hardiness zone: 5–9
Height: 25cm (10in)
Spread: 15cm (6in)
Grow for: flowers from mid-spring to late summer; ornamental foliage; AGM

This pretty little plant proves that small is beautiful. It forms a neat cushion of ivy leaf-shaped foliage that is velvety and moss-green with brown markings along the central vein. Delicate pale pink buds in dainty spikes open to reveal tiny flowers, their long stamens creating a shimmering haze; every one is a twinkling star! Beth Chatto, the knowledgeable and discerning plantswoman, grows it alongside *Ophiopogon planiscapus* 'Nigrescens', the emerald velvet foliage contrasting with the black leaves. *Tiarella* is from the Greek word *tiara* or small crown, referring to the shape of the seed capsule.

There have been many selections from this and other species, chosen for their colour and the marking on their leaves; many are spreading. *Tiarella wherryi* 'Bronze Beauty' has dark, red-bronze leaves, turning darker in winter. *Tiarella* 'Skid's Variegated' has cream-mottled, pink-tinted foliage. *T.* 'Ninja' has deeply lobed leaves with a central blotch of dark chocolate which become almost totally plum-purple in winter. 'Heronswood Mist' was a chance seedling found at the legendary Heronswood Nursery in Washington state, USA. The foliage is marbled and blotched in cream and pink – a spectacular plant! *T. polyphylla* is a good gap filler with marbled leaves and pink flowers.

They need cool, moist, humus-rich soil in shade. Dig in plenty of well-rotted organic matter if necessary before planting. Cut back foliage and mulch in spring. They dislike waterlogging in winter. Sow seed of species in spring or as soon as ripe; divide in spring. Slugs can damage the leaves. **MB**

Trachelospermum jasminoides
STAR JASMINE

Type: frost-hardy, evergreen, twining climber
Soil & situation: well-drained, moisture-retentive, free-draining soil/sun/shelter
North American hardiness zone: 7–10
Height & spread: 9m (30ft)
Grow for: glossy leaves and fragrant waxy flowers from mid- to late summer; AGM

This plant provided one of my life's most memorable moments! I was visiting a garden in the centre of Blandford Forum in Dorset, when I was overwhelmed with a glorious scent that encapsulated the heady sensation of summer. There several metres away, bathed in sunshine was the most wonderful *Trachelospermum jasminoides* I have ever seen. How thankful I am that it was introduced by Robert Fortune from Shanghai in 1844 – what a wonderful legacy!

The oval, glossy, dark green leaves provide the perfect contrast to the pure white, waxy flowers 3cm (1in) across that are produced from mid- to late summer. It is hardy in all but the coldest parts of the UK, where it needs the protection of a conservatory or can be grown in a container and taken outdoors in summer. Train it up canes or grow it through a trellis.

T. asiaticum reaches 6m (20ft) each way. Its flowers are creamy white with a buff yellow centre, it is neater and more compact but less fragrant and, in my opinion, is not quite as beautiful. The leaves of the varieties listed below become

Trachelospermum jasminoides

crimson with winter's chilling touch. *T. jasminoides* 'Japonicum' is vigorous, grows taller and has larger leaves; the leaves of *T. j.* 'Variegatum' are splashed and margined with creamy white; *T. j.* 'Wilsonii' has attractively veined leaves.

Grow in well-drained, moderately moisture-retentive soil in a sheltered, sunny position. Dig in plenty of well-rotted organic matter before planting, mulch in spring and feed with general fertilizer. Lightly prune in spring to remove dead or weak growth or to keep within its allotted space. Propagate by semi-ripe cuttings in late summer and layering. **MB**

Bunny adds:
Do not be put off by the hardiness zone – I have found this plant perfectly hardy in my East Midlands garden for a good ten years now. I did put up some fleece to keep off a few degrees of frost during cold nights in the first winter, but have not bothered since. It is my favourite climber, and I regularly use it on many schemes. Not only is it smart looking but it grows fast too. The leaves are up to 8cm (3½in) long, an oval-lanceolate shape and mine colours up very strongly in the winter. Right now (late winter) it is a strong ruby-red nearly all over. This is on a south wall, whereas the ones on a shadier, east-facing wall are still a smart racing green. As you may notice I have gone big on this splendid plant. I am training them quite formally up to the top of the ground floor windows along an elegant-looking Georgian part of the house. The scent penetrates the keyhole of the front door reminding you, that if only you opened the door, the whole room would be filled with fragrance. I have seen ready-made arches of this plant imported from Italy, which you can just 'pop over' your front door to form an evergreen, sweet-smelling entrance – no planning needed but deep pockets essential. They are quick-growing, so get the extra satisfaction of training your own!

Trachycarpus fortunei
Plant of the Week (see page 383)

Tricyrtis formosana
TOAD LILY

Type: hardy, rhizomatous perennial
Soil & situation: moist, well-drained, humus-rich soil/partial or deep shade
North American hardiness zone: 6–9
Height: 90cm (36in)
Spread: 45cm (18in)

Tricyrtis formosana

Grow for: happy in deep shade; an interesting, different-looking flower; AGM

This is a very useful perennial for planting in deep shade. It is late flowering with a most unusual flower, shaped like a starfish. The erect, soft hairy stems tend to zigzag with 10cm (4in) long, lance-shaped leaves. They are dark green with purple-green spots on the surface. The upward facing, 3cm (1in) wide flowers appear in autumn. They are pinkish-purple on a white background, with red-purple spots on the inside and white stigmas with red spots. The base of the tepals is a pale yellow.

I can grow this plant in a peat bed with no added soil where it quickly spreads by underground stolons. Avoid areas exposed to biting, cold, drying winds. Apply an annual deep mulch of coarse bark every winter after flowering is finished. Propagation is by seed sown as soon as it is ripe and over-wintered in a cold frame with protection from frost. Young plants may be planted out after all risk of frost is over. Divide established clumps in early spring before growth starts. Take precautions against slugs and snails in spring as the new shoots appear. **JC**

Trachycarpus fortunei   November

CHUSAN PALM, HEMP PALM

Type: evergreen palm
Soil & situation: tolerates a range of soils/appreciates free drainage conditions/full sun or partial shade/looks best in a place free from strong winds, which lacerate the foliage
North American hardiness zone: 8–9
Height: 20m (66ft)
Spread: 2.5m (8ft), trunk diameter to 1m (3ft)
Grow for: the air of tropical luxuriance conveyed by its exciting, huge – up to 1.2m (4ft) – evergreen fan-shaped leaves; will tolerate temperatures down to –10°C (14°F). Few plants look this good at this time of year; AGM

I have grown this palm in my East Midlands courtyard for a good ten years or so. The plants are in huge pots and too massive to move now, but they have 'lived out' from the word go when they were under a foot high, so that is not a problem. Now one of them strokes its leaves against my first-floor bedroom window in breezy weather. Visitors often arrive and on encountering my palms remark on what an amazingly warm courtyard it must be. No way! It is just that these palms are far tougher than most people think. They grow well in containers too, looking even more dramatic in massive pots, and have amazingly small root systems compared to their height. On one job we had to transplant one with a digger; it was about 4m (13ft) high, but the roots were hardly 60cm (24in) in diameter. It transplanted very easily, which is nearly always the case with these great plants.

These could be protected with fleece in the early years if you are planting them in colder areas. Good, free-draining conditions undoubtedly help them get through cold periods. No pruning is required apart from cutting off any of the lower leaf bases to make the trunk more visible as it is curious clothed with the fibrous remains of the old leaf bases. The yellow flowers (interesting and odd, but not what I would call beautiful) grow on quite young plants in huge quantities in terminal panicles and sometimes male and female flowers occur on the same tree. The fruits are like dark, midnight-blue marbles. They freely seed around and this is an easy way to propagate them.   **BG**

Trollius x *cultorum* 'Lemon Queen'
GLOBEFLOWER

Type: hardy, herbaceous perennial
Soil & situation: moist, damp soil/sun or partial shade
North American hardiness zone: 5–8
Height: 1m (3ft)
Spread: 60cm (24in)
Grow for: attractive leaves and bold flowers from late spring to mid-summer

I love these big bold buttercups with their deeply cut leaves and globular flowers like giant lollipops. Forget your temperamental flouncy summer specials, these yeomen of the garden are tough, no-nonsense herbaceous plants with attractive leaves and cheerful flowers. Robust and jolly, they are happy to wallow up to their knees in damp soil by ponds or streams, in boggy borders or naturalized in meadows and drink all day! The flowers, up to 6cm (2½in) across, appear from late spring to mid-summer. There are some wonderful selections, but the clear tones of *Trollius* x *cultorum* 'Lemon Queen' are just perfect, although 'Alabaster', which flowers slightly ahead of the others, with clear, pale yellow blooms, 7cm (3in) across, is not far behind. From the Swiss-German name *Trollblume*, Latinized as *Trollius flos* or rounded flower, it's linked to the Middle English *troll*, to trundle or roll. You'd expect them to come rolling home!

There are about 30 cultivars of *T.* x *cultorum* available, most flowering from mid-spring to early summer. 'Commander-in-Chief' has large, glowing

Trollius x *cultorum* 'Lemon Queen'

Tropaeolum 'Strawberries and Cream'

orange flowers. 'Golden Monarch' has warm orange flowers, 'Fire Globe' (also known as 'Feuertroll') is rich orange-yellow and the early-flowering 'Heleos' has orange globes. 'Orange Princess' has wonderful, large, double, orange-gold flowers in late spring and early summer. 'Superbus' has greeny-yellow flowers from late spring to mid-summer.

They need moist, deep, fertile, preferably heavy soil that never dries out; happy in full sun or shade or wet, heavy clay. Cut back in spring and mulch with well-rotted organic matter. Divide in spring or immediately after flowering. **MB**

Tropaeolum 'Strawberries and Cream'
NASTURTIUM

Type: hardy, annual climber
Soil & situation: impoverished, moist, well-drained soil/full sun
North American hardiness zone: annual
Height: 20–30cm (8–12in)
Spread: 30cm (12in)
Grow for: a lovely-looking plant – and every bit edible

All parts of this plant are edible. I wonder if I am starting to write like Bob Flowerdew! Its leaves are spicy, the seeds, which can be pickled, are hot and the flowers are colourful in salads.

The 5cm (2in) wide, rounded, light green leaves have wavy edges. The flowers are produced from summer to autumn with long spurs and creamy-yellow petals each with a red blotch at the base. They are double and up to 5cm (2in) across. *Tropaeolum* 'Strawberries and Cream' is a non-trailing variety ideal for annual bedding or growing in containers on a patio.

When grown in 'poor' soil without nutrients they flower more readily. Fertile soils produce more leaves at the expense of flowers. Where the soil is fertile feed with a high-potash liquid fertilizer weekly to encourage more flowers. Seed can be sown in late spring *in situ*. Propagation is by seed which is quick to germinate. Tip cuttings can be rooted in a gritty compost in early summer and over-wintered in a cool greenhouse. **JC**

Tulipa 'Artist'

Type: hardy, bulbous perennial
Soil & situation: fertile, well-drained soil/full sun/shelter from strong winds
North American hardiness zone: best treated as an annual with the bulbs lifted each year
Height: 45cm (18in)
Spread: 15cm (6in) for a single plant
Grow for: an impressive display when planted en masse; AGM

I love tulips. My favourites are the long-stemmed varieties that stand on parade, proud and to attention. The mid-green, lance-shaped leaves of *Tulipa* 'Artist' (which belongs to the Viridiflora Group) are lower than the flowerheads. The single flowers are cup shaped, appearing in late

Tulipa 'Artist'

spring. Before they fully open the petal margins are crimped and salmon-pink with a greenish-purple stripe on the outside of each petal. When fully open the inside of each flower is green flushed salmon-pink. It makes a wonderful display when the bulbs are planted in a mass in the border or as a mixed planting underplanted with yellow wallflowers. An added bonus is that they make excellent, long-lasting cut flowers.

After flowering remove the dead heads before they set seed. Allow the foliage to yellow before cutting it down. Lifting the bulbs isn't essential but there is more chance of losing them to slugs or rot if they are left in the ground over winter. Avoid planting in wet ground. Plant at least 10–15cm (4–6in) deep and space the bulbs 8cm (3½in) apart. Tulips may be planted out as late as November. Earlier planting may encourage the disease tulip fire. **JC**

Tulipa 'Magier'
Plant of the Week (see page 177)

Tulipa 'Queen of Night'

Type: hardy, bulbous perennial
Soil & situation: good garden loam/sunny position
North American hardiness zone: 3–8
Height: 60cm (24in)
Spread: 15cm (6in) for a single plant
Grow for: dark purple, velvety flowers in late spring

I first saw these tulips growing in the late John Codrington's front garden: they were planted with equal quantities of white tulips, and generous masses of them were threaded through extensive clumps of low-growing, cottage-garden plants. This exuberant planting almost totally filled the space between the cottage and the road, a width of about 8m (25ft).

These tulips are such a bold, yet subtle colour, that you can afford to be equally bold with your planting and make quite a statement. They are ideal for using in repeated clumps, to stock all those spare gaps that will later be filled with expanding foliage or plants not yet in place. The first year you plant them they are tall, but if you leave them *in situ* they are usually slightly shorter with smaller flowers in subsequent years. I prefer them like this. Either way, they give several weeks of colour.

Tulipa 'Queen of Night'

For a simpler life, you can leave these tulips *in situ*, rather than treating them as bedding tulips. Whichever way you choose, plant them by early winter (or if you are desperate up until early spring) and do plant them deeply, with a good 20cm (8in) of soil above them. This helps to prevent slug damage and also helps them give a better performance in subsequent years, as does a good summer baking. Plant them about 10cm (4in) apart. **BG**

Ulex europeaus 'Flore Pleno'
Plant of the Week (see page 111)

Vaccinium corymbosum
HIGHBUSH BLUEBERRY

Type: very hardy, deciduous shrub
Soil & situation: moist, acid soil/sun/shelter
North American hardiness zone: 3–7
Height: 1.5m (5ft)
Spread: unpruned to over 4m (13ft)
Grow for: pretty flowers in late spring to early summer; edible fruit in mid- to late summer; and brilliant autumn colour; AGM

I still can't decide which stirs my passions more, their autumn leaves aflame in tones of red and yellow, or a bowl heaped with delicious blueberries, submerged in lashings of cream!

Pretty white flowers, like dainty lampshades appear in late spring and early summer and are pleasing to the eye, but it is the blue-black fruit that makes my heart beat faster. Grow at least two varieties for a worthwhile crop.

Will it be *Vaccinium* 'Bluecrop', the top all rounder with brilliant autumn colour, heavy crops and good drought resistance; *V.* 'Earliblue' with its eye-catching autumn colour and moderate crops; or *V.* 'Herbert' who's more subdued in autumn but with an unbeatable flavour? The choice is yours! Blueberry pies, blueberry muffins, blueberries with blueberries and yet more cream! Stand aside, strawberries, your reign is over; all hail, blueberries, king of summer fruit!

Blueberries need shelter, sunshine or light shade and a moist, free-draining soil with a pH of 4–5.5. Grow in raised beds or pots in a 50:50 mix of ericaceous compost and grit. Water with rainwater and never let the soil dry out. Feed with ericaceous plant food and mulch to 15cm (6in) deep with sawdust, bark or ericaceous compost. Harvest every four to five days.

Prune in early spring; two-to-three-year-old wood is the most productive. In the first two years remove weak, diseased or damaged shoots and fruit buds; thereafter cut out old wood at the base or to strong outward facing shoots. Propagate by semi-ripe cuttings. Protect the fruit from birds using netting. **MB**

Vaccinium corymbosum

Bob adds:

I never used to grow blueberries, then I got a taste for them with yoghurt so now I have to grow them. Despite living in a dry village on a lime-filled, sandy soil they have proved fairly easy in large containers; these are usefully carried into the greenhouse or fruit cage for getting the ripening fruits away from the birds. They also like company, as the more plants I get the more each one bears as they seem to need cross-pollinators although are theoretically self-fertile.

Blueberries are not water plants but marginals, i.e. they like wet, not waterlogged, soil, and can drown! Otherwise they are easy in any acid soil or compost and need no special treatment. Ideal for the edge of a ditch or pond or under a rainwater drainpipe. They will become parched in a hot dry place but do not crop well in heavy shade. They can be sown in winter or divided in early spring; alternatively, with some care, summer softwood cuttings can be rooted. They suffer no special problems other than a dislike for both lime and lime-filled, chlorinated tapwater.

Veratrum album
FALSE HELLEBORE

Type: hardy, herbaceous perennial
Soil & situation: most soil/partial sun to heavy shade
North American hardiness zone: 5–9
Height: 1.2m (4ft)
Spread: 30cm (12in)
Grow for: attractive, ribbed, hosta-like leaves and a tall spike of green outside white inside, small flowers

Veratrum album

I am fond of poisonous plants. I started as a child, probably with unpleasant motives, and still find them fascinating. Although every part of the false hellebore is toxic, it is a beautiful stately plant with few problems and combines well, under an arch of laburnum and yew, with monkshood and foxgloves in a little corner dedicated to matrimonial harmony.

Veratrum is the Old Latin name as this plant was known to the Romans. It was long used as a pesticide for killing obstinate pests such as gooseberry sawfly caterpillars but is now obsolete. There are a few other species, all of which make stately garden plants, though they are not in favour at the time of writing – possibly due to their poisonous properties!

It seems to grow almost anywhere though is happiest in dappled shade with a moist, leafmould-enriched soil. It can be tidied after flowering to prevent seed setting, though this is unusual. It can be grown from seed but is slow to germinate and grow. Old plants can be divided in autumn or spring. It is slug immune, so should be grown among hostas to confuse them.   **BF**

Verbascum bombyciferum 'Polarsommer'

Type: biennial to perennial
Soil & situation: dry, free-draining soil/sun
North American hardiness zone: 4–8
Height: up to 1.8m (6ft)
Spread: up to 1m (3ft)
Grow for: a fun plant that will self-seed but not so prolifically as to become a nuisance; brightens up an area of gravel, paving or border; saucer-shaped, pale yellow flowers throughout the summer on the large candelabra-shaped spikes; huge basal rosettes of the young plants which maintain their presence throughout the winter

There are several different verbascums to choose from. This one has exceptional foliage – rosettes of silver-grey, woolly leaves in its first year, which are set off by its pale flowers. It has strong growth so the flower spikes do not need supporting unless grown on very rich soil. It is an architectural plant I would not want to be without and invariably settles into pleasantly surprising, new spots each year. For instance, one year in my garden it formed a strong line all the way along the north side of a massive stone barn. Happily it has remained there, although I would have thought it was too cool and dark, providing a highlighted band of dazzling silver amongst the gravel. Of all

Verbascum bombyciferum 'Polarsommer'

the plants which require little maintenance, this must be one of the most eye-catching.

My husband loathes this plant, as on returning home late from work, he accidentally brushes his dark suit against it in the dark, and only notices when colleagues comment on his woolly appearance the next morning.

This plant requires little attention apart from, perhaps, the removal of the flower spike after it has set seed, assuming you wish to produce more. Even the dead spikes do not look unattractive and in frost they are positive stars. They are short-lived though and generally die after flowering, but I find it safe just to let them carry on and do their own thing, as self-sown seedlings can usually be relied upon to be similar to type. Alternatively, seed can be sown in late spring or early summer. If sown earlier it may flower in its first year. Root cuttings may also be taken in winter.   **BG**

Verbascum nigrum
DARK MULLEIN

Type: hardy, semi-evergreen perennial
Soil & situation: infertile, well-drained, alkaline soil/full sun
North American hardiness zone: 5–8
Height: 90cm (36in)
Spread: 60cm (24in)
Grow for: tall spikes of orange-yellow flowers in summer

I surprised myself when I first decided to recommend this mullein. Normally I extol the virtues of the giant *Verbascum olympicum* and *V. bombyciferum*, and rightly so. However, the dark mullein wins on flower colour and ultimate size. It isn't an embarrassment in a windy autumn when other taller types need support.

The mid-green, long-stalked, scalloped basal leaves form a rosette. They can be 15–45cm (6–18in) long, becoming smaller up the flowering stem. The slender, upright racemes of flowers, up to 60cm (24in) long, appear in summer and early autumn. The saucer-shaped flowers are deep orange-yellow with violet-coloured filaments and are clustered tightly on the stem. They open at different times, appearing in batches up and down the stalk.

Mulleins tolerate impoverished soil and will germinate and grow in the cracks in the patio or path. In fertile soil they tend to become large and more liable to wind damage. They are not long-lived perennials, often dying after the second year of flowering. Propagation is by seed in early summer. Pot up the seedlings and plant out the following spring to flower the same year. Every year since the millennium all my mulleins have suffered from moth caterpillar attacks. The simple remedy has been to pick them off and introduce them to a heavy boot. **JC**

Verbascum nigrum

Viburnum carlesii

Viburnum carlesii

Type: hardy, deciduous shrub
Soil & situation: moisture-retentive soil/sun or partial shade
North American hardiness zone: 5–8
Height & spread: 2m (6½ft)
Grow for: pink buds and domed clusters of white, fragrant flowers from mid- to late spring

This compact, dense shrub is impeccably attired in oval, irregularly toothed leaves, which often turn red in autumn. Domed flowerheads appear from mid- to late spring, the clusters of bright pink buds bursting open, revealing white- or pink-flushed flowers with a strong daphne-like fragrance followed by red fruits that ripen to black.

This genteel plant has inspired several selections and hybrids all with the same glorious perfume. 'Aurora' has red buds and pale pink flowers. Its young leaves are light green, some flushed with copper. 'Charis' is vigorous, the buds are red, and the flowers pink fading to white. 'Diana' is also vigorous with red buds, but the young leaves have chocolate tints. Many argue that the hybrids are more beautiful. *Viburnum* x *burkwoodii* (*V. carlesii* x *V. utile*) is a medium-sized evergreen, with clusters of fragrant pink flowers from mid-winter (if it is mild) but usually mid- to late spring. It is hardy, beautiful and easy to raise from semi-ripe cuttings. *V.* x *carlcephalum* (*V. carlesii* x *V. macrocephalum*) is deciduous with flower clusters up to 15cm (6in) across which are impressive but rather overpowering. It often has good autumn colour. *V.* x *juddii* (*V. bitchiuense* x *V. carlesii*) is a floriferous, small- to medium-sized shrub which is robust and less susceptible to the attentions of aphids.

Prune after flowering to retain the shape. Propagate by softwood cuttings and evergreens from semi-ripe in summer. Viburnum aphid damages the leaves of *V. carlesii* which stay distorted for the rest of the season. Spray colonies before they disfigure the leaves. **MB**

Viburnum davidii

Type: hardy, evergreen shrub
Soil & situation: moist, well-drained soil/full sun or light shade
North American hardiness zone: 7–9
Height & spread: 1.5m (5ft)
Grow for: attractive evergreen foliage and winter fruit; AGM

For a reliable winter show plant a group of three, spaced 2m (6½ft) apart. It forms a dome-shaped, compact plant with 15cm (6in) long, shiny, dark green leaves. They are marked with three, deep, parallel veins.

Panicles of small, tubular, white flowers appear in late spring and are followed in autumn by clusters of metallic, deep blue fruits which will remain on the plant for most of the winter months. It is necessary to grow male and female plants together to guarantee fruit.

Pruning is not normally necessary once the framework of branches has been achieved. Propagation is by seed sown in autumn in a cold frame and over-wintered. Semi-ripe cuttings taken in late summer will root in a heated propagator. **JC**

Viburnum davidii

Taxus baccata '*Fastigiata Aurea*'

GOLDEN IRISH YEW

Type: evergreen tree
Soil & situation: well-drained, fertile soil/any position
North American hardiness zone: 7–8
Height: after ten years 2m (6½ft) and eventually to 8m (25ft)
Spread: 60cm (24in)
Grow for: good looks all year round, so it's particularly welcome in the botanical doldrums of mid-winter.

If you want a plant that will behave itself and scorn any maintenance, then grow this yew. It retains its golden-yellow foliage for 12 months of the year, and becomes bright yellow in a sunny site. An added bonus is, being female, it produces dusky red fruit which contrast with the gold. It will retain its linear leaves to ground level with stiff upright shoots, giving the tree its columnar appearance. This yew makes a wonderful dot plant in a bed of low-growing heathers or is perfect for giving stature to a rock area.

Like most yews, it will tolerate acid or alkaline soil situated in full sun or a shaded site. It prefers a well-drained, fertile soil. If necessary old, sprawling yew trees may be rejuvenated to their former glory by pruning hard in spring, followed by regular watering and liquid feeds.

Warning: every part of the plant, with the exception of the seed coat, is poisonous. It is recommended that it isn't planted in the vicinity of grazing animals. **JC**

Viburnum farreri

Viburnum farreri

Type: hardy, deciduous shrub
Soil & situation: fertile, moist, well-drained soil/full sun or partial shade
North American hardiness zone: 6–8
Height: 3m (10ft)
Spread: 2.5m (8ft)
Grow for: clusters of very fragrant flowers; bright red fruit; AGM

This beautiful shrub used to be called *Viburnum fragrans*. It was a much better and more descriptive name and I wouldn't dream of correcting anyone who hasn't heard of the new one.

It forms an erect shrub with 10cm (4in) long, young bronze leaves, turning dark green and finally a rich red-purple in autumn. Dense clusters of very fragrant, white or white tinged pink, tubular flowers are produced in late autumn, before leaf fall, and throughout the winter. Small, vivid red fruits follow. *V. farreri* 'Candidissimum' has pure white flowers followed by bright yellow fruit. The young leaves are pale green, turning mid-green.

An annual mulch of composted bark in spring will conserve moisture close to the plant's surface roots. Pruning of young plants is seldom necessary. Old, neglected plants can be hard pruned in spring. Cut half the old branches with flaking bark as close to the ground as possible to encourage new shoots from the base. The following year cut

the remaining branches. Propagation is by semi-ripe cuttings in mid-summer. Cover them with horticultural fleece until they are rooted. Don't transplant newly rooted cuttings until the following spring before they come into leaf. **JC**

Viburnum opulus
GUELDER ROSE, WATER ELDER

Type: hardy, deciduous shrub
Soil & situation: damp soil/dry soils too/sunny or light shade/will tolerate shadier sites
North American hardiness zone: 4–8
Height: 5m (16ft)
Spread: 4m (13ft)
Grow for: attractive but unassuming plant; ideal for use in woodlands, hedgerows and thickets where a more natural landscape is required; white flowers in late spring/early summer

This thicket-forming shrub produces rather showy flowers, white, lace-cap-like, up to 8cm (3½in) across and reminiscent of hydrangeas. They appear in late spring to early summer. The dark green leaves are usually three-lobed and maple-like, and colour up in autumn to burning reds and purples. Bright, glistening, red, fleshy fruits are produced in autumn and are on display well into winter. It is an easy plant to grow. I find it tolerates extremes from virtual hardcore to bogs and, although native, it looks pretty and ornamental. It is useful mixed into broad, natural plantings, perhaps to form a woodland edge or screen for some children's play area. Onc established it will recover from trampling or being used as a general stalking ground.

I also use *Viburnum lantana*, the wayfaring tree, for these types of spaces. It is perhaps more ornamental, the leaves are very different – broadly ovate, pale creamy-green and velvety when they come out – as are the young shoots. It is not so versatile in wet areas as *V. opulus*, but tolerates very shallow, limy, exposed conditions without batting an eyelid.

On planting these tough natives, I make sure there is no weed competition till they are well established. In wilder areas, weed control can take the simplest, least expensive method: many sheets of old newspaper, hidden and kept in place with grass clippings. I plant them bare-rooted in autumn or late winter, trim them right back to 50cm (20in) from the ground and never bother with rabbit-proof guards. I often mix them up, in groups of threes and fives, in native hedges with *Acer campestre*, *Crataegus monogyna*, *Ligustrum vulgare* and a little wild rose and holly, with the

hawthorn (*Crataegus*) forming maybe 40 per cent, as it knits it all firmly together. A wonderful, colourful, natural, countryside boundary. **BG**

Viburnum rhytidophyllum

Type: hardy, evergreen shrub
Soil & situation: fertile, moist, well-drained soil/full sun or partial shade
North American hardiness zone: 6–8
Height: 5m (16ft)
Spread: 4m (13ft)
Grow for: large deeply veined evergreen leaves and late spring flowers

'Big and bold' sums up this useful evergreen. Generally trouble free, it quickly forms a dense screen for privacy or shelter. The 20–25cm (8–10in) long, lance-shaped leaves have wavy edges. They are glossy, dark green and deeply veined. Large, terminal clusters of small white flowers are produced in late spring, followed by bright red fruit ripening to shiny black.

It is tolerant of most soils except the extremes of wet and dry. Provide young plants with shelter from cold, drying winds. It dislikes being transplanted so it is better to purchase small container-grown plants. Apply a deep mulch of composted bark in autumn.

Viburnum opulus

Viburnum rhytidophyllum

Pruning where necessary to thin out crov
branches should be completed before spr.
old branches to ground level to encourage
strong shoots from the base. Propagation is
semi-ripe cuttings in summer. Shorten the leaves
by half to reduce transpiration until the cuttings
form roots. Pot the young rooted plants up the
following spring. **JC**

Vicia faba 'Stereo'
BROAD BEAN

Type: half-hardy, annual vegetable
Soil & situation: best on deep, fairly heavy but
well-drained land/acceptable crops on a wide
range of soils
North American hardiness zone: annual
Height: 50cm (20in)
Spread: 60cm (24in)
Grow for: a milder taste than many conventional
broad beans; is delicious cooked or raw

I am a big broad bean fan and grow quite a
quantity of different types: dwarf ones, such as
this; Longpods, which are very hardy; and
Windsors, which have broader pods and more
flavour. The sweeter, more delicate flavour of
'Stereo' makes it stand out from the crowd in
terms of flavour, but in stature it is smaller. This
means staking is usually unnecessary. It is a good
bean in terms of productivity too, though due to
the short pods you usually only get five or six
beans in one pod, and they are small and whitish.
There is no way I would ever tire of broad beans,
but for those more easily bored there are different
ways to enjoy them. You can pick them small (no

bigger than your little finger), cook them in their
shells and eat pod and all – delicious but extravagant
with the young pods. Another favourite way is to
remove the 'jackets' from the bean itself, revealing a
shinier, darker bean which you usually cook unless
the bean is young, and then you can use them in
salads. I like them raw best of all.

These shorter-podded beans do better with a spring
sowing as opposed to an autumn one. They can be
sown at about three-week intervals from early to
late spring. Early spring sowings will probably have
ore losses in terms of actual plants, but the
ulting yields will be higher because of the extra
wing time gained. Fleece helps tremendously in
ing up success rates, especially for early
ngs. It certainly prevents the birds from
ng out the seeds too. Black bean aphids are a
ce, congregating on the growing tip in mid-
r. They are dealt with by pinching out the
he plant (about 7cm/2³⁄₄in) as the early
rt to develop. **BG**

Vicia faba 'Stereo'

Vinca minor
LESSER PERIWINKLE

Type: hardy, evergreen ground cover
Soil & situation: one of the most tolerant plants/
will grow in any soil, in any aspect/extremely
tolerant of temperature extremes
North American hardiness zone: 4–9
Height: 10–20cm (4–8in)
Spread: indefinite
Grow for: colonizing ground; attractive bright blue
flowers from spring to early summer and from then
on at odd intervals till the autumn

When you look at this plant in the garden centre
your heart probably won't leap into your mouth

with excitement. But when you see sheets of it
studded with its penetratingly blue flowers and
mixed in with a few other old favourites such as
foxgloves and bluebells in a modest, lightly-
shaded orchard, then I reckon it might well do. It
is such an obliging plant, and does not take over,
as its big brother, *Vinca major*, does. It looks well
furnished, with small, neat, trailing shoots that
root as they go. It is perfect for growing with
many bulbs as it takes your eye off the decaying
foliage of plants such as erythroniums, daffodils
and the like. In short, it is one of those plants
that is common, dead common, but that is
because it is good – use it well and it is stunning.
If you like something a little on the flash side
then opt for *Vinca minor* 'Argenteovariegata'
(AGM) with creamy-white, variegated leaves.

Needless to say, there really is not much you have
to do to this plant. For ground cover, I usually
plant at a rate of 8 per square metre or square
yard, making sure the ground is as weed free as
possible first. Plants in full sun flower best. I
would normally grow them by division just
popping in any shoot with roots where you intend
it to go, anytime from autumn to spring. Or, if I
was shorter of material, cuttings taken virtually
anytime of year will grow but semi-ripe cuttings in
summer are quickest. **BG**

Vinca minor

Vinca minor 'Atropurpurea'

Vinca minor 'Atropurpurea'
LESSER PERIWINKLE

Type: hardy, herbaceous perennial
Soil & situation: most soils/sun or shade
North American hardiness zone: 4–9
Height: 20cm (8in)
Spread: indefinite
Grow for: swirling stems and flowers from spring to autumn; AGM

At some point in their careers, most gardeners have used ultra-vigorous evergreen *Vinca major* 'Variegata'. Freely available in garden centres, you can buy as many as you want, the flower colour is tempting and well, it seems like a good idea at the time. There's plenty of time to repent at leisure when you're stumbling through 'spaghetti'; few have not been upended by its looping, rolling stems. It's fine for naturalizing on banks or when wandering through woodlands but in genteel borders, never!

Consider instead one of its enthusiastic but more civilized relatives. *V. minor* understands all of your needs, is more refined yet still ground covering, and floriferous yet more discreet. Its trailing shoots and fine glossy leaves offer the perfect background for the beautiful flowers.

Here are some of its varieties: 'Blue Cloud', 'Blue Drift', 'Blue Moon', 'Azurea Flore Pleno' provide a myriad of shades of blue, but 'Gertrude Jekyll', 'Alba' and 'Bowles' White' with pink buds all produce white flowers.

The variegated leaf forms are 'Argenteovariegata' with creamy margins and 'Alba Variegata' with a yellow edge. My favourite is 'Atropurpurea': the flowers are a deep-plum purple or, if you prefer, a deep burgundy – which, of course, I do!

It may become invasive but cutting back hard in early spring keeps it under control. Choose the planting location carefully and allow it space to spread. It flourishes in full sun, where it will flower prolifically, or partial shade in any soil except those that are very dry. Divide from autumn to spring. Stems naturally root at the nodes. **MB**

Viola odorata
ENGLISH VIOLET, SWEET VIOLET

Type: hardy, semi-evergreen, spreading, perennial rhizome
Soil & situation: moist, well-drained, humus-rich soil/full sun or partial shade
North American hardiness zone: 6–9
Height: 20cm (8in)
Spread: 40cm (16in)
Grow for: dainty, sweetly scented flowers from late winter to early spring

This little gem is native to southern England and widely spread throughout England and Wales although less so in Scotland and Ireland. The

Viola odorata

Victorians used bunches of violets as a love token and at funerals, which meant the plant was always in demand. It is ironic that in the wild, white rather than violet is the most common colour. Sweet violet is a great standby for the cottage border and makes an early splash of colour in the wild garden.

The runners or stolons spread rapidly, rooting as they go with long-stalked, bright green, heart-shaped rosettes of leaves. The sweetly scented, solitary flowers are carried on 5–10cm (2–4in) stalks from late winter until late spring. Usually white, there are forms with violet, purple, lilac or pink flowers. In milder areas the plant may flower again in the autumn.

There is no difficulty propagating this plant as it freely seeds all over the garden and can become a bit of a weed – but a nice one. Large clumps may be divided in autumn or in colder areas in spring.

For such harmless and useful plants they suffer a lot of ailments. Slugs, snails, red spider and greenfly love them and they can be affected by rust and powdery mildew. **JC**

Vitex agnus-castus
CHASTE TREE, MONKS' PEPPER

Type: hardy, open, spreading, aromatic, deciduous shrub
Soil & situation: well-drained soil/sun
North American hardiness zone: 6–9
Height & spread: 8m (25ft)
Grow for: leaves and late autumn flowers

This is a very pretty shrub; the leaves are made up of dark green, rounded leaflets that line the elegant, grey, downy shoots. The flowers are a beautiful soft lilac to dark blue on slender spikes up to 18cm (7in) long and appear at the tip of the current year's shoots in early and mid-autumn. *Vitex agnus-castus* 'Alba' has white flowers. *V. negundo* is similar but with smaller violet-blue flowers.

This aromatic native of the Mediterranean and southwest and central Asia grows in riverbeds often with tamarisk and oleander and is said to have been cultivated in the UK since 1570. The Greeks knew it as *agnos*, or chaste, and it was the symbol of chastity in ancient Greece, though the seeds were also used to treat venereal disease – presumably after the chaste became chased! It is still used as a hormone regulator for women.

Vitex agnus-castus

Pliny, the Roman natural historian (AD 23–79), spoke of using the plant to promote menstruation, purge the uterus and encourage the flow of milk in new mothers; recent research suggests that he may well have been right.

It needs shelter and sunshine on free-draining soil. It flowers best on sunny walls after a long hot summer. Once the framework has been established, prune back the previous summer's growth to two to three buds from the old wood in early spring once the danger of frost is over. Grow from seed in autumn or spring, or semi-ripe cuttings in summer. **MB**

Vitis coignetiae

Type: hardy, deciduous climber
Soil & situation: humus-rich, neutral to alkaline soil/sun or partial shade
North American hardiness zone: 5–9
Height & spread: 15m (50ft)
Grow for: architectural foliage and brilliant autumn colour

This spectacular plant challenges the Russian vine for vigour and easily beats it for beauty. It is a woody climber, with twining tendrils. The young shoots are covered with a loose grey down and the huge leathery, very shallowly three- to five-lobed, heart-shaped leaves, to 30cm (12in) diameter, are just magnificent. Sunken veins create a rough texture on the upper surface, underneath there's thick rusty-brown felt that feels like suede. Forget the insignificant green flowers in the summer and the small, black, inedible grapes with a purple bloom appearing in autumn – they don't even make wine! Admire instead the spectacular autumn colour creating a colourful cloak of scarlet, mahogany and orange; bathed in autumn sunshine, its awesome! When planting, ensure you have enough space, grow it along a wall, let it wrap its tendrils round the branches and shin up the tallest trees, but beware of growing it over your house: it will disappear!

It needs well-drained, humus-rich, preferably neutral to alkaline soil in full sun or partial shade. The best colours are on poorer soil or a restricted root run where the plant is grown 'hard'; do not let the soil dry out or the leaves will be smaller. Prune to keep it within its allotted space (oh, yes?) by shortening the young shoots in summer. It is difficult to propagate – try layering in autumn. It may suffer from powdery mildew and honey fungus. **MB**

Bunny adds:
The leaves of this plant are such a visual treat – I like them situated on a horizontal surface at eye level, so you can ogle them at close quarters. My mother has sited one perfectly in her garden, on a rather tumbled-down, low stone wall that surrounds an old pig sty.

Although I agree with Matt that the berries are not tasty in their raw form, in Japan I regularly drink a juice made from them. It is the best juice in the world, sort of bitter sweet. I would think quantities of sugar must be added. Next time I'll get the label translated.

Vitis coignetiae needs a good, hefty support system to carry its considerable weight. The permanent framework of the plant becomes a feature in its own right, beautifully gnarled and knobbly.

To renovate, you could risk cutting it all down to 30–45cm (12–18in) and then selecting the strongest three or four shoots that are produced from each stem to develop the new structure, cutting out the rest. Ideally, to shock the plant less, you would thin out over two or three years, reducing the older stems by a half, removing weak and dead growth, and thinning half of the remaining stems to about 5–10cm (2–4in).

Vitis coignetiae

Vitis vinifera 'Muscat Hamburg'

Vitis vinifera 'Muscat Hamburg'
GRAPE, UNDER COVER

Type: hardy, deciduous climber
Soil & situation: rich compost/sun
North American hardiness zone: 6–9
Height: 2.2m (7ft)
Spread: 60cm (24in)
Grow for: attractive climber with typical vine leaves colouring well in autumn; insignificant scented flowers, but the tastiest dessert grape

I grow many indoor grapes, now mostly in tubs as those in the ground have been too much effort to control and rife with problems. Those in containers just keep on cropping year after year with just a spring top dressing. I grow nearly a dozen and a half indoor varieties, and most are

excellent, bearing bigger sweeter fruits than outdoor sorts, and out of all of these 'Muscat Hamburg' (not 'Black Hamburg', which is good but not as good) is the finest flavoured; a black oval fruit with a spicy aromatic, sweet flavour.

Indoor grapes are a peculiarly European development that occurred during the Victorian period when hot houses were common. Most vines are far too vigorous for modern, small greenhouses or conservatories unless grown in containers; this allows them to be kept compact and by spending winter outdoors most pests and diseases are eliminated.

Ideally do not grow an indoor grape in the border inside or out but in a container. This reduces the pruning, the pests and diseases and ensures reliable crops every year. Plant in big tubs of rich compost and grow in full sun trained up poles.

These will be very long lived; mine are still cropping after two decades in the same tubs! In autumn prune back all the growth leaving just a stub of each with a couple of buds on a short framework and put the tubs out for the winter. In spring bring the tubs inside. In summer tie six shoots to the pole, removing the rest; later cut them off when they reach the top, and nip out sideshoots. Cuttings can be taken in autumn. The only common problems are wasps and there's nothing you can do about those. **BF**

Vitis vinifera 'Phoenix'

Type: hardy, deciduous climber
Soil & situation: reasonably fertile but well-drained soil with a pH between 6 and 7.5/warm, sunny wall or trained on a support system
North American hardiness zone: 6–9
Height: it can grow a good 4m (13ft) in a season, depending on the rootstock
Spread: indefinite
Grow for: good disease-resistant variety; ideal for an amateur; grapes are delicious for eating, but it is commercially grown for winemaking

I have only grown this vine for about six months but it has been highly recommended to me by Simon Day, a leading viticulturalist, and several others who have been growing vines commercially for many years. It is a fairly new variety (it was registered in Germany in 1984) and has been grown experimentally in the UK from the early 1990s, but in the last three or four years has really gained in popularity, as growers and amateurs are realizing its potential. It is outstanding for gardeners because of its disease resistance and because it has delicious grapes which ripen to a lovely, pale, golden colour. Of all the wine varieties, they are one of the tastiest to eat (more delicious than any I have ever bought from a supermarket). They are about as large as the smallest supermarket eating grape and they do have pips, but the skin is not tough.

Too rich a soil encourages masses of vegetative growth as opposed to fruit. I grow my vines trained up walls where they look wonderful as well as being highly productive. They can of course also be grown over pergolas, arches and garden fences, all to great effect. You can choose between several different systems of training them: the Double Guyot system is quite popular but it depends what best suits you and your structure. This variety is vigorous, so do make sure that your trellis, wires or support system is man enough to cope with it, otherwise you can end up carrying out excessive summer pruning and canopy management. If you want to pick the grapes to eat then leave them on the vine longer than you would normally, as this allows the acid level to drop. **BG**

Vitis vinifera 'Purpurea'
Plant of the Week (see page 319)

Vitis vinifera 'Siegerrebe'
GRAPE, OUTDOOR

Type: hardy, deciduous climber
Soil & situation: low lime soil/sun
North American hardiness zone: 6–9
Height & spread: unlimited
Grow for: attractive climber with typical vine leaves colouring well in autumn; insignificant scented flowers and some of the best tasting rosy-red grapes you have ever tried

I adore grapes; I went grape picking as a student and love wine too. But I prefer the fresh juice and can drink much more of it. I grow many outdoor grapes, over a dozen and a half, but few are much good most years in the open. Some varieties such as *Vitis* 'Boskoop Glory' are reliable but not well flavoured; many others, like the *V.* 'Strawberry Grape', crop well but taste poor. However, *V. vinifera* 'Siegerrebe' is not a bad cropper given a warm site, it comes early and is staggeringly delicious! A red fruit with a spicy aromatic flavour and very sweet.

Grapes are the one of oldest plants in cultivation and are mentioned in the book of Genesis. Thought to have been brought to the UK by the Romans, grapes were only sporadically cultivated here until recent times when new varieties made it possible to grow outdoor grapes without a wall or cloches – though good results still come more often with the aid of a wall! This variety is used to

Watsonia 'Stanford Scarlet'

make an excellent wine – I've had some from a vineyard in Devon.

Ideally put an outdoor grape on a warm wall in full sun; otherwise train it on poles and wires to get as much sun as possible. It will be very long lived, so do a good job on the supports and siting. Prune back all the new growth in autumn, leaving just a stub of each with a couple of buds on the framework. In summer nip out all shoots to five leaves after a bunch and thin the bunches by half. Cuttings can be taken in autumn. The only common problems are cold, wet summers, wasps and birds and you can do ****** all about all save the last. **BF**

Watsonia 'Stanford Scarlet'

Type: half-hardy, cormous perennial
Soil & situation: open, gritty, well-drained soil/full sun
North American hardiness zone: 9–10
Height: 80–120cm (32–48in)
Spread: 15cm (6in)
Grow for: long, sword-like foliage; striking orange-red flowers; excellent form

Watsonias are strikingly beautiful with their tall, symmetrical spikes of brightly coloured flowers which are held horizontally to the stem. They resemble gladiolus with panache.

The mid-green, sword-like leaves are up to 1m (3ft) long, not reaching the height of the flower spike. In late spring and early summer, each unbranched spike carries up to 12 tubular, orange-red flowers. When fully open, the tepals are spread wide. Watsonia is native to South Africa, where in the wild it grows in areas prone to bush fires, appearing immediately after a burn. Where they can be left in the ground mulch them with wood ash after the foliage has died down or top dress container-grown plants. They will love it.

Plant the corms 15cm (6in) deep, at the base of a sheltered, sunny wall in a very free-draining soil. Protect them from frost and in a few years they will form a clump. They will flower better if they are left undisturbed. In less ideal situations the corms should be lifted in autumn and stored in a dry, frost-free place over the winter for planting out in spring. Propagation is by division in autumn. When grown from seed it may take five years to produce flowering-sized corms.

Watsonia pillansii flowers in summer and autumn with branched spikes bearing up to 20 tubular, bright orange-pink flowers. **JC**

Weigela middendorffiana

Weigela middendorffiana

Type: hardy, deciduous shrub
Soil & situation: fertile, well-drained soil/partial shade
North American hardiness zone: 5–7
Height & spread: 1.5m (5ft)
Grow for: showy, bell-shaped flowers surrounded by bright green foliage

When you are used to shades of pink and red there is something nice about a change of colour and this weigela does it with panache. When mature it forms an upright shrub with the older branches arching. The 8cm (3½in) long, pointed, bright green leaves turn golden-brown in autumn. The bell-shaped, sulphur-yellow flowers have conspicuous, dark orange markings on the lower lobes and are continually produced from mid-spring until mid-summer.

It prefers to be planted in a sheltered situation in partial shade and protected from cold winds. When grown in full sun the flowers quickly fade to a pale yellow. Prune after flowering by cutting back shoots which have flowered to strong, healthy buds lower down the stem. Old plants may be rejuvenated by removing a third of the oldest branches as close to the soil level as possible. New strong shoots will be produced from the base. Continue to prune over a three-year period until all the old branches have been replaced with flowering shoots.

Propagation is easy using softwood cuttings in early summer. Pot the rooted plants before autumn to ensure there is a root run through the compost. Hardwood cuttings taken in winter root well outside in a sheltered position. They will be ready for planting out the following winter. **JC**

Acer pensylvanicum

SNAKE-BARK MAPLE, MOOSE WOOD

Type: hardy, deciduous tree
Soil & situation: moist, well-drained loam; dislikes chalk/prefers a sheltered position
North American hardiness zone: 3–7
Height & spread: 6m (20ft); occasionally as tall as 10m (33ft)
Grow for: compact profile; autumn colour; beautiful bark in winter, which is why I have allocated it to December; AGM.

It was love at first sight when I saw this gorgeous tree with her elegant upswept branches and a fine cloak of large trilobed leaves; she simply oozes grace and style. Stepping into the limelight in autumn, she coyly sheds her soft yellow garments to reveal delicately marked, 'snake skin' stems. The silvery-white pattern, highlighted by the jade-green background, is intense on young growth and she looks stunning basking in the spotlight of the low winter sun. Her relative *Acer pensylvanicum* 'Erythrocladum' is more glamorous but not as robust. A stunning, candy-pink when young, she fades to orange-red with age; it's the difference between a real and fake tan! A restorative face-lift by hard pruning every other year brings back much of her appeal, but as far as I'm concerned, *A. pensylvanicum* with her charm and lasting beauty is the ultimate 'it' tree!

It needs a cool, moist, well-drained, acid soil and must be protected from scorching sunlight and cold winds. Plant at the same level as it is in the pot; water well until settled in. Young plants are cheaper to buy and establish more rapidly than mature ones.

Prune only if necessary when branches are small, in early summer or late autumn; don't prune in spring or the cuts will bleed. Propagation is by sowing seed of the species in spring after a period of chilling over winter. Drought and frost cause bark splitting and late frosts can damage the shoot tips. Plant in a sheltered spot. It can suffer from coral spot; remove affected stems with sharp secateurs. **MB**

Wisteria sinensis

Wisteria sinensis 'Alba'

Wisteria sinensis

CHINESE WISTERIA

Type: hardy, deciduous, twining climber
Soil & situation: deep, moist, well-drained
soil/full sun
North American hardiness zone: 5–8
Height: 9m (30ft)
Spread: to 1.5m (5ft) or more
Grow for: trailing garlands of fragrant flowers

If you have been putting off planting a wisteria
because those you have seen have grown all over
their support and are totally bare of flower then
read on. They are one of the most spectacular
flowering climbers, fully hardy in all but the
coldest of gardens. The secret of success is in the
pruning and that is easily explained.

The mid-green, pinnate leaves are carried on
twining stems. In late spring and early summer the
plant is smothered in 30cm (12in) long, pendent
racemes of fragrant, pea-like, lilac-blue to white
flowers, which are followed in autumn by 15cm
(6in) long, velvety green, bean-like seedpods. The
variety *W. s.* 'Sierra Madre' has very fragrant,
lavender-blue flowers flushed white. *W. s.* 'Alba' has
long, pendent racemes of pure white flowers.

Given support, wisteria is ideal for growing on a
sunny wall. At planting don't enrich the soil with
manure, which will encourage growth at the
expense of flowers. Avoid a cold, windy site.

Prune twice a year. In summer cut the new sideshoots back to four or five leaves from the older
branches. In winter further reduce these shoots
to two or three buds. At the same time, shorten
the main leading shoots to leave 1m (3ft) of new
growth. This builds up a framework of branches
with lots of short 'spurs' which carry the flowers.
Wisterias scrambling through trees are not
pruned. I have no difficulty rooting layers. After
18 months they are ready to plant out or pot up.

How do you tell a Chinese wisteria from a
Japanese wisteria? Easy. *Wisteria sinensis* (Chinese)
twines anti-clockwise. *W. floribunda* (Japanese)
twines clockwise. **JC**

Yucca filamentosa 'Bright Edge'

ADAM'S NEEDLE

Type: hardy, evergreen shrub
Soil & situation: well-drained soil/sunny position
North American hardiness zone: 5–10
Height: 75cm (30in)
Spread: 1.5m (5ft)
Grow for: architectural plant with striking dark
green leaves edged with yellow stripes; AGM

This is a stemless yucca and has several good
attributes. It always looks striking and smart, with
its erect, brightly coloured, lance-shaped leaves.
This is in part due to its degree of hardiness. *Y.
filamentosa* is hardy to about −15°C (5°F) and so it
takes an extremely severe winter to make it suffer.
When I first realized its robustness, I was
surprised – it looks such an exotic beast. Tall
panicles of creamy-white flowers, rising to about
1.2m (4ft), are produced in mid- to late summer.
They are pretty dramatic and remain looking
good for a fair few weeks. And, usefully for
impatient gardeners, they bloom at a young age.

In many situations I like the plain green *Yucca
filimentosa* as much as, if not more than, its rather
brash-looking, gold and green relative. Particularly
when it comes to flowering, the simplicity of the
plain green looks more stylish, with just the green
and white coming into play. As ever, it all depends
on the effect you are driving at.

With many yuccas the tips of the leaves are very
pointed, so if you have young children it is worth
cutting off the tips of the leaves as soon as they –
children or plants – arrive. As they tolerate dry
conditions and are so hardy, *Y. filimentosa* are
perfect container plants. They often look better
raised up nearer to eye level and are extremely
tolerant of negligence, for those that tend to be
idle with the watering can. Propagate by
removing rooted suckers in spring or by root
cuttings in winter. **BG**

Yucca filamentosa 'Bright Edge'

Yucca gloriosa

Yucca gloriosa
SPANISH DAGGER

Type: frost-hardy, evergreen shrub
Soil & situation: well-drained soil/full sun
North American hardiness zone: 7–10
Height & spread: 2m (6½ft)
Grow for: its form, foliage and flowers; AGM

Yucca gloriosa grows in at least five locations in my garden. I love its shape, leaves and flowers. I have one particular plant with an attitude problem. It insists on sending up enormous flower spikes in mid- to late autumn. When they do manage to flower there is often a coating of frost on the flowers. It has carried on like this for 12 to 15 years and even managed to be in full bloom one Christmas.

When mature it forms an erect shrub with thick, bare stems. The broad, sword-like leaves with dangerously sharp points are clustered near the top of the branches. The young leaves arc blue-green maturing to dark green. The 5cm (2in) long, pendent, bell-shaped, ivory-white flowers are often tinged with purple. They are carried on stiff, 2m (6½ft) long, upright panicles during late summer and autumn.

After flowering remove the whole stalk, cutting it as close to the leaf rosette as possible. I have never seen seed form and I'm told it is necessary to pollinate the flowers by hand. Where there are people, especially children, coming in contact with the leaves it is necessary to remove the sharp tips. This is easily done with nail clippers and it will never be noticed. Remove the dying leaves as

they yellow by pulling downwards from the stem one at a time.

Y. gloriosa hates wet ground. At planting time incorporate extra coarse grit to the planting hole. Choose a sheltered site in full sun. Propagation is by seed sown in spring in a propagator. Rooted suckers may be carefully removed in spring and potted up for a year before planting out in the garden. Root cuttings may be taken in winter and rooted in a free-draining compost.   **JC**

Zaluzianskya capensis
NIGHT OR CAPE PHLOX

Type: half-hardy annual
Soil & situation: any soil/sun
North American hardiness zone: annual
Height: 30cm (12in)
Spread: 15cm (6in)
Grow for: prolific, scented, white flowers opening in the evening

Night phlox is slightly heather-like until the flowers appear; these resemble campions rather than phloxes and are chocolate-brown inside, opening purest white in the cool of the evening and giving off an addictive lemony-vanilla fragrance that is so intoxicating. Named after a 16th-century botanist from Prague, this South African beauty is little known, which is probably because it comes at the end of the catalogue. There are three dozen species.

Night phlox is good as bedding in most soils and sites but not heavy shade or cold. It does well in pots and containers. As a half hardy-annual it is best sown in the warmth early in spring and planted out as soon as the frosts are over. Do not take pots into a warm room to enjoy their perfume, as they lose it inside.   **BF**

Zaluzianskya capensis

Zaluzianskya ovata

Zaluzianskya ovata
SOUTH AFRICAN PHLOX

Type: half-hardy perennial
Soil & situation: moist, free-draining soil/sun
North American hardiness zone: 9–10
Height: 25cm (10in)
Spread: 60cm (24in)
Grow for: beautiful flowers from early summer to mid-autumn

I once met a beautiful woman who ate chocolate and wore raspberry; I'm sure she would adore this plant. Like a tiny jewel, each facet glistening, the deep raspberry-red bud unfurls revealing pure white, saucer-shaped flowers with heart-shaped petals backed with that same sumptuous colour. They shy away from bright sunlight, opening only when the light is low; in early morning, on dull days or at dusk when glistening in the twilight, the night air is laden with their sweet and sensuous perfume. I planted mine by a window so the fragrance of romance drifted through; yours may be on a moonlit terrace or by a tranquil pool; choose carefully, then linger long, and dream of tropical climes.

Z. ovata 'Semonkong' from Lesotho is hardier, flowers for longer, is less compact and becomes straggly later in the season. *Z. capensis* (see previous entry) is taller with narrower lobes and is good as a gap-filler in the front of the border.

All need a warm, sheltered position on moist, humus-rich, free-draining soil; water well in summer. Dead-head regularly and they will flower until the first frosts. Cut back hard after flowering. They are not frost hardy, so lift and pot up in autumn or grow in containers and over-winter in a cool, bright, frost-free place. Plants are short lived; propagate regularly from tip cuttings in summer, over-winter under glass and plant out when danger of frost has passed. Prone to botrytis in damp conditions.   **MB**

Zantedeschia aethiopica 'Crowborough'
ARUM LILY

Type: hardy, tuberous perennial
Soil & situation: humus-rich, moist soil/full sun
North American hardiness zone: 8–10
Height: 90cm (36in)
Spread: 45cm (18in)
Grow for: elegant spathes; arrow-shaped glossy foliage; makes a big impression in a clump; AGM

I have mixed feelings about the arum lily. I appreciate its tolerance of wet, boggy conditions, making it ideal for the pool edge. I love the pure white, upturned trumpet-shaped spathe. Against that, it is associated with funerals. Although that hasn't stopped me planting six or seven clumps in various areas of my garden.

Zantedeschia aethiopica 'Crowborough'

It quickly forms a clump, remaining evergreen in mild locations. The 45cm (18in) long, glossy, dark green leaves are arrow shaped. They stand almost vertical well into autumn. The wide-throated, ivory-white spathes with a long, golden spadix are produced in succession from late spring through to mid-summer. *Z. a.* 'Green Goddess' has a similar habit of growth but its flowers are pale green with a white-and-green-splashed throat. Very striking. Arums are great as cut flowers, lasting for long periods in water.

It may be used as a marginal plant in the pond tolerating up to 30cm (12in) of water. In the border it dislikes soils which dry out in summer. In gardens prone to frosts the foliage will die down in winter. It is advisable to cover the crown with a deep mulch of bark or straw, which can be removed when risk of frost is past. Propagation is by division in spring. Take care not to damage the fleshy roots.   **JC**

Zea mays
SWEET CORN

Type: half-hardy annual crop
Soil & situation: rich, moist soil/sun
North American hardiness zone: annual
Height: 3m (10ft)
Spread: 60cm–1m (2–3ft)
Grow for: architectural statuesque plants with cobs of delicious sweet kernels; some with decorative colours

Sweet corn has to be fresh to be really sweet, and I mean fresh; I run in with the cobs and throw them into the already boiling water. You don't believe me – well pick one half an hour early and another and boil them immediately and you'll see the difference. I grow lots of varieties, which is hard as they need to be kept apart, but they are all delicious. There are also some ornamental cultivars with coloured cobs and of course popcorn.

Originally grown by the American Natives there are no wild species known but countless cultivars. They grew it as one of three sisters, planting sweet corn, squashes and beans in hillocks together, which is an early example of effective companion gardening. It gets its name from the Greek for another cereal entirely!

Sweet corn needs a moist soil enriched with a handful of chicken pellets or similar. A dead fish is traditional. Give full sun as any shade leads to no cobs. Water heavily and grow in a block, not a long row, to ensure (wind) pollination, and do not mix varieties or plant them adjacently. In the warmer parts of the UK you can sow *in situ* in late spring or early summer and hope to get a crop; in colder regions it is best started under cover in individual pots and planted out after the last frosts. Other than our miserable summers and two-legged rats (adults of the species *Homo criminalis*) there are no problems with sweet corn. **BF**

Zea mays

Zingiber officinale

Zingiber officinale
GINGER

Type: tender rhizomatous perennial
Soil & situation: well-drained compost/dappled shade to light sun/under cover
North American hardiness zone: 10–11
Height: 60cm (24in) vertical blade
Spread: 60–120cm (2–4ft)
Grow for: curiosity and as a crop

I love to grow anything I can eat or sniff and this is a real challenge; not so much in the maintenance but just to get it going. Then it needs a long season to do well, so it has to be started in late winter when the light is a bit too low. None the less, most years I make my own stem ginger in syrup for Christmas and have plenty of root ginger for my cooking. I use ginger and garlic in most fried dishes as the former offsets the bad breath engendered by the latter.

Ginger was known to the ancients; it originated on the Pacific rim and from there went to central Asia; indeed the name comes from the Indian via the Greek and Latin. It was brought to England by the Romans and it is in many old Anglo-Saxon recipes. Traded since as one of the most important spices, it was sea-faring merchants' search for its roots that led to the discovery of the rest of the world. Galangal (*Alpinia officinarum*) is very similar but actually a different plant.

Grow in a gritty, rich, moist compost. It needs to be in bright light but full sun parches it, so I find it does well at the back of the greenhouse. The initial root needs warmth to spur it into growth and the tall grass-like stems do not seem to do much. However, in autumn they die down and if they are in a big pot you will find a much bigger root or hand. If it is harvested while the leaves are still green it is more succulent and known as stem ginger, which you can preserve in sugar syrup. Other than needing warmth, ginger is fairly easy once it gets going. **BF**

Sarcococca confusa

CHRISTMAS BOX, SWEET BOX

Type: hardy, evergreen shrub
Soil & situation: humus-rich, moist, well-drained soil/deep or partial shade
North American hardiness zone: 6–9
Height: 2m (6¹/₂ft)
Spread: 1m (3ft)
Grow for: the most incredible winter fragrance from clusters of small, white flowers; happy in shade. I couldn't feature the Christmas box in any other month! AGM.

This perfectly behaved shrub deserves to be planted in every garden in the country. There is no excuse. It is small, evergreen and trouble free, with flowers, fruit and the most exquisite winter fragrance imaginable. You don't have to bury your nose in the flowers: you can be 6m (20ft) away and its perfume will still stop you in your tracks.

It forms a bushy shrub with 5cm (2in) long, glossy, dark green leaves. The tiny, pure white, very fragrant flowers appear in winter in clusters of five. They are followed by shiny black fruit. Other species include *Sarcococca hookeriana*, which is similar and grows to 1.5m (5ft); and *S. humilis*, which has fragrant, white flowers tinged with pink, and is more compact, growing to 60cm (24in).

In gardens where the soil remains moist in summer *S. confusa* may be grown in sun, otherwise it will perform best in deep shade and is ideal in woodland. Providing it is sheltered from cold, drying winds, the Christmas box will grow against a shady wall or fence.

Older plants can become straggly. In spring, after flowering is finished, remove any long growths that are spoiling the shape. Propagation is by seed, sown in spring, in pots outside. Semi-ripe, 5cm (2in) long cuttings taken in late summer will root in a peaty compost. Grow the rooted plants in a container for a year before planting out in the ground.   **JC**

Some Practical Tips

Planting

When planting trees dig a big hole – do not be mean, make it wide and deep, break up the subsoil but do not mix it with the topsoil. Do not put loads of fertilizer or much else in the hole! It is better to apply muck, fertilizer and so on as mulches in later years than to confine it to the planting hole now, as the roots will not need it for a year or two. Hammer in the stake to support the tree. Spread out the roots in their natural layers as you refill the hole, tread the soil in firmly, embedding each root in its own portion. Make sure the tree is not buried too deep or too shallow – set it to its original level, indicated by a dirty mark on the trunk. After refilling and refirming the soil, tie the tree to the supporting stake, then mulch around it well and keep a big circle weed free for the first year or three. It is far better to plant into moist soil, i.e. ground that was well watered previously, than to water the holes just before or worse, to water on top.

Planting out shrubs is much the same as for trees, but without the need for a stake or as careful teasing out of roots. Obviously the smaller the shrublet the smaller the hole needs be, but bigger holes are always worth the effort and smaller plants well planted soon outgrow bigger ones no matter how well the latter are treated. The same goes for herbaceous plants. However, as these grow much smaller and so are planted more densely than most shrubs, their entire bed should be prepared and enriched before planting. Herbaceous plants usually look better grouped in threes, fives and sevens. Biennials and bedding plants should be treated as herbaceous plants with their whole bed prepared and enriched beforehand and they will need more assiduous watering to help them establish as they are often moved when in growth. Many annuals do not perform well if their soil is rich and do best sown *in situ* in poor soil; only a few do not resent being transplanted. Bulbs are fussy about how they are planted – requirements vary enormously from species to species, so read the instructions on the packet carefully or seek the advice of an expert.

Watering

Water control is crucial. Too little and the plants desiccate, too much and their roots drown; unfortunately the symptoms are the same in both cases with drooping, flagging leaves. In pots it is safest to keep the compost only just moist, if not actually dry all winter, and then to water more and more generously as the year warms up. Rather than pouring water on top to run through the container, you may immerse pots in water and then drain them, but *never, ever* leave any specimen standing in water unless you want to lose it! In hot weather big plants in small pots need watering at least three times daily. Plants in the ground need watering from the day they are planted if the weather and soil are dry, the more so if it is also windy. It is almost impossible to over-water plants in the ground, especially during the growing season. Foliage, bog and salad plants need even more water than most other groups if they are to perform well. If you must skimp on watering, leave out the lawn and concentrate on the plants.

Soil type

Your basic soil type will affect your success with many sorts of plants. If it's a sticky, heavy clay you may drown plants in water-filled planting holes, but, once tempered, clay will produce luxuriant growth and is best suited to permanent planting such as trees, shrubs and bog gardens. In a chalky soil you will not be able to grow acid-loving lime-haters such as heathers or camellias, and you will need to feed and water often. In a sandy soil you will probably be able to grow acid-loving plants and will also need to feed and water often. In most common garden, loamy soils you can grow the majority of plants fairly well and weeds most luxuriantly. To improve all soil types add more organic material as muck and compost and mulch really heavily.

If you don't know whether your soil is acid or alkaline, assume it is alkaline unless everyone around you is growing rhododendrons. **BF**

Pests and Diseases

Pests and diseases can be controlled by chemical sprays, good hygiene and management, or by using 'biological controls', natural predators that parasitize or prey on the pest.

Following these few simple rules will improve your chances of producing healthy plants:

• Check plants regularly, preferably daily, for signs of pests and diseases; treat them before they become established and spread to nearby plants.

• Provide good growing conditions so that your plants are strong, healthy and disease resistant. Choose disease-resistant cultivars where possible.

• Encourage natural predators to your garden, such as lacewings, ladybirds and blue tits to control aphids. Provide an 'anvil' stone so that song thrushes can smash snail shells and eat the contents. Encourage hedgehogs.

• Use environmentally friendly sprays and physical barriers such as horticultural fleece to control pests and diseases.

• Buy a specialist book to help you identify problems correctly.

• Use companion planting and sacrificial crops to discourage predators. Bob Flowerdew's *Complete Book of Companion Planting*, also published by Kyle Cathie, will tell you all you need to know!

• Legislation governing chemical controls is constantly changing, so check what's available at your retailer and always follow the manufacturer's instructions. Most controls either work on contact or are translocated through the sap system.

Here is some basic advice on combating specific pests and diseases mentioned in this book.

Pests

Aphids are sap sucking and come in many colours and sizes. Many have summer and winter hosts; others, like viburnum aphid, are specific to a particular group. They debilitate and disfigure young growth, transmit viruses and secrete 'honeydew', encouraging sooty mould (see below). Don't overfeed with nitrogen.

Use contact or translocated organic or inorganic sprays, physical barriers such as horticultural fleece and encourage predators like ladybirds, lacewings and blue tits.

Woolly aphids hide among the cracks and crevices in the bark of pyracantha, cotoneaster and apples, and are covered with a white, protective 'wool'. It can be cleaned off with a scrubbing brush and water, blasted off with a hose (taking care not to damage the plant tissue), hanging bird food in the tree so that the birds waiting their turn at the feeding station feed on the nearest available insects, or spraying.

Lily beetles are bright red with black heads. The larvae cover themselves with excrement as a protection from predators – it's revolting but effective! Adults and larvae eat leaves, flowers and seedpods, devastating lilies and fritillarias. They appear from spring until autumn and are becoming more widespread throughout Britain. Pick off the adults by hand – they tend to drop off the leaf just as you are about to pick them up, so cup your hand and place it below the leaf to catch them or temporarily cover the ground below with white plastic so that they are easy to spot once they fall. Alternatively, spray with contact insecticide or wipe off the larvae by hand – or get someone else to do it!

Asparagus beetles appear from late spring and eat the leaves and bark from the stems, which then turn yellow and die. They're black with six yellow blotches on their back. There are two generations between late spring and autumn. Seek and destroy by burning over-wintering asparagus stems, remove by hand or spray at dusk so that bees are not affected.

Flea beetles are shiny beetles about 2mm ($^1/_{12}$in) long that jump off the leaves when disturbed; there are several species, appearing from late spring to mid-summer, that leave anything from rocket to stocks covered in tiny holes that can 'check' growth or kill. Cover with horticultural fleece, use contact insecticide.

Capsid bugs are pale green and about 6mm ($^1/_4$in) long with toxic saliva that disfigures leaves and shoot tips and causes puckering on apples and other fruit. Check plants regularly from late spring to late summer and spray with contact insecticide.

Mealy bugs look like tiny woodlice covered in white fluff. Spray with insecticidal soap or use biological control indoors.

Carrot fly leaves the roots of carrots and its relatives riddled with holes. There are three generations between late spring and early autumn. Grow resistant varieties such as 'Sytan' or 'Flyaway', surround the crops with barriers, cover with horticultural fleece, thin crops on damp days or sow in clusters at the final spacing, thus reducing the need to thin the crops.

Whitefly cluster on the underside of leaves to suck the sap, flying up when disturbed. They also produce 'honeydew' that encourages black, disfiguring sooty mould (see below). Use contact or translocated sprays, physical barriers or biological control.

Big bud affects a number of plants, most commonly currants. The buds become swollen and fail to develop because they are packed with microscopic mites. These can be found at any time of year. The disease is most serious on blackcurrants; remove affected stems immediately and, in bad cases, destroy the whole plant.

Caterpillars may be solitary or in clusters. Many are alarmingly voracious; some, like those of 'webber' moths, cover themselves with a fine web to protect themselves from predators. Sawfly larvae are eating machines that can defoliate plants at an alarming rate, particularly Solomon's seal (*Polygonatum* spp.) and berberis. Larger specimens such as the caterpillars of grey, yellow and black mullein moth can be picked off by hand; prune out the affected stems of plants attacked by webber moths or spray with the biological control *Bacillus thuringiensis*. Make sure that you spray the pests and not butterfly caterpillars – *Bacillus thuringiensis* is non-selective. Other caterpillars can damage fruit, notably the codling moth, the 'maggot' in your apples. Pheromone traps catch enough males on isolated trees to reduce the population; otherwise spray in early summer before the caterpillars enter the developing fruit.

Two-spotted or red spider mites are tiny and difficult to spot with the naked eye; they are a problem in summer, or all year round under glass. A magnifying glass reveals all! Symptoms include mottling and fine webbing over the leaf. Increase humidity; use contact or translocated sprays or biological control.

Scale insects hide under a protective hemispherical shell on leaves and stems, sucking sap and secreting 'honey dew'. Spray with translocated insecticide, soft soap or use biological controls.

Eelworms are microscopic nematodes living within the plant with a variety of hosts from narcissus to onion and phlox. Others nibble root hairs and transmit viruses. Affected narcissus have distorted leaves and stems; onions become stunted, swollen and may rot; phlox have swollen, stunted stems that often split. Dispose of affected plants immediately; do not grow vulnerable plants on infected sites, buy 'clean' stock, rotate crops.

Slugs and snails damage leaves, shoots and flowers. Pick them off by hand, encourage predators, remove decaying organic matter, use traps, barriers and biological controls.

Wasps damage soft fruit such as plums, but on apples and pears cause secondary damage, usually after the birds have taken their pick. Protect ripening fruit with netting or bags made from old nylon tights or muslin. Destroy nests but remember too that wasps they are valuable predators of aphids and help the gardener.

Vine weevil adults are black with orange spots and cut notches from the edge of leaves, particularly on plants such as rhododendrons. The larvae are white, fat and slightly curved, and eat the roots of a wide range of plants, especially in containers; the worst damage is between autumn and mid-spring. Use biological controls or physical barriers, squash adults, use drench or compost containing imidacloprid.

Diseases
Black spot appears as dark blotches on rose leaves with yellowing patches – in severe cases they join together and can defoliate plants. Spray, rake up and destroy infected leaves, prune out infected wood in winter and destroy, mulch in autumn and grow resistant cultivars. It is worse in damp seasons.

Grey mould comes in several guises and includes peony wilt. Fuzzy, grey fungal growth appears on infected parts; any soft tissue of living and dead plant material is vulnerable. Isolate dead and injured plants before they become infected, prune back infected areas to healthy growth, remove all plant debris immediately, spray with fungicide.

Coral spot appears as orange pustules on dead and sometimes on living material. Remove infected parts back to healthy material immediately the disease appears and burn; destroy garden debris that harbours the disease.

Blight appears in several forms. Potato blight causes browning and collapsing of the plant, tubers become rotten and evil smelling. Spray with copper-based fungicide, grow resistant varieties; also affects tomatoes. The symptoms of box blight are yellowing leaves and death; remove affected plants immediately. Fire blight leaves the flowers, foliage and stems looking as though they have been too close to a bonfire. It affects Rosaceae with apple-like fruit, including *Sorbus* and *Cotoneaster* spp., though some varieties are more susceptible than others. Remove infected parts immediately, cutting well back into healthy wood, sterilize tools after use, burn pruned material.

Honey fungus causes die back on susceptible plants from trees to perennials; honey-coloured mushrooms appear at the base of the plant in autumn; white mycelium (fungus roots) can be found below the bark at the base of woody plants; 'boot lace' rhizomorphs are found in the ground. Grow non-susceptible plants, install physical barriers, remove all stumps and as much root as possible from felled or infected trees. Keep plants healthy and stress free.

Iris ink disease is so called because of the blue-black streaks that appear on the bulb. The whole bulb may turn black and rot and any foliage is striped yellow with red tints. Dispose of bulbs immediately, grow plants in a new location.

Leaf spots can be bacterial or fungal; bacterial spots often have a bright yellow 'halo', fungal spots may join together, forming patches. Both show that plants are under stress or have other problems. Remove infected leaves, rake them up and dispose of them at the end of the season, improve plant health. Treat fungal spots with fungicide.

Powdery mildew appears like a whitish powdery layer on leaves; young shoots may distort and fruit is blemished. Encourage air circulation, keep plants well watered, prune out affected branches immediately, avoid high-nitrogen fertilizers, spray with fungicide, grow resistant varieties.

Silver leaf affects notably plums and cherries (*Prunus* spp.). The symptoms are silvering of the leaves, failure to leaf in spring and 'die back'; stems more than 2.5cm (1in) wide have a central reddish stain. The fungus enters through pruning cuts or damage. Prune vulnerable plants throughout the summer months, never in winter. Some control may be gained by pruning infected boughs to at least 15cm (5in) past stained wood or by using biological control.

Tulip fire causes emerging foliage to wither, distort and become mouldy. Buds may develop but not open; if they do flower the petals are blotched. Horrible! Remove infected plants immediately, buy from a reputable source, do not plant tulips on the site for three years.

Willow anthracnose is manifested by curling yellowing leaves that fall early; stems are covered with rough cankers and may die back. It is worse in wet seasons. Fungus over-winters in the cankers, on bud scales and leaves. Prune out infected stems immediately and rake up leaves. Bordeaux mixture may help.

Green alga covers the surface of the leaves and the sunless side of trees and shrubs, particularly in damp areas; if it becomes unsightly, it can be rubbed off or washed off with slightly soapy water. Improve air circulation and reduce dampness.

Sooty mould is a black fungus that lives on the sugary exudate from scale, whitefly, aphids, mealy bug and other 'suckers'. Treat the cause, then wipe off the mould carefully with a soft, damp, slightly soapy cloth.

Phytophthora root rot causes rotting at the collar of woody plants, foliage is sparse and becomes yellow, stems die back; often the whole plant dies. Look at the roots: affected fibrous roots are dead, others discoloured. Remove the bark at the base and you will find a reddish-brown stain. Remove and destroy infected plants and the soil around them, improve drainage.

Rots can be bacterial or fungal. Bacterial such as *Brassica* bacterial soft rot affects roots, fruits, tubers and rhizomes. Discoloured areas develop, then sink as the rot spreads. The bacteria enter via wounds and are spread by pruning tools. Infection spreads rapidly; destroy damaged tissue immediately and disinfect tools.

Fungal rots such as brown rots are manifested by soft brown rotting tissue; fruits fall off or become 'mummified'. Avoid damage to plants, remove infected material immediately and prune out mummified fruits with a small portion of wood.

Rusts appear on leaves and stems as bright orange or brown pustules; infected parts often wither and die. Some have alternative hosts for the winter; others only one. Remove infected leaves, spray, grow resistant varieties.

Scabs can appear on potatoes or apples and fit their description perfectly. Apples crack or split, are small or misshapen, affected leaves fall early. It can occur on any apple or relative. Rake up fallen leaves, prune out cracked or scabby shoots; grow resistant varieties.

Viruses stunt and distort the whole plant – leaves develop streaks or mosaic patterns, flowers develop colour breaks, some plants are simply weakened, not showing external symptoms. Plants affected include cucumbers and tobacco. Viruses can be spread by sap-sucking insects. Dispose of affected plants, buy virus-free stock, control sap-sucking insects, do not plant similar varieties in the same location, wash hands and tools after use, don't propagate from infected plants. **MB**

Pruning

The difference between simply cutting a plant and pruning it properly is knowledge and common sense. Anyone can cut a shrub or tree, but to prune it you need to understand the plant's reaction to the treatment. If you bear in mind that pruning promotes growth you will naturally go easy with the cutting equipment.

Throughout this book there are many examples of shrubs which can be rejuvenated by a hard

pruning, leaving the stumps of branches. Escallonias, rhododendrons and *Taxus* (yew) will recover fully from such drastic action. Where time allows it is easier on the plant and the eye if you work on them over a two-year period, cutting 50 per cent of the old stems in the first year. But dish out the same treatment to a lavender or *Cytisus* (broom) and it will probably die. Another group of plants does not require pruning other than to restrict their size or to change the shape: camellias, pieris, kalmias, magnolias and azaleas are happy to grow and flower year after year without input from the owner.

The golden rule with all pruning is to remove any diseased or rubbing branches first. After that, try to retain the shape of the plant without it becoming one-sided or gappy.

With small branches try to prune immediately above a bud, sloping the cut so that water will run away from the bud. Always make a clean cut with a sharp blade. Where a saw has left roughened bark, smooth it by trimming with a knife. When diseased branches are removed, clean the blade before cutting healthy wood.

The majority of shrubs deserve and in some cases demand an annual prune to encourage flowers, leafy growth, coloured bark or fruit. With these plants it is necessary to know and recognize their habit of growth. When they flower and the age of the stems they flower on are crucial to the type and time of pruning:

• Winter-flowering deciduous shrubs do not normally need to be pruned except to remove diseased branches or those that are growing towards the centre of the plant.

• Those that flower in spring and early summer should be pruned as soon as flowering is finished. First remove any diseased or thin shoots, then cut all the branches that flowered back to within a few buds of the base. Leave the new shoots to flower next year.

• Prune late summer-flowering shrubs in spring when all risk of frost has passed. Again, remove diseased and thin shoots and prune out last year's flowering shoots, allowing the new shoots to grow away and flower next year.

• Evergreen shrubs should be pruned in early summer to avoid any risk of frost damage. Again, the priority is to remove diseased, thin and spindly shoots, and to maintain a balanced and attractive shape.

A few specific examples:

Forsythias flower early in the year on growth made the previous summer. Prune immediately after they have finished flowering, removing all of the branches which produced blossom. The new shoots will grow during the summer and flower next spring.

Bush roses flower on this year's growth but as they are prone to spring frost damage do not prune them until spring; they will then come into flower from mid-summer onwards.

Apple trees fruit best on wood which is at least two years old. In spring last year's growths should be shortened by half to encourage more shoots. The remainder of the stem will produce fruit buds in winter and fruit the following summer.

Wisterias are best pruned twice each year. Cut the excess new growth in summer, leaving 10–15cm (4–6in). Sideshoots will form. In winter shorten the hardening stems back to 5–7cm (2–3in). Flower buds will appear on the remaining stem.

To thicken a young hedge, clip it lightly in late spring. This causes the stems to form sideshoots. After a few cuts there will be an extensive branch system.

The young growths of the red-stemmed *Cornus alba* '**Sibirica**' have the best colour and are most visible in winter after leaf fall. In early spring cut all the branches to within a few centimetres of soil level. They will quickly regrow with good colour for the coming winter. Gather up the prunings and shred or burn them.   **JC**

Propagation

Being naturally frugal, I got into propagation at an early age, but apart from saving huge sums of money, it has other big benefits too. It totally changes the way you approach planting design because it enables you to grow larger quantities of plants, encouraging you to plant generous interlocking drifts or repeated groups of one plant. Almost inevitably the overall effect is far more cohesive than the spotty results often achieved by garden-centre buyers who are able to indulge in only one of each type. It also, especially in the case of box, can prevent you importing noxious diseases that inevitably come with certain plants.

The simplest methods of propagation are seed, cuttings and division. Division is generally the easiest: you dig up the clump that is to be divided and either tease it apart by hand or prise it using two garden forks. Replant as soon as possible in weed-free soil and water the plants in to settle the soil around the roots.

If you are propagating from seed, far better success rates are achieved if you can sow seeds with some protection from the elements and pests, such as in a greenhouse, cold frame or on the window sill. The majority of my spring vegetable seed I now get going inside first, as external factors can be so extreme at this time of year. I tend not to use seed trays – having little spare time, I go for the most time-efficient method possible. I find the special dried pellets, such as the Jiffy -7, which come in reusable plastic trays, extremely easy to use. You soak the peat and coir pellets in their trays for 30 minutes and then sow one or two seeds per cell, thinning them out to one after germination. As soon as I see the plants roots at the base of the pellet, I start hardening them off (putting them outside for longer and longer each day) to acclimatize them to the real world; then I plant them out as soon as the temperature permits. The little netting bag they come in is left intact and degrades quickly in the soil. To water them I tend to soak the entire tray, every few days or as necessary. Many plants need warmer temperatures for germination (but not necessarily high light levels), but will not tolerate lower light levels as soon as leaves start to emerge, so if your window sill is overloaded you can put the trays near a radiator initially and then move them to a cooler, lighter place once they have germinated.

Propagating by cuttings is extremely simple for many plants, but like many things it can be made complicated. You can take softwood cuttings, from fresh new growth, semi-ripe cuttings from the later growth when the shoots are starting to firm at the base or hardwood cuttings later on towards the end of the year. Some plants are best taken as basal cuttings (through the base of the young shoot where it joins the parent branch, cutting through the slight swelling); heeled cuttings (formed by tugging off the young shoot complete with a small piece of parent plant that can be trimmed up); nodal cuttings (immediately below a leaf bud); or internodal (between two leaf buds). There are other types too, but these four will cover many, many plants. I almost invariably take heeled or nodal cuttings, which are quick, simple and effective. Once detached from the plant the softer, younger growth will wilt quickly, so have a plastic bag ready to put the cuttings in as soon as you take them, keeping them well away from sunlight.

I find a mix of 50 per cent grit and 50 per cent compost works well as a rooting medium for most plants and I generally use seed trays and put the cuttings fairly close together – depending on the size of the material, I will often get a hundred or so cuttings from one seed tray. You can put many, easily rooted cuttings straight into the soil outside, but I still find them easier to handle in trays.

Once you have inserted the cuttings into the tray, softwood cuttings or more difficult subjects may require a plastic bag over the container and/or being kept in a shaded place initially, to keep the cuttings in good condition. I also mist them with a mist sprayer, if they look on the point of flagging. The cold frame or greenhouse is the ideal place for rooting cuttings, but many work outside too. I rarely use hormone powder because its shelf life is quite short and most months I will be taking cuttings of something and I am not organized enough to have fresh supplies to hand. It does seem to speed up rooting and improve success rate in some cases, but I compensate by taking larger quantities to allow for possible failures.

Many other factors affect success too. The vigour of the parent plant is a significant one, so if it is an old favourite on its last legs that you want to retain, give it a good boost with feed, water and murmur a few sweet nothings to it to encourage it to put on a great spurt of new life ready for you to take advantage of, rather than selecting some slothful old shoot. Bottom heat – wonderful term – speeds things up no end, and you can achieve this by running soil-warming cables through the compost, or buying a special metal tray which heats up to stand the seed trays on. (Also handy for speeding up germination). This is my latest toy, and my success rates are very satisfying. Bottom heat is well worth putting on your Christmas list.

There are other ways of propagating – grafting, which is largely used for trees; and layering, which is particularly useful for climbers and involves encouraging a branch to shoot by covering it with soil while it is still attached to the parent plant, are just two of many to which there is not space to do justice here. All fascinating. but requiring a bit more expertise and less used than cuttings and seeds. Even so, they are well worth having a go at, just to see what amazing things you can do with plants. Micropropagation is becoming increasingly popular, but is limited to specialists with the necessary knowledge and equipment.   **BG**

Index of Plants by Type

Plants are listed in ascending order of height. Some plants occur in more than one category.

Index of Plants by Common Name

Photographic Acknowledgements

Key

AL = Andrew Lawson
AZ = A–Z Botanical Collection
CN = Clive Nicholls
EC = Eric Crichton
HA = Heather Angel
GP.com = GardenPhotos.com
GPL = Garden Picture Library
GWI = Garden World Images
Holt = Holt Studios International Ltd
JB = Jonathan Buckley
JF = John Fielding
JG = John Glover
JH = Jerry Harpur
MHa = Marcus Harpur
MH = Marijke Heuff
LeSM = Le Scanff-Mayer
MM = Marianne Majerus
PH = Photos Horticultural
PPW = Plant Portraits Worldwide
SH = Sunniva Harte
SaxH = Saxon Holt
SO = S & O Mathews

t = top
b = bottom
c = centre
l = left
r = right

page 1 JB (Great Dixter, East Sussex; design: Christopher Lloyd); 2/3 MH; 4/5 (l) LeSM; 7 MH (Barnsley House, Gloucestershire); 11 CN (Eastgrove Cottage, Worcester); 12 EC; 15 JB (Great Dixter; design: Christopher Lloyd); 16 MM; 17 JB (Lady Farm, Somerset; design: Judy Pearce); 18 (l) JG; (r) JH; 19 (l) MM; (r) JG; 20 (l) GPL/Neil Holmes; (r) MHa; 21 (l) MM; (c) Holt/Jean Hall; 22 (l) JG; (c) JG (RHS Garden, Wisley); (r) JG; 23 (l) JG; (r) EC; 24 Holt/ Nigel Cattlin; 25 PH; 26 (tl) AL; (bl) JB; (r) JB; 27 (l) PH; (r) JB (Glen Chantry, Essex); 28 (l) MM; (c) MH; (r) JB (Great Dixter; design: Christopher Lloyd); 29 (l) JG; (r) AZ/Adrian Thomas; 30 (l) JB; (c) PH; (r) GPL/Neil Holmes; 31 (l) GPL/Jerry Pavia; (r) JG; 32 JH; 33 JG; 34 (l) Oxford Scientific Films; (r) JG; 35 (l) JG; (r) GPL/Rex Butcher; 36 (l) GP.com/Judy White; (r) CN; 37 (l) PH; (c) GPL/François de Heel; (r) JB; 38 (l) MM (design: Piet Oudolf); (tr) Holt/Nigel Cattlin; (br) GPL/Christopher Fairweather; 39 (l) JG; (r) GPL/Bob Challinor; 40 GPL/Steven Wooster; 41 MHa; 42 (l) MM; (r) JB (Glen Chantry; design: Sue & Wol Staines); 43 (l) GPL/Christopher Fairweather; (r) JH; 44 (l) JG; (c) MM; (r) JG; 45 (l) MM; (r) SO; 46 (l) PH; (r) MHa; 47 (l) PH; (c) SaxH; (r) AL; 48; (l) MM; (c) AL; (r) SaxH; 49 (l) JG; (c) MHa; (r) JB (Perch Hill; design: Sarah Raven); 50; (l) LeSM (les Jardins de Bellevue); (r) JH; 51 (l) JB (Great Dixter; design: Christopher Lloyd); (r) JB; 52 (l) MHa (design: Beth Chatto); (r) MM; 53 (tl) MM; (bl) JG; (r) PH; 54 JG; 55 SaxH; 56 (l) MM; (r) EC; 57 (l) SH; (r) SH; 58 (l) GWI; (c) GPL/Howard Rice; (r) JG; 59 (l) EC; (r) AZ/Adrian Thomas; 60 MHa; 61 MHa; 62 (l) JH; (r) PH; 63 (l) GPL/ Howard Rice; (r) PPW; 64 (l) JB; (r) Andrea Jones 65 GPL/ Michael Howes; 66 JB (Great Dixter); 67 JG; 68 JG; 69 (tr) JH; (br) JH; 70 Holt/ Richard Anthony; 71 (l) JG; (r) JB; 72 (l) GPL/ Jerry Pavia; (r) GPL/Neil Holmes; 73 (l) GPL/ Sunniva Harte; (c) JB (Alan Titchmarsh's garden); (r) PH; 74 GPL/Sunniva Harte; 75 JB (Hinton Ampner, Hampshire); 76 (l) ; (c) JG; (r) JB; 77 (l) JG; (r) JG; 78 JG; 79 (tr) JG; (br) JG; 80 (l) PH; (r) MHa; 81 (l) JG; (c) JB; (r) GPL/ Didier Willery; 82 (l) GPL/Howard Rice; (c) JG; 83 (l) Richard Bloom; (c) AL; (r) JG; 84 (l) MHa; (r) JH; 85 (l) JB; (r) GPL/ Christi Carter; 86 GPL/ Howard Rice; 87 GPL/David Cavagnaro; 88 (l) JG; (r) SO (Hilbarn House); 89 (l) JG; (c) JH (design: Beth Chatto); (r) MHa; 90 (l) JH; (c) JG; (r) JH; 91 (l) JB; (r) JB (Upper Mill Cottage, Kent; design: David & Mavis Seeney); 92 (l) JG; (r) JB (Hollington Herbs, Berks; design: Simon Hopkinson); 93 (l) JH; (r) GPL/John Ferro Sims; 94 MHa; 95 JB (design: Beth Chatto); 96 (l) Bob Flowerdew; (r) JB (Ketley's, East Sussex; design: Helen Yemm); 97 (l) Jane Nichols; (r) GPL/Howard Rice; 98 (l) JG; (c) JG; (r) JG; 99 (l) JB (Great Dixter); (r) JB (Glen Chantry; design: S & W Staines); 100 (l) MM; (c) Holt/Primrose Peacock; (r) PH; 101 JG; 102 (l) MM; 103 SaxH; 104 (l) GPL/Christi Carter; (r) JG; 105 (l) Holt/Nigel Cattlin; (r) GPL/Howard Rice; 106 (l) GPL/Densey Clyne; (r) PH; 107 (l) MM; (c) MM; (r) JG; 108 (l) JG; (r) LeSM (Ellebore, France); 109 (l) JG; (r) MM; 110 Oxford Scientific Films/Geoff Kidd; 111 Sunniva Harte; 112 (l) GPL/JG; (r) JG; 113 (l) JG; (tr) JH; (br) CN; 114 (l) JH (design: Beth Chatto); (r) MM (RHS Garden, Wisley); 115 (l) Andrea Jones Location Photography; (r) JB (RHS Garden, Wisley); 116 (l) LeSM; (r) John Cushnie; 117 (l) SaxH; (r) LeSM; 118 LeSM (Les Jardins du Prieuré Notre Dame d'Orsan Maisonnais (18) France); 119 Bob Gibbons; 120 (l) SO; (tr) Holt/Willem Harinck; (br) MM; 121 (l) MHa; (r) JH; 122 (l) PH; (c) JG; (r) PH; 123 (l) JG; (r) MH; 124 (tr) MM; (br) Derek St Romaine; 125 (l) EC; (r) Andrew N. Gagg's PHOTO FLORA; 126 JB (design: Beth Chatto); 127 GPL/Howard Rice; 128 (l) CN; (r) JF; 129 (l) MM; (r) JB (Great Dixter); 130 (l) MHa; (r) JB (Glen Chantry); 131 (l) PH; (c) PH; (r) LeSM; 132 (l) JB; (r) CN (Stourton House, Wilts); 133 (l) PH; (c) JH; (r) JG; 134 JB (design: Beth Chatto); 135 HA; 136 (l) JB (Abbey Dore, Herefordshire); (c) MM (r) JH; 137; (l) GPL/Lamontagne; (r) MM; 138 JH; 139 (l) GPL/Philippe Bonduel; (r) MHa; 140 (l) JB; (c) PH; (r) JB; 141 (l) JG; (r) GP.com/Judy White; 142 (l) JG; (r) GPL/David England; 143 (l) SaxH; (r) GPL/LeSM; 144 GPL/Michael Howes; 145 EC; 146 (l) Holt/Alan & Linda Detrick; (c) MHa; (r) MM; 147 (l) JH; (r) GPL/Mark Bolton; 148 (l) CN; (c) MHa; (r) JB (Sissinghurst); 149 (l) MH; (r) GP.com/Graham Rice; 150 (l) GPL/J S Sira; (r) MHa; 151 (l) MM (Urn Cottage, Charfield; design: Lesley Rosser; (r) GPL/Lamontagne; 152 JG; 153 LeSM (Jardin des Fournials Ossart- Maurières, France); 154 (l) JG; (r) JB (design: Beth Chatto; 155 (l) GP.com/ Graham Rice; (r) LeSM; 156 (l) GPL/ Lamontagne; (c) JH; (r) JG; 157 (l) CN; (c) JG; (r) JH; 158 (l) CN; (r) MHa (design: Beth Chatto); 159 (l) MM; (r) MHa; 160 LeSM (Les Jardins de Bellevue); 161 MM; 162 (l) PH; (r) PH; 163 (l) GPL/Didier Willery; (c) JG; (r) JB (Great Dixter); 164 (l) GPL/Henk Dijkman; (r) Holt/Nigel Cattlin; 165 (l) MM; (r) GPL/Marie O'Hara; 166 (l) CN; (c) JG; (r) PH; 167 (c) MM; (r) GPL/Brian Carter; 168 (l) JG; (c) GPL/Juliette Wade; (r) PH; 169 (c) JB (RHS Garden, Wisley); (r) MH (design: Mrs G Lauxtermann, Holland); 170 JB; 171 JG; 172 (l) PH; (c) MM; 173 (l) JB; (c) CN (design: Jill Billington); (r) GPL/Steven Wooster; 174 (l) MHa; (r) JF; 175 (l) JB; (r) JG; 176 GPL/Chris Burrows; 177 MM; 178 (l) JB (Glen Chantry); (r) SaxH; 179 (l) JG; (c) MM; (r) PH; 180 (l) MM; (r) JG; 181 (l) JB; (r) JB (Magdalen College, Oxford); 182 (l) JB; (c) JG; (r) GPL/Sunniva Harte; 183 (l) AL; (r) JG; 184 GPL/Howard Rice; 185 (l) JH; (r) JH; 186 (l) MHa; (c) PH; (r) MM; 187 (l) JG; (r) MM; 188 (l) JG; (c) JG; (r) MHa; 189 (l) JB; (r) JG; 190 (l) JH; (c) JB; 191 (l) JB; (c) SaxH; (tr) LeSM; (br) JG; 192 GPL/Christi Carter; 193 GPL/Stephen Robson; 194 (l) PH; (c) SaxH; (r) JG; 195 (l)

PH; (r) MM (Chesil Beach); 196 (l) GPL/Howard Rice; (r) JB; 197 (l) PH; (r) JG; 198 (l) MHa (RHS Garden, Wisley); (c) JG; (r) PH; 199 (l) GPL/Sunniva Harte; (r) EC; 200 JH; 201 MM; 202 (l) SaxH; (r) JF; (r) GPL/Jerry Pavia; 203 MM; 204 (l) EC; (r) CN; 205 (l) MHa; (c) GPL/Howard Rice; (r) GPL/Jerry Pavia; 206 (l) JG; (c) AZ/Martin Land; (r) CN; 207 (c) GPL/J S Sira; (r) JH; 208 JB; 209 LeSM (Les Jardins de Bellevue (76) France); 210 (l) GWI; (c) Holt/Nigel Cattlin; (r) JB; 211 (l) SO; (r) JG; 212 (l) GPL/Howard Rice; (c) MM; 213 (l) AZ/A Young; (r) GPL/Howard Rice; 214 (l) GPL/Lamontagne; (r) JB; 215 (l) PH; (c) Plant Portraits Worldwide (r) JB (Great Dixter); 216 JB; 217 JH; 218 (l) SO; (r) GPL/Jerry Pavia; 219 (l) GWI; (r) JG; 220 (l) JG; (c) GPL/Howard Rice; (r) MHa; 221 MHa; 222 (l) JH; (c) JH; (r) JG; 223 (l) JG; (r) JB (Glen Chantry); 224 JG; 225 JB (Coton Manor, Northants; design: Susie Pasley-Tyler); 226 (l) AL; (c) PH; (r) GWI; 227 (l) SaxH; (r) PH; 228 (l) Thompson & Morgan; (r) JG; 229 (l) SaxH; (r) MHa; 230 (l) GPL/David Russell; (c) JG; (r) LeSM (Les Jardins de Bellevue (76) France); 231 (l) MHa; (r) JB (Great Dixter); 232 JG; 233 JH; 234 (l) Geoff Hayes; (c) JG; (r) JG; 235 (c) JG; (r) JG; 236 (l) Holt/Bob Gibbons; (c) GPL/Howard Rice; (r) JG; 237 (l) JH; (r) JG; 238 (l) JG; (r) JF; 239 (l) JB; (r) GPL/Brian Carter; 240 MHa; 241 JB; 242 (l) JG; (r) PH; 243 (l) JG; (c) MHa (design: Beth Chatto); (r) JG; 244 (l) JG; (r) JB; 245 (l) JH; (r) PH; 246 (l) JG; (c) JG; (r) MM; 247 (l) JB (East Ruston, Old Vicarage, Norfolk; design: Alan Gray & Graham Robeson; (r) LeSM; 248 CN; 249 Geoff Hayes; 250 (l) JG; (r) MHa; 251 (l) GPL/Didier Willery; (c) JG; (r) GPL/Neil Holmes; 252 (l) GPL/LeSM; (r) SO; 253 (l) JH; (r) GPL/LeSM; 254 (l) GWI; (r) JG; 255 (l) SO; (r) JG; 256 GPL/JG; 257 SO; 258 (l) GPL/Brian Carter; (r) JG; 259 (l) LeSM (Domaine de St Jean de Beauregard); (r) JG; 260 (l) AZ/Nick Wiseman; (r) PH; 261 (c) JB; (r) MHa; 262 (c) PH; (r) GPL/ Sunniva Harte; 263 (l) EC; (c) MM; (r) EC; 264 CN; 265 (tr) GPL/Brigitte Thomas; (br) GPL/

David Cavagnaro; 266 (l) JG; (c) EC; 267 (tl) SaxH; (bl) MM; (r) SaxH; 268 (l) GP.com/Judy White; (c) PH; (r) JB (Great Dixter); 269 (tr) PH; (br) MM; 270 (l) JB (RHS Garden, Wisley); (r) EC; 271 (l) EC; (r) LeSM; 272 JB (design: Gay Wilson); 273 JG; 274 (l) JH; (r) GPL/Erika Craddock; 275 (l) JG; (c) PH; (r) PH; 276 (l) JB (Great Dixter); (c) GPL/Jerry Pavia; (r) MH; 277 (l) JB (Ketley's, East Sussex; design: Helen Yemm); (r) JG; 278 (l) GPL/Jerry Pavia; (r) CN; 279 (l) MM; (r) JH; 280 MM; 281 JG; 282 (l) GWI; (c) MM (design: Tom Stuart-Smith); 283 (tl) SaxH; (bl) GPL/Sunniva Harte; (r) JG; 284 (l) JG; (c) CN; (r) JG; 285 (l) LeSM (Les Jardins de Bellevue (76) France); (r) AZ/Carol Casselden; 286 (l) JG; (c) MM; (r) MHa; 287 (l) JB (Great Dixter); (r) JF; 288 JG; 289 JB; 290 (l) JG; (r) JB (design: Anthony Goff); 291 (l) PH; (r) EC; 292 (l) AL; (c) MM; 293 (l) MM; (c) MH; (r) MM; 294 (l) PH; (r) GP.com/Judy White; 295 (l) MHa; (c) JH; 296 JG; 297 JB; 298 (l) SaxH; (c) PH; (r) JH; 299 (l) JG; (c) JG; (r) PH; 300 (l) MM; (r) PH; 301 (l) EC; (c) CN; (r) GPL/JG; 302 (l) GWI; (c) GPL/David Cavagnaro; 303 (l) PH; (c) MHa; (r) JB; 304 AL; 305 SO; 306 (l) PH; (r) JG; 307 (l) MHa; (r) AL; 308 (l) LeSM; (c) JG; 309 (l) PH; (r) JG; 310 PH; 311 (tr) SO; (br) JG; 312 (l) GPL/ Micky White; (c) EC; 313 (l) MM; (c) JG; (r) MHa; 314 (l) GPL/ Philippe Bonduel; (c) Holt/Inga Spence; (r) GPL/Jerry Pavia; 315 (l) MHa; (r) PH; 316 (l) JB (Great Dixter); (r) EC; 317 (l) JG; (r) MHa; 318 Holt/Primrose Peacock; 319 GPL/Howard Rice; 320 (l) EC; (r) MHa; 321 (l) JB; (c) PH; 322 (l) JG; (r) JG; 323 (l) GWI; (c) MM; (r) PH; 324 (l) PH; (c) GPL/ Sunniva Harte; (r) EC; 325 leSM; 326 JG; 327 JB; 328 (l) GPL/Howard Rice; (c) MM; (r) SaxH; 329 (l) GPL/ Howard Rice; (r) JB (Great Dixter); 330 (l) JH; (c) JG; (r) JG; 331 (l) GPL/J S Sira; (r) LeSM; 332 (l) GPL/David Russell; (c) EC; (r) GPL/David Askham; 333 MM; 334 (l) SaxH; (c) LeSM; (r) PH; 335 (l) MM; (c) David Austin Roses Ltd; (r) PH; 336 JB (design: Jackie McLaren); 337 MM; 338 (l) GPL/J S Sira; (c) GWI; (r) JB (Lady Farm, Somerset; design:

Judy Pearce); 339 (c) JB (Hollington Herbs); (r) JG; 340 (l) JB (Perch Hill; design: Sarah Raven); (r) JB (design: Robin Green & Ralph Cade); 341 (l) MHa; (r) PH; 342 (l) JG; (c) JG; (r) MM; 343 (l) AL; (r) JB; 344 JB; 345 JB; 346 (l) JG; (c) MHa; 347 (c) GPL/Mark Bolton; (r) PH; 348 (l) SO; (c) Holt/Bob Gibbons; (r) JG; 349 (l) LeSM; (c) Geoff Hayes; (r) MHa; 350 (l) JG; (r) JG; 351 (l) EC; (r) EC; 352 MM; 353 Wildlife Matters; 354 (l) Geoff Hayes; (r) PH; 355 (l) GPL/Didier Willery; (c) Holt; (r) PH; 356 MM; 357 GPL/JG; 358 (l) MM; (c) GPL/J S Sira; (r) PH; 359 (l) MM; (r) PH; 360 AL; 361 SO; 362 (l) MHa; (c) JG; (r) JG; 363 (l) GPL/Howard Rice; (c) GP.com/Graham Rice; 364 (l) PH; (r) JG; 365 (l) JG; (r) CN; 366 AL; 367 JH; 368 MM; 369 PH; 370 (l) PH; (c) JH; (r) JG; 371 (l) GPL/J S Sira; (r) MM; 372 (l) GPL/Neil Holmes; (r) JB (design: Judy Pearce); 373 (l) MH; (c) GPL/Neil Holmes; (r) SaxH; 374 (l) GPL/Neil Holmes; (c) JG; (r) EC; 375 (c) JG; (r) JH; 376 JG; 377 JB; 378 (l) JG; (r) GPL/Howard Rice; 379 (l) MM; (c) JF; (r) JG; 380 (l) MM (The Herbalist Garden, RHS Chelsea 1998; design: Bunny Guinness); (r) GPL/J S Sira; 381 (l) MM; (r) JB (design: David & Mavis Seeney); 382 JG; 383 MM; 384 (l) JB; (c) JF; (r) JB; 385 (c) JH; (r) AZ/Gary Newport; 386 (l) AZ/Lino Pastorelli; (r) MM (design: Tom Stuart-Smith); 387 (l) GPL/Neil Holmes; (c) GPL/Howard Rice; (r) SaxH; 388 GPL/Steven Wooster; 389 (tr) JG; (br) GPL/Gillian McAlmont; 390 (l) JB; (r) JB; 391 (l) JH; (r) JG; 392 (l) JG; (c) MM; 393 (l) Robin B. Cushman; (r) JG; 394 Holt/Jean Hall; 395 (l) SO; (r) MHa; 396 EC; 397 CN; 398 (l) GPL/JG; (c) GPL/JG; (r) PH; 399 (l) JH; (r) GWI; 400 (l) MHa; (r) MHa; 401 (l) MHa; (r) Holt/Inga Spence; 402 JG; 403 LeSM (Les Jardins de Bellevue (76) France)